ASHE Reader
ON COMMUNITY COLLEGES

Edited by BARBARA TOWNSEND and DEBRA BRAGG

THIRD EDITION

PEARSON
Custom
Publishing

Cover Art: *Racing Machine,* by Angela Sciaraffa.

PEARSON
Custom
Publishing

PEARSON CUSTOM PUBLISHING
75 Arlington Street, Suite 300, Boston, MA 02116
A Pearson Education Company

ASHE READER ON COMMUNITY COLLEGES

Part I: THE VARIETIES OF COMMUNITY COLLEGES

Part II: THEORETICAL FOUNDATIONS

Part III: FINANCE, GOVERNANCE, AND ADMINISTRATION

Smart, J. C., Kuh, G. D., & Tierney, W.G. (1997). The roles of institutional cultures and decision approaches in promoting organizational effectiveness in two-year colleges. *Journal of Higher Education, 68*(3), 256–280.

Amey, M. J., VanDerLinden, K. E., & Brown, D. F. (2002). Perspectives on community college leadership: Twenty years in the making. *Community College Journal of Research and Practice, 26* (7–8), 573–589.

Zamani, E. M. (2003). African American student affairs professionals in community college settings: A commentary for future research. *NASAP Journal, 6*(1), 91–103.

Part IV: CURRICULAR MISSIONS

Townsend, K. (2001). Redefining the community college transfer mission. *Community College Review, 29*(1), 29–42.

Floyd, D. (2005). The community college baccalaureate in the U.S. In D. Floyd, M. Skolnik, & K. Walker (Eds.), *The community college baccalaureate* (pp. 25–47). Sterling, VA: Stylus Press.

Bragg, D. D. (2001). The past, present, and future role of federal vocational legislation in U.S. community colleges. *Journal of Applied Research in the Community College, 9*(1), 57–76.

Grubb, W. N., Badway, N., & Bell, D. (2003). Community colleges and the equity agenda: The potential of noncredit education. In K. Shaw & J. Jacobs (Eds.), Community colleges: New environments, new directions. *The Annals of the American Academy of Political and Social Science,* Vol. 586.

Deil-Amen, R., & Rosenbaum, J. (2002, July). The unintended consequences of stigma-free remediation. *Sociology of Education, 75,* 249–268.

Perin, D. P. (2002). The location of developmental education in community colleges: A discussion of the merits of mainstreaming vs. centralization. *Community College Review, 30*(1), 27–44.

Maxwell, W., Hagedorn, L. S., Cypers, S., Moon, H. S., Brocato, P., Wahl, K., & Prather, G. (2003). Community and diversity in urban community colleges: Coursetaking among entering students. *Community College Review, 30*(4), 21–46.

Tinto, V. (1997). Classrooms as communities: Exploring the educational character of student persistence. *Journal of Higher Education, 68*(6), 599–623.

Johnson, S. D., Benson, A. D., Duncan, J., Shinkareva, O. N., Taylor, G. D., & Treat, T. (2004). Internet-based learning in postsecondary career and technical education. *Journal of Vocational Education Research, 29*(2), 101–119.

Part V: FACULTY

Twombly, S. B. (2004). Looking for signs of community college arts and science faculty professionalization in searches: An alternative approach to a vexing question. *Community College Review, 32*(1), 21–39.

Wolfe, J. R., & Strange, C. C. (2002). Academic life at the franchise: Faculty culture in a rural two-year branch campus. *The Review of Higher Education, 26*(3), 343–362.

Perna, L. (2003, April). The status of women and minorities among community college faculty. *Research in Higher Education 44*(2), 205–240.

Roueche, J. E., Roueche, S. D. & Milliron, M. D. (1996). In the company of strangers: Addressing the utilization and integration of part-time faculty in American community colleges. *Community College Journal of Research & Practice, 20*(2), 105–118.

Akroyd, D., Jaeger, A., Jackowski, M., & Jones, L. C. (2004). Internet access and use of the web for instruction: A national study of full-time and part-time community college faculty. *Community College Review, 32*(1), 40–51.

Part VI: STUDENTS

Adelman, C. (April/May 2003). A growing plurality: The 'traditional age community college dominant' student. *Community College Journal*, 27–30, 32.

Laden, B. V. (1999). Celebratory socialization of culturally diverse students through academic programs and support services. In K. M. Shaw, J. R. Valadez, and R. Rhoades (Eds.), *Community colleges as cultural context* (pp. 173–194). Albany: State University of New York Press.

Rendón, L. I. (2002). Community College Puente: A validating model of education. *Educational Policy, 16*(4), 642–667.

Sanchez, J. R., Laanan, F. S., & Wiseley, W. C. (1999). Postcollege earnings of former students of California community colleges: Methods, analysis, and implications. *Research in Higher Education, 40*(1), 87–113.

Averett, S., & Dalessandro, S. (2001). Racial and gender differences in the returns to 2-year and 4-year degrees. *Education Economics, 9*(3), 281–292.

Pascarella, E., T., Edison, M., Nora, A., Hagedorn, L. S., & Terenzini, P. T. (1998). Does community college versus four-year college attendance influence students' educational plans? *Journal of College Student Development, 39*(2), 179–193.

Pascarella, E., Bohr, L., Nora, A., & Terenzini, P. (1995). Cognitive effects of 2-year and 4-year colleges: New evidence. *Educational Evaluation and Policy Analysis, 17*(1), 83–96.

Strauss, L.C., & Volkwein, J. F. (2002). Comparing student performance and growth in 2- and 4-year institutions. *Research in Higher Education, 43*(2), 133–161.

CONTENTS

Debra D. Bragg and Barbara K. Townsend, Senior Editors

Berta Vigil Laden, Associate Editor

Rebecca D. Cox and Alexander C. McCormick

Barbara K. Townsend

Paul Gallagher and John D. Dennison

Kevin J. Dougherty, Associate Editor

Burton R. Clark

Stephen Brint and Jerome Karabel

COPYRIGHT ACKNOWLEDGMENTS

"The Status of Women and Minorities Among Community College Faculty," by Laura W. Perna, reprinted from *Research in Higher Education* 44, no. 2 (April 2003), by permission of Springer Science and Business Media.

"In the Company of Strangers: Addressing the Utilization and Integration of Part-Time Faculty in American Community Colleges," by John E. Roueche, Suanne D. Roueche, and Mark D. Milliron, reprinted from *Community College Journal of Research & Practice* 20, no. 2 (1996), by permission of Taylor & Francis Group, LLC. Copyright © 1996 by John E. Roueche, Suanne D. Roueche, and Mark D. Milliron.

"Internet Access and Use of the Web for Instruction: A National Study of Full-time and Part-time Community College Faculty," by Duane Akroyd et al., reprinted by permission from *Community College Review* 32, no. 1, (2004).

"A Growing Plurality: The 'Traditional Age Community College Dominant' Student," by Clifford Adelman, reprinted from *Community College Journal*, (April-May 2003), American Association of Community Colleges.

"Celebratory Socialization of Culturally Diverse Students Through Academic Programs and Support Services," by Berta Vigil Laden, reprinted from *Community Colleges as Cultural Texts: Qualitative Explorations of Organizational and Student Culture*, edited by Kathleen M. Shaw, James R. Valdadez, and Robert A. Rhoads, (1999), State University of New York Press.

"Community College Puente: A Validating Model of Education," by Laura I. Rendón, reprinted from *Educational Policy* 16, no. 4 (2002), by permission of Sage Publications. Copyright © 2002 by Laura I. Rendón.

"Postcollege Earnings of Former Students of California Community Colleges: Methods, Analysis, and Implications," by Jorge R. Sanchez, Frankie Santos Laanan, and W. Charles Wiseley, reprinted from *Research in Higher Education* 40, no. 1 (1999), by permission of Springer Science and Business Media.

"Racial and Gender Differences in the Returns to 2-Year and 4-Year Degrees," by Susan Averett and Sharon Dalessandro, reprinted from *Education Economics* 9, no. 3 (2001), by permission of Taylor & Francis Ltd.

"Does Community College Versus Four-Year College Attendance Influence Students' Educational Plans?" by Ernest T. Pascarella et al., reprinted by permission from the *Journal of College Student Development* 39, no. 2 (1998).

"Cognitive Effects of 2-Year and 4-Year Colleges: New Evidence," by Ernest Pascarella et al., reprinted from *Educational Evaluation and Policy Analysis* 17, no. 1 (spring 1995), by permission of the American Educational Research Association. Copyright © 1995 by the American Educational Research Association.

"Comparing Student Performance and Growth in 2- and 4-Year Institutions," by Linda C. Strauss and J. Fredericks Volkwein, reprinted from *Research in Higher Education* 43, no. 2 (April 2002), by permission of Springer Science and Business Media.

EDITORIAL ADVISORY BOARD

ASHE Reader on Community Colleges in the 21st Century: Introduction

Debra D. Bragg and Barbara K. Townsend

The community college is an astounding institution, perhaps the greatest educational innovation of the 20th century, according to Clark Kerr. In this *ASHE Reader on Community Colleges in the 21st Century*, we seek to provide an overview of the community college from its origins at the turn of the 20th century through its various permutations in that same century and up to its current manifestations as the primary vehicle for access to higher education for millions of people who could not and would not otherwise attend college. More than 1,100 public and private community colleges operate in the United States, with 1,600 independent campuses (Phillippe & Patton, 2000). Well over five million students enroll in credit-generating courses in community colleges annually, approaching half of all students enrolled in higher education in the United States. Added to this official count is an unknown but undoubtedly large and growing number of students enrolled in non-credit offerings. Ranging from its historic roots in liberal arts and transfer to its modern-day emphasis on a comprehensive curriculum, community colleges have taken on their own unique and important role in higher education, both domestically and internationally.

In this introduction, we will trace the development of community colleges, with special focus on their curricular functions and open access mission, and briefly discuss assessment of their impact on higher education. In terms of the Reader itself, we provide an overview, review how the readings were selected, and describe the organization by reviewing each of the six sections. We then move to a discussion of what is missing from the Reader (because it is missing in the research about community colleges) and suggest what needs to be researched to provide a fuller, more accurate portrait of the community college.

Development of the Community College

Community colleges began near the turn of the 20th century as transfer institutions, hence the name junior colleges, with many of the public ones starting as extensions of high schools. At the urging of university leaders such as William Rainey Harper of the University of Chicago and David Starr Jordan of Stanford University, junior colleges were conceived, at least in part, as a mechanism for relieving senior institutions from the burden of teaching first- and second-year students. Junior colleges provided an educational institution where students could remain close to home to pursue higher education (Cohen & Brawer, 2003). Widely acknowledged as the first public junior college in the United States, Joliet Junior College exemplifies this history, with its beginnings in the local high school where Joliet students received advanced standing upon entrance to the University of Chicago. Harper, considered by some scholars as the father of the junior college, conceived of the associate degree as an academic credential for students completing the first two years of college. Recipients of the associate degree could matriculate to a four-year college to pursue the baccalaureate or they could exit the junior college, having completed an adequate amount of higher education to secure viable employment.

Other curricular functions.   As various social, economic and political forces exerted influence over junior colleges, vocational education emerged (Brint & Karabel, 1989). Several advocates of the early junior college, people such as Walter Crosby Eells and Leonard Koos, were adamant supporters of a broader mission that would go beyond transfer. They suggested that vocational programs should prepare students for immediate employment in semi-professional occupations after completing two years of college. Indeed, Eells' (1931) vision was widely adopted, resulting in many junior colleges expanding their focus to address four functional areas: popularization, preparatory education, terminal education, and guidance. For Eells the fact that students didn't follow the curricular tracks that he prescribed was not especially problematic; if students graduated from junior colleges in terminal programs and then decided to transfer to senior institutions to continue their education at the four-year college or university level, he considered that an unanticipated success. In fact, this early phenomenon of vocational students transferring to pursue baccalaureate degrees foreshadowed a transfer pattern that is one among several ways modern-day students transfer between and among community colleges and four-year colleges and universities today, according to Townsend (2001).

Even with calls for increased emphasis on terminal education, junior colleges maintained their primary emphasis on transfer and liberal arts education before the mid-century. In the 1950s Jesse Bogue (1956) endorsed the transfer and vocational missions of what he called the community junior college, and he added the third function of continuing education to offer students the opportunity for part-time education. His description of continuing education was particularly insightful because of how well he anticipated the expanded role of community colleges in addressing community and business needs, including envisioning their offering training for persons seeking job advancement and opportunities to learn about new technological developments undoubtedly stimulated by the industrial developments of WWII. Bogue was one of the first national figures to speak actively about the notion of the comprehensive community college, recommending the expansion of curriculum to extend instruction to more students while emphasizing a more careful integration of the liberal arts and vocational education.

Several functions have emerged since the 1960s when the proliferation of community colleges was so extensive, at one time resulting in the opening of at least one college campus per week (Cohen & Brawer, 2003). As the number of institutions grew—almost doubling from about 400 to just under 800 nationally by the early 1970s—the notion of a comprehensive mission became widely accepted as encompassing liberal arts for transfer and vocational education in preparation for employment, along with newer functions. As Bogue (1956) predicted, the comprehensive mission of the community college expanded to include a whole host of forms of continuing education and community service, but it also grew to include remedial services and developmental education (see, for example, Grubb and Associates, 1999). Though earlier estimates of the size of the remedial function are difficult to come by, current national figures consistently place enrollment at nearly 50% or even higher for entering students to the community college (Adelman, 1996; National Center for Education Statistics, 1996), with mathematics, reading, and writing literacy dominating the remedial agenda of most two-year institutions.

Open access mission.   After WWII, federal and increasingly state policies created a gradual shift in the mission of the higher education system overall, resulting in junior colleges later called community colleges playing an increasingly important role in the system. Besides the GI Bill, which had an indelible impact on college enrollments post-World War II, a major report on higher education issued immediately after the WWII and referred to widely as the Truman Commission Report (U.S. President's Commission on Higher Education, 1948) made a bold statement in support of junior colleges as critical to expanding access to higher education for America's citizens. The Commission advocated that junior colleges become an avenue to enhance access and used the term *community college* to convey the intent of these institutions offering the comprehensive curricular mission that permeates community colleges today. Another policy statement advocating this perspective was the Carnegie Commission on Higher Education's *The Open-Door Colleges: Policies for Community Colleges* (1974). Referring to these two-year colleges as serving a democratizing role in American higher education, both these documents make clear the necessity for community colleges to provide open access. The Carnegie Commission (1974) advocated "universal access for those who want to enter institutions of higher education, [so they] are able to make reasonable progress after enrollment, and benefit from enrollment" (p. 17). For the Carnegie Commission, the community college was the institution of choice to increase access for minority and low-income groups through the creation of a stratified approach to higher education that placed community colleges at the bottom rung of the academic ladder.

To a great extent, community colleges have fulfilled this charge by becoming the primary portal to higher education for minority and low-income groups. Persons of color make up about 30% of all participants in community colleges compared to approximately 24% in four-year institutions (National Center for Education Statistics, 1999). More than half of persons of Hispanic origin and African Americans who enroll in higher education attend a community college. These two minority groups are the largest minority groups represented in community colleges; however, persons of Asian/Pacific Islander background and Native Americans are also represented in significant numbers.

For minority and low-income students, community colleges are viewed as the gateway to four-year colleges and the baccalaureate degree, either immediately after high school or later in life. In large part this perspective has come about because policy makers and policy influencers such as the Carnegie Commission on Higher Education have advocated for a system that would achieve this goal. Dougherty (1994) has pointed to the important role of public officials and private-sector leaders in influencing the evolution of the community college mission, both promoting and constraining policy through competing market, political, and ideological forces. His research recognizes that community college enrollment occurs through the choices individuals make, but also because of the political choices made for them by government officials, politicians, and business leaders. As a consequence, community colleges have been designated and have been largely accepted as the starting point for higher education for minority and low-income students.

Assessing the impact of community colleges.   Debate about how to appropriately portray the impact of community colleges rages among scholars, practitioners, policy makers, and even accreditation agencies. The diversity of functions and programs offered by community colleges creates an overwhelmingly complex terrain for assessing outcomes without first recognizing that the students who seek higher education at community colleges are themselves extremely diverse. Community colleges serve students of traditional age and background as well as many more who are nontraditional in terms of their age, economic background, race/ethnicity, and prior experiences with the educational system. Unable to deal with such complexity, most researchers judge the value of a community college education through the lenses of the four-year college and university. From this perspective, student outcomes such as persistence, program completion, transfer, and post-program employment rise to the surface as of greatest importance. It is on these terms that a substantial body of evidence has accumulated, both lauding the openness and inclusivity of community colleges but also condemning them for inadequate results. Thus without fully considering the institution's unique and important characteristics, it is easy to cast the community college as a "second best" higher education institution (Zwerling, 1976).

While comparisons between community colleges and other forms of higher education are convenient and almost automatic, all too often they result in a portrayal of the community college as inadequate and even inferior because it does not measure up when a four-year college yardstick is used. Such simplistic comparisons are unfortunate because they undermine the community college as an important form of higher education with its own unique mission and agenda. Cursory comparisons between two-year and four-year higher education do not fully account for fundamental differences between these institutions. This is not to say community colleges are without fault or imperfection. Indeed, to advocate for community colleges without accounting for their liabilities as well as their assets perpetuates uncertainty about these institutions and clouds understanding of their present and future possibilities. Rather than advocate or make ill-informed judgments, we need to examine community colleges for their own intentions, functions and features to ascertain their actual and potential benefits.

An Overview of the Reader

Our goal in developing this new ASHE Reader was to provide a contextualized picture of community colleges, having their own history, their own place within the contemporary higher education system, and their own future trajectory. Our selections of readings do not place community colleges on a pedestal, nor do they attempt to condemn. They offer a rich array of perspectives, theoretical frameworks and research-based evidence drawn from quantitative and qualitative investigations to give readers a fuller understanding of these distinctive and increasingly pivotal institutions of higher education.

This Reader is different from any other ASHE Reader because it focuses on a specific institutional type—the community college. One of the reasons this book is so necessary is because other Readers that focus on higher education generally include few selections on community colleges, despite their enormous contribution to the higher education enterprise in the U.S. and their growing importance internationally. In fact, these institutions are barely visible in the core higher education journals (Townsend, Bragg, & Kinnick, 2002; Townsend, Donaldson, & Wilson, 2005). Thus, this Reader on community colleges is an important means to convey information about this institution to higher education scholars as well as practitioners.

The literature acknowledges the continuing evolution that has characterized the community college from its beginning. Far more than 13 years ago when the last ASHE Reader on the community college was compiled, the current literature continues historical, conceptual, and empirical work that enriches and deepens knowledge of these two-year institutions. Less afraid to question or critique than in earlier days, this literature offers greater depth and meaningful insights pertaining to organizational goals and structures, philosophical stances and viewpoints, curricular missions, and the characteristics and perspectives of faculty and students who are or should be engaged.

To best illustrate community colleges' present form and emphasize their currency, this book draws upon a few classic scholarly pieces but concentrates mostly on cutting-edge empirical research and valuable thought pieces. Our intent is to remind readers of what community colleges used to be and to give them a deeper and richer understanding of what the community college is becoming in the 21st century. Except for a couple of exceptional classic pieces, all selections in this Reader were published no earlier than 1995, and, in fact, well over half of the writings were published since 2000. A variety of research approaches as well as a diversity of voices and perspectives was chosen purposefully, ranging from structural functionalists to critical theorists. Though impossible to include all of the literature relevant to portraying the community college as it is now and how it may be in the future, the selections contained herein represent a sampling of some of the most valued knowledge and perspectives on the community college written to date.

This book is designed for two major audiences: (1) faculty and graduate students in courses that focus on the community college, and (2) individual scholars and practitioners who are interested in an overview of the community college. Master's and doctoral programs for general higher education administrators, community college faculty and administrators, and student affairs administrators can use the Reader to supplement various higher education courses. If used in a course that focuses specifically on the community college, it can be used in conjunction with the standard textbook for an introductory course on the community college such as Cohen and Brawer's (2003) *The American Community College*. Other texts that are likely companion texts are W. Norton Grubb's (1999), *Honored but Invisible*, and Barbara Townsend and Susan Twombly's (2001), *Community Colleges: Policy in the Future Context*. Because we anticipate these texts to be used by faculty offering graduate instruction on the community college, we chose not to include chapters from these volumes. Instead, we urge graduate faculty to use these texts because of their high compatibility with this book.

For the second group of individual scholars and practitioners, scholars new to the study of community colleges can learn about major issues dominating the study of community colleges and the diverse perspectives from which the institutions are viewed. Practitioners such as members of the American Association of Community Colleges (AACC), the Association of Community College Trustees (ACCT), and community college faculty and administrators can use the book to become acquainted with current research on the institutions in which they work. They can benefit from reading and understanding the wide range of perspectives associated with community colleges, from highly critical to neutral to complimentary. They can understand and appreciate more fully that not all research finds fault with the community college nor is the research consistently laudatory.

Method for Selecting Readings

Once our proposal was accepted by the ASHE board in the fall of 2004, we created an advisory board comprised of community college scholars and practitioners from throughout the country. Once selected, advisory board members selected from these groups were queried to nominate published works, primarily refereed journal articles and book chapters, to be included in the Reader. In addition the editors solicited nominations from other university faculty not members of the aforementioned groups, community college practitioners, and others known to be interested in research on community colleges.

In addition to these methods, the editors of this Reader conducted searches of the literature using multiple search engines and databases. Source material from these searches was combined with nominations from advisory board members to create an extensive list of possibilities. Each inclusion was read and given serious consideration, both to provide an overall, comprehensive understanding of the literature and to consider entries for this particular Reader. Also, from this comprehensive list, we were able to create logical schema for categorizing the literature that would make sense to various readers that we anticipated using the book. Through this iterative process that took place over nearly a six-month time period, the editors solicited, reviewed, and compiled successive rounds of source material into lists, until the final lists of selections that appear in this Reader were compiled into this book, organized by chapters of full-text, recommended and electronic resources.

Organization of the Reader

The reader is organized into six sections. The sections are sequenced as follows: (1) the varieties of community colleges; (2) theoretical perspectives on the community college; (3) institutional and systemic aspects of governance, finance, and administration; (4) the institution's curricular missions; (5) the characteristics, experiences, and perspectives of faculty; and (6) the diversity of students, including who they are, how they behave, and what outcomes they attain. Each section includes the full text of a small, select number of publications with an equal number and sometimes more recommended readings that were considered by the editors to be especially pertinent to the topic. Sometimes their inclusion as a full text was not possible simply because of copyright costs. In addition to these, the editors identified electronic resources that address the key themes of the Reader, including monographs, technical reports, conference papers, and other readings not widely available in text. By utilizing these various sources and media, we have attempted sought to compile a set of up-to-date and highly valuable publications on the community college. Each section of the Reader is described briefly below.

Section One: The Varieties of Community Colleges.   Three selections illustrate the variety of community colleges that exist in North America, showing how the idea of the U.S. community college evolved during the 20th century throughout the states and Canada. The section provides a description of the rich diversity that characterizes community colleges as unique higher education institutions with a firm commitment to expanding educational opportunity and educating students of different age, race/ethnic, cultural and economic backgrounds. Various classification schemes and models are discussed to show the range and breadth of two-year colleges operating in the U.S. The section also discusses two-year colleges dedicated to serving students with particular characteristics, cultures and interests such as Historically Black Colleges, Hispanic-Serving Colleges, Tribal Colleges, women's colleges, and religious colleges. The historical development of two-year colleges in Canada is the third selection in this section, portraying the structural, organizational, and operational decisions that resulted in an entirely new sector of postsecondary education in Canada. All selections in this section are conceptual and theoretical, often drawing upon history to provide context for this contemporary writing.

Section Two: Theoretical Perspectives.   This section presents six publications and additional recommended readings organized with an analytical framework proposed by Dougherty (1994) with four perspectives: functionalism, instrumental Marxism, institutionalist theory and state relative autonomy. Providing a historical perspective, the section begins with a classic piece by Burton Clark (1960) on cooling out to illustrate the functionalist perspective. In this seminal work, Clark posits that community colleges fulfill an essential function relative to universities, allowing four-year colleges to be selective. A second piece demonstrates the functionalism associated with the community college's vocational function of preparing future employees. The instrumental Marxist perspective offers the harshest criticism of community colleges, arguing that community colleges are instruments of the capitalist class to train the working class for low paid jobs, reserving space for elites in selective universities and ultimately high paid jobs. The institutionalist perspective is most evident in Brint and Karabel's (1989) *Diverted Dream* book where they portray a number of groups working in concert to vocationalize community colleges. Institutional factors play an important role in this argument, with criticism launched at advocates who unknowingly or unwillingly support a vocationalization agenda. State relative autonomy is the fourth perspective, observing some of the same phenomenon as Brint and Karabel (1989) but coming to the conclusion that political forces play an important role in explaining how community colleges have evolved. Two additional selections round out this section, one offering insights into the community college as a vehicle for enhancing access and social mobility, and the other offering insights into the community college's contemporary mission and foci at the end of the 21st century. Drawing heavily from the historical and philosophical literature, readings in this section offer insights into ways to conceive of the community college as its own unique institution.

Section Three: Governance, Finance, and Administration.   This section presents seven readings and a number of additional recommended readings that help characterize the community college according to the way it is governed, including modes of institutional governance; financed with public, private and individual funding; and administered, including internal governance. Concerns associated with ownership, referring to public or private control, are addressed as well as the fluidity with which state governance is changing as a result of growing enrollments and increasing state funding problems. Finance is considered from the standpoint of the federal, state and local governments as well as tuition and fees, private payments and contributions, endowments, and other sources. Student aid is treated as a separate issue because of its importance to students who are disadvantaged in relation to students attending public and private four-year institutions in terms of the amount of payment they receive. The rise of performance-based funding is another dimension of the discussion in this section; this approach to funding demonstrates ways states are attempting to control institutional behavior by tying funding more closely to outcomes. Issues and difficulties associated with performance-based funding are explored in this section, including the significant costs associated with documenting and distributing accountability data to external constituents and, more seriously, potential threats to the open access mission of the community college. Noting the complexity of external governance, this section also points out the complications of internal governance and administration. The wide range of organizational structures, institutional cultures, decision-making modalities, and staffing patterns that characterize community colleges is discussed in these selections and the recommended readings associated with this section. Drawn from conceptual and empirical literature, primarily large surveys, secondary analysis of existing data sets, and case studies, this section describes some of the essential elements of the inner workings and external relationships of the core operations of community colleges.

Section Four: Curricular Missions.   Nine selections appear in this section on the curricular missions of the community college, along with a good number of recommended publications. These readings are organized into four groupings, beginning with two selections that examine the alignment of community college curriculum with traditional undergraduate education, focusing on preparing students to transfer to the university or staying at the community college in pursuit of the bachelor's degree. These two writings offer insights into changes occurring in the transfer function, though the old definitions of transfer need to be reconsidered because of the realities of what students expect of higher education and how they actually experience it. The next two articles offer perspectives on curriculum associated with vocational education and other offerings available to students for noncredit. These conceptual pieces, drawing on historical but mostly public policy, consider how community colleges have evolved with respect to the comprehensive curriculum and how they can and should meet the needs of diverse learners. This section offers two readings on remedial and developmental education, considering the controversy that swirls around remedial education as a legitimate part of higher education. Both articles reference the negative stigma that remediation carries, and they examine the organization of remedial instruction and support services with respect to preparing students for college-level study. These articles also offer a micro perspective on curriculum by drawing upon extant literature for insights; one of these offers data from two cases conducted over an extensive amount of time. Finally three articles look deeper at curriculum, exploring courses, classrooms and alternative delivery modes to understand what community colleges do to promote teaching and learning and enhance access for students. All three of these pieces are empirical works conducted in the U.S., with one involving transcript analysis of a sizeable sample of students in a large urban community college system, another utilizing multiple methods in yet another urban community college, and the third based on a national survey of a random sample of community colleges across the country.

Section Five: Faculty.   The fifth section of this Reader focuses on faculty. The diverse selection of readings highlights the characteristics of faculty as both full-time and part-time, male and female, and white and non-white instructional employees of the community college. Chapters in this section portray faculty by disciplinary foci, particularly academic and vocational, and according to the instructional methods and assessment strategies they use. The characteristics and experiences of women and minority faculty are highlighted in selections included in full text and in the recommended readings. The extent to which faculty participate in faculty development and the amount of attention they pay to accessing the Internet is considered, as well as whether states require that faculty be formally prepared to teach and hold certification in their specialty field or in teaching, an issue particularly pertinent to faculty teaching highly technical subject matter. Though not plentiful, a number of quantitative and qualitative studies inform us about what is known about community college faculty, with older studies providing a framework for more recent research. For example, national datasets including data on two-year college faculty have been exploited by several researchers listed in this section, providing descriptive information about faculty and their work. More can be done with national datasets, particularly if they continue to be refined to fit the particulars of community college faculty. Thus the research reported in this section is promising because of its contributions to enriching understanding of a vital aspect of the community college, its faculty.

Section Six: Students.   The last section of the Reader emphasizes community college students in terms of who they are, how they experience college, and what benefits they attain from participation. Eight chapters appear in this section; additionally, several related readings are listed in Chapter 42 as recommended readings. Some readings in this section pay particular attention to the unique needs and experiences of racial and ethnically diverse students, including exploring ways 2-year higher education institutions organize and construct the learning experiences to address particular learning needs. The relationship between academics and the social aspects of a collegiate education are examined and in at least two selections particular programs and strategies are proposed for enhancing students' educational experiences and personal growth. Economic benefits are the focus of the next two chapters wherein the authors attempt to answer questions about the economic value of vocational certificates and degrees and how earnings vary by educational attainment. Earnings by gender and racial/ethnic origin are considered as well, with these studies showing positive benefits for women and African American men attending 2-year colleges. Finally, the section chapter looks at outcomes associated with 2-year college attendance on students' educational plans, academic performance, and personal growth. Results of these studies show some positive outcomes for women and minority males who attend 2-year colleges relative to their 4-year college counterparts, though some outcomes are superior for 4-year college students. This mixed picture leaves readers with ways in which 2-year and 4-year college students' outcomes differ, yet these results rarely account fully for the 2-year students' experiences and outcomes since the quantitative research that produced them is often limited by data that appear in national data sets that are themselves constructed with assumptions and definitions more consistent with 4-year than 2-year colleges.

What's Missing?

By combing the literature and considering its ability to speak to different aspects of the community college, we were able to survey and categorize the varied literature that has emerged, particularly over the past couple of decades. Though our claim is certainly not that we uncovered every written document on the community college, we feel relatively confident about the comprehensiveness of our search and about what it reveals about the historical development and contemporary status of the community college.

Through this undertaking, we learned not only about what appears in the literature but what is missing. Despite a growing body of literature, we were struck by how little is known about two-year colleges besides the comprehensive community college. For example, almost no literature portrays technical colleges, though a number of states dedicate substantial resources to technical education in these institutions. We were also surprised by how little is written about community colleges outside the United States. Some literature focuses on Canada, as various selections in this Reader show, but there is very little literature on two-year colleges outside North America, particularly literature that has an empirical base.

We also found that historical and philosophical writing about the community college tends to be sporadic and dominated by a few elite voices, generally white males in highly selective, often private universities. Increasingly, sociological, political, and economic lenses are used to portray the community college, but these writings are not plentiful. Many of them continue to fail to consider the community college as distinctive from four-year colleges and universities. After so many years of study of the community college, it is unfortunate that we still do not see research using multiple methods that would allow for the examination of the complex social impact of community colleges on the lives of their diverse student populations. This is not to say some studies of this type are not evident, but it is to say the field would benefit enormously if more were conducted.

Surprisingly, we had difficulties locating solid studies about the core administrative functions of the community college, including finance, governance and leadership. Almost no national research addresses these important and interrelated topics, relying on state-level studies and case studies, often single institution studies. Given the importance of finance and governance in particular, it is unfortunate that there are so few studies examining the federal perspective. It is equally frustrating to have so few multi-state analyses to learn about how different policies, structures, and approaches play out and impact various stakeholders of the system. Theoretical frameworks are limited but sorely needed to help describe and assess community colleges with respect to financing education, organizing and administering these educational institutions and leading curricular functions most central to their mission.

Though not at all adequate, other aspects of the community college mentioned in this Reader have gained more attention as the subject of research and scholarly writing. For example, various curricular missions, including transfer and vocational education, have been the focus of quantitative and qualitative studies on the national, state, and local levels. Studies of faculty and students grounded in a range of methodological approaches, particularly national surveys and case studies, are evident though not nearly as plentiful as we would like. It is unfortunate, however, that so much of the research on student outcomes positions community college students at a deficit in comparison to four-year students without adequately accounting for differences in personal and culture background. Even so, the extant research addressing these issues begins to establish a baseline of knowledge that can and should be expanded in the future. We urge researchers to tackle problems associated with the curriculum, faculty and students in ways that deepen understanding of the context and substance of the community college; we also urge them to pursue studies with sophisticated research designs that avoid the limitations of non-theoretical research and single-institution quantitative studies that continue to dominate the literature. National studies or multi-state investigations utilizing multivariate statistical designs, and qualitative or mixed-method comparative case study designs are needed to provide additional insights into how the community college works and how it operates the teaching and learning process, and how it impacts students and other stakeholders. These types of investigations were identified by Bailey and Alfanso's (2005) review of literature on program effectiveness pertaining to student persistence and completion. Critical of the dominant use of student integration or engagement theories, these authors call for theories attentive to the particular characteristics of community college students and programmatic responses of community colleges rather than the traditional-age university students for which these theories were originally designed.

Conclusion

More than ever, we are knowledgeable about the growing scope and depth of the literature on the community college. Without question there has been an enormous growth of published material since the last *ASHE Reader on Community Colleges* was reissued in 1994. Though gaps remain in the knowledge base, the amount and more importantly the quality of the literature on the community college has advanced. Still, even with richer detail and substance, questions remain unanswered, as they probably always will, about these uniquely distinctive higher education institutions. It is our hope that the contents of this Reader reveal much of the essence of what is known about the community college up to this point in time, revealing them to be distinctive higher education institutions devoted to the education and training of a vast number of diverse students in the United States and around the world. While some questions are answered by the conceptual and empirical works illustrated in this Reader, others remain obscured, awaiting attention from the students and scholars of the higher education community. Given the charge of the ASHE Board for which we are enormously grateful, we hope our goals of stimulating understanding, encouraging additional research, and enhancing possibilities for improved practice through the production of a well-researched volume on the community college has been fulfilled. We encourage its use to enhance teaching and learning for and about the community college, and we take pride in our accomplishment.

References

Adelman, C. (1996, October 4). The truth about remedial work. *Chronicle of Higher Education,* p. A56.

Bailey, T. R., & Alfanso, M. (2005). *Paths to persistence: An analysis of research on program effectiveness at community colleges.* New York: Community College Research Center, Teachers College, Columbia University.

Bogue, J. (1956). *American junior colleges.* Washington, D.C.: American Council on Education.

Brint, S., & Karabel, J. (1989). *The diverted dream: Community colleges and the promise of educational opportunity in America: 1900–1985.* New York: Oxford University Press.

Carnegie Commission on Higher Education. (1974). *A digest of reports of the Carnegie Commission on Higher Education.* New York: McGraw Hill.

Clark, B. (1960). The open door college. New York: McGraw-Hill.

Cohen, A., & Brawer, F. (2003). *The American community college* (4th ed.). San Francisco: Jossey-Bass.

Dougherty, K. J. (1994). *The contradictory college.* Albany, NY: SUNY Press.

Eells, W. C. (1931). *The junior college.* Boston: Houghton Mifflin.

Grubb, W. N. & Associates. (1999). *Honored but invisible.* New York: Routledge.

National Center for Education Statistics. (1996). *Remedial education at higher education institutions in fall 1995.* Washington, D.C.: Office of Educational Research and Improvement, U.S. Department of Education.

National Center for Education Statistics. (1999). *Integrated postsecondary education data system (IPEDS) fall enrollment survey.* Washington, D.C.: U.S. Department of Education.

Phillippe, K., & Patton, M. (2000). *National profile of community colleges: Trends and statistics* (3rd ed.). Washington, D.C.: American Association of Community Colleges.

Townsend, B. (2001). Redefining the community college transfer mission. *Community College Review, 29*(1), 29–42.

Townsend, B., & Twombly, S. (Ed.). (2001). *Community colleges: Policy in the future context.* Westport, CT: Ablex Publishers.

Townsend, B., Bragg, D., & Kinnick, M. (2002). Who writes the most about community colleges? An analysis of selected academic and practitioner-oriented journals. *Community College Journal of Research and Practice, 27,* 41–49.

Townsend, B. K., Donaldson, J., & Wilson, T. (2005). Marginal or monumental? Visibility of community colleges in selected higher education journals. *Community College Journal of Research and Practice, 29*(2), 123–135.

U.S. President's Commission on Higher Education. (1948). *Higher education for democracy.* New York: Harper Bros. Originally released on December 11, 1947.

Part I

THE VARIETIES OF COMMUNITY COLLEGES

INTRODUCTION

BERTA VIGIL LADEN

At the beginning of the twenty-first century, United States and Canadian community colleges continue to exemplify the historic core values embedded in their mission statements to provide educational access and opportunity within their communities to all residents who wish to benefit from their extensive curricular offerings. In the U.S., approximately 1,200 community colleges currently enroll approximately 40 percent of all students and approximately half of all students from diverse racial and ethnic backgrounds enrolled in postsecondary institutions. As has been the case since their emergence at the turn of the twentieth century as a new type of postsecondary system, the American community colleges serve as a vital gateway and entry access point into higher education for a vast number of individuals, particularly increasingly so for women and students of color.[1] In the mid 1960s, Canadian provincial governments responded to the post World War II population explosion and the public's demand for greater access to mass education by creating community colleges in their jurisdictions. Forty years later, there are 176 community colleges across Canada's ten provinces and two territories.[2] Like their American counterparts, Canadian colleges also enroll over a third (34%) of all students who attend higher education institutions.[3]

As the concept of the community colleges has expanded across North America, so has the variety of how they have evolved in response to community needs and demands. The three selections offered in Part I of this Reader illustrate some of the rich diversity and differentiation that has emerged among community colleges in the U.S. and Canada in their continuing efforts to expand educational opportunity and better serve and educate their students.

The first selection, Chapter 1, is by Rebecca D. Cox and Alexander C. McCormick. It is the final chapter from a New Directions in Community Colleges volume entitled *Classification Systems for Two-Year Colleges* (2003), which they edited. In this chapter, Cox and McCormick offer an overview of the five proposed classification models of two-year colleges presented in earlier chapters of the volume and discuss the practical results and implications of the models as applied to a common sample of colleges. The authors note that while the movement to establish classification schemes for two-year colleges is still in its infancy, their hope is that the models and the ensuring discussions will generate further development and application of such classification schemes. However, Cox and McCormick—who directs the Carnegie Classification of Higher Education Institutions—also warn that "the intent of classifying colleges is not to make quality judgments or to induce ambitions for colleges to change categories. This has been a thorny issue for the Carnegie Classification among four-year institutions, as particular categories are sometimes thought to imply institutional quality or status."[4] Nonetheless, the classification models reveal the breadth and range of colleges as they continue to offer innovative ways to provide access, retain, and assist their students to successfully achieve their educational and career goals.

Barbara K. Townsend introduces the next selection, Chapter 2, which is the first chapter of a book she edited entitled *Two-Year Colleges for Women and Minorities* (1999). In this chapter, Townsend provides a brief historical overview and patterns of two-year special focus colleges, distinctive institutions that strive to create a climate conducive to academic success for their students, namely, students who are often marginalized population groups in many higher education institutions. These include African American, Hispanic, Native American, women, and religious students. This chapter discusses the emergence, significance, and implications of such postsecondary institutions as Historically Black Colleges, Hispanic-Serving Colleges, Tribal Colleges, women's colleges, and religious colleges. Moreover, this publication as a whole represents a seminal effort to identify, describe, analyze the findings, and discuss the future of these unique institutions that had not been the subject of attention by most scholars until this publication. These special focus colleges, also increasingly referred to as Minority-Serving Institutions, are finally receiving much greater attention by researchers.

In Chapter 3, Paul Gallagher and John D. Dennison introduce Canada's college system in an article that is part of a special edition of the *Community College Journal of Research and Practice* focused on Canada. Gallagher, a former college president in British Columbia, and Dennison, professor emeritus, combine their expertise to present an overview of the distinct public polices in each province that led to the creation of the colleges. The authors offer insights into the provincial underpinnings and structural, organizational, and operational decisions that resulted in the development of an entirely new sector of postsecondary education in Canada. Gallagher and Dennison discuss the five models that emerged across the provinces and how each developed since their founding. How the American model was considered in the different provinces, then adopted or adapted, varied considerably. The

authors reveal how contextual factors, like the influence of universities or specific politically inclined individuals, influenced the college models that finally emerged in each province and how each subsequently developed. Canada's colleges today are much more diverse in light of such influences as partnerships and collaborations with universities and industry, emergence of applied degrees, and the development of college-university models on shared campuses.

These three selections are by no means meant to be definitive representations of the variety of community colleges that exist, either in North America, or elsewhere, but to serve as illustrations of how the idea of the American community college born at the end of the nineteenth century has evolved over a hundred years later. Thus, also included in Chapter 4 are other relevant readings that can be found on the Internet and offer additional perspectives.

[1] Laden, B. V. Introduction. In B. V. Laden (Ed.), *Serving Minority Populations.* New Directions for Community Colleges, 127, Fall 2004.

[2] Orton, L. *A new understanding of postsecondary education in Canada: A discussion paper.* Statistics Canada, September 2003.

[3] Statistics Canada. *Community college postsecondary enrollment by provinces and territories.* Catalogue No. 81-229XIB. Statistics Canada, 2004.

[4] McCormick, A. C. & Cox, R. D. Classifying two-year colleges: Purposes, possibilities, and pitfalls. In *Classification systems for two-year colleges*, Cox, R. D. & McCormick, A. L. (Eds.). New Directions for Community Colleges, 122, Summer 2003, p. 9.

CHAPTER 1

CLASSIFICATION IN PRACTICE: APPLYING FIVE PROPOSED CLASSIFICATION MODELS TO A SAMPLE OF TWO-YEAR COLLEGES

REBECCA D. COX, ALEXANDER C. MCCORMICK

This chapter illustrates the practical results of the five classification proposals. Each classification model has been applied to a common sample of colleges, and the authors review the key implications of this collective exercise.

In the interest of presenting a practical illustration of the five proposed classification models, each was applied to a randomly-selected set of two-year colleges. The resulting categorizations are presented in Exhibits 1.1 through 1.6, and offer the opportunity to compare and contrast the way each classification scheme arrays the colleges.

Exhibit 1.1 provides an overview of the five proposals, identifying the actual classifications that individual colleges would receive under each of the five schemes. In conjunction with the other exhibits in this chapter, which display the distinct groupings that result from each proposal, it illuminates additional practical complications of the classification enterprise. The intent is to provide a concrete illustration of the proposed models, calling attention to points of convergence and divergence, thereby suggesting directions for further conceptualization and refinement. This chapter summarizes several issues that have emerged in this analysis.

The set of 114 colleges selected for this exercise is a sample of public and private degree-granting Title IV–eligible two-year colleges drawn from the Integrated Postsecondary Education Data System (IPEDS) of the U.S. Department of Education's National Center for Education Statistics. These 80 public and 34 private colleges comprise a common sample for putting each classification model into practice. Exhibit 1.1 lists only the 64 public institutions that could be classified in all schemes and the 30 private colleges categorized by the two schemes that included private colleges. The other exhibits contain every sampled college that could be classified.

EXHIBIT 1.1

A Comparison of Illustrative Classifications (Arranged Alphabetically by Control)

Institution	State	Katsinas (Chapter Two)	Schuyler (Chapter Three)	Cohen (Chapter Four)	Merisotis and Shedd (Chapter Five)	Shaman and Zemsky (Chapter Six)
Public Institutions						
Belleville Area College	IL	Public: suburban, multicampus	Large liberal arts	Large	Community megaconnector	Mixed focus
Belmont Technical College	OH	Public: rural, small	Small and medium	Small	Community connector	Degree focus
Bismarck State College	ND	Public: rural, small	Small and medium	Medium	Community connector	Degree focus
Cape Cod Community College	MA	Public: rural, large	Small and medium	Medium	Community connector	Course focus
Carl Sandburg College	IL	Public: rural, large	Small and medium	Small	Community connector	Mixed focus
Central Piedmont Community College	NC	Public: urban, multicampus	Large liberal arts	Large	Community megaconnector	Course focus
Chattanooga State Technical Community College	TN	Public: urban, single-campus	Large liberal arts	Large	Community megaconnector	Course focus
Chesapeake College	MD	Public: rural, small	Small and medium	Small	Community connector	Course focus
Cincinnati State Technical and Community College	OH	Public: urban, single-campus	Small and medium	Large	Community connector	Mixed focus
College of Marin	CA	Public: suburban, multicampus	Large liberal arts	Large	Community megaconnector	Course focus
Community College of Rhode Island	RI	Public: suburban, multicampus	Large liberal arts	Large	Community megaconnector	Course focus
Cuesta College	CA	Public: rural, large	Large liberal arts	Large	Community megaconnector	Mixed focus
Danville Area Community College	IL	Public: rural, large	Small and medium	Small	Community connector	Mixed focus
Eastern Iowa Community College District	IA	Public: urban, multicampus	Small and medium	Large	Community connector	Degree focus
Fayetteville Technical Community College	NC	Public: rural, large	Large liberal arts	Large	Community megaconnector	Mixed focus
Germanna Community College	VA	Public: rural, large	Small and medium	Medium	Community connector	Course focus
Hawaii Community College	HI	Public: rural, small	Small and medium	Small	Community connector	Degree focus
Helena College of Technology of University of Montana	MT	Public: rural, small	Small and medium	Small	Community development and career	Degree focus
Henry Ford Community College	MI	Public: suburban, multicampus	Large liberal arts	Large	Community megaconnector	Course focus
Hocking Technical College	OH	Public: rural, large	Small and medium	Medium	Community connector	Degree focus
Holyoke Community College	MA	Public: rural, large	Small and medium	Medium	Community connector	Mixed focus
Jefferson Davis Community College	AL	Public: rural, small	Small and medium	Small	Community connector	Degree focus
Jefferson State Community College	AL	Public: suburban, single-campus	Small and medium	Medium	Community connector	Course focus
John Wood Community College	IL	Public: rural, small	Small and medium	Small	Community connector	Degree focus
Kellogg Community College	MI	Public: rural, large	Small and medium	Medium	Community megaconnector	Degree focus

College	State	Type		Size	Function	Focus
Labette Community College	KS	Public: rural, small	Small and medium	Small	Community connector	Mixed focus
Lenoir Community College	NC	Public: rural, small	Small and medium	Small	Community connector	Degree focus
Linn-Benton Community College	OR	Public: rural, large	Small and medium	Medium	Community megaconnector	Mixed focus
Lower Columbia College	WA	Public: rural, large	Small and medium	Medium	Community connector	Degree focus
Mercer County Community College	NJ	Public: suburban, multicampus	Large liberal arts	Large	Community megaconnector	Mixed focus
Metropolitan Community College Area	NE	Public: urban, multicampus	Large liberal arts	Large	Community megaconnector	Course focus
Mississippi Gulf Coast Community College	MS	Public: rural, small	Large liberal arts	Large	Community megaconnector	Mixed focus
Monroe Community College	NY	Public: urban, multicampus	Large liberal arts	Large	Community megaconnector	Degree focus
Montgomery Community College	NC	Public: rural, small	Small and medium	Small	Community development and career	Degree focus
Napa Valley College	CA	Public: suburban, single-campus	Large liberal arts	Medium	Community megaconnector	Mixed focus
Nassau Community College	NY	Public: suburban, single-campus	Large liberal arts	Large	Community megaconnector	Degree focus
New Hampshire Community Technical College-Manchester/Stratham	NH	Public: rural, large	Small and medium	Medium	Community connector	Course focus
New Hampshire Community Technical College-Nashua	NH	Public: rural, small	Small and medium	Small	Community development and career	Degree focus
New Mexico Military Institute	NM	Special-use institutions	Small and medium	Small	Community development and career	Degree focus
North Lake College	TX	Public: urban, multicampus	Small and medium	Large	Community megaconnector	Course focus
Northeastern Junior College	CO	Public: rural, large	Small and medium	Medium	Community megaconnector	Course focus
Northwestern Connecticut Community-Technical College	CT	Public: suburban, single-campus	Small and medium	Small	Community connector	Mixed focus
Norwalk Community-Technical College	CT	Public: suburban, single-campus	Small and medium	Medium	Community connector	Course focus
Oklahoma City Community College	OK	Public: urban, single-campus	Large liberal arts	Large	Community megaconnector	Course focus
Pierce College	WA	Public: suburban, single-campus	Small and medium	Large	Community megaconnector	Mixed focus
Pulaski Technical College	AR	Public: suburban, single-campus	Small and medium	Medium	Community connector	Course focus
Reid State Technical College	AL	Public: rural, small	Small and medium	Small	Community development and career	Degree focus
Rend Lake College	IL	Public: rural, large	Small and medium	Medium	Community megaconnector	Degree focus
Rock Valley College	IL	Public: rural, large	Large liberal arts	Large	Community megaconnector	Degree focus
Saint Johns River Community College	FL	Public: suburban, single-campus	Small and medium	Medium	Community connector	Course focus

EXHIBIT 1.1 (Continued)

A Comparison of Illustrative Classifications (Arranged Alphabetically by Control)

Institution	State	Katsinas (Chapter Two)	Schuyler (Chapter Three)	Cohen (Chapter Four)	Merisotis and Shedd (Chapter Five)	Shaman and Zemsky (Chapter Six)
Southwest Mississippi Community College	MS	Public: rural, small	Small and medium	Small	Community connector	Degree focus
Southwest Virginia Community College	VA	Public: rural, large	Small and medium	Medium	Community connector	Mixed focus
Spokane Falls Community College	WA	Public: urban, multicampus	Large liberal arts	Large	Community megaconnector	Course focus
Springfield Technical Community College	MA	Public: urban, single-campus	Large liberal arts	Large	Community connector	Mixed focus
Texarkana College	TX	Public: rural, large	Small and medium	Medium	Community connector	Mixed focus
Three Rivers Community-Technical College	CT	Public: suburban, single-campus	Small and medium	Medium	Community connector	Mixed focus
Treasure Valley Community College	OR	Public: rural, small	Small and medium	Small	Community connector	Mixed focus
Trenholm State Technical College	AL	Public: rural, small	Small and medium	Small	Community development and career	Degree focus
Tri-County Technical College	SC	Public: rural, large	Small and medium	Medium	Community connector	Degree focus
Trinity Valley Community College	TX	Public: rural, large	Small and medium	Medium	Community connector	Degree focus
University of Pittsburgh-Titusville	PA	Public: rural, small	Small and medium	Small	Community development and career	Course focus
Vernon Regional Junior College	TX	Public: rural, small	Small and medium	Small	Community connector	Degree focus
Volunteer State Community College	TN	Public: rural, large	Large liberal arts	Large	Community connector	Course focus
Western Oklahoma State College	OK	Public: rural, small	Small and medium	Small	Community connector	Course focus
Private Institutions						
Cambria Rowe Business College	PA	Private, proprietary	—	—	Career connector	—
Chatfield College	OH	Private, nonprofit	—	—	Connector	—
Denver Academy of Court Reporting-Main Campus	CO	Private, proprietary	—	—	Career connector-	—
ECPI College of Technology	VA	Private, proprietary	—	—	Career connector	—
Ellis Hospital School of Nursing	NY	Special-use institutions	—	—	Allied health	—
Gallipolis Career College	OH	Private, proprietary	—	—	Career connector	—
Hallmark Institute of Technology	TX	Private, proprietary	—	—	Career connector	—
Helene Fuld College of Nursing	NY	Special-use institutions	—	—	Allied health	—
Hesston College	KS	Private, nonprofit	—	—	Connector	—

Institution	State	Type				Connector
Indiana Business College	IN	Private, proprietary	—	—	—	Career connector
Interboro Institute	NY	Private, proprietary	—	—	—	Career connector
ITT Technical Institute	OH	Private, proprietary	—	—	—	Career connector
ITT Technical Institute	TX	Private, proprietary	—	—	—	Career connector
Lincoln Technical Institute	PA	Private, proprietary	—	—	—	Career connector
Mary Holmes College	MS	Private, nonprofit	—	—	—	Connector
Morrison Institute of Technology	IL	Special-use institutions	—	—	—	Connector
Mountain West College-Salt Lake City	UT	Private, proprietary	—	—	—	Career connector
Newport Business Institute	PA	Private, proprietary	—	—	—	Career connector
Nielsen Electronics Institute	SC	Private, proprietary	—	—	—	Career connector
Plaza Business Institute	NY	Private, proprietary	—	—	—	Career connector
Ranken Technical College	MO	Private, nonprofit	—	—	—	Connector
Rochester Business Institute	NY	Private, proprietary	—	—	—	Career connector
Saint Catharine College	KY	Private, nonprofit	—	—	—	Connector
Southern College	FL	Private, proprietary	—	—	—	—
Southwest School of Electronics	TX	Private, proprietary	—	—	—	Career connector
Spartanburg Methodist College	SC	Private, proprietary	—	—	—	Connector
Triangle Tech Incorporated-Dubois	PA	Private, proprietary	—	—	—	Career connector
Trocaire College	NY	Private, nonprofit	—	—	—	Connector
Utica School of Commerce	NY	Private, proprietary	—	—	—	Career connector
Wyoming Technical Institute	WY	Private, proprietary	—	—	—	Career connector

Note: Exhibit includes only institutions that could be classified in all relevant schemes.

TABLE 1.2
Illustrative Classification Corresponding to Katsinas's Proposal in Chapter Two
(Arranged Alphabetically by State and College Name)

I. Publicly Controlled Institutions
Rural, Small

Jefferson Davis Community College	AL
Reid State Technical College	AL
Trenholm State Technical College	AL
Lassen Community College	CA
Hawaii Community College	HI
John Wood Community College	IL
Ivy Tech State College-Wabash Valley	IN
Labette Community College	KS
Ashland Community College	KY
Owensboro Community College	KY
Chesapeake College	MD
Mississippi Gulf Coast Community College	MS
Southwest Mississippi Community College	MS
Helena College of Technology of University of Montana	MT
Montana State University College of Technology-Billings	MT
Montana Tech College of Technology	MT
Lenoir Community College	NC
Montgomery Community College	NC
Bismarck State College	ND
New Hampshire Community Technical College-Nashua	NH
Belmont Technical College	OH
Western Oklahoma State College	OK
Treasure Valley Community College	OR
University of Pittsburgh-Titusville	PA
Vernon Regional Junior College	TX

Rural, Large

Cuesta College	CA
Northeastern Junior College	CO
Carl Sandburg College	IL
Danville Area Community College	IL
Rend Lake College	IL
Rock Valley College	IL
Cape Cod Community College	MA
Holyoke Community College	MA
Kellogg Community College	MI
Fayetteville Technical Community College	NC
New Hampshire Community Technical College-Manchester/Stratham	NH
University of New Mexico-Gallup Campus	NM
Hocking Technical College	OH
Linn-Benton Community College	OR
Tri-County Technical College	SC
Volunteer State Community College	TN
Texarkana College	TX
Trinity Valley Community College	TX
Germanna Community College	VA
Southwest Virginia Community College	VA
Community College of Vermont	VT
Lower Columbia College	WA

TABLE 1.2 (*Continued*)
Illustrative Classification Corresponding to Katsinas's Proposal in Chapter Two
(Arranged Alphabetically by State and College Name)

Suburban, Single-Campus

Jefferson State Community College	AL
Pulaski Technical College	AR
Napa Valley College	CA
Northwestern Connecticut Community-Technical College	CT
Norwalk Community-Technical College	CT
Three Rivers Community-Technical College	CT
Saint Johns River Community College	FL
Nassau Community College	NY
Pierce College	WA

Suburban, Multicampus

College of Marin	CA
Belleville Area College	IL
Montgomery College of Germantown	MD
Henry Ford Community College	MI
Mercer County Community College	NJ
Community College of Rhode Island	RI

Urban, Single-Campus

Ventura College	CA
Springfield Technical Community College	MA
Cincinnati State Technical And Community College	OH
Oklahoma City Community College	OK
Northampton County Area Community College	PA
Chattanooga State Technical Community College	TN

Urban, Multicampus

Columbia College	CA
Porterville College	CA
San Diego Miramar College	CA
Eastern Iowa Community College District	IA
Dundalk Community College	MD
Central Piedmont Community College	NC
Metropolitan Community College Area	NE
Monroe Community College	NY
North Lake College	TX
Salt Lake Community College	UT
Spokane Falls Community College	WA

II. Privately Controlled Institutions
Nonprofit

Hesston College	KS
Saint Catharine College	KY
Ranken Technical College	MO
Mary Holmes College	MS
Trocaire College	NY
Chatfield College	OH

TABLE 1.2 (Continued)
Illustrative Classification Corresponding to Katsinas's Proposal in Chapter Two
(Arranged Alphabetically by State and College Name)

Proprietary

Heald College Schools of Business and Technology-Hayward	CA
Denver Academy of Court Reporting-Main Campus	CO
Southern College	FL
Indiana Business College	IN
Institute of Electronic Technology	KY
Mid-State College	ME
Interboro Institute	NY
Plaza Business Institute	NY
Rochester Business Institute	NY
Utica School of Commerce	NY
Gallipolis Career College	OH
ITT Technical Institute	OH
Cambria Rowe Business College	PA
Lincoln Technical Institute	PA
Newport Business Institute	PA
Triangle Tech Incorporated-Dubois	PA
Nielsen Electronics Institute	SC
Spartanburg Methodist College	SC
Hallmark Institute of Technology	TX
ITT Technical Institute	TX
Southwest School of Electronics	TX
Mountain West College-Salt Lake City	UT
ECPI College of Technology	VA
Wyoming Technical Institute	WY

III. Federally Chartered and Special-Use Institutions[a]

Special-Use Institutions

Morrison Institute of Technology	IL
Mid-America College of Funeral Service	IN
New Mexico Military Institute	NM
Ellis Hospital School of Nursing	NY
Helene Fuld College of Nursing	NY

[a]There were no tribal colleges in this sample.

Defining Boundaries

Ultimately, all five schemes are consistent in defining the two-year college sector with two mutually exclusive categories: public and private. Three proposals do so by excluding the private colleges altogether, while the two that include private colleges—both proprietary and nonprofit—explicitly differentiate them from the public colleges. Despite this consensus, the issue of boundaries is not entirely resolved. Phillippe and Boggs note that the AACC definitions require that community colleges be regionally accredited. Acknowledging the importance of including the wider universe of two-year colleges, they assert that accreditation status should be an important consideration in classification. Another question of definition is illustrated by

the categorization of the New Mexico Military Institute (NMMI). Katsinas's model identifies NMMI as a "special-use institution," although in the rest of the models NMMI is grouped with other public colleges. Katsinas's separation of NMMI from the rest of the public colleges in the sample raises questions of whether, or in what ways, NMMI and similar institutions are comparable to the other public colleges.

Phillippe and Boggs suggest an additional way of approaching the public-private divide. They contend that classification by organizational structure is especially useful for state-level policymaking, but not in isolation from categorization based on colleges' curricular or programmatic offerings. Programmatic categories, they assert, could help distinguish the colleges within the "special-use" class. Indeed,

TABLE 1.3
**Illustrative Classification Corresponding to Schuyler's Proposal in
Chapter Three (Arranged Alphabetically by State and College Name)**

Small and Medium

College	State
Jefferson Davis Community College	AL
Jefferson State Community College	AL
Reid State Technical College	AL
Trenholm State Technical College	AL
Pulaski Technical College	AR
Columbia College	CA
Lassen Community College	CA
Porterville College	CA
Northeastern Junior College	CO
Northwestern Connecticut Community-Technical College	CT
Norwalk Community-Technical College	CT
Three Rivers Community-Technical College	CT
Saint Johns River Community College	FL
Hawaii Community College	HI
Eastern Iowa Community College District	IA
Carl Sandburg College	IL
Danville Area Community College	IL
John Wood Community College	IL
Rend Lake College	IL
Ivy Tech State College-Wabash Valley	IN
Labette Community College	KS
Ashland Community College	KY
Owensboro Community College	KY
Cape Cod Community College	MA
Holyoke Community College	MA
Chesapeake College	MD
Dundalk Community College	MD
Montgomery College of Germantown	MD
Kellogg Community College	MI
Southwest Mississippi Community College	MS
Helena College of Technology of University of Montana	MT
Montana State University College of Technology-Billings	MT
Montana Tech College of Technology	MT
Lenoir Community College	NC
Montgomery Community College	NC
Bismarck State College	ND
New Hampshire Community Technical College-Manchester/Stratham	NH
New Hampshire Community Technical College-Nashua	NH
New Mexico Military Institute	NM
University of New Mexico-Gallup Campus	NM
Belmont Technical College	OH
Cincinnati State Technical and Community College	OH
Hocking Technical College	OH
Western Oklahoma State College	OK
Linn-Benton Community College	OR
Treasure Valley Community College	OR
Northampton County Area Community College	PA
University of Pittsburgh-Titusville	PA
Tri-County Technical College	SC
North Lake College	TX

perhaps a consideration of the instructional programs at private colleges could inform the instructional classification of public ones. As Shaman and Zemsky suggest in their analysis, the two-year educational market encompasses multiple instructional services, blurring the lines between credit and noncredit or academic and occupational.

TABLE 1.3 (*Continued*)
Illustrative Classification Corresponding to Schuyler's Proposal in
Chapter Three (Arranged Alphabetically by State and College Name)

Texarkana College	TX
Trinity Valley Community College	TX
Vernon Regional Junior College	TX
Germanna Community College	VA
Southwest Virginia Community College	VA
Community College of Vermont	VT
Lower Columbia College	WA
Pierce College	WA
Large Liberal Arts	
College of Marin	CA
Cuesta College	CA
Napa Valley College	CA
San Diego Miramar College	CA
Ventura College	CA
Belleville Area College	IL
Rock Valley College	IL
Springfield Technical Community College	MA
Henry Ford Community College	MI
Mississippi Gulf Coast Community College	MS
Central Piedmont Community College	NC
Fayetteville Technical Community College	NC
Metropolitan Community College Area	NE
Mercer County Community College	NJ
Monroe Community College	NY
Nassau Community College	NY
Oklahoma City Community College	OK
Community College of Rhode Island	RI
Chattanooga State Technical Community College	TN
Volunteer State Community College	TN
Salt Lake Community College	UT
Spokane Falls Community College	WA

TABLE 1.4
Illustrative Classification Corresponding to Cohen's Proposal in
Chapter Four (Arranged Alphabetically by State and College Name)

Small	
Jefferson Davis Community College	AL
Reid State Technical College	AL
Trenholm State Technical College	AL
Northwestern Connecticut Community-Technical College	CT
Hawaii Community College	HI
Carl Sandburg College	IL
Danville Area Community College	IL
John Wood Community College	IL
Ivy Tech State College-Wabash Valley	IN
Labette Community College	KS
Chesapeake College	MD
Southwest Mississippi Community College	MS
Helena College of Technology of University of Montana	MT
Lenoir Community College	NC
Montgomery Community College	NC
New Hampshire Community Technical College-Nashua	NH
New Mexico Military Institute	NM
University of New Mexico-Gallup Campus	NM

TABLE 1.4 (*Continued*)
Illustrative Classification Corresponding to Cohen's Proposal in
Chapter Four (Arranged Alphabetically by State and College Name)

Belmont Technical College	OH
Western Oklahoma State College	OK
Treasure Valley Community College	OR
University of Pittsburgh-Titusville	PA
Vernon Regional Junior College	TX
Medium	
Jefferson State Community College	AL
Pulaski Technical College	AR
Napa Valley College	CA
Northeastern Junior College	CO
Norwalk Community-Technical College	CT
Three Rivers Community-Technical College	CT
Saint Johns River Community College	FL
Rend Lake College	IL
Cape Cod Community College	MA
Holyoke Community College	MA
Kellogg Community College	MI
Bismarck State College	ND
New Hampshire Community Technical College-Manchester/Stratham	NH
Hocking Technical College	OH
Linn-Benton Community College	OR
Northampton County Area Community College	PA
Tri-County Technical College	SC
Texarkana College	TX
Trinity Valley Community College	TX
Germanna Community College	VA
Southwest Virginia Community College	VA
Community College of Vermont	VT
Lower Columbia College	WA
Large	
College of Marin	CA
Cuesta College	CA
Ventura College	CA
Eastern Iowa Community College District	IA
Belleville Area College	IL
Rock Valley College	IL
Springfield Technical Community College	MA
Henry Ford Community College	MI
Mississippi Gulf Coast Community College	MS
Central Piedmont Community College	NC
Fayetteville Technical Community College	NC
Metropolitan Community College Area	NE
Mercer County Community College	NJ
Monroe Community College	NY
Nassau Community College	NY
Cincinnati State Technical and Community College	OH
Oklahoma City Community College	OK
Community College of Rhode Island	RI
Chattanooga State Technical Community College	TN
Volunteer State Community College	TN
North Lake College	TX
Salt Lake Community College	UT
Pierce College	WA
Spokane Falls Community College	WA

Functional Differences Among Classifications

Despite their shared focus on distinguishing colleges by enrollment and related characteristics, the proposals in other chapters have discrepant results when applied to the sample. For example, Cohen notes the importance of the curriculum in distinguishing community colleges, reiterating Schuyler's finding that the higher the enrollment, the larger the proportion of classes in the traditional liberal arts. This holds true for most, but not all, of the colleges sampled for this project. Four colleges designated as "large" colleges in terms of enrollment are not part of the "large liberal arts" category. What are the practical implications for Eastern Iowa Community College District, Cincinnati State Technical and Community College, North Lake College, and Pierce College? Do these four exceptions indicate a need for more precise categories?

Furthermore, comparison of Schuyler's proposal with Shaman and Zemsky's reveals distinct variance between the two conceptual

TABLE 1.5

Illustrative Classification Corresponding to Merisotis and Shedd's Proposal in Chapter Five (Arranged Alphabetically by State and College Name)

Community Development and Career Institutions	
Reid State Technical College	AL
Trenholm State Technical College	AL
Helena College of Technology of University of Montana	MT
Montgomery Community College	NC
New Hampshire Community Technical College-Nashua	NH
New Mexico Military Institute	NM
University of Pittsburgh-Titusville	PA
Community Connector Institutions	
Jefferson Davis Community College	AL
Jefferson State Community College	AL
Pulaski Technical College	AR
Lassen Community College	CA
Porterville College	CA
Northwestern Connecticut Community-Technical College	CT
Norwalk Community-Technical College	CT
Three Rivers Community-Technical College	CT
Saint Johns River Community College	FL
Hawaii Community College	HI
Eastern Iowa Community College District	IA
Carl Sandburg College	IL
Danville Area Community College	IL
John Wood Community College	IL
Labette Community College	KS
Cape Cod Community College	MA
Holyoke Community College	MA
Springfield Technical Community College	MA
Chesapeake College	MD
Dundalk Community College	MD
Southwest Mississippi Community College	MS
Lenoir Community College	NC
Bismarck State College	ND
New Hampshire Community Technical College-Manchester/Stratham	NH
Belmont Technical College	OH
Cincinnati State Technical and Community College	OH
Hocking Technical College	OH
Western Oklahoma State College	OK
Treasure Valley Community College	OR
Tri-County Technical College	SC
Volunteer State Community College	TN
Texarkana College	TX
Trinity Valley Community College	TX
Vernon Regional Junior College	TX
Germanna Community College	VA
Southwest Virginia Community College	VA
Lower Columbia College	WA

TABLE 1.5(*Continued*)
Illustrative Classification Corresponding to Merisotis and Shedd's Proposal in Chapter Five (Arranged Alphabetically by State and College Name)

Community Megaconnector Institutions

College of Marin	CA
Cuesta College	CA
Napa Valley College	CA
Northeastern Junior College	CO
Belleville Area College	IL
Rend Lake College	IL
Rock Valley College	IL
Henry Ford Community College	MI
Kellogg Community College	MI
Mississippi Gulf Coast Community College	MS
Central Piedmont Community College	NC
Fayetteville Technical Community College	NC
Metropolitan Community College Area	NE
Mercer County Community College	NJ
Monroe Community College	NY
Nassau Community College	NY
Oklahoma City Community College	OK
Linn-Benton Community College	OR
Community College of Rhode Island	RI
Chattanooga State Technical Community College	TN
North Lake College	TX
Pierce College	WA
Spokane Falls Community College	WA

Allied Health Institutions

Ellis Hospital School of Nursing	NY
Helene Fuld College of Nursing	NY

Connector Institutions

Morrison Institute of Technology	IL
Hesston College	KS
Saint Catharine College	KY
Ranken Technical College	MO
Mary Holmes College	MS
Trocaire College	NY
Chatfield College	OH
Spartanburg Methodist College	SC

Career Connector Institutions

Denver Academy of Court Reporting-Main Campus	CO
Southern College	FL
Indiana Business College	IN
Interboro Institute	NY
Plaza Business Institute	NY
Rochester Business Institute	NY
Utica School of Commerce	NY
ITT Technical Institute	OH
Gallipolis Career College	OH
Cambria Rowe Business College	PA
Lincoln Technical Institute	PA
Newport Business Institute	PA
Triangle Tech Incorporated-Dubois	PA
Nielsen Electronics Institute	SC
Hallmark Institute of Technology	TX
ITT Technical Institute	TX
Southwest School of Electronics	TX
Mountain West College-Salt Lake City	UT
ECPI College of Technology	VA
Wyoming Technical Institute	WY

Note: There were no certificate institutions in this sample.

approaches. For instance, of the eighteen colleges designated "large liberal arts" by Schuyler, eight are "course focus" colleges, seven are "mixed," and three are "degree focus," according to Shaman and Zemsky. A similar divergence appears in Merisotis and Shedd's approach.

Such differences in grouping patterns may be analytically instructive. Conversely, they may simply cause confusion. In examining the exhibits in this chapter, one reviewer noted that the classification of Fayetteville Technical Community College among "large liberal arts" colleges is entirely inconsistent with its statutory mission and would likely cause considerable consternation among its institutional or system leaders. This observation calls attention to the limitations of classification according to empirical criteria that substitute for the phenomenon of genuine interest. The classification serves as a simplification, but as Schuyler found, this can result in misclassifications in either direction (what in other applications might be called false positives and false negatives). One implication is that classification should not be confused with identity, nor should more authority be attributed to it than is justified by the underlying methodology. Thus classification according to site visits and intensive analysis—while not practical for a comprehensive classification—might justifiably claim greater authority.

However, examining each scheme simply to uncover contradictions is not particularly constructive. As Cohen notes, it is very likely that any *single* classification scheme will be deemed inadequate by community college stakeholders. In fact, none of the proposed classifications meet the full set of assessment criteria outlined in de los Santos's commentary. These categories do not offer nuanced descriptions of individual colleges; rather they function as heuristics for thinking about the entire landscape of two-year colleges. At this preliminary stage, the differences among these classifications and the patterns that emerge across schemes are important because they offer a foundation for the next iteration of the classification discussion.

Consider, for example, Shaman and Zemsky's "degree focus" classification. Within the sample of colleges selected for this volume, the size of the degree focus colleges varies: in Cohen's classification, eleven are "small," seven are "medium," and four are "large." A more telling pattern, however, arises from applying Katsinas's categories. With the exception of five

colleges in this sample, the "degree focus" colleges correspond to a single geographical designation: "rural." Is there something to be gained from this information—either about "degree focus" colleges or "rural" colleges?

Unfortunately, the most significant implications of this practical exercise are revealed by absences. Each classification is presented and critiqued with a fundamental caveat: adequate classification is severely compromised by the data currently available. In some instances, the goal of each classification scheme and the proxies relied on to circumvent the gaps in data are not tightly linked.

Even seemingly straightforward categories, such as rural, urban, or suburban setting, present complications. Katsinas mentions a few when explaining how he identified colleges serving "the urban core" of metropolitan areas, thereby distinguishing between urban and suburban colleges. Fundamentally, this is an issue of demographics—not only of each college's service area but also of the college's student population. In reporting findings from a large-scale study of community colleges, Vanessa Smith Morest (2003) describes two contrasting types of "urban" colleges. Her comparison of racial demographics of the community with those of the student population revealed that some colleges have a substantially greater proportion of white students enrolled than live in the surrounding area. Alternatively, in other colleges the pattern is reversed. Additional factors distinguish these "urban" colleges, including different access to resources and relationships to nearby four-year colleges. As a result, these two types of "urban" community colleges differ in multiple, significant ways. While Katsinas recognizes the differences among urban colleges and attempts to limit the definition to colleges that serve the "core" of America's central cities, his parameters do not address the interrelated matrix of demographics, funding, and four-year college proximity.

Even the potential simplicity of classification by size obscures the range of variation among two-year colleges. Although the cut-off numbers for small, medium, and large colleges used in the classification proposals create groups of roughly equal size, these three categories may need refinement. In particular, the "large" category encompasses colleges with student enrollments from 7,000 to nearly 30,000.

Every author included in this volume has noted shortcomings in the available data. The

TABLE 1.6

Illustrative Classification Corresponding to Shaman and Zemsky's Proposal in Chapter Six (Arranged Alphabetically by State and College Name)

Degree Focus

Jefferson Davis Community College	AL
Reid State Technical College	AL
Trenholm State Technical College	AL
Lassen Community College	CA
Hawaii Community College	HI
Eastern Iowa Community College District	IA
John Wood Community College	IL
Rend Lake College	IL
Rock Valley College	IL
Kellogg Community College	MI
Southwest Mississippi Community College	MS
Helena College of Technology of University of Montana	MT
Montana Tech College of Technology	MT
Lenoir Community College	NC
Montgomery Community College	NC
Bismarck State College	ND
New Hampshire Community Technical College-Nashua	NH
New Mexico Military Institute	NM
Monroe Community College	NY
Nassau Community College	NY
Belmont Technical College	OH
Hocking Technical College	OH
Northampton County Area Community College	PA
Tri-County Technical College	SC
Trinity Valley Community College	TX
Vernon Regional Junior College	TX
Lower Columbia College	WA

Mixed Focus

Columbia College	CA
Cuesta College	CA
Napa Valley College	CA
Northwestern Connecticut Community-Technical College	CT
Three Rivers Community-Technical College	CT
Belleville Area College	IL
Carl Sandburg College	IL
Danville Area Community College	IL
Ivy Tech State College-Wabash Valley	IN
Labette Community College	KS
Owensboro Community College	KY
Holyoke Community College	MA
Springfield Technical Community College	MA
Mississippi Gulf Coast Community College	MS
Fayetteville Technical Community College	NC
Mercer County Community College	NJ
Cincinnati State Technical and Community College	OH
Linn-Benton Community College	OR
Treasure Valley Community College	OR

TABLE 1.6 (*Continued*)
**Illustrative Classification Corresponding to Shaman and Zemsky's Proposal in
Chapter Six (Arranged Alphabetically by State and College Name)**

Texarkana College	TX
Salt Lake Community College	UT
Southwest Virginia Community College	VA
Pierce College	WA
Course Focus	
Jefferson State Community College	AL
Pulaski Technical College	AR
College of Marin	CA
Porterville College	CA
San Diego Miramar College	CA
Ventura College	CA
Northeastern Junior College	CO
Norwalk Community-Technical College	CT
Saint Johns River Community College	FL
Ashland Community College	KY
Cape Cod Community College	MA
Chesapeake College	MD
Dundalk Community College	MD
Montgomery College of Germantown	MD
Henry Ford Community College	MI
Central Piedmont Community College	NC
Metropolitan Community College Area	NE
New Hampshire Community Technical College-Manchester/Stratham	NH
University of New Mexico-Gallup Campus	NM
Oklahoma City Community College	OK
Western Oklahoma State College	OK
University of Pittsburgh-Titusville	PA
Community College of Rhode Island	RI
Chattanooga State Technical Community College	TN
Volunteer State Community College	TN
North Lake College	TX
Germanna Community College	VA
Community College of Vermont	VT
Spokane Falls Community College	WA

most often cited concerns include the need for adequate information on curricular offerings, including noncredit courses; funding structures, such as formulas for state and local appropriations; and characteristics of the communities that two-year colleges serve.

Indeed, the role of local contexts in shaping community colleges' missions, structures, and outcomes demands a more sophisticated database at the national level. In this regard, it is worth reiterating Bailey's remark, that if the classification process were to result in the collection of currently inaccessible data, "the process would represent a significant advance for research."

The movement to establish classification schemes for two-year colleges is in its infancy. The classification models assembled in this volume illustrate a range of possible approaches to the problem, each with strengths and weaknesses. The insights generated by the contributors offer an informed basis for the next stage of conceptualizing and refining the classification of two-year colleges.

References

Morest, V. S. *Community College Missions.* New York: Community College Research Center, Teachers College, Columbia University, 2003.

Rebecca D. Cox is a Ph.D. candidate in education at the University of California, Berkeley.

Alexander C. McCormick is a senior scholar at The Carnegie Foundation for the Advancement of Teaching, where he directs the Carnegie Classification of Institutions of Higher Education.

CHAPTER 2

COLLECTIVE AND DISTINCTIVE PATTERNS OF TWO-YEAR SPECIAL-FOCUS COLLEGES

BARBARA K. TOWNSEND

Within the constellation of approximately 1,500 American non-profit two-year colleges are clusters of schools that enroll women students only or primarily enroll black, Hispanic, or Native American students. These clusters include women's colleges, historically black and predominantly black colleges, tribal colleges and predominantly Native American colleges, and predominantly Hispanic institutions. Some of these colleges are also church-affiliated schools, where commitment to a particular Christian denomination guides service to the distinctive student body. As of 1996–1997, 97 institutions or about 7 percent of two-year schools enrolled women students only or had a student body numerically dominated by black, Hispanic, or Native Americans students (50 percent or more of the student enrollment).

These colleges comprise an intriguing and little studied phenomenon within higher education. Like most two-year schools, they expand educational access to non-traditional students. What differentiates these colleges from most two-year colleges is a focus on non-white students or on women only. Called special-focus colleges in this book, many of these, distinctive institutions strive to create a climate conducive to the academic success of their particular racial or ethnic student body or their all-female student body. Some of the colleges have even established a curriculum and use pedagogy designed specifically for their students. Although there are limited data about the outcomes of these schools, what evidence there is indicates that many have been quite successful in advancing their students' educational achievement. Coeducational, predominantly white institutions have much to gain from understanding what these special-focus colleges are and how they facilitate students' academic attainment.

This chapter profiles each of the four types of special-focus schools: (1) women's colleges, (2) historically black colleges and predominantly black institutions, (3) tribal colleges and predominantly Native American schools, and (4) predominantly Hispanic-serving institutions. The chapter also glances at approximately 150 other two-year schools whose student body is between 25 percent and 49 percent black, Hispanic, or Native American. These schools, known as black-serving, Hispanic-serving, and Native American-serving institutions,[1] deserve recognition because in them the isolating, stress-filled effect of being a minority is "less exaggerated" (Kanter, 1977, p. 209; see also Hurtado, 1994) in these schools than in colleges where almost all the students are white. Since church-affiliation has been a critical factor in the development of special-focus colleges, the chapter also includes a description of the few remaining church-affiliated special-focus colleges. How all these schools fit within the development of American higher education is then described. The chapter concludes with speculations about the future of each type of special-focus college.

Women's Colleges and Predominantly Female Schools

As of 1996–1997 there were 83 women's colleges, of which eight were two-year colleges. Collectively, these institutions (see Table 2.1) enrolled over 1,700 students in 1996–1997. Enrollments ranged from a low of 24 students at Assumption College for Sisters (a training institution for nuns) to a high of 459 in Peace College. Except for Assumption College, where 60 percent of its students were Asian or Pacific Islanders in 1996–1997, and Lexington College, where 50 percent of the students were nonwhite, two-year women's colleges have a predominantly white student body.

The ranks of two-year women's colleges have shifted somewhat since 1996–1997, with some colleges leaving and one entering. Among those leaving is St. Mary's College, which was founded in 1842 and established its junior college program in 1927. In 1996–1997 it only enrolled 142 women in its junior college program, so it closed this program and continues as a high school for girls. Leaders of the two Aquinas Colleges, both sponsored by the Congregation of Sisters of Saint Joseph, decided in 1997 to consolidate into one institution in order to save administrative costs. Peace College has changed into a four-year college, and Fisher College will become coeducational in fall 1998 and also establish a four-year degree program in management. However, Harcum College, a women's college that became coeducational in the 1970s, decided in 1997 to return to serving women students only. Thus, as of fall 1998, there will be only five women's two-year schools: Assumption College for Sisters, which is only for Catholic sisters; Aquinas College, with its two campuses; Cottey College; Harcum College; and Lexington College.

TABLE 2.1
Single-Sex Two-Year Schools in 1996–1997

School	State	Control
Women's Colleges		
Aquinas College at Milton	Massachusetts	Catholic
Aquinas College at Newton	Massachusetts	Catholic
Assumption College for Sisters	New Jersey	Catholic
Cottey College	Missouri	Private
Fisher College	Massachusetts	Private
Lexington College	Illinois	Private
Peace College	North Carolina	Presbyterian
St. Mary's College	North Carolina	Episcopalian
Men's Colleges		
Deep Springs College	California	Private
Don Bosco Technical Institute	California	Catholic
Mid-America Baptist Theological Seminary (specialized)	Tennessee	Southern Baptist
The Williamson Free School of Mechanical Trades	Pennsylvania	Private
Valley Forge Military College	Pennsylvania	Private

Although two-year colleges for men are not examined in this book, as of 1996–1997, there were five two-year colleges for men only, enrolling over 750 students (see Table 2.1). Enrollments ranged from a low of 24 students at Deep Springs College in Deep Springs, California, to a high of 254 at the Williamson Free School of Mechanical Trades in Media, Pennsylvania. Don Bosco Technical Institute, open only to graduates of Don Bosco Technical High School, is a predominantly Hispanic institution: in 1996–1997: 66 percent of its students were Hispanic. The Williamson Free School of Mechanical Trades, established in 1888, is the oldest, and the specialized Mid-America Baptist Theological Seminary, established in 1972, is the newest.

Historically Black Colleges, Predominantly Black Colleges, and Black-Serving Institutions

Several types of two-year institutions have a sizable enrollment of black students. The most obvious are the two-year historically black colleges, institutions established before 1965 as segregated schools. Another type is integrated institutions, including colleges which once primarily or only enrolled white students but now have a student body that is at least 50 percent black. This second type is labeled predominantly black institutions, to differentiate them from historically black colleges. Finally, there are black-serving institutions, where black students constitute between 25 to 49 percent of the students.

Established during the time when education was segregated in the south, two-year historically black colleges are clustered in the Southeast.[2] As of 1996–1997, there were nine two-year historically black colleges created before 1954, the year when the U.S. Supreme Court ruled that segregation in education was unconstitutional. Five more schools are also classified as historically black colleges even though they were created after 1954, because they were established in states which continued to maintain segregated schools (see Table 2.2). These five colleges include three public community colleges with one or more branch campuses that were once black two-year schools. For example, the Utica campus of Hinds Community College was once the site of the black Utica Junior College. Excluding these three institutions, as enrollment figures were not available by branch campuses, histor-

ically black colleges enrolled over 7,000 students in 1996–1997. Enrollments ranged from 191 at Lewis College of Business in Detroit, Michigan, to 1,701 in Lawson State Community College in Birmingham, Alabama. Not all of the students served by these schools are black. In the ten single-campus schools, the percentage of black students ranged from 21 percent at St. Philip's College to 97 percent at Lawson State. Thus St. Philips, officially an HBC, is not even a black-serving institution, for less than 25 percent of its student body is black. However, it is currently an Hispanic-serving institution, because 46 percent of its students in 1996–1997 were Hispanic.

In 1996–1997 the oldest existing two-year historically black college was Shorter College in North Little Rock, Arkansas. Founded as Bethel University in 1886, it became Shorter College in 1901. In 1955 it went from being a four-year school to a two-year school (*Shorter College Catalog*, 1994–1998). Unfortunately, the college lost its accreditation in spring 1997 and its survival is unsure ("Shorter College," April 24, 1998). The most recently established two-year single-campus historically black college is Lawson State Community College, founded in 1965 in Birmingham, Alabama. Additionally, another college, the Valley Street Campus of Gadsden State Community College in Gadsden, Alabama, was recognized in 1997 as an historically black college. It started in 1960 as a private vocational school.

In 1996–1997 there were also 26 predominantly-black institutions, colleges whose student body is at least 50 percent black. Collectively, these 26 institutions enrolled almost 100,000 students in 1996–1997, with the percentage of black students ranging from 51 percent to 95 percent. Three of these schools were also Hispanic-serving institutions: Bronx Community College in the City University of New York System, Compton Community College in California, and Roxbury Community College in Massachusetts. Individual enrollments ranged from 162 students at the specialized institution Long Island College School of Nursing in New York and 319 at the comprehensive Berean Institute in Pennsylvania to 11,696 at Prince George's Community College in Maryland. All are coeducational, with enrollment of women ranging from 42 percent to 96 percent. The oldest predominantly black school is Peirce College, founded in 1865, and the newest is Metropolitan Community College in East St. Louis, Illinois, established in 1996. The college is a replacement for State Community College, abol-

TABLE 2.2
Historically Black Two-Year Colleges in 1996–1997

School	State	Control
Bishop Community College, Carver Campus and Southwest Campus	Alabama	Public
Coahoma Community College	Mississippi	Public
Concordia College	Alabama	Private
Denmark Technical College	South Carolina	Public
J.F. Drake State Technical Institute	Alabama	Public
C.A. Fredd Campus, Shelton State Community College	Alabama	Public
Hinds Community College, Utica Campus	Mississippi	Public
Lawson State Community College	Alabama	Public
Lewis College of Business	Michigan	Private
Mary Holmes College	Mississippi	Private; Presbyterian
St. Philip's College	Texas	Public
Shorter College	Arkansas	Private; African Methodist Episcopal
Southern University, Shreveport, Bosier City Campus	Louisiana	Public
Trenholm State Technical College	Alabama	Public

ished in 1994 by vote of the citizens in its district. Predominantly black two-year schools are primarily in the Southeast (nine) and Mideast (nine) and are often located in major cities such as New York (three) and Chicago (three).

In predominantly black colleges and most historically black colleges, black students find themselves in the majority. In all other institutions they are in the minority but far less so in institutions labeled black-serving institutions, schools where black students constitute between 25 to 49 percent of the student body. There were 95 two-year black-serving institutions in 1996–1997, including five specialized institutions. Four of the black-serving institutions are also Hispanic-serving institutions: Borough of Manhattan Community College; Richard J. Daley College in Chicago; Los Angeles Trade-Technical College; and Mountain View College in Dallas, Texas. One institution, the private Kelsey Junior College in California, is also a predominantly Hispanic school.

Collectively, these institutions enrolled over 330,000 students in 1996–1997. Two private schools had the lowest enrollments: 79 at the specialized Commonwealth Institute of Federal Service in Texas, and 202 at the private comprehensive Kemper Military School and College in Missouri. The highest enrollments were at public institutions: 16,186 at City University of New York's Borough of Manhattan Community College, and 18,713 students at Community College of Philadelphia.

All the black-serving institutions are coeducational, with female enrollments ranging from 3 percent at the Franklin Institute to 79 percent at Martin Community College in North Carolina. The oldest private black-serving institution is Kemper Military School and College, founded in 1844; the oldest public one is Middle Georgia College, founded in 1884. The most recently founded black-serving institution is Arkansas's Mid-South Community College, founded in 1993. Almost 70 percent of the schools were founded since 1960. Since blacks constitute the largest minority group in the South (Nettles, 1991), over half (52) are located in the Southeast or in contiguous states.

Predominantly Hispanic and Hispanic-Serving Institutions

There are two categories of schools with a large Hispanic enrollment: predominantly Hispanic schools, whose student body is 50 percent or more Hispanic, and Hispanic-serving institutions, whose enrollment is between 25 percent and 49 percent Hispanic.

During the 1996–1997 academic year, there were 21 predominantly Hispanic schools (see Table 2.3), with a collective enrollment of over 175,000 students. Hispanic enrollment in these schools ranged from 52 percent at Delmar College in Texas to 95 percent at St. Augustine's College in Illinois. As indicated earlier, one of the schools, Kelsey Junior college in California, is also a black-serving institution. All but one predominantly Hispanic school are coeducational, with the enrollment of women ranging from 47

percent at Texas State Technical College to 79 percent at Hostos Community College of City University of New York in the Bronx. Kelsey Junior College is the oldest predominantly Hispanic school, founded in 1888. The most recently founded school is Palo Alto College, founded in Texas in 1987. Half the schools have been founded since 1960. Since over 60 percent of Hispanics live in California, and Texas (Nettles, 1991), it is not surprising to find that 60 percent of predominantly Hispanic schools are in these states. Over 20 percent of Hispanics live in four other states, each of which has a predominantly Hispanic two-year school: New Mexico, Illinois, Florida, and New York. Arizona is the only other state besides these to have a predominantly Hispanic two-year college.

Unlike Hispanic students in predominantly Hispanic schools, most Hispanics who attend college do not find themselves in the majority.

TABLE 2.3
Predominantly Hispanic Two-Year Schools in 1996–1997

School	State	Control
Bee County College	Texas	Public
Cohise College	Arizona	Public
Delmar College	Texas	Public
Don Bosco Technical Institute	California	Private; Roman Catholic
East Los Angeles College	California	Public
El Paso Community College	Texas	Public
Heald College, School of Business	California	Private
Hostos Community College of City University of New York	New York	Public
Imperial Valley College	California	Public
Kelsey Jenney College	California	Private
Laredo Community College	Texas	Public
Los Angeles Mission College	California	Public
Miami-Dade Community College	Florida	Public
Northern New Mexico Community College	New Mexico	Public
Palo Alto College	Texas	Public
Palo Verde College	California	Public
Rio Hondo College	California	Public
Saint Augustine's College	Illinois	Private
Southwestern College	California	Public
Southwest Texas Junior College	Texas	Public
Texas State Technical College-Harlingen	Texas	Public

However, if they attend Hispanic-serving institutions, they will at least find between 25 and 49 percent of the student body is Hispanic. In 1996–1997 there were 52 two-year Hispanic-serving institutions with a collective enrollment of over 400,000. Enrollments ranged from 52 students at the all female Lexington College in Illinois to 32,000 at Mt. San Antonio College in California. Besides Mt. San Antonio, three other schools had enrollments of over 20,000 students: Cerritos College and Pasadena City College, both in California, and Pima Community College in Arizona. Almost all Hispanic-serving institutions are coeducational, with the percentage of women students ranging from 15 percent at the predominantly male Heald College, School of Technology in California, to 68 percent at University of New Mexico-Valencia.

A few schools classified as Hispanic-serving institutions are also classified as schools serving many black students. St. Philip's College is not only Hispanic-serving (46 percent in 1996–1997) but is also an historically black college. Bronx Community College, Compton Community College in California, and Roxbury Community College in Massachusetts are also predominantly black institutions. Finally, the Borough of Manhattan Community College of the City University of New York is also a black-serving institution. The oldest Hispanic serving institution is Heald College, School of Technology, founded in 1863. The newest is Santa Fe Community College, founded in 1983. Approximately 30 percent of these schools were established since 1960. Hispanic-serving institutions are found in only ten states, with most located in the Southwest.

Tribal Colleges, Predominantly Native American Institutions, and Native American-Serving Institutions

Tribal colleges are schools established to serve Native American Indians and controlled by the federal government and the founding tribe. The first tribal college, Navajo Community College (now Dine College), was established in 1968. Almost 30 years later there are 26 tribally controlled American colleges.

In 1993, over 14,500 students, most of whom were Native Americans, were enrolled in tribal colleges (Philippe, 1997, personal communica-

tion). For the 21 two-year institutions listed in *Peterson's Guide to Two-Year Colleges* 1998 (1997) for which enrollment figures were included, all but two enrolled fewer than 1,000 students in 1996–1997. Enrollments ranged from 123 students (98 percent Native American), at Cankdeska Cikana Community College (formerly Little Hoop Community College) in North Dakota, to 1,718 at Navajo Community College in Arizona (93 percent Native American). Women constituted anywhere from 44 to 73 percent of the student body. The two-year and predominantly two-year schools are largely in the Southwest and Rocky Mountain states or in the Plains.

There are also three Native American colleges that are federally controlled or supported. Haskell Indian Nations University in Kansas (which primarily awards the associate's degree but also awards the bachelor's degree); the Institute of American Indian Arts in New Mexico; and Southwest Indian Polytechnic Institute in New Mexico. Haskell's roots stretch back to 1884, when it was founded as a nonreservation boarding school. In 1996–1997 all of its 809 students were Native American. Similarly, Southwest, founded in 1971, enrolled only Native American students (638) that same year. The Institute of American Indian Arts, founded in 1962, had a more diverse student body. Of its 240 students in 1996–1997, 90 percent were Native American, 2 percent were Hispanic, and 8 percent were white.

There are also five schools whose student body is at least 25 percent Native American (see Table 2.4). Primarily located in the Southwest, these schools collectively enrolled over 11,000 students in 1996–1991. Bacone College, founded in 1880, is the oldest nontribal, Native American-serving school. The newest is Northland Pioneer College, founded in 1974.

Church-Affiliated Colleges

Denominational support of colleges for women and minorities has been vital to their creation and existence. After the Civil War, various denominations, including African Methodist Episcopals, Baptists, and Presbyterians (Anderson, 1997), founded and supported southern black liberal arts colleges. Religious denominations also established many women's academies, forerunners of numerous women's colleges. By 1970, most remaining women's colleges were

TABLE 2.4.
Predominantly Native American and Native American-Serving Two-Year Institutions in 1996–1997

School	State	Control
Bacone College	Oklahoma	Private; American Baptist Churches
Central Indian Bible College (specialized)	South Dakota	Private; Assemblies of God
Northland Pioneer College	Arizona	Public
Robeson Community College	North Carolina	Public
San Juan College	New Mexico	Public

church-affiliated, primarily Roman Catholic (Rice & Hemmings, 1988). By the early 1990s, of the 76 institutions identified by the Department of Education as women's colleges, over half were Catholic (25) or Protestant (14).

Religious sponsorship is clearly seen in the development of the two-year school. Koos (1925/1970) found that about half of the two year schools in 1921–1922 were "operating under the auspices of some church or other religious group" (p. 9). The Catholic church often sponsored two-year schools as "sister-training institutions and seminaries" for its various orders (Tremonti, 1951, p. 7). Thus around 1950, 18 of the 43 Catholic two-year schools served this purpose (p. 7); as does one today (Assumption College for Sisters).

Only a dozen of the two-year special-focus colleges existing in 1996–1997 were church-affiliated, with almost half being Roman Catholic. Each of these schools enrolled fewer than 1,000 students, for a collective enrollment of under 3,000 students in 1996–1997. Enrollments ranged from a low of 24 students (all sisters) at Assumption College for Sisters to a high of 459 at Peace College. Andrew College, a black-serving institution in Cuthbert, Georgia, is the oldest school, with roots stretching back to 1854. The newest is Central Indian Bible College, founded in 1970.

The Role of Special-Focus Two-Year Schools in the Development of American Higher Education

The development of almost 100 two-year special-focus colleges illustrates several patterns in the development of American higher education: (1) the need for groups other than white males to develop their own colleges in order to enter higher education in large numbers, (2) the evolution of two-year special-focus schools into four-year special-focus schools, and (3) the demise of special-focus colleges as majority-culture or predominantly white institutions become more receptive to minority-culture students.

Development of colleges for women and minorities

When groups other than white Protestant males have wanted more than token access to American higher education, they have first had to develop their own schools. Catholics began this pattern in the eighteenth century, women and blacks did so in the nineteenth century, and Native Americans in the twentieth century.

Education of women. When the first colonists came to America, they did not view educating women as a priority. In fact, many colonists believed women should not be educated beyond the ability to read the Bible (Power, 1958/1987, p. 114). Women were to have one role in society-service as wives and mothers, and this service did not necessitate much education.

As the new country began to develop, so too did a belief that women (that is, white women) needed more education so they could educate their sons as good citizens. Consequently, female academics were formed in the late 1700s and female seminaries in the early 1800s (Palmieri, 1987/1997). Building upon the elementary-level education offered women in the dames' schools and grammar schools, tile academies and seminaries offered a secondary-level education. Subjects included skills considered necessary for refined women, such as watercolor painting, drawing, music, and sewing, but also included subjects found in male seminaries, such as English, French, grammar, history, and geography (Power, 1958/1987, p. 116). With few exceptions before the Civil War, the academies and seminaries were the only recourse for parents seeking education beyond the elementary level for their daughters.

The South led the United States in establishing institutions as women's colleges. The first college to award a degree to women was Wesleyan Female College of Macon, Georgia, in 1836. Two years later Judson College was established in Alabama. Mary Sharpe College was founded in Tennessee in 1852 (Brubacher & Rudy, 1968, p. 67). Women's colleges also gained prominence in the East, partly because the male colleges tenaciously clung to their single-sex status (Brubacher & Rudy, 1968). Thus a number of prominent four-year women's colleges, such as Vassar, Wellesley, and Bryn Mawr, were established. Early Eastern women's colleges included Elmira Female College, established in 1855, and Ingham Collegiate Institute, converted in 1852 from a seminary to a college and relabeled in 1857 as Ingham University (Wing, 1991, p. 67).

Ingham's history illustrates the path of many higher education institutions in the nineteenth century. Beginning as secondary-level seminaries often with a preparatory department, they added a teacher preparation department or normal school and some collegiate instruction, equivalent, to the first year or two of today's four-year schools. Eventually they were able to offer the entire four years of an undergraduate degree. This pattern of development may be a factor in the uncertainty about how many two-year colleges existed in the 1800s. According to Kelly and Wilbur (1970), there were at least 50, but only eight of these still existed by 1900. How many of these enrolled women only is unknown.

By 1898 over 61,000 women, including almost 1,800 black women, attended college (O'Malley, 1898/1987, p. 1), primarily at coeducational institutions: Almost 72 percent of colleges and universities were coeducational in 1900 (Brubacher & Rudy, 1968, p. 70). However, women's colleges were still the norm for educating women in the Northeast and in the South.

In 1901 there were 119 women's colleges (Brubacher & Rudy, 1968, p. 69), of which some may have been two-year schools. By the early 1920s there were about 60 women's two-year schools (Koos, 1925/1970). Most likely, all were private institutions, and many were church-affiliated. During this period junior colleges for women often served as feeder schools for four-year women's colleges or as finishing schools for middle-class women planning to marry and raise children. As coeducation became more acceptable and eventually mandatory in public institutions after the Civil Rights Act in 1964, the number of women's colleges, both two and four-year, declined drastically so that in 1998 only a handful of two-year women's colleges remained.

Education of blacks.   Prior to the Civil War, most blacks lived in the South. If they desired higher education, they had to attend college in the North as it was illegal in the South to educate black slaves and, in some states, freed blacks. If they went North, they would find a few black colleges such as Avery College and Lincoln University in Pennsylvania, or Wilberforce University in Ohio (Lucas, 1994, pp. 158–159). Only a few white schools, such as Oberlin, Amherst, and Bowdoin, admitted blacks.

After the Civil War, many black colleges were created, especially in the South. Given that only about 10 percent of blacks could read when the Civil War started (Holmes, 1936/1970), these were colleges largely in name only. Rather, they taught elementary and high school-level subjects to bring their students to the college level. Very few schools actually offered four years of college-level work (Roebuck & Murty, 1997). By 1900 there were approximately 100 black colleges (Lucas, 1994, p. 207).

As with white colleges, two-year black colleges were largely a product of the twentieth century. According to Lane (1933), "the first 'pure' junior college" (p. 277) for blacks was the now defunct Walden College in Nashville, Tennessee, which existed from 1919–1929. Like many white two-year schools, when two-year black schools developed, they were usually associated with high schools. By 1932 there were 19 two-year black colleges, of which 18 had some connection with a high school. All the two-year schools were in the South. Fourteen were private, including 12 affiliated with various Protestant denominations (Lane, 1933). The high school connection was maintained in Florida, when the legislature established the state's black two-year college system in the 1950s. All these colleges *were* developed as extensions of black high schools (Smith, 1994, p. xxiii).

The number of black two-year schools was never large. According to Walker (1960), there were just 19 between 1950 and 1957; 13 were private. Florida's decision to establish black junior colleges added 10 more public schools between 1958 and 1966. In the southern and border states in 1961, 19 two-year schools had an entirely or predominantly black student body (Miller, 1962). McGrath (1968) identified 36 black two-year schools as of 1963–1964, of which 16 were public. Collectively, they enrolled about 7,000 students as compared to 100,000 enrolled in the four-year predominantly black schools (pp. 12–13).

With the exception of those in Florida, black two-year schools did not generate much appeal to black families or garner much support from four-year black colleges, at least during the 1960s (Commission on Higher Educational Opportunity, 1967; McGrath, 1968). McGrath (1968) found that black students were hesitant to go to two-year schools because they wanted to "go away" to college, in part to "escape from the southern setting" and a life of "privation and social restrictions" (p. 40). Blacks also viewed two-year schools unfavorably because of their emphasis on occupational education, instead of the liberal education "associate[d] with students' education" (p. 41). Also, most four-year HBCs "seem[ed] to consider the two-year [predominantly black] colleges beneath college grade" (p. 13). The senior institutions often refused to give transfer credit for courses taken at two-year black colleges, probably because many of the schools were unaccredited (p. 13).

The federal government's decision in 1972 to provide student financial aid only for attendance at accredited colleges affected the number of two-year black schools. Many were unable to gain accreditation and therefore disappeared. As of fall 1998 only 14 two-year historically black colleges existed, including four that are branch campuses of public two-year schools.[4]

Education of Native Americans.   Just as blacks and women sought more than token access to higher education in the nineteenth century, so too did Native Americans and Hispanics in the twentieth century. For Native Americans, the creation of tribal colleges has been a result.

Educating Native Americans was at least a nominal concern of the first colonial colleges. Both Harvard and the College of William and Mary included in their charters the education of Native Americans (called Indians), with the intent of converting them to Christianity. Dartmouth also sought to educate Native Americans and is considered to be "the first college founded primarily for the education of American Indians" (Oppelt, 1990, p. 5). However, as Wright (1997) states, "the colonial experiments in Indian higher education were not simple expressions of unblemished piety." Instead they served as a means "to further [the colleges') own political, economic, and educational agendas" (p. 78). For example, educating Indians engendered a lot of financial support from English people, desirous of converting the Indians to Christianity. By the end of the eighteenth century, American colleges effectively ceased efforts to recruit and educate Native Americans. Few had enrolled; even fewer had graduated. Given that attending these schools required Native Americans to assimilate to white, Protestant values and forego their own values and culture, it is understandable why they were little interested in attending college at this time (Oppelt, 1990).

As Native Americans continued to be displaced from their lands, they declined in numbers and were forced onto reservations. At this point they were educated first at government boarding schools, which were often denominationally operated, and later at day schools on their own reservation. Some schools were also created off the reservation.

Whether in nonreservation or reservation classrooms, Native American students faced hostility to their language and culture. Teachers hired by the Bureau of Indian Affairs could be fired "if they incorporated in their teaching any of the rich and ancient heritage of the vast oral tradition" (Hill, 1995, p. 33) of the Native Americans. The experience was no different for the very few who went on to college.

Native American students also faced cessation of their education after attainment of a high school diploma. The U.S. government, through its Bureau of Indian Affairs, "decided early to terminate the schooling of Indian youths at the secondary-school level (Brubacher & Rudy, 1968, p. 80). Rarely were Native Americans sent on to receive a college education.

The 1930s initiated some positive changes in the education of Native Americans. The Indian

Reorganization Act was passed in 1934, under Franklin Roosevelt. Among other provisions, this act provided loans for Native Americans to attend college. As a result, by 1935 over 500 were in postsecondary education. In the 1940s the GI Bill also facilitated the education of Native American veterans of World War II. In the 1960s creation of the Bureau of Indian Affairs Higher Education Grant programs also added to the number of Native American college graduates (Hill, 1995, pp. 33–34).

Although more Native Americans were attending college by the 1960s, they were doing less well than most other students. They also had a higher dropout rate than any other group of students. These facts contributed to the establishment of tribal colleges, institutions locally owned and controlled by Native American tribes but supported with federal funds through the Tribally Controlled Community College Assistance Act of 1978. These institutions were committed to preserving the tribe's culture and educating the students in ways consonant with that culture. In 1968 the first tribal college, Navajo Community College in Arizona, was established. By 1980 16 more had been created. Currently there are 26 in America and one in Canada. All began as two-year schools, although two, Salish Kootenai College in Montana and Oglala Lakota, now offer bachelor's degrees in addition to two-year degrees, and one school, Standing Rock College in North Dakota, offers a master's degree.

Education of Hispanics. Like tribal colleges, Hispanic-serving institutions also began to be established in the late 1960s. Some were created as two-year and some as four-year schools. As of 1994 there were 133 Hispanic-serving institutions in 16 states. By 1996–1997, there were at least 73 non profit, two-year schools whose student body was at least 25 percent Hispanic (*Peterson's Guide to Two-Year Schools 1998*, 1997).

Where Hispanic-serving institutions and predominantly Hispanic institutions differ from the other minority-culture schools is that two-year institutions serving Hispanics were usually not created specifically for that mission. Rather, two-year Hispanic-serving and predominantly Hispanic institutions have typically been created as part of the expansion of community colleges in the 1960s and 1970s. Built in areas where many Hispanics lived, these schools became Hispanic-

serving and predominantly Hispanic institutions by demographic default.

Deliberately developing schools to serve Hispanics did not occur until the 1960s. Olivas (1997) has written about the development of colleges for two Hispanic subgroups, Mexican Americans and Puerto Ricans. According to Olivas, unlike the situation with blacks and Native Americans, "no governmental or religious groups founded colleges for Mexican Americans" (p: 680). However, like blacks and Native Americans, Mexican Americans suffered from a lack of adequate elementary and secondary schooling, although the situation was exacerbated for Mexican Americans because so many were migrant workers. With the growing interest in civil rights and minority groups in the 1960s, Chicanos were able to develop six Chicano colleges during the late 1960s and early 1970s. One of these schools, D-Q University, is now a tribal college. At its inception, it was a Chicano-Indian college. Only it and one other of the original six Chicano colleges (Colegio Cesar Chavez in Mt. Angel, Oregon) now exist (Olivas, 1997).

Puerto Ricans, "the most educationally disadvantaged subgroup" (Olivas, 1977, p. 683), also saw the establishment of historically Puerto Rican colleges during the late 1960s and early 1970s. With the advent of open admissions in the City University of New York (CUNY) system in the 1960s, Hostos Community College was founded in 1969 in the Bronx as a CUNY school. In 1973 Boricua College, a four-year school, was established in Brooklyn.

Since the 1960s and 1970s, at least one two-year school was consciously founded to serve Hispanics. Established in Chicago in 1980 under the auspices of the Episcopal church, St. Augustine College does not list itself as church-affiliated in *Peterson's Guide to Two-Year Colleges* 1998 (1997); hence it is not listed in this chapter as a church-affiliated school.

Evolution into four-year schools

Two-year special-focus colleges are unique in demonstrating another pattern in the history of higher education. Like many two-year majority-culture or predominantly white schools, some developed into four-year schools, a change which diminishes the number of special-focus two-year schools but provides an alternative educational opportunity for the groups they represent. A stage in this development is to offer a baccalaureate degree while still offering associate degrees. Schools in this stage are known as predominantly two-year schools because the majority of their enrollment is in two-year programs. A few of the women's colleges examined in this book illustrate this path.

Women's colleges also provide examples of two-year schools that have become four-year schools. For example, the two-year Midway College in Kentucky, affiliated with the Disciples of Christ, became a four-year school in 1989. The change has resulted in greatly increased enrollments for the school. In 1985 it enrolled approximately 300 women; in 1997 it enrolled 1,100 (Fiore, 1997, p. A25). Also, the women's college, Bay Path College in Longmeadow, Pennsylvania, was a two-year school until recently (Carnegie Foundation, 1994).

The demise of single-sex and historically black colleges

Another pattern in the development of American higher education is the decline of special-focus colleges as majority-culture institutions become more receptive to minority-culture students. This pattern is again well illustrated by women's colleges. Once the idea of educating women at the collegiate level began to be accepted in the nineteenth century, coeducation was rapidly accepted at many institutions. Over 70 percent were coeducational by the turn of the century. The elite private Northeastern schools like Harvard and Yale were among the last to become coeducational, holding out until the late 1960s and early 1970s. When all elite male schools became coeducational, women's colleges saw their enrollments decline, sometimes to the point where institutions had to close. In 1960 there were 233 women's colleges; in 1997 there were less than 90 with only eight of them being two-year schools.

Just as with women's colleges, historically black colleges have also declined in number as majority-culture institutions began to recruit black students. During much of their existence, historically black colleges were the primary, or in the South the only, venue for blacks to enter higher education. With the mandated integration of higher education in the 1960s through the Civil Rights Act of 1964 and the Supreme Court order in 1969, the primary reason for the existence of black colleges evaporated. Prior to the 1954 Supreme Court decision (*Brown v. Board of Education of Topeka, Shawnee County, Kansas*) that "separate but equal" was unconstitutional, historically black colleges had educated over 90 percent of black students in higher education. By 1987 less than 20 percent of black college students went to historically black colleges (Roebuck & Murty, 1993, pp. 669–700).

Historically black and single-sex colleges are, of course, not the only two-year schools to have expired. Some two-year schools serving only white students have also closed because they could not attract enough students. Often these schools were private and sometimes church-affiliated, for example, Felician College (renamed Montay College) in Chicago, Illinois. This Catholic two-year institution was open to both women and men, but had to close its doors in the early 1990s due to lack of enrollment.

Future Directions

The future of these two-year schools varies according to the group(s) they serve. Two-year women's colleges and historically black colleges are dying out largely because both women and black students are now sought after by majority-culture institutions. Two-year women's colleges may well be extinct as an institutional type within a decade if their current pattern of converting to four-year schools and/or admitting men continues.

Private, two-year historically black colleges may also die as an institutional type, although the public ones will remain as a historical reminder of de jure and de facto segregation. The private HBCs are hard pressed to compete for students when there are currently so many public, two-year predominantly black and black-serving institutions with newer facilities and more financial resources to serve black students. As far back as 1967, this point was made by the Commission on Higher Educational Opportunity in the South, which stated, "Most church related [black] junior colleges began as missionary efforts to serve disadvantaged students for whom no other resources were available. Now, public, institutions are gradually assuming this function" (p. 28).

A major factor in the demise of private two-year historically black colleges and women's colleges is their being private. According to Hoffman (1990), the private two-year school "is an endangered species" (p. 9), largely due to the growth of the public two-year college. In 1963 there were 278 private junior colleges; in 1989 there were 89 (Woodruff, 1990, p. 92). Reasons for their decline include their high cost to students and their small size. Around 1990, almost 60 percent of the schools enrolled under 500 students. Institutions operating with so few students annually usually "operate more inefficiently, with total costs per enrolled students greatly exceeding competitive sectors" (Woodruff, 1990, p. 86). Thus the private sponsorship of two-year women's colleges and most historically black colleges, combined with majority-culture schools' interest in recruiting their students, works against the continuation of these schools as institutional types.

Collectively, tribal colleges are alive and well and should continue as a success story for many decades. Existing ones will grow in enrollment and levels of degrees offered; almost all have plans to offer a four-year degree. Also, more tribal colleges will be created. However, failure of the federal government to fund tribal colleges to the extent promised in the 1978 legislation hurts these institutions.

Predominantly Hispanic and Hispanic-serving institutions will also grow in number and size as the Hispanic population increases in America. The number of 18- to-24-year-old Hispanics is projected to increase to approximately 20 percent of the American population by 2020, as compared to 13 percent in 1995 (Justiz, Wilson, & Bjoork, 1994). As Hispanics seek higher education, they will change the demographic makeup of individual schools, with the result that a number of today's majority-culture two-year schools will become Hispanic-serving or even predominantly Hispanic in a few decades. Because of the growth in the percentage of Hispanics in America, "the community college student populations are slowly but surely becoming more Hispanic" (Padron, 1994, p. 86).[5]

Two-year church-affiliated schools are currently in decline and will probably continue to decline, partly because of the previously mentioned problems associated with private control. In 1921 there were approximately 100 church-affiliated two-year schools (Koos, 1970, pp. 8–9), mostly single-sex institutions and some black colleges. In 1996 1997 there were almost 60 church-affiliated two-year schools.

Conclusion

As indicated above, diversity within the types of special-focus two-year schools may well decline in the coming decades. At the micro level the death of individual colleges causes grief to the parties involved, but from a macro perspective, the near or total death of, some types of special-focus schools may portend well for the groups they were created to serve. Two-year women's colleges and two-year historically black colleges have declined partly because these schools are no longer the only ones eager to serve women and blacks. Both groups are now readily accepted in almost all higher education institutions, both two-year and four-year. Also, some two-year women's colleges have become or are becoming four-year schools, which from both a micro and macro level is considered success for those schools even though this evolution diminishes the ranks of two-year schools. Similarly, some two-year historically black colleges became four-year schools.

Although two-year women's colleges and two-year historically black colleges are dying out, two new kinds of minority-culture or special-focus colleges have emerged since the 1960s. Tribal colleges and predominantly Hispanic and Hispanic-serving; institutions serve groups that have been seriously neglected by the entire educational system, not just higher education. Through the emergence of these schools, the number of college-educated Native Americans and Hispanics has grown significantly in the past three decades and will continue to grow. The major difference between these two institutional types is that tribal colleges were deliberately created to serve Native Americans, whereas most predominantly Hispanic and Hispanic-serving institutions have had this mission thrust upon them because of the initial or changing demographics in their service area. The same can be said of predominantly black and black-serving colleges. However, many of these schools now consciously embrace the mission of educating minority students.

Two-year schools whose student body is primarily or entirely female or black, Hispanic, or Native American have much to teach most faculty and administrators in predominantly white or majority-culture schools. Minority-culture colleges have recognized populations hungry for higher education and given those populations an opportunity to succeed. With their legacy of serving groups initially ignored by or excluded from higher education, these schools can serve as models of how to educate students whose cultural heritage differs significantly from that of the white, male students for whom American higher education was originally designed.

Notes

1. Four sources have been used to identify the colleges discussed in this chapter; (1) *Peterson's Guide to Two-Year Colleges* 1998 (1997), (2) *Peterson's Guide to Four-Year Colleges* 1998 (1997), (3) the American Association of Community Colleges, and (4) the Carnegie Foundation's technical report, *A Classification of Institutions of Higher Education,* 1994 edition.

   Peterson's Guide to Two-Year Schools 1998 lists all "accredited [regional or specialized] institutions in the United States and U.S. territories that award the associate degree as their most popular undergraduate degree" (p. 18). It also includes "some non-degree granting institutions, usually branch, campuses of a multicampus system, that offer the equivalent of the first two years of a bachelor's degree, transferable to a bachelor's-degree-granting institution" (pp. 8–19). The 1998 guide contains data submitted voluntarily from the institutions during the 1996–1997 academic year. Thus figures about the percentage of minority and female students at a particular school were provided by the institution. Each entry in Peterson's was read to determine if the school was one of the five types of schools examined in this book. Occasionally, a school did not submit information about the percentage of female and male students or minority students. Thus it is possible that some minority-culture two-year schools have not been included because of lack of information about the student body they serve. Also, some schools fit into two or more categories. For example, Bronx Community College of the City University of New York is both a predominantly black and a Hispanic-serving institution.

   The American Association of Community Colleges (AACC) provided assistance through Kent Philippe, Research Associate. He provided AACC's lists of historically black colleges, Hispanic-serving schools, and independent colleges. The AACC lists were cross-checked with the lists derived from the two *Peterson's Guide* books and from the Carnegie 1994 *Classification* to develop the lists used in this book. When a school on one of the AACC lists could not be found in the *Peterson's Guide to Two-Year Schools,* the Carnegie 1994 *Classification* report were checked. If the school was classified by the Carnegie Foundation as a four-year school, the institution was not included in this study.

   Only non-profit schools were included, although it is important to note that many of the for-profit schools could be classified as predominantly black, black-serving, predominantly Hispanic, or Hispanic-serving. Some of these for-profit schools are also among the highest producers of associate degrees. For example, the main campus of the proprietary Monroe College in New York City was 20th among 50 institutions that conferred the highest number of associate degrees to African Americans in 1994–1995, and 16th among those conferring associate degrees to Hispanic Americans (*Community College Week,* July 14, 1997, p. 11).

2. The regional schema used is that used in *The Two-Year College and Its Students* (The American College Testing Program, 1969). The New England region includes Connecticut, Maine, Massachusetts, New Hampshire, Rhode Island and Vermont. The Mideast region includes Delaware, District of Columbia, Maryland, New Jersey, New York, and Pennsylvania. The Great Lakes region includes Illinois, Indiana, Michigan; Ohio, and Wisconsin. The Plains region includes Iowa, Kansas, Minnesota, Missouri, Nebraska, North Dakota, and South Dakota. The Southeast region includes Alabama, Arkansas, Florida, Georgia, Kentucky, Louisiana, Mississippi, North Carolina, South Carolina, Tennessee, Virginia, and West Virginia. The Southwest and Rocky Mountains region includes Arizona, Colorado, Idaho, Montana, New Mexico, Oklahoma, Texas, Utah, and Wyoming. The Far West region includes Alaska, California, Hawaii, Nevada, Oregon, and Washington.

3. The names of the colleges in this list are the names used in *Peterson's Guide to Two-Year Colleges* 1998 (1997). Two of the colleges have since changed their names as indicated in Chapter 4, Tribal Colleges.

4. The 14 historically black colleges still in existence in Fall 1998 do not include Shorter College, since it lost its accreditation in Spring 1998. The list does include the Valley Street Campus of Gadsen State Community College, recognized in 1997 as an historically black college.

5. Padron (1994) also notes the growing number and percentage of Asian community college students. Although this chapter does not include predominantly Asian/Pacific Islander or Asian/Pacific Islander-serving institutions as a type of minority-culture school, there are at least 20 non-profit two-year schools in *Peterson's Guide to Two-Year Colleges* 1998 (1997) that enroll 25 percent or more Asian/Pacific Islanders.

References

Anderson, J. D. (1997). Training the apostles of liberal culture: Black higher education, 1900–1935. In L. Goodchild & H. Weschler (Eds.), *The history of higher education* (2nd ed.) (pp. 432–458). Needham Heights, MA: Simon and Schuster. (Original work published 1988).

Basinger, J. (1998, January 27). Another all-female college in Mass. decides to admit men. *Chronicle of Higher Education,* p. A9.

Brubacher, J. S., & Rudy, W. (1968). *Higher education in lransilion.* New York: Harper & Row.

Carnegie Foundation for the Advancement of Teaching. (1994). *A classification of instilulions of higher education.* Princeton, NJ: Author.

Chronicle of Higher Education 1997–1998 *Almanac Issue* (1997, August 29). XLIV (1), p. 5.

Cohen, A. (October, 1992). Tracking the transfers: State policy and practice. National Center for Academic Achievement and Transfer. Working papers 3 (7).

Commission on Higher Educational Opportunity in the South. (1967, August). *The Negro and higher education in the South.* Atlanta: Southern Regional Education Board.

Damann, Mother Grace, R. S. C. J. (1987). The American Catholic college for women. In M. J. Oates (Ed.), *Higher education for Catholic women: An historical anthology* (pp. 149–172). New York: Garland. (Original work published 1942).

Davis, J. (1992). Factors contributing to post-secondary achievement of American Indians. *Tribal College Journal,* 4 (2), 24–30.

Deveric, C. (1997, November 3). Study shows where to get most for your Hope-scholarship money. *Community College Week,* p. 3.

Fiore, M. (1997, August 1). The thinning ranks of private 2-year colleges. *Chronicle of Higher Education,* A 25.

Gadsen State Finally Gets HBCU Designation. (1998, February 9). *Community College Week,* p. 17.

Galluzzi, W. E. (1979). Haskell Indian Junior College-Serving a special need. In F. Gilbert (Ed.), *Minorities and community colleges: Data and discourse* (pp. 22–23). Washington, DC: American Association of Community and Junior Colleges.

Godbold, D. H. (1979). Efficacy of community colleges for minorities. In F. Gilbert (Ed.), *Minorities and community colleges: Data and discourse.* Washington, DC: American Association of Community and Junior Colleges, 24–25.

Hazzard, T. (1988, June). *Attitudes and perceptions of while students attending historically black colleges and universities.* ERIC Document. ED298806.

Hill, M. J. (1995, Summer). Tribal colleges: Their role in U. S. higher education. In J. Killacky & J. R. Valadez (Eds.), *Portrait of the rural community college.* New Directions for Community Colleges, no. 90 (pp. 31–41). San Francisco: Jossey-Bass.

Hoffman, N. M., Jr. (1990, Spring). The private junior college in higher education's future. In R. H. Woodruff (Ed.), *The viability of the private junior college.* New Directions for Community Colleges, no. 69 (pp. 9–17). San Francisco: Jossey-Bass.

Holmes, D. O. W. (1970). *The evolution of the Negro college.* New York: AMS Press. (Original work published 1936).

Hurtado, S. (1994). The institutional climate for talented Latino students. *Research in Higher Education,* 35, 21–41.

Justiz, M. J., Wilson, R., & Bjork, L. (1994). *Minorities in higher education.* Phoenix: American Council on Education & Oryx Press.

Kanter, R. M. (1977). *Men and women of the corporation.* New York: Basic Books.

Kelley, W., & Wilbur, L. (1970). *Teaching in the community-junior college.* New York: Appleton-Century-Crofts Educational Division, Meredith Corporation.

Koos, L. (1970). *The junior college movement.* Westport, CT: Greenwood Press. (Original work published 1925).

Lane, D. A., Jr. (1933). The junior college movement among Negroes. *The Journal of Negro Education,* 2, 272–283.

Lucas, C. (1994). *America higher education: A history.* New York: St. Martin's Press.

McGrath, E. (1968). *The predominantly Negro colleges and universities in transition.* Teachers College, Columbia, NY: Institute of Higher Education.

Miller, C. L. (1962). The Negro publicly-supported junior college. *The Journal of Negro Education,* 31 (3), 386–395.

National Center for Education Statistics. (1997): *Findings from the condition of education 1996: Minorities in higher education.* Washington, DC: Office of Educational Research and Improvement, no. 9.

Nettles, M. T. (1991). *Assessing progress in minority access and achievement in American higher education.* Denver: Education Commission of the States.

O'Malley, A. (1987). College work for Catholic girls. In M. I. Oates (Ed.), *Higher education for Catholic women: An historical anthology* (pp. 161–167). New York: Garland. (Original work published 1898).

Olivas, M. A. (1997). Indian, Chicano, and Puerto Rican colleges: Status and issues. In L. Goodchild & H. Weschler, (Eds.), *The history of higher education* (2nd ed.) (pp. 677–698). Needham Heights, MA: Simon and Schuster. (Original work published 1982).

Oppelt, N. T. (1990). *The tribally controlled Indian college: The beginnings of self determination in Ameri-*

can Indian education. Tsaile. AZ: Navajo Community College Press.

Padron, E. J. (1994). Hispanics and community colleges. In G. Baker (Ed.). *A handbook on the community college in America* (pp. 82–93). Westport, CT: Greenwood Press.

Palmieri, P. A. (1997). From Republican motherhood to race suicide: Arguments on the higher education of women in the United Slates. 1820–1920. In L. Goodchild & H. Weschler, (Eds.), *The history of higher education* (2nd ed.) (pp.] 73–182). Needham Heights, MA: Simon and Schuster. (Original work published 1987).

Peterson's Guide to Two-year Colleges 1998. (1997). Princelon, NJ: Author.

Peterson's Guide to Four-Year Colleges 1998. (1997). Princeton, NJ: Author.

Power, E. J. (1987). Catholic higher education for women in the United States. In M. J. Oates (Ed.), *Higher education for Catholic women: An historical anthology* (pp. 114–135). New York: Garland. (Original work published 1958).

Rice, J. K., & Hemmings, A. (1988). Women's colleges and women achievers: An update. *Signs. /3* (31), 546–559.

Roebuck, J. B., & Murty, K. S. (1997). Historically black colleges and universities: Their place in American higher education. In L. Goodchild & H. Weschler (Eds.), *The history of higher education* (2nd ed.) (pp. 667–676). Needham Heights, MA: Simon and Schuster. (Original work published (993).

Shorter College (1994). *Shorter College Catalog, 1994–1998.* Little Rock, AK: Author.

Shorter College loses accreditation. (1998, April 24). *Chronicle of Higher Education,* p. A8.

Smith, W. L. (1994). *The magnificent twelve: Florida's black junior colleges.* Winter Park, FL: Four-G Publishers, Inc.

Solomon, B. M. (1985). *In the company of educated women.* New Haven, CT: Yale University Press.

Tremonti, Rev. J. B. (195 1). *The status of Catholic junior colleges.* Washington, DC: The Catholic Education Press.

Walker, G. H. (1960, January). Analysis of Negro junior college growth. *Junior College Journal, 3D,* 264–267.

Wing, R. (1991). Requiem for a pioneer of women's higher education: The Ingham University of LeRoy, New York, 1857–1892. *History of Higher Education Annual,* 61–79.

Woodruff, R. H. (1990). Doubts about the future of the private liberal arts junior college. In R. H. Woodruff (Ed.), *The viability of the private junior college.* New Directions for Community Colleges, no. 69 (pp. 83–93). San Francisco: Jossey-Bass.

Wright, B. (1997). "For the children of the infidels"? American Indian education in the colonial college. In L. Goodchild & H. Weschler (Eds.), *The history of higher education* (2nd ed.) (pp. 72–79). Needham Heights, MA: Simon and Schuster. (Original work published 1988).

Youn, T. I. K., & Loscocco, K. A. (1991). Institutional history and ideology: The evolution of two women's colleges. *History of Higher Education Annual,* 21–44.

CHAPTER 3

CANADA'S COMMUNITY COLLEGE SYSTEMS: A STUDY OF DIVERSITY

PAUL GALLAGHER
VANCOUVER, BRITISH COLUMBIA, CANADA

JOHN D. DENNISON
DEPARTMENT OF ADMINISTRATIVE, ADULT, AND HIGHER
EDUCATION, UNIVERSITY OF BRITISH COLUMBIA,
VANCOUVER, BRITISH COLUMBIA, CANADA

Diversity is central to Canada's community colleges. For example, Ontario created vocationally oriented colleges of applied arts and technology, British Columbia and Alberta opted for locally governed comprehensive colleges with university transfer, Saskatchewan developed "colleges without walls," Quebec's colleges of general and vocational education incorporated tuition-free technical and preuniversity streams, and Newfoundland, Manitoba, New Brunswick, the Yukon, and the Northwest Territories established technical colleges with a strong accent on short-term work-entry training. This article describes the rich diversity found within Canada's systems of community colleges, as well as the reasons for and consequences of this diversity.

With "too much geography and not enough history,"[1] Canada is the world's second largest land mass, but supports a population of less than 30 million people, most of whom live within 200 miles of the United States. Contemporary Canada has evolved into a dynamic G-7 country from an original confederation of four British colonies.[2] The federal government, and those of its 10 provinces[3] of greatly differing sizes and populations, share constitutionally established powers. Historically, each of this nation's provinces (and vast northern territories) has developed uniquely, with differences of culture, language, religion, resources, and geography all coming into play. In fact, equitable redistribution of the nation's wealth has been one of the most important responsibilities of Canada's federal government.

This diversity is reflected in all aspects of Canadian life, including the organization, structure, and operation of postsecondary education and, in particular, in the variations among its community college systems. In this article, we describe the development of these systems. We also discuss the consequences of this rich diversity and identify the key challenges these systems face as Canada enters a postindustrial era of rapid technological change and economic restructuring.

Constitutional Context for Education

Consistent with the distinctive characters of the original provinces, the 1867 division of powers between the federal and provincial governments under Canada's constitution saw education clearly and solely as a matter of provincial jurisdiction.[4] This arrangement continues to apply to all fields of education, including the postsecondary sector. Thus, Canada has no federal office of education, no federal minister (or secretary), no national goals, and no national standards. Yet, with typically Canadian tolerance for ambiguity, few constitutional sensitivities are raised when the federal government engages in three education-related areas: the funding of research, postsecondary student financial assistance, and adult training.

Both levels of government have seen training, as distinct from education, as a dimension of economic development and therefore a legitimate area of shared jurisdiction, and neither the federal government nor the provinces have seen it in their interests to draw a fine line between what is education and what is training. One consequence is that public funds for vocational training have historically come almost exclusively from the federal treasury, but have been managed under joint agreements between the two levels of government.

Until 1960, postsecondary education was effectively limited to a university sector (Gregor, 1992). Churches had originally played the primary role in establishing denominational degree-granting colleges, except in the western provinces where public universities were created by provincial governments. Plagued by financial uncertainties, virtually all denominational colleges and universities became public institutions by 1970 (Cameron, 1991). Public postsecondary technical and vocational training opportunities were very limited until the 1960s, as these forms of education were quickly encumbered with the stigma of low status and were viewed as a second-order choice for young people who could not aspire to attend a university (Anisef, 1982; Young, 1992). Both formal and informal adult education developed impressively but variably across the country, particularly in the years immediately preceding and following World War II (Selman & Dampier, 1991).

In the early 1960s, a number of significant factors converged to prompt a dramatic change of public policy and practice with respect to the design and function of postsecondary education in all regions of Canada. The first was the influence of human capital theory, which persuaded governments that investment in people could be the key to economic growth (Denison, 1962; Economic Council of Canada, 1964; Schultz, 1961). The second was a disturbing prediction by a number of social scientists (Sheffield, 1962; Zsigmond & Wennas, 1970) that an unprecedented wave of students would soon demand access to postsecondary education. The third factor was the popular acceptance of the view that Canada's prosperity would now increasingly depend on the technical skills of its work force. Manpower training was seen as crucial to fueling the economic engine, particularly when the long-standing policy of importing technically skilled individuals from other countries became a less practical course of action.

Community College Systems

It was in this setting that governments in Canada developed an entirely new sector of postsecondary education. The Sheffield (1962) study noted that only an enormous expansion of facilities could accommodate anything close to the number of students who would soon knock on university doors. Many university leaders observed that significant expansion could inadvertently prompt these institutions to diffuse their energies and resources, and could put at risk the traditional mission of the university as a center of liberal education and research. So the search for new kinds of postsecondary institutions began as a way of relieving an anticipated demand on the established universities and of expanding technical training throughout the country.

As talk of new kinds of postsecondary institutions spread informally across Canada in the early 1960s, the Canadian Association for Adult Education did its best to encourage people and organizations to share information in the hope that a nationwide perspective on a postsecondary alternative to universities might emerge (Dennison & Gallagher, 1986). The sociopolitical contexts and economic opportunities of the provinces were so different, however, that a nationwide approach was soon seen as unrealistic. There then began the search for regionally and culturally specific ways of providing a broader range of postsecondary education and training opportunities to a much larger segment of the population in each province and territory. It was this search that led to the creation of several different college systems. Five significantly different models for the organization of postsecondary education in different parts of Canada were developed in the 1965–75 period (Dennison & Gallagher, 1986). In characteristically Canadian fashion, there were also internal variations within each of these five models.

In the most and least populated provinces (Ontario and Prince Edward Island), a kind of college new to Canada was developed to complement the university sector in each of these provinces. In Ontario, new institutions were formally called colleges of applied arts and technology, in part to make sure that they would not be confused with either the more traditional degree-granting institutions or the postsecondary institutes specializing in fields such as agriculture or medical technologies. On Prince Edward Island, the lone college was not given a similar label but was expected, as in Ontario, to be a postsecondary institution for young people who were not eligible for university admission. In both of these provinces, locally designated boards were given governance responsibilities.

In Ontario, this kind of college—an alternative to university for less academically able high school graduates—was the model promoted by the politically powerful Committee of Presidents of Provincially Assisted Universities, who wanted to make sure that no new institutions would threaten their stature or support. In both provinces, it was also recognized that these new colleges could serve additionally as adult education centers to provide both retraining programs for people in the work force interested in new career opportunities and community and general education for people whose objectives were less career oriented.

A quite different model was developed in the two most western provinces. Alberta and British Columbia opted for California-style locally governed, comprehensive community or regional colleges with transfer programs to universities as a major curriculum component. In these provinces, in which the populations were very dispersed and geographic access to the few universities was very difficult for students who did not live in the larger population centers, the intention was not to segregate the university-bound students from other postsecondary students, as

in Ontario and Prince Edward Island. Rather, the vision was to provide both technical–vocational programming and university transfer courses on the same campuses, giving many secondary school graduates the choice of either immediate university entrance or admission to a college program that would provide transfer credits for up to 2 years of university undergraduate study. In both of these provinces, the establishment of institutes of technology and other specialized postsecondary institutes, in addition to community or regional colleges, added further to student choice.

In British Columbia, the California influence was also evident from its adoption of the notion that community colleges could concurrently serve as second-chance institutions and enhance adult education opportunities of all kinds. In Alberta, most second-chance students were still directed to government-run vocational centers established throughout the province.

The third model that emerged might best be described as the postsecondary vocational–technical college, without any transfer function and with a much stronger accent on shorter term work-entry training programs than on more advanced technological education. The early years of college development in Manitoba, New Brunswick, the Yukon and Northwest Territories, and Newfoundland broadly fit this model, but the need for a greater variety of programming soon became evident in all of these jurisdictions.

Newfoundland later incorporated transfer education into its college curriculum and maintained a number of specialized postsecondary institutes in addition to the colleges and its only university. Articulation arrangements between the colleges in the two northern territories and universities in the southern provinces became a quite effective and realistic alternative to the establishment of additional universities in the north. As in the other provinces and models, enhancing adult education opportunity was seen as a secondary justification for establishing all of these new postsecondary institutions.

A fourth and distinctive model developed in Saskatchewan, where people in sparsely populated agricultural regions wanted locally responsive learning opportunities of many kinds, whereas those in the growing urban areas insisted on the need for more technical and industrial training opportunities. Community colleges without walls were established, chiefly in rural areas, with the expectation that they would serve as brokers rather than as service providers. As brokers, their primary responsibilities would be to arrange for the provision of educational services by other institutions and community agencies. In the more urban areas, vocational and technical education programs were to be provided by technical institutes, with the two universities of that province remaining the sole institutions providing postsecondary academic and professional courses and programs.

The original Saskatchewan broker model was effectively set aside in the late 1980s when four previously independent technical institutes were reconstituted as a new multicampus Saskatchewan Institute of Applied Science and Technology and the more rural community colleges began to provide, as well as broker, educational services. Decentralization of that multicampus institute has been underway for more than 2 years, as postsecondary education in this province—as in others—adjusts to changing economic circumstances and political exigencies.

The fifth and most distinctive model exists in Quebec, which launched a sweeping social and economic revolution in the early 1960s. As part of that mostly quiet revolution, a new public multicampus university was established, and the properties of many old private colleges were used to form the physical nucleus for a new college system that was to be accessible to all young people in that province.

That system of colleges of general and vocational education borrowed from the experience of European as well as North American approaches to postsecondary education. Its special distinction was that all postsecondary students would be required to complete the equivalent of at least 1 year of general education, regardless of career or educational choices after college. Accordingly, the Quebec college curriculum was designed to have two main streams: one of 2 years for students planning to proceed to university study, the other of 3 years for students needing technical education before work force entry. Thus, the Quebec college was conceived of as preparation for some students for admission to university (which offered for college graduates 3-year undergraduate degree programs in virtually all fields of study) and as contemporary preparation for others wishing to enter the skilled work force immediately after college.

The Quebec college model was unique in other respects as well. Three of those distinctions are particularly notable. One, unlike colleges in other Canadian jurisdictions, Quebec colleges were not originally intended to place significant emphasis on adult education (but most soon became very active adult education centers anyway). Two, they were not to provide entry-level vocational training (that was to be provided by secondary schools, for both secondary school students and adults who might wish that kind of training). Three, full-time college study was to be tuition free as an incentive to young Quebeckers to continue their studies beyond the secondary school level (and that tuition policy has been maintained to this day despite extraordinary pressures to find new sources of revenue for college operations).

The Quebec college system has operated in a more centralized fashion than other systems in Canada, yet partially elected institutional boards play a significant role in shaping the curriculum and community responsiveness of each college. In uniquely Quebec style, that province subsidizes a number of private colleges of general and vocational education in addition to maintaining a full complement of almost 50 public colleges and a very accessible public university system. Over the years, there have been several major reviews and reassessments of the effectiveness of the Quebec approach to college education. In each of these cases, areas for improvement have been identified, but the core values and underpinnings of that system have been validated time and time again (Conseil des Colleges, 1992; Ministere de l'Education, 1993).

Evolution of College Systems

Diversity and differentiation have been further accentuated in the quarter century in which the original college systems have evolved. In some jurisdictions, unique expertise has been developed in the field of distance education to cope with the Canada's vastness and to capitalize on its international leadership in some fields of telecommunications (Sweet, 1989). In all provinces and territories, special attention has been paid to the development and refinement of more open, nonconventional learning systems, as student and client populations have become more diverse over the years. Custom-designed training, off-campus delivery systems, and technological applications to various forms of college learning have produced even further diversity of institutions within already diverse systems (Paul, 1990).

Despite their differences, Canada's colleges and college systems have had many features in common. Without exception, these systems have been seen as instruments for the implementation of government policy rather than as quasi-autonomous institutions. Provincial and territorial governments have often felt free to impose on their colleges in ways that would never go unchallenged by universities. The federal government has on occasion been quite insensitive by unilaterally introducing policy changes that have had significant influence on the colleges' capacity to function effectively (Gallagher, 1990).

Patterns of governance have called for balance between local or regional authority to enhance community responsiveness and central decision making to ensure system coherence. That balance has shifted in all jurisdictions over the years (Dennison & Levin, 1989). It is safe to assume that this trend will continue as part of the dynamic of these vibrant systems.

Canadian colleges have remained faithful to their original mission as teaching institutions responsible for providing a broad range of instructional programs. Although the range of programming has always varied from one institution and system to another, the notion of comprehensiveness of programming in colleges has been preserved throughout the country.

It is particularly significant to note that, until very recently, few colleges have sought the formal redefinition of their roles or status, unlike many newer postsecondary institutions in, for example, the United Kingdom and Germany. Alternatively, in the past few years, the British Columbia government has seen fit to designate some of its community colleges as university colleges and has asked them to become centers for 4-year undergraduate programs in a variety of areas of study, in addition to their more traditional mandates (Dennison, 1992). In the same province, novel cooperative working arrangements between the Open University[5] and several community colleges have led to new degree programs of several kinds as well as to much greater variety in industry-based training programs. Equally, in neighboring Alberta, some colleges have recently sought degree-granting status, in some cases to respond more effectively to demand for greater access to university studies. In other cases, this new status has been proposed to permit the offering of more extended instructional programs in applied fields of study now that the traditional 2-year college program is insufficient to meet labor market needs in several program areas as structural changes take place in the Canadian economy. Elsewhere in the country, there has been little agitation for a redefinition of the roles of public colleges. Rather, the call has been for all postsecondary institutions to do a better and more responsive job of achieving their historic mandates.

Similarly, Canada's colleges have retained their original commitment to open admission policies and to the provision of a range of student services necessary for institutions that accept students of diverse backgrounds and abilities. In fact, there is growing concern that admission policies may be too liberal. In British Columbia, there is a new emphasis on improving success rates in all postsecondary institutions. In Quebec, there has been a recent decision to introduce tuition fees for full-time students who continue to be unsuccessful in college studies. In other jurisdictions, the need to match programming to applicants' capabilities as well as to labor market needs has prompted an expansion of adult basic education instruction and other programs for underprepared students.

Most college personnel are now unionized. In some cases, this is a statement of ideology, in others it is a response to restrictive institutional management or tight government controls or budgets, and in yet other cases it is simply a decision to be consistent with a pattern of public sector unionization across the country. In any event, college employees who recall an era of relatively tranquil internal relationships have become more militant (or more resigned) as they face wage rollbacks, more onerous working conditions, and demands for higher productivity. College faculty groups, in particular, are now demanding more meaningful participation in the governance of their institutions and systems, and terms such as *comanagement* and *codetermination* have become much more a part of college governance vocabulary in recent years.

People in the colleges and college systems across Canada also still speak the same educational language, read the same professional literature, and try to stay on top of the same issues. Organizational culture, human resource development, leadership styles, global competition and interdependence, knowledge-based and technology-driven economics, social equity, public deficits and debt, and world sustainability are some of the topics that provoke active debate in colleges and their communities from sea to sea.

Consequences of Diversity

On balance, Canada's college systems have over the years become more dissimilar than similar as they have responded to different economic, social, and political circumstances. For example, Ontario has recently experienced one of the longest and deepest recessions in its history, and British Columbia has continued to expand economically as it capitalizes on its strategic Pacific Rim status. Newfoundland has at least temporarily lost the fishery base of its economy. Although support for a politically independent Quebec remains strong, concern about an economy that is anything but robust competes for public attention in that province. New Brunswick sticks out its determined chin and insists that its citizens will have a better future. The Northwest Territories proceed methodically with their political realignment and growing sense of self-confidence. Both public service reductions and demands for greater social equity have prompted public policy change in the western provinces.

One of the most telling consequences of increasing diversity has been a declining opportunity for these systems and institutions to learn much from one another. Several examples may be appropriate. In the area of labor relations, frameworks for collective bargaining differ, as labor legislation is specific to each jurisdiction. In some provinces, there is centralized bargaining; in others, institution-based bargaining is the practice. In some jurisdictions, college staff are government employees; in others, they are college employees. Patterns of governance are equally diverse. The composition and powers of college boards vary so much that, for example, board development programs at a national level have had marginal value at best.

In some provinces and territories, there are deliberate efforts to incorporate traditional and nontraditional students pursuing the same credentials into the same courses, classrooms, and shops. In other jurisdictions, there are still marked differences in the ways in which learning for younger and more mature students, for example, is organized. To illustrate, British Columbia and Quebec colleges generally see the distinction between full- and part-time students as an awkward but necessary administrative device with little educational significance, whereas colleges elsewhere still frequently establish separate programs, with the same objectives and content, for part-time and full-time students.

The measure of institutional entrepreneurship also varies considerably. Ontario colleges have traditionally been very effective in reaching out to employers and in providing work site, custom-designed training programs. In the northern territories, the vast distances and scattered populations have prompted their multisite colleges to be particularly innovative in finding ways to reach and support potential adult learners. Yet, in the western provinces, campus-based education and training is still the customary practice for most colleges.

Equally, the degree of differentiation of institutions within each college system also varies considerably. In Quebec, Ontario, and Nova Scotia, colleges tend to be duplicates of one another, varying largely in size and in peripheral activities, such as involvement in workplace-based training or international education. In Alberta and British Columbia, colleges now identify their own quite separate mandates and styles in systems that have become increasingly differentiated. In other provinces, institutional roles within postsecondary systems have not yet settled into discernible patterns, as systems continue to evolve.

College Diversity: A Projection

Relatively new external influences suggest that major change must be embraced by public colleges and systems, or they will soon find themselves in serious trouble. Four of these influences are of special importance.

First, all postsecondary institutions now operate in a world that has become increasingly interdependent, that is economically structured to favor the highly competitive, and that favors uniformity rather than diversity. The notion of a community college to train young people for jobs in that community is no longer realistic. In an economic environment in which an increasing amount of employment is no longer place specific, Canadians in all parts of the country now have needs that are far more common than different, and providing all learners with similar learning opportunities is now realistic and feasible. In a very real sense, there is no longer a need for college systems that are so different one from another, because all people now need much the same knowledge, skill, and behavior for economic and social purposes, wherever they may live. It is only a modest exaggeration to assert that we now need world-oriented colleges rather than community colleges.

Second, the shift from an industrial mentality to postindustrial, knowledge-based economies and rapid technological change means that many standard college instructional programs are as obsolete as many of our industrial practices. In particular, the traditional distinction between general transfer programs and specific technical or vocational ones is an industrial age perspective. Needed now are completely revamped programs that combine applied technical learning with new approaches to general education. Colleges need to enable their students to acquire generic workplace skills as well as nontechnical skills so that they will have the foundation for continuous workplace-specific training and be able to take charge of their own future learning.

Third, the range of needs in every jurisdiction is now so great that colleges, and all other postsecondary institutions, will have to develop their own distinctive market niches. The day of the college trying to be all things to all students at all times has been over for some time. It should be anticipated that postsecondary systems or networks will soon emerge in which the comprehensiveness and responsiveness that so characterized community colleges in the past will now be ensured through the system or network of unique institutions rather than through numerous comprehensive institutions. Individual institutions will come to be judged on their distinctive merits, regardless of category or class.

Fourth, a traditional but artificial distinction between public and private sectors of postsecondary education in Canada is no longer useful. In the first instance, most postsecondary institutions labeled as private are not so, unlike most in the United States. They sustain themselves by taking on government-subsidized training programs, and really serve as alternative public institutions in disguise, unencumbered by the bureaucracy and regulation associated with mainstream postsecondary institutions. Also, private institutions are rarely in competition with public ones. Rather, many of them serve disadvantaged students turned away by public institutions (Sweet, 1993). The time has come for the variety of private institutions, with their own mandates and responsibilities, to be welcomed into the new postsecondary networks as full partners.

Summary

In the vast Canadian federation that has consistently valued multiculturalism, bilingualism, and regionalism, it should not be surprising that there is no single, coherent college system. Rather, each political jurisdiction has developed its own approaches to postsecondary education. As postsecondary systems in all developed nations now adjust to new international economic and social realities, Canadian postsecondary education retains a variety of models of governance, labor relations, curriculum, and virtually every other feature of college activity. However, all these models are themselves in transition. There is every indication that the diversity evident in Canadian postsecondary education in the past will be no less apparent in the future, but that the form and shape of that diversity will be driven more by the imperatives of a postindustrial world than by the dynamics of local or regional communities in which most of Canada's college systems were originally established.

Notes

[1]This observation has been attributed to William L. MacKenzie King, a former prime minister of Canada.

[2]Canada became an independent confederation in 1867.

[3]Canadian provinces are roughly equivalent to the U.S.'s states.

[4]Although Canada adopted a renewed constitution in 1982, that constitution incorporated the original British North America Act of 1867 and made no change to the constitutional status of education.

[5]Open University and Open College are two components of The Open Learning Agency of British Columbia.

References

Anisef, P. (1982). *Losers and winners.* Toronto: Butterworth.

Cameron, D. M. (1991). *More than an academic question: Universities, government, and public policy in Canada.* Halifax, Nova Scotia, Canada: Institute for Research on Public Policy.

Conseil des Colleges. (1992). *College education: Priorities for renewal,* Quebec City, Quebec, Canada: Gouvernement du Quebec.

Denison, E. F. (1962). *The sources of economic growth in the U.S. and the alternatives before us.* New York: Committee for Economic Development.

Dennison, J. D. (1992). The university college idea: A critical analysis. *Canadian Journal of Higher Education, 22*(1), 109–123.

Dennison, J. D., & Levin, J. S. (1989). *Canada's community colleges in the nineteen eighties: Responsiveness and renewal.* Toronto: The Association of Canadian Community Colleges.

Dennison, J. D., & Gallagher, P. (1986). *Canada's community colleges: A critical analysis.* Vancouver, British Columbia, Canada: UBC Press.

Dennison, J. D., & Levin, J. S. (1989). *Canada's community colleges in the nineteen eighties: Responsiveness and renewal.* Toronto: The Association of Canadian Community Colleges.

Economic Council of Canada. (1964). *Annual review.* Ottawa, Ontario, Canada: Information Canada.

Gallagher, P. (1990). *Community colleges in Canada: A profile.* Vancouver, British Columbia, Canada: Vancouver Community College Press.

Gregor, A. D. (Ed.). (1992). *Higher education in Canada.* Ottawa, Ontario, Canada: Supply & Services Canada.

Ministere de l'Education et de la Science, Quebec. (1993). *Des colleges pour le Quebec du XXIe siecle [Colleges for a 21st Century Quebec].* Quebec City, Quebec, Canada: Ministry of Education and Science.

Paul, R. H. (1990). *Open learning and open management.* New York: Nichols.

Schultz, T. W. (1961). Investment in human capital. *American Economic Review, 5*(1), 1–17.

Selman, G., & Dampier, P. (1991). *The foundations of adult education in Canada.* Toronto: Thompson Educational.

Sheffield, E. F. (1962). *Education in Canada.* Ottawa, Ontario, Canada: Statistics Canada.

Sweet, R. (Ed.). (1989). *Post-secondary distance education in Canada.* Athabasca, Alberta, Canada: Athabasca University and The Canadian Society for the Study of Education.

Sweet, R. (1993). A profile of vocational training schools. *Canadian Journal of Higher Education, 23*(3), 36–62.

Young, D. R. (1992). *An historical survey of vocational education in Canada* (2nd ed.). North York, Ontario, Canada: Captus Press.

Zsigmond, Z. E. & Wennas, C. J. (1970). *Enrollment in educational institutions by province 1951–52– 1980–81.* Ottawa, Ontario, Canada: Economic Council of Canada.

CHAPTER 4

WEB-BASED RESOURCES

Eller, R., et al. (1998). *The rural community college initiative I: Access: Removing barriers to participation.* Washington, DC: American Association of Community Colleges. *http://www.aacc.nche.edu/Template.cfm?Section= Project_Briefs1&template=/ContentManagement/ContentDisplay.cfm&ContentID=5541&InterestCategoryID=220& Name=Project%20Briefs&ComingFrom=InterestDisplay*

Fann, A. (2002). *Tribal colleges—An overview.* ERIC Digest. EDO-JC-02-01. Los Angeles, CA: University of California at Los Angeles, ERIC Clearinghouse for Community College. *http://www.gseis.ucla.edu/ ccs/digests/dig0201.htm*

Katsinas, S. G. (2004). *Community colleges and rural America: Progress and prospects.* Denton, TX: Bill Priest Center, University of North Texas. *http://www.AACC.nche.edu/Content/NavigationMenu/ResourceCenter/ Clearinghouses/Rural_Issues/COMMUNITY_COLLEGES_AND _RURAL_AMERICAREV.pdf*

Kisker, C. (2002). Capturing the complexity: Classification systems for community and two-year colleges. EDO-JC-03-08. Los Angeles, CA: University of California at Los Angeles, ERIC Clearinghouse for Community College. *http://www.gseis.ucla.edu/ccs/digests/digest0308.htm*

Phipps, R. A., Shedd, J. M., & Merisotis, J. P. (June 2001). *A classification system for 2-year postsecondary institutions.* U.S. Department of Education: Office of Educational Research and Improvement, NCES 2001-167. *http://nces.ed.gov/pubsearch/pubsinfo.asp?pubid=2001167*

Part II

THEORETICAL FOUNDATIONS

INTRODUCTION

KEVIN J. DOUGHERTY

The community college has been subject to vigorous debate for the past thirty years over what is its mission, impact, and origins. This debate has reached a fairly high theoretical level, as questions have been posed about the fundamental nature of U.S. society and the place of the community college within it. In this part, we have included several of the classic contributions to this debate, as well as some more recent viewpoints. At the end, we describe elements of the community college mission that have not been sufficiently explored by scholars.

Typically, the debate over the social role of the community college is framed dualistically, as one between defenders and critics of the community colleges. But this simplistic frame misses very important nuances. Instead, I wish to use an analytic framework contrasting four perspectives: functionalism, instrumentalist Marxism, institutionalist theory, and state relative autonomy.

Functionalism

Most advocates of the community college fit under this theoretical position, even if they are not always aware of it. What holds them together is a set of tenets that are logically organized and closely resemble functionalist theory in the social sciences. These advocates describe the community college as serving several central needs of society: providing college opportunity, training middle-level workers, and preserving the academic excellence of our universities. Community colleges, functionalists claim, democratize college access by being plentiful, nearby, and inexpensive, by offering vocational education and adult education in addition to more traditional college offerings, and by adhering to an "open door" admissions policy that imposes few entry requirements. As a result, they argue, community colleges attract many students who are not capable of or interested in attending more traditional colleges either because as students, they have poor academic records, have strongly vocational interests, or are beyond traditional college age. Meanwhile, traditional college students who happen to attend the community college have the option to take university parallel courses and eventually transfer to a four-year college. Besides democratizing college access, functionalists argue, the vocational emphasis of the community college also serves the needs of the economy by training "middle level" workers. Finally, the community college has helped our leading state universities preserve their academic excellence. By drawing off younger and less able students, it has allowed the universities to concentrate their resources on juniors and seniors and more able students (Clark, 1960, 1980; Cohen & Brawer, 2002; Gleazer, 1968; Monroe, 1972).

These arguments closely resemble functionalist theory in social science. This theory typically focuses on the social "functions" of institutions, that is, how they serve fundamental needs of society as a whole. In the case of the schools, functionalists stress that the educational system inculcates the fundamental values and norms of society, prepares and certifies people for jobs, allows social mobility, and (through universities) creates new knowledge (Clark, 1962).

This section includes two articles that provide striking statements of a functionalist theory of the community college. The first is by the eminent sociologist, Burton Clark. His article, "The 'Cooling Out' Function in Higher Education" (Chapter 5), analyzes the organizational implications of the community college's open door admissions policy, diffuse social mission, allegiance more to the secondary school than the university, and dependence on other educational institutions. Clark posits that the community college is profoundly shaped by its unselective admissions policy, which brings it many students with baccalaureate ambitions but sub-baccalaureate abilities. In order to preserve its academic status, the community college responds by "cooling out" weak but ambitious students by diverting them toward terminal sub-baccalaureate degrees. What makes his analysis functionalist is that Clark sees this task as a necessary, albeit dirty, job: while it is dirty because cooling out must be done behind students' backs in order to be effective, it is also necessary because universities' selectivity must be preserved in order to meet society's need for advanced expertise (Clark, 1960).

Clark's analysis was subject to very sharp attack by holders of other perspective, but it has by no means been replaced. He strikingly restated his thesis two decades later (Clark, 1980). Moreover, in recent years, the functionalist analysis has been picked up by economists who argue that the community college is an effective response to societal needs for college opportunity and labor training (Kane & Rouse, 1999; Rouse, 1998). In "The Community College: Educating Students at the Margin between College and Work" (Chapter 9), Thomas Kane and Cecilia Rouse argue that the community college arose in response to societal demands for college opportunity and vocational education. They review the evidence on economic returns to community college training, finding that community college students receive significantly higher payoffs from their degrees than do students who finish their education with high school. And they conclude that the community college is an excellent, cost-efficient way of meeting popular demand for higher education because of the significant economic returns to community college training and because states with large numbers of community colleges have higher rates of college going than states without (Kane and Rouse, 1999).[1]

Instrumentalist Marxism

The functionalist celebration of the community college received a powerful rebuke by the early 1970's. Picking up Burton Clark's cooling out concept, Jerome Karabel (1972) used it to develop a conflict, rather than functionalist, theory of the community college. Whereas Clark saw the community college's role as a painful but necessary resolution of the contradiction between the American values of educational opportunity and educational excellence, Karabel saw the community college as a weapon deployed by the capitalist class against the working class in the class struggle over life chances. He noted that those cooled out were largely working class and non-white, while those upholding the putative value of educational quality were the privileged classes. For Karabel, the community college's emphasis on vocational education arises from a class stratified capitalist society. In this society, the demand for good jobs outstrips the supply, requiring the elite to find ways of defusing this politically explosive contradiction. In addition, capitalist elites—centered in business, the selective universities, and prestigious foundations—support the vocationalized community college because it provides business with publicly subsidized employee training and selective universities with a covert means of deflecting the enrollment demands of less desirable students. Community college leaders have acquiesced to these capitalist imperatives, according to Karabel, because vocationalization affords their institution a unique identity: that of a "community" college that is no longer "junior" to the university. However, community college students, particularly minority students, have resisted vocationalization just as workers have resisted capitalist work demands. Karabel backed up his argument by citing evidence that community colleges and their vocational programs disproportionately enroll working class students, that few community college aspirants to a baccalaureate degree ever receive one, and that a key basis of this result is that community college students are pressured to enroll in vocational courses (a process that Karabel termed "cooling out").

Karabel's (1972) arresting argument—which was joined by Fred Pincus (1974)—set the terms for much subsequent research on the community college. This research has strongly buttressed most of Karabel's statements about the community college's effects, while calling into question his instrumentalist Marxist analysis of the community college's origins (Dougherty, 1994, 2002). Sociologists coming after Karabel and Pincus significantly shifted the terms of the debate over why community colleges arose and later moved in a sharply vocational direction. The main element was to recast business influence more in terms of indirect constraint rather than direct intervention and to highlight the important role as well of other actors. This new approach took two forms: institutionalist theory and state relative autonomy theory.

Institutionalist Theory

In *The Diverted Dream* (1989), a portion of which is excerpted in this section (Chapter 6), Steven Brint and Jerome Karabel (1989) substantially reoriented Karabel's (1972) analysis of why the community college was vocationalized. In contrast to Karabel, Brint and Karabel (1989) find much less evidence of a direct business role in the rise and vocationalization of the community college; instead business's influence had been mostly indirect, based on its control of jobs that community colleges seek to fill. Moreover, Brint and Karabel argue that the internal dynamics of the field of higher education—particularly entrepreneurial activity by community colleges—played an even greater role than Karabel suggested in 1972. Drawing on institutional theory within organizational sociology, Brint and Karabel portray higher education as an "organizational field" composed of colleges competing for prestige and resources. Within this Darwinian universe, universities are at the top of the food chain, securing the best students, the most revenues, and the greatest prestige. Their chief concern has been to protect their academic and social exclusivity and thus the exchange value of their credentials in the face of the clamor for admissions by less privileged but ambitious students. In order to avoid throwing their doors open to the teeming masses, the universities supported the expansion of an alternative, the vocationalized community college.

Community colleges, in the meantime, collaborated with this university thrust, according to Brint and Karabel (1989). Seeing that the universities and four-year colleges had snapped up the best occupational-training markets, community colleges began many years ago to carve out a market of their own, supplying middle level or semiprofessional occupations. Beginning in the 1920s, the American Association of Community Colleges (AACC) conceived of and then militantly proselytized for a vocationalized community college. And in time, this vision persuaded not only AACC members but also external supporters such as state university heads, government officials, business, and foundations (Brint & Karabel, 1989).

State Relative Autonomy Theory

Finally, Kevin Dougherty (1994) developed an analysis that both converges with and diverges from Brint and Karabel's. The main features of this analysis are summarized in an article excerpted in this book (Chapter 7), "The Community College: The Origin, Impact, and Future of a Contradictory Institution" (2004).

Like Brint and Karabel, Dougherty (1994) finds that students entering the community college attain significantly fewer baccalaureate degrees and total years of education than do comparable students (in background, aspirations, and academic preparation) entering four-year colleges. But where Dougherty particularly diverges from their argument in his analysis of why the community arose and has taken on the particular missions that it has.

While Brint and Karabel (1989) advance a largely organizational explanation, Dougherty's (1994) analysis is grounded more in political sociology. The crux of Dougherty's argument is that government officials took the lead in establishing and vocationalizing the community college, but they did so within the constraints set by a democratic polity and a capitalist economy. Like Brint and Karabel, Dougherty concludes that direct student or business demand is insufficient to explain the rise and vocationalization of the community college. However, contrary to Brint and Karabel, Dougherty finds that governmental initiative went well beyond the actions of state university and community college officials. A wide variety of government officials supported the establishment and vocationalization of community colleges, in part out of a sincere belief in educational opportunity but also out of more self-interested reasons. At the local level, school superintendents and high school principals instigated local drives to found community colleges in good part because this would bring them prestige as educational innovators and the opportunity to become college presidents. At the state level, governors, state legislators, and state education departments joined state universities in pushing for state aid for community colleges because, among other things, they saw the community college as a cheap way to meet the demand for college access and to stimulate politically popular economic growth through publicly subsidized training for business. And at the national level, Presidents and Congress members supported federal aid for the community college for much the same reasons as their state counterparts.

But if business's direct role in establishing and vocationalizing community colleges was only secondary, Dougherty (1994) finds that its indirect role—based on its economic and ideological hegemony—has been quite strong. Dougherty agrees with Brint and Karabel (1989) that one aspect of this indirect influence has been the fact that business controls jobs that community college officials seek to fill. But Dougherty also argues that business's power to constrain governmental initiative goes further. Business also controls capital for investment and thus the pace and distribution of economic growth. Realizing that capital investment is key to economic growth and therefore their own political prospects, public officials have taken the initiative to offer business publicly subsidized vocational education in order to secure business investment in their jurisdictions. Furthermore, business has constrained government initiative not only economically but also ideologically. Government officials subscribe to values and beliefs—such as the importance of economic growth and that this growth must come through an expansion of jobs in the private rather than public sector—that have made them ready to serve business interests with little prompting (Dougherty, 1994).

For Dougherty (1994), an awareness of the community college's complex origins allows us to see how the community college could powerfully, and yet, largely unintentionally, hinder the baccalaureate opportunities of its students. The fact that most community colleges lack dormitories contributes to their higher dropout rate, but the reason they lack dormitories is because this made community colleges cheaper to operate, a potent consideration in the minds of the local educators founding them and the state officials financing them. The fact that community colleges are heavily vocational lessens their students' desire to transfer,[2] but they are so strongly vocational not in order to track students but to meet business's need for trained employees and government officials' desire for an attractive incen-

tive to secure business's political support and economic investment. The fact community colleges are two-year schools discourages students from pursuing a baccalaureate degree, because they have to transfer to separate four-year institutions with different academic standards. But the reason community colleges are two-year schools is largely because university heads did not want the competition of many more four-year schools, state officials did not want the financial burden of myriad four-year colleges, and local educators believed it would be easier to establish two-year rather than four-year colleges. The precipitate of these varying desires is an institutional structure that, unfortunately and largely unintentionally, often subverts the educational ambitions of baccalaureate aspirants entering community college, even as it opens up opportunities for students with nonbaccalaureate ambitions.

Subsequent Analyses

Since these publications, several scholars have been applying elements of both functionalist theory and the critiques of functionalist theory to analyze the community college. In an article excerpted in this book, "Educational Access and Social Mobility in a Rural Community College," (Chapter 8), James Valadez studies decision making by low-income students in a rural community college. He shows how the community college does not take advantage of those students' skills and knowledge, but at the same time he holds out hope that the community college could genuinely be an instrument of democratic access. On a more macroscopic scale, John Levin (2001) discusses the effects of globalization on seven community colleges in the U.S. and Canada. Mixing both a functionalist analysis and implicit elements of conflict theory, he examines how the growing exposure of the community colleges and their localities to wider economic, cultural, and demographic forces (what he calls globalization) has led the colleges to put more emphasis on efficiency and productivity, workforce training and economic development, and responsiveness to government and business demands.

Poorly Charted Dimensions of the Community College Role

The debate over the social role of the community college has focused on issues of access and graduation. Students' educational and economic attainment have gotten the lion's share of attention, because they fit nicely with the functionalist emphasis on social mobility and meeting the needs of the economy and critical theory's interest in social stratification. Yet community colleges have other important goals besides shaping students' life chances, and unfortunately the content and effectiveness of these other goals have been little studied. (For more on the points below, see Dougherty, 2002).

Remedial Education

As portals into higher education for students that four-year colleges would turn away as unprepared, community colleges have long provided remedial education to many students. In 1995, 41% of freshmen in public two-year colleges were enrolled in remedial courses either in reading, writing, or arithmetic, as compared to 29% of college students generally (U.S. National Center for Education Statistics, 1997). And this role promises to become even larger, as state legislators and four-year college boards continue to push to have remedial education reduced or even eliminated at four-year colleges and instead relegated to community colleges (Shaw, 1997). We need to know more about the forces behind this redefinition of institutional responsibilities for remedial education, what impact it will have on students and their colleges (both two-year and four-year), and how well community colleges actually do remediate (Dougherty, 2002).

Education for Civic Participation

Under the rubric of general education, the community college has long been committed to the nonvocational education of its students for citizenship and social participation (Cohen and Brawer, 1996: chap. 12). But we have little rigorous data on how effective it is in this role. For example, how much general education do students in vocational majors get and how much impact does it have? We also do not know how the community college's contribution to civic education is being affected by its growing role in workforce preparation and economic development (Dougherty, 2002).

Community Building

Community colleges are an important means of generating a vibrant "civil society," by providing a place for citizens of diverse backgrounds to come together, whether as students in courses or participants in public events on campus (such as art performances and exhibitions or public affairs forums). In coming together, diverse citizens learn about each other and can search for over-arching commonalities (Cohen & Brawer, 1996; Rhoads & Valadez, 1996). Community colleges are better able to do this than either four-year colleges or high schools because their student bodies are typically more socially diverse than those of four-year colleges and more chronologically diverse than those of high schools. Moreover, community colleges typically have a stronger commitment to serving their local communities. Yet this community-building function, though much described and celebrated by community college observers, has not been systematically studied except in recent research by Howard London and Kathleen Shaw (1998). We need to investigate the degree to which these community-building efforts do enhance civic consciousness and social solidarity in the community and how the community college contribution compares to that of churches, volunteer groups, clubs, and so on (Dougherty, 2002).

Endnotes

[1]However, entrants to community colleges are considerably less likely to receive bachelors' degrees than are four-year college entrants, even with controls for student background, aspirations, and academic preparation (Dougherty, 1994; Pascarella & Terenzini, 2005). As a result of this "diversion effect," states with large community college systems—though they have significantly greater college-going rates—do not have significantly higher baccalaureate attainment rates than states with small community college systems.

[2]In recent years, the argument has been made that vocational students transfer at the same rate as academic majors. But a recent study using the National Educational Longitudinal Study of the Eighth Grade (NELS: 88) and the Beginning Postsecondary Student (BPS:90) survey found that enrolling in a vocational major had a statistically significant negative effect on transfer—even after controlling for student background, academic preparation, educational and occupational aspirations, marital and parental status at time of college entry, and attendance status (Dougherty and Kienzl, forthcoming).

References

Brint, S., & Karabel, J. (1989). *The diverted dream: Community colleges and the promise of educational opportunity in America, 1900–1985.* New York: Oxford University Press.

Clark, B. R. (1960). The 'cooling out' function in higher education. *American Journal of Sociology, 65*(6), 569–576.

———. (1980). The "cooling out" function revisited. In G. Vaughan (Ed.), *Questioning the community college role* (pp. 15–32). New Directions in Community Colleges, No. 32. San Francisco: Jossey-Bass.

Cohen, A. M., & Brawer, F. B. (2002). *The American community college.* (4th ed.) San Francisco: Jossey-Bass.

Dougherty, K. J. (1994). *The contradictory college: The origins, impacts, and futures of the community college.* Albany, NY: State University of New York Press.

Dougherty, K. J. (2002). The evolving role of community colleges: Policy issues and research questions. In J. Smart & W. Tierney (Eds.), *Higher education: Handbook of theory and research,* Vol. 17 (pp. 295–348). New York: Kluwer, 2002.

Dougherty, K. J. (2004). The community college: The impact, origin, and future of a contradictory institution. In J. Ballantine & J. Spade (Eds.), *Schools and society: A sociological approach to education.* Belmont, CA: Thomson/Wadsworth.

Dougherty, K. J., & G. S. Kienzl. Forthcoming. It's not enough to get through the open door: Inequalities by social background in transfer from community colleges to four-year colleges." *Teachers College Record*

Gleazer, E. G., Jr. (1968). *This is the community college.* Boston: Houghton-Mifflin.

Kane, T. J., & Rouse, C. E. (1999). The community college: Educating students at the margin between college and work. *Journal of Economic Perspectives, 13* (Winter), 63–84.

Karabel, J. B. (1972). Community colleges and social stratification. *Harvard Educational Review 42,* 521–562.

Levin, J. (2001). *Globalizing the community college: Strategies for change in the twenty-first century.* New York: Palgrave.

Medsker, L. L. (1960). *The junior college.* New York: McGraw-Hill

Monroe, C. R. (1972). *A profile of the community college.* San Francisco: Jossey-Bass.

National Center for Education Statistics. 1997. *Remedial education at higher education institutions in fall 1995.* NCES 97-584. Washington, DC: Author.

Pascarella, E. F., & Terenzini, P. T. (2005). *How college affects students.* (Vol. 2). San Francisco: Jossey-Bass.

Pincus, F. L. (1974). Tracking in community colleges. *Insurgent Sociologist, 4* (Spring), 17–35.

Rhoads, R., & Valadez, J. (1996). *Democracy, multiculturalism, and the community college.* New York: Garland.

Rouse, C. E. (1998). Do two-year colleges increase overall educational attainment? Evidence from the states. *Journal of Policy Analysis and Management, 17*(4), 595–620.

Shaw, K. (2001). Reframing remediation as a systemic phenomenon. In B. Townsend & S. Twombly (Eds.), *Community colleges: Policy in the future context* (pp. 193–222). New York: Ablex.

Shaw, K., & London, H. (2001). Culture and ideology in keeping transfer commitment. *Review of Higher Education, 25*(4), 91–114.

CHAPTER 5

THE "COOLING-OUT" FUNCTION IN HIGHER EDUCATION[1]

BURTON R. CLARK

Abstract

The wide gap found in many democratic institutions between culturally encouraged aspiration and institutionally provided means of achievement leads to the failure of many participants. Such a situation exists in American higher education. Certain social units ameliorate the consequent stress by redefining failure and providing for a "soft" denial; they perform a "cooling-out" function. The junior college especially plays this role. The cooling-out process observed in one college includes features likely to be found in other settings: substitute achievement, gradual disengagement, denial, consolation, and avoidance of standards.

A major problem of democratic society is inconsistency between encouragement to achieve and the realities of limited opportunity. Democracy asks individuals to act as if social mobility were universally possible; status is to be won by individual effort, and rewards are to accrue to those who try. But democratic societies also need selective training institutions, and hierarchical work organizations permit increasingly fewer persons to succeed at ascending levels. Situations of opportunity are also situations of denial and failure. Thus democratic societies need not only to motivate achievement but also to mollify those denied it in order to sustain motivation in the face of disappointment and to deflect resentment. In the modern mass democracy, with its large-scale organization, elaborated ideologies of equal access and participation, and minimal commitment to social origin as a basis for status, the task becomes critical.

The problem of blocked opportunity has been approached sociologically through means-ends analysis. Merton and others have called attention to the phenomenon of dissociation between culturally instilled goals and institutionally provided means of realization; discrepancy between ends and means is seen as a basic social source of individual frustration and recalcitrance.[2] We shall here extend means-ends analysis in another direction, to the responses of organized groups to means-ends disparities, in particular focusing attention on ameliorative processes that lessen the strains of dissociation. We shall do so by analyzing the most prevalent type of dissociation between aspirations and avenues in American education, specifying the structure and processes that reduce the stress of structural disparity and individual denial. Certain components of American higher education perform what may be called the cooling-out function,[3] and it is to these that attention will be drawn.

The Ends-Means Disjuncture

In American higher education the aspirations of the multitude are encouraged by "open-door" admission to public-supported colleges. The means of moving upward in status and of maintaining high status now include some years in college, and a college education is a prerequisite of the better positions in business and the professions. The trend is toward an ever tighter connection between higher education and higher occupations, as increased specialization and professionalization insure that more persons will need more preparation. The high-school graduate, seeing college as essential to success, will seek to enter some college, regardless of his record in high school.

A second and allied source of public interest in unlimited entry into college is the ideology of equal opportunity.[4] Strictly interpreted, equality of opportunity means selection according to ability, without regard to extraneous considerations. Popularly interpreted, however, equal opportunity in obtaining a college education is widely taken to mean unlimited access to some form of college: in California, for example, state educational authorities maintain that high-school graduates who cannot qualify for the state university or state college should still have the "opportunity of attending a publicly supported institution of higher education," this being "an essential part of the state's goal of guaranteeing equal educational opportunities to all its citizens."[5] To deny access to college is then to deny equal opportunity. Higher education should make a seat available without judgment on past performance.

Many other features of current American life encourage college-going. School officials are reluctant to establish early critical hurdles for the young, as is done in Europe. With little enforced screening in the precollege years, vocational choice and educational selection are postponed to the college years or later. In addition, the United States, a wealthy country, is readily supporting a large complex of colleges, and its expanding economy requires more specialists. Recently, a national concern that manpower be fully utilized has encouraged the extending of college training to more and different kinds of students. Going to college is also in some segments of society the thing to do; as a last resort, it is more attractive than the army or a job. Thus ethical and practical urges together encourage the high-school graduate to believe that college is both a necessity and a right; similarly, parents and elected officials incline toward legislation and admission practices that insure entry for large numbers; and educational authorities find the need and justification for easy admission.

Even where pressures have been decisive in widening admission policy, however, the system of higher education has continued to be shaped partly by other interests. The practices of public colleges are influenced by the academic personnel, the organizational requirements of colleges, and external pressures other than those behind the open door. Standards of performance and graduation are maintained. A commitment to standards is encouraged by a set of values in which the status of a college, as defined by academicians and a large body of educated laymen, is closely linked to the perceived quality of faculty, student body, and curriculum. The raising of standards is supported by the faculty's desire to work with promising students and to enjoy membership in an enterprise of reputed quality—college authorities find low standards and poor students a handicap in competing with other colleges for such resources as able faculty as well as for academic status. The wish is widespread that college education be of the highest quality for the preparation of leaders in public affairs, business, and the professions. In brief, the institutional means of the students' progress toward college graduation and subsequent goals are shaped in large part by a commitment to quality embodied in college staffs, traditions, and images.

The conflict between open-door admission and performance of high quality often means a wide discrepancy between the hopes of entering students and the means of their realization. Students who pursue ends for which a college education is required but who have little academic ability gain admission into colleges only to encounter standards of performance they cannot meet. As a result, while some students of low promise are successful, for large numbers failure is inevitable and *structured*. The denial is delayed, taking place within the college instead of at the edge of the system. It requires that many colleges handle the student who intends to complete college and has been allowed to become involved but whose destiny is to fail.

Responses to Disjuncture

What is done with the student whose destiny will normally be early termination? One answer is unequivocal dismissal. This "hard" response is found in the state university that bows to pressure for broad admission but then protects standards by heavy drop-out. In the first year it weeds out many of the incompetent, who may number a third or more of the entering class.[6] The response of the college is hard in that failure is clearly defined as such. Failure is public; the student often returns home. This abrupt change in status and in access to the means of achievement may occur simultaneously in a large college or university for hundreds, and sometimes thousands, of students after the first semester and at the end of the freshman year. The delayed denial is often viewed on the outside as heartless, a slaughter of the innocents.[7] This excites public pressure and anxiety, and apparently the practice cannot be extended indefinitely as the demand for admission to college increases.

A second answer is to sidetrack unpromising students rather than have them fail. This is the "soft" response: never to dismiss a student but to provide him with an alternative. One form of it in some state universities is the detour to an extension division or a general college, which has the advantage of appearing not very different from the main road. Sometimes "easy" fields of study, such as education, business administration, and social science, are used as alternatives to dismissal.[8] The major form of the soft response is not found in the four-year college or university, however, but in the college that specializes in handling students who will soon be leaving—typically, the two-year public junior college.

In most states where the two-year college is a part of higher education, the students likely to be caught in the means-ends disjuncture are assigned to it in large numbers. In California, where there are over sixty public two-year colleges in a diversified system that includes the state university and numerous four-year state colleges, the junior college is unselective in admissions and by law, custom, and self-conception accepts all who wish to enter.[9] It is tuition-free, local, and under local control. Most of its entering students want to try for the baccalaureate degree, transferring to a "senior" college after one or two years. About two-thirds of the students in the junior colleges of the state are in programs that permit transferring; but, of these, only about one-third actually transfer to a four-year college.[10] The remainder, or two out of three of the professed transfer students, are "latent terminal students": their announced intention and program of study entails four years of college, but in reality their work terminates in the junior college. Constituting about half of all the students in the California junior colleges, and somewhere between one-third and one-half of junior college students nationally,[11] these students cannot be ignored by the colleges. Understanding their careers is important to understanding modern higher education.

The Reorienting Process

This type of student in the junior college is handled by being moved out of a transfer major to a one- or two-year program of vocational, business, or semiprofessional training. This calls for the relinquishing of his original intention, and he is induced to accept a substitute that has lower status in both the college and society in general.

In one junior college[12] the initial move in a cooling-out process is pre-entrance testing: low scores on achievement tests lead poorly qualified students into remedial classes. Assignment to remedial work casts doubt and slows the student's movement into bona fide transfer courses. The remedial courses are, in effect, a subcollege. The student's achievement scores are made part of a counseling folder that will become increasingly significant to him. An objective record of ability and performance begins to accumulate.

A second step is a counseling interview before the beginning of the first semester, and before all subsequent semesters for returning students. "At this interview the counselor assists the student to choose the proper courses in light of his objective, his test scores, the high school record and test records from his previous schools"[13] Assistance in choosing "the proper courses" is gentle at first. Of the common case of the student who wants to be an engineer but who is not a promising candidate, a counselor said: "I never openly countermand his choice, but edge him toward a terminal program by gradually laying out the facts of life." Counselors may become more severe later when grades provide a talking point and when the student knows that he is in trouble. In the earlier counseling the desire of the student has much weight; the counselor limits himself to giving advice and stating the probability of success. The advice is entered in the counseling record that shadows the student.

A third and major step in reorienting the latent terminal student is a special course entitled "Orientation to College," mandatory for entering students. All sections of it are taught by teacher-counselors who comprise the counseling staff, and one of its purposes is "to assist students in evaluating their own abilities, interests, and aptitudes; in assaying their vocational choices in light of this evaluation; and in making educational plans to implement their choices." A major section of it takes up vocational planning; vocational tests are given at a time when opportunities and requirements in various fields of work are discussed. The tests include the "Lee Thorpe Interest Inventory" ("given to all students for motivating a self-appraisal of vocational choice") and the "Strong Interest Inventory" ("for all who are undecided about choice or who show disparity between accomplishment and vocational choice"). Mechanical and clerical aptitude tests are taken by all. The aptitudes are directly related to the college's terminal programs, with special tests, such as a pre-engineering ability test, being given according to need. Then an "occupational paper is required of all students for their chosen occupation"; in it the student writes on the required training and education and makes a "self-appraisal of fitness."

Tests and papers are then used in class discussion and counseling interviews, in which the students themselves arrange and work with a counselor's folder and a student test profile and, in so doing, are repeatedly confronted by the accumulating evidence—the test scores, course grades, recommendations of teachers and counselors. This procedure is intended to heighten self-awareness of capacity in relation to choice and hence to strike particularly at the latent terminal student. The teacher-counselors are urged constantly to "be alert to the problem of unrealistic vocational goals" and to "help students to accept their limitations and strive for success in other worthwhile objectives that are within their grasp." The orientation class was considered a good place "to talk tough," to explain in an *impersonal* way the facts of life for the overambitious student. Talking tough to a whole group is part of a soft treatment of the individual.

Following the vocational counseling, the orientation course turns to "building an educational program," to study of the requirements for graduation of the college in transfer and terminal curriculum, and to planning of a four-semester program. The students also become acquainted with the requirements of the colleges to which they hope to transfer, here contemplating additional hurdles such as the entrance examinations of other colleges. Again, the hard facts of the road ahead are brought to bear on self-appraisal.

If he wishes, the latent terminal student may ignore the counselor's advice and the test scores. While in the counseling class, he is also in other courses, and he can wait to see what happens. Adverse counseling advice and poor test scores may not shut off his hope of completing college; when this is the case, the deterrent will be encountered in the regular classes. Here the student is divested of expectations, lingering from high school, that he will automatically pass and, hopefully, automatically be transferred. Then, receiving low grades, he is thrown back into the counseling orbit, a fourth step in his reorientation and a move justified by his actual accomplishment. The following indicates the nature of the referral system:

Need for Improvement Notices are issued by instructors to students who are doing unsatisfactory work. The carbon copy of the notice is given to the counselor who will be available for conference with the student. The responsibility lies with the student to see his counselor. However, experience shows that some counselees are unable to be sufficiently self-directive to seek aid. The counselor should, in such cases, send for the student, using the Request for Conference blank. If the student fails to respond to the Request for Conference slip, this may become a disciplinary matter and should be referred to the deans.

After a conference has been held, the Need for Improvement notices are filed in the student's folder. *This may be important* in case of a complaint concerning the fairness of a final grade.[14]

This directs the student to more advice and self-assessment, as soon and as often as he has classroom difficulty. The carbon-copy routine makes it certain that, if he does not seek advice, advice will seek him. The paper work and bureaucratic procedure have the purpose of recording referral and advice in black and white, where they may later be appealed to impersonally. As put in an unpublished report of the college, the overaspiring student and the one who seems to be in the wrong program require "skillful and delicate handling. An accumulation of pertinent factual information may serve to fortify the objectivity of the student-counselor relationship." While the counselor advises delicately and patiently, but persistently, the student is confronted with the record with increasing frequency.

A fifth step, one necessary for many in the throes of discouragement, is probation: "Students [whose] grade point averages fall below 2.0 [C] in any semester will, upon recommendation by the Scholarship Committee, be placed on probationary standing." A second failure places the student on second probation, and a third may mean that he will be advised to withdraw from the college altogether. The procedure is not designed to rid the college of a large number of students, for they may continue on probation for three consecutive semesters; its purpose is not to provide a status halfway out of the college but to "assist the student to seek an objective (major field) at a level on which he can succeed."[15] An important effect of probation is its slow killing-off of the lingering hopes of the most stubborn latent terminal students. A "transfer student" must have a C average to receive the Associate in Arts (a two-year degree) offered by the junior college, but no minimum average is set for terminal students. More important, four-year colleges require a C average or higher for the transfer student. Thus probationary status is the final blow to hopes of transferring and, indeed, even to graduating from the junior college under a transfer-student label. The point is reached where the student must permit himself to be reclassified or else drop out. In this college, 30 per cent of the students enrolled at the end of the spring semester, 1955–56, who returned the following fall were on probation; three out of four of these were transfer students in name.[16]

This sequence of procedures is a specific process of cooling-out;[17] its effect, at the best, is to let down hopes gently and unexplosively. Through it students who are failing or barely passing find their occupational and academic future being redefined. Along the way, teacher-counselors urge the latent terminal student to give up his plan of transferring and stand ready to console him in accepting a terminal curriculum. The drawn-out denial when it is effective is in place of a personal, hard "No"; instead, the student is brought to realize, finally, that it is best to ease himself out of the competition to transfer.

Cooling-Out Features

In the cooling-out process in the junior college are several features which are likely to be found in other settings where failure or denial is the effect of a structured discrepancy between ends and means, the responsible operatives or "coolers" cannot leave the scene or hide their identities, and the disappointment is threatening in some way to those responsible for it. At work and in training institutions this is common. The features are:

1. *Alternative achievement.*—Substitute avenues may be made to appear not too different from what is given up, particularly as to status. The person destined to be denied or who fails is invited to interpret the second effort as more appropriate to his particular talent and is made to see that it will be the less frustrating. Here one does not fail but rectifies a mistake. The substitute status reflects less unfavorably on personal capacity than does being dismissed and forced to leave the scene. The terminal student in the junior college may appear not very different from the transfer student—an "engineering aide," for example, instead of an "engineer"—and to be proceeding to something with a status of its own. Failure in college can be treated as if it did not happen; so, too, can poor performance in industry.[18]

2. *Gradual disengagement.*—By a gradual series of steps, movement to a goal may be stalled, self-assessment encouraged, and evidence produced of performance. This leads toward the available alternatives at little cost. It also keeps the person in a counseling milieu in which advice is furnished, whether actively sought or not. Compared with the original hopes, however, it is a deteriorating situation. If the individual does not give up peacefully, he will be in trouble.

3. *Objective denial.*—Reorientation is, finally, confrontation by the facts. A record of poor performance helps to detach the organization and its agents from the emotional aspects of the cooling-out work. In a sense, the overaspiring student in the junior college confronts himself, as he lives with the accumulating evidence, instead of the organization. The college offers opportunity; it is the record that forces denial. Record-keeping and other bureaucratic procedures appeal to universal criteria and reduce the influence of personal ties, and the personnel are thereby protected. Modern personnel

record-keeping, in general, has the function of documenting denial.

4. *Agents of consolation.*—Counselors are available who are patient with the over-ambitious and who work to change their intentions. They believe in the value of the alternative careers, though of lower social status, and are practiced in consoling. In college and in other settings counseling is to reduce aspiration as well as to define and to help fulfil it. The teacher-counselor in the "soft" junior college is in contrast to the scholar in the "hard" college who simply gives a low grade to the failing student.

5. *Avoidance of standards.*—A cooling-out process avoids appealing to standards that are ambiguous to begin with. While a "hard" attitude toward failure generally allows a single set of criteria, a "soft" treatment assumes that many kinds of ability are valuable, each in its place. Proper classification and placement are then paramount, while standards become relative.

Importance of Concealment

For an organization and its agents one dilemma of a cooling-out role is that it must be kept reasonably away from public scrutiny and not clearly perceived or understood by prospective clientele. Should it become obvious, the organization's ability to perform it would be impaired. If high-school seniors and their families were to define the junior college as a place which diverts college-bound students, a probable consequence would be a turning-away from the junior college and increased pressure for admission to the four-year colleges and universities that are otherwise protected to some degree. This would, of course, render superfluous the part now played by the junior college in the division of labor among colleges.

The cooling-out function of the junior college is kept hidden, for one thing, as other functions are highlighted. The junior college stresses "the transfer function," "the terminal function," etc., not that of transforming transfer into terminal students; indeed, it is widely identified as principally a transfer station. The other side of cooling-out is the successful performance in junior college of students who did poorly in high school or who have overcome socioeconomic handicaps, for they are drawn into higher edu-

cation rather than taken out of it. Advocates of the junior college point to this salvaging of talented manpower, otherwise lost to the community and nation. It is indeed a function of the open door to let hidden talent be uncovered.

Then, too, cooling-out itself is reinterpreted so as to appeal widely. The junior college may be viewed as a place where all high-school graduates have the opportunity to explore possible careers and find the type of education appropriate to their individual ability; in short, as a place where everyone is admitted and everyone succeeds. As described by the former president of the University of California:

> A prime virtue of the junior college, I think, is that most of its students succeed in what they set out to accomplish, and cross the finish line before they grow weary of the race. After two years in a course that they have chosen, they can go out prepared for activities that satisfy them, instead of being branded as failures. Thus the broadest possible opportunity may be provided for the largest number to make an honest try at further education with some possibility of success and with no route to a desired goal completely barred to them.[19]

The students themselves help to keep this function concealed by wishful unawareness. Those who cannot enter other colleges but still hope to complete four years win be motivated at first not to admit the cooling-out process to consciousness. Once exposed to it, they again will be led not to acknowledge it, and so they are saved insult to their self-image.

In summary, the cooling-out process in higher education is one whereby systematic discrepancy between aspiration and avenue is covered over and stress for the individual and the system is minimized. The provision of readily available alternative achievements in itself is an important device for alleviating the stress consequent on failure and so preventing anomic and deviant behavior. The general result of cooling-out processes is that society can continue to encourage maximum effort without major disturbance from unfulfilled promises and expectations.

Notes

[1]Revised and extended version of paper read at the Fifty-fourth Annual Meeting of the American Sociological Association, Chicago, September 3–5,

1959. I am indebted to Erving Goffman and Martin A. Trow for criticism and to Sheldon Messinger for extended conceptual and editorial comment.

[2]"Aberrant behavior may be regarded sociologically as a symptom of dissociation between culturally prescribed aspirations and socially structured avenues for realizing these aspirations" (Robert K. Merton, "Social Structure and Anomie," in *Social Theory and Social Structure* [rev. ed.; Glencoe, Ill.: Free Press, 19571, p. 134). See also Herbert H. Hyman, "The Value Systems of Different Classes: A Social Psychological Contribution to the Analysis of Stratification," in Reinhard Bendix and Seymour M. Lipset (eds.), *Class, Status and Power: A Reader in Social Stratification* (Glencoe, Ill.: Free Press, 1953), pp. 426–42; and the papers by Robert Dubin, Richard A. Cloward, Robert K. Merton, and Dorothy L. Meier, and Wendell Bell, in *American Sociological Review*, Vol, XXIV (April, 1959).

[3]I am indebted to Erving Goffman's original statement of the cooling-out conception. See his "Cooling the Mark Out: Some Aspects of Adaptation to Failure," *Psychiatry*, XV (November, 1952), 451–63. Sheldon Messinger called the relevance of this concept to my attention.

[4]Seymour Martin Lipset and Reinhard Bendix, *Social Mobility in Industrial Society* (Berkeley: University of California Press, 1959), pp. 78–101.

[5]*A Study of the Need for Additional Centers of Public Higher Education in California* (Sacramento: California State Department of Education, 1997), p. 128. For somewhat similar interpretations by educators and laymen nationally see Francis J. Brown (ed.), *Approaching Equality of Opportunity in Higher Education* (Washington, D.C.: American Council on Education, 1955), and the President's Committee on Education beyond the High School, *Second Report to the President* (Washington, D.C.: Government Printing Office, 1957).

[6]One national report showed that one out of eight entering students (12.5 per cent) in publicly controlled colleges does not remain beyond the first term or semester; one out of three (31 per cent) is out by the end of the first year; and about one out of two (46.6 per cent) leaves within the first two years. In state universities alone, about one out of four withdraws in the first year and 40 per cent in two years (Robert E. Iffert, *Retention and Withdrawal of College Students* [Washington, D.C.: Department of Health, Education, and Welfare, 1958], pp. 15–20). Students withdraw for many reasons, but scholastic aptitude is related to their staying power: "A sizeable number of students of medium ability enter college, but . . . few if any

of them remain longer than two years" (*A Restudy of the Needs of California in Higher Education* [Sacramento: California State Department of Education, 1955], p. 120).

[7]Robert L. Kelly, *The American Colleges and the Social Order* (New York: Macmillan Co., 1940), pp. 220–21.

[8]One study has noted that on many campuses the business school serves "as a dumping ground for students who cannot make the grade in engineering or some branch of the liberal arts," this being a consequence of lower promotion standards than are found in most other branches of the university (Frank C. Pierson, *The Education of American Businessmen* [New York: McGraw-Hill Book Co, 1959], p. 63). Pierson also summarizes data on intelligence of students by field of study which indicate that education, business, and social science rank near the bottom in quality of students (*ibid.*, pp. 65–72).

[9]Burton R. Clark, The *Open Door College: A Case Study* (New York: McGraw-Hill Book Co., 1960), pp. 44–45.

[10]*Ibid.*, p. 116.

[11]Leland L. Medsker, *The Junior College: Progress and Prospect* (New York: McGraw-Hill Book Co., 1960), chap. iv.

[12]San Jose City College, San Jose, Calif. For the larger study see Clark, *op. cit.*

[13]San Jose Junior College, Handbook for Counselors, 1957–58, p. 2. Statements in quotation marks in the next few paragraphs are cited from this.

[14]*Ibid.*, p. 20.

[15]Statement taken from unpublished material.

[16]San Jose junior College, "Digest of Analysis of the Records of 468 Students Placed on Probation for the Fall Semester, 1956," September 3, 1956.

[17]Goffman's original statement of the concept of cooling-out referred to how the disappointing of expectations is handled by the disappointed person and especially by those responsible for the disappointment. Although his main illustration was the confidence game, where facts and potential achievement are deliberately misrepresented to the "mark" (the victim) by operators of the game, Goffman also applied the concept to failure in which those responsible act in good faith (*op. cit, passim*). "Cooling-out" is a widely useful idea when used to refer to a function that may vary in deliberateness.

[18]*Ibid.*, p. 457; cf. Perrin Stryker, "How To Fire an Executive," *Fortune*, L (October, 1954), 116–17 and 178–92.

[19]Robert Gordon Sproul, "Many Millions More," *Educational Record*, XXXIX (April, 1958), 102.

CHAPTER 6

COMMUNITY COLLEGES AND THE AMERICAN SOCIAL ORDER

STEPHEN BRINT AND JEROME KARABEL

From the earliest days of the Republic, Americans have possessed an abiding faith that theirs is a land of opportunity. For unlike the class-bound societies of Europe, America was seen as a place of limitless opportunities, a place where hard work and ability would receive their just reward. From Thomas Jefferson's "natural aristocracy of talent" to Ronald Reagan's "opportunity society," the belief that America was—and should remain—a land where individuals of ambition and talent could rise as far as their capacities would take them has been central to the national identity. Abraham Lincoln expressed this deeply rooted national commitment to equality of opportunity succinctly when, in a special message to Congress shortly after the onset of the Civil War, he described as a "leading object of the government for whose existence we contend" to "afford all an unfettered start, and a fair chance in the race of life."[1]

Throughout much of the nineteenth century, the belief that the United States was a nation blessed with unique opportunities for individual advancement was widespread among Americans and Europeans alike. The cornerstone of this belief was a relatively wide distribution of property (generally limited, to be sure, to adult white males) and apparently abundant opportunities in commerce and agriculture to accumulate more. But with the rise of mammoth corporations and the closing of the frontier in the decades after the Civil War, the fate of the "self-made man"—that heroic figure who, though of modest origins, triumphed in the competitive marketplace through sheer skill and determination—came to be questioned. In particular, the fundamental changes then occurring in the American economy—the growth of huge industrial enterprises, the concentration of propertyless workers in the nation's cities, and the emergence of monopolies—made the image of the hardworking stockboy who rose to the top seem more and more like a relic of a vanished era. The unprecedented spate of success books that appeared between 1880 and 1885 (books bearing such titles as *The Law of Success, The Art of Money Getting, The Royal Road to Wealth,* and *The Secret of Success in Life*) provide eloquent, if indirect, testimony to the depth of the ideological crisis then facing the nation.[2]

Clearly, if belief in the American dream of individual advancement was to survive under the dramatically changed economic and social conditions of the late nineteenth century, new pathways to success had to be created. No less a figure than the great steel magnate Andrew Carnegie recognized this. Indeed, in 1885, just one year before the bitter labor struggle that culminated in the famous Haymarket affair, Carnegie conceded in a speech to the students of Curry Commercial College in Pittsburgh that the growth of "immense concerns" had made it "harder and harder . . . for a young man without capital to get a start for himself." A year later, in his widely read book, *Triumphant Democracy,* Carnegie forthrightly acknowledged that opportunities to rise from "rags to riches" had declined with the rise of the giant corporation (Carnegie 1886; Perkinson 1977, pp. 120–121).

Carnegie's solution to the problems posed by the great concentration of wealth was not, however, its redistribution, as was being called for by an increasing number of Americans. On the contrary, in 1889, Carnegie wrote that the "Socialist or Anarchist" who proposes such solutions "is to be regarded as attacking the foundation upon which civilization itself rests." Nevertheless, the man of wealth has a responsibility to administer it in the interest of all so as to promote "the reconciliation of the rich and poor." Perhaps the most effective means of doing so, Carnegie suggested, was to follow the example of such educational benefactors as Peter Cooper and Leland Stanford. The result of such judicious and farsighted philanthropy would be, he noted, the construction of "ladders upon which the aspiring can rise" (Carnegie 1889, pp, 656, 660, 663).

Yet when Carnegie wrote, the nation's educational institutions were poorly suited to provide such ladders of ascent. In 1890, the average American had not been educated beyond the fifth grade. Moreover, the prevailing assumption—among both businessmen and the population at large—was that an ordinary common school training would provide the skills necessary for economic advancement. The nation's colleges and universities, still largely encrusted by traditional notions of cultural transmission and professional training, stood well to the side of the pathways to business success. As late as 1900, 84 percent of the prominent businessmen listed in *Who's Who in America* had not been educated beyond high school (Wyllie 1954, p. 95). In the late nineteenth century, getting ahead in America thus largely remained a matter of skill in the marketplace, not in the classroom.

If education remained peripheral to the attainment of the American dream, this was in part because, as late as 1890, there was a sense in which no educational system as such had yet been constructed. To be sure, the widely accessible common school had been one of the distinguishing features of American democracy, and one of its tasks was to provide those who attended it with the tools for economic success. But the primary purpose of the common school had been to train citizens for life in a democratic society, not to select workers and employees for their future positions in an increasingly complex and hierarchical division of labor. For this task, a differentiated rather than a common educational system needed to be constructed whose hierarchical divisions would mirror those of the larger society.

The "ladders of ascent" that Carnegie advocated presupposed basic structural changes in the organization of American education. The loose array of high schools, colleges, universities, and professional schools attended in the late nineteenth century by the increasing, though still limited, numbers of students who continued beyond elementary school was not really a system at all. There was not even a clear sequential relationship among the various types of educational institutions. Professional schools did not require the completion of four years of college, and colleges did not require the completion of four years of high school (Collins 1979, pp. 109–130). As a consequence, high schools, colleges, and professional schools sometimes even competed for the same students.[3] For its part, business was largely contemptuous of the diplomas awarded by high schools and especially colleges; in fact, many businessmen contended that college training was positively harmful to young men, in that it made them unfit for the harsh and practical world of commerce and industry (Wyllie 1954, pp, 101–105).

Yet despite the chaotic and relatively undifferentiated organization of American education in 1890, by 1920 the outlines of the orderly and highly stratified educational system that remains with us today were already visible.[4] The emergence of a hierarchically differentiated educational system closely linked to the labor market provided an alternative pathway to success in an era when the traditional image of the self-made man who rose to riches through success in the competitive marketplace was becoming less and less plausible. The creation of "ladders of ascent" through education thus gave new life to the American ideology of equality of opportunity at the very moment when fundamental changes in the economy threatened to destroy it.

In a context of increasing inequality between rich and poor and growing challenges to the established order, the importance of a new pathway to economic advancement is difficult to overestimate. America's large and open educational system now provided an alternative means of getting ahead. Vast inequalities of wealth, status, and power though there might be, the ladders of opportunity created by the new educational system helped the United States retain its national identity as a land of unparalleled opportunities for individual advancement.

Today, the idea that the education system in general, and higher education in particular, should provide ladders of upward mobility is so familiar as to be taken for granted. Yet viewed from a comparative perspective, the emphasis in the United States on individual mobility through education is quite remarkable.[5] To this day, no other society—not Japan, not Canada, not Sweden—sends as many of its young people to colleges and universities as the United States does (Organization for Economic Cooperation and Development 1983). *The vast and expensive system of educational pathways to success that has been constructed in this country is both the institutional embodiment of this commitment to the ideology of equality of opportunity and a constant source of reinforcement of this ideology.* The shape of today's enormous system of colleges and universities—a system in which in recent years almost half the nation's young people have participated—is incomprehensible apart from this commitment.

Central to this distinctive system of higher education is an institution—the two-year junior college (or community college, as it came to be called)—that came into being just when the American educational system was being transformed so as to provide new ladders of ascent. The two-year college, whose pattern of historical development will be the subject of this book, has from its very origins at the turn of the century reflected both the egalitarian promise of the world's first modern democracy and the constraints of its dynamic capitalist economy. Enrolling fewer than ten thousand students in 1920, the American junior college had by 1980 grown to enroll well over four million students (Eells 1931a, p. 70; U.S. Bureau of the Census 1987, p. 138).[6] The most successful institutional innovation in twentieth-century American higher education, the two-year college has in recent years spread beyond the United States and established roots in a growing number of foreign countries, among them Japan, Canada, and Yugoslavia.

Community Colleges and Democratic Ideology

With over one-half of all college freshmen now enrolled in two-year institutions (U.S. Department of Education 1986, p. 111), the community college has come to be an integral feature of America's educational landscape. Yet as recently as 1900, the junior college was no more than a dream in the minds of a few administrators at a handful of America's leading universities. Enrolling under 2 percent of all college freshman in 1920 (U.S. Office of Education 1944, pp. 4, 6), the year in which the American Association of Junior colleges (AAJC) was founded, the junior college came to play an increasingly pivotal role in the transformation of the nation's system of colleges and universities. Perhaps more than any other segment of postsecondary education, the community college was at the forefront of the postwar demographic expansion that changed the face of American higher education.

The transformation of American higher education was organizational as well as demographic. For the birth of the two-year college marked the arrival of an entirely new organizational form in the complex ecological structure of American postsecondary education. In terms of sheer numbers, no other twentieth-century organizational innovation in higher education even begins to approach the success of the two-year college, which grew from a single college in 1901 to over 1,200 institutions in 1980, representing almost 40 percent of America's 3,231 colleges. In 1984, over 4.5 million students were enrolled in two-year colleges nationwide (U.S. Bureau of the Census 1987, p. 138).

When the junior college, first appeared, the outlines of a hierarchical system of colleges and universities were already becoming visible. Nonetheless, the emergence of the junior college fundamentally altered the shape of American higher education, for it introduced a new tier into the existing hierarchy. Thus the two-year institution was not simply another of the many lower-status colleges that dotted America's educational landscape; it was a different type of institution altogether. Unlike even the humblest four-year institution, it failed to offer what had come to be considered the sine qua non of being an "authentic" college—the bachelor's degree.

What was behind the birth of this new institutional form with roots in both secondary and higher education? What explains the extraordinary growth of the two-year college during the twentieth century? And why has the provision of terminal vocational education—a function that, as we shall see, was for decades peripheral to the mission of the junior college—come to occupy an increasingly central place in the community college? The answers to these questions require an understanding of the peculiar political and ideological role that education has come to play in American life.

American Education and the Management of Ambition

All industrial societies face the problem of allocating qualified individuals into a division of labor characterized by structured inequalities of income, status, and power. Since occupying the superordinate positions in such systems provides a variety of material and psychological gratifications not available to those who occupy subordinate positions, the number of individuals who aspire to privileged places in the division of labor not surprisingly tends to surpass, often by a considerable margin, the number of such slots that are available. In advanced industrial societies, all of which have renounced to one or another degree the ideologies that have historically legitimated the hereditary transmission of positions, this problem of a discrepancy between ambition and the capacity of the opportunity structure to satisfy it is endemic. All such societies face, therefore, a problem in what might be called the *management of ambition*.[7]

In the United States, the management of ambition is a particularly serious dilemma, for success—as Robert Merton (1968, pp. 185–214) and others have pointed out—is supposed to be within the grasp of every individual, no matter how humble his (and, more recently, her) background.[8] Moreover, ambition and hard work have been held in more unambiguously high regard in America—a society that was bourgeois in its very origin—than in many European societies, with their aristocratic residues. From Benjamin Franklin to Norman Vincent Peale, the desire to succeed and the willingness to work hard to do so have been seen by Americans as among the highest moral virtues. One consequence of this belief that the "race of life" is both open and well worth winning is that more Americans from subordinate social groups harbor aspirations of making it to the top.

To be sure, not all Americans have joined the race to get ahead. Educational and occupational aspirations are systematically related to social class (Kerckhoff 1974, Spenner and Featherman 1978), and some segments of the population, especially in the racial ghettos of the nation's inner cities, have withdrawn from the competition all together (Ogbu 1978, 1993).[9] Even among those individuals who do harbor hopes of upward mobility, the depth of their commitment is highly variable and shifts in aspirations are common. Upward mobility has real social and psychological costs, and not everyone is willing—or able—to pay them. For many Americans, hopes of a "better life" crumble in the face of obstacles; consigned to low-status jobs, they nonetheless find fulfillment in the private sphere of family and friends. Moreover, aspirations to move ahead are often accompanied by a belief in the legitimacy of inequalities that are based on genuine differences in ability and effort[10]—*and* by doubts about whether one measures up.

The problem of managing ambition is particularly difficult in the United States. In 1980, for example, over half of high school seniors "planned" (not "aspired to") careers in professional/technical jobs. But in that same year, only 13 percent of the labor force was employed in such jobs (Wagenaar 1984). Even if one assumes that there will be a considerable increase in the number of such jobs in the future and that there is significant uncertainty in many of these "plans," it seems clear nonetheless that American society generates far more ambition than its structure of opportunity can satisfy.

As early as the 1830s, there was a powerful popular demand for free schooling, although it should be noted that the early workingmen's organization of New York, Boston, and Philadelphia looked on the provision of free, public education not as a way of getting ahead but as indispensable to the exercise of their rights as democratic citizens (Welter 1962, pp. 46–47).[11] By the middle of the nineteenth century, free elementary education in America's "common schools" had become a reality in many states. Much as the early granting of "universal" suffrage (limited in fact to while males) promoted the incorporation of American working people into the existing political order, so too did the early provision of free public schools (Katznelson and Weir 1985).

As schools became more relevant to economic success and correspondingly more attractive to ambitious young men and women during the early twentieth century, popular demand for the expansion of education intensified. Between 1920 and 1940, over 20 percent of the age-eligible (fourteen to seventeen) population in the United States was enrolled in secondary schools; in eleven European countries, including Great Britain, France, Germany, and Sweden, the proportions nowhere surpassed 8 percent (Rubinson 1986, p. 522). The same pattern could also be seen in rates of attendance in higher education. An examination of statistics regarding college enrollments in twenty-two countries, including Japan and Russia as well as the major nations of Western and Central Europe, reveals that no country enrolled even half as many students as did the United States during the period 1913 and 1948 (Ben-David 1966, p. 464). From a sheer demographic perspective, then, the educational system has nowhere been as central to the life experiences of the population as it has been in the United States.

In light of the extraordinary emphasis in the United States on individual economic success and on the role of education as a pathway to it, it is hardly surprising that there has been such a powerful demand from below to expand the educational system. What is perhaps more difficult to understand is the readiness of the state to provide the additional years of schooling demanded by the populace. After all, one can well imagine the state trying to control public expenditures by limiting the amount of education. Yet for the most part, governing elites have joined in a broad national consensus that favored the construction of an educational system of unparalleled dimensions.

There have been many sources of elite support for the expansion of education, among them adherence to the classic Jeffersonian view that a democratic citizenry must be an educated one, and a related commitment to the task of nation building (Meyer et al. 1979). But also critical, we wish to suggest, has been the implicit recognition that a society that promises its subordinate classes unique opportunities for individual advancement needs to offer well-developed channels of upward mobility.

No one could deny the inequalities of wealth and power in the United States. But what made these inequalities tolerable, perhaps, was that everyone—or so the national ideology claimed—had a chance to advance as far as his ability and ambition would take him. And once education became established as the principal vehicle of this advancement, it became politically difficult for any group to oppose its expansion.

The result of this interplay of popular demand and elite response was the creation of a huge but highly differentiated educational system, with unequaled numbers of students enrolled in it. America's commitment to the idea of equal opportunity guaranteed that there would be a tremendous amount of ambition for upward mobility among the masses; somehow the educational system would have to find a way to manage the aspirations that its own relative openness had helped arouse. The junior college was to play a critical role in this process, and it is to the complex pressures it has faced both to extend and to limit opportunity that we now turn.

The Contradictory Pressures Facing the Junior College

From its very beginnings, the junior college has been subjected to contradictory pressures rooted in its strategic location in the educational system in a society that is both democratic and highly stratified. Its growth in substantial part a product of the responsiveness of a democratic state to demand from below for the extension of educational opportunity, the junior college's trajectory has also been shaped by the need to select and sort students destined to occupy different positions in the job structure of a capitalist economy. In the popular mind—and in the eyes of the many dedicated and idealistic men and women who have worked in the nation's two-year institutions—the fundamental task of the junior college has been to "democratize" American higher education, by offering to those formerly excluded an opportunity to attend college. But the junior college has also faced enormous pressure to limit this opportunity, for the number of students wishing to obtain a bachelor's degree—and the type of professional or managerial job to which it has customarily led—has generally been far greater than the capacity of the economy to absorb them. Poised between a burgeoning system of secondary education and a highly stratified structure of economic opportunity, the junior college was located at the very point where the aspirations generated by American democracy clashed head on with the realities of its class structure.

Like the American high school, the community college over the course of its history has attempted to perform a number of conflicting tasks: to extend opportunity and to serve as an agent of educational and social selection, to promote social equality and to increase economic efficiency, to provide students with a common cultural heritage and to sort them into a specialized curriculum, to respond to the demands of subordinate groups for equal education and to answer the pressures of employers and state planners for differentiated education, and to provide a general education for citizens in a democratic society and technical training for workers in an advanced industrial economy.[12]

Burton Clark, in a seminal article on "The 'Cooling-Out' Function in Higher Education," put the dilemma facing the junior college well: "a major problem of democratic society is inconsistency between encouragement to achieve and the realities of limited opportunity" (Clark 1961, p. 513). By virtue of its position in the structure of educational and social stratification, the junior college has confronted the necessity of diverting the aspirations of students who wish to join the professional and managerial upper middle class, but who are typically destined by the structure of opportunity to occupy more modest positions. In such a situation, Clark now bluntly, "for large numbers failure is inevitable and *structured*" (Clark 1961, p. 515, emphasis his).

The junior college has thus been founded on a paradox: the immense popular support that it has enjoyed has been based on its link to four-year colleges and universities, but one of its primary tasks from the outset has been to restrict the number of its students who transfer to such institutions. Indeed, the administrators of elite universities who developed the idea of the junior college (and who later gave the fledgling organizational form crucial sponsorship) did so, as we shall show in Chapter 2, with the hope that it would enable them to divert from their own doors the growing number of students clamoring for access to higher education. These university administrators recognized that the democratic character of American culture and politics demanded that access to higher education be broad; in the absence of alternative institutions, masses of ill-prepared students would, they feared, be clamoring at their gates.[13]

The junior college thus focused in its early years on offering transfer courses reason was simple: Students who attended two-year institutions did so on the basis of their claim to be "real" colleges, and the only way to make this claim convincing was for them to offer liberal arts courses that would in fact receive academic credit in four-year institutions. For the first three decades of their existence, the junior colleges thus concentrated on constructing preparatory program that, as the catalogues of the two-year

institutions were fond of characterizing them, were of "strictly collegiate grade."

There was almost a missionary zeal among the predominantly small-town Protestant men who presided over the early junior college movement; their task as they saw it was to bring the blessings of expanded educational opportunity to the people. Proudly referring to their institutions as "democracy's colleges," they viewed the two-year institution as giving thousands of worthy students who would otherwise have been excluded a chance to attend higher education. Yet they were also aware that the educational and occupational aspirations of their students outran their objective possibilities by a substantial margin; while some of their students had great academic promise, well under half of them, they knew, would ever enter a four-year college or university. Something other than college preparatory courses, therefore, would have to be provided for them if they were to receive an education appropriate for their future place in the division of labor.

The solution that the leaders of the junior college movement devised bore a striking resemblance to the one developed earlier by the administrators of secondary education at the point when the high school was transformed from an elite to a mass institution: the creation of a separate vocational education track. The underlying logic of the vocational solution is perhaps best captured in a speech given in 1908 by Dean James Russell of Teachers College, Columbia University, to a meeting of the National Education Association. Entitling his presentation "Democracy and Education: Equal Opportunity for All," Russell asked:

> How can a nation endure that deliberately seeks to raise ambitions and aspirations in the oncoming generations which in the nature of events cannot possibly be fulfilled? If the chief object of government be to promote civil order and social stability, how can we justify our practice in schooling the masses in precisely the same manner as we do those who are to be our leaders? (quoted in Nasaw 1979, p. 131)

Russell's answer was unequivocal: The ideal of equal education would have to be forsaken, for only *defferentiated education*—education that fit students for their different vocational futures—was truly democratic. Paradoxically, then, if mass education were to realize the promise of democracy, separate vocational tracks had to be created.

In a society that generated far more ambition for upward mobility than its structure of opportunity could possibly satisfy, the logic of vocationalism, whether at the level of secondary or higher education, was compelling. The United States was, after all, a class-stratified society, and there was something potentially threatening to the established order about organizing the educational system so as to arouse high hopes, only to shatter them later. At the same time, however, the political costs of turning back the popular demand for expanded schooling were prohibitive in a nation placing so much stress on equality of opportunity. What vocationalism promised to do was to resolve this dilemma by, on the one hand, accepting the democratic pressure from below to provide access to new levels of education while, on the other hand, differentiating the curriculum to accommodate the realities of the economic division of labor. The aspirations of the masses for upward mobility through education would not, advocates of vocationalization claimed, thereby be dashed; instead, they would be rechanneled in more "realistic" directions.[14]

The leaders of the junior college movement enthusiastically embraced the logic of vocationalism and, by the 1930s, had come to define the decided lack of student enthusiasm for anything other than college-transfer programs as the principal problem facing the two-year institution. Their arguments in favor of expanding terminal vocational education in the junior college were essentially identical to those used by advocates of vocational education in the high school: Not everyone could be a member of the elite; vocational programs would reduce the high dropout rate; and occupational training would guarantee that students would leave the educational system with marketable skills.

At times, junior college leaders were remarkably forthright about the fate that awaited these students in the labor market. For example, Walter Crosby Eells, founder of the *Junior College Journal* and executive secretary of the American Association of Junior Colleges from 1938 to 1945, noted that while universities tend to train leaders, democratic societies also needed "educated followership" and so proposed junior college terminal education as a particularly effective vehicle for training such followers (Eells 1941b, p. 29). Under Eells's leadership, by 1940 a consensus had been reached among key junior college leaders

that between two-thirds and three-fourths of junior college students should be enrolled in terminal vocational education programs.

Yet the junior college leaders who advocated vocationalization faced a formidable obstacle: the widespread and persistent lack of interest among their own students. Despite encouragement from local administrators and counselors, no more than 25 to 30 percent of junior college students had ever enrolled in vocational programs. Their chances of getting ahead in a nation increasingly obsessed with educational credentials depended, they believed, on transferring to a four-year institution. The students realized that junior college occupied the bottom rung of higher education's structure. But as long as they were enrolled in college-parallel transfer programs, the possibility that they could obtain a professional or upper managerial job survived. Faced with the energetic efforts of junior college administrators to expand occupational education, the students—many of whom were of modest social origins—sensed that the attempt to vocationalize their institutions threatened to divert them from their educational and occupational aspirations.

This pattern of student opposition to vocational programs continued after World War II. The enrollment target of vocational education advocates remained two-thirds to three-quarters of junior college students, but at no time from the mid-1940s to the late-1960s did the proportion of two-year college students in the vocational track surpass one-third of the entire enrollment. Remarkably, this pattern of resistance to vocational education continued despite a dramatic increase in the number of students enrolled in community colleges, from just over 200,000 students in 1948 to almost 1.3 million in 1968 (U.S. Bureau of the Census, 1975, p. 383). Throughout this period, approximately two-thirds of community college students continued to be enrolled in college preparatory programs; of these, fewer than half ever transferred to a four-year institution (Medsker 1960, Medsker and Tillery 1971).

After decades of student resistance, enrollments in community college vocational programs finally surged after 1970, following a decline in the market for college graduates. By the mid-1970s the percentage of students in programs specifically designed to provide occupational training had risen to at least 50 percent, and by 1980, the proportion had grown to approximately 70 percent.[15] Simultaneously, transfer rates fell drastically (Baron 1982, Cohen and Brawer 1982, Friedlander 1980, Lombardi 1979).

Although it would be misleading to hearken back to a mythical "golden age" when the junior college catapulted the majority of its students onto the pathway of educational and occupational success, the community college has historically provided a ladder of upward mobility to at least some of its students.[16] Especially in an institution that claimed as its *raison d'être* the democratization of American higher education, the sharp rise in vocational enrollments and the corresponding decline in the rate of transfer warrant careful examination. Increasingly, it seems, the community college has become a vocational-training institution, more and more divorced from the rest of academia, with potentially serious consequences for the life chances of its students.[17]

Curricular Change in the Community College

Observers of the transformation of the community college from an institution oriented to college-preparatory transfer programs to one emphasizing terminal vocational training have tended to focus on one of two forces as the principal cause: either the changing preference of student "consumers" of community college education or, alternatively, the decisive influence of business elites. In the first, which might be called the *consumer-choice model*, institutions of higher education are regarded as responding exclusively to students' curricular preferences: what the consumers of higher education demand, they receive. In the second, which we shall refer to as the *business-domination model*, the curricular offerings of the community colleges are seen as reflecting the imprint of powerful business interests, which prefer programs that provide them with technically trained workers. Drawing, respectively, on classical liberal and Marxist approaches to the problem of institutional change, each of these models provides a theoretically plausible explanation for the trajectory of community college development, and, accordingly, commands our attention.

The Consumer-Choice and Business-Domination Models

The consumer-choice model is an application of the more general "rational-choice" model of human behavior popular among economists (see, for example, Becker 1983) and an increasing number of social scientists in neighboring disciplines. This model sees students' preferences as based on perceptions of the labor market "returns" that are yielded by different programs (Freeman 1971, 1976). According to this perspective, the enormous growth in community college vocational programs reflects the shift in the preference of hundreds of thousands of educational consumers. The aggregate consequence of all these individual shifts is the increasing predominance of occupational training in the two-year colleges.

The consumer-choice model views students as highly rational economic maximizers.[18] They wish to obtain the highest possible rates of return for the lowest cost in time, effort, and expense. Consequently, as the rate of return to liberal arts education begins to decline and opportunities for relatively high returns to low-cost vocational education increase, students make the rational choice: they begin to invest more heavily in vocational education, and colleges in turn expand their vocational course offerings to meet the increased demand. Especially in light of the widely publicized decline in the early 1970s in the economic returns for a college degree, the consumer-choice model offers a parsimonious explanation of the community college's vocationalization.

The unit of analysis in the consumer-choice model is not the group or the institution but, rather, the individual. As with the other approaches embodying "methodological individualism," the underlying assumption of this model is that social processes can be reduced to individuals' preferences and activities (Lukes 1968).

The other explanation of the community colleges' vocationalization, the business-domination model, emphasizes the power of large corporations to shape the educational system to serve their own interests. This perspective is in many ways an application to education of a broader Marxist "instrumentalist" theory of the role of the state in advanced capitalist societies.[19] Advocates of this view see the rise of vocationalism as primarily caused by the active intervention of business in shaping the community college's curricular offerings. Seeing in vocational education an opportunity to train at public expense a labor force of narrowly educated but technically competent middle-level specialists, big business has moved—through private donations, control of boards of trustees, and influence on trend-setting private foundations—to tailor the community college to its particular needs. In the business-domination model, the primary unit of analysis is social class, viewed in the Marxist framework as embedded in a capitalist mode of production.

Given the historical enthusiasm of the business community for vocational training (Lazerson and Grubb 1974) and its often-expressed concern in recent years about the tendency of four-year colleges and universities to produce masses of "over-educated" workers, the role attributed by the business-domination model to large corporations in the process of vocationalization seems plausible. According to this perspective, community colleges are seen as eager "to do the errands of business interests," having "no broader conception of education . . . than one that narrowly serves these interests" (Pincus and Houston 1978, p. 14). Bowles and Gintis, authors of *Schooling in Capitalist America*, believe that the increasingly vocationalized community college is well designed to produce that particular combination of technical competence and social acquiescence that is required to occupy skilled but powerless positions in the corporate economy: "The social relationships of the community college classroom increasingly resemble the formal hierarchical impersonality of the office or the uniform processing of the production line" (Bowles and Gintis 1976, p. 212)[20]

Both the consumer-choice and the business-domination perspectives capture something important, we believe, about the forces shaping community college development. Market forces have influenced student preferences, and the downturn in the labor market for college graduates in the early 1970s was indeed a major factor in the rapid community college vocationalization of the following years. And especially since the mid-1970s, business has influenced (occasionally directly, but more often indirectly) the shape and content of the curricula from which community college students select their programs.

Today student "consumers" eagerly enroll in community college occupational programs that they hope will lead them into relatively high-paying, secure jobs with opportunities for advancement. These choices, though based, we shall argue, on imperfect labor market information, are in part logical responses to the over-crowded market for college-trained persons and the difficulties of competing in such a market. The programs in which these occupational students enroll, in turn, are determined in part by industry's needs for particular types of "middle-level" manpower.

We believe that the indirect influence of business on community college curricula has always been great. The colleges have for some time sought to keep pace with manpower developments in the private economy. Indeed, the more enterprising two-year college administrators have studied regional and national labor projections almost as if they were sacred texts. Arthur Cohen, now director of the ERIC Clearinghouse for Junior Colleges at the University of California at Los Angeles, was hardly exaggerating when he wrote that "when corporate managers . . . announce a need for skilled workers . . . college administrators trip over each other in their haste to organize a new curriculum" (Cohen 1971, p. 6).

Yet despite the consumer-choice and business-domination models' contributions to our understanding of recent developments in the community college, neither is an adequate guide to the past. Rather, they are most useful for the period since 1970, the year of the first signs of decline in the labor market for college graduates—and of little help for the period before that year. Since some of the most influential community college officials have been attempting to vocationalize their institutions since at least 1930, that leaves forty years of history almost entirely unaccounted for by either model. Moreover, we shall argue, neither model captures some of the key dynamics of the process of vocationalization since 1970.

Before 1970, our study reveals, neither students nor businessmen were very interested in vocational programs. Most students (and their families) desired the prestige of a baccalaureate degree and resisted terminal vocational training. But despite the students' overwhelming preference for liberal arts programs, the leaders of the American Association of Junior Colleges and their allies pursued a policy of vocationalization for over four decades before there was any notable shift in the students' preferences. This policy decision cannot be explained by the consumer-choice model.

Similarly, most members of the business elite were indifferent to community colleges before the late 1960s. Indeed, for almost another decade after that, business interest in the community colleges remained modest and picked up only in the late 1970s, after the colleges had already become predominantly vocational institutions. The indifference of business people to programs ostensibly developed in their interests cannot be readily explained by the business-domination model. An adequate explanation of the community college's transformation thus requires a fundamental theoretical reformulation.

Toward an Institutional Approach

The framework that we propose to account for the transformation of American community colleges may be called, albeit with some oversimplification, an *institutional model.* Inspired in part by the classical sociological tradition in the study of organizations,[21] this approach can, we believe, illuminate processes of social change beyond the specific case of education. Perhaps the model's most fundamental feature is that it takes as its starting point organizations themselves, which are seen as pursuing their own distinct interests. Within this framework, special attention is focused upon "organizational fields" (e.g., education, medicine, journalism), which may be defined as being composed of "those organizations that, in the aggregate, constitute a recognized area of institutional life: key suppliers, resource and product consumers, regulatory agencies, and other organizations that produce similar services or products" (DiMaggio and Powell 1938, p. 148).[22] Relations among organization within the same field are often—but not always—competitive; accordingly, understanding the historical trajectory of a particular organization generally requires an analysis of its relationship to other organizations offering similar services. The dynamics of specific institutions, in turn, are rooted in their relationships to other major institutions. For example, the educational system must be analyzed in relation to the state and the economy. If the focus of the consumer-choice and the business-domination models is on the individual and the class respectively, the focus of this approach will be, accordingly, on the institution.

According to this perspective, neither the consumer-choice nor the business-domination model pays sufficient attention to the beliefs and activities of the administrators and professionals who typically have the power to define what is in the "interest" of the organizations over which they preside. Much of our analysis will focus, therefore, on explaining why these administrators chose to vocationalize despite what we shall document was the opposition of the student consumers (an opposition that casts doubt on the consumer-choice model) and the indifference of potential sponsors in the business corporations (which in turn undermines the business-domination model). Our analysis assesses the beliefs and organizational interests of those who pursued the vocationalization policy and the techniques they used to implement this policy over time. It also examines the forces, both external and internal to the community college movement, that facilitated or hindered implementation of the policy at different historical moments.

In skeletal form, our basic argument is that the *community colleges chose to vocationalize themselves, but they did so under conditions of powerful structural constraints.* Foremost among these constraints was the subordinate position of the community college in the larger structure of educational and social stratification. Put more concretely, junior colleges were hampered by their subordinate position in relation to that of the older and more prestigious four-year colleges and universities and, correspondingly, a subordinate position in the associated competition to place their graduates into desirable positions in the labor market.

Perhaps the best way to capture this dual structural subordination is to think of the structure of stratification faced by community colleges in terms of two parallel but distinct components—one a structure of labor market stratification and the other a structure of institutional stratification in higher education. From this perspective, educational institutions may be viewed as competing for training markets—the right to be the preferred pathway from which employers hire prospective employees. Access to the most desirable training markets—those leading to high-level professional and managerial jobs—is, and has been for decades, dominated by four-year colleges and, at the highest levels, by elite graduate and professional schools. Community colleges, by their very location in the structure of higher education, were badly situated to compete with better-established institutions for these training markets. Indeed, it is not an exaggeration to say that by the time that two-year colleges established a major presence in higher education, the best training markets were effectively monopolized by rival institutions.

Training markets are critical to the well-being of higher-education institutions. In general, those that have captured the best markets—for example, the top law, medical, and management schools—are the institutions with the most resources, the greatest prestige, and the most intense competition for entry. Viewed historically, community colleges had lost the most strategic sectors of this market before they could enter the competition. The best that the community colleges could hope to do, therefore, was to try to situate themselves favorably for the next available market niche. Therein resided the powerful organizational appeal of the two-year college's long-standing vocationalization project, a project that, as we shall show, had become widely accepted among community college administrators long before there was any decline in the demand for graduates of four-year colleges or any demand for vocational programs from the community college students themselves.

Because of their precarious position in the competition for training markets, community colleges tried desperately to fit themselves to the needs of business despite the absence of direct business interest in the colleges. Indeed, far from imposing on the community colleges a desire for a cheap docile labor force trained at public expense, as the business-domination model would have it, big business remained indifferent to the community colleges for the first sixty years of their existence. Yet because of the structural location of business in the larger political economy—and, in particular, its control of jobs—community colleges had little choice but to take into account the interests of their students' future employers. Thus business exerted a profound influence over the direction of community college affairs and pushed them in the direction of vocationalization without any direct action whatsoever. This capacity to exert influence in the absence of direct intervention reflects the *structural power* of business.[23]

Reduced to its essentials, then, our argument is that the community colleges found themselves in a situation of structured subordination with respect to both other higher-education institutions and business. Within the constraints of this dual subordination, the vocationalization project was a means of striking the best available bargain. We refer in the text to this deference to the perceived needs of more powerful institutions—even when such institutions made no conscious efforts to control their affairs—as *anticipatory subordination.*

This anticipatory subordination was rooted in the recognition by the community colleges that if they tried to compete with the existing better-endowed, higher-status institutions on their own terrain, they would face certain defeat. A far better strategy, it was determined after much internal debate with the junior college movement, was to try to capture an unexploited—albeit less glamorous—market in which they would not compete directly with institutions with superior resources. In return for accepting a subordination that was, in any case, inherent in their structural location, the community colleges would use vocationalization to bring a stable flow of resources linked to a distinctive function, a unique institutional identity, and above all, a secure—indeed, expanding—market niche. Only the students' resistance stood in the way of this project's realization.

The Outline of This Volume

Our study of the American junior college is divided into two sections. Part I is a historical analysis of the origins of the two-year institution, its growth and development, and its transformation into a predominantly vocational institution. The focus of Part I is on developments at the national level, and it attempts to trace the spread of junior colleges during this century from a few states in the Midwest and West to every corner of the United States. We shall pay particular attention in Part One to the trajectory of junior college development in the state that for decades was the uncontested leader of the national movement: California. For California was not only the first state to develop a coherent "master plan" for higher education; as late as 1968, it enrolled over one-third of all the junior college students nationwide (Carnegie Commission 1970, p. 59).[24]

Part II is a detailed case study of the development of community colleges in Massachusetts. The history of junior colleges in this stale encapsulates, in telescoped fashion, developments at the national level. Founded initially as institutions primarily devoted to the provision of liberal arts-transfer programs, Massachusetts's community colleges were transformed during the 1970s into overwhelmingly vocational institutions. Broadly representative of national trends ever the past two decades, the case of Massachusetts's community colleges will illuminate the dynamics which have led to the triumph of vocationalism in so many other states.[25]

We have included both national-level and state-level studies because of our conviction that each is critical to understanding junior college development. The study of national-level events is crucial for tracing the rise to prominence of the two-year college. By 1920, with the founding of the AAJC, the junior college movement had become nationwide, and developments in national institutions often had major consequences for two-year colleges at state and local levels. In particular, the national level was where the campaign for vocationalization originated and gained momentum; indeed, it is hard to imagine that the "comprehensive model" of the community college, with its strong emphasis on vocational programs, would have been embraced by state systems from Florida to Washington without the help of such national organizations as the American Association of Junior Colleges and the Carnegie Foundation.

Yet an analysis of national-level forces and developments can tell us only part of the story of the two-year colleges' transformation. Although it can illuminate the historical evolution of program preferences, it cannot give us a detailed account of the reactions to these pref-erences at the state and local levels, the independent sources of change at these levels, or the means through which policy preferences were implemented on specific community college campuses. Such issues require both archival data and field work for the purposes of examining processes of change in state coordinating bodies and on individual community college campuses. A case study was thus necessary, we believed, to complement and give texture to our broader analysis of national trends, and it is for this reason that we examined the rise and transformation of Massachusetts community colleges.

Finally, in the last chapter, we attempt to bring together the findings of our national-level study and our case study of Massachusetts and to identify the theoretical implications of our investigation. The development of junior colleges reveals much about not only the educational system but also the character of American society: the two-year college has been a distinctively American creation, and nowhere else has it attained such prominence. How and why this peculiar institution developed—and through what processes it was fundamentally transformed—will be the subject of the remainder of the book.

CHAPTER 7

THE COMMUNITY COLLEGE: THE IMPACT, ORIGIN, AND FUTURE OF A CONTRADICTORY INSTITUTION

KEVIN J. DOUGHERTY

Kevin J. Dougherty discusses the development of the community college and its role in American society. In doing so, he explores what he calls "the contradictory functions" of community colleges and considers the future of this important, but often neglected, part of higher education. As you read through this piece, consider how educational trajectories and future work careers are shaped by the type of educational institution you attend.

Questions to consider as you read this selection:

1. What are the functions of community colleges? In what sense are they contradictory?
2. What is the role of community colleges in maintaining inequality in society?
3. How did business and government affect the growth of community colleges?
4. Was the impact of business and government on community colleges different from that on research universities?

Community colleges are one of the most important sectors of U.S. higher education. They are important because of their great number, their critical role in providing college opportunity (especially for nontraditional students), and the essential function that they play in providing postsecondary vocational training. These public two-year colleges (excluding branches of state four-year colleges) comprise over one-quarter of all higher educational institutions in the United States, numbering nearly one thousand (American Association of Community Colleges, 2000: 11).[1] Community colleges enroll over one-third of all college students (some 5.3 million in fall 1999).[2] This enrollment share is even greater for nontraditional students, whether older, part-time, minority, or disadvantaged (American Association of Community Colleges, 2000: 28–29, 36–37; U.S. National Center for Education Statistics, 2002: 231, 242, 245, 248). Finally, community colleges are important as key sources of post secondary vocational education. Vocational enrollees at community colleges comprise over half of all students in all forms of postsecondary vocational training and provide a large share of our nation's graduates in such important occupations as nursing, computer operations, and auto repair (Dougherty, 1994: 5; Dougherty and Bakia, 2000; Grubb, 1996: 54–56).

Yet, because of this very importance, community colleges are contradictory institutions. Community colleges have taken on a host of different social functions, but some of these functions are partially incompatible. In this piece I explore these contradictory functions in closer detail.

Contradictory Functions and Impacts

Most community colleges are "comprehensive" institutions, offering a wide variety of programs to a diverse student clientele. In most community colleges, a majority of students are enrolled in workforce preparation and economic development programs. However, three-quarters of all first-time community college students (including adults) aspire to get at least a baccalaureate degree and one-quarter transfer to a four-year college within five years of entering a community college (Kojaku and Nunez, 1998: 7; McCormick, 1997: 32, 41). In addition, community colleges operate sizable programs in remedial education, nonvocational or adult education, and entertainment and other programs for the general community (Cohen and Brawer, 2002). Examining these functions in greater detail allows us to better understand the ways in which they are compatible or incompatible, synergistic or contradictory.

Workforce Development

The community college role in workforce preparation and economic development ranges from preparing students for their first job to retraining unemployed workers and welfare recipients, upgrading the skills of employed workers, assisting owners of small businesses, and helping communities with economic development planning (Dougherty and Bakia, 1999, 2000; Grubb, 1996).

In terms of initial job preparation, community colleges play a central role in supplying trained workers for "middle level" or "semiprofessional" occupations such as nurses, computer operators, and auto mechanics. In fact, about one-fifth of recent labor force entrants began at a community college (Grubb, 1996: 54–56). These vocational graduates receive substantial economic payoffs. For example, students earning a vocational associate's degree from a community college earn 20 to 30% more than high school graduates of similar race and ethnicity, parental education, marital status, and job experience (Grubb, 2002).[3] Still, the economic payoffs to community college degrees are, on average, not as good as those for baccalaureate degrees. Granted, community college degrees can have greater payoffs than baccalaureate degrees, if we are comparing, for example, an associate's

degree in engineering and a baccalaureate degree in humanities. However, we should not let this overlap in payoffs lead us—as it does some observers—to simply state that a community college degree pays as well as a bachelor's degree. Looking across all fields of study, the average baccalaureate degree pays about 40% more than the average high school degree, considerably more than the average vocational or academic associate's degree (Dougherty, 1994: 61; Grubb, 2002).

The community college's role in job retraining, small business assistance, and economic development planning—though less heralded than its role in job preparation—is growing rapidly in importance. Today, almost all community colleges retrain workers for new jobs or new tasks in existing jobs. In addition, many colleges assist small business owners by sponsoring small business development centers or simply offering courses that provide advice and training in management and personnel practices, marketing, finance, procuring contracts with government agencies, introducing new production technologies and work practices, and adapting to new government regulations. Finally, community colleges promote economic development by assisting local economic development planning efforts. A number of community colleges actively scan the economic environment for social and economic trends, emerging work practices, and new regulations and then pass this information on to employers, government agencies, civic groups, and the public. In addition, some community colleges actively participate in efforts to create or shape their locality's response to those economic and social trends. For example, community colleges often join local economic planning organizations and local and state initiatives to attract employers to the region or, in the absence of such organizations, themselves convene local political and economic leaders to discuss what actions to take (Dougherty and Bakia, 1999, 2000).

While the community college's role in workforce preparation and economic development is very useful, it also can cause the community college considerable difficulties. Community colleges with very active workforce preparation programs can lose money on unpopular training programs, flood the market with too many graduates, provoke criticism by competing training providers, and give employers too much influence over the college curriculum (Dougherty,

1994; Dougherty and Bakia, 2000). Moreover, an active workforce preparation effort can interfere with other functions of the community college such as preparing students for transfer to four-year colleges and providing students with a general education. Let us address these issues below.

College Access and Opportunity

The community college is not just a job trainer. It is also a central avenue into higher education and toward the baccalaureate degree, particularly for working class, nonwhite, and female students. Many baccalaureate recipients, particularly in states such as California and Florida, got their start at community colleges. In fact, several studies find that states and localities that are highly endowed with community colleges have significantly higher college attendance rates than states and localities with a smaller community college presence (Dougherty, 1994: 50–51; Rouse, 1998).

Several features of community colleges make them great avenues of college access. Community colleges are widely distributed across the country, located in urban, suburban, and rural areas. They are cheaper to attend than four-year colleges: Their tuitions are usually low, and they are nearby, so that dormitory residence is not necessary (or possible). And because of their open-door admissions ideal, they are more willing to take "nontraditional" students: high school dropouts, the academically deficient, vocational aspirants, and adults interested in leisure education.

However, we must attach a major qualification to this finding about the community college's openness. Many different studies find that entering a community college rather than a four-year college significantly lowers the probability that a student will attain a baccalaureate degree (Dougherty, 1994: 52–61; Pascarella and Terenzini, 1991: 372–373, 506–507).[4] Clearly, this gap in baccalaureate attainment could be simply due to the fact that community college students *on average* tend to be less well off, less prepared academically, and less ambitious educationally and occupationally than are four-year college entrants. But even when we compare community college entrants and four-year college entrants with the same family background, academic aptitude, high school grades, and educational and occupational aspirations, the community college entrants on average attain 11

to 19% *fewer* baccalaureate degrees than their four-year college peers (Dougherty, 1994: 52–61; and Pascarella and Terenzini, 1991: 372–373, 506–507). How do we explain this?

On closer inspection we find that—quite apart from the qualities students bring to college—entering the community college puts obstacles in the way of the pursuit of the baccalaureate degree. All other things being equal, baccalaureate aspirants who begin at a community college are more likely than comparable four-year college entrants to drop out during the first two years of college, not move on to become juniors at a four-year college, and drop out in the junior or senior year (Dougherty, 1994: chap. 4). Let's examine each of these three obstacles. Community college students more often drop out in the first two years of college because community colleges are less able to academically and socially integrate their students into the life of the college through such devices as living in campus dorms and being surrounded by academically oriented students and teachers. In addition, fewer community college students go on to the junior year at four-year colleges because, in comparison to four-year college entrants, they receive weaker encouragement to pursue a bachelor's degree (largely due to the emphasis that community colleges place on occupational education), less adequate financial aid, and less interest by four-year colleges in admitting them to popular campuses and programs. Finally, community college students who do successfully transfer to a four-year degree are more likely to drop out than their four-year college peers because former community college students lose credits in transfer, find it more difficult to secure financial aid, receive a poorer preparation in the freshman and sophomore years for the academic demands of upper-division courses, and often encounter inadequate efforts by universities to socially integrate community college transfers (Dougherty, 1994: chap. 4).

As noted above, a major reason why community college entrants attain fewer baccalaureate degrees than four-year college entrants lies in the fact that community colleges are so committed to occupational education. A number of studies show that the more vocational a community college is, the lower its transfer rate and the lesser the likelihood that its students will go on to get bachelor's degrees. Furthermore, the more vocational a state's community college system is, the lower the proportion of its high school graduates who will receive baccalaureate degrees ten years later, even when studies control for differences between the states in population characteristics and labor market conditions (Dougherty, 1994: 94).

But how precisely does the fact that a community college is very vocationally oriented make it less likely that its students will transfer? One way is by pulling more students into programs that have low transfer rates. Another is by undercutting the quality of the academic programs that have higher transfer rates.

Strongly vocational community colleges pull many students who enter with baccalaureate ambitions or are undecided into occupational education. These colleges spread before students a vast array of well designed vocational programs in attractive fields such as medical technology, computer operations, and engineering technology. These programs are advertised in college catalogs and brochures that are abundant, glossy, and well placed, in contrast to the often paltry, poorly printed, and poorly displayed advertisements for the academic transfer programs. The vocational programs are often housed in more modern facilities than the academic programs. And the colleges loudly and frequently proclaim that vocational-education graduates do as well as baccalaureates (although on the whole this is not true) (Dougherty, 1994: 95, 207–208).

Once in vocational programs, students are not as strongly encouraged to consider transfer. The main goal of these programs is still to prepare students for immediate employment. The teachers and administrators in these programs are often recruited from the trades for which they train students and have relatively little interest in and knowledge about transfer. This is not to say that enrolling in a vocational program is an insurmountable hurdle to transferring. To be sure, many community college vocational students do transfer to four-year colleges (Cohen and Brawer, 2002). But national data on transfer rates also show that community college students enrolled in vocational programs transfer at a substantially lower rate than do students majoring in academic subjects (Bradburn, Hurst, and Peng, 2001: 23).[5]

The community college's commitment to occupational education has also undercut transfer by weakening the quality of the academic program. As the community college has steadily increased its interest in and spending on vocational education over the last three decades, the liberal arts curriculum has steadily shriveled, with many fields abandoned and sophomore or post-introductory courses becoming rare. As a result, fewer students have been getting the academic associate degree, the traditional route to the baccalaureate. Instead, they "mill" around with no particular major or direction (Cohen and Brawer, 2002, Dougherty, 1994: 95–96; Grubb, 1991).[6]

Remedial Education

From the beginning, community colleges have been gateways into higher education for students whom four-year colleges would turn away as unprepared for college. As a result, community colleges have long provided remedial education to many of their students (Cohen and Brawer, 2002). In 1995, 41% of freshmen in public two-year colleges were enrolled in remedial courses either in reading, writing, or arithmetic, as compared to 29% of college students generally (U.S. National Center for Education Statistics, 1997: 102). And this role promises to become even larger, as state legislators and four-year college boards increasingly push to have remedial education reduced or even eliminated at four-year colleges and relegated instead to community colleges (Shaw, 1997).

This diversion of remediation into the community college seems to make sense if, as many believe, community colleges do a better job of remediation than four-year colleges. However, there is no conclusive evidence that this is the case.[7] And even if it were true, it would still pose a deep dilemma, one rooted in the contradictory effects of the community college. As shown above, community colleges hinder students' chances of getting baccalaureate degrees. As a result, the many states now pushing students needing remediation out of four-year colleges into community colleges may be exposing those students to contradictory impacts. On the one hand, academically deficient students pushed into community colleges may attain more education by perhaps receiving better remediation and occupational education than they would at four-year colleges. But on the other hand, their long-run educational attainment may be harmed by receiving less assistance in pursuing a baccalaureate degree.

General Education

A longstanding commitment of American education has been general education, whether defined as transmitting a common culture or fostering skills of broad utility in a person's life, such as critical thinking and communication skills. But this commitment is also partially contradicted by the community college's other commitments, particularly to occupational education.

Community colleges have made a major commitment to general education. For example, an analysis of the catalogs of 32 community colleges found that all of them had some kind of general education requirement for their transfer programs and at least 90% had a general education requirement for their nontransfer programs. But though these figures are impressive, they also exaggerate the actual degree to which community college students receive a general education. For example, among the 90% of those 32 community colleges that had core curriculum requirements for their nontransfer programs, only half required taking even one course in U.S. government and only one-fifth required a course in ethnic studies or multiculturalism (Zeszotarski, 1999).

These apparent gaps in the provision of general education are not surprising because community colleges face great difficulties in providing general education for all their students. The rise of occupational education has meant that community colleges now enroll many students whose primary purpose is likely to be preparation for a job rather than preparation for a variety of life roles. This problem is exacerbated if employers are paying for the training. Contract training programs typically are narrowly focused on providing skills and usually devote little or no attention to broader social knowledge and life skills (Dougherty, 2002; Dougherty and Bakia, 2000).

The Origins and Later Development of Community Colleges

Befitting their multiple and contradictory functions, community colleges have had equally mixed and contrasting origins, which is rarely acknowledged in the standard accounts of how community colleges were founded and later developed. Typically, these conventional accounts state that community college was founded in response to calls by students, parents, and publicly interested educators and government officials for more college opportunities. And later, community colleges moved from an emphasis on academic education to a stress on occupational education primarily in response to the needs of students and employers for vocational training (Cohen and Brawer, 2002; Monroe, 1972).

But some observers—particularly sociologists—have pointed out how these conventional chronicles miss much of the real history of the community college. For example, while these accounts mention the key role of state universities, they often misanalyze it. The state universities pushed the founding of community colleges not just to expand college opportunity, as is typically claimed, but also to keep the universities academically selective by channeling less able students toward the community colleges. Moreover, the universities unwittingly spurred the vocationalization of the community college by monopolizing greater status as "senior" colleges that trained for the most prestigious professional and managerial occupations. In order to escape the status of "junior" colleges, community colleges began in the 1920s to carve out an independent role as suppliers of a distinct training market of their own, the "middle level" or semiprofessional occupations such as technicians, nurses, etc. (Brint and Karabel, 1989; Dougherty, 1994).

Local and state government officials also played a key role in the establishment and later vocationalization of community colleges, motivated not just by a sincere belief in educational opportunity but also by self-interest. At the local level, school superintendents and high school principals were the prime instigators of local drives to found community colleges. While they were certainly moved by a commitment to expand college opportunity, they were also driven by the desires to earn prestige as college founders and to secure jobs as presidents of the new colleges (Dougherty, 1994).

At the state level, governors, state legislators, and state education departments strongly pushed the expansion and later vocationalization of community colleges. Again, their support was prompted by more than just a desire to widen college access. State officials were mindful that building more community colleges, rather than expanding existing four-year colleges, could meet the great demand for college access in the 1960s and 1970s at a much lower cost to state government. Unlike the four-year colleges, community colleges would not require expensive dormitories, libraries, and research facilities. These savings would translate either into lower taxes or more state funds for other politically popular programs, both of which would make elected government officials more popular. In addition, community colleges, because of their strong commitment to vocational and technical education, could help stimulate the growth of state economies by attracting business firms with the carrot of publicly subsidized training of employees. This economic growth in turn would enhance the reelection chances of officials when they ran again for political office (Dougherty, 1994).

Business firms usually did not play a powerful direct role in founding or vocationalizing community colleges. But business played a powerful indirect role, based on business's central position within the United States's economic and ideological systems. Economically, business controls jobs and investment capital. Hence, in order to get their graduates access to the jobs employers control, community college officials on their own initiative will develop occupational programs that employers find useful, even without business demand for such programs (Brint and Karabel, 1989; Dougherty, 1994). Business also owns investment capital and thus largely controls the pace and distribution of economic growth. Realizing that capital investment is key to economic growth and therefore their own political prospects, elected officials have taken the initiative to offer business publicly subsidized vocational education in order to secure business investment in their jurisdictions. Ideologically, business influences government officials because those officials subscribe to values and beliefs—such as that economic growth is vital and that this growth must come primarily through an expansion of jobs in the private rather than public sector—that have made them ready to serve business interests (Dougherty, 1994).

From Complex Origins to Contradictory Effects

An awareness of the community college's complex origins allows us to see how community colleges have come to powerfully hinder the baccalaureate opportunities of their students without this necessarily being an intended result. Because they lack dormitories, community colleges are less likely to keep their students in college by enmeshing them in a vibrant campus social life. But the reason community colleges lack dormitories is because this made the colleges cheaper to operate, a potent consideration in the minds of the local educators founding them and the state officials financing them. Because community colleges are heavily vocational, their transfer rate is lower than it might otherwise be. But a major reason community colleges are so strongly vocational is that this was a means of meeting elected officials' desire for economic investment and community college officials' desire for political support from business and jobs for their graduates. Finally, because community colleges are two-year schools, students are discouraged from pursuing a baccalaureate degree because they have to transfer to separate four-year institutions with different academic standards. But the reason community colleges are two-year schools is largely because university heads did not want the competition of many more four-year schools, state officials did not want the financial burden of myriad four-year colleges, and local educators felt two-year colleges would be easier to establish and be staffed by local educators. The precipitate of these many different interests is an institutional structure that, unfortunately and largely unintentionally, often subverts the educational ambitions of baccalaureate aspirants entering community college, even as it opens up opportunities for students with nonbaccalaureate ambitions. In short, the complex origins of the community college have created a contradictory institution: one serving many, often conflicting, missions.

The Future of the Community College

The community college will not remain static. It will continue to change, perhaps sharply, due to its diffuse institutional mission and high responsiveness to its economic, social, and political environments (Brint and Karabel, 1989; Clark, 1960; Dougherty, 1994). As it is, this environment is changing rapidly and rather chaotically. Economically, as our economy further globalizes, the occupational composition, class distribution, and employment stability of the U.S. population are being transformed. Semi-skilled jobs in factories and offices are being killed or moved abroad, and class inequality has been increasing. Meanwhile, high immigration is bringing many people who require acculturation and preparation for high-skill jobs. Hence, community colleges are stepping up their efforts at job preparation and economic development (Dougherty and Bakia, 1999, 2000). Meanwhile, the drive to reform welfare by moving people rapidly into jobs is bringing the community college many students for short-term job training, but it is also depriving the community college of other students who have to leave college to take jobs either to make up for the loss of welfare benefits or to meet work requirements in order to retain them (Mazzeo, Rab, and Eachus, 2003). Finally, the community college faces a more hostile political environment, with government becoming more stingy in its appropriations, demanding greater accountability, and more frequently denouncing remedial education in the community college (Dougherty, Hong, and Kim, 2003).

Beyond affecting the number and kind of students the community college gets, these same external pressures are also shaping the programs it offers. Occupational and remedial education are rising, but so might transfer education if financially strapped states increasingly rely on community colleges to offer the beginning of a baccalaureate education at a cheaper cost to the state. Teaching may change dramatically if the promised revolution in educational technology, such as internet courses, indeed takes place. But this much ballyhooed phenomenon may not develop as promised if it provides a less effective education—especially for less prepared students who may need a lot of hands-on contact with teachers—than claimed (Dougherty, 2002).

All in all, the community college—now an American classic—will keep changing, adding new missions and revising old ones. This very inclusiveness of mission will continue to keep the community college a very important, but also very contradictory, institution.

Notes

I would like to thank Floyd Hammack and Joan Spade for their comments on this chapter.

1. The 968 community colleges in 1998 did not include two-year branches of state universities. In 1985, the latest year for which these figures are reported, there were 67 such branches (American Association of Community Colleges, 2000: 11; U.S. National Center for Education Statistics, 2002: 290).

2. Though community colleges enrolled 37% of all college students in 1999, they enrolled 44% of all minority students, 44% of all students age 25 and older, and 56% of all part-time students (Ameri-

can Association of Community Colleges, 2000: 28–29, 36–37; U.S. National Center for Education Statistics, 2002: 231, 242, 245, 248). The figures are for degree-credit enrollments and do not include the many students in nondegree credit courses in adult education and contract training.

3. Lower degrees receive smaller payoffs. Students receiving one-year certificates outpace high school graduates by only about 10% in annual earnings, and students who attend community college but do not receive a certificate or degree lead high school graduates by only 5 to 10% in earnings for every year of community college. Moreover, the payoff to a given community college credential varies by the student's social background, major, and job placement. For example, women make more from associate's degrees and certificates than do men but make less when they have secure no credential. The payoff is considerably higher for associate's degrees in engineering and computers, business, and (for women) health than in education or humanities. Finally, community college students get much better returns if they find employment in fields related to their training, than if they do not (Grubb, 1996: 90, 95, 99, 102; 2002).

4. Partially counterbalancing this diversionary effect is the finding (which is tentative and by no means conclusive because it is based on only a few studies) that community colleges are more helpful than four-year colleges to students who do not aspire to a bachelor's degree and come from disadvantaged backgrounds (Dougherty, 1994: 56; Whitaker and Pascarella, 1994).

5. It may be that much of the difference in transfer rate between academic and vocational majors may be due to differences in their family background, academic aptitude and preparation coming out of high school, and educational and occupational aspirations. This is a question that merits close investigation.

6. Besides the demoralizing impact of the community college's growing vocationalization, the liberal arts were also weakened by the decline in the academic aptitude and academic interest of entering students, the revolt against curricular restrictions in the late 1960s, and the desire of community colleges to hold on to students under the enrollment-driven funding system in place in the 1970s (Cohen and Brawer, 2002; Grubb, 1991).

7. Despite the importance of remedial education, we have little hard data on how well community colleges actually remediate. We do not know what proportion of remedial students go on to graduate from college. We also do not know what role unsuccessful remediation plays in the poorer educational attainment of working-class and minority students.

References

American Association of Community Colleges. (2000). *National profile of community colleges: Trends and statistics, 1997–1998*. Washington, DC: Author.

Bradburn, E., Hurst, D., and Peng, S. (2001). *Community college transfer rates to 4-year institutions using alternative definitions of transfer. NCES 2001–197*. Washington, DC: U.S. National Center for Education Statistics.

Brint, S. G., and Karabel, J. B. (1989). *The diverted dream*. New York: Oxford University Books.

Clark, B. (11960). *The open door college*. New York: McGraw Hill.

Cohen, A. C., and Brawer, F. B. (2002). *The American community college*, 4th ed. San Francisco: Jossey-Bass.

Dougherty, K. J. (1994). *The contradictory college: The conflicting origins, impacts, and futures of the community college*. Albany: State University of New York Press.

———. (2002). The evolving role of the community college: Policy issues and research questions. In J. Smart and W. Tierney (eds.), *Higher education: Handbook of theory and research*. Vol. 17. New York: Algora Press, pp. 295–348

———, and Bakia, M. F. (1999). *The new economic development role of the community college*. New York: Community College Research Center, Teachers College, Columbia University.

———, and Bakia, M. F. (2000). Community colleges and contract training: Content, origins, and impacts. *Teachers College Record* 102 (Feb.), 198–244.

———, Hong, E., and Kim, J. (2003). *Performance accountability and community colleges: Forms and impacts*. New York: Community College Research Center, Teachers College, Columbia University.

Grubb, W. N. (1991). The decline of community college transfer rates: Evidence from national longitudinal surveys." *Journal of Higher Education* 62 (2), 194–217.

———. 1996. *Working in the middle*. San Francisco: Jossey-Bass.

———. (2002). Learning and earning in the middle, Part 1: National studies of pre-baccalaureate education. *Economics of Education Review* 21 (4): 299–32 1.

Kojaku, L. and Nunez, A. (1998). *Descriptive summary of 1995–96 beginning postsecondary students. NCES 1999–030*. Washington, DC: U.S. National Center for Education Statistics.

Mazzeo, C., Rab, S., and Eachus, S. (2003). "Work-first or Work-only: Welfare reform, state policy, and access to postsecondary education." *Annals of the American Academy of Political and Social Science*.

McCormick, A. (1997). *Transfer behavior among beginning postsecondary students: 1989–94. NCES 97–266*. Washington, DC: U.S. National Center for Education Statistics.

Monroe, C. (1972). *A profile of the community college*. San Francisco: Jossey-Bass.

Pascarella, E. T., and Terenzini, P. T. (1991). *How college affects students*. San Francisco: Jossey-Bass.

Rouse, C. E. (1998). Do two-year colleges increase overall educational attainment? Evidence from the states. *Journal of Policy Analysis and Management* 17 (4), 595–620.

Shaw, K. M. (1997). Remedial education as ideological battleground: Emerging remedial education policies in the community college. *Educational Evaluation and Policy Analysis* 19 (Fall 1997), 284–296.

United States National Center for Education Statistics. (1997). *The condition of education, 1997*. Washington, DC: U.S. Government Printing Office.

———. (2002). *Digest of education statistics, 2001. NCES 2002–130*. Washington, DC: Government Printing Office.

Whitaker, D. G., and Pascarella, E. L. (1994). Two-year college attendance and socioeconomic attainment. *Journal of Higher Education* 65 (March/April), 194–210.

Zeszostarski, P. (11999). Dimensions of general education requirements. In G. Schuyler (ed.), *Trends in community college curriculum*. New Directions for Community Colleges #109. San Francisco: Jossey-Bass.

CHAPTER 8

EDUCATIONAL ACCESS AND SOCIAL MOBILITY IN A RURAL COMMUNITY COLLEGE

JAMES R. VALADEZ

Community colleges are commonly linked with the democratic ideals of equal opportunity and open access (Brint and Karabel 1989; Cohen and Brawer, 1990). Open-door admission policies and relatively low cost help to promote the community college's image as "democracy's colleges." Critics, however, have argued that although community colleges provide access they have not necessarily provided opportunity for lower socioeconomic groups to achieve social mobility. In her study of African American students, Lois Weis (1985) argued that while community colleges are set up to offer mobility and opportunity to poor and working-class students, students produced a collective culture that kept them from achieving success and insured a return to the streets. Howard London (1978) argued that cultural conflict between students and the faculty and administration contributed to the problems of high student attrition and low academic achievement among working-class students. More recently, he (1989) detailed the cultural conflict between the students' own social and cultural background and the culture of the community college. London suggested that students experienced a "breaking away" in which they must make choices between conflicting cultures and posited that they enter the often mysterious and foreign world of higher education with a great deal of ambivalence.

Dennis McGrath and Martin Spear (1991) argued similarly that Students enter a culture that is strange and unintelligible. Community college administrators fail to recognize or respect the students' cultural backgrounds and impose rigid organizational structures to force students to conform to the college culture. Ken Kempner (1990) also cited the role of institutional culture in facilitating or hindering the learning of community college students. Other critics claim that, rather than fostering the social mobility of these groups, community colleges actually contribute to the reproduction of existing class differences (Grubb 1984; Karabel 1972, 1986, Pincus 1980; Zwerling 1976).

There is little disagreement that the expansion of the community colleges during the last two decades has provided increased access for disadvantaged students. The available evidence however, shows that this expanded access has not translated directly into increased opportunities for minority and working-class students (Olivas 1979; Velez 1985). While more minorities and working-class students enter the community colleges, few graduate or transfer to four-year colleges (Nora 1993). Valerie Lee and Ken Frank (1990) showed that it was the most academically prepared and the least economically stressed students who used the Community College to their best advantage. Students who are better prepared are often the ones who graduate from two-year programs or transfer to four-year colleges. The more poorly prepared students, not surprisingly, have more difficulty in completing their studies.

Arthur Cohen attempted to counter the critics by explaining that "minority students tend to be from lower socioeconomic groups and have lower educational aspirations and lower academic ability" than white middle-class students (1988, 187). He and Francis Brawer (1990) argued further that it was not the role of the community colleges to provide the means for social mobility for lower socioeconomic groups but rather their mission was to allow individuals to take advantage of the offerings of the community college to pursue academic or career goals. The evidence however, shows that relatively few minorities and working-class students pursue those goals (Brint and Karabel 1989; Dougherty 1991; Karabel 1972, 1986; Nora 1993; Nora and Rendon 1990; Pincus 1980).

The critics' portrayal of the community college as a sorting mechanism that pushes high-ability students toward high-status careers and low-ability students toward vocational degrees fails to address the interactions within the institution that influence students' decisions about their careers. Ethnographic studies have added to our understanding of the ways in which gender, class, and race or ethnicity shape the experience and decisions made by students in school. Paul Willis (1977) explained how a group of working-class students "chose" working-class jobs by outlining a careful structural analysis of the school and the society in which their choices emerged. He explained how students produce both resistance to and compliance with the dominant social relationships to arrive at their decisions. In this case study, I emphasize the interactions within the community college by examining how the culture of the institution framed student aspirations.

The first part of this article introduces the theoretical perspective. I have used Pierre Bourdieu's ideas about the role of social class position and its impact on student achievement and aspirations, Admittedly, Bourdieu's ideas are more complex than can be outlined here; but for the purposes of this article, I focus on one central topic—that of cultural capital. Following the discussion of the theoretical perspective, I describe a case study of a community college. I discuss how the culture of the institution shapes the beliefs and assumptions of the students concerning their academic and career aspirations.

The culture of the institution may be defined in a number of ways. Most definitions of institutional culture would include the practices, rituals, traditions, values, knowledge, and the taken-for-granted attitudes that shape the behavior of the members of the organization (Schein 1985). I will concentrate on four pertinent cultural practices and beliefs associated with community college culture: (1) assumptions about what students need to know about college-going behavior (school knowledge) (2) the significance of placement exams, (3) academic and career advising, and (4) attitudes about the world of work.

Cultural Capital

The concept of cultural capital is central to understanding Bourdieu's (1977) theory of cultural reproduction. Cultural capital refers to the different sets of linguistic and cultural competencies that individuals inherit from the social location of their families. More specifically, children incorporate a set of meanings, qualities of style, modes of thinking, and behaviors that are assigned a certain social value and status. Robert Rist (1977), Jean Anyon (1981), and Hugh Mehan (1978) demonstrated that white middle-class children display linguistic forms, style, and values that are acknowledged as a privileged form of cultural capital. This cultural capital is honored by those dominant groups in society that define and legitimate the meaning of success in education (Giroux 1983). In contrast, students who exhibit characteristics outside the mainstream of society (e.g., speech patterns, unusual dress), or who reject academic knowledge that is based on historical perspectives in opposition to their own experiences and values, are at a decided cultural disadvantage compared to middle-class white students (Aronowitz and Giroux 1991). Working-class students enter territory where their own cultural resources and values are not celebrated or even recognized, and consequently their resources remain subordinate to the preferred cultural capital of the white middle class (Hanson 1994).

Educational institutions play a particularly important role in legitimizing and reproducing the dominant culture (Apple 1990; Giroux 1983, 1992). Legitimizing the cultural capital of upper socioeconomic groups occurs by assigning privileged status to middle-class values; this process is reinforced through the institution's preference for and selection of particular textbooks, teaching styles, curricula, and classroom discourse. The culture transmitted by the school is related to the various cultures that make up the wider society in that it confirms and sustains the culture of dominant groups while marginalizing and silencing the culture of subordinate groups of students (Cherryholmes 1988). These institutional preferences and practices define what counts as knowledge and authorize those who may speak about it. Conversely, by authorizing those who may speak, it silences those who have been marginalized throughout the history of higher education. Minorities and working-class students in particular have found that their views and perspectives have not been heard with equal authority in education (Apple 1990; Fine 1991; Giroux 1992).

In this study I argue that educational institutions arrange their policies and practices to take advantage of the cultural resources of the white middle class. The analysis, however, is unfinished without considering the social interactions within the institution that influence student academic and career aspirations. An explanation would be incomplete without including the voices of students as they explain how they are attempting to rise above their positions in society and improve the conditions in which they work, live, and learn (Giroux 1983).

The Case Study

The Setting

Approximately 2,500 students attend Eastlake Community College (pseudonym), 20 percent of whom are African American. The community college is located in a small rural county (pop. 76,000) in a largely rural state. According to the 1990 U.S. census, whites comprise 68 percent, African Americans 31 percent, and other ethnic groups less than 1 percent of the county's population. The source of income for most employed people in the county derives from service, manufacturing, and agricultural industries. Median family income for whites in the county is approximately $31,000 compared to the median family income of $19,500 for African Americans. The fact that Eastlake is a rural community college has significance because of its position in the educational System within the state. Rural communities face extraordinary social problems, including poor health care, inadequate funding

for education, high rates of illiteracy, and few job opportunities. As the center of educational and cultural activities, Eastlake is seen as a vital community resource. The college is expected not only to provide education and job training but also, in the view of many, to be a catalyst for economic development.

Method

I based the findings of this report on data from an earlier study of institutional influences on student academic achievement (Valadez 1993) and data collected over an additional period of eight months at the community college. The original study examined the institutional culture of the community college and probed the varying influences of that culture on student achievement. My intent in the earlier study, therefore, differed from examining the process by which students made decisions about their future lives.

I used a case study approach because it facilitated the understanding of the social, historical, and cultural context that influenced the interpretation of the events that occurred at the site (Yin 1994). The case study approach was also compatible with the critical perspective I took in the study that allowed participants to reconstruct events and to elaborate on the meanings they assigned to those events.

The data for the study consisted of interviews, institutional documents including statistical reports, college catalogs, and other miscellaneous documents, and field notes from direct observations of events and classroom interactions over a period of fourteen months. I conducted 106 formal interviews with faculty, administrators, and students. Sixty-six of the participants were students enrolled in developmental studies courses in mathematics, reading, and language. I selected twenty-eight faculty members from a variety of programs throughout the community college. I interviewed the college president, vice president, dean of academic affairs, and the dean of students. I also interviewed the directors of the following units: institutional research, developmental studies, college transfer, and student support services. In addition to these administrators, I interviewed the business officer, registrar, information officer, two staff counselors, and the coordinator of the tutorial program. Besides formal interviews, I conducted numerous informal interviews with the college president, chief academic officer, faculty, staff, and students over the course of the study.

I analyzed the transcripts of the interviews and the field notes using the constant comparative method suggested by Barney Glaser and Anselm Strauss (1967). The point of this method is to examine events, incidents, and observations, and to compare them With data collected over the course of the study. This constant comparison leads the investigator toward the discovery of an emerging framework for interpreting the data. The interpretive framework that emerged from this study led to the formulation of four higher level themes (school knowledge, placement exams, advisement, and the world of work) used to explain the students' academic and career decisions and their aspirations.

The procedures used for strengthening the validity of the study follow Harry Wolcott's admonition for "not getting it all wrong" (1990, 127). I attempted to construct an accurate picture of the participants' views through the recurrent nature of the data collection process, including multiple interviews, observations and extensive document reviews. In addition, I shared the findings and my interpretations with the participants throughout the study. At the conclusion of the study, I conducted a final field check with a panel of the participants including administrators, faculty, and students. I reported my findings and my interpretations to the panel and invited their feedback.

School Knowledge

Besides skills needed to succeed in the classroom, there was an expectation at Eastlake that students would master the skills associated with being a successful student. What assumptions and beliefs did community college personnel have about college students, and what were their expectations for college student behavior and attitudes toward education? Predictably, I found that many of these skills were essential for mastering the course material, such as note-taking and study skills, but other skills were associated with cultural competencies. As an example, faculty expected certain styles of communication associated with academic discourse, such as the give and take in a discussion or the defense of an argument. Many Eastlake faculty believed that students should have already learned these skills in elementary and high school and had them reinforced by parents, counselors, and

peers. Yet many Eastlake students who did not have access to these mainstream cultural values did not exhibit these competencies. The result was that students lacked essential knowledge for achieving success in the classroom. A faculty member discussed his experience:

> Some of these students don't even know how to take notes. I tell them that if I write it on the board they should be writing it in their notes because there's a good chance that this information will be on the test. These are skills they should have picked up in high school. . . . The skills that they need compared to what they have is really shocking. . . . Somewhere along the line they didn't get it, and it goes beyond not knowing math or English but just the responsibilities that a student should take for their education . . . time management, turning in their assignments, coming to class. . . . I really give them a lot of slack if they have responsibilities to take care of . . . [but] they need to let me know that they can't be in class. . . . Frankly they let things get in their way. . . . The problems seem insurmountable . . . but there are so many things. . . . It's like one little thing will interfere, like car trouble and they won't come to class.

The instructor contrasted these students with other students who "come to class prepared" and "know what they have to do to pass the course." He noted that these students had "more stable home lives" and "fewer distractions."

Many students lacked basic skills because of poor advice or because of the generally inferior quality of their earlier schooling. As an example, of the sixty-six students I interviewed, thirty-seven had never taken high school algebra. Some of these students were advised not to take high school algebra, while others simply bypassed the opportunity. It was not unusual for developmental studies students to have selected high school courses without sufficient knowledge about the implications of their choices for the future of their academic careers. Sixty of the sixty-six students I interviewed did not have parents who attended college, and few of their peers had college experience. High school counselors, when available did not always give students accurate information about courses needed to prepare for college. The following is an excerpt from an interview with Kelly, an eighteen-year-old white female student:

I was working in a doctor's office . . . filing, waiting on patients when they came into the office . . . typing. It was not the kind of thing I wanted to do forever. . . . I was going to school part-time, but I quit my job because it was just too much doing both. . . . I wasn't prepared for college . . . the courses . . . the math . . . I didn't take math . . . or not much math in high school. . . . I never took algebra. . . . The teacher I talked to in the ninth grade, he asked if I was going to college; and at that time I didn't think I was, so he said I should take consumer math. . . . Algebra sounded hard so I took the easiest way out. . . . I wish I had known. . . . Now all those years in high school seem like such a waste. . . . There was no one else. . . . My mother—my parents are divorced—she never went to college so she really couldn't tell me much and I don't think she ever thought about me going to college. It was just something that never came up. . . . She went to high school and then got married. . . . She has worked as a secretary. . . . I suppose she thought it was something that was out of reach.

Mark, an eighteen-year-old African American explained that he also "never took algebra. I was in the ninth grade, I think it was, I took a test and they placed you." Kelly had to make an important decision early in her academic career with inadequate information about the consequences, Mark had the decision taken out of his hands. The impact has been significant for both students. Mark or Kelly will find it difficult to enter math-based curricula because of their inadequate high school preparation. Kelly made a decision she regretted, but at the time she did not have family members who could counsel or advise her. The advice she did get from her teacher was not helpful. For Mark, the situation was equally problematic. His early placement effectively derailed any hope for a college preparatory curriculum. He also did not have family members to counsel him, nor did his family understand schools well enough to advocate for him or question the decision to place him in special education classes.

Mark and Kelly's experiences were symptomatic of those of many working-class students who did not have families with sufficient knowledge of higher education to guide them through the educational system. The students' own store of knowledge, along with their values and cultural perspectives, often conflicted with the expectations of faculty members. Some faculty members regarded themselves as the standard bearers for the values and traditions of the college and demanded firmly that students conform to the standards of the institution. Elizabeth, an English instructor was firm in her belief that "you have to maintain standards and I won't lower mine. Students need to learn that when they go out into the world of work they are not going to be spoon-fed."

Bourdieu (1977; Bourdieu and Passeron 1977) proposed that the policies and practices of higher education, and the expectations of faculty concerning the cultural and social competencies of students, favored individuals from middle- and upper-income families. At Eastlake, the lack of school knowledge worked against lower-income students, but the situation was perhaps not as deterministic as Bourdieu suggested. Many students challenged existing conditions and called for the organization to make adjustments. Several of the African American students I interviewed questioned the lack of minority faculty and cultural sensitivity in their courses. Women students called for greater attention toward the unique needs of working-class women, particularly concerning advisement, support services, financial aid for reentry women, and the expansion of child care services. These requests were not unheeded, and there was evidence of some organizational change. Courses were scheduled to meet the needs of working students, and more services were provided in the evenings to accommodate all students. There was some resistance to changes from the faculty and staff, but students struggled for recognition and for changes in the institution.

Placement Exams

Placement exams, which were widely used at Eastlake, had an important impact on students' academic decisions. Placement tests are an institutional practice used by nearly all community colleges to assess student skills in mathematics, language, and reading and to assign students to appropriate curricular levels. Use of the exams is simply assumed as an essential part of student advisement. Staff at Eastlake community college voiced the prevailing attitude toward the use of placement exams in comments such as "it's for their own good" or "it wouldn't be fair to the students to put them in a course they couldn't handle." The institution placed a great deal of weight on these exams, and faculty and administrators maintained that the exams provided a fair measure of students' abilities. However, despite their utility and the good intentions behind their use, these tests have the inadvertent effect of creating barriers for students in achieving their educational and occupational goals.

A developmental studies administrator commented on the impact of the placement exam on admissions to the various college curricular programs:

> We are an open-door institution. We don't leave anybody out. As long as students can pass the placement test they are allowed into the college transfer courses. The curriculum is not limited, . . . but first they have to take the placement test—or they can take the SAT and get a minimum of 400 of both tests. If they don't pass the placement test, then they need to enroll in the developmental courses. After they take the developmental courses, they can retake the placement test; and if they get the score they need, they can enroll in the college transfer courses . . . then we're open door.

The community college admits nearly all students who apply, but all students are not free to enroll in any course they choose. This became most apparent to me as I walked through the nursing department where photographs of graduating classes adorned the corridors. I noticed that each class of approximately twenty-five consisted almost entirely of women and that only one or two per class were African American. Nursing was among the most popular programs at the college, with long waiting lists, but the process for entering the program eliminated many students. If a student failed the placement exam, he or she had to take developmental courses and retake the examination, receiving above the cutoff score, to prove his or her competence in reading, math, and language.

Though the institution placed a great deal of importance on the exam, not all students understood its significance. Charles, an eighteen-year-old African American student, recognized that the exam was necessary but may not have realized all of its implications. He said:

> I took the placement test. . . . Everybody takes it. I got something in the mail about the courses I was supposed to be in. I didn't think about talking to anybody about the courses. I just got the letter in the mail and these are the courses I'm supposed to take.

> I want to take algebra because I never took it before. My math teacher says I need to take this course and this other one before I can take algebra. The placement test was . . . I don't know . . . it was timed and I just didn't have enough time and I had to rush. I know these are the courses I'm supposed to take because I want to transfer . . . I want to transfer in two years.

Charles accepted the idea that the exam assessed his educational skills and that he would need to take a series of courses before he could enroll in college transfer courses. When I asked Charles whether he knew if these developmental courses could be transferred to a four-year institution for credit, he did not know but he thought they could. When I asked if he still believed he could transfer to a four-year college in two years even if he had to take one year of developmental courses in math and English, he replied that he thought he could. Charles's case is not unusual in that it reflects the lack of understanding that some working-class and minority students have about the procedures of college life, the impact of institutional practices such as testing, or even the types of questions college students need to ask about their futures. The placement exam had an enormous impact on Charles's life because his first year in community college consisted of taking developmental courses, none of which could be used toward graduation and none of which will be accepted by an accredited four-year institution.

Not all minority and working-class students were unaware of the importance of the placement test. One student I spoke to, Cheryl, challenged the validity of the test and successfully argued that she should be allowed to retake it. She did, passed it, and was placed in college transfer courses. Other students who did not question or challenge the results of the test invested a year or more going through the developmental series. Anita explained: "I feel like I'm in high school again. It's not like I'm in a real college. Even though I'm in these courses I know I shouldn't be in them." In contrast, Maria, a thirty-five-year-old developmental student talked about her placement: "I'm really enjoying being in college. It's been seventeen years since I've been in high school."

Maria and Anita revealed some of the varying opinions regarding testing and placement. Many of the students however, did not believe that the exam was a true indicator of their abilities.

Some students expressed surprise at their low scores. Most blamed the pressure of the testing setting. Others talked about the years they had been away from formal education and the "rustiness" of their skills. Bill, a thirty-one-year-old disabled man, explained:

> I don't have complete use of my hand. . . . I had an industrial accident. . . . I worked in construction. . . . I've been on disability. I've always wanted to come back to school. I was never a good student in high school. . . . I was just interested in having a good time, being with my friends. I didn't take school seriously . . . ; but I was in this room and it was crowded. . . . I told them about my hand so they gave me some extra time, but still, you know, there's only so much I can do and I can only go so fast. . . . The test was timed, still . . . I just couldn't do all of it. You would think that, you know, with my hand the way it is . . .

Academic and Career Advisement

The prevailing sentiment among teachers and administrators was definitely that students should be encouraged to pursue their goals and aspirations. I heard no reports from students and observed no attempts by faculty to dissuade students from pursuing their goals. I was more apt to hear faculty expressing positive feelings about their students. A typical statement was: "We have a lot of good students here." A nursing instructor was particularly pleased about "the high quality and industriousness of the nursing students." Faculty members, however, characterized developmental studies students as "unrealistic" about their career aspirations. "The trouble is [they want] to come in here and be in college transfer." A widespread feeling among the faculty and staff was that developmental studies students, because of poor high school preparation or their "disadvantaged backgrounds" were long shots for academic success. As a faculty member said, "If we can train them for a job, get them to become contributing members of society, then we have been successful."

Danny typified many developmental studies students. He was twenty-nine and a high school dropout, who had recently lost his construction job because of a disabling injury and come back to school. He was married with three children. He said: "[Returning to school] was something I had always wanted to do. When I was in high school I didn't put much effort in

it. I quit and I went into the military when I was seventeen. Then I got married, had kids. I'd been working in construction and I was making nine dollars an hour. Then I had this accident. I've been on disability and now I've got the time to go back."

Danny's story is not unusual because there were many other students who had returned to school because they had lost their jobs or were stuck in low-skilled, low-paying occupations. They entered Eastlake believing they "would get retrained" for jobs that promised better pay and a chance for social mobility. Danny, and other students like him, who had never planned or given much thought to higher education, found themselves in situations where they were expected to make critical academic decisions with limited experience. Danny was the first person in his family to go to college, and he did not have family members or friends he could go to for academic advice. His family, in fact, "discouraged him from going to college." He was determined, however, and depended on faculty and staff at the college to guide him. Danny talked about his interactions with his adviser:

> I leave it up to him. . . . He helps me with classes I need to take. I decided on a curriculum, architectural technology, and he tells me what I need to take. He is careful not to overload me. I knew it was going to be tough in the beginning. When I got here I didn't even know how to divide. I've been doing well though and everyone is surprised. My parents always thought that there was something wrong with me because I had an accident when I was young and I injured my head.

Because of their limited experience with higher education, first-generation college students like Danny may not even know the right questions to ask and frequently suffer the consequences of an ill-informed decision. Tameka, for instance, was enrolled in a physical therapy program and wanted to transfer to a four-year program at a nearby state institution. She was disappointed to learn that her courses "wouldn't be accepted."

It is not clear to students, and it is not always clear to faculty which courses will be accepted by four-year institutions. Articulation agreements between community colleges and four-year institutions have not been completed, and the transferability of courses has been a source of confusion. Consequently, students who selected particular curricula often did not know whether their courses would be accepted at other institutions. A faculty member talked about advising students on course selection: "If they want to go to [State], then I advise them to go into college transfer. If they choose a particular curriculum, then I advise them on the courses they need to take. If they are in [the architectural technology] curriculum, there's little chance that [State] will accept our credits. The way I see it is, if they can complete four curriculum] then maybe they [can complete the college transfer] curriculum."

Many of the faculty I interviewed recognized that student advisement, especially for developmental studies students, was an area that needed improvement. Teaching responsibilities and heavy advising loads limited the time that faculty could spend with students, and they frequently expressed frustration: "There's only so much that we can do" or "so many [students] fall through the cracks." A faculty member lamented that Eastlake had "only two full-time counselors over in student services" to provide career counseling and information on college transfer. Resources were limited, but the college provided services to students, including tutoring, computer-based instruction, and other study aids. Faculty talked about the "frustration levels" associated with losing students because they could not spend enough time with them. One faculty member sighed: "If [only] we had the time or resources to work with them. They need encouragement. So many of them have the desire to complete but they get lost in the shuffle. If I even had the time to make a phone call to the students—find out why they didn't reregister—it might make a difference."

The World of Work

What were the attitudes and assumptions of college personnel and students about the "world of work" outside Eastlake? If the institution's participants saw its mission as primarily economic or one that prepared students for the workforce, how did that impact the career and academic decisions made by students? Some faculty at Eastlake believed that they helped students to develop as individuals, but many saw their role as preparing students to become competitive in the workforce. This attitude was particularly prevalent in the developmental and vocational areas where the college ethos was to "prepare

students for the world of work." The faculty were committed to inculcating the students with the "values associated with getting a job, keeping a job . . . showing up on time, knowing how to dress, how to talk." One faculty member I talked to was concerned that "some of these students frankly don't know anything about that." She felt responsible for "teaching students about the values for getting prepared for a job. When they get a job they're not going to have anybody who is going to tell them these things."

In addition to this well-articulated concern from faculty that students acquire job skills, students felt pressure from families to complete their studies and to begin work. The faculty knew that students were pressured to find work and were sometimes frustrated by the dilemma. A faculty member commented that it was "tough to reach the students and convince them that they need to stay in school" and lamented that "the lure of the job was too great."

Often students came to college with the a goal of getting a good job; and if a job was offered, they could not pass up the opportunity. Delores, a twenty-nine-year-old African American pre-nursing student, explained:

> I have three kids. . . . I have a Pell grant and I can get money for childcare. My books [and] tuition are paid and the tutors are free . . . but I'm barely making it and my kids need clothes. . . . When my little girl needs shoes, I got to tell her we don't have the money and I want to have those things. . . . [When I entered] I thought I could go for my bachelor's but [now] I just want to get out of this program and start working. . . . Right now I'm in school all day long. . . . I start early in the morning and I'm not finished until five. Then I got to go home and study. My kids miss me and sometime they don't understand . . . the little one especially. If I can get a job [where] the pay is good. . . . I can go back to school when I get established, but right now I got to finish this degree and get a job.

The community college provided opportunities for job training, which was attractive to many students because of the promise of job placement or the availability of scholarships. As an example, the college developed partnerships with industry and designed customized training programs to train employees to perform specific tasks. Customized programs had obvious appeal to students because of the possibility of job placement after completion of the training. Norton Grubb and David Stem (1989) have characterized industry partnerships as having something for everyone: Students get training and placement in jobs, firms get part of their training subsidized by the community college, educational institutions increase their enrollments, community services are enhanced, and the colleges strengthen their ties to the employers. When I asked a community college dean about these partnerships, he cited an example of a scholarship program sponsored by a local employer:

> The scholarship is for students who can go into the car dealership [and] understand how to use the equipment for auto repair. Their equipment is technical, sophisticated and they need people who can come out of the classroom ready to work. The students who qualify for the scholarship learn how to use the equipment. . . . They get very good training; and when they get out of here, they step into good jobs. You have to understand car dealerships. . . . They don't want to wait around for four years for a graduate. . . . It would be great for the students to get a degree, but you don't need a four-year degree to work at a car dealership. . . . Maybe down the road these companies will pay for a [four-year] program like that, but right now these companies need jobs and our students benefit from stepping into good-paying jobs.

The college, through its relationships with business and industry presented students with access to numerous opportunities and devoted considerable resources by which students could acquire specific skills for entering the workforce. This partnership program contrasted sharply with the limited resources available to developmental students for advisement or for the improvement of their academic skills. A developmental studies instructor commented: "We get the short end. . . . It's like we're invisible. We do not have the resources, the ability to reach students who need the extra push."

Discussion

Students at Eastlake entered the college with aspirations for finding good jobs and improving their social positions. Many of these students viewed the community college hopefully, as the institution that would transform their lives. Faculty and administrators agreed that the community college provided opportunity to students, particularly those who ordinarily would

not attend college. The faculty and staff, however, expressed different ideas about how they wanted to help students achieve their goals. Faculty supported student goals but raised doubts that students could achieve their lofty ambitions. As one faculty member said: "Everyone is college transfer. . . . Their goals are unrealistic."

Faculty attitudes toward student goals reflected the class and cultural differences between faculty and students. Faculty believed that developmental students were not prepared for college-level work and were unlikely to ever attain those standards. Although the developmental studies program was designed to remediate students and lift them to standards acceptable to the social and cultural norms of the institution, the dropout and failure rate for developmental students remained high. Faculty attitudes conveyed that students had little probability of attaining the standards needed for advanced college study and would achieve a measure of success if they could be trained for a job. Burton Clark's (1960) notion of "cooling out" can be extended here as we examine these structural processes that reserve higher level college majors for the more academically prepared students and also serve society by assuring that the economic sector is not overburdened with students with baccalaureate degrees. The evidence suggests that while structures favor middle-class students, the social interactions within the institution also have a significant impact on decisions made by students.

Students were driven by economic needs and measured their own success by the type of job they could get. The students, however, did not always understand fully the consequences of their academic decisions. Many Eastlake students maintained a desire to pursue baccalaureate degrees but did not understand that their decision to enter a vocational track could prevent them attaining a four-year degree. Eastlake students, particularly developmental studies students, did not always have access to the information to help them make the most beneficial academic decisions. Bourdieu (1977) proposed that social class influenced the type of information available to students through their social interactions, activities, and the social networks they formed. At Eastlake, middle-class students had access to information that produced a higher social profit than that available to working-class students because of the privileged status of middle-class culture. In particular middle-class culture provided the students with experience and practice in the discourse and behaviors that eased their transition to higher education. Middle-class students drew upon these experiences and relied on their social networks to help them with educational decisions. Working-class students did not have access to networks or sources of cultural capital to help them make informed academic decisions. Instead, working-class students at Eastlake made their own decisions or relied on the services provided by the institution to guide them through the system. The scarcity of resources however, often meant that students had limited access to services to help them with career and academic plans.

Preparing students to join the workforce is a prime objective for the community college, but this mission raises the question of the community college's responsibility as a democratic institution. Does the community college fulfill that responsibility by training students to get jobs? As a democratic institution, the community college must not lose sight of its responsibility to develop students into creative thinkers, responsible citizens, and contributing members of society. The community college administrators felt they were serving society and the needs of their students by providing them with jobs. It is also true that many students were being trained to enter highly paid and skilled professions, but were they also learning to become full participants in a democratic society?

Conclusion

The findings of this study agree with assertions made by other researchers that social-class position and class culture become a form of cultural capital in higher education (Bourdieu, 1977; Bourdieu and Passeron 1977; Lareau 1987). Clearly, students bring different social and cultural skills to the college, and educators interpret these skills in a variety of ways. A student's social class position, however, influences the type of cultural knowledge he or she accumulates and how he or she displays that knowledge. Educators interpret the knowledge exhibited by students, make judgements, and categorize students according to those assessments. Not surprisingly, the knowledge presented by middle-class students matches more closely the expectations of community college educators. Working-class students also have cultural knowledge and skills, but this type

of knowledge is often overlooked or, worse, is devalued and even diagnosed as a deficit by educators. These judgements made by community college faculty reflect their own social class positions and their perceptions of what counts as knowledge in the community college.

The findings of this study demonstrate that the institutional practices of the community college—assessments, advisement, and placement—are not organized to take advantage of the skills and knowledge of working-class students but instead work to the benefit of the middle class. This finding agrees with Bourdieu's (1977; Bourdieu and Passeron 1977) position on the role of cultural capital in the cultural reproduction of society. My point, however, is that to understand the role of the institution in influencing the decisions and aspirations of students, we must, as Mehan (1992) suggests, examine the social construction of these arrangements. Unless we analyze the interactions among the institutional actors (students, faculty and staff), we are left with a highly structured account of the relationship between social origins, schooling, and subsequent achievement.

Institutional arrangements and structures influence student achievement and the decisions they make about their lives, but students also have a voice in determining their life outcomes. Students in this study recognized that a role of the community college was to provide them with skills to get a good job. We also know that the forces of the economy and society have an impact on student decisions. In this respect, I extend Bourdieu's theory by affirming that students are not merely bearers of cultural capital but that they also play an important role in defining and claiming the knowledge they need to achieve their goals.

Even if we acknowledge that working-class students claim the knowledge they need and do not follow a predetermined path toward working-class jobs, we are still left with the vexing problem of the stratified nature of the community colleges. As Kerckhoff (1993) noted, it may be unreasonable to expect educational institutions to prepare an undifferentiated group of students because students have different abilities, levels of motivation, and aspirations. It is not unreasonable, however, to expect community colleges to reduce the inequality of opportunity among its students. Presently, white middle-class students congregate in the higher status majors (nursing, college transfer, physical therapy), while working-class students gravitate toward vocational programs. Reducing inequality would require that we examine the structures and arrangements that influence achievement and also those arrangements that affect students' academic and career decisions. Using the concept of cultural capital would turn our attention toward an examination of those arrangements that favor the knowledge, values, traditions, and skills of middle-class over working-class students and help us learn how to develop and activate the strengths of the working class as a form of cultural capital that would be useful in higher education settings.

Bibliography

Anyon, Jean. "Social Class and School Knowledge," *Curriculum Inquiry* 11 (Winter 1981):3–42.

Apple, Michael W. *Ideology and Curriculum.* New York. Routledge, 1990.

Aronowitz, Stanley, and Henry Giroux. *Postmodern Education.* Minneapolis: University of Minnesota Press. 1991.

Bourdieu, Pierre. *Outline of a Theory of Practice.* Cambridge: Cambridge University Press, 1977.

Bourdieu, Pierre, and Jean-Claude Passeron. *Reproduction in Education, Society, and Culture.* London: Sage, 1977.

Brint, Steven, and Jerome Karabel. *The Diverted Dream.* New York: Oxford University Press 1989.

Cherryholmes, Cleo H. *Power and Criticism: Poststructural Investigations in Education.* New York, Teachers College, Columbia University, 1988.

Clark, Burton, *The Open Door College.* New York: McGraw-Hill, 1960.

Cohen, Arthur. "Degree Achievement by Minorities in Community Colleges." *Review of Higher Education* 11 (Summer 1988): 383–402.

Cohen, Arthur, and Francis Brawer, *The American Community College.* San Francisco: Jossey-Bass, 1990.

Dougherty, Kevin. "The Community College at the Crossroads: The Need for Structural Reform." *Harvard Educational Review* 61 (Summer 1991): 311–36.

Fine, Michelle. *Framing Dropouts.* Albany: State University of New York Press, 1991

Giroux, Henry A. *Theory and Resistance in Education.* New York: Bergin and Garvey. 1983.

———. *Border Crossings.* London: Routledge Press, 1992.

Glaser, Barney, and Anselm, Strauss. *The Discovery of Grounded Theory: Strategies for Qualitative Research.* New York: Aldine de Gruyter, 1967.

Grubb, Norton. "The Bandwagon Once More: Vocational Preparation for High-Tech Occupations." *Harvard Educational Review* 54 (Fall 1984): 429–51.

Grubb, Norton, and David Stem. *Separating the Wheat from the Chaff: The Role of Vocational Education in Economic Development.* Berkeley: University of California, National Center for Research in Vocational Education, 1989.

Hanson, Sandra L. "Lost Talent: Unrealized Educational Aspirations and Expectations Among U.S. Youths." *Sociology of Education* 67 (Summer 1994):159–83.

Karabel, Jerome. "Community Colleges and Social Stratification." *Harvard Educational Review* 4 (Fall 1972): 521–62.

———. "Community Colleges and Social Stratification in the 1980s." In *The Community College and Its Critics,* edited by Steven Zwerling. New Directions for Community Colleges, No. 54. San Francisco: Jossey-Bass, 1986.

Kempner, Ken. "Faculty Culture in the Community College: Facilitating or Hindering Learning?" *The Review of Higher Education* 13 (Winter 1990): 215–35.

Kerckhoff, Alan C. *Diverging Pathways: Social Structure and Career Deflections.* Cambridge: Cambridge University Press, 1993.

Lee, Valerie, and Ken Frank. "Student Characteristics That Facilitate the Transfer from Two-Year to Four-Year Colleges," *Sociology of Education* 63 (Summer 1990): 178–93.

Lareau, Annette. "Social Class Differences in Family-School Relationships." *Sociology of Education* 60 (1987): 73–85, London, Howard. *The Culture of the Community College.* New York: Praeger, 1978.

———. "Breaking Away: A Study of first-Generation College Students and their Families." *American Journal of Education* 97, no. 2 (1989): 144–70.

McGrath, Dennis, and Martin Spear. *The Academic Crisis of the Community College.* Albany: State University of New York, 1991.

Mehan, Hugh. "Structuring School Structure." *Harvard Educational Review* 48 (Winter 1978): 32–64.

———. "Understanding Inequality in Schools: The Contribution of Interpretive Studies." *Sociology of Education* 65 (Winter 1992): 1–20.

Nora, Amaury. "Two-Year Colleges and Minority Students' Educational Aspirations: Help or Hindrance?" In *Higher Education: Handbook of Theory and Research,* Vol. 9, edited by John Smart, 212–47. New York: Agathon Press, 1993.

Nora, Amaury, and Laura Rendon. "Determinants of Predisposition to Transfer Among

Community College Students: A Structural Model." *Research in Higher Education* 31 (Summer 1990): 235–55.

Olivas, Michael. *The Dilemma of Access.* Washington, D.C.: Howard University Press, 1979.

Pincus, Fred L. "The False Promise of Community Colleges: Class Conflict and Vocational Education." *Harvard Educational Review* 50 (Summer 1980), 332–61.

Rist, Robert. *The Urban School: A Factory for failure.* Cambridge: M.I.T. Press, 1977.

Schein, Edgar. *Organizational Culture and Leadership.* San Francisco: Jossey-Bass, 1985.

Valadez, James. "Cultural Capital and Its Impact on the Aspirations of Nontraditional Community College Students." *Community College Review* 21, no. 3 (Winter 1993): 30–43.

Velez, William. "Finishing College: The Effects of College Type." *Sociology of Education* 58 (Summer 1985): 191–20.

Weis, Lois. *Between Two Worlds: Black Students in an Urban Community College.* Boston: Routledge & Kegan Paul, 1985.

Willis, Paul. *Learning to Labor How Working Class Kids Get Working Class Jobs.* New York: Columbia University Press, 1977.

Wolcott, Harry F. "On Seeking—and Rejecting—Quality in Qualitative Research." In *Qualitative Inquiry in Education,* edited by Elliot Eisner and Alan Peshkin, 121–52. New York: Teacher College Press, 1990.

Yin, Robert K. *Case Study Research: Design and Methods.* 2d ed. Newbury Park: Sage, 1994.

Zwerling, L. Steven. *Second Best.* New York: McGraw-Hill, 1976.

CHAPTER 9

THE COMMUNITY COLLEGE: EDUCATING STUDENTS AT THE MARGIN BETWEEN COLLEGE AND WORK

THOMAS J. KANE AND CECILIA ELENA ROUSE

Community colleges have assumed an increasingly central role in the nation's education and training system. Between 1980 and 1994, the proportion of 18 to 24 year-olds enrolled in college grew by more than one-third, from 26 to 36 percent. Nearly half of this increase in enrollment was absorbed at community colleges (U.S. Department of Education, 1997, Tables 178 and 186, p. 188, 196). Yet despite the increasing interest in community colleges among both students and policymakers as a potential source of education for workers seeking to upgrade their skills, relatively little is known about them.

We have four goals in this paper. The first is to provide background on the history and development of community colleges in the United States in the last half century. Second, we survey the available evidence on the impacts of community colleges on educational attainment and earnings. Third, we weigh the evidence on the impact of public subsidies on enrollment at community colleges and explore some weaknesses in the current higher education financing structure. Finally, we reflect on how the students who have been responding to the rise in the payoff to education are to be absorbed by our postsecondary training institutions.

The History and Development of Community Colleges

In the late 19th century, when William Rainey Harper, founding president of the University of Chicago, developed a plan to separate the first two years of college from the second two years, he started a movement that would revolutionize higher education. The plan, modeled after the German "Gymnasium," was to create university-affiliated six-year high schools and two-year colleges, called "junior colleges," that would teach students the lower-division "preparatory" material. Although their evolution differed across the country, junior colleges were generally designed to increase access to higher education without compromising and burdening the existing four-year colleges. These colleges are generally defined as "any institution accredited to award the associate's in arts or science as its highest degree" (Cohen and Brawer, 1982, pp. 5–6). This definition includes comprehensive two-year colleges and many technical institutes (both public and private), but it excludes publicly funded vocational schools, adult education centers, and most proprietary schools. In this article, we use the terms "community college," "junior college," and "two-year college" interchangeably.[1]

The first phase in the expansion of junior colleges began after World War II when millions of former military personnel were given a tuition voucher under the GI Bill to attend college. Between

1944 and 1947, enrollments in junior colleges nearly doubled. The end of the Korean War brought another similar increase in junior college enrollments (Witt et al., 1994). The final phase in the expansion occurred in the 1960s, when the first baby boomers began to reach college age, Vietnam War veterans began to return home, and Americans enrolled in college to avoid the military draft. Over the 1960s, the number of junior colleges more than doubled and enrollments quadrupled (Witt et al., 1994). This immense expansion led Clark Kerr, an architect of the California higher education system, to term the junior college the great innovation in American higher education in the 20th century (Brint and Karabel, 1989, p. v).

Originally, junior colleges focused on what is termed the "transfer function": students would complete two years of a general undergraduate education and earn an associate's degree (AA) at the two-year college, and those who wanted and were capable would transfer to a four-year college to complete a bachelor's degree. Since then, two-year colleges have broadened their mission to include vocational degree programs, continuing adult education programs, and workforce, economic and community development programs. In addition, community colleges have traditionally striven to increase access to higher education through an open admissions policy—often not even requiring a high school diploma—and low, or no, tuition. In 1996–97, full-time students paid, on average, $1,283 for annual tuition and required fees at public two-year colleges compared to $2,986 at public four-year colleges (U.S. Department of Education, 1997).

Although private junior colleges were common at the turn of the century—at that time, only 26 percent of two-year colleges were public—

96 percent of the 5.5 million students enrolled in two-year colleges in 1995 were enrolled in public institutions (U.S. Department of Education, 1997). These 5.5 million students represent 38 percent of enrollments in all postsecondary institutions and 48 percent of enrollments in public institutions (U.S. Department of Education, 1997). Figure 1 shows the importance of community colleges by graphing the proportion of first-time first-year students enrolled in public two-year colleges from 1955 through 1995. In 1955, only 17 percent of all such students were enrolled in a public two-year college; today, that percentage has grown to 44 percent.

This explosion in enrollment in community colleges was powered primarily by the growth in part-time students. Part-time enrollments in public two-year colleges increased 222 percent between 1970 and 1995, compared to an increase of 63 percent in full-time enrollments. Today, roughly 65 percent of community college students attend part-time.

Although community colleges exist nationwide, they are not equally represented in all states. In California, which enrolls one-fifth of all students enrolled in public two-year colleges, 47 percent of all college enrollments are in public two-year colleges—compared to Louisiana and Montana which each have less than 7 percent. States with more developed four-year college systems tend to have less developed two-year college systems, and vice versa, suggesting that states choose to invest in one system or the other (Rouse, 1998).

The faculty at two-year colleges also differs from that at four-year colleges. The master's degree is the highest degree of 64 percent of full-time faculty in public community colleges, while 68 percent of four-year comprehensive college

Figure 1

Proportion of First-time First-year Students in Public Two-year Colleges

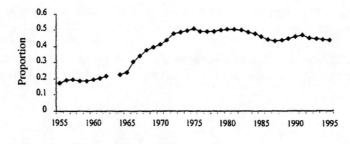

Source: *Digest of Education Statistics* (1997).

faculty have doctorates. Almost two-thirds (60 percent) of the faculty at public two-year colleges teach part-time, compared to one-third of comprehensive four-year college faculty. Only 32 percent of the full-time faculty at public two-year colleges hold a rank of either associate or full professor, compared to over 60 percent at public four-year universities. Instead, community colleges rely more heavily on non-tenure track faculty; 40 percent of community college faculty hold a rank of instructor or lecturer and 11 percent have no rank; for comparison, 11 percent of faculty at comprehensive and 8 percent at public research universities hold the rank of instructor or lecturer, and fewer than 1 percent have no rank (U.S. Department of Education, 1997). Of course, the heavy reliance on part-time and adjunct faculty help maintain community colleges' flexibility to respond to changing educational needs in the community.

Community college faculty also spend far more time on teaching than their four-year college counterparts. Two-year college faculty spend 69 percent of their time teaching and 4 percent of their time conducting research or scholarship (the bulk of the rest of their time is spent on administration, non-teaching service, and professional development), while faculty at comprehensive public four-year colleges spend 60 percent of their time teaching, and faculty at public research universities spend 40 percent of their time teaching. Similarly, 58 percent of faculty at community colleges teach more than 15 hours per week, compared to 18 percent of faculty at comprehensive four-year colleges and 7 percent of faculty at public research universities (U.S. Department of Education, 1997). The focus on teaching both lowers the educational costs and is hailed by many students as an advantage of attending a community college, particularly for those who seek more personal attention in the classroom.

Who Goes to Community College?

About one-third of all high school graduates will attend a community college at some point in their lives (Rouse, 1994). Compared to students who first enroll in a four-year college, community college students are more likely to be the first in their family to attend college and are much less likely to have parents who have graduated from a four-year college. The combined student body of community colleges is 70 percent white, 11 percent black, and 11 percent Hispanic. Almost 36 percent of community college students are at least 30 years old, compared to only 22 percent of public four-year college students. As noted above, most community college students attend part-time.

A community college education appeals to many students because of the lower costs of attendance. The average tuition is less than one-half that at public four-year colleges, and because community colleges are located in most towns and cities, many students can live at home while attending college.[2] Community colleges have also lowered other costs of attendance. Courses are not only offered during the "traditional" daytime hours, but also at night and on weekends. Many community colleges offer courses at work sites, or via audio, video, or computer technologies. As a result, 84 percent of community college students work while also attending college compared to 78 percent of students attending public comprehensive four-year colleges. Although the proportion of students reporting some employment is comparable at two-year and comprehensive four-year colleges, roughly one-half of those attending a community college who are employed report work as their primary activity, compared to only one-quarter of those attending public comprehensive four-year colleges (Horn, Becktold and Malizio, 1998).

Do the attractively low tuition and neighborhood convenience of community colleges divert students from four-year colleges? Or do they provide a place in higher education for those who would not have otherwise attended college? Of course, the social importance of this issue ultimately depends on the extent to which the type of institution one attends affects one's educational attainment, as we discuss below. The few studies that attempt to address such issues tend to find that community colleges draw both types of students, although it appears that slightly more than half of community college students are non-traditional students who probably would not have attended four-year institutions (Grubb, 1989; Rouse, 1995, 1998). This suggests that community colleges have increased overall educational attainment, and that a major role of community colleges is to provide a place in higher education for those not traditionally served by the four-year college system.

The Changing Shape of a Community College Education

Originally, students at community colleges completed courses that mimicked the first two years of a university curriculum before transferring to a four-year college. As a result, most students followed an academic curriculum delivered in a traditional manner. Today, however, community college courses have taken a variety of other approaches.

A significant fraction of community college students enroll in terminal (usually vocational) degree programs. Community colleges also serve an important remediating function within our higher education system. In 1995, almost all public two-year colleges provided remedial courses, compared to 81 percent of public four-year institutions (Lewis, Farris and Greene, 1996). About 41 percent of community college students took at least one remedial course compared to only 22 percent of public four-year college students. There seems to be an increased interest in limiting the amount of remediation done at four-year colleges; for example, the trustees of the City University of New York (CUNY) voted in May 1998 to deny admission to students who cannot pass reading, writing, and mathematics proficiency tests (Arenson, 1998). If educational offerings of four-year colleges are limited in this way, the remediation role of community colleges is likely to increase.

As another example of their flexibility in adapting to labor market conditions, a growing number of community colleges are providing contract training—that is, classes offered to employees of a business, industry, labor union, or public agency—often at a site designated by the contracting agency. As of the late 1980s, 94 percent of community colleges provided at least one course by contract. The most common form of contract training was teaching the job-specific skills needed to perform a job, to improve current performance, or to prepare for advancement on a contract basis with firms; 93 percent of community colleges provided such courses (Lynch, Palmer and Grubb, 1991). Sixty percent of community colleges provided contract courses in basic reading, writing, or math skills. The median ratio of contract enrollment (in 1988–89) to regular credit enrollment was 0.22, indicating that at one-half of colleges there was one or fewer contract students for every five or so regularly enrolled students (Lynch, Palmer and

Grubb, 1991). Krueger and Rouse (1998) evaluated one such workplace education program in which a community college provided basic literacy education to employees at a manufacturing company and a service company. They reported positive and significant effects of the training on the wage growth and job progression of employees at the manufacturing company, but no such effects at the service company.

The Net Effect of Community Colleges on Educational Attainment

One concern among observers of community colleges is that as they provide education services in non-traditional ways, the quality of such services may suffer. Critics point to the fact that community college students typically do not complete many college credits. Figure 2 shows the distribution of credits completed at two-year colleges.[3] The credits have been divided by 30 so as to represent years of enrollment on the horizontal axis. The figure shows that a majority of students who ever enroll in a two-year college complete one year or less; 35 percent of students complete only one semester or less.

Similarly, Table 1 shows degree attainment, 10 years after high school, by whether students first attended a two- or four-year college.[4] Of all students who enroll in a two-year college, over one-half do not complete any degrees. About 15 percent complete a certificate, another 16 percent attain an associate's degree and about 16 percent complete at least a bachelor's degree. In contrast, nearly 60 percent of four-year college entrants complete at least a bachelor's degree. The remaining columns of the table refer to opinions that the students expressed about their own future while seniors in high school. While the percentages of students who complete a degree increases among two-year college students who would either be "disappointed if they do not complete college," or feel they are "'definitely' able to complete college," or for whom "a bachelor's degree is the lowest level of education with which they would be satisfied," degree completion still lags considerably behind that of four-year college students.

The skewed distribution of completed credits and the relatively small proportion of students who complete degrees raises an important question: Do two-year college students simply

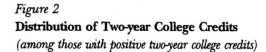

Figure 2

Distribution of Two-year College Credits

(among those with positive two-year college credits)

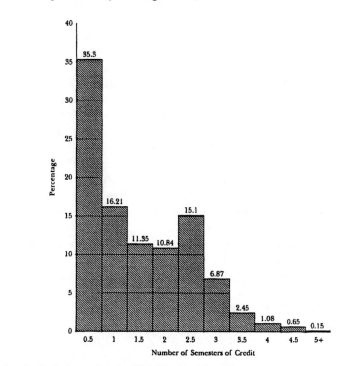

Source: Authors' calculations using the *High School and Beyond.*

maintain modest educational objectives or is there some aspect of two-year colleges that discourages students from completing more courses? Policymakers in certain states, such as California and New York, are considering limiting enrollment at four-year colleges and encouraging students to begin at a two-year college (Trombley, 1991; Kelley, 1998, p. 2). A key question is whether such a policy will affect the educational attainment of those students denied admission to a four-year college. If educational outcomes of students who begin in a community college only differ from those who begin in a four-year college because the two-year college students desire less education, then students who begin at a two-year college with a certain level of desire for schooling should fare as well as those who begin at a four-year college. However, if it appears that some aspect of community college discourages otherwise equally motivated and prepared students from completing more courses, which is one possible interpretation of Table 1, policymakers might ask why.

One could argue that two-year college students attain less education than four-year college students because, although two-year and four-year college students have the same aspiration levels while seniors in high school, their desired level of schooling changes over time and this change is unrelated to the type of institution that the individuals attend. Of course, if this is the case, policymakers need not be concerned about differences in educational attainment between the two types of institutions. However, it is also possible that the difference is due to some effect of community colleges. Clark (1960) and Brint and Karabel (1989) argue that the vocational education and terminal degree programs of community colleges are not conducive to completing four years of college, even for those who aspire to a four-year college degree. Their thesis is that two-year colleges are not appropriate institutions for students interested in completing a four-year degree because transferring can be costly and burdensome; conversely, they argue, the four-year college environment helps to keep students focused on the bachelor's degree. Essentially these authors argue that many students lack the necessary information to make an informed decision between two- and four-year colleges, and so they do not fully realize in attending a two-year college that they are reducing their chances of completing a four-year degree.

The potential importance of starting at a two-year or four-year college on eventual educational attainment is an empirical issue. But the effect is difficult to estimate, because desired levels of schooling and academic preparation are difficult to measure. Some authors have concluded that students who begin at a two-year college complete less education, on average, than similar students who begin at a four-year college (Alba and Lavin, 1981; Anderson, 1981; Breneman and Nelson, 1981; Dougherty, 1987; Velez, 1985). However, these studies limit their analysis to students who have already started at a college. As a result, they not only miss an important component of the mission of community colleges—to include students who ordinarily would not attend college—but they also bias their estimates of the effect of having been diverted from a four-year college on educational attainment. Rouse (1995) accounts for all students, not just those who have started college, and also uses college proximity as an instrumental variable that

is correlated with the type of college first attended, but hypothetically uncorrelated with educational attainment (conditional on the type of college attended). As with other authors, she finds that students who begin at a two-year college (and who otherwise would have attended a four-year college) complete less schooling—about three-quarters of a year—than those who begin at a four-year college. However, unlike the previous literature, she also finds that starting at a two-year college does not appear to affect the likelihood of attaining a bachelor's degree for those diverted from a four-year college. Therefore, it appears there is some negative effect of starting at a two-year college on years of education completed for an individual who would otherwise have attended a four-year college, perhaps because with so few students living on campus, peer effects are not as strong as on four-year campuses and because transferring from a two-year to a four-year college can be difficult and burdensome.

TABLE 9.1
Degree Attainment by Type of First College Attended and by
Degree Aspirations in the 12th Grade
(Among high school seniors in 1982/degree attainment as of 1992)

Highest Degree Attained	All	Disappointed if Do Not Complete College	"Definitely" Able to Complete College	BA+ is Lowest Level of Education With Which Would be Satisfied
		Two-year College Students		
None	53.7	47.8	60.1	44.9
Certificate	14.6	12.8	12.9	8.5
Associate's Degree	16.1	18.7	14.8	12.8
Bachelor's Degree	14.8	19.5	11.3	31.0
Graduate Degree	0.8	1.1	0.8	2.9
All		68.0	73.4	17.9
		Four-year College Students		
None	29.4	26.7	39.4	22.5
Certificate	5.3	3.8	6.1	2.5
Associate's Degree	6.4	6.1	7.7	2.8
Bachelor's Degree	48.5	52.2	41.8	56.8
Graduate Degree	10.4	11.3	5.0	15.5
All		87.1	83.5	56.0

Note: Authors' calculations using the High School and Beyond sophomore cohort (self-reported postsecondary attendance and degree attainment). The cells represent percentages of the column. All percentages are weighted using the fifth follow-up panel weight. "Two-year Students" are those who started at a two-year college; "Four-year Students" are those who started at a four-year college.

Labor Market Payoffs to Community College

Despite the fact that community colleges enroll a large share of those starting college—and an even larger share of those persuaded by public subsidies to enter college—we know relatively little about the relationship between community college coursework and future earnings. The standard educational attainment question used by the U.S. Bureau of the Census inquires about years of schooling completed (or, more recently, degrees received)—not about the type of institution one attended. The resulting lack of data has been a serious limitation for research on community colleges.

Evidence from Panel Survey Data

The handful of available analyses of the labor market payoffs to community colleges has relied on panel surveys beginning with high school-age youth, which follow respondents through college and beyond, eventually observing sample members' earnings in the years after college. Table 2 summarizes the results from six papers estimating the relationship between community college attendance and earnings.[5] Five of the papers attempt to control for prior differences in academic preparation between college entrants by using either a standardized test score or high school class rank (or both) as regressors. The paper by Jacobson, LaLonde and Sullivan (1997) uses information on earnings prior to college entry to "control for" such differences.

One could draw two primary generalizations from the results reported in Table 2. First, as reported by Leigh and Gill (1997) and Kane and Rouse (1995), the average community college entrant (who never attended a four-year college), who enrolls but does not complete a degree, earns 9 to 13 percent more than the average high school graduate with similar high school grades and/or test scores between the age of 29 and 38. Second, Kane and Rouse (1995), Grubb (1995), and Monk-Turner (1994) estimate that each year of credit at a community college is associated with a 5–8 percent increase in annual earnings—which happens to be the same as the estimated value of a year's worth of credit at a four-year college.

Most of the above results are based on the labor market experiences of those who entered community college soon after high school. How-ever, given the recent policy interest in retraining for older workers, the earnings impacts for older adults is of particular interest. The papers by Leigh and Gill (1997) and by Jacobson, LaLonde and Sullivan (1997) provide what evidence we have on this issue. Leigh and Gill test for differences in the educational wage differentials for those entering college at different ages, and do not find evidence that the earnings differentials associated with associate degrees or with community college coursework are any different for the one-third of those who attend community college after age 25. Jacobson, LaLonde and Sullivan's analysis of samples of displaced workers suggests that the earnings differential associated with a year of community college coursework is approximately 2–5 percent. How-ever, the authors estimate substantially larger returns (on the order of 15 percent per year) for courses in more quantitatively or technically-oriented courses such as vocational health, technical/professional, and technical trade courses, and science and math academic courses, but find negligible returns to non-quantitative courses like sales/service, non-technical vocational, social science/humanities, health/physical education/consumer-oriented, and basic education. Despite these gains, the average earnings of displaced workers did not return to pre-displacement levels.

Evidence from Differentials by State and Over Time

An alternative approach to analyzing the labor market effects of community colleges is to use evidence on historical differences in the prevalence of community and four-year colleges between states and over time. We used the microdata from the 1990 census to estimate the difference in each state in the log of annual earnings between high school graduates (with no postsecondary training) and those with "some college, no degree," for 25–34 year-old males.[6] (In an attempt to categorize the men by the states in which they were trained, the income differentials were measured by the state in which men were living five years earlier.) In Figure 3, we then plot these state average earnings differentials by the proportion of enrollment in each state in community colleges. If those attending community colleges were receiving lower earnings differentials from college attendance than those attending four- year colleges, we might expect

TABLE 9.2
Summarizing Research on Labor Market Effects of Community College Education

Authors:	Data Sources:	Covariates:	A.A. Degree Holders:	Some College No Degree:	
			Annual Earnings Differential: (relative to high school graduates)		
Leigh and Gill (1997)	NLSY (1993)	*Ability Measure:* AFQT Score *Other Covariates:* Race, ethnicity, age, gender, work exp., region, part-time emp.	.235 (.040) (No sig. diff. over age 25)	2-Yr Coll 4-Yr Coll	.118 (.031) .093 (.035)
Kane and Rouse (1995)	NLSY (1990)	*Ability Measure:* AFQT Score *Other Covariates:* Race, ethnicity, age, gender, work exp., region, part-time emp., parents' education.	.271 (.038)	2-Yr Coll 4-Yr Coll	.100 (.030) .125 (.036)
	NLS-72 (1986)	*Ability Measure:* H.S. Class Rank, NLS-72 Test Score *Other Covariates:* Race, ethnicity, gender, work exp., region, part-time employment, parental income.	.159 (.034) (Differential larger for women)	*Per Year:* 2-Yr Coll 4-Yr Coll	.061 (.016) .061 (.012)
Grubb (1995)	NLS-72 (1986)	*Ability Measure:* NLS-72 Test Scores, H.S. Grades *Other Covariates:* Race, ethnicity, parental income, an index of parental socio-economic status, work experience, tenure on current job, indicators for firm-provided training.	Voc. AA .106 (.033) Acad AA −.021 (.044)	*Per Year:* Voc 2-Yr Voc 4-Yr Acad 2-Yr Acad 4-Yr	.046 (.042) .120 (.025) .047 (.025) −.012 (.014)
Jacobson, LaLonde and Sullivan (1997)	Displaced workers in PA and WA.	*Ability Measure:* Person Fixed-Effects *Other Covariates:* Prior industry, age	—	2-Yr, PA 4-Yr, WA	.015 (.004) .052 (.005)
Monk-Turner (1994)	Parnes NLS	*Ability Measure:* IQ Score (on H.S. Transcript) *Other Covariates:* Race, gender, parental educ., region, work exp. marital status, educational plans.		*Per Year:* 2-Yr Coll 4-Yr Coll	.054 (.02) .079 (.01)
Heineman and Sussna (1977)	HS Graduates (Class of 1964 and 1967)	*Ability Measure:* H.S. Class Rank *Other Covariates:* Race, age, gender, work exp., parental family income, parental education, religion, military service.	.150	—	

Note: In the studies which report impacts by year or by gender, the above estimates represent weighted averages using sample sizes as weights. Standard errors for the pooled estimates were calculated under the assumption of independence. Where impacts were reported in dollars, we divided by the relevant average annual earnings to convert to percentages. Where impacts were reported in units of log earnings, we reported log earnings differentials, which approximate percentage differences.

to see a downward sloping graph. As is apparent from Figure 3, there is no strong relationship between the "some college" earnings differential and the proportion of enrollment in community colleges.[7] In fact, the "some college/high school graduate" earnings difference in California—

with relatively large community college enrollments—is higher than the national average. Moreover, as we reported in Kane and Rouse (1995), there is no evidence that the "some college" earnings differential has fallen over time as community college enrollments have risen.

Experimental Evidence

The non-experimental evidence summarized to this point suggests substantial effects of community college training on annual earnings. However, experimental evaluations of training programs have offered a much less optimistic appraisal of the impacts of classroom training for the unemployed and out-of-school youth.[8] For instance, in 1986, the U.S. Department of Labor commissioned an experimental evaluation of training provided to adults and out-of-school youth under the Job Training Partnership Act. Because many of the training providers under the Job Training Partnership Act (JTPA) were community colleges—indeed, over one-half of community colleges receive JTPA funds (Lynch, Palmer and Grubb, 1991)—the results of the JTPA evaluation provide another indirect assessment of the labor market value of a community college education.

The primary difference between the non-experimental results summarized above and the results of the typical randomized controlled experiment lies in the fact that the experiments can only estimate the incremental impact of a new opportunity for training—not the value of the training itself. For instance, many members of the control group in the JTPA experiment received classroom training at the very same institutions where the treatment group members received their training—they just paid for the training themselves or took advantage of other government programs, such as the federal Pell Grant program, to help pay the cost. Thus, the experimental evidence provides no direct evidence on the value of training vs. no training, but rather estimates only the difference between the training opportunities provided to the treatment group and the training opportunities available elsewhere. The more similar JTPA training was to training available elsewhere, the more likely one would find a zero incremental impact of the JTPA program.

Indeed, this may explain the divergence between the results of the JTPA evaluation and the non-experimental estimates cited above. The impacts of the JTPA program on earnings were not statistically distinguishable from zero for several subgroups—leading some observers to conclude that classroom training had little impact. However, the differences in the amount of classroom training received by the treatment and control groups were also quite small.

Figure 3

The "Some College" Wage Differential and Community College Enrollment by State

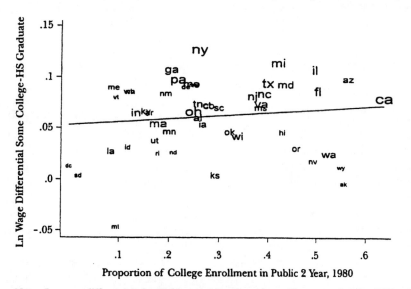

Proportion of College Enrollment in Public 2 Year, 1980

Note: Ln wage differentials for 25-34 year-old males estimated by state using the 1990 5% PUMS. The wage differentials were estimated with separate log wage equations for each state, including regressors for age (10 categories), race/ethnicity, and category of educational attainment. The size of the symbol for each state reflects the reciprocal of the standard error on the estimated coefficient.

Source: Kane and Rouse (1995).

In fact, if one translates the point estimates of the educational wage differentials arising out of the JTPA experiment into the framework we have been using, the results are quite comparable in magnitude. For example, during the final year of the JTPA evaluation follow-up, the average adult woman assigned to classroom training earned $282 (5.1 percent) more than those in the control group (Orr et al., 1994). They also received 147 hours more training than those in the control group. If there are 420 hours of classroom training in a typical academic year (that is, 14 weeks per semester, 15 classroom hours per week, and two semesters a year), then our point estimate would be that receiving an academic year's worth of training would have been associated with an annual earnings differential per year of 14.6 percent. Similar results hold for the adult male and female youth groups, although the impacts for male youth were smaller than the 5 to 8 percent differential implied by the nonexperimental estimates. In other words, even though the JTPA experimental estimates were generally not statistically distinguishable from zero, because alternative training opportunities were so readily available to the control group, the implied estimates of the differential per year of training received were generally on the high end of the non-experimental estimates above. Heckman, Hohmann, Khoo and Smith (1997) have used the JTPA data to generate non-experimental estimates of the value of classroom training. Their results also suggest substantial private internal rates of return to classroom training, albeit with more ambiguous social returns.

The Payoff to Completing an Associate's Degree

With only about 16 percent of community college entrants completing an associate's degree, the incremental value of degree completion itself has been central to the policy debate over community colleges. While the evidence presented in the last section suggests there are returns to completing community college credits, some argue that the main return to attending a community college comes with completing an associate's degree.

The evidence in Table 2 reports the total earnings differential between associate's degree recipients and high school graduates, inclusive of any credits completed. (One exception: the associate's degree effects reported for Grubb

(1995) should be interpreted as incremental to the number of credits completed.) Completing an associate's degree appears to be associated with a 15 to 27 percent increase in annual earnings. Since estimates suggest that two years of community college credit is associated with a 10 to 16 percent increase in earnings (that is, the 5 to 8 percent annual gain times two), there appears to be some additional gain to the associate's degree itself. The evidence also suggests that this differential is larger for women, largely reflecting the value of nursing degrees where the earnings gain is especially pronounced (Kane and Rouse, 1995; Grubb, 1995).[9]

Discontinuities in the relationship between average log earnings and years of schooling completed at 14 and 16 years of schooling have traditionally been interpreted as reflecting the value of completing an associate's or bachelor's degree (Hungerford and Solon, 1987).[10] However, before 1992, the standard Census Bureau question on educational attainment did not allow one to distinguish between those who had completed an associate's or bachelor's degree and those who had completed 14 or 16 years of schooling without degrees. To assess whether the return to the associate's degree reflects a "sheepskin effect" or the effect of having completed two years of college, Jaeger and Page (1996) exploit a 1992 change in the Census Bureau educational attainment question; the earlier question focused solely on years of schooling completed, while the new one inquires about degree completion. After matching responses in the March 1991 *Current Population Survey* (including the question regarding years of schooling completed) and March 1992 survey (with data on degree completion), they found that white men with associate's degrees earn 8–19 percent more than men reporting similar years of schooling completed, but no degrees, and white women with associate's degrees earn 24–31 percent more than women reporting similar years of schooling completed, but no degrees. Again, it seems that nursing degrees account for much of the importance of associate's degrees for women (Kane and Rouse, 1995).

However, such estimates likely overstate the direct effect of degree completion for two reasons. First, the estimates are not adjusted for prior differences in family background and ability between degree completers and dropouts—because such information is not available on the Current Population Survey. It appears that those completing degrees not only have higher earnings than others with similar years of schooling, but they also seem to have higher prior test scores and more advantaged family backgrounds as well, and so controlling for these other factors would shrink the effect of degree completion.

Second, the magnitude of sheepskin effects may partially reflect the nature of measurement error in self-reported measures of educational attainment. Kane, Rouse and Staiger (1997) develop a technique for estimating the amount of measurement error in both self-reported and transcript-reported schooling in the NLS-72. Their findings suggest that respondents are more likely to misreport the number of years of college they have completed than they are to misreport degrees completed. While more than 95 percent of those who report a bachelor's degree 7 years after graduating from high school are estimated to be reporting accurately, one-third of those who report 3 years of college credit are estimated to have completed only 0, 1 or 2 years of college. Similarly, among those who report 1 year of college, 30 percent are estimated to actually have 0, 2 or 3 years of college. As a result, estimates based on self-reported schooling are likely to provide an accurate estimate of the earnings of those with a bachelor's degree and underestimate the differences in earnings per year of college for those without a bachelor's degree. Any discontinuity of earnings between those reporting 3 years of college and those reporting a bachelor's degree is likely to be exaggerated. In other words, the "sheepskin" effects reported in the literature may well be due in part to the nature of the reporting error in educational attainment.

Finally, even what remains of the "sheepskin" effect, after controlling for individual heterogeneity and measurement error, overstates the relative value of degrees and understates the anticipated value of postsecondary entry for those who do not complete degrees. There may be an option value to college entry for those uncertain of their prospects for finishing (Manski, 1989; Altonji, 1991; Comay et al., 1973). If the returns to education are uncertain or if youth are uncertain as to whether they are "college material," youth may gain some information in the first few months of college which helps to resolve the uncertainty. The wage differentials only reflect later monetary payoffs to college attendance. However, to the extent that the decision to enroll in college is an experiment for many, the anticipated outcome of that experiment may be sufficient to justify the public and private investments required, even if, after running the experiment, students do not finish the degree. This argument also suggests that we might wish to avoid proposals which seek to limit aid to those who complete degrees, as is occasionally suggested as a policy response to the high noncompletion rates at community colleges (for example, Fischer, 1987).

A Rough Approximation of the Private and Social Rates of Return

How do the earnings differentials associated with a year at a community college compare to the costs of attendance? Using the average annual earnings of current 25–64 year-old workers (employed full-time, full-year) to estimate future earnings and employing a discount rate of 6 percent, the present value of expected lifetime earnings for the average male high school graduate in 1992 would have been $480,500 (in 1997 dollars).[11] The present value of a 5 to 8 percent increase in lifetime earnings for someone with career income of $480,500 would be $24,000 to $38,400 before taxes or $15,600 to $25,000 after taxes (assuming a combined federal and state tax rate of 35 percent).

The full cost to a family of a year at a community college includes both the earnings foregone by students as well as the cost of tuition. (We have left out room and board, since individuals would have to eat even if they were not in school). In 1992, the average income of a male 18–24 year-old high school graduate working full-time, full-year was $19,400 (in 1997 dollars). Foregoing nine months at that salary would imply costs of $14,600 before taxes or $9,500 after taxes. As mentioned above, a minority of students actually seem to forego nine months of full-time earnings, since a majority of both two-year and four-year college students work while they are in school. Nevertheless, such calculations provide a rough approximation of the "unit price" of a year of full-time schooling, even if relatively few students decide to "purchase" a full nine months away from work.

Adding in the private cost of tuition at the average public two-year college, the rise in after-tax lifetime income of $15,600 to $25,000 would be larger, but not dramatically larger, than the estimated private cost of $10,800

($9,500 in foregone after-tax earnings plus $1,300 per year for tuition).

Calculations along these lines also reveal why it may not be surprising that the earnings differential associated with a year at a community college is similar in magnitude to that associated with a year at a four-year college. Although the tuition charges at community colleges are typically lower ($1,300 per year compared to $3,000 at the average public four-year institution), the vast majority of the private cost of attendance is foregone earnings, not tuition. To the extent that students are choosing on the margin between two-year and four-year colleges, we might expect students to attend each type of college to the point where the payoffs were similar.

Given the size of the public subsidies directed at community colleges, the average tuition families face ($1,300) is considerably less than the actual cost of a year of full-time education. Rouse (1998) estimates that average variable cost of a year in community college is $6,300 (in 1997 dollars).[12] However, this figure does not include capital costs, which Winston and Lewis (1997) estimate to be an additional $1,700 per student (27 percent of expenditures per student). To the extent that the private cost families face is considerably lower than the actual cost of the resources required to produce a year at a community college, we might fear students would over-invest in post-secondary education. However, even if we were to count only the earnings increases associated with community colleges (and ignore any of the other hard-to-measure benefits, such as civic participation or greater social mobility), the estimated 5 to 8 percent earnings differential would imply gains roughly the same as the full cost of the resources used: the combined cost of pre-tax earnings and expenditures per pupil of $22,600 is comparable in magnitude to the $24,000 to $38,400 estimate of the present value of future earnings differentials.

Although these back-of-the-envelope calculations can of course be subjected to criticism on many dimensions, it thus appears possible that a year of community college increases earnings by an amount roughly equal to the value of the resources used to produce that year.

Student Financing Issues

Community colleges are heavily dependent upon public subsidies for their operations; 62 percent of current-fund revenues are appropriated by state and local governments (U.S. Department of Education, 1997, Table 328, p. 344). Because students must be enrolled at least half-time to qualify for many federal aid programs such as the guaranteed student loan programs, only a quarter of community college students report receiving state or federal grant aid to help cover the cost of tuition and fees (U.S. Department of Education, 1992–93, Table 3.1a, p. 62).

Future demographic trends are likely to strain the ability of states to maintain this commitment in coming years. The size of the traditional college-age population (that is, 15- to 24-year-olds) has declined by 15 percent since 1980, partially relieving the cost pressure produced by rising college enrollment rates. However, this college-age population is now projected to rise by one-fifth over the next 15 years (Campbell, 1994). The rise is projected to be particularly dramatic in California, where the number of 15- to 24-year-olds is projected to increase at roughly twice the national rate. If the labor market wage premiums favoring college entry persist, and college enrollment rates remain high, states are likely to be forced to choose between raising tuition and increasing public expenditures on higher education.

Should states decide to increase tuition, it is likely to have an unusually large impact on community college enrollments. The demand elasticities with respect to upfront costs of college entry are quite high. After reviewing 25 estimates of tuition price responses, Leslie and Brinkman (1988) reported a median estimate of a 4.4 percentage point difference in post-secondary entry for every $1,000 difference in tuition costs (in 1997 dollars).[13] A number of others have found similar results, including Cameron and Heckman (1998b), Rouse (1994), Kane (1995), Kane (1994) and McPherson and Schapiro (1991). Enrollment at two-year colleges appears to be particularly sensitive to tuition changes (Kane, 1995; Rouse, 1994; Manski and Wise, 1983).

In addition, students seem to be more sensitive to tuition changes than to changes in future wage differentials. While the payoff to college was rising dramatically during the 1980s, the proportion of high school graduates entering college within two years of high school rose by only 7 percentage points, from 65 to 72 percent (U.S. Department of Education, *Condition of Education*, 1997, p. 64). Using the estimates of tuition sensitivity described above, a tuition increase of

$1500 would have been enough to have wiped out that rise in college entrance rates—even though the present value of the college earnings differential rose by far more than $1500 during the 1980s.

One potential explanation for the sensitivity of students to the tuition costs at community colleges is that they face borrowing constraints in the private capital market. Indirect evidence on this point is provided by Card (forthcoming), who summarizes evidence suggesting higher marginal returns to schooling for disadvantaged groups than for the population as a whole. Such findings may result from the fact that lower-income families have more difficulty arranging financing for college. In a similar vein, most studies find that large differences in college entry by family income remain, even among those with similar test scores and academic performance in high school.[14]

The most obvious constraints which limit family borrowing for community college are the explicit limits on student borrowing in the federal student loan programs. Since 1992, the most a dependent student could borrow under the Stafford loan program has been $2,625 during the freshman year, $3,500 during the sophomore year and $5,500 per year thereafter. Independent students who are married, have dependents, are veterans or are over age 24 can borrow an additional $4,000 per year during their first two years and an additional $5,000 per year thereafter. However, such amounts may not be sufficient to pay living expenses on top of tuition bills. Some states and institutions have their own loan programs, but in 1992–93, less than 1 percent of undergraduates received either a state loan (0.5 percent) or an institutional loan (0.4 percent); in contrast, 20 percent of undergraduates received federal loans. A third source of borrowing constraints may be the confusing nature of the application process. Several studies cited in Orfield (1992) suggest that low-income families are often unaware of eligibility rules and procedures.

An important challenge will be to create a financing structure that will allow community colleges to expand in the next few years to meet the training needs of the population—and then eventually to contract as the relevant population declines. The current system of "backward-looking" means-testing, which looks back at the parents' income to determine student eligibility for financial aid, is more appropriate for the student of traditional college age and is less well-suited to the population of community college entrants. If community colleges are to remain an engine of innovation in postsecondary education, we will require similarly creative and flexible financing strategies to match. As an alternative to the current form of financing with several advantages would be greater reliance on income-contingent loans—that is, loans where the amount of repayment depends to some extent on future income earned—as discussed in this journal in Krueger and Bowen (1993). The expected subsidy implicit in an income-contingent loan is lower than the cost of a dollar in appropriations to public institutions, which in turn means that families and youth would have a stronger incentive to allocate society's educational resources in a prudent manner. Moreover, the means-test implicit in income-contingent loans does not involve the same difficulty in distinguishing students who are "dependent" on parents' resources from those who are "independent."

Conclusion

For the past five decades, the debate over access to higher education and the role of higher education in economic development has implicitly been a debate about community colleges. In any discussion involving marginal incentives, community colleges have been the margin. They have been the gateway for those on the verge of enrolling in college: older students, those who cannot afford to attend full-time, and those who need to develop their basic skills. Ironically, though, we know less about community colleges than about other sectors of higher education. The evidence we do have, as summarized above, suggests that community colleges increase aggregate educational attainment, and are associated with higher wages, even for those not completing degrees.

If current labor market conditions persist, we can expect significant increases in demand for postsecondary training slots in the future, due to the projected growth in college-age cohorts. Historically, community colleges have been the buffer, absorbing much of the increase in enrollment when veterans returned from war or when demand for skilled labor outpaced supply. Enrollment at community colleges also has swelled much more dramatically than at other institutions during economic downturns, when opportunity costs of such investments in training are lowest (Betts and McFarland, 1996).

Recent technological developments in distance learning will likely allow colleges to be even more responsive to changes in demand for higher education and have raised hopes of improving productivity in instruction.[15] Community colleges are participating in this growing trend. In 1995, 58 percent of public two-year colleges were offering distance learning courses serving over 400,000 students (or about 7 percent of their total enrollment).[16] However, community colleges are not the only institutions turning to distance learning: two-thirds of public four-year colleges offered such courses in 1995 and an additional 25 percent were planning to offer such courses by 1998. To the extent that geographic accessibility and flexible scheduling have been a traditional source of community colleges' market niche, the technological revolution may allow other institutions, such as four-year colleges and private for-profit institutions, to compete more effectively in the markets traditionally served by community colleges.[17] The net result of these technological changes—whether they lead to an increasing or decreasing role for community colleges in the future—remains to be seen.

- *We thank Lauren Brown for expert research assistance, Mark López for help with some calculations, and Brad De Long, Alan Krueger, John Siegfried, Timothy Taylor, and participants at the JEP Symposium on Higher Education held at Macalester College on June 26, 1998 for helpful comments. Kane acknowledges the generous support of the Andrew W. Mellon Foundation.*

Notes

[1]Although we use the terms interchangeably, we know of no private "community" colleges while "junior" and "two-year" colleges are both public and private.

[2]Rouse (1994) shows that college proximity is an important determinant of college attendance. We discuss the literature on the effects of tuition below.

[3]Figure 2 is based on authors' calculations from the *High School and Beyond Post-secondary Transcript* file, which is for students who were sophomores in 1980 (the "sophomore cohort"). The figure includes only students who had a complete set of (cumulative) transcripts and who had earned any credits at a two-year college as of 1992; the distributions are weighted by the post-secondary transcript weight. If the sample is limited to those

who have no four-year credits, the distribution looks quite similar.

[4]Proprietary schools were not counted as college for this exercise; therefore, if a student first attended a proprietary school and then attended either a two- or four-year college, we count the two- or four-year college as the "first" school attended.

[5]Hollenbeck (1993) and Surette (1997) also report results consistent with those in Table 2 using the National Longitudinal Study of the Class of 1972 (NLS-72) and the National Longitudinal Survey of Youth (NLSY) respectively.

[6]To match as closely as possible the state where the person was educated, sample members were categorized by their state of residence in 1985, when they would have been 20 to 29. The regressions also adjusted for race/ethnicity and year of age.

[7]Weighting by the reciprocal of the standard error of each estimate, the slope coefficient in Figure 3 was .038 with a standard error of .029, meaning that for every 10 percentage point increase in the proportion of students in the state enrolled in community colleges, the estimated wage differential is estimated to rise by a statistically insignificant third of a percentage point.

[8]For instance, in a recent summary in this journal, LaLonde (1995) concluded: "Finally, the National JTPA Study found that . . . those men assigned to a strategy that offered classroom training did not appear to benefit from JTPA services."

[9]The estimated earnings differential for associate's degree completion for women falls by one-third when one includes a dummy variable for nurses.

[10]In contrast, studies of the relationship between log earnings and the number of years of schooling suggest that the percentage increase in earnings between the 13th and 14th years of schooling is similar to that between the 12th and 13th years of schooling; there is no discontinuity (for example, Park, 1994).

[11]This may be a conservative estimate since we are implicitly assuming no real wage growth. However, it may also be overly optimistic, since the continuing increases in college enrollment may eventually lead to a decline in earnings differentials.

[12]Excluding "fixed costs" such as research, administration, student services and admissions, her estimate would be $4,200.

[13]Leslie and Brinkman's (1988, appendix table 6) actual estimate was that a $100 increase in tuition in 1982–83 dollars was associated with a .7 percentage point decline in enrollment among 18–24 year-olds. We have converted to 1997 dollars in the text.

[14]Kane (1998), Manski and Wise (1983) and Hauser and Sweeney (1997) report differences in post-

secondary entry by family income, conditioning on both parental education and student test scores. Using the NLSY, Cameron and Heckman (1998a) find differences in college entry by family income to be greatly reduced, but not eliminated, after including controls for AFQT scores.

[15]The Department of Education defines distance learning as ". . . education or training courses delivered to remote (off-campus) locations via audio, video, or computer technologies" (Lewis et al., 1997).

[16]The most common form of the distance learning is one-way pre-recorded video classes (67 percent), although half of public two-year colleges also offer two-way interactive video.

[17]We thank Michael Rothschild for pointing out the potential vulnerability of community colleges as the technology for distance learning improves.

References

Alba, Richard D. and David E. Lavin. 1981. "Community Colleges and Tracking in Higher Education." *Sociology of Education.* 54, pp. 223–37.

Altonji, Joseph. 1991. "The Demand for and Return to Education When Education Outcomes are Uncertain." National Bureau of Economic Research. Working Paper No. 3714, May.

Anderson, Kristine L. 1981. "Post-High School Experiences and College Attrition." *Sociology of Education.* 54, pp. 1–15.

Arenson, Karen W. 1998. "CUNY To Tighten Admissions Policy at Four-Year Schools." *New York Times.* May 27, Section A, Page 1.

Barbett, Samuel F., Roslyn Korb and MacKnight Black. 1988, *State Higher Education Profiles: 1988 Edition.* Washington, D.C.: National Center for Education Statistics.

Betts, Julian and Laurel McFarland. 1996. "Safe Port in a Storm: The Impact of Labor Market Conditions on Community College Enrollments." *Journal of Human Resources.* 30:4, pp. 742–65.

Bloom, Howard S. et al. 1994. *National JTPA Study Overview: Impacts, Benefits and Costs of Title II-A: A Report to the U.S. Department of Labor.* Bethesda: Abt Associates, January.

Breneman, David W. and Susan C. Nelson. 1981. *Financing Community Colleges: An Economic Perspective.* Washington, D.C.: The Brookings Institution.

Brint, Steven and Jerome Karabel. 1989. *The Diverted Dream: Community Colleges and the Promise of Educational Opportunity in America, 1900–1985.* New York: Oxford University Press.

Bruno, Rosalind R. and Andrea Curry. 1996. *School Enrollment—Social and Economic Characteristics of Students: October 1994.* U.S. Bureau of the Census, Current Population Reports, P20–487. Washington, D.C.: U.S. Government Printing Office.

Cameron, Stephen V. and James J. Heckman. 1998a. "Life Cycle Schooling and Dynamic Selection Bias: Models and Evidence for Five Cohorts of American Males." *Journal of Political Economy.* 106:2, pp 262–333.

Cameron, Stephen V. and James J. Heckman. 1998b. "The Dynamics of Educational Attainment for Blacks, Hispanics, and Whites." Working Paper, Columbia University Department of Economics, September.

Campbell, Paul R. 1994. Population *Projections for States, by Age, Race and Sex: 1993–2020.* U.S. Bureau of the Census, Current Population Reports, P25–1111. Washington, D.C.: U.S. Government Printing Office.

Card, David E. Forthcoming. "The Causal Effect of Education on Earnings," in *Handbook of Labor Economics, Volume 3.* Orley Ashenfelter and David E. Card, eds. New York, NY: North-Holland.

Clark, Burton R. 1960. "The 'Cooling-Out' Function in Higher Education." *American Journal of Sociology.* 65, pp. 569–76.

Cohen, Arthur M. and Florence B. Brawer. 1982. *The American Community College.* San Francisco: Jossey-Bass Publishers.

Comay, Y., A. Melnick and M. Pollatschek. 1973. "The Option Value of Education and the Optimal Path for Investment in Human Capital." *International Economic Review.* 14, pp. 421–35.

Dougherty, Kevin. 1987. "The Effects of Community Colleges: Aid or Hindrance to Socioeconomic Attainment?" *Sociology of Education.* 60, pp. 86–103.

Fischer, Frederick. 1987. "Graduation-Contingent Student Aid." *Change.* November/December, pp. 40–47.

Griliches, Zvi. 1977. "Estimating the Returns to Schooling: Some Econometric Problems." *Econometrira.* 45, pp. 1–22.

Grubb, W. Norton. 1993. "The Varied Economic Returns to Postsecondary Education: New Evidence from the Class of 1972." *Journal of Human Resources.* 28:3, pp. 365–82.

Grubb, W. Norton. 1995. "Postsecondary Education and the Sub-Baccalaureate Labor Market: Corrections and Extensions." *Economics of Education Review.* 14:3, pp. 285–99.

Grubb, W. Norton. 1988. "Vocationalizing Higher Education: The Causes of Enrollment and Completion in Public Two-year Colleges, 1970–1980." *Economics of Education Review.* 7, pp. 301–19.

Grubb, W. Norton. 1989. "The Effects of Differentiation on Educational Attainment: The Case of

Community Colleges." *Review of Higher Education,* 12, pp. 349–74.

Hauser, Robert M. and Megan Sweeney. 1997. "Does Poverty in Adolescence Affect the Life Chances of High School Graduates?" In *Consequences of Growing Up Poor.* Greg J. Duncan and Jeanne Brooks-Gunn, eds. New York: Russell Sage.

Heckman, James J. et al. 1997. "Substitution and Drop Out Bias in Social Experiments: A Study of an Influential Social Experiment." University of Chicago Working Paper, August.

Heineman, Harry N. and Edward Sussna. 1977. "The Economic Benefits of a Community College." *Industrial Relations.* 16:3, pp. 345–54.

Hollenbeck, Kevin. 1993. "Postsecondary Education as Triage: Returns to Academic and Technical Programs." *Economics of Education Review.* September, 12:3, pp. 213–32.

Horn, Laura J., Jennifer Berktold and Andrew G. Malizio. 1998. *Profile of Undergraduates in U.S. Postsecondary Education Institutions: 1995–96.* Washington, D.C.: National Center for Education Statistics.

Hungerford, Thomas and Gary Solon. 1987. "Sheepskin Effects in the Returns to Education." *Review of Economics and Statistics.* 69:1, pp. 175–77.

Jaeger, David AL and Marianne E. Page. 1996. "Degrees Matter: New Evidence on Sheepskin Effects in the Returns to Education." *Review of Economics and Statistics.* 78:4, pp. 733–40.

Jacobson, Louis S., Robert J. LaLonde and Daniel G. Sullivan. 1997. "The Returns from Community College Schooling for Displaced Workers." Federal Reserve Bank of Chicago, WP–97–16, June.

Kane, Thomas J. October 1994. "College Attendance By Blacks Since 1970: The Role of College Cost, Family Background and the Returns to Education." *Journal of Political Economy.* 102:5, pp. 878–911.

Kane, Thomas J. 1995. "Rising Public College Tuition and College Entry: How Well Do Public Subsidies Promote Access to College?" National Bureau of Economic Research Working Paper No. 5164, April.

Kane, Thomas J. 1998. "Are College Students Credit Constrained?" Working Paper, Kennedy School of Government, Harvard University, May.

Kane, Thomas J. and Cecilia Elena Rouse. 1995. "Comment on W. Norton Grubb, 'The Varied Economic Returns to Postsecondary Education: New Evidence from the Class of 1972'." *Journal of Human Resources.* Winter, 30:1, pp. 205–21.

Kane, Thomas J. and Cecilia Elena Rouse. 1995. "Labor-Market Returns to Two- and Four-Year College." *American Economic Review.* June, 85:3, pp. 600–14.

Kane, Thomas J., Cecilia Elena Rouse and Douglas Staiger. December 1997. "Estimating Returns to Schooling When Schooling is Misreported. " Unpublished paper, Kennedy School of Government, Harvard University.

Kelley, Pam. 1998. "Free K-14 Could Become the Standard in North Carolina." *Community College Week.* June, 10:22, p. 6.

Krueger, Alan B. and William G. Bowen. 1993. "Policy Watch: Income Contingent Loans." *Journal of Economic Perspectives.* 7:3, pp. 193–201.

Krueger, Alan B. and Cecilia Elena Rouse. 1998. "The Effect of Workplace Education on Earnings, Turnover, and Job Performance" *Journal of Labor Economics.* January, 16:1, pp. 61–94.

LaLonde, Robert J. 1995. "The Promise of Public Sector-Sponsored Training Programs. *Journal of Economic Perspectives.* Spring, 9:2, pp. 149–68.

Leigh, Duane E. and Andrew M. Gill. 1997. "Labor Market Returns to Community Colleges: Evidence for Returning Adults." *Journal of Human Resources.* Spring, 32:2, pp. 334–53.

Leslie, Larry and Paul Brinkman. 1988. *Economic Value of Higher Education.* New York: Macmillan.

Lewis, Laurie, Elizabeth Farris and Bernie Greene. 1996. *Remedial Education at Higher Education Institutions in Fall 1995.* Washington, D.C.: U.S. Department of Education, National Center for Education.

Lewis, Laurie et al. 1997. *Distance Learning in Higher Education Institutions.* Washington, D.C.: U.S. Department of Education, National Center for Education.

Lynch, Robert, James C. Palmer, and W. Norton Grubb. 1991. *Community College Involvement in Contract Training and Other Economic Development Activities.* Berkeley, CA: National Center for Research in Vocational Education, October.

Manski, Charles F. 1989. "Schooling as Experimentation: A Reappraisal of the Postsecondary Dropout Phenomenon." *Economics of Education Review.* 4, pp. 305–12.

Manski, Charles F. and David A. Wise. 1993. *College Choice in America.* Cambridge, MA: Harvard University Press.

McPherson, Michael S. and Morton Owen Schapiro. 1991. "Does Student Aid Affect College Enrollment? New Evidence on a Persistent Controversy." *American Economic Review.* 81, pp. 309–18.

Monk-Turner, Elizabeth. 1994. "Economic Returns to Community and Four-Year College Education," *Journal of Socio-Economics.* 23:4, pp. 441–47.

Orfield, Gary. 1992. "Money, Equity and College Access." *Harvard Educational Review.* Fall, 72:3, pp. 337–72.

Orr, Larry L. et al. 1994. *National JTPA Study: Impacts, Benefits and Costs of Title II-A.* Draft report to the U.S. Department of Labor, March.

Orr, Larry L. et al. 1996. *Does Training for the Disadvantaged Work?* Washington, D.C.: Urban Institute.

Park, Jin Heum. 1994. "Returns to Schooling: A Peculiar Deviation from Linearity." Princeton University Industrial Relations Section Working Paper No. 335, October.

Pincus, Fred L. 1980. "The False Promises of Community Colleges: Class Conflict and Vocational Education." *Harvard Educational Review.* 1980, 50, pp. 332–61.

Rouse, Cecilia Elena. 1994. "What To Do After High School? The Two-year vs. Four-year College Enrollment Decision." In *Contemporary Policy Issues in Education.* Ronald Ehrenberg, editor. Ithaca, NY: ILR Press, pp. 59–88.

Rouse, Cecilia Elena. 1995. "Democratization or Diversion? The Effect of Community Colleges on Educational Attainment." *Journal of Business Economics and Statistics.* April, 13:2, pp. 217–24.

Rouse, Cecilia Elena. 1998. "Do Two-year Colleges Increase Overall Educational Attainment? Evidence from the States." *Journal of Policy Analysis and Management.* Fall, 17:4, pp. 595–620.

Surette, Brian J. 1997. "The Effects of Two-Year College on the Labor Market and Schooling Experi-

ences of Young Men." Working paper, Finance and Economics Series, Washington, D.C.: Federal Reserve Board, June.

Tinto, Vincent. 1985. "College Proximity and Rates of College Attendance." *American Educational Research Journal.* 10, pp. 277–93.

Trombley, William. 1993. "College Running Out of Space, Money." *Los Angeles Times.* October 18, 3A.

U.S. Department of Education. 1997. *Condition of Education 1997.* Washington, D.C.: National Center for Education Statistics.

U.S. Department of Education. 1997. *Digest of Education Statistics 1997.* Washington, D.C.: National Center for Education Statistics.

U.S. Department of Education. *Student Financing of Undergraduate Education, 1992–93.* U.S. Government Printing Office: National Center for Education Statistics.

Velez, William. 1985. "Finishing College: The Effects of College Type." *Sociology of Education.* 58, pp. 191–200.

Winston, Gordon C. and Ethan G. Lewis. 1997. "Physical Capital and Capital Service Costs in U.S. Colleges and Universities: 1993." *Eastern Economic Journal.* Spring, 23:2, pp. 165–89.

Witt, Allen A. et al. 1994. *America's Community Colleges: The First Century.* Washington, D.C.: The Community College Press.

CHAPTER 10

RECOMMENDED READINGS AND WEB-BASED RESOURCES

Recommended Readings

Bragg, D. D. (2001). Community college access, mission, and outcomes: Considering intriguing intersections and challenges. *Peabody Journal of Education, 7* (1), 93–116.

Diener, T. (1986). *Growth of an American invention: From junior to community college.* Westport, CT: Greenwood Press.

Levin, J (2001). The revised institution: The community college mission at the end of the 21st century. *Community College Review, 28* (2), 1–25.

Pincus, F. L. 1980. The false promises of community colleges: Class conflict and vocational education. *Harvard Educational Review, 50,* 332–361.

Web-Based Resources

Bailey, T., & Morest, V. S. (2004). *The organizational efficiency of multiple missions for community colleges.* New York: Community College Research Center. *http://www.tc.columbia.edu/Publication.asp?UID=7*

Boswell, K., & Wilson, C. (Eds.). (2004). *Keeping America's promise: A report on the future of the community college.* Denver, CO: Education Commission of the States. *http://www.communitycollegepolicy.org/pdf/KeepingAmericasPromise.pdf*

Community College Journal (1930–present) and *Community College Times* (1988–Present) *http://www.aaccarchives.org/*

Early Public Junior Colleges: A Resource for Graduate Students and Researchers. This site includes copies of primary sources that describe the organization, governance, curriculum, funding, and student culture of junior colleges established between 1900 and 1940. *http://junior-college-history.org*

Part III

FINANCE, GOVERNANCE, & ADMINISTRATION

INTRODUCTION

KEVIN J. DOUGHERTY

All too often, discussions of the finance, governance, and administration of higher education institutions tend to be based on the model of four-year colleges, particularly universities. This model fails to do justice to community colleges, which are substantially different from four-year colleges on all three counts. In what follows, I review key elements of the governance, finance, and administration of community colleges, including modes of institutional governance (under which will be brought finance) and the organization and administration of community colleges, including internal governance. Along the way, I will note how the readings reproduced in this section shed light on these questions.

Governance

Governance focuses on the external control of higher education organizations, particularly public ones. Typically, the focus has been on what state bodies govern or coordinate public colleges. However, governance needs to be put in more general terms of the external control of organizations by a variety of actors, not just public bodies, and a variety of modes of control. Four such modes come to mind: ownership; finance; legal regulation; and ideological and professional influence.

Ownership. One of the most fundamental characteristics of higher education institutions is whether they are publicly or privately controlled. This has enormous implications for who selects their leaders, sets their policies, finances them, etc. Clearly, community colleges are publicly owned institutions but that public ownership can take many different forms. They can be sponsored and directly controlled by the state or they can be locally sponsored and controlled, though with great state voice. The nature of that state role has been the subject of several different studies of governance (Lovell & Trouth, 2002; Richardson & de los Santos, 2001; Tollefson et al., 1999).

The Lovell and Trouth selection (Chapter 13) in this volume describe a variety of classifications of state governance structures for community colleges that have been developed in recent years. All grapple with whether states try to directly govern the community colleges or rather try to coordinate them, leaving direct governance to local bodies. Moreover, whatever the state role, does the state body focus on community colleges alone or does it also encompass four-year colleges or even elementary and secondary education? As it happens, in 23 states, the state directly governs the community colleges, whether through a board specifically for community colleges or one that also covers four-year colleges. This direct governance involves appointment and removal of president, day-to-day management and operations, and so forth (Richardson & de los Santos, 2001). However, in another 12 states, the state coordinates the system, but leaves day-to-day governance to local boards. And in 16 states, the state provides little or no state coordination, much less direct control (Richardson & de los Santos, 2001).[1]

As the Lovell and Trouth selection notes, these governance arrangements are not static. Many states are reviewing their governance arrangements. The impetus is coming from such forces as rising enrollment demand but yet continued financial stress on the states, rapid changes in educational technology, and the steady movement toward a seamless K-12 system (a facet of which is the rise of dual enrollment on the one hand and the community college baccalaureate on the other).

Finance. A key means by which community colleges are controlled is through how they are financed. In 2000–01, community college revenues for current operations came from these sources: 20% from student tuition and fees; 6% from the federal government (not including financial aid, which shows up in the tuition and fees column);[2] 45% from state government; 20% from local government;[3] 1% from private gifts and contracts; 6% from sales and services (including educational activities); less than 1% from endowment; and 4% from other sources (National Center for Education Statistics, 2003).

The state funding is complicated because it comes in several different forms. It includes formula funding primarily driven by enrollments, but also negotiated budgets and performance based funding (Cohen & Brawer, 2003; Education Commission of the States, 2000). We will review performance funding in greater detail below.

Student aid. A key facet of community college finance is student aid. Such aid plays an important role in whether students can enter the community college (particularly as tuition has risen sharply in the last decade) and then transfer to four-year colleges. Community college students have sharply increased their share of Pell grants from 25% in 1973–74 to 33% in 1997–98 (Cohen & Brawer, 2003). However, the excerpt from F. King Alexander's article, "Direct Student Aid, Public Community Colleges, and their Students" (Chapter 11), shows that community college students are still less likely to receive federal and state student aid grants than are students at private two-year colleges or at public and private four-year colleges. And while community college students are more likely to receive federal direct student loans, the amount they receive is lower than that received by students at private two-year colleges.

Besides the amount of aid overall, there are other student aid issues that face community college students, particularly less advantaged ones. Over the last decade, an increasing proportion of state aid has been given on the basis of "merit," that is, test scores and grades, which tend to advantage already advantaged students. Moreover, the many part-time students attending community colleges do not have the same access to student aid as full-time students. And undocumented immigrants very rarely receive student aid, though efforts are stirring in some states to provide it (Dougherty, Nienhusser, and Reid, forthcoming; National Center for Education Statistics, 2003: 376).

Performance based funding. In the 1990's performance accountability burst into the awareness of higher education policymakers. The hope was that performance accountability—particularly if institutions' funding was tied to it—would lead colleges and universities to become much more effective and efficient, doing better despite lagging or even dropping state funding (Burke & Associates, 2002; Dougherty and Hong, forthcoming; Laanan, 2001).

Joseph Burke and his colleagues have developed a useful typology of performance accountability (PA) systems: performance funding, performance budgeting, and performance reporting (Burke and associates, 2002). Both performance funding and performance budgeting focus on variations in funding as the prod to institutional change. Where they differ is in the tightness of connection between funding and performance. Performance funding connects state funding directly and tightly to institutional performance on individual indicators. A formula is created in which specific institutional outcomes such as graduation rates are translated into discrete amounts of funding. In the case of performance budgeting, the connection between institutional performance and funding is more contingent. State government bodies (such as governors, legislators, and coordinating or system boards) announce that they will consider institutional achievements on performance indicators as one factor in determining their allocations to those institutions. As of 2003, 15 states have performance funding and 21 have performance budgeting (Burke & Minassians, 2003).

As the selection by Hudgins and Mahaffey, "When Institutional Effectiveness and Performance Funding Coexist" (Chapter 12), notes, the rise of performance funding brings both promise and peril for community colleges. It brings them opportunities to demonstrate their contribution to the public weal and improve their effectiveness. But that promise can be sapped if states use measures and methods that are poorly related to actual institutional quality and if performance funding creates destructive competition among colleges.

A recent study of five states (Florida, Texas, Illinois, California, and Washington) sheds further light on the impacts of performance accountability (Dougherty & Hong, forthcoming). It finds that performance accountability does result in making local community college officials more aware of state priorities and interested in their own college's performance. As a result, those college officials have changed their colleges' structures and operations in order to achieve such state goals as more student retention, improved remediation, greater numbers of graduates, and better job placement rates. However, the evidence is only moderately strong that states with seemingly stronger accountability systems (performance funding as versus performance reporting) have indeed produced stronger student outcomes. In part, this is due to the fact that existing performance accountability systems pose several obstacles to community colleges: poorly designed measures of success; funding that is unstable and does not keep pace with increasing enrollments; and inequalities in institutional capacity. In addition, unintended impacts also crop up. They include significant costs to institutions of complying with accountability demands, a weakening of academic standards in order to keep up retention and graduation rates, and more speculatively, a constriction of open door admissions in order to get students more likely to graduate and a narrowing of institutional mission to those outcomes that are being measured (Dougherty & Hong, forthcoming).

Legal Regulations

The third mechanism of governance is government regulation. As with all institutions, community colleges must be chartered by the states and their degrees and programs approved (Berdahl & McConnell, 1999). In addition, they are subject to a wide variety of regulations covering such things as protection of freedom of speech, nondiscrimination toward students and staff, collective bargaining, environmental practices, and work safety. Many of these emanate from the federal government, which does not own the community colleges (Lovell, 2001).

Ideological and Professional Influence

A final potent form of governance is one available to private as well as public actors: influencing the attitudes and beliefs both of community colleges and their stakeholders. Groups as diverse as state and local officials and agencies, professional and accrediting associations, the mass media, business, and community based organizations try to influence what community college do by trying to shape what is regarded as the mission of the community college and what are appropriate practices with regard to such things as admissions, student support, curriculum, hiring and promotion, and so forth (Berdahl & McConnell, 1999; Cohen & Brawer, 2003; Dougherty, 1994).[4]

These different modalities of governance allow public and private actors many different ways of trying to influence community colleges. They can try to get certain kinds of people appointed to state and local governing or coordinating boards and these in turn can shape who heads community colleges and what systemwide regulations are put in place. They can try to shape the amount and kind of funding community colleges get. They can try to have certain legal regulations written. And they can try to frame how community colleges and their publics conceptualize the colleges' mission and practices.

Administration and Internal Governance

If community colleges are complicated in their external governance, they are also complicated in their internal governance and administration. We will review findings about their organizational structures, institutional cultures and modes of decisionmaking, and staffing.

Organizational structures. Community colleges vary greatly in organizational structure. Some are multi-campus districts offering a wide variety of programs and organized in very complex ways, but others are single campus institutions with a fairly narrow range of offerings and a simple organizational structure. Some are organized by discipline and others by multi-disciplinary units. Some keep their credit and noncredit operations quite separate, while others combine them (Cohen and Brawer, 2003: 107–112).

Institutional cultures and modes of decision making. This variety of organizational forms may explain the depiction of institutional cultures of community colleges to be found in the Smart, Kuh, and Tierney selection, "The Role of Institutional Cultures and Decision Approaches" (Chapter 14). They apply Cameron and Ettington's typology of four main types of institutional cultures: bureaucratic, clan, adhocracy, and market. Based on responses from 639 administrators and faculty at 30 community colleges, they find that 30% of the colleges predominantly have a bureaucratic culture, 27% a clan culture, 27% an adhocracy culture, and 17% a market culture. Moreover, they find that community colleges with a predominantly clan or adhocracy culture are significantly more likely to exhibit a rational/collegial as versus autocratic/political style of decisionmaking and that the former style is significantly associated in turn with greater institutional effectiveness (in the judgment of their administrative and faculty respondents).[5]

A key component of institutional decisionmaking that often goes unanalyzed is the role of collective bargaining. Over 60% of community colleges have collective bargaining contracts in force. While collective bargaining agreements do focus on pay, hours, and benefits, a wide variety of organizational matters are and have been bargainable, including class sizes, personnel policies, text book selection, and so forth (Cohen & Brawer, 2003).

Staffing. The staffing of community colleges has been changing greatly, as colleges have grown in size, multiplied their offerings, and diversified their student bodies. Though community colleges are still led primarily by white men, the selection by Amey, VanDerLinden, and Brown (Chapter 15) notes that the gender complexion of top administrators has changed significantly over the last twenty years. Based on a sample of nearly 850 administrators at community colleges nationwide, they find that women and persons of color have increased their share of top administrative positions. For example, between 1985 and 2000, the proportion of female presidents jumped from 3% to 27%, and the proportion of presidents who are persons of color

doubled from 6% to 14%. Amey et al. find other changes as well in the form of shorter presidential tenures and less recruitment from the public school ranks. Women make up 49% of the instructional faculty staff at community colleges, a higher proportion than for higher education as a whole (41%). However, people of color are only very slightly better represented among community college faculty than faculty generally (National Center for Education Statistics, 2003).

One of the most important changes in faculty has been the great rise in the proportion who are part-time. Between 1973 and 2001, the proportion part time of senior instructional staff (that is, excluding teaching assistants) in public two-year colleges rose from 41% to 62%. Meanwhile, the proportion part time at all higher education institutions was 43% in 2001 (Cohen & Brawer, 2003; National Center for Education Statistics, 2003).

Nonfaculty professionals have increased their importance over time as offices devoted to business and finance, student support, distance education, etc. have grown. As of 2001, nonfaculty professionals made up 9% of the total staff of public two-year institutions (and nearly one-eighth of professional staff) (National Center for Education Statistics, 2003). The selection by Eboni Zamani (Chapter 16) addresses the role of African-American student personnel staff. She notes that they can play an important role as community colleges grow more diverse in their student bodies, given the evidence that African-American students are more comfortable and perform better at predominantly white institutions with a strong minority presence among student service professionals, as well as students and faculty. Moreover, the presence of more African-American student service professionals is important as community colleges face a major leadership transition as the previous generation of presidents and top administrators—heavily white and male—is retiring, at the same time as the student body is diversifying.

Notes

[1] The cases add up to more than 50 because New York shows up in two different categories, due to the different structures of the State University and City University systems.

[2] This figure also does not include federal tax credits insofar as they underwrite private grants and contracts (Lovell, 2001: 25–27)

[3]The local share varies greatly, with several states having no local funding and yet Arizona having 57% coming from local sources (Education Commission of the States, 2000: 10–11).

[4]This ideological and professional influence is a form of what Dougherty (1994) calls "ideological constraint," a form of power that does not require interest groups to actively monitor and intervene in community college decisions.

[5]Based on a much smaller sample of 70 faculty at 10 Midwestern colleges, Thaxter and Graham (1999) find that faculty tend to see their community colleges as more autocratic in functioning than the administrators and faculty in Smart et al. (1997).

References

Berdahl, R., & McConnell, T. R. (1999). Autonomy and accountability. In P. Altbach, R. Berdahl, and P. Gumport (Eds.), *American higher education in the twenty-first century*. Baltimore, MD: Johns Hopkins University Press.

Burke, J. C. & Associates. (2002). *Funding public colleges and universities for performance: Popularity, problems, and prospects*. Albany, NY: Rockefeller Institute Press.

Burke, J. C., & Minassians, H. (2003). *Performance reporting: "Real" accountability or accountability "lite": Seventh annual survey 2003*. Albany, NY: State University of New York, Rockefeller Institute of Government.

Cohen, A. M., & Brawer, F. B. (2003). *The American community college* (4th ed.). San Francico: Jossey-Bass.

Dougherty, K. (1994). *The contradictory college: The origins, impacts, and futures of the community college*. Albany, NY: State University of New York Press.

Dougherty, K., & Hong, E. (in press). Performance accountability as imperfect panacea: The community college experience. In T. Bailey & V. Smith Morest (Eds.), *Defending the community college equity agenda*. Hoboken, NJ: John Wiley & Sons, Inc.

Dougherty, K. H., Nienhusser, K., & Reid, M. (in press). *State policies affecting community college access and success in five states*. New York: Community College Research Center, Teachers College, Columbia University.

Education Commission of the States (2000). *State funding for community colleges: A 50 state survey*. Denver, CO: Author.

Hines, E. (1997). State leadership in higher education. In L. Goodchild, C. D. Lovell, E. R. Hines, & J. I. Gill (Eds.), *Public policy and higher education* (pp. 376–409). Boston: Allyn and Bacon.

Laanan, F. (2001). Accountability in community colleges. In B. Townsend & S. Twombly (Eds.), *Community colleges: Policy in the future context* (pp. 57–76). Westport, CT: Ablex.

Lovell, C. D. (2001). Federal policies and community colleges. In B. Townsend and S. Twombly (Eds.), *Community colleges: Policy in the future context* (pp. 23–38). Westport, CT: Ablex.

Lovell, C. D., & Trouth, C. (2002). State governance patterns for community colleges. In New Directions for Community Colleges, Vol. 117 (pp. 91–100). San Francisco: Jossey Bass.

National Center for Education Statistics. (2003). Digest of Education Statistics, 2003. Washington, DC: Author.

Richardson, R.C., Jr., & de los Santos, G. (2001). Statewide governance structures and community colleges. In B. Townsend & S. Twombly (Eds.), *Community colleges: Policy in the future context* (pp. 39–56). Westport, CT: Ablex.

Thaxter, L. P., & Graham, S. W. (1999). Community college faculty involvement in decision-making. *Community College Journal of Research and Practice, 23*, 655–674.

Tollefson, T. A., Garrett, R. L., Ingram, W. G., & Associates. (Eds.). (1999). *Fifty state systems of community colleges: Mission, governance, funding and accountability*. Johnson City, TN: The Overmountain Press.

CHAPTER 11

THE FEDERAL GOVERNMENT, DIRECT FINANCIAL AID, AND COMMUNITY COLLEGE STUDENTS

F. KING ALEXANDER
MURRAY STATE UNIVERSITY, MURRAY, KENTUCKY, USA

Direct Student Aid, Public Community Colleges, and Their Students

For community college leaders, it is important to understand how institutions that maintain low-cost accessibility are disadvantaged by the federal and state direct student aid programs. The final section of this article presents recent data to show how economic incentives inherent in most federal and state direct student aid policies impact low-cost public community colleges when compared to other high-cost institutional sectors. Much of the recent research on direct student aid relies on institutional data and information collected through the National Postsecondary Student Aid Study (NPSAS). NPSAS uses a base sample of thousands of students from hundreds of postsecondary institutions in the United States and is a comprehensive, accurate source for determining average student aid awards and the percentage of students that receive student aid from federal, state, and institutional sources.

For the purposes of this study, federal grant and subsidized loan programs and state direct student aid grant programs were considered, because these resources emanate from the public domain and taxpayers. Average direct student aid awards and the percentage of students receiving aid awards were compared by institutional sector. In measuring the fiscal equity of student aid by institutional sector, it is important to compare just how much student aid was distributed to students from similar family income levels enrolled at comparable higher education institutions. Too, this article recognizes that as students progress to higher levels of collegiate attendance in many disciplines, institutional and student costs tend to increase. Therefore, most federal and state student aid programs consider academic level in the formula for determining aid awards.

To identify similar types of postsecondary education institutions, this study used 1994 Carnegie Classifications to contrast the ways aid was distributed to lower-income students. In this analysis, five types of public and private classifications were used including research, doctoral, comprehensive, baccalaureate, and associate of arts. Proprietary institutions were included in separate categories.

The results of the study reveal a number of important findings. For students seeking associate of arts degrees, federal grant aid awards were relatively comparable, however the percentage of lower-income students receiving federal aid awards significantly favored private proprietary and non-profit

2-year students and institutions (see Table 1). When analyzing the equitable distribution of federal grants to dependent undergraduate students from families earning less than $30,000, the average federal grant allocation to students attending private "non-profit" 2-year institutions constituted only 18% more than the average grant awards to public community college students. More importantly, however, over 65% of the lowest income students enrolled at private "nonprofit" 2-year institutions received federal grants and 74% of lower-income students from private "for-profit" 2-year institutions receive federal grant aid while only 34% of lower-income students at public community colleges received aid awards. Comparable disparities in the percentage of public community college students receiving federal grant aid also were present among dependent students with family incomes of $30,001 to $60,000 (see Table 1).

Despite the obvious important distinctions between 2- and 4-year institutions, when comparing public community college students with private 4-year institutions, the average federal grant allocation to students attending public community colleges was 49% lower than federal awards granted to private baccalaureate institution students. Also, only one in three public community college students from the lowest income group received federal grant aid while three out of every four students at private baccalaureate institutions received this aid.

When comparing the equitable distribution of federal subsidized loan aid per recipient, lower-income students enrolled at private institutions consistently received much larger awards than comparable students attending public institutions. Table 2 shows the aggregate amount of federal subsidized loan aid per recipient. The public subsidy that accompanies these awards is commensurate with the amount of loan aid distributed. As Table 2 shows, lower-income students enrolled at private research and doctoral universities received the most federal subsidized loan aid per recipient, constituting nearly 32% and 57% more than lower-income students at public research and doctoral universities. Also, a higher percentage of lower-income students enrolled at private institutions received federal subsidized loan aid than lower-income students at comparable public institutions in all classifications.

Among 2-year institutions, federal subsidized loan aid to students attending public and private institutions did not differ significantly for dependent students from families with incomes of $30,000 or less (see Table 2). For dependent students with family incomes of $30,001 to $60,000, however, students attending private "for-profit" 2-year institutions received an average of 21% more aid than similar students attending public community colleges. When analyzing the percentage of students receiving federal subsidized loan aid, very great disparities emerged.

As Table 2 shows, over 63% of the dependent students from private "for-profit" institutions and 49% of the students from private "nonprofit" institutions received federal loan aid assistance while only 9% of public community college students from the same income group received federal loan aid.

When comparing student aid awards from state government programs, the data show even more severe fiscal disparities (see Table 3). By comparing average aid awards and the percentage of lower-income students receiving state grant aid, lower-income students enrolled at private proprietary 2-year institutions received 130% more in state grant aid per recipient than lower-income students at public 2-year institutions. Lower-income students enrolled at private "non-profit" 2-year institutions were awarded over twice the average amount of state grant aid than lower-income students at public 2-year institutions. About 42% of lower-income students attending private "nonprofit" 2-year institutions and 24% of students enrolled at proprietary 2-year institutions received state grant student aid, while only 12% of lower-income students at public 2-year institutions received such state aid.

For dependent undergraduate lower-income students from families earning up to $60,000, Table 3 shows that wide differences exist in the distribution of federal and state direct student aid. These data also show greater fiscal variations in the distribution of federal subsidized loans and state grant aid as compared to federal grant program aid.

Do these findings suggest equity or inequality in federal and state student aid distribution to lower-income students? According to Grubb and Tuma (1999), "an obvious conception of equity is that access to aid should not be a function of the type of institution in which a student chooses to enroll" (p. 376). Yet, as these figures demonstrate, students who select lower-cost public institutions

TABLE 1

Federal Direct Student Aid Grants for Dependent Undergraduate Students

Institutional Carnegie Classification	Income of $30,000 or less		Income of $30,001–$60,000	
	Award	Percentage	Award	Percentage
Research				
Private	$2,808	49%	$1,423	13%
Public	$2,005	55%	$1,090	10%
Doctoral				
Private	$2,152	59%	$1,352	13%
Public	$1,754	57%	$1,141	11%
Comprehensive				
Private	$2,235	62%	$1,438	N/A
Public	$1,875	60%	$1,175	12%
Baccalaureate				
Private	$2,337	74%	$1,357	18%
Public	$1,684	58%	$1,198	10%
Associate of Arts				
Private non-profit	$1,846	65%	$1,170	17%
Private for-profit	$1,590	73%	$1,010	12%
Public	$1,567	34%	$941	5%

Note: Federal grants included Pell, SEOG, and SSIG.
Source: NPSAS 1995–1996.

TABLE 2

Federal Direct Student Aid Subsidized Loans for Dependent Undergraduate Students

Institutional Carnegie Classification	Income of $30,000 or less		Income of $30,001–$60,000	
	Award	Percentage	Award	Percentage
Research				
Private	$3,644	52%	$3,534	49%
Public	$3,823	69%	$3,143	43%
Doctoral				
Private	$3,467	54%	$2,970	43%
Public	$3,358	58%	$3,359	91%
Comprehensive				
Private	$2,891	51%	$2,463	52%
Public	$2,562	71%	$2,377	9%
Baccalaureate				
Private	$3,655	48%	$3,239	36%
Private for-profit	$3,722	58%	$2,915	40%
Public	$3,467	58%	$2,940	38%
Associate of Arts				
Private non-profit	$3,431	59%	N/A	N/A
Private for-profit	$2,747	38%	$2,590	49%
Public	$2,812	63%	$2,320	9%

Note: Subsidized Federal Loans include FFEL and Direct Loans.
Source: NPSAS 1995–1996.

TABLE 3
State Direct Student Aid Grants for Dependent Undergraduate Students

Institutional Carnegie Classification	Income of $30,000 or less		Income of $30,001 to $60,000	
	Award	Percentage	Award	Percentage
Research				
Private	$2,882	23%	$1,885	14%
Public	$2,413	28%	$1,947	13%
Doctoral				
Private	$3,267	49%	$2,235	32%
Public	$1,934	24%	$1,451	11%
Comprehensive				
Private	$2,594	38%	$2,067	33%
Public	$1,723	29%	$1,182	16%
Baccalaureate				
Private	$2,188	43%	$1,846	39%
Private for-profit	$3,359	N/A	N/A	N/A
Public	$1,496	20%	$992	10%
Associate of Arts				
Private non-profit	$2,075	42%	$2,174	32%
Private for-profit	$2,279	24%	N/A	13%
Public	$995	12%	$781	5%

Source: NPSAS 1995–1996.

will receive less federal and state aid than those who choose comparable private institutions. These data also show that the likelihood of qualifying for student aid is greatest at high-cost proprietary and private "non-profit" institutions, while students attending low-cost public community colleges are the least likely to receive federal and state grant and loan aid.

Conclusion

The findings presented in this article show a number of problematic trends. First, due to substantial variations in institutional tuition and other costs, access to federal and state direct student aid resources varied significantly between students enrolled at comparable public and private institutions. Lower-income students from comparable economic backgrounds who enrolled in higher cost institutions were more likely to receive federal and state aid while receiving disproportionately larger average aid awards. Second, proprietary institutions disproportionately benefit more than other comparable institutional sectors from federal and state direct student aid program resources despite the rhetoric that the survival of these institutions is the economic marketplace. This may explain the recent proliferation of over 6,000 proprietary institutions throughout the country during the last two decades. Third, due to an egalitarian commitment promoted by state government interests to maintain low cost postsecondary education opportunities, students attending public community colleges are the least likely to receive federal and state direct student aid assistance.

As long as college costs continue to rise, federal and state governments will face continued pressure to increase funding to direct student aid programs with little consideration for the issue of fiscal equity. Evidence from a variety of sources indicate that lower income students still predominantly enroll in low-cost institutions while big-cost institutions struggle to retain about the same percentage of these students. Unfortunately, the majority of lower-income students who still attend public community colleges remain disproportionately disadvantaged by the current federally initiated system. This has led many public and private 4-year institutions to abolish low cost strategies to ensure that their students receive a proportionate share of federal and state direct student aid resources. Without considering the fiscal inequities and the inefficiencies that are inherent in the manner that direct student aid resources are distributed, public community colleges and their students may never fully benefit from federal and state government direct student aid policies.

Reference

Grubb, W. N., & Tuma, J. (1999). Who gets student aid? Variations in access to aid. *The Review of Higher Education,* 14(3), 359–381.

CHAPTER 12

WHEN INSTITUTIONAL EFFECTIVENESS AND PERFORMANCE FUNDING CO-EXIST

JAMES L. HUDGINS
JEAN MAHAFFEY
MIDLANDS TECHNICAL COLLEGE (SC)

Just as the higher education community was gaining comfort and proficiency with assessing its performance in order to improve its services, the notion of using the performance data for funding began to spread among state governing agencies. Performance funding is not an inherently bad idea. The challenge is to Implement funding based on performance without compromising the catalytic value of the data to affect changes within the Institution. Using the South Carolina example (enacted legislation that, by 1999, will allocate all state funds to higher education based on performance data), this chapter describes the challenges which arise when institutional effectiveness and performance funding co-exist. The authors suggest some strategies for helping the process achieve its goal of quality, cost-effective higher education.

Over the past decade, higher education has accepted the challenge of accrediting agencies to show evidence that the performance of colleges and universities corresponds with their lofty statements of purpose. This process of assessing the effectiveness of an institution's educational intentions and actual outcomes has slowly but surely gained acceptance among administrators and even faculty, particularly in the community colleges. Educators' needs to repeatedly cite the litany of reasons why the instructional process and its effects cannot and should not be measured have actually decreased. However, even before this self-imposed process of assessing student learning has become institutionalized, a new trend is emerging; state policy makers ate calling upon public colleges to use data to report their efficiency and productivity with numerical precision. In fact, based on a September 1997 survey conducted by The Washington State Board for Community and Technical Colleges, only ten states reported having "no statewide performance efforts." In a number of states, performance data are being collected, analyzed, and rated as a formula for allocating state operating funds.

While institutional improvement and external accountability have similarities, the two are fundamentally different in their purposes and their measurements. This chapter discusses the similarities and differences between these evaluation processes, paying special attention to an emerging trend of using performance data as the basis for funding public colleges.

External Demands for Accountability

Concerns about the quality and cost-effectiveness of higher education, which are currently being discussed by most state policy-makers, can be traced to two issues: (1) the rising cost of public higher education in competition for limited state resources, and (2) a rising tide of concern about the academic preparation and competency of college graduates entering an increasingly sophisticated global workplace. Elected officials are asking questions about the returns-on-investment of educational dollars, such as: *Why offer duplicate high-cost academic majors within a small geographic area? Why are colleges repeating instruction in basic skills before students can qualify for college courses? What is the productivity of faculty in terms of workload and availability to student? How many non-reaching employees does it take to support the teaching faculty? How many students graduate? . . . transfer? . . . find employment in their major fields? How much does it cost to educate one student in each major at a given college?*

These are valid questions for assessing fiscal accountability and institutional effectiveness, and they are typical of questions that are being asked in legislative bodies, newspaper editorials, corporate boardrooms, and in family discussions across the country.

Under a variety of titles—institutional effectiveness, total quality management, right sizing, and educational improvement—most colleges are somewhere on the continuum of enhancing educational processes and outcomes through assessment. However, as colleges are becoming increasingly comfortable with assessing their services to students for the purpose of improvement, many state legislatures are linking at least some state appropriations for higher education to an institution's performance on specific outcome measures. Of the 40 states in which higher education institutions report measurements of performance to governing agencies, 15 states plan to fund the institutions in part or whole based on the performance data. Further information may be accessed at: http://www.sbctc.ctc.edu.

As an example, by 1999, South Carolina will appropriate 100 percent of state funds to 33 public colleges and universities based on their performance on 37 indicators of effectiveness (Critical Success Factors and Performance Indicators Act, 1996), whereas other states, including

Louisiana, Missouri, and Tennessee, will "provide incentives for improvement without penalties for failure to improve" (Washington State Board for Community and Technical Colleges, 1997). Plans for performance funding in other states fall somewhere between impacting total appropriation and providing incentives for improvement.

Institutional Effectiveness vs. Performance Funding

As funding agencies increasingly view higher education as a strategic investment and move toward the performance funding model, the similarities and differences between measuring an institution's effectiveness for improving teaching and learning (institutional effectiveness) and correlating its effective performance with its funding (accountability) need to be considered. The following definitions help to clarify the discussion:

Institutional Effectiveness—an internal process of planning, evaluating, and modifying intended to assure that the performance of a college matches its purpose. Institutional effectiveness is self-examination (without fear of reprisal) for the purpose of improving performance by increasing positive outcomes and decreasing ineffective behaviors.

Accountability—taking responsibility for the outcomes of services and actions. Accountability relates to external relationships and deals with the responsibility of college leaders to demonstrate the cost-effective implementation of the college's mission to its various publics.

While both of these concepts purport to improve the quality of outcomes in higher education, these evaluation concepts have fundamentally different values. Institutional effectiveness is formative, while accountability is summative. Institutional effectiveness emphasizes effective learning outcomes; accountability focuses more on efficiency and cost effectiveness. Institutional effectiveness considers both process and product, whereas accountability is mote interested in product. Institutional effectiveness measurements include both qualitative and quantitative data, while accountability measurements are mostly quantitative. Finally, institutional effectiveness measures trends, patterns, and profiles over a long period of time;

accountability takes its measurements at a discrete point in time.

Both approaches to measuring effectiveness are outcomes based, can serve as catalysts for change, and provide valuable information for self-assessment. The fundamental difference between them is the breadth and scope of the data that is collected.

Performance funding models tend to rely on accountability data because their quantitative, point-in-time measurements lend themselves to comparative statistics which can be electronically generated to produce arithmetic formulas for allocating dollars in a predictable time frame. The more inclusive institutional effectiveness data, with their longitudinal, anecdotal, and subjective measurements, are too imprecise to be used in a formula for distributing funds among a state's institutions. In order to make the distribution of funds fair and equitable, the complex enterprise of educating students gets reduced to objective, quantifiable measurements. Therein lies the challenge in using performance data for allocating funds.

Opportunities with Outcomes Based Evaluation

The current attention being directed nationally at higher education offers community colleges three unparalleled opportunities to tell their stories in a context which both defines and distinguishes them.

(1) The Opportunity to Do the Right Thing

Because education is about teaching and learning, preparing for life and influencing values, educators should not be surprised to be held accountable. The real surprise should be over higher education's earlier resistance to the accountability movement and the need for it to be forced from outside the institution rather than being proactively advocated internally. The American public that invests more than $400 billion a year in education has a right to call for a report card—even from higher education.

A 1996 report issued by the Joint Commission on Accountability (comprised of representatives from the American Association of Community Colleges, the American Association of State Colleges and Universities, and the Association of State Universities and Land-Grant Universities) offers colleges and universities important guidelines by which they ran answer effectively the most common accountability questions. The report concludes that accountability reporting is essentially the right thing to do and argues that credibility with the public is suffering as the result of a paucity of understandable, straight-forward and comparable information. The overarching question can no longer be: "Should we be accountable?" but rather: "How shall we demonstrate accountability?"

(2) The Opportunity to Demonstrate Value

Community colleges have lived in the shadow of the research university since their inception a century ago, In several high-profile national studies, community colleges have been measured by university standards with the results being generally unfavorable to the community college—not because the standards were too high, but because they were the wrong standards (Clark, 1960; Zwerling, 1976; Picus, 1994). The premise of thew studies has been that the primary purpose of higher education is to earn a baccalaureate degree. When community colleges are measured on these traditional standards, including graduation rates, transfer rates, and length of time to earn a baccalaureate degree, the mission of the community college is truncated because education for a professional career is discounted. On the other hand, the people who provide the resources for public higher education—businesses, industries, government, tax payers—are interested in students being educated in specific career opportunities that support local economic development.

Harvey and Immerwahr (1995) conducted a study for the American Council on Education to determine the public's perception of higher education. They analyzed all of the public surveys of higher education between 1989–1992 and organized focus groups around the country. They confirmed that the general public believes the purpose of a college education is to acquire a credential for employment, and that community and business leaders believe that the principal role of colleges and universities is to prepare a highly educated workforce.

These perceptions match the mission of the community college. As taxpayers and elected officials talk about "returns on investment" and appeal to public agencies for suggestions for cost effective solutions to social, fiscal, and technological challenges, community college leaders have their greatest opportunity to promote the relevance and responsiveness of their institutions. For example, approximately 68 percent of associate degrees awarded by community colleges are in career fields that prepare graduates for immediate entry into the local job market with the option to continue their studies as their careers progress (Phillippe, 1996). This measure, when extrapolated for each community college, provides powerful evidence of the college's value to its community.

(3) The Opportunity to Improve Community Colleges

Community colleges have had a longstanding commitment to student success. They are in the vanguard of institutions asking substantive, analytical questions about what and how much students are learning and using the results of their queries to improve the quality of their programs and services to students.

In many community colleges, the measurement of the effects of teaching and learning has been incorporated into the routine behavior of individual faculty, of clusters who teach a particular course, and of academic departments. For example, at Midlands Technical College, conducting classroom research is a way of life for faculty as they measure the effect of a wide variety of instructional variables (teaching methods, types of delivery systems, appropriateness of prerequisite courses, technology-aided instruction, tutorial assistance, etc.) on students' academic successes. Faculty use the results of their studies to make changes in their teaching processes which ate again studied for their effectiveness in helping students learn. Classroom research is institutionalized as a part of annual action strategies which support priority initiatives aligned with the college's five-year goals. Inherent in this process is the sharing of information, both what worked and what did not work, across the college community in both private and public forums.

Midlands is far from alone in its use of outcomes based evaluations to improve performance. In *Embracing the Tiger,* Johnson (1997) reports that a national survey found that 64% of community colleges have linked outcome indicators to the college's mission statement and 34% are routinely monitoring outcomes data.

Challenges of Using Performance Data to Allocate Funds

While there are unprecedented opportunities for community colleges to use performance data to demonstrate value and effectiveness, the use of these data for allocating funds provides several unique challenges.

Integrity of the Data

When used for summative purposes like funding, performance data must have integrity, meaning they must measure what they are intended to measure and they must take their measurements consistently. The assessment data used for institutional improvement may lack the precision and validity to serve simultaneously as the measurements upon which funding is based, In describing the Netherlands' decade-long experience with performance funding for its universities, Vroeijenstijn (1995) observes that the performance funding model presupposes three essential premises: that quality can be defined; that performance indicators are related to quality; that quality can be quantified and objectified.

In practice, these assumptions am very difficult to validate. For example, a common measurement of an institution's effective performance is the quality of its faculty. However, since the quality must be "quantified and objectified" to produce a statistic that can be incorporated into a funding formula, the subjective but real measurements of classroom performance (spellbinding lectures, multimedia presentations, collaborative learning exercises, student presentations of capstone competencies, classroom research) do not factor into the equation. Instead, quality of faculty is reduced to summary data of their academic credentials, their compensation, their availability to students, and the presence of a faculty review system. Do these indicators adequately define the quality of faculty?

Another frequent measurement of an institution's effectiveness that is used in performance funding is graduation rates. This indicator begs the question of whether or not it measures what the recipients of the data think it measures. For example, when an entering cohort of students is tracked to determine graduation rates without considering each student's goal upon entering the college, graduation rates are not an accurate reflection of the college's success. If a community college has strong articulation agreements with senior colleges, many students will choose to transfer or be dually enrolled prior to earning an associate degree. While the community college might have a low graduation rate, in actuality it may have been very successful in helping students reach their goal of attaining a baccalaureate degree.

When accountability data are used in a dramatic, summative manner, special efforts should be given to assure the fairness and equity of the relative weight that these carry in determining the institution's funding. Comparative disclosures need to include clear explanations of their meaning.

The Limitations of Assessment Instruments and Methodologies

No assessment instruments can precisely measure student learning and, to their credit, most performance funding models do not pretend to assume so. Instead, instructional quality is measured by such variables as class size, student-teacher ratios, faculty teaching loads, and program accreditations. What conclusions can be drawn from these about the quality of instruction in the classroom?

At best, academic testing can identify broad, and usually subjective, bands of student performance. Classroom research, such as correlating the course content and students' grades in a prerequisite course with their success in a sequel course, can strengthen instruction. Opinion surveys can suggest trends in students' perceptions, attitudes, and values.

Based on his experience with performance funding, Vroeijenstijn (1995) concludes that "we have no yard stick at our disposal to measure the quality of education" (p. 18). He further states that "it is impossible to identify one set of criteria or standard for the quality of higher education" (p. 17). Assessment tools currently available to educators are inadequate for use as the primary indicator of the quality of instruction at an institution.

Some state performance funding plans include a wide variety of worthy but practically unmeasurable indicators of effectiveness. For example, partnerships among higher education institutions and between the academy and industry are quantified for the purpose of performance funding. While such partnerships are valuable assets for the participating institutions

and their students and add much value to the educational experiences of students, what is being measured? Service to the community? Fiscal efficiency of the institution? Aggressiveness or popularity of the institution in garnering partnerships? Nevertheless, in performance funding, the number generated by this measurement goes into the formula for allocating dollars to the institution.

The Variable Quality of Entering Students

Assessing the effectiveness of higher education is modeled on quality control processes in manufacturing industries where repetitive defects can be detected and corrected. Manufacturers, however, have complete control over the quality of their raw material, which is the single most important factor in product quality. Community colleges take pride in their democratic mission to provide open access to postsecondary education for students with widely varying academic preparation. But 41% of entering community college students require remedial education prior to enrolling in college-level work (National Center for Educational Statistics, 1996). Many community college students must begin their studies in nondegree credit courses which prepare them to perform successfully in college-level courses. If graduation rates are calculated on 150% of the program time, the community college's statistic is not impressive even though it is successfully accomplishing its mission of open access.

The Dynamic Nature of Student Bodies

Student learning measures are further complicated by multiple nonacademic factors influencing personal behavior and cognitive development. Families, jobs, peers, personal crises and numerous other factors either enhance or impede student learning and development. Because community college students flow in and out of the educational system with greater frequency than senior college students, external factors are magnified.

To be equitable, performance funding models must factor in the variables that are beyond the control of the institutions. For example, Midlands Technical College routinely conducts follow-up studies of students in an attempt to eliminate institutional-based causes for attrition. A 1996 survey of nonreturning students in the

1992 entering cohort found that 88% of the students indicated that attendance at the College, had assisted them in attaining their educational goals and that they would consider attending the College again. The three primary reasons for students' leaving prior to earning a degree were cited as: (1) attainment of the job skill for which they enrolled; (2) early transfer to a senior college; and (3) personal issues such as job changes, financial problems, and child care. These students are appropriately using the community college as a resource to meet their lifelong goals; however, a statistical snapshot of the retention rate of the 1992 entering cohort does not take into account these qualitative data and shows a very different and negative picture.

Competition among Institutions

The institutional improvement process has generated cooperation and sharing among all sectors of higher education. Since institutional effectiveness is a process that enables everyone to win, all colleges, regardless of size, location, or resources can share their experiences without fear of reprisals. Performance funding, on the other hand, has the potential to promote competition over cooperation and to create both winners and losers.

An institution competing with a sister institution for limited funds is less likely to share ideas which could enhance the other institution's relative position in the funding formula. For instance, sharing courses and programs through distance delivery of instruction is a fiscally efficient way to expand academic offerings to meet the local community's needs. But to thrive, distance education requires a cooperative environment. If a state's performance funding model rewards institutions for their outreach, what incentive exists for an institution to allow its competitors to broadcast courses into its service area instead of teaching those courses and programs itself? Likewise, if one institution discovers intervention strategies to retain more engineering technology students, will that institution share the information with sister institutions with whom it competes for a better retention statistic in the funding formula? Quality assessment will surely fail if it is part of a zero-sum game between institutions competing for resources in a culture of compliance.

When Institutional Effectiveness and Performance Funding Coexist

Over time, it is inevitable that funding based on performance will be incorporated into most state appropriation systems for public colleges and universities. It is incumbent upon educators and elected officials to collaborate in making this new funding model achieve the most desirable ends for institutions and funding agencies alike: quality, cost-effective delivery of higher education that meets the needs of consumers. The process must be a win-win opportunity for the funding agencies and the educational institutions.

Gaither (1997) reviewed experiments with performance funding and warns: ". . . state level or top-down models do not normally produce the constructive, substantive and sustained results that campus-initiated performance systems produce. Externally imposed systems are rarely accepted by internal stake-holders such as faculty" (p. 2). If they are to succeed, colleges and universities must commit to making these seemingly incompatible evaluations of outcomes coexist within the college's own culture.

First and foremost, the collection of data or fear of its results must not be allowed to subsume the college's mission of teaching and learning. In reality, an institution's effectiveness is still measured by its success in helping students achieve their educational goals. As the same time, the college community must collectively accept performance funding issues as critical to the college budget. The college community can coalesce around learning to effectively use the process of performance funding. It can maintain its integrity and protect its resources. The college can also strengthen its external relationships by partnering with other higher education institutions to use their collective wisdom to identify more accurate definitions and more effective measurements of the educational experience. Finally, the college community must be diligent in helping policy makers, elected officials, the business community, and the general public understand the complexity of the higher education experience.

Higher education can proudly demonstrate its effectiveness when it is measured on standards that are consistent with its mission of teaching and learning. When performance funding is used as incentive for improving an institution's effectiveness rather than as punishment for less favorable statistical results than competitor institutions, the potentially negative impact of using performance data for funding is ameliorated. Incentive funding reduces competition and supports the time-honored and highly valued collegiality among institutions. Perhaps most important of all, incentive funding sends the message to the faculty and staff of each institution that the governing and funding agencies understand the complexity of the educational process and recognize that it cannot be reduced to statistical measurement. Incentive funding indicates that governing and funding agencies really are trying to be supportive partners in helping institutions improve. Is that not the goal of all of this effort anyway? As Marchese (1994, p. 4) pointed out in *Change* when describing accountability: "This movement is not about the reporting of statistics; it's about our commitment to academic values, self-examination, and change."

References

Critical success factors and performance indicators Act, 59 SC Code Ann. § §59–103–30 (1976 & Supp., 1996).

Clark, B. R. (1960). The "cooling-out" function in higher education. *American Journal of Sociology, 63*(6), 569–576.

Deming, W. E. (1986). *Out of the crisis.* Cambridge, MA: Massachusetts Institute of Technology, Center for Advanced Engineering Study.

Gaither, G. (1997). Performance indicator systems as instruments for accountability and assessment. *Assessment Update, 9*(1), 1–15.

Harvey, J., & Immerwahr, J. (1995). *The fragile coalition: Public support for higher education In the 1990s.* Washington, DC: American Council on Education.

Johnson, L. F. (1997). Surveying institutional effectiveness in North American community colleges. In J. E. Roueche, L. F. Johnson, & S. D. Roueche (Eds.), *Embracing the tiger: The effectiveness debate & the community college* (pp. 27–50). Washington, DC: Community College Press.

Joint commission an accountability reporting. *The JCAR Technical Conventions Manual.* Washington, DC: American Association of State Colleges and Universities, 1996.

Marchese, T. (1994). Accountability. *Change, 26*(6), 4.

Midlands Technical College (1996). *Midlands Technical College non-returning student survey.* Columbia, SC: Author.

National Center for Educational Statistics. (1996). *Remedial education at higher education institutions In fall 1995* (NCES Publication No. 97–584). Washington, DC: U.S. Department of Education.

Phillippe, K. (1996). *National profile of community colleges: Trends and statistics 1997–1998.* Washington, DC: American Association of Community Colleges.

Pincus, F. L. (1994). How critics view the commu nity college's role in the twenty-first century. In G. Baker (Ed.), *A handbook in the community college in America* (pp.). Westport, CT: Greenwood Press.

Vkroeijenstijn, A. I. (1995). *Improvement and accountability: Navigating between Scylla and Charybdis.* Melksham, Wiltshire, Great Britain: Cromwell Press.

Washington State Board for Community and Technical Colleges. (1997, September 23). *Performance activities by state as of fall 1997.* Olympia, WA: Author. (Retrieved September 24, 1997 from World Wide Web: http://www.sbctc.ctc.edu/)

Zwerling, L. S. (1976). *Second best: The crisis of the community college.* New York: McGraw-Hill.

CHAPTER 13

STATE GOVERNANCE PATTERNS FOR COMMUNITY COLLEGES

CHERYL D. LOVELL, CATHERINE TROUTH

The many governance patterns developed for community college systems reveal the complex relationships states have evolved with these institutions. Policy issues for community colleges demonstrate that these relationships are still in the process of changing.

Community colleges have shaped the landscape of higher education for one hundred years. The community college system has evolved from one Illinois institution founded in 1901 to over a thousand institutions in 1999 (Tollefson, 2000). This remarkable past has been chronicled from both inside and outside the community college movement. Even with the well-documented history, relatively few discussions have been presented about statewide governance patterns, and even fewer have examined the factors that influence the existing governance systems.

This chapter presents a brief overview of the different types of statewide governance practices and patterns that exist in today's community colleges, followed by a discussion of the factors that influence these statewide governance practices. We then present state and federal policies that affect community colleges at the institutional level and conclude with a discussion of future statewide governance issues.

State Governance Practices, Definition, and Patterns

Community college governance is characterized by a complex web of relationships and arrangements that have evolved over the years. Before specifically examining community college governance structures, it is useful to define the terms used in describing statewide governance. *Governance* is the decision-making authority for an organization, which is typically controlled by boards. Governing boards usually appoint the chief executive of the institution or system, establish policies and approve actions related to faculty and personnel, ensure fiscal integrity, and perform other management functions (Education Commission of the States, 1997).

Governing boards are responsible for the specific operation of their institutions or campus systems, but they are only part of the picture of state governance. Statewide coordination is also necessary to ensure that state postsecondary institutions and systems work collectively toward the state interest (Education Commission of the States, 1997). *Statewide coordination* is the formal mechanism that states use to organize higher education. The responsibilities of coordinating boards include statewide planning and policy leadership; defining the mission for each postsecondary institution in the state; academic program review and approval; resource allocation; providing financial aid to students; information, assessment, and accountability systems; and implementing statewide projects (McGuinness, 1997).

Four governing taxonomies have been proposed to help define the many ways in which states have developed statewide organizational structures that apportion governance and coordination responsibilities across institutional types. A brief overview is presented here, but readers wanting a comprehensive discussion should consult the *State Postsecondary Structures Sourcebook,* published by the Education Commission of the States (ECS) (1997).

The first taxonomy classifies states as consolidated governing board states, coordinating governing board states, and planning or service agency states (Education Commission of the States, 1997). Consolidated governing board states assign coordinating responsibilities to a board that also has primary responsibilities to govern the institutions under its jurisdiction. Coordinating board states have boards that serve as coordinating agencies between the state government and the governing boards of the institutions. Governance is decentralized in these states. Finally, planning or service agency states have no statutory entity with coordinating authority but may have an entity to ensure good communication among the institutions or sectors in postsecondary education.

In the second taxonomy, Tollefson (2000) classifies states into five models of state-level coordination and governance similar to the ECS taxonomy. Each state is classified according to which type of state board has responsibility for community colleges. In the first model in Tollefson's taxonomy, the state board of education is responsible for community colleges. This board usually has minimal control, and local boards remain autonomous. In the second model, responsibility for community colleges resides in a state higher education board or commission. In the third model, statewide community college coordinating boards exercise responsibility for community colleges. In the fourth model, there is a state community college governing board with direct control over the community college operations. In the final model, a state board of regents is responsible for community colleges.

The third taxonomy defines statewide structures for all postsecondary institutions in terms of federal systems, unified systems, and seg-

mented systems (Richardson, Baracco, Callan, and Finney, 1998). A federal system organizes institutions under a range of governing boards that are required to work directly with a statewide coordinating board. A unified system places all institutions under a single governing board that works directly with the governor and legislature in budgeting, program planning and approval, articulation, and information collection and reporting. A segmented system has two or more governing boards that supervise single institutions or groups of institutions. In a segmented system, there is no single statewide agency with statutory authority in the areas of budgeting, program planning and approval, articulation, and information collection and reporting.

Building on this third taxonomy, Richardson and de los Santos (2001) suggest a fourth typology: the state community college governance structures typology. This new typology posits seven categories for describing the array of statewide governance systems in place today specifically for community colleges: federal-federal, federal- unified, federal-segmented, unified, segmented-federal, segmented-unified, and segmented-segmented states.

Federal-federal states have local governing boards for colleges, a coordinating board for all higher education institutions, and a separate statewide coordinating structure for community colleges. *Federal-unified states* have one statewide coordinating board for all higher education and a single statewide governing board for community colleges. *Federal-segmented states* have a statewide board that coordinates all higher education and several community colleges or technical institutions that each have their own governing arrangements. *Unified states* have one governing board for all higher education institutions in the state.

Segmented-federal states have two or more governing boards for higher education and either a coordinating board or governing board for community colleges. *Segmented-unified states* have two or more statewide governing boards for higher education, and one of these boards will have responsibility for community colleges. Finally, *segmented-segmented states* have two or more governing boards for higher education, but no board has overall responsibility for community colleges, which in these states are governed by local community college governing boards. These seven categories define the interplay between governing and coordinating boards and the placement of the community college system within the entire higher education community of each state.

Why Model Community College Governance Structures?

These models and taxonomies shed light on the complex relationships states have developed with community colleges. The historical development of community colleges in part explains these complex patterns. Community colleges have been seen at various times as an extension of high school and therefore part of secondary education; as the first two years of a college system; and as a unique educational enterprise separate from both secondary and higher education (Diener, 1994). As the interpretation of the community college changed, governance and coordination patterns also changed, reflecting the move toward placing community colleges firmly in the postsecondary community (Tollefson and Fountain, 1994). Governance patterns continue to change as the definition of the community college evolves.

By understanding governance and coordination systems, leaders can anticipate strengths and weaknesses of the systems for meeting future challenges. For instance, where statewide boards supervise both two- and four-year colleges, two-year colleges are often overlooked by board members, who concentrate on what they perceive as more pressing issues at the four-year institutions. Yet these systems may be well positioned to respond to demands for improved articulation and collaboration in a K-16 postsecondary model (Richardson and de los Santos, 2001).

These taxonomies also help define the placement of community colleges within a state system. Depending on its place in the state system, a community college may face many levels of governance and coordination, which can create problems. Conflicts between state and local boards or between boards and the state legislature can arise when there is a dispute or some ambiguity over which entity has governing responsibilities. The existence of multiple levels of governance may also contribute to these misunderstandings about responsibilities. For example, a recent California study found that twenty-two different agencies and offices shared community college governance responsibilities (Davis, 2001).

Factors Influencing Statewide Governance

Several factors affect statewide governance systems for community colleges today. The most important factors include board composition, articulation issues, and collective bargaining agreements.

Board Composition.   Board composition has far-reaching consequences for a community college. Studies conducted on boards of trustees for all types of institutions show that governing board members are usually white, over age fifty, and male, although women and minorities are represented on governing boards of public institutions in slightly greater proportions than on those of private institutions (Hines, 1997). The ethnic and gender composition of boards often do not reflect the diverse constituencies they serve, though the question remains open as to how this affects policy decisions or whether the symbolism of a board's composition influences decisions such as students' choosing to enroll or taxpayers' willingness to support the institution.

Members of both governing and coordinating boards can be appointed or elected. Popular election is practiced for local community college boards in at least twenty states (Hines, 1997). One might assume that board members elected by popular vote might legitimately represent the interests of diverse stakeholders, but with low voter turnouts at some elections, it might be easier for special-interest groups to influence the outcome of the election (Davis, 2001).

At public institutions in which board members are appointed, the governor usually makes the appointments. Board agendas may change whenever a new political party wins the governor's office. Sometimes the appointment of a single board member can lead to an abrupt change in direction for the institution (Davis, 2001). Davis suggests that irresponsible board members should be subject to recall, whether they are appointed or elected. A well-designed provision for recall that protects good members from attacks for unpopular decisions would encourage board members to hold themselves to high standards of governance.

Articulation Issues.   One of the oldest missions of community colleges is to provide the first two years of education for students seeking a bachelor's degree (Rifkin, 1998). States have approached articulation between community colleges and other institutions in different ways. Most states have promoted voluntary articulation agreements, meaning that institutions are encouraged to negotiate agreements among themselves. Other states have legislated policies that enhance articulation, such as a common course-numbering system or a core general education curriculum (Rifkin, 1998). Voluntary articulation agreements put this governance issue in the hands of local boards, while legislative policies place this issue in the hands of state-level boards.

Recently, Illinois created a new means of articulation through the Illinois Articulation Initiative (IAI). This initiative created a statewide general education core curriculum as well as several model lower-division curricula in a number of majors. Faculty panels from public and private two-year and four-year institutions review course syllabi from participating institutions to determine which institutional courses are "equivalent to," and therefore satisfy, the IAI general education or major-specific courses (Rifkin, 1998). The IAI approach makes articulation a joint concern of both community college and higher education boards at the state level.

Collective Bargaining Agreements.   Collective bargaining agreements, which may exist at the college or statewide level, have important effects on governance. The statewide agreements—those encompassing all community colleges in the state—have considerable influence over governance systems. Unions represent 51 percent of full-time faculty at public two-year institutions and 27 percent of part-time faculty (National Center for Education Statistics, 2001). Many of these agreements can limit the span of management control of governing or coordinating boards as the issues are decided in the contract negotiations rather than at the board level.

State and Federal Policies

Since both federal and state policies affect community colleges, governing boards must be aware of the effect of these policies and work with both state and federal governments to shape policies that further the goals of their institutions. Three areas of particular interest are federal financial aid, workforce preparation, and state funding.

Federal Financial Aid.   Probably one of the most important federal influences on American higher education is the federal financial aid program. Federal financial aid regulations raise issues for community colleges that other institutions do not face (Lovell, 2001). For example, in many states, community colleges provide the bulk of remediation for students. Since federal regulations limit the amount of financial aid that may be used for remedial coursework, campus administrators must monitor course-taking patterns of students on a larger scale than baccalaureate institutions (Lovell, 2001). There are also ability-to-benefit (ATB) requirements in place that pertain to institutions with open access. Open access is one of the primary characteristics of community colleges, so these requirements have a particularly large impact on these institutions. These requirements are in place to ensure that a student receiving federal financial aid has the potential to successfully complete a program, which places additional monitoring and reporting constraints on participating institutions. A final area of concern for community colleges is that federal financial aid policies limit aid to part-time students. This is a critical issue for community colleges because many of their students attend on a part-time basis.

Workforce Preparation.   Recent federal legislation created a number of federal and state school-to-work and vocational preparation programs. The Workforce Investment Act and the reauthorized Perkins Vocational Act were passed in 1998. These legislative acts tied federal funding to workforce training offered on campuses and were intended to build a competitive workforce (Lovell, 2001). Workforce preparation is already one of the primary goals of community colleges. Federal funding regulations and state interpretations of federal legislation, as they pertain to federal funds that flow through states to individual institutions, shape and influence how local institutions develop and deliver their programs. Workforce preparation funding requires statewide governance vigilance, as stewardship of these preparation measures is necessary to ensure adequate support programs for citizens in the state. As Debra Bragg discusses in Chapter Three, little is yet known about the actual impact of many federal workforce preparation initiatives.

State Funding.   While community colleges in many states still collect support through local taxes, usually property taxes, the trend for the past three decades has been for states to fund an increasing percentage of community college operating costs (Education Commission of the States, 2000). This raises the question as to whether there will then be a shift away from local governance control toward greater state governance or coordination for community colleges. One study found that while the authority resided with the state boards, much of that authority was delegated to local community colleges (Tollefson, 1996). Community colleges have so far retained much of their local governance control, but there is no guarantee that states will continue to delegate their authority to the local boards.

Emerging Issues for Statewide Governance and Policy

As noted, community colleges have just recently celebrated their hundredth year as part of America's higher education system. As they prepare for their next hundred years, several policy issues will challenge those who govern community colleges.

Changing Statewide Structures for Community College Governance and Coordination.   From 1963 to 1989, major changes in the types of state-level boards for community colleges occurred, including an increase from thirty-eight to forty-nine states with statewide community college systems and an increase from six to twenty-two states with separate state boards specifically for community colleges (Tollefson, 1996). While there have not been as many changes in statewide governance structures since 1989, a number of states have recently considered such changes. Florida provides the most prominent example of reorganization. In 2000, the Florida legislature eliminated most of the state's postsecondary boards, including the state's Board of Community Colleges, in favor of one board of education for the entire school system in Florida. The purpose of this reorganization is to redefine the educational system in Florida as one seamless K–20 system. Since the change will not be completed until 2003, it is not yet clear how this change will affect the community colleges in the state.

Other states in the process of reviewing their statewide governance systems for postsecondary education are Arizona, California, Colorado, Iowa, Pennsylvania, and West Virginia. Changes are usually intended to improve the effectiveness and responsiveness of state systems. For example, in Iowa, legislators introduced a bill to establish a task force to study the restructuring of governance in order to make community colleges run more cooperatively, effectively, and efficiently as a state system. In Colorado, a report from the Northwest Education Research Center recommended that Colorado consider certain structural realignments in its governance system to increase the potential for responsiveness to community and regional higher education needs.

Seamless K–16 System.   Many states are calling for a seamless K–16 educational system to better prepare and serve their citizens and the states' needs. Creating such systems could have far-reaching consequences for the governance of community colleges. The integration of K–12 and postsecondary systems may require states to reconsider the traditional separation of K–12 and higher education governance (Boswell, 2000). Florida's education reorganization eliminates this separation. In three other states, Ohio, Maryland, and Georgia, higher education board members at both the local and state levels are working on K–16 councils aimed at establishing reform (Boswell, 2000).

Technology.   As access to technology increases, students may choose a community college on the basis of cost and range of offerings rather than geographical proximity (Mingle and Ruppert, 1998). This could profoundly affect community colleges, which are dependent on attracting students from the local geographical area. For example, in 1997, Colorado created the Colorado Community College Online, a collaborative effort to offer degrees from thirteen community colleges and one university on the Internet (Mingle and Ruppert, 1998). The interconnection of a state's community colleges on-line may increase the trend away from local governance and toward greater state governance and coordination. As the geographical boundaries of community colleges erode, it is harder to define the constituency of the college and therefore harder to establish a governing body that reflects that constituency.

Redefining the community college mission is also a potential concern to statewide governance. Some leaders have discussed possible transformations of the role of community colleges, such as transforming community colleges into four-year colleges or changing them into two-year university branch campuses. The current literature is contradictory, weak, or inconclusive regarding the extent to which the mission of community colleges should be redefined; some have called for recasting the community college as a noncollegiate institution concerned primarily with vocational education. If the mission of community colleges changes, then changes in statewide systems for coordination and governance will be required as well. Yet the literature is also contradictory about what constitutes an appropriate model of governance for community colleges. What seems most evident is that multiple models exist, there is no single "best" model, and patterns of governance are shaped by multiple influences related to all levels of education and to state-specific issues and politics.

Conclusion

Community college governance has undergone tremendous changes in the past hundred years. As community colleges enter their second century, they face issues that will continue to redefine their place in the American educational system. These changes seem to be redefining community colleges more as state-level than local institutions. Community college leaders often need training in facing these changes and in understanding their relationship to various constituents, including the state.

Many organizations provide support for these leaders. The Association of Community College Trustees provides trustee education and assists boards in developing and affecting public policy. The American Association of Community Colleges also provides information on legislation affecting community colleges and actively promotes the goals of community colleges in Washington, D.C. The Education Commission of the States recently established the Center for Community College Policy to conduct research on policy issues affecting community colleges and to organize workshops on the issues community colleges face.

Local board members, faculty, and staff at community colleges should be proactive in reviewing state systems. They need to ensure that states carefully consider the purposes of community colleges before deciding on system changes. At the same time, community college leaders will want to understand the legitimate needs of the state in helping to coordinate their institutions. This means understanding the whole system of statewide coordination and understanding where their particular institution belongs in this system.

References

Boswell, K. "Building Bridges, Not Barriers: Public Policies That Support Seamless K–16 Education." In Center for Community College Policy (ed.), *Community College Policy Handbook*. Denver: Education Commission of the States, 2000.

Davis, G. "Issues in Community College Governance." Issue paper for "New Expeditions: Charting the Second Century of Community Colleges," an A. W. K. Kellogg Foundation Initiative sponsored by the American Association of Community Colleges and the Association of Community College Trustees. 2001 [http://www.aacc.nche.edu/intitiatives/newexpeditions/White_Papers/governancewhite.htm]

Diener, T. "Growth of an American Invention: From Junior to Community College." In J. L. Ratcliff, S. Schwarz, and L. Ebbers (eds.), *Community Colleges.* (2nd ed.) Boston: Allyn & Bacon, 1994.

Education Commission of the States. *State Postsecondary Structures Sourcebook: State Coordinating and Governing Boards.* Denver: Education Commission of the States, 1997.

Education Commission of the States. *State Funding for Community Colleges: A 50-State Survey.* Denver: Education Commission of the States, 2000.

Hines, E. R. "State Leadership in Higher Education." In L. F. Goodchild, C. D. Lovell, E. R. Hines, and J. I. Gill (eds.), *Public Policy and Higher Education.* Boston: Allyn & Bacon, 1997.

Lovell, C. D. "Federal Policies and Community Colleges: A Mix of Federal and Local Influences." In B. K. Townsend and S. B. Twombly (eds.), *Educational Policy in the 21st Century, Vol. 2: Community Colleges: Policy in the Future Context.* Westport, Conn.: Ablex, 2001.

McGuinness, A. "The Function and Evolution of State Coordination and Governance in Postsecondary Education." In Education Commission of the States. *State Postsecondary Structures Sourcebook: State Coordinating and Governing Boards.* Denver: Education Commission of the States, 1997.

Mingle, J. R., and Ruppert, S. S. "Technology Planning: State and System Issues." In Center for *Community College Policy, Community College Policy Handbook.* Denver: Education Commission of the States, 1998.

National Center for Education Statistics. *Institutional Policies and Practices: Results from the 1999 National Study of Postsecondary Faculty, Institution Survey.*

Washington, D.C.: U.S. Department of Education, 2001.

Richardson, R., and de los Santos, G. "Statewide Governance Structures and Two-Year Colleges." In B. K. Townsend and S. B. Twombly (eds.), *Educational Policy in the 21st Century, Vol. 2: Community Colleges: Policy in the Future Context.* Westport, Conn.: Ablex, 2001.

Richardson, R. C., Baracco, K. R., Callan, P. M., and Finney, J. E. *Designing State Higher Education Systems for a New Century.* Westport, Conn.: Oryx Press, 1998.

Rifkin, T. "Improving Articulation Policy to Increase Transfer." In Center for Community College Policy, *Community College Policy Handbook.* Denver: Education Commission of the States, 1998.

Tollefson, T. A. "Emerging Patterns in State-Level Community College Governance: A Status Report." 1996. (ED 437 076)

Tollefson, T. A. "Martorana's Legacy: Research on State Systems of Community Colleges." Paper presented at the annual meeting of the Council for the Study of Community Colleges, Washington, D.C., Apr. 2000. (ED 443 461)

Tollefson, T. A., and Fountain, B. E. In J. L. Ratcliff, S. Schwarz, and L. Ebbers (eds.), *Community Colleges.* (2nd ed.) Boston: Allyn & Bacon, 1994.

CHAPTER 14

THE ROLES OF INSTITUTIONAL CULTURES AND DECISION APPROACHES IN PROMOTING ORGANIZATIONAL EFFECTIVENESS IN TWO-YEAR COLLEGES

JOHN C. SMART
GEORGE D. KUH
WILLIAM G. TIERNEY

The effectiveness of a college or university is a function of how it responds to external forces and internal pressures in fulfilling its educational mission. Most of the research on institutional effectiveness has focused on four-year institutions. Yet, two-year institutions comprise the single largest institutional sector of American higher education with over twelve hundred of these institutions serving more than five million students (Pincus & Archer, 1989). This article focuses on the organizational effectiveness of two-year colleges.

Background

Cameron (1978; 1986) identified nine dimensions of organizational effectiveness that can be used to evaluate the performance of all forms of postsecondary institutions. The nine dimensions are: student educational satisfaction, student academic development, student career development, student personal development, faculty and administrator employment satisfaction, professional development and quality of faculty, system openness and community interaction, ability to acquire resources, and organizational health. From their study of a sample of two-year colleges, Smart and Hamm (1993b) concluded that Cameron's nine dimensions of organizational effectiveness represent key management and institutional performance indicators of two-year colleges. They also demonstrated that the organizational effectiveness of two-year colleges is a function, in part, of their mission priorities (e.g., transfer/college parallel, technical/career, adult/continuing, and other goals).

Cameron's dimensions of organizational effectiveness encompass a wide range of important variables. However, they do not include other factors that also affect institutional performance, such as decision-making approaches, institutional culture, and the nature of relations among faculty, administrators, and students (Birnbaum, 1988, 1992; Senge, 1990; Weick, 1979; Whetten, 1984). These variables become increasingly important as turbulent and unpredictable economic cycles, competitiveness, and shifting priorities for public support threaten the viability of many postsecondary institutions

(Ashar & Shapiro, 1990; Cameron, 1986; Finn & Manno, 1996; "To Dance With Change," 1994). In these circumstances institutions often adopt structural patterns (e.g., centralization of functions) and management practices (e.g., autocratic decision-making processes) that frequently result in inflexible patterns of behavior, which over time may have a negative influence on institutional performance (Cameron, 1983; Cameron, Whetten, & Kim, 1987; Zammuto & Cameron, 1985). Indeed, much of the most recent literature on high performance in organizations calls for exactly the opposite kind of structural patterns and organizing processes; "postmodern" organizations, argue researchers, need less autocracy, more flexibility, and greater creativity (Handy, 1989; Senge, 1990; Tierney, forthcoming).

The research is unclear about whether certain decision-making approaches are related to enhanced institutional effectiveness (Baldridge, 1971; Chaffee, 1983; Cohen & March, 1974). Nonetheless, many organizational theorists argue that participative decision processes are associated with higher levels of organizational performance (Birnbaum, 1992; Child, 1973; Meyer, 1979; Peters, 1987; Senge, 1990; Sutton & D'Aunno, 1989). Consensual, participative decision processes seem to be more strongly associated with the organizational effectiveness of four-year colleges and universities than are centralized decision processes (Cameron & Tschirhart, 1992). The nature of administrative and faculty relations also can influence decision making and, in turn, institutional effectiveness (Cameron, 1982, 1985). Cameron (1982) found that institutions with collective bargaining agreements scored lower than non-unionized campuses on eight of the nine organizational effectiveness dimensions.

An institution's culture is thought to mediate how an institution deals with external forces and internal pressures (Chaffee & Tierney, 1988; Kuh & Whitt, 1988). Culture is formed over decades, as institutions "learn" how to respond to challenges associated with their establishment, survival, and growth (Clark, 1970; Schein, 1985). There are many ways to conceptualize and define institutional culture. For the purpose of this article culture is the patterns of interpretations people form about the manifestations of their institutions' values, formal rules and procedures, informal codes of behavior, rituals, tasks, jargon, and so on (Martin, 1992). In this sense, "culture is reflected in what is done, how

it is done, and who is involved in doing it. It concerns decisions, actions, and communication" (Tierney, 1988, p. 127). The plural form of the word "pattern" suggests that no single interpretation or view can accurately represent the perspectives of all faculty, staff, and students, because people do not see the institution in the same way (Martin, 1992). Indeed, a college can be host to many cultures or subcultures (Van Maanen & Barley, 1985). At the same time it is possible to deduce some general themes of organizational life about which people can generally agree, such as preferred approaches to decision making (Quinn & McGrath, 1985).

How one thinks about organizational life also suggests the manner in which strategy gets enacted and defined. As Chaffee and others have noted, an organization's culture, then, implies a particular stance toward strategy (Chaffee, 1984; 1989; Chaffee & Tierney, 1988). A cultural view of the organization suggests that strategy is a process, not a product, a means to ask appropriate questions rather than a series of answers. In effect, a cultural strategy—often called interpretive strategy—is a way for leaders to think about, look at, and define their organization. In contrast, previous uses of strategy—usually called linear—were hierarchial in nature and expected a small group of an institution's leaders to develop an efficient mechanism that would manipulate the predictable components of the organization. The environment was seen as a series of understandable properties "out there"; an effective manager was one who was able to react to the complex set of forces in the environment. Administrators assessed goals and planned actions that achieved definable ends. Such a strategic orientation often has been seen as too rigid because it overlooks the dynamic aspects at work within the organization and in the environment.

In reaction to linear strategy, some critics utilized adaptive strategy. Rather than thinking of the organization as machinelike, adaptive strategists thought of it more as an organism that adapted to environmental trends and demands. The external environment received prominence. Whatever the environment needed was seen as the goal of the organization. Organizational values were ignored or subordinated to the demands of the environment. A leader was someone who could read the environment accurately and adapt the organization to the press of external forces. The concern with this approach was that the overriding purpose or ethos of the organization often became lost, constituents were unsure of their tasks, and any sense of organizational glue came unhinged; long-range stability was put in jeopardy for perceived short-range needs.

In the cultural approach, people receive, process, and send messages. To be sure, goals and results are as important in the cultural approach as they are in linear strategy. The environment is also critical, as it is with the adaptive strategy. However, in the cultural approach organizational values are central. How individuals interpret the organization to themselves and to outsiders becomes the key task as they struggle to meet the challenges and demands of the marketplace. Such a strategy works from the assumption that the organization plays a role in creating its structure and its environment.

Studies of institutional effectiveness have typically employed conventional regression procedures to examine the relationships between organizational structures and processes. Regression analyses take into account only direct effects of independent variables (e.g., environmental conditions, mission priorities, institutional culture) on the dependent measure of organizational effectiveness. There is also reason to believe that the external postindustrial environments (Cameron & Tschirhart, 1992) of two-year colleges may have significant negative indirect, as well as direct, effects on organizational performance. For example, as mentioned earlier, institutions often centralize managerial functions and processes in response to external threats to their viability (Cameron, 1983; Cameron & Tschirhart, 1992; Zammuto & Cameron, 1985). To discover how the external environment and an institution's culture, mission, preferred decision-making approaches, and collective bargaining status work together to influence the performance of two-year colleges, both indirect and direct effects must be estimated.

Purpose

This study examines the relationships between institutional culture, decision-making approaches, and organizational effectiveness of two-year colleges. It differs from most of the related research on postsecondary institutional effectiveness in three respects. First, the study focuses on two-year institutions, a sector of American higher education in which such inquiries are relatively rare. Second, most studies of the culture of postsec-

ondary institutions (e.g., Clark, 1970; Chaffee & Tierney, 1988; Kuh, Schuh, Whitt & associates, 1991; Kuh & Robinson, 1995) have employed an integration perspective (Martin, 1992); that is, people are assumed to interpret organizational arrangements and activities pretty much the same way (i.e., cultural properties are interpreted consistently by all institutional members). In contrast, the idea of "equifinality" is that members may subscribe to similar goals, but the reasons they desire to achieve such goals and/or how they interpret the goals may vary. Accordingly, in this study we acknowledge that multiple interpretations of institutional life are not only possible but likely, and that certain events and actions (e.g., decision-making approaches) may be ambiguous even though the data-collection methods employed suggest otherwise (Martin, 1992).

Finally, the study uses causal modeling procedures to estimate the contributions of factors considered important to organizational effectiveness in two-year colleges. The advantage of causal modeling procedures over conventional regression techniques is that they take into account both direct and indirect influences of predictor variables, thus producing a more robust estimate of the total influence of variables in the model. In addition, they reveal the dynamic process by which the predictor variables exert influence by identifying salient intervening or mediating variables (Wolfle, 1985).

Methods

Sample

A two-stage process was used to select the sample. First, 30 public two-year colleges, stratified according to size, were randomly selected using the 1990 AACJC membership directory. Then, all full-time administrators and a random sample of full-time faculty members at these institutions were invited to participate in the study ($n = 1332$). Approximately twice as many faculty were selected as administrators at each college. A 54% response rate ($n = 698$) was realized. The administrator response rate (63%) was greater than that for faculty members (47%). The results are based on the responses of 639 individuals who had complete data on the variables described below.

The Causal Model

The causal model estimated for this study (Table 1) uses Cameron's nine dimensions of organizational effectiveness to produce a global measure of institutional performance. The inclusion of decision-making approaches in the model reflects their reputed importance to organizational performance (Child, 1973; Meyer, 1979; Peters, 1987; Sutton & D'Aunno, 1989). The model also assumes that the missions, cultures, and external environmental conditions of two-year colleges differ. Mission priorities and environmental conditions interact with the institutional culture in unknown ways and shape institutional decision-making and management approaches. Taken together, all these variables are thought to influence the global organizational effectiveness of two-year colleges.

Therefore, four sets of variables are ordered in a causal sequence in the model. The first set is comprised of seven exogenous variables reflecting (1) college size in terms of head count enrollment, (2) college financial health in terms of deteriorating funding and revenue patterns, (3) college enrollment health in terms of declining student enrollments, (4) college transfer emphasis in terms of the percentage of total enrollment in college parallel programs, (5) college career emphasis in terms of the percentage of total enrollment in technical/career programs, (6) college continuing education emphasis in terms of the percentage of total enrollment in adult/continuing education programs, and (7) collective bargaining status based on whether

or not the campus is unionized. These exogenous variables are included in the model to control for their demonstrated relationship to the organizational effectiveness of colleges and universities noted earlier.

The second set was comprised of measures of the four types of institutional cultures developed by Cameron and Ettington (1988) and used in previous studies of the effectiveness of two- and four-year postsecondary institutions (Cameron & Ettington, 1988; Fjortoft & Smart, 1994; Smart & Hamm, 1993a; Smart & St. John, 1996; Zammuto & Krakower, 1991). The four culture types are clan, adhocracy, beureaucracy, and market. *Clan cultures* are characterized by norms and values that foster affiliation, encourage member participation in decision making, and emphasize talent development as an institutional goal. Faculty and staff are motivated by trust, tradition, and their commitment to the institution. The clan's strategic orientation is to use consensus to make decisions; interpretive strategy is utilized. *Adhocracy cultures* assume that change is inevitable; individuals are motivated by the importance and ideological appeal of the tasks to be addressed. A prospector-type strategic orientation is used to acquire resources to ensure institutional vitality and viability. Adaptive and interpretive strategies are called on to make decisions. A *bureaucratic culture* seeks stability; its strategic orientation is to maintain the status quo. Formally described roles dictate the activities performed by various individuals and the nature of relations among people; individual compliance with organizational mandates is governed

TABLE 1
Casual Model to be Estimated

Exogenous Variables	Institutional Cultures	Decision Approaches	Institutional Effectiveness
College size			
	Clan		
Financial health			
		Rational/Collegial	
Enrollment health			
	Adhocracy		
Transfer emphasis			Global Effectiveness
	Market		
Career emphasis			
		Autocratic/Political	
Adult emphasis			
	Bureaucratic		
Union status			

by rules and regulations, and linear strategy is the mode of operation. *Market cultures* are achievement oriented and emphasize planning, productivity, and efficiency in developing strategy; again, linear strategy is the modus operandi. Faculty and staff performance is assured through rewards for competence and contributions to organizational effectiveness. Appendix A explains the analytical procedures used to derive the four culture scores.

These four culture types represent ideal forms. They differ in terms of the degree to which they emphasize the importance of: (1) people or the organization, (2) stability and control or change and flexibility, and (3) means or ends. Most institutions probably reflect properties of more than one of these types. At the same time, colleges manifest different combinations of attributes that evolve into distinctive institutional cultures that "are reflected in idiosyncratic manifestations: organization-specific rituals, symbols, languages, and the like. But while specific manifestations of individual cultures may be unique, their meaning content across organizations will be similar to the extent that the underlying value systems are similar" (Quinn & Kimberly, 1984, p. 300).

The hypothesized link between organizational effectiveness and institutional cultures has been substantiated in several recent studies. For example, Cameron and Ettington (1988) and Cameron and Freeman (1991) found that four-year colleges with a dominant clan culture have higher levels of performance on internal morale performance criteria, those with a dominant adhocracy culture are more effective in promoting academic development, and those with a dominant market culture are more successful in their interactions with the external environment (e.g., acquiring resources).

The third set of variables in the model was comprised initially of how respondents characterized the manner in which resource allocation decisions at their institution were made (Baldridge, 1971; Cohen & March, 1974; Chaffee, 1983). The six decision approaches are: (a) collegial, based on consensus, (b) rational, based on supporting data, (c) bureaucratic, based on structured administrative patterns, (d) political, based on self-interest and power, (e) organized anarchy, based on serendipity, and (f) autocratic, based on the preference of a single, powerful individual. Because these measures have unknown psychometric properties, factor analytic procedures

were used to determine their construct validity. The results (Appendix B) pointed to two prevalent decision approaches. The first is *rational/collegial,* in which resource allocation decisions are the result of "group discussion and consensus," based on the use of "a standard set of procedures," and criteria reflecting "what objectively seems best for this institution overall." The second is *autocratic/political,* in which resource allocation decisions are customarily made by "one individual at this institution," in a political manner "based on the relative power of those involved" and without any "particular pattern" characterizing the criteria used.

The fourth set is a single dependent variable reflecting the global organizational effectiveness of the 30 participating two-year colleges. The organizational effectiveness scale was created by summing the mean scores for all respondents on the nine effectiveness dimensions developed by Cameron (1978; 1986). These perceptual measures of effectiveness have external validity in that they are consistently and positively correlated with indices characteristic of high performing organizations (e.g., financial health, student enrollment, ratings of academic quality) (Cameron, 1978; 1986). Table 2 provides operational definitions and reliability estimates (where appropriate) for all measures used in the study.

Analyses. Institutional culture factor scores were computed to identify a dominant culture type for each institution. This was done by classifying institutions according to their highest score across each of the four culture factors. The results indicated that 9 (30%) have a dominant bureaucratic culture, 8 (27%) represent a dominant adhocracy culture, 8 (27%) reflect a dominant clan culture, and 5 (17%) have a dominant market culture. Appendix A shows that the corresponding factor score for each dominant culture type is about a half standard deviation above the grand mean (standardized at 0) and that each dominant culture type has a substantially higher mean score on its corresponding factor. Thus, faculty and administrators perceive that their institutions have distinctive profiles consistent with the culture factor labels.

A preliminary analysis was conducted to determine if administrators and faculty members differed in the factors they perceived to influence the global measure of effectiveness of two-year colleges. This was accomplished by

TABLE 2
Variable Names and Variable Definitions

Names	Definitions
Exogenous Variables:	
College size	Total number of full-time equivalent students.
Financial health	A two-item scale indicating the extent to which "Financial resources have become more difficult to obtain in the last year" and "Revenue for the college, adjusted for inflation, decreased over the last year." (alpha = 0.84)
Enrollment health	A single item indicating the extent to which "Full and part-time student enrollments have decreased over the last year."
Transfer emphasis	Percent of total enrollment in transfer-college parallel programs.
Career emphasis	Percent of total enrollment in technical-career programs.
Adult emphasis	Percent of total enrollment in adult-continuing education programs.
Union status	A dichotomous variable indicating whether the faculty are unionized. The variable was coded: 0 = nonunionized; 1 = unionized.
Institutional Cultures (see Appendix A):	
Clan culture	A factor score defined primarily by the extent to which respondents *agree* that their campuses are characterized as (1) being held together by loyalty and tradition (0.76), (2) with an emphasis on human resources (0.51), and (3) where the leader is generally considered to be a mentor, a sage, or a father or mother figure (0.36), and *disagree* with the perception that there is a strong production orientation with an emphasis on tasks and goal accomplishment (−0.74).
Adhocracy culture	A factor score defined primarily by the extent to which respondents *agree* that their campuses are characterized (1) by a commitment to innovation and development with an emphasis on being first (0.71), (2) where people are willing to stick their necks out and take risks (0.70), (3) there is an emphasis on growth and the acquisition of new resources (0.51), and (4) the leader is generally considered to be an entrepreneur, an innovator, or a risk taker (0.50), and *disagree* with the perception that there is an emphasis on permanence and stability (−0.62).
Market culture	A factor score defined primarily by the extent to which respondents *agree* that their campuses are characterized as (1) being production oriented and where people aren't very personally involved (0.70), (2) the leader is considered to be a producer, a technician, or a hard driver (0.62), and (3) emphasizing competitive actions, achievement, and measurable goals (0.43), and *disagree* with the perceptions that (a) the campus is a personal place where people seem to share a lot of themselves (−0.70) and (b) the leader is generally considered to be a coordinator, an organizer, or an administrator (−0.58).
Bureaucratic culture	A factor score defined primarily by the extent to which respondents *agree* that their campuses are characterized as (1) a very formalized and structured place where bureaucratic procedures generally govern what people do (0.89) and (2) held together by formal rules and policies with the maintenance of a smooth running institution being very important (0.71), and *disagree* with the perspective that the campus is a very personal place where people seem to share a lot of themselves (−0.65).
Decision Approaches (see Appendix B):	
Rational/collegial	A factor score defined primarily by the extent to which respondents agree with the following statements regarding resource-allocation decisions on their campuses: (1) "Resource-allocation is a matter for group discussion and consensus" (0.71), (2) "Resource-allocation decisions are based on what objectively seems best for the college overall" (0.54), and (3) "The college has a standard set of procedures it uses to make resource decisions" (0.53).
Autocratic/political	A factor score defined primarily by the extent to which respondents agree with the following statements regarding resource-allocation decisions on their campuses: (1) "One individual at the college makes all resource decisions of any consequence" (0.60), (2) "Resource-allocation decisions

TABLE 2(*Continued*)
Variable Names and Variable Definitions

Names	Definitions
	are political, based on the relative power of those involved" (0.54), and (3) "No particular pattern characterizes the process by which resource-allocation decisions are made at this college" (0.39).
Institutional Effectiveness:	
Global effectiveness	The mean score of respondents on the nine dimensions of organizational effectiveness developed by Cameron (1978). The nine dimensions are: Student Educational Satisfaction; Student Academic Development; Student Career Development; Student Personal Development; Faculty and Administrator Employment Satisfaction; Professional Development and Quality of Faculty; System Openness and Community Interaction; Ability to Acquire Resources; and Organizational Health. (alpha = 0.80)

NOTE: Numbers in parentheses for the institutional culture and decision-approach descriptions are the structure loading weights derived from the factor analyses (see Appendices A and B, respectively).

regressing the organizational effectiveness measure on all causally antecedent variables in the model plus a set of interaction terms that were the cross-products of employment status (i.e., administrator, faculty member) and each of the predictor variables. The results showed trivial differences in the amount of variance explained, indicating that the influence of variables in the model was comparable for both administrators and faculty members.

A two-step process was used to estimate the direct and indirect effects represented in the model (Table 1). First, ordinary least squares regression procedures were used to estimate the coefficients in the seven structural equations defining the full model. Each endogenous variable was regressed on the exogenous variables and all causally antecedent endogenous variables. This produced seven sets of regression coefficients representing the direct effects of the causal factors on organizational effectiveness. Second, GEMINI (Wolfle & Ethington, 1985) was used to calculate and test the statistical significance of indirect effects implied in the model.

Results

Table 3 presents the means, standard deviations, and intercorrelations for all variables. Table 4 presents the structural equations derived from the model. The regression coefficients in Table 4 may be interpreted as the direct effects of individual predictor variables on the dependent variable while holding constant the influence of all other predictors in the equations.

The final structural equation in Table 4 indicates that the variables in the model explain 44% of the variance in organizational effectiveness of the 30 two-year colleges. We are unable to contrast this percent with earlier research findings

because they have customarily employed analysis of variance procedures and have not reported an equivalent statistic (i.e., percent of variance explained among groups). Nonetheless, it is unusual to account for such a large amount of the variance in a dependent variable as complex as organizational effectiveness. This suggests that the collective influence of the independent variables in the model are powerful predictors of the organizational effectiveness of two-year colleges.

Table 5 presents a summary of the direct, indirect, and total effects of all variables in the model on the global measure of organizational effectiveness for the combined sample of administrators and faculty members. These are standardized coefficients and may be used to interpret the relative influences of variables in the causal model.

The results indicate that organizational effectiveness of two-year colleges is a function of the interaction among the external environment, institutional culture, and preferred decision-making approach. Two measures of the external environment (financial health, enrollment health), all four culture types, and both decision approaches (rational/collegial, autocratic/political) have significant total effects on organizational effectiveness (Table 5). Furthermore, several predictor variables have significant indirect effects that are consistent with the effects discovered by other researchers (Cameron, 1981; Cameron & Tschirhart, 1992; Zammuto & Cameron, 1985). The results are presented according to the three sets of predictor variables in the causal model shown in Table 1.

Preexisting conditions (Exogenous Variables) The organizational effectiveness of two-year colleges is negatively affected by deteriorating financial conditions and enrollment declines, for

TABLE 3

Means, Standard Deviations, and Correlations

	1	2	3	4	5	6	7	8	9	10	11	12	13	14
1. Effectiveness	1.00													
2. Financial health	-0.30	1.00												
3. College size	0.19	-0.19	1.00											
4. Enrollment health	-0.27	0.18	-0.20	1.00										
5. Union status	0.02	-0.01	0.01	0.10	1.00									
6. Transfer emphasis	0.03	-0.11	0.22	-0.10	0.06	1.00								
7. Career emphasis	-0.08	0.09	-0.23	0.11	-0.05	-0.57	1.00							
8. Adult emphasis	0.08	0.01	0.05	0.03	0.01	-0.22	-0.30	1.00						
9. Bureaucratic	-0.28	0.04	0.02	0.06	-0.04	-0.03	0.06	-0.03	1.00					
10. Adhocracy	0.42	-0.23	0.23	-0.22	-0.01	0.06	-0.09	0.06	0.17	1.00				
11. Market	-0.18	0.03	0.17	0.04	-0.14	0.05	0.01	-0.04	-0.08	-0.11	1.00			
12. Clan	0.06	0.01	0.03	0.01	-0.06	0.07	-0.09	0.05	0.19	-0.02	0.14	1.00		
13. Rational/collegial	0.34	-0.08	0.10	-0.09	0.04	0.04	-0.09	0.05	-0.21	0.17	-0.16	0.04	1.00	
14. Autocratic/political	-0.18	0.16	-0.05	0.10	-0.03	-0.07	0.06	0.03	0.06	-0.12	0.06	-0.06	0.03	1.00
Means	0.00	3.37	4864.39	1.50	1.55	33.78	44.75	19.57	-0.01	0.01	0.01	0.00	0.00	0.00
Standard deviations	0.50	0.90	3832.71	0.87	0.50	18.49	19.79	13.73	1.00	0.98	0.98	0.99	0.81	0.74

TABLE 4
Structural Equations: Standardized Regression Coefficients

Independent Variables	Dependent Variables (Standardized Direct Effects)						
	8	9	10	11	12	13	14
Exogenous Variables:							
1. College size	0.01	0.16***	0.19***	0.05	0.09*	0.00	0.08**
2. Financial health	0.02	−0.18***	−0.01	0.03	−0.02	0.13**	−0.17***
3. Enrollment health	0.02	−0.16***	0.10*	0.06	0.00	0.05	−0.11***
4. Transfer emphasis	0.07	−0.01	0.05	0.00	−0.02	−0.01	−0.02
5. Career emphasis	−0.04	−0.01	0.05	0.05	−0.04	0.02	0.05
6. Adult emphasis	0.05	0.05	−0.03	−0.01	−0.01	0.04	0.05
7. Union status	−0.07	0.02	−0.15***	−0.04	0.01	−0.02	−0.01
Institutional Cultures:							
8. Clan					0.11**	−0.09*	0.15***
9. Adhocracy					0.17***	−0.08	0.35***
10. Market					−0.19***	0.08	−0.17***
11. Bureaucratic					−0.28***	0.09*	−0.34***
Decision Approaches:							
12. Rational/collegial							0.15***
13. Autocratic/political							−0.06*
Dependent Variable:							
14. Institutional effectiveness							
R^2	0.01	0.12***	0.06***	0.01	0.14***	0.06***	0.44***

*$p < 0.05$.   **$p < 0.01$.   ***$p < 0.001$.

both these variables have significant negative direct, indirect, and total effects on organizational effectiveness. Approximately one-third of the total effect of financial health and enrollment health is exerted indirectly (see Table 5). Understanding of the primary mediating variables that carry the significant, negative indirect influences for financial health and enrollment health may be seen from inspection of Table 4. For example, both of these conditions have significant, negative effects on the presence of an adhocracy culture (see results for equation number 9 in Table 4). In addition, financial health has a positive contribution to the use of autocratic/political decision approaches (see results for equation number 13), and enrollment health has a positive influence on the presence of a market culture (see equation number 10).

Institutional size has a significant positive direct ($p < 0.05$) and total ($p < 0.01$) influence on effectiveness (see Table 5); that is, larger two-year colleges are perceived by both administrators and faculty members to be more effective than smaller institutions. Neither mission emphasis (transfer, career, adult learning) nor collective bargaining status are related to organizational effectiveness when controlling for the influence of other variables in the model.

Culture types. All four institutional culture factors have significant direct and indirect influ-

ences on effectiveness. In fact, the total effects column in Table 5 shows that the two most powerful influences on the organizational effectiveness of two-year colleges are culture measures (i.e., adhocracy and bureaucratic). Adhocracy (total effect = 0.39) and clan (total effect = 0.21) cultures are positively associated with effectiveness, whereas bureaucratic (total effect = -0.39) and market (total effect = -0.18) cultures are negatively related. Moreover, the significant negative indirect effects of external conditions (i.e., financial and enrollment health) on organizational effectiveness are minimized by the presence of a strong adhocracy culture (see the equation for variable number 9, adhocracy, in Table 4). The significant negative indirect effect of enrollment health is exacerbated in institutions with a strong market culture (see the equation for variable number 10, market, in Table 4).

Decision approaches. Both the rational/collegial and autocratic/political decision approaches have significant direct and total effects on organizational effectiveness; the former is positive (0.15; $p < 0.001$), the latter is negative (-0.06; $p < 0.05$). The influence of the rational/collegial variable in the model, however, goes well beyond its significant direct influence on effectiveness, because it also serves as the primary mediating variable for the positive indirect effects of clan and adhocracy culture types and the negative

TABLE 5
Standardized Direct, Indirect, and Total Effects on Organizational Effectiveness

	Standardized Effect Sizes (Beta Weights)		
	Direct	Indirect	Total
Exogenous Variables:			
1. College size	0.08**	0.05	0.13**
2. Financial health	−0.17**	−0.08***	−0.25***
3. Enrollment health	−0.11***	−0.08***	−0.19***
4. Transfer emphasis	−0.02	0.00	−0.02
5. Career emphasis	0.05	−0.04	0.01
6. Adult emphasis	0.05	0.03	0.08
7. Union status	−0.01	0.02	0.01
Institutional Cultures:			
8. Clan culture	0.15***	0.06***	0.21***
9. Adhocracy culture	0.35***	0.04***	0.39***
10. Market culture	−0.17***	−0.01	−0.18***
11. Bureaucratic culture	−0.34***	−0.05***	−0.39***
Decision Approaches:			
12. Rational/collegial	0.15***		0.15***
13. Autocratic/political	−0.06*		−0.06*

* = $p < 0.05$.   ** = $p < 0.01$.   *** = $p < 0.001$

indirect effects of market and bureaucratic cultures. That is, clan and adhocracy cultures appear to foster the use of a rational/collegial decision approach, which has a significant positive influence on effectiveness (see *positive* effects in the equation for variable 12, rational/collegial, in Table 4). Conversely, the negative effects in the equation for variable 12 in Table 4, rational/collegial, indicate that bureaucratic and market cultures obviate rational/collegial approaches to decision making. The negative indirect influence of the financial health measure is exacerbated at institutions using an autocratic/political decision approach (see *positive* effect in the equation for variable 13 in Table 4).

Discussion

The findings from this study confirm and extend previous research on the influence of the external environment and institutional cultures on organizational effectiveness. The results also lend some insight into the dynamic manner by which potentially debilitating factors in the external environment indirectly influence organizational effectiveness. For example, the key mediating variable for both enrollment and financial health is an adhocracy culture. It seems that colleges with a strong adhocracy culture are able to minimize the impact of difficult enrollment and financial conditions, perhaps by enabling the institution to adapt to changing external condi-

tions and internal pressures. These institutions also are considered by their faculty and administrators to be more effective overall. Consistent with other research (Cameron & Freeman, 1991; Cameron & Tschirhart, 1992; Fjortoft & Smart, 1994; Smart & Hamm, 1993a), declining enrollment and financial conditions and bureaucratic and market cultures are negatively related to effectiveness.

These findings suggest that the relative influence of these measures may have been previously underestimated as they now appear to have important indirect, as well as direct, influences on the organizational performance of two-year colleges. This is especially the case in terms of financial and enrollment health where approximately a third of their total effects on organizational performance are indirect in nature (see Table 5). The potentially debilitating influences of declining enrollment and financial conditions on organizational performance seem to be muted in part by leadership styles and decision approaches that are congruent with adhocracy and clan cultures. Leaders in institutions with an adhocracy culture prefer to be proactive with regard to trends and forces in the external environment through external positioning, long-term time frames, and achievement-oriented activities. Turning inward and focusing on internal management issues is inconsistent with their prospector, externally oriented style of administration and leadership, which is associated with enhanced organizational performance. Therefore, it seems advisable that two-year college administrators adopt a leadership style and advocate for managerial processes that will develop and sustain a culture that permits some measure of entrepreneurism in its interactions with the external environment.

According to Schein, "The only thing of real importance that leaders do is to create and manage culture" (1985, p. 2). In fact, the most common mistake made by new presidents is acting in ways that are counter to their institution's culture (Birnbaum, 1992). The results of this study confirm that becoming competent In discovering and managing culture is a critical skill for institutional leaders (Dill, 1982; Kuh & Whitt, 1988; Lundberg, 1990). "The symbolic role of leadership," writes Tierney, "is to communicate and interpret the values and goals of the community" (1992, p. 17). Thus, it appears prudent that community college leaders employ interpretive strategies aided by an adaptive view of the environment (Bensimon, 1989; Bensimon, Neumann, A., & Birnbaum, 1989; Neumann, 1989).

Most scholars who use cultural perspectives in their work are hesitant to endorse certain forms of cultures as "better" than others (Martin, 1992; Kuh & Whitt, 1988; Van Maanen & Barley, 1985). They argue that although cultures have different properties, they do not differ in relative worth. However, the results of this study indicate that institutions with adhocracy or clan cultures are advantaged when dealing with potentially debilitating conditions in the external environment (Cameron & Ettington, 1988; Cameron & Freeman, 1991; Fjortoft & Smart, 1994). Almost half of the institutions in this study have dominant cultures classified as bureaucratic or market, types that are negatively associated with institutional effectiveness. Bureaucratic cultures, for example, are generally considered to be among the most difficult to respond purposefully and adroitly to external forces and internal pressures (Birnbaum, 1988).

Leadership styles, bonding mechanisms, and strategic emphases vary by culture types. For example, in clans the dominant leadership style is that of a mentor or facilitator, the bonding among organizational members is based on loyalty and tradition, and the strategic emphases focus on human resources and cohesion. The attributes of a clan culture may take longer to cultivate, especially if the dominant culture type is bureaucratic. Alternatively, in adhocracies the prevalent leadership style is that of an entrepreneur or innovator, the bonding among organizational members is based on innovation and development, and strategic emphases focus on growth and the acquisition of additional resources. Such institutions emphasize concern for the welfare of employees and the maintenance of flexibility, individuality, and spontaneity (Cameron & Ettington, 1988). In general, organizations that exhibit a clan culture are places where people seem to share a lot of themselves, while those that exhibit an adhocracy culture are regarded as being very dynamic and entrepreneurial places in which people are wining to stick their necks out and take risks. Both of these forms of institutional culture are superior to market and bureaucratic cultures: the former is characterized by a production orientation and an emphasis on competitive actions and achievement, where leaders are regarded as hard drivers or producers and in which the bonding among organizational members is based on task and goal accomplishment, whereas the latter is characterized by structured and formalized rules and regulations and an emphasis on permanence and stability, where leaders are regarded as organizers or coordinators, and the bonding among organizational members is based on adherence to formal procedures.

Leaders in clans and adhocracies utilize interpretive strategies which assume that the organization and environment are not preexisting and determined realities with a singular interpretation. Instead, leaders make sense of the organization and the environment to constituents. Clan leaders call more on the use of historical ideologies, whereas adhocracies interpret the environment. In this sense, adhocracies, are more adaptive to the needs of the marketplace; nonetheless, they still focus on interpretation. Bureaucratic and market cultures, however, subscribe to a singular notion of organizational reality and assume that structural responses are adequate.

Administrators at two-year colleges with strong bureaucratic and market cultures should consider ways to "bend" their college's culture in order to make the institution more responsive and adaptable to external forces and internal pressures, thereby insuring institutional survival. At some institutions this may require that administrators approach their work in Janusian fashion, centralizing some functions while at other times encouraging participative decision-making practices in ways that might become compatible with their institution's culture. Recall that the rational/collegial decision approach has a significant *positive* influence on organizational performance and is the primary mediating variable for the significant indirect effects of the four culture types; the autocratic/political approach has a significant *negative* influence on organizational performance and mediates the significant indirect effect of the financial health external threat.

These two decision approaches represent sharply contrasting ways of making resource allocation decisions. The differences in the approaches can be characterized by three key features: (a) degree of membership participation, (b) institutional focus of decision criteria, and (c) procedural orderliness. Rational/collegial processes are characterized by higher levels of membership participation in decision making through an emphasis on group discussion and consensus, a stronger focus on institutional priorities when making resource allocation decisions, and more consistency achieved through the use of a standard set of procedures to reach decisions. At the other extreme, autocratic/political processes manifest less membership participation in that one individual tends to make all important decisions, special interest groups influence decisions as much as institutional priorities, and there is ambiguity in how decisions are reached. The findings of this study clearly suggest that efforts to enhance the organizational performance of two-year colleges would be advised to incorporate the approach of the rational/collegial process in critical resource allocation decisions.

Finally, an institutional strategy must be developed that will help forge an emergent institutional culture with priorities of an adhocracy and clan so that the external environment becomes "more munificent and supportive of the institution's activities" (Cameron, 1983, p. 375) and internal processes encourage active participation. Such a strategy will likely reflect a combination of what Miles and Cameron (1982) called domain defense, offense, and creation. Domain defense activities (e.g., activate support groups, form lobbying organizations, develop consortia) are intended to generate support from important external constituencies, to buffer the institution from environmental threats, to buy time to clarify those threats, and to formulate domain offense strategies. The objectives of

domain offense activities (e.g., expanding current markets or student groups, aggressive recruiting, active public relations programs) are to enable institutions to expand activities they already perform, to broaden institutional appeal, and to increase slack resources. Domain creation activities (e.g., establishing new programs in high demand areas, capital investments, new public service ventures) are intended to create "new opportunities for institutional success while minimizing the risk of being overspecialized in areas where resources are decreasing" (Cameron, 1983, p. 375).

It is not possible to describe a culture-bending strategy that will work in every two-year college. Administrators and faculty are encouraged to consult Schein (1985), Lewin (1958), Lundberg (1985), Goodstein and Burke (1991), and others as they seek ways to infuse the complementary values of adhocracy and clans in their own institutional cultures and decision-making approaches. For example, Schein (1985, pp. 270–296) describes twelve mechanisms that have been employed successfully to modify cultures depending on the institution's stage of organizational development. And Lundberg (1985) provides a conceptual framework to understand the process of cultural change that is grounded in organization learning theory and incorporates internal and external contingencies that facilitate and hinder efforts to intervene in the culture change cycle.

Limitations

This study has several limitations that must be taken into account when interpreting the results. First, although this is a multiple institution study, 30 randomly selected institutions is but a small fraction of the more than 1,200 two-year colleges in the United States. Thus, caution must be exerted when attempting to generalize from this sample to other two-year institutions.

The selection of external environmental measures (financial and enrollment health) may have affected the results in unknown ways. The use of other indices (e.g., changing local employment conditions or tax base) might have influenced perceptions of institutional effectiveness differently. In addition, these measures may not necessarily reflect factors that are independent of the institution as portrayed in the causal model. That is, it is possible that a college creates enrollment problems by treating students poorly or through its inability to offer high-demand programs.

Some of the measures of the global organizational effectiveness index may be contaminated by perceived environmental threats. For example, because enrollment has declined recently, faculty and staff may assume students are less satisfied and that the institution is doing other things wrong as well.

Interpreting the relationships between decision approaches and effectiveness is complicated by the possibility that respondents' perceptions of their institution's approach to resource allocation decisions affect their views of organizational effectiveness. For example, because rational and collegial approaches to decision making as described in the survey instrument are more congruent with academic values than autocratic and political approaches, faculty may perceive institutions that use rational or collegial approaches to be more effective. We are not able in this study to separate and parse causally respondents' values about good decision making and their perceptions about institutional effectiveness.

In addition, the measures used to determine institutional culture profiles are not sensitive to many cultural properties that may have a bearing on institutional effectiveness (e.g., trust, history of managing well threats to institutional survival). Also, it is not clear whether preferred approaches to decision making shape the institutions' culture profiles, or whether the distinctive institutional culture essentially dictates which approaches could be used. That is, what comes first: A culture that supports rational decision-making approaches? Or is rational participative decision making a fundamental property of clan and adhocracy cultures? This is a nontrivial distinction. It may be possible for administrators to modify decision-making processes through technical adjustments. However, when implemented, the new processes may be seen by faculty and others as countercultural and subsequently become counterproductive. As we have suggested, if culture shapes decision making, then institutional leaders must focus more on interpretive strategies (Chaffee, 1985) when explaining the institution's relationship to its external environment and symbols and meaning making (Dill, 1982) in internal communications.

Furthermore, the work is a snapshot of an organization at a particular point in time. One potential for further investigation pertains to how cultures change over the organizational life cycle. Perhaps new organizations need cultures

that are bureaucratic, for example, in order to implement basic structural processes. At what point in its history is an organization capable of becoming clan-like? Further research is needed to answer these and related questions.

Conclusion

This study confirms and extends earlier research on the relative influence of factors in the external environment, institutional culture, and internal decision and managerial approaches on the organizational effectiveness of postsecondary institutions. The findings of this study suggest that the influences of these factors may have been underestimated in the past by not taking into account indirect influences on effectiveness. In addition to providing more accurate estimates of the effects of these forces, the results also suggest how the negative influences of declining enrollments and financial health may be partially muted through attention to institutional cultures and decision approaches. These two components of the overall managerial strategy of two-year colleges appear to be powerful mechanisms in efforts to enhance organizational performance in an era where the credibility of colleges and universities is being challenged and their environments are less munificent.

Appendix A

Institutional Culture Measures: Factor Analytic Procedures and Results

Factor Procedures: The survey instrument contained the original 16 items used by Cameron and Ettington (1988) to measure four distinct but related types of campus cultures. Theoretically, there are 4 items intended to measure each of the four campus cultures. Factor analytic procedures using an oblique rotation were used to assess the validity of the proposed factor structure and, subsequently, to obtain factor scores used in the path analysis. Four factors were derived, given the underlying four-dimensional conceptual framework of the survey instrument developed by Cameron and Ettington (1988).

Factor Results: The results of the analysis produced the factor loadings presented in Table A. The table presents the pattern and structure weights used to interpret the substantive meaning of the four derived factors. The *pattern weights* are similar to regression coefficients, whereas the *structure coefficients* represent the correlations of the variables with the factor scores. Overall, the four-factor solution accounts for 57.6% of the variance among the 16 variables. In addition, 12 of the 16 items load most highly on the factor to which they are theoretically related. None of the 4 items that do not conform to theoretical expectations (items 1, 7, 12, and 15 in Table A) load in a positive manner on any other factor; rather,

they tend to have a strong negative loading on another factor and a weak positive loading on the factor to which they are theoretically related.

The *first factor* represents the *bureaucratic culture* and is defined primarily in a positive sense by 2 items associated with the bureaucratic scale (no. 3 and no. 11), and in a negative sense by a single item (no. 1) associated with the clan culture. The 2 items that were assumed to be mea-

TABLE A
Institutional Culture Factor Results: Pattern and Structure Weights

Institutional Culture Items	Factor Number			
	I	II	III	IV
Institutional Characteristics Items:				
1. This is a **personal place**. It is like an extended family. People seem to share a lot of themselves. (Clan item)	−0.55 (**−0.65**)	0.04 (0.09)	−0.62 (**−0.70**)	0.08 (0.33)
2. This is a very **dynamic and entrepreneurial** place. People are willing to stick their necks out and take risks. (Adhocracy item)	−0.13 (−0.26)	0.67 (**0.70**)	0.07 (0.08)	0.12 (0.17)
3. This is a very **formalized and structured** place. Bureaucratic procedures generally govern what people do. (Bureaucracy item)	0.87 (**0.89**)	−0.15 (−0.29)	0.05 (0.14)	0.05 (−0.17)
4. This is a **production-oriented** place. A major concern is with getting the job done. People aren't very personally involved. (Market item)	−0.20 (0.04)	−0.44 (−0.36)	0.70 (**0.70**)	−0.29 (−0.39)
Institutional Leader Items:				
5. Our leader is generally considered to be a **mentor, a sage, or a father or mother figure**. (Clan item)	−0.09 (−0.17)	−0.07 (−0.05)	−0.05 (−0.13)	0.34 (**0.36**)
6. Our leader is generally considered to be an **entrepreneur, an innovator, or a risk taker**. (Adhocracy item)	−0.06 (−0.15)	0.47 (**0.50**)	0.23 (0.23)	0.18 (0.17)
7. Our leader is generally considered to be a **coordinator, an organizer, or an administrator**. (Bureaucracy item)	0.04 (0.09)	−0.27 (−0.34)	−0.63 (**−0.58**)	−0.35 (−0.25)
8. Our leader is generally considered to be a **producer, a technician, or a hard driver**. (Market item)	0.06 (0.15)	−0.03 (0.01)	0.60 (**0.62**)	−0.04 (−0.17)
Institutional "Glue" Items:				
9. The glue that holds this college together is **loyalty and tradition**. Commitment to this college runs high. (Clan item)	−0.35 (−0.47)	−0.21 (−0.12)	0.01 (−0.18)	0.68 (**0.76**)
10. The glue that holds this college together is **commitment to innovation and development**. There is an emphasis on being first. (Adhocracy item)	−0.07 (−0.20)	0.70 (**0.71**)	−0.05 (0.00)	−0.02 (0.03)
11. The glue that holds this college together is **formal rules and policies**. Maintaining a smooth-running institution is important here. (Bureaucracy item)	0.67 (**0.71**)	−0.25 (−0.38)	−0.07 (−0.01)	−0.03 (−0.18)
12. The glue that holds this college together is the emphasis on **tasks and accomplishment**. A production orientation is commonly shared. (Market item)	−0.24 (−0.01)	−0.16 (−0.13)	0.12 (0.22)	−0.77 (**−0.74**)
Institutional Emphases Items:				
13. This college emphasizes **human resources**. High cohesion and morale are important. (Clan item)	−0.33 (−0.46)	−0.00 (0.04)	−0.32 (−0.43)	0.37 (**0.51**)
14. This college emphasizes **growth and acquiring new resources**. Readiness to meet new challenges is important. (Adhocracy item)	0.06 (0.05)	0.54 (**0.51**)	−0.05 (0.07)	−0.36 (−0.34)
15. This college emphasizes **permanence and stability**. Efficient, smooth operations are important. (Bureaucracy item)	0.19 (0.27)	−0.59 (**−0.62**)	0.04 (0.00)	0.12 (0.05)

TABLE A (*Continued*)

| Institutional Culture Items | Factor Number | | | |
	I	II	III	IV
16. This college emphasizes **competitive actions and achievement**. Measurable goals are important. (Market item)	0.04 (0.11)	0.09 (0.11)	0.39 **(0.43)**	−0.16 (−0.24)

NOTES: *Factor Titles:* Factor I: Bureaucratic Culture; Factor II: Adhocracy Culture; Factor III: Market Culture; Factor IV: Clan Culture.

Emphases (highlighted words) in the items are in the original instrument.

Structure coefficients are given in parentheses. Those highlighted were used to define the factors.

sures of the bureaucratic culture but did not load strongly on the first factor (no. 7 and no. 15), load more highly with negative weights on other factors and have weak positive loadings on this factor. The *second factor* is defined primarily by the strong positive loadings of the 4 items related theoretically to the *adhocracy culture* (no. 2, no. 6, no. 10, no. 14) plus the negative loading of 1 item (no. 7) theoretically associated with the bureaucratic culture. The *third factor* is defined primarily by the positive loadings of 3 of the 4 items theoretically related to the *market culture* (no. 4, no. 8, no. 16) and the negative loadings of 2 items theoretically associated with clan (no. 1) and bureaucratic (no. 7) cultures. The *fourth factor* is defined primarily by the positive loadings of 3 of the 4 items theoretically related to the *clan culture* (no. 5, no. 9, no. 13) and the negative loading of I item (no. 12) theoretically associated with the market culture.

"Dominant" Culture Type: The four factor scores above are used throughout the article to reflect the degree to which individuals perceive their colleges as manifesting the four institutional cultures developed by Cameron and Ettington (1988). All prior studies have classified institutions by their "dominant" culture type; that is, an institution is classified as having a dominant clan culture if the institution's score on the clan scale, regardless of the magnitude of the difference, is higher than its score on the three remaining culture scales.

We were interested in determining what the *dominant* culture *type* would be for each of the 30 institutions in this study, given this tradition in prior research. This was done by classifying institutions according to their highest score across each of the four culture factors. The results indicate that 9 (30%) have a dominant bureaucratic culture, 8 (27%) represent a dominant adhocracy culture, 8 (27%) reflect a dominant clan culture, and 5 (17%) have a dominant market culture.

The following is the mean score on all four culture scales for colleges clasified by their dominant culture type.

Inspection of the above indicates that the mean for each dominant culture type is about a half standard deviation above the grand mean (standardized at 0) and that each dominant culture type has a substantially higher mean score on its corresponding factor: for example, the mean for colleges with a dominant market culture on the market culture factor is 0.52. Thus, faculty and administrators perceive that their institutions have "unique profiles" consistent with the dominant culture type labels.

Appendix B

Decision-Approach Measures: Factor Analytic Procedures and Results

Factor Procedures: The survey instrument included 6 items to assess the nature by which resource-allocation decisions were made on the 30

| Dominant Culture Type | Means on Four Culture Factor Scores | | | |
	Bureaucratic	Adhocracy	Market	Clan
Bureaucratic (*n* = 9)	+0.43	−0.35	−0.17	−0.01
Adhocracy (*n* = 8)	−0.04	+0.53	−0.06	−0.06
Market (*n* = 5)	−0.03	−0.28	+0.52	−0.07
Clan (*n* = 8)	−0.21	−0.28	−0.12	+0.39

TABLE B
Decision-Approach Measures: Factor Analytic Procedures and Results

Decision-Approach Variables	Factor Number	
	I	II
1. Resource allocation is a matter for group discussion and consensus	0.71 (0.71)	−0.11 (−0.17)
2. Resource-allocation decisions are based on what objectively seems best for this college	0.55 (0.54)	0.07 (0.02)
3. The college has a standard set of procedures it uses to make resource decisions	0.54 (0.53)	0.01 (−0.04)
4. Resource allocation-decisions are political, based on the relative power of those involved	0.11 (0.06)	0.61 (0.60)
5. No particular pattern characterizes the process by which resource-allocation decisions are made at this college	−0.08 (−0.13)	0.54 (0.54)
6. One individual at this college makes all resource allocations of any consequence	−0.01 (−0.05)	0.38 (0.39)

Note: Structure coefficients are given in parentheses.

campuses. The dimensionality of the 6 items shown in Table B was explored through the use of factor analytic procedures with oblique rotation.

Factor Results: The results of the analysis yielded two factors with eigenvalues of 1.0 or greater. Overall, the two-factor solution accounts for 54.2% of the variance among the six decision-approach variables. Table B reports the pattern and structure weights used to interpret the substantive meaning of the two factors obtained from the analysis. The first factor is defined primarily by the first 3 items and was given the label of "rational/collegial" decision approach; the second factor is defined primarily by the last 3 items and was given the title of "autocratic/political" decision approach.

References

Ashar, H., & Shapiro, J. Z. (1990). Are retrenchment decisions rational? *Journal of Higher Education, 61,* 121–141.

Baldridge, J. V. (1971). *Power and conflict in the university.* New Haven, CT: J. Wiley.

Bensimon, E. (1989). The meaning of good presidential leadership. *Review of Higher Education, 12,* 107–123.

Bensimon, E., Neumann, A., & Birnbaum, R. (1989). *Making sense of administrative leadership: The L word in higher education.* ASHE-ERIC Higher Education Report (#1). Washington, D.C.: Association for the Study of Higher Education.

Birnbaum, R. (1988). *How colleges work.* San Francisco: Jossey-Bass.

Birnbaum, R. (1992). *How academic leadership works.* San Francisco: Jossey-Bass.

Cameron, K. S. (1978). Measuring organizational effectiveness in institutions of higher education. *Administrative Science Quarterly, 23,* 604–632.

Cameron, K. S. (1982). The relationship between faculty unionism and organizational effectiveness. *Academy of Management Journal, 25,* 6–24.

Cameron, K. S. (1983). Strategic responses to conditions of decline: Higher education and the private sector. *Journal of Higher Education, 54,* 359–380.

Cameron, K. S. (1985). Investigating the causal association between unionism and organizational effectiveness. *Research in Higher Education, 23,* 387–411.

Cameron, K. S. (1986). A study of organizational effectiveness and its predictors. *Management Science, 32,* 87–112.

Cameron, K. S., Whetten, D. A., & Kim, M. U. (1987). Organizational dysfunctions of decline. *Academy of Management Journal, 30,* 126–138.

Cameron, K. S., & Ettington, D. R. (1988). The conceptual foundations of organizational culture. In J. C. Smart (Ed.), *Higher education: Handbook of theory and research* (vol. 4, pp. 356–396). New York: Agathon Press.

Cameron, K. S., & Freeman, S. J. (1991). Cultural congruence, strength, and type: Relationships to effectiveness. *Research in Organizational Change and Development, 5,* 23–58.

Cameron, K. S., & Tschirhart, M. (1992). Postindustrial environments and organizational effectiveness in colleges and universities. *Journal of Higher Education, 63,* 87–108.

Chaffee, E. E. (1983). *Rational decision making in higher education.* Boulder, CO: National Center for Higher Education Management Systems.

Chaffee, E. E. (1984). Successful strategic management in small private colleges. *Journal of higher Education, 55,* 212–241.

Chaffee, E. E. (1985). The concept of strategy: From business to higher education. In J. C. Smart (Ed.), *Higher education: Handbook of theory and research* (vol. 1, pp. 133–172). New York: Agathon.

Chaffee, E. E. (1989). Strategy and effectiveness in systems of higher education. In J. C. Smart (Ed.), *Higher education: Handbook of theory and research* (vol. 5, pp. 1–30). New York: Agathon.

Chaffee, E. E., & Tierney, W. G. (1988). *Collegiate cultures and leadership strategies.* New York American Council on Education: Macmillan.

Child, J. (1973). Predicting and understanding organizational structure. *Administrative Science Quarterly, 18,*168–185.

Cohen, M. D., & March, J. G. (1974). *Leadership and ambiguity: The American college president.* New York: McGraw-Hill.

Clark, B. R. (1970). *The distinctive college: Reed, Antioch, and Swarthmore.* Chicago: Aldine.

Dill, D. (1982). The management of academic culture: Notes on the management of meaning and social integration. *Higher Education, 11,* 303–320.

Finn, C. E., & Manno, B. V. (1996). Behind the curtain. *The Wilson Quarterly, 20,* 44–53.

Fjortoft, N., & Smart, J. C. (1994). Enhancing organizational effectiveness: The importance of culture type and mission agreement. *Higher Education, 27,* 429–447.

Goodstein, L. D., & Burke, W. W. (1991). Creating successful organization change. *Organizational Dynamics, 19*(4), 5–17.

Handy, C. (1990). *The age of unreason.* Boston: Harvard Business School Press.

Kuh, G. D., & Whitt, E. J. (1988). *The invisible tapestry: Culture in American colleges and universities.* ASHE-ERIC Higher Education Report, No. 1. Washington, D.C.: Association for the Study of Higher Education.

Kuh, G. D., Schuh, J. S., Whitt, E. J., Andreas, R. E., Lyons, J. W., Strange, C. C., Krehbiel, L. E., & MacKay, K. A. (1991). *Involving colleges: Successful approaches to fostering student learning and personal development outside the classroom.* San Francisco: Jossey-Bass.

Kuh, G. D., & Robinson, B. R. (1995), Friends, brothers, and some sisters: Using cultural research to guide the merger of two seminaries. *Review of Higher Education, 19,* 71–92.

Lewin, K. (1958). Group decisions and social change. In E. E. Maccobby, T. M. Newcomb, & E. L. Hartley (Eds.), *Readings in social psychology.* New York: Holt, Rinehart and Winston.

Lundberg, C. C. (1985). On the feasibility of cultural intervention in organizations. In P. J. Frost, L. F. Moore, M. R. Louis, C. C. Lundberg, & J. Martin (Eds.), *Organizational culture* (pp. 169–185). Beverly Hills: Sage.

Lundberg, C. C. (1990). Surfacing organizational culture. *Journal of Managerial Psychology, 5*(4), 19–26.

Martin, J. (1992). *Cultures in organizations: Three perspectives.* New York: Oxford University Press.

Meyer, M. W. (1979). *Change in public bureaucracies.* Cambridge, MA: Cambridge University Press.

Miles, R. H., & Cameron, K. S. (1982). *Coffin nails and corporate strategies.* Englewood Cliffs, NJ: Prentice-Hall.

Neumann, A. (1989). Strategic leadership: The changing orientations of college presidents. *Review of Higher Education, 12,* 137–151.

Peters, T. J. (1987). *Thriving in chaos: Handbook for a management revolution.* New York: Knopf.

Pincus, F. L., & Archer, E. (1989). *Bridges to opportunity.* New York: College Entrance Examination Board.

Quinn, R. E., & Kimberly, J. R. (1984). Paradox, planning, and perseverance: Guidelines for managerial practice. In R. H. Hall & R. E. Quinn (Eds.), *Managing organizational translations* (pp. 295–313). Homewood, IL: Dow Jones-Irwin.

Quinn, R. E., & McGrath, M. (1985). The transformation of organizational cultures: A competing values perspective. In P. J. Frost, L. F. Moore, M. R. Louis, C. C. Lundberg, & J. Martin (Eds.), *Organizational culture* (pp. 315–334). Beverly Hills, CA: Sage.

Schein, E. H. (1985). *Organizational culture and leadership.* San Francisco: Jossey-Bass.

Senge, P. (1990). *The fifth discipline: The art and practice of the learning organization.* New York: Doubleday.

Smart, J. C., & Hamm, R. E. (1993a). Organizational culture and effectiveness in two-year colleges. *Research in Higher Education, 34,* 95–106.

Smart, J. C., & Hamm, R. E. (1993b). Organizational effectiveness and mission orientations of two-year colleges. *Research in Higher Education, 34,* 489–502.

Smart, J. C., & St. John, E. P. (1996) Organizational culture and effectiveness in higher education: A test of the "culture type" and "strong culture" hypotheses. *Educational Evaluation and Policy Analysis, 18,* 219–241.

Sutton, R. I., & D'Aunno, T. (1989). Decreasing organizational size: Untangling the effects of people and money. *Academy of Management Review, 14,* 194–212.

Tierney, W. G. (1988). Organizational culture in higher education: Defining the essentials. *Journal of Higher Education, 59,* 2–21.

Tierney, W. G. (1992). Cultural leadership and the search for community. *Liberal Education, 78,* 16–21.

Tierney, W. G. (forthcoming). *The responsive university: Restructuring for high performance.* Baltimore: Johns Hopkins University Press.

"To Dance With Change" (1994). *Policy Perspectives, 5*(3), A1–12.

Van Maanen, J., & Barley, S. R. (1985). Cultural organization: Fragments of a theory. In P. J. Frost, L. F. Moore, M. R. Louis, C. C. Lundberg, & J. Martin (Eds.), *Organizational culture* (pp. 31–53). Beverly Hills, CA: Sage.

Weick, K E. (1979). *The social psychology of organizing* (2nd ed.). Reading, MA: Addison-Wesley.

Whetten, D. A. (1984). Effective administrators: Good management on the college campus. *Change, 16,* 38–43.

Wolfle, L. M. (1985). Application of causal models in higher education. In J. C. Smart (Ed.), *Higher education: Handbook of theory and research* (vol. 1, pp. 381–413). New York: Agathon.

Wolfle, L. M., & Ethington, C. A. (1985). GEMINI: Program for analysis of structural equations with standard errors of indirect effects. *Behavior Research Methods, Instruments and Computers, 17,* 1581–1584.

Zammuto, R. F., & Cameron, K. S. (1985). Environmental decline and organizational response. *Research in Organizational Behavior, 7,* 223–262.

Zammuto, R. F., & Krakower, J. Y. (1991). Quantitative and qualitative studies of organizational culture. *Research in Organizational Change and Development, 5,* 83–114.

CHAPTER 15

PERSPECTIVES ON COMMUNITY COLLEGE LEADERSHIP: TWENTY YEARS IN THE MAKING

MARILYN J. AMEY
KIM E. VANDERLINDEN
DENNIS F. BROWN
MICHIGAN STATE UNIVERSITY, EAST LANSING, MICHIGAN, USA

Findings from a national study of community college administrative careers, examining issues of position, gender and race/ethnicity are reported. Career path data also are compared with an earlier national study, showing that paths to the presidency have changed since 1985. Implications for recruitment into senior positions and leadership diversity are discussed.

Since the early 1980s, community colleges have grown in number, size, and organizational complexity, The "comprehensive community college" of the late 1990s and early twenty-first century offers a wide array of credit, non-credit, and lifelong learning experiences across a seemingly endless array of disciplinary and technical foci. The strength and size of occupational education/vocational education units, and the development of new and enhanced infrastructure administrative systems such as business-industry incubators, continuing education units, instructional technology centers, and centers for teaching excellence are among the many collegiate innovations that have taken hold in the last 20 years. In the midst of such increased organizational diversification, the colleges also are experiencing the beginning of unprecedented faculty, staff, and administrative turnover, without a clear sense of emergent replacements.

Similar to their four-year counterparts, community college leaders seem caught in the currency of leadership succession patterns, still assuming traditional paths into senior administrative positions. These assumptions may not necessarily be consistent with labor market trends and the sector's growth and change during the last three decades. Developing a new generation of leaders at all administrative levels is imperative if community colleges are to be successful in an increasingly complex environment (Hockaday & Puyear, 2000), and leadership may be the key variable in determining organizational engagement in effective renewal or slipping into decline (Amey & Twombly, 1992). Who are the future leaders willing to guide community colleges through this challenging period? Is the leadership experience changing, and thus coinciding with the changing environment on the community college campus? These questions lie at the heart of the research study described in this chapter.

A plethora of information exists on community college presidents. Pierce and Pedersen (1997) report that between 1989 and 1995, more than 150 books, monographs, articles, and reports focused on community college presidents. These informative studies provided insight into presidents' life experiences, career paths, priorities, relationships, and leadership styles. Yet studies of presidents only illuminate those who have arrived at the most senior leadership position. There are few empirical studies that go below the presidential level to thoroughly examine the lives and careers of other community college administrators and leaders on campus, though some authors do suggest the existence of a clear presidential pipeline or pathway via the senior academic officer's position (Twombly, 1988; Vaughan, 1990). Less consideration is given in the literature as to why and how certain administrative paths evolve, or what organizational strategies might be appropriate for developing and supporting alternative trajectories. It is therefore important to gain a better understanding of the broader array of administrative leadership paths in their own right, including those that may be part of "new" staffing patterns of the practitioner cadre from which future senior community college leaders may come. Such examination is especially important in light of the onset of massive retirements, when "atypical "hires may be needed to ensure new leaders.

Can community colleges, with their diverse missions and constituencies, afford to maintain narrow definitions of leadership, limited criteria of acceptable experiences, and traditional professional constructions of leadership? If calls for diversity and leadership access are to be answered (e.g., Amey, 1999; DiCroce, 1995; Townsend, 1995; Twombly, 1995), it seems particularly important to look *inside* the community college organization and examine not only traditional administrative labor markets, such as academic vice presidents and academic deans, but also non-traditional and growth administrative markets in areas of the colleges that are more newly organized or gaining in status. Many scholars have noted that while women and administrators of color may fare better at gaining initial employment at community colleges and even leadership opportunities, they start their actual career paths on the organizational periphery or in experimental or temporary positions (Moore, Martorana, & Twombly, 1985;

Townsend, 1995; Winship & Amey, 1992). Changes in organizational mission and function can sometimes shift internal labor market forces and elevate in status and power that which was once deemed tangential, thereby affording different leadership opportunities for administrators of such units. We wanted, in part, to examine this assumption and see the extent to which it might be true in today's community colleges.

The Study

The most comprehensive snapshot of the full range of career pathways for administrators in community colleges remain the study by Moore, Martorana, and Twombly, *Today's Academic Leaders* (Moore et al., 1985). Their survey data, which provided systematic analyses of two-year college administrative careers, led to various follow-up analyses of internal and external labor market issues (Twombly 1986, 1988). Data presented below comes from a national survey designed to, in part, replicate the 1984 Moore et al. survey.[1] Our instrument consisted of 34 open-ended, closed-ended, and Likert scale questions. The Moore et al. survey was adapted for language and terminology for direct comparison. Additional questions were constructed to represent current trends, issues, and foci of community college leaders based on an extensive literature review of key administrative studies and instruments.

Our instrument was piloted with community college administrators, two peer reviewers, and a panel of experts from the American Association of Community Colleges (AACC). A stratified random sample of 1700 community college administrators across 14 position codes was drawn from the AACC data bank, providing representation by geographic location (urban and rural), and single and multi-campus sites. Letters of introduction and survey packets were mailed, extensive electronic and telephone follow-ups were conducted, and a second mailing distributed, yielding a response rate of 54% usable surveys. Quantitative variables were analyzed using descriptive statistics, and open-ended responses were content analyzed.

Administrative Careers

Survey results are presented first by position, so that the career trajectories and profiles of more discrete groups is of administrators can be better understood. Some administrators chose not to provide complete career information, so percentages do not always equal 100%.

President's Career Paths

Profiles

Demographically, our presidents are more diverse than those found in the 1985 Moore et al. survey. Twenty-seven percent of the respondents were women, compared with 3.1% in the earlier study, and of those who identified a racial/ethnic profile other than Caucasian, 14% were presidents of color as opposed to only 6.3% in 1985. Presidents in our study were somewhat more likely to hold the doctorate than those responding to Moore et al. (86% versus 79.3%). A far greater percentage of presidents holding the doctorate had a Ph.D. in 2000 (50%) than did in 1985 (39.5%), with men being somewhat more likely than women to hold a Ph.D. as opposed to an Ed.D. The mean age of college presidents increased slightly from 52.4 years in 1985 to 55.5 years in 2000, and the mean age of male presidents is slightly higher (56 years) than that of their female counterparts (55 years).

Career Trajectories

Presidents had more diversified paths to the senior leadership position than their counterparts in 1985 (Twombly, 1988). Twenty-two percent were promoted into the presidency from within their present institution, while an additional 66% were hired into their current positions from other community colleges. The remainder moved into a presidency from other sectors.

Tenure in the position from which presidents were hired was five years or less for 66% of respondents, with similar proportions of presidents (between 60–70%) holding positions throughout their careers for averages of five years or less. The fairly rapid turnover in the community college presidency mirrors research that indicates presidential tenure has dropped from its earlier high of 10 years to a norm of 5 years (Dudertstadt, 2000). Forty-five percent of responding presidents had served at their present institution for 10 years or more, while another 45% were employed at their present institution for less than 5 years. This implies a very mixed internal/external labor market for CEOs. While it is possible to be promoted from

within, it is just as likely that one needs to move in order to secure a presidency.

The largest percentage of presidents in our study indicated that their immediate past position was as a president at another community college (25%). Other responding presidents indicated a traditional senior leadership path—37% indicating immediate prior service as provost and 15% as an Associate, Assistant, Academic Dean/Dean of Instruction (15%). These percentages are higher than those found in the Moore et al. (1985) study (16.6%, 8.8%, and 15.6%, respectively), although a similar percentage were most recently academic deans. Three percent of those in the present study came from Dean or Assistant Dean/Director positions in Continuing/Vocational Education, while 12% held other administrative positions, including senior student affairs offices and vice presidents for institutional planning or advancement. This represents a significant increase since 1985, when just 3.6% of presidents came to their positions from other types of administrative positions. In 2000, 2% of respondents came from community college system boards, and 2% directly from public school administration. Two percent were promoted directly from faculty ranks, whereas in 1985, 5.2% of responding presidents came directly from the faculty.

Nearly one-third of all presidents indicated that they had held positions earlier in their careers at four-year institutions, often as faculty or department chairs/program directors before switching to the community college sector. This is a slightly higher percentage than found in the 1985 Moore et al., study. We also found a lower percentage (17%) of those with public school backgrounds than in the earlier study, perhaps reflecting the transition from "junior" college to community college.

Gender Differences

There is not a significant gender difference between the career trajectories of male and female leaders. Around half of each group followed "traditional" paths to the presidency, and the rest had backgrounds reflecting a myriad of other administrative configurations. An almost equal percentage of men and women indicated prior service as community college presidents (26% compared to 23%, though the number of women is very small), and slightly more women than men were promoted from within their institution into the presidency (23% compared to 20%, but again the number of women is very small). Both men and women, with the exception of those in student affairs, built careers by moving between institutions rather than developing a single-institution career. One finding of note was a difference between women and men in both the reported length of time in position and at their present institution. Women presidents were in their positions an average of 4 years, while men were in their positions an average of 7 years. Similarly, women were at their present institution for a shorter period of time compared to their male counterparts, 6 years compared to 10 years.

Themes

Over the past 20 years, governing boards and presidential search committees appear more inclined to hire presidents with substantial administrative experience, including other presidencies. That a president may have completed two, three, or even four presidencies prior to assuming their current role is not atypical in the 2000 data, and suggests a strong preference towards hiring persons with extensive experience rather than providing "on the job training." Even the growth in previous administrative experience in positions other than president suggests a realization that the role of community college president, while perhaps still "first among equals," in fact has multiple and conflicting responsibilities for which management, administration, and leadership skills gained through particular and extended experiences is important. College presidents continue to be one of few position categories most likely to have any public school teaching experience in their background (17%), but this percentage dropped substantially since 1985 when almost 60% reported work in K-12 organizations. This indicates a shift away from a "junior college" mentality.

The data raise interesting career and mobility questions. Community college presidents in this study appear to be reaching their first presidency in their early 40s, and then proceed through multiple presidencies with an average duration of under five years. That a person could have been president three or four times by the ripe old age of 55 suggests a series of career and professional development concerns among this population, as well as administrative access

issues for those coming along behind. This picture of presidential succession is clearly quite different than that portrayed in the early 1980s.

Chief Academic Officers

Profiles

While women now represent 42% of the responding Chief Academic Officers (CAOs), up from 15.9% in the earlier Moore et al. (1985) study, the racial and ethnic diversity of CAOs remains largely the same. In 2000, slightly more respondents identified themselves as Caucasian than in 1985, 89% as compared to 86.2%. The mean age of CAOs has also increased since 1985, from 49.1 years to 54 years. This could be attributed to the growth of women in the position category, stereotypically categorized as entering the workforce at an older age and progressing in rank more slowly. It also is possible that the multiple presidential career pattern impedes CAO advancement. Those holding the doctorate remain fairly constant at 74%. As compared to presidential demographics, the number of respondents with a Ph.D. dropped between the study periods, from a high of 48.5% in 1985 to 40% in 2000.

Career Trajectories

CAOs had more diversified career paths than their counterparts in 1985 (Twombly, 1988). Fifty-two percent were promoted into the CAO position from within their present institution, while 28% were hired from another community college. Slightly over half of the CAOs were at their present institution for 10 years or more, yet almost 40% of the remaining half were employed at their present institution less than five years. This suggests a very mixed internal/external labor market for CAOs.

The career paths of CAOs were marked by holding positions for relatively short periods of time. Seventy-four percent of CAOs were in their current position for less than five years, and 54% less than three years. Almost 60% of CAOs had held their immediate past positions for five years or less, with similar proportions of CAOs holding positions throughout their careers for averages of 4–5 years or less.

The largest percentage of CAOs' immediate past positions were those that would be thought of as traditionally leading to the senior academic officer's position—similarly titled senior positions (8%); Associate, Assistant, or interim CAO (8%); Assistant, Associate, or Academic Dean or Dean of Instruction (31%); or Department Chair (4%), for a total of 51%. This represents a significant change from 1985, when Moore et al. found 65% of CAOs came through the route of "traditional" academic ladders. Ten percent of CAOs in our study had immediate prior service as Deans, Assistant Deans, or Directors in Continuing/Vocational Education, and 18% held other administrative positions, including senior student affairs officers and vice presidencies for institutional planning or development (up from 12% in the Moore et al. study). A smaller percentage came from outside academe in the present study (6% in 2000 compared to 11% in 1985), with basically comparable percentages promoted to the CAO position directly from faculty ranks in 2000 and in 1985 (7% and 9%, respectively). Over one-fourth of all CAOs held positions earlier in their careers at four-year institutions, often as faculty or department chairs/program directors before switching to the community college sector.

Gender Differences

Women CAOs' career paths mirrored those of their male counterparts, with the largest percentage having traditional academic administrative careers, beginning as faculty. Some women (14%) began their paths in student affairs, staying almost exclusively in that division until becoming CAO, typically with a title of provost or Vice President for Academic and Student Affairs. A similar percentage (14%) came through continuing education, while 19% had careers as instructional support/technology and faculty developers. A small percentage (6%) was in other non-academic administrative careers, apart from student affairs, including institutional research, institutional development, and grants administration. Women were more likely than men to be promoted from within the institution (58% compared to 43%, respectively). Similar to the college presidents, we found that women CAOs were in their present positions for a shorter period of time than CAOs who were men (3.6 years on average, compared to 5.2 years). They also were likely to have been at their current institutions for less time, an average 10.5 years compared to 13.4 years. This pattern again mirrored that of women presidents.

Themes

Traditional academic credentialing still appears to be an important aspect of promotion into CAO positions, however the emergence of a strong administrative background in continuing and vocational education, student affairs, and non-academic administration suggests that an acceptable alternative career trajectory has emerged. The challenge for analysis lies in the interpretation of such change. It is conceivable that leadership in organizational growth areas such as vocational education may present search committees with differently viable candidates to be institutional CAOs. The presence of student affairs backgrounds in the career paths of CAOs might also be a function of institutional reorganizations that have become so prevalent during the last decade, as financial resources have tightened. While they may or may not have served at one time as faculty, over 40% of CAOs come to their positions from areas other than the traditional academic hierarchy of chair, director, associate dean, and/or dean. This apparent trend is worthy of close observation, not only for understanding the perspectives of people assuming the senior academic leadership position of CAO, but also for the implications it has on the potential pool of future presidents.

Other Positions of Note

Given the varied career paths of presidents and chief academic officers, it is important to briefly describe the positions that directly fed into these senior leadership roles. In this way, a more complete picture of the backgrounds of current and prospective community college leaders is presented.

Senior Student Affairs Officers

Over half (54.8%) of Senior Student Affairs Officers (SSAOs) were women, and a fifth (19.4%) were administrators of color, representing the greatest demographic diversity among the senior positions studied. Higher levels of gender and ethnic diversity for SSAOs were also found in 1985 (41.3% and 13.1%, respectively). The average age of SSAOs was 52 years, and almost 47% held doctorates. SSAOs were in their present position approximately seven years on average. It is clear that at community colleges, women have gained their greatest stronghold within the student affairs ranks. It is also clear that while diversity has significantly increased for SSAOs in the last 20 years, movement into the presidency is still not common. Such clustering into one position gives rise to the argument that at community colleges, leadership diversity has become an organizational "silo."

SSAOs followed the traditional career path of being promoted from within the division. Immediate past positions included dean or vice president for student affairs (9%), associate/assistant dean or vice president of student affairs (25%), counseling (16%), or other student services positions (19%). Eleven percent came directly from academic positions, including deans of instruction, while an almost equal percentage (12%) was in other administrative positions such as continuing education, development, and institutional research.

An overwhelming 70% of responding SSAOs were employed at the same community college for 10 years or more (on average, 16 years), indicating the presence of a strong internal labor market. The data also suggested a relatively quick rise to the senior leadership position for at least two-thirds of respondents, in that 62% were in their immediate past positions for less than five years, and 67% were in their second previous position for less than five years. Women SSAOs worked at their present institutions longer than men, and held their current position for less time, perhaps suggesting women were promoted less quickly into the SSAO position than their male colleagues. It is clear that once in this professional track, SSAOs build traditional careers within community colleges. Still, about 15% had four-year college experience, 10% public school experience, and 17% experience in the private sector, often early in their careers.

This profile of the SSAO career path is different than that described by Moore et al. (1985), even though they also depicted a traditional career trajectory. In 1985, 19% came to the SSAO position in a lateral move from another SSAO position, over twice the percentage we found. The pattern of movement from assistant/associate positions into the SSAO was just the opposite: 8% in 1985 compared to 25% in 2000. Fewer came from counseling positions in the earlier study (5% compared to 16%) while around 15% held a variety of other positions in student affairs as opposed to 19% who did so in our study. Another striking point of comparison was that 14% came to the SSAO from public schools in

1985, while only 2% did so in our study. Positions were held longer in the earlier study (40% having been in their position five years or less) and a much lower proportion of administrators were promoted from within the same institution (53.4%).

Business/Fiscal Officers

The majority of Chief Business/Fiscal Officers (CFO) followed a career path within the financial network. Respondents held various job titles including business manager, accountant, controller/comptroller, auditor, analyst, or finance officer throughout their careers, including in the most senior position. Seventy percent of the CFOs were male and nearly 90% were white. The majority of CFOs held the master's as their highest degree (59%), over half of which were MBAs. The mean age for a CFO was 50 years old; women were younger on average (47 years old) than men (52 years old).

More than 60% of CFOs held immediate past positions at community colleges (approximately 40% at the same and 23% at a different community college). Thirteen percent came directly from private-sector business and financial jobs, and 5% came from financial jobs in public schools. Fifty-five percent of CFOs were new to the position, in place three years, or fewer, although the average length of service at their current institutions was 12 years, suggesting the presence of a strong internal labor market. Many CFOs (44%) held at least one position in the private sector at some point in their careers, and 18% had worked in a public school setting, often as business teacher or in a financial or business office.

Drawing any significant conclusions regarding gender differences in career trajectories is premature, given the relatively small number of women in this category, and further intensive study is warranted. Women served at the same institution for shorter periods of time than men (7.6 years versus 13 years, respectively), and women held the CFO position for only an average of three years at the time of the survey, compared to an average of eight years for their male counterparts. Women CFOs had served in the private sector more recently than their male colleagues, with as high as 37% holding such positions as recently as their third previous job, compared to only 14% of men. One could interpret this to mean that once entering the community college sector, women advanced to become

CFOs more quickly than men. Again, the numbers here were small so it would be appropriate to look more closely at this potential labor market issue than to draw decisive conclusions here.

Director of Continuing Education

Women Directors of Continuing Education (CE) were better represented in the respondent pool than in some other job categories we studied, but men still comprised 55% of the CEs. The mean age of CEs was 51 years old, and by degree earned, 65% held master's degrees and 30% held doctorates. Men CEs were twice as likely as women CEs to hold doctorates.

The career path of CEs were varied. Most held titles of director, coordinator, or manager of one or more educational programs such as economic development, continuing education, off-campus center, and nontraditional credit programs. Most held immediate past positions at community colleges (50% at the same community college and 8% at a different community college), and 13% came directly from private-sector jobs such as manager and center director. Twenty-nine percent of CEs had held private-sector jobs at least once in their careers, and 15% had worked in a public school, often as an adult educator.

On average, CEs were in their current positions for 7 years and a majority (58%) had worked at the same institution for 10 or more years, suggesting an internal labor market. Women were employed at the same college longer than men (15 versus 12 years), and men were more likely than women to have been in the community college sector already when promoted to CE (72% compared to 52%, respectively).

Occupational/Vocational Education Leaders

A unique contribution of our data set was the opportunity to look closely within the occupational/vocational education (OVE) division of community colleges to get a sense of career paths for those in charge of this organizational growth area. This allows for a more complete picture of this career path than was possible in the Moore et al. (1985) study, which did not present comparable data.

The terminology of career education has never been exact (Cohen & Brawer, 1996), and indeed the variety of job titles of our respondents reveals that career education still has many descriptors at community colleges, including vocational, occupational, professional, vo-tech, and workforce/career education. While job titles vary, as do career paths, this administrative position is marked by a lack of gender and ethnic diversity, similar to that found among CFOs. Occupational/Vocational Vice Presidents, Deans, and Directors were predominently male (70%), and only two people responding to the survey self-reported that they were people of color (1 Hispanic, 1 Native American). Respondents had a mean age of 53, and had served at their current institution an average of 14 years. Over 63% were in their current position for five years or less. Fifty-nine percent held a master's as the highest degree obtained (of which 9% had an MBA), while 37% held a doctorate; women were more likely than men to hold the terminal degree.

Over two-thirds of occupational/vocational leaders held their first previous position at community colleges, with 61% being employed at the same community college, and 23% moving from a different community college into their current position. Nineteen percent of respondents made lateral jumps inter- or intra-institutionally from a dean's position to their current position, and 41% were in traditional positions leading to dean or vice president (e.g., department chair or associate dean). Another large percentage (19%) advanced directly from instructor or faculty ranks. Few (5%) came from private sector jobs and few (5%) assumed their positions directly from a public school setting. The remainder of the occupational/vocational leaders held various other administrative responsibilities prior to their present position.

More complete career trajectories help illuminate the professional paths of occupational/vocational leaders. Twenty percent held positions at four-year colleges at some point in their careers, albeit for usually a short duration as a faculty member or adjunct instructor. Close to 50% had once served as community college faculty, 27% had public school experience, 9% had military backgrounds, and 11% had nursing or medical technology backgrounds. Perhaps surprising was the small number of respondents who indicated working in the private sector at some point in their career history. Eleven percent indicated jobs in the private sector as consultants, human resources managers, trainers, or engineers.

The small number of women in this position makes it difficult to generalize or even discuss the career trajectories into senior occupational/vocational positions. Some observations include that women respondents had fewer administrative positions in their career histories than their male counterparts and the majority of women had faculty/instructor, nursing, or public school teaching backgrounds. Closer examination of this position category over time is warranted to draw more substantive conclusions.

Discussion and Implications for Practice

Several points are worth reiterating that may affect leadership succession within community colleges and warrant further investigation.

Career Paths are Changing

Paths to the presidency are clearly changing. Prior presidential or other significant administrative experience is much more the norm than before, and this includes non-academic positions within higher education institutions other than the chief academic officer. Although the growth in administrative background is not quite as dominant among CAOs, it is still strong. This suggests that even when a president is hired from the position that most believe to be the traditional stepping stone, it is quite likely that the background of the new president is different than it was in 1985. Fewer presidents and senior leaders come with public school backgrounds, and the emergent administrative office positions that feed the presidency, such as occupational/vocational education officers, have quite varied backgrounds. Although administrators still build careers largely in the community college sector, there remains sufficient variation to suggest that movement between four-year and two-year colleges and between public and private sectors is more fluid than before (Moore, 1988). Further exploration of these differences is worthwhile to determine the impact, if any, on the perspectives, values, and the meaning of experiences of those entering the pool of potential presidents. As backgrounds of community college administrators change, so too might leadership priorities and understandings of current issues (as well as strategies to address them).

Rethink Assumptions About Searches

The Moore et al. study in 1985 spurred numerous recommendations to improve the diversity of hiring pools and methods by which they were generated (Moore, 1988; Twombly, 1986, 1988). We encourage hiring committees to think again about the assumptions they make in structuring administrative searches. Traditional assumptions for advertising open positions and generating candidate pools remain the norm and need reconsideration. Relying solely upon advertisements in *Community College Times, The Chronicle of Higher Education,* and *Community College Week,* and nominations from academics may be insufficient to fill senior positions. Headhunters, more common of late, and broader networks may be necessary to solicit interested candidates with the breadth and depth of experience required to lead community colleges—not only in the presidency but in other senior leadership positions as well. Community college boards of trustees, faculty, and administrative leaders are encouraged to rethink the structure of their administrative search processes.

Gender Differences

In many of the positions we studied, women were better represented than in 1985, although in some areas women remain severely underrepresented. Our data show in many cases that women reach a senior position earlier than men, but the gender age gap diminishes the more central the position. By the time a woman reaches the presidency, she may be the same age as a man if not older, given the rate of promotion.

Of particular note was the extent to which women were more strongly represented among CAOs compared to 1985. This would seem positive for increasing leadership diversity, but the advancement of women into presidencies is not yet the same as their male counterparts. Their relative lack of representation among emergent positions feeding the presidency is important in that, if the future path to the presidency shifts toward positions in which they are underrepresented (such as occupational/vocational education or CFOs), women (and people of color) may be again disadvantaged in promotions. Being mindful of organizational silos for white women and administrators of color, particularly in the senior student affairs area, seems important to avoid the trap of appearing to promote greater diversity in community college leadership, when in fact such positions remain at the periphery.

As noted throughout the study, we had hoped to be able to show a similar growth in the number of administrators of color across the senior positions. Although administrators of color who responded provided valuable information, the numbers were insufficient in most cases to conduct any specific analyses by race or ethnicity. Quite often, we found little substantive variation in career trajectory as explained by position title between men and women. Where administrators followed traditional academic administrative career paths (assistant, associate, dean/director), by and large the pattern held for men and women; where administrators' paths fell away from discernable patterns based on position titles, they fell away for both men and women. We had expected the paths of women to be different from the paths of men throughout the college hierarchy, especially given other research on college administrators; closer examination of other configurations of data is needed to see if more subtle differences emerge. For example, by examining only position paths, we did not account for how one becomes a candidate for a position or the reasons for taking the position. When looking at highest degrees earned, we did not examine whether an administrator received a terminal degree prior to significant promotions or after. Such factors related to career mobility, and factors such as mentoring and hiring practices, institutional policies, partners and family issues, and so forth all deserve further close examination. More complex analyses of the study data may provide better understanding of career enactment and the issues associated with it, than simply studying the series of jobs that make up one's resume (VanDerLinden & Amey, 2001).

Labor Market Observations

It appears that an internal labor market provides the dominant model of leader succession, if defined as being at the same institution for 10 years or more. This timeframe represented, on average, at least two inter-institutional job promotions and sometimes three across all job categories in our study. The exceptions to the dominant internal labor market were presidents and chief academic officers, whose pathways indicated a mixed internal/external labor market.

Conclusion

Much has changed nationally in the 20 years since the Moore et al. (1985) study. Enrollment growth has continued unabated—by the fall of 1999, 10.4 million students were enrolled at publicly controlled community colleges, of whom nearly half, 5.0 million, were enrolled in noncredits courses. Perhaps we should expect that community colleges would appear to be opening their doors to administrative leadership in newer ways than they did in their early "great man" years. Yet, as represented in these data, there is much work to be done in generating diverse candidate pools for senior positions, in preparing younger generations of administrators with the skills and experiences that assist in promotion, and in promoting equity for the most senior positions. Boards of trustees and internal faculty and administrative search committees need education regarding changing definitions of requisite experiences for leadership and new definitions of leaders. Succession planning suggests a reason to more fully understand the labor market and career trajectories, so that false assumptions are not the basis of future hiring and personnel policies and decisions. It is hoped that by providing a clearer picture of pathways to senior level administrations in community colleges, this contributes to that under standing.

Notes

[1] The study was originally supported with funding from the Center for the Study of Advanced Learning Systems and the Office of University Outreach, University Provost's Office, Michigan State University.

References

Amey, M. J. (1999). Navigating the raging river: Reconciling issues of identity, inclusion and administrative practice. In K. M. Shaw, J. R. Valadez, & R. A. Rhoads (Eds.), *Community colleges as cultural texts: Qualitative explorations of organizational and student cultures* (pp. 59- 82). Albany, NY. SUNY Press.

Amey, M., & Twombly, S. (1992). Re-visioning leadership in community colleges. *The Review of Higher Education, 15*(2), 125–150.

Cohen, A., & Brawer, F. (1996). *The American community college.* San Francisco: Jossey-Bass.

DiCroce, D. (1995). Women and the community college presidency. In B. K. Townsend (Ed.), *Gender and power in the community college.* New Directions for Community Colleges, No. 89 (pp. 79–88). San Francisco: Jossey-Bass.

Duderstadt, J. (2000). *A university for the 21st century.* Ann Arbor, MI: University of Michigan Press.

Hockaday, J., & Puyear, D. (2000). *Community college leadership in the new millenium.* New Expeditions Issues Paper No. 8. Washington, DC: Community College Press, American Association of Community Colleges.

Moore, K. M. (1988). Administrative careers: Multiple pathways to leadership positions. In M. F. Green (Ed.), *Leaders for a new era: Strategies for higher education* (pp. 159–180). New York: American Council on Education and MacMillan.

Moore, K., Martorana, S. V., & Twombly, S. (1985). *Today's academic leaders: A national study of administrators in two-year colleges.* University Park, PA: Center for the Study of Higher Education.

Pierce, D. R., & Pedersen, R. P. (1997). The community college presidency: Qualities for success. In I. Weissman & G. Vaughan (Eds.), *Presidents and trustees in partnership:* New roles and leadership challenges. New Directions for Community Colleges, No. 98. San Francisco: Jossey-Bass, 13–20.

Townsend, B. (1995). *Gender and power in the community college.* New Directions for Community Colleges, No. 89. San Francisco: Jossey-Bass.

Twombly, S. (1986). Boundaries of an administrative labor market. *Community College Review,* 13, 34–44.

Twombly, S. (1988). Administrative labor markets. *Journal of Higher Education, 59* (6), 668–689.

Twombly, S. B. (1995). Gendered images of community college leadership: What messages they send. In B. K. Townsend (Ed.), *Gender and power in the community college.* New Directions for Community Colleges, No. 89 (pp. 67–78). San Francisco: Jossey-Bass.

Vaughan, G. B. (1990). *Pathways to the presidency: Community college deans of instruction.* Washington, DC: The Community College Press.

VanDerLinden, K., & Amey, M. (2001). *Women administrators: Their investments in human capital.* Paper presented at the annual meeting for the Association for the Study of Higher Education, Richmond, VA.

Winship, S. W., & Amey, M. J. (1992). Gender differences in the position pathing of community college presidents. *American Association of Women in Community and Junior Colleges Journal,* 21–25.

CHAPTER 16

AFRICAN AMERICAN STUDENT AFFAIRS PROFESSIONALS IN COMMUNITY COLLEGE SETTINGS: A COMMENTARY FOR FUTURE RESEARCH

EBONI M. ZAMANI, PH.D.

Abstract

Student affairs is one facet within colleges and universities that is generally thought to be at the forefront in responding to the changing nature of collegiate life. Correspondingly, student affairs practitioners are expected to provide for a host of various student backgrounds. Although the role of student affairs continues to expand as two- and four-year institutions are more heterogeneously populated, little is known about African American student affairs professionals in two-year settings. This commentary provides an overview of the extant literature concerning postsecondary participation of African American students as well as the role and functions of student affairs in community college settings with particular attention paid to African American student affairs professionals.

As the landscape of higher education is presently shifting due to increasing diversity among college students, two-year institutions[1] have been responsive in opening the doors to postsecondary study for diverse student groups (Cohen & Brawer, 2002; Dungy, 1999). While access may be readily granted via community college's open admissions, the full promotion of student success and learning (particularly among commonly marginalized groups) is debatable (Brint & Karabel, 1989; Dougherty, 1994). Higher education personnel in student affairs[2] roles are frequently charged with facilitating the social, developmental, and academic needs of diverse students. It is hard to ignore the difficulty of reaching all college students because racially/ethnically diverse student affairs professionals are few and far between (Stewart, Russell & Wright, 1997; Turrentine & Conley, 2001) often making the learning context intricate, less inclusive, and more difficult to navigate for students of color (e.g., transition, retention, and matriculation).

Given the multiplicity of needs and range of postsecondary participants, greater consideration should be paid to student affairs in concert with staff diversity (Jackson & Flowers, in press). Ideally, faculty and support staff would mirror the overall student body. Yet despite the demographic shifts of those currently enrolled, there continues to be disproportionately low numbers of faculty and administrative leaders from racially/ethnically diverse backgrounds (Amey & VanDerLinden, 2001; Colby & Foote, 1995).

Recent research has indicated a looming leadership crisis facing two-year institutions of higher education due to impending retirements (American Association of Community Colleges, 2002; Amey & VanDerLinden, 2001; Shults, 2001). Although the approaching retirements before community colleges are distressing, this projected deficit is fundamentally disconcerting when coupled with an overrepresentation of African American students in community colleges and a paucity of African American faculty, mid-level and senior student affairs administrators in the pipeline. Furthermore, Shults (2001) suggests that not only is the pool of leaders thin, but programs specializing in two-year issues in addition to promoting the professional development of community college leaders are lacking.

Student services are thought to be one of the top priorities at an institution that merges academic and student affairs functions in providing comprehensive educational programs for students (Deegan, 1982; Flynn, 1986; Ender, Chand, & Thornton, 1996; Kellogg, 1999). Student services are important contributors to the success of students given the capacity to enhance campus life and college environment, especially for those from marginalized and underrepresented groups (Jackson, 2002). This commentary sought to advance a research agenda focused on African Americans in student affairs at two-year institutions. This is important, because little over two-fifths of African American students enroll in community colleges annually (Phillippe & Patton, 2000). Concurrently, this commentary sought to address how critical involvement of African American student affairs professionals is for student advancement.

Students, Faculty and Administrative Leadership in Community Colleges

During the last five to ten years, estimates of minorities enrolled in two-year institutions have ranged from 30 to 47%[3] (Cohen & Brawer, 2002; Phillippe & Patton, 2000; Rendon & Hope, 1996). Two-year institutions have long been the institution students of color have looked to as the conduit to higher education, particularly those who may not otherwise gain admittance to college due to financial constraints, family obligations, ill preparedness, and/or proximity. The open admissions policies of community colleges guarantee access with the expressed purpose of helping students succeed in meeting whatever the educational goal (Zamani, in press). Focusing on African American college enrollment over the last two decades, approximately 43% of African Americans were attending a public or private two-year institution in 1980; by 1999 that figure fell slightly to 41%.

While there are 14 historically Black community colleges, predominantly White two-year institutions register the preponderance of African American community college attendees (Guyden, 1999). Further, greater numbers of African American faculty and staff are found at historically Black Colleges and Universities (HBCUs) in contrast to those employed at predominantly White institutions (Fleming, 1985). Literature examining campus climate and institutional culture posits that the environment at predominantly White institutions is often not thought to be inclusive of racial/ethnic minority students (Hurtado, Milem, & Clayton-Pedersen, 1999; Stewart, Russell, & Wright, 1997). HBCUs are generally considered to have a better campus ecology (e.g., more inclusive and nurturing) for African American students (Brown, 1998; Brown & Davis, 2001). Studies have supported the idea of acknowledging cultural differences as they can be a powerful means of socialization in acclimating to a new educational environment as well as the importance of the person-environment fit (Kee, 1999; Laden, 1999). One way of affirming African American students' sense of belonging is through active recruitment

TABLE 1
African American Public and Private Two-year College Enrollment and Degrees Conferred by Selected Years

	1980	1990	1999	Total Associate Degrees 1996-97
African American				
Public Two-year	437,900	481,400	637,700	41,532
Private Two-year	34,600	42,900	41,000	

Source: Phillippe & Patton (2000) and U.S. Department of Education (1999)

and consistent staffing of diverse professionals in academic and student affairs (Zamani, 2000). Nonetheless, open to discussion is whether community colleges in keeping with their commitment to admit large percentages of African American students, have been as steadfast in hiring and promoting African American faculty leaders or student affairs officers.

Nearly 13% of faculty of color are employed at public four-year institutions and fewer than 3% of faculties of color are at private two-year institutions (Colby & Foote, 1995). However, in searching the NCES report generated on Fall Staff in Postsecondary Institutions 1997, information specifically detailing professional and/or nonprofessional status by race/ethnicity, gender or institutional type was not available, though percentages of full-time faculty participation presented by race/ethnicity were included. It is important to note that African American student affairs professionals comprise 8.4% of the total number of those in student affairs administrative positions. However, an estimated 11.7% of the total population of African American student affairs administrators are employed at community colleges (Jackson, 2003).

In concentrating on African American administrators, it is essential to note while student diversity is at its peak in community colleges, there is a disproportionately lower representation of full-time faculty and administrators of color making two-year colleges, like their four-year counterparts, not representative of the students served. This further exacerbates the crisis in the profession of furnishing leaders that can serve as role models for a more diverse student population (Martinez, 1991; Vaughan, 1996).

Research on Student Affairs Personnel and African Americans

While research on the role of student affairs in two-year colleges is limited, studies examining African American professionals in student services are virtually nonexistent. Then again, the dearth of research and national data available disclose that the overwhelming majority of faculty as well as chief student affairs administrators are White males. Whether or not this can be attributed to a lack of concern as related to diversity of student services personnel and/or no responsiveness to meeting the needs of students of color is arguable but in desperate need of change.

Student services is one segment of community colleges where students can feel a sense of belonging, be culturally affirmed, and have their academic aspirations fueled (Becherer & Becherer, 1995; Laden, 1999). Student affairs professionals should be more cognizant of the cultural, economic, and social barriers that face African American students in postsecondary education, particularly those endemic to African American males (Cuyjet, 1997). Research-to-date suggests alternative methods are needed for constructing experiences that bear greater utility for students of color (Brown, 1998; Fleming, 1985; Mattox & Creamer, 1998; Poock, 2000; Rendon & Hope, 1996). Some examples of making student affairs more comprehensive and tailoring programs for African American college students include: (1) organizing services to smooth the progress of African American students (i.e., recruitment, retention, advising, etc.); (2) evaluating program effectiveness and (3) responsiveness for all student groups, in addition to mentoring and fostering relationships with students as they may have difficulty making transitions to college (Stewart, Russell, & Wright, 1997; Zamani, 2000).

Relative to college transition, Grubb (1999) reported that up to 80% of high school graduates entering community colleges require remedial education in at least one of three areas (i.e., English, Math, and Reading). Also worthy of mention is the fact that African American college students are disproportionately placed in remedial courses at a higher rate than their White counterparts (Shaw, 1997). Often the assessment of whether students are college ready (i.e., course placement services) falls under the auspices of student affairs divisions. Wagener and Lazerson (1995, p. 60) noted, "Staff members in student services argue that students have become their responsibility by the default of the faculty . . ." (As cited in Ender, Newton, & Caple, 1996). Besides, when it comes to curricular matters in two-year institutions student affairs professionals have customarily had a minimal role in the planning process (Barke, 1999; Ender, Chand, & Thornton, 1996; Freas, 1987; Kellogg, 1999). For that reason there is confusion, reluctance, and resistance on the part of faculty and student affairs professionals to interact in ways that do not portray the other as the enemy. Accordingly, it is inconclusive as to whether student affairs can successfully impact the learning of under prepared college students or be willing to assume the responsibility for doing so.

Burley and Butner (2000) surveyed 180 senior student affairs officers at community colleges regarding what degree of involvement student affairs should have in remediation. Sixty percent completed usable surveys yielding 108 respondents, of which the vast majority were White, male, with an average age of 49 years old. The findings illustrated among occupying senior student affairs positions, people of color, females and those under age 49, expressed greater favor toward involvement in remediation efforts. Perhaps senior student affairs administrators of color found remedial education to be a relevant responsibility for student services divisions given the disproportionately higher percentage of African American college students in remedial education in contrast to White students (Lewis & Greene, 1996). Student affairs services are crucial in nurturing African American student retention and matriculation at the community college and beyond. Having African Americans in the role of senior student affairs officer as well as other student affairs positions could further influence and support the progress of students. Not to suggest that at the absence of African American student affairs professionals that African Americans are not receiving the educational necessities; however, research has illustrated that African American students have a higher degree of academic growth, a greater sense of belonging, and receive degrees at greater rate where larger numbers of African American faculty and administrators are employed (Brown, 1998; Brown & Davis, 2001; Fleming, 1985).

Opp (2001) assessed how to enhance recruitment success for community college students of color merging data from the National Center for Education Statistics (NCES) with national survey data of senior student affairs officers on recruitment barriers and strategies for student of color. He found statistical significance that supports urban two-year institutions and those having a senior student affairs officer of color being better positioned in drawing students of color. Even more telling was Opp's reporting of the percentages of administrators and faculty of color plus the quantity of contact senior student affairs officers have with racially/ethnically diverse students; both were found to be the strongest predictors of increasing the proportion of students of color as community colleges with greater numbers of faculty and administrators of color interact more with students of color and create a climate that is perceived to be inclusive by diverse students, Nevertheless, in this study and previous literature, specific information regarding the impact of African American student affairs professionals on African American student enrollment growth and two-year campus climate were not explicitly examined.

Changing of the Guard? Threats to Leadership Continuity

Much of what is symbolic and expressed in terms of an educational organizations' culture and climate is greatly shaped by the leaders at the helm of the institution. In the very near future, community colleges will witness a transformation relative to leadership or lack thereof (Amey & VanDerLinden, 2001). It is anticipated that the number of projected community college leaders retiring from upper-level management (e.g., senior level administrators and faculty leaders) and presidential positions will far exceed those with the requisite skill set and credentials for assuming vacant administrative posts (American Association of Community Colleges, 2002). According to Christopher Shults (2001), the following trends are occurring nationally:

- More than two-fifths of current presidents intend to retire by 2007

- The average age of community college presidents is increasing (e.g., 51 years of age in 1986 and 57 years old by 1998)

- There has been a 78% decrease in the number of advanced graduate degrees in community college administration from 1982 to 1997

- In 1999, over half of faculty ages 55 to 64 reported plans to retire by 2004

The aforementioned data coupled with little diversity among senior administrators, increasingly diverse student bodies and many new community college presidents reportedly feeling unprepared for effectively carrying out key functions of presidential administration leaves the future of two-year leadership in peril. With the doctorate increasingly becoming the preferred if not required degree for community college senior-level administrative posts and presidential positions, partial responsibility for producing a critical mass of community college leaders falls on graduate degree granting institutions.

Recruiting and Promoting African American Student Affairs Administrators at Community Colleges

In terms of the characteristics of community college leaders, research by Amey and VanDer-Linden (2001) examined the career paths and backgrounds of community college leaders finding that women and minorities were underrepresented in administrative posts and suggesting that aspiring college leaders have an earned doctorate. Advanced graduate study is mounting in importance for individuals that desire upper-level administrative positions and/or the community college presidency (Vaughn, 1996). In looking at African American students' choice to enroll in higher education administration doctoral programs, Poock (2000) examined seven doctoral programs (across institutional types and regions) in higher education surveying African American students that began doctoral study between fall 1995 and fall 1996 yielding a total net sample of 390. The study had a 46% survey return rate with a total of 180 students responding.

Five major themes emerged and were identified as important factors influencing their decision to apply and subsequently attend doctoral study in higher education administration: (1) a seamless process from application to admission and attendance; (2) highly rated program quality (e.g., school standing, program reputation, rigor and faculty expertise); (3) an academic infrastructure that supports student progress in the degree program (e.g., library collections, technological facilities, and flexible course offerings); (4) an environment or climate at the institution that is sensitive to the needs of students of color and invites input from students; and (5) positive encounters with faculty that are suggestive of a welcoming departmental culture. In sum, the findings of Poock's study indicate that the recruitment process clearly should accentuate all of the above in successfully attracting African American students in undertaking doctoral study in higher education administration/community college leadership.

Although many leadership posts in two-year colleges are expected to be available in the near future, the specific figures for student affairs positions (particularly for senior-level officers) have not been projected. Rapp (1997) ascertained that racial/ethnic minorities are underrepresented in student affairs offices, particularly in senior positions. Even so, one has to be presented with a point of entry before rising to a senior level position in a student affairs division.

The pipeline of available African American candidates has not been fully tapped as there is still a lack of African American administrators. Turrentine and Conley (2001) studied the diversity of the labor pool for entry-level utilizing multiple data sources (i.e., IPEDS data, and survey of ACPA/NASPA on-line directories of student affairs preparation programs in higher education administration, counseling education, and college student personnel). Sixty programs responded to the survey stemming from the ACPA/NASPA on-line directories. The total master's level enrollment in 1998–1999 for those 60 programs was 2,289. Nationally, African Americans were 15.4% of the total students enrolled in student affairs programs. Their findings imply that the small pool of racially/ethnically diverse professionals do not correspond with the projected growth of minority undergraduate student groups, particularly when considering the uneven enrollment of African American students in two-year versus four-year institutions.

Implications for Research and Practice in Student Affairs

This commentary explored the functions of student affairs in community colleges and addressed the paucity of literature examining African American student affairs administrators. While there is evidence to indicate that student personnel services are critical in African American student recruitment, retention, and matriculation, research has also revealed the significance of having senior student affairs officers that are persons of color in mitigating the many factors that present barriers to students of color in two-year colleges. The literature points to inclusive campus climates as crucial in helping African American students reach their goals. Likewise, institutional culture and climate are gravely important in attracting, retaining, and advancing African American administrators within student affairs divisions or other campus units.

Two- and four-year colleges concerned with the growing diversity of students should be distressed with the disproportionate number of African Americans and other racial/ethnic minority groups in leadership positions. More than a decade ago, Brown and Globetti (1991) surveyed the perceptions and experiences of 42 African American student affairs professionals. The participants of their study expressed support for affirmative action programs and policies as a means of remedying hiring inequities and felt that their colleges were being proactive in appealing to candidates of color.

Taking into consideration the small number of studies that specifically look at issues surrounding African American student affairs professionals, particularly in two-year settings, it becomes obvious that more models are needed of institutions with proven success as witnessed in the philosophy, programs and policies that insure African American administrators are seriously regarded as valuable to the whole academic community (Jackson, 2002; Jackson & Flowers, in press; Martinez, 1991). Perhaps through scrutinizing multiple data sources a more complete picture of African American student affairs professionals can be attained. To date, no fine distinctions can be drawn from this small number of African American student affairs professionals in two-year institutions (e.g., public versus private or for-profit colleges, professional staff designations and primary responsibilities, salary, years of experience, and career ladder).

National professional groups such as American Association of Community Colleges (AACC), American College Personnel Association (ACPA), National Association for Student Affairs Professionals (NASAP) and the National Association of Student Personnel Administrators (NASPA) are avenues that could be tapped in voicing as well as actively addressing the concerns regarding the dearth of diversity in student affairs. Each of these organizations has subgroups or components that address student affairs in a two-year context. More should be done using these professional associations to further student affairs research.

In sum, as this topic is under researched, greater social inquiry on student affairs practice in two-year institutions is needed to further enlighten the supportive role this unit plays at these campuses, and approaches to creating more opportunities for African Americans aspiring higher leadership positions at community colleges. As there is little empirical scholarship on this topic, research is needed on several important issues related to the nature of student affairs work and African American administrators at community colleges including but not limited to the following:

- Research that pays greater attention to programs and services for special populations and underrepresented students in correspondence with institutional efforts to achieve administrative diversity at two-year colleges would extend the extant literature.

- Studies constructed to examine the impact of changing legislation and the effects of affirmative action policies on identifying and recruiting African Americans to administrative positions in student affairs divisions in two- and four-year institutions would prove timely given the present public discourse.

- Additionally, inquiry that advances theoretical perspectives and assesses the heuristic value of previous models investigating the influence of African American student affairs administrators on African American student gains, retention, graduation and transfer rates.

Given the dearth of available information and the small numbers of African Americans in leadership positions at two-year colleges, greater attention should be paid to leadership development opportunities and graduate programs in advancing effective student affairs leaders and staff. Moreover, community college presidents should give more consideration to determining how to attract more persons of color to senior student affairs officer roles, which in turn illustrates an institutional commitment to diversity and promoting an inclusive educational environment for students and staff. Lastly, it is important for African American student affairs professionals in two-year colleges to move from the margins to mattering in educational research. By initiating studies that explicitly gauge the experiences of community college African American student affairs professionals, we can better determine if, and how, the unique needs of African American students at these institutions are being served.

Notes

[1]In this paper, two-year institutions are used interchangeably with community colleges.

[2]In this paper, student affairs is used interchangeably with student personnel services and student services.

[3]Estimates may vary across sources due to some enrollment data for all selected years not covering accredited degree-granting institutions eligible to participate in federal student aid programs or recognizing enrollment status.

References

American Association of Community Colleges (2002). *AACC Professional Development: Characteristics of Community College Leaders*. Retrieved on September 12, 2002 from http://www.aacc.nche.edu/Content/NavigationMenu?ResourceCenter/LeadershipProgram

Amey, M. J., & VanDerLinden, K. E. (2001). *Career paths for community college leaders, leadership series report no. 2*. Washington, DC: American Association of Community Colleges.

Barke, V. (1999 April). The path of least resistance: Programming with academic support on two-year campuses. *Campus Activities Programming*, 62–65.

Becherer, J. J. & Becherer, J. H. (1995). Programs, services, and activities: A survey of the community college landscape. *New Directions for Student Services, 69*, 63–75.

Brint, S., & Karabel, J. (1989). *The diverted dream: Community colleges and the promise of educational opportunity in America, 1900–1985*. New York: Oxford University.

Brown, C. L., & Globetti, E. C. (1991). Perceptions and experiences of African-American student affairs professionals. *College Student Affairs Journal, 11*(2), 3–10.

Brown, II, M. C. (1998). African American college student retention and the ecological psychology of historically Black colleges. *NASAP Journal*, 50–66.

Brown, II, M. C., & Davis, J. E. (2001). The historically Black college as social contract, social capital, and social equalizer. *Peabody Journal of Education, 76*, 31–49.

Burley, H. E., & Butner, B. K. (2000). Should student affairs offer remedial education? *Community College Journal of Research and Practice, 24*, 193–205.

Caple, R. B. (1996). Student affairs professionals as learning consultants. *New Directions for Student Services, 75*, 33–43.

Cohen, A. M., & Brawer, F. B. (2002). *The American community college, 4th edition*. San Francisco, CA: Jossey-Bass.

Colby, A. & Foote, E. (1995). *Creating and maintaining a diverse faculty, ERIC Digest*. Los Angeles, CA: ERIC Clearinghouse for Community Colleges. (ERIC Documents Reproduction Service No. ED386261)

Cuyjet, M.J. (1997). African American men on college campuses: Their needs and their perceptions. *New Directions for Student Services, 80*, 5–16.

Deegan, W. L. (1982). *The management of student affairs programs in community colleges: Revamping processes and structures, Horizons issues monograph series*. Washington, DC: American Association of Community Colleges (ERIC Documents Reproduction Service No. ED223297).

Dougherty, K. J. (1994). *The contradictory college: The conflicting origins, impacts, and future of the community college*. New York: State University of New York.

Dungy, G. J. (1999). View from community colleges. *New Directions for Student Services, 85*, 33–45.

Ender, K. L., Chand, S., & Thornton, J. S. (1996). Student affairs in community college: Promoting student success and learning. *New Directions for Student Services, 75*, 45–53.

Ender, S. C., Newton, F. B., & Caple, R. B., (1996). Contributions to learning: Present realities. *New Directions for Student Services, 75*, 5–17.

Fleming, J. (1995). *Blacks in college*. San Francisco, CA: Jossey-Bass.

Flynn, R. T. (1986). The emerging role for community college student affairs personnel. *NASPA Journal, 24*, 36–42.

Fress, H. J. (1987). *The role of student affairs personnel in curriculum planning in the community college curriculum*. Unpublished thesis, Nova University (ERIC Documents Reproduction Service No. ED284141).

Grubb, W. N. (1999). *Honored but invisible*. New York: Routlege.

Guyden, J. A. (1999). *Two-year historically Black colleges*. In B. K. Townsend (Ed.), *Two-year colleges for women and minorities: Enabling access to the baccalaureate* (pp. 85–112). New York: Falmer Press.

Hurtado, S., Milem, J. F., & Clayton-Pedersen, A. (1999). *Enacting diverse learning environments: Improving the climate for racial/ethnic diversity in higher education*. Washington, DC: ASHE-ERIC Higher Education Report.

Jackson, J.F.L. (2003). Engaging, retaining, and advancing African Americans in student affairs administration: An analysis of employment status. *NASAP Journal, 6*(1), 9–24.

Jackson, J. F. L. (2002 Fall). Retention of African American administrators at predominantly White institutions: Using professional growth factors to inform the discussion. *C & U*, 11–15.

Jackson, J. F. L. & Flowers, L. A. (in press). Retaining African American student affairs administrators: Voices from the field. *Journal of College Student Affairs, 22*.

Kee, A. M. (1999). *Campus climate: Perceptions, policies and programs in community colleges*. Washington,

DC: American Association of Community Colleges (ERIC Documents Reproduction Service No. ED430597).

Kellogg, K. (1999). *Collaboration: Student affairs and academic affairs working together to promoted student learning, ERIC Digest.* Los Angeles, CA: ERIC Clearinghouse for Community Colleges (ERIC Documents Reproduction Service No. ED432940).

Laden. B. V. (1999). Celebratory socialization of culturally diverse students through academic program and support services. In K. M. Shaw, J. R. Valadez and R. A. Rhoads (Eds.) *Community colleges as cultural texts: Qualitative explorations of organizational student culture,* 173–194. New York: State University of New York Press, Albany.

Lewis, L., Farris, E., & Greene, B. (1996, October). *Remedial education at higher education institutions in fall 1995.* Washington, D.C.: U.S. Department of Education.

Martinez, R. L., Jr. (1991). A crisis in the profession: Minority role models in critically short supply. *Vocational Education Journal, 66,* 24–25, 46.

Mattox, R. E., & Creamer, D. G. (1998). Perceptions of the scope and quality of student services functions in two-year colleges. *Community College Review, 25*(4), 3–20.

Opp, R. D. (2001). Enhancing recruitment success for two-year college students of color. *Community College Journal of Research and Practice, 25,* 71–86.

Phillippe, K., & Patton, M. (2000). *National profile of community colleges: Trends and statistics, 3rd edition.* Washington, D.C.: Community College Press.

Poock, M. C. (2000). African American students and the decision to attend doctoral programs in higher education administration. *College Student Affairs Journal, 19,* 51–60.

Rapp, J. L. (1997). Staff diversity: The need for enhancing minority participation in student affairs. *College Student Affairs Journal, 16*(2), 73–84.

Rendon, L. I., & Hope, R. O. (1996). *Educating a new majority: Transforming American's educational system for diversity.* San Francisco, CA: Jossey-Bass.

Shaw, K. (1997). Remedial education as ideological battleground: Emerging remedial education policies in the community college. *Educational Evaluation and Policy Analysis, 19*(3), 284–296.

Shults, C. (2001). *The critical impact of impending retirements on community college leadership* (Research Brief 01–5). Washington, D.C.: American Association of Community Colleges.

Stewart, G. L., Russell, R. B., & Wright, D. (1997). The comprehensive role of student affairs in African-American student retention. *Journal of College Admission, 154,* 6–11.

Turrentine, C. G., & Conley, V. M. (2001). Two measures of the diversity of the labor pool for entry-level student affairs positions. *NASPA Journal, 39,* 84–102.

U.S. Department of Education (1999). College enrollment by racial and ethnic group, selected years. Retrieved August 30, 2002 from http://www.ed.gov.

Vaughan, G. B. (1996). Paradox and promise: Leadership and the neglected minorities. *New Directions for Community Colleges, 94,* 5–12.

Zamani, E. M. (2000). Sources and information regarding effective retention strategies for students of color. *New Directions for Community Colleges, 112*(4), 95–104.

Zamani, E. M. (in press). Affirmative action attitudes of African American community college students: The impact of educational aspirations, self-interest and racial affect. In C. Camp Yeakey, R. D. Henderson, and M. Shujaa (Series Eds.), *Research on African American Education,* Volume One. Greenwich, CT: Information Age Publishing, Inc.

CHAPTER 17

RECOMMENDED READING AND WEB-BASED RESOURCES

Recommended Reading

Anderson, P., Murray, J. P., & Olivarez, Jr., A. (2002). The managerial roles of public community college chief academic officers. *Community College Review, 30*(2), 1–26.

DiCroce, D. M. (1995). Women and the community college presidency: Challenges and possibilities. In B. Townsend (Ed.), *Gender and power in the community college. New Directions for Community Colleges,* Vol. 89 (pp. 79–88). San Francisco: Jossey-Bass.

Floyd, D. (2003). Distance learning in community colleges: Leadership challenges for change and development. *Community College Journal of Research and Practice, 27,* 337–347.

Kempner, K. (2003). The search for cultural leaders. *Review of Higher Education, 26*(3), 363–385.

Marcus, L. R. (1999). Professional associations and student affairs policy. *Journal of College Student Development, 40*(1), 22–31.

Miller, M. T. (1999). The department chair as speaker of the house: Shared authority in the community college department. *Community College Journal of Research and Practice, 23,* 739–74.

Vaughan, G. B., & Weisman, I. M. (1997). Selected characteristics of community college trustees and presidents. In I. M. Weisman, & G. Vaughan (Eds.), *Presidents and trustees in partnership* (pp. 5–12). New Directions for Community Colleges, No. 98. San Francisco: Jossey-Bass.

Web-Based Resources

American Association for Community Colleges. (2003). *Summary analysis: 2003 community college tuition survey.* Washington, DC: Author. http://www.aacc.nche.edu/Template.cfm?Section=NewsandEvents& template=/ ContentManagement/ContentDisplay.cfm&ContentID=11101&InterestCategoryID=272.

Amey, M. J., & VanDerLinden, K. E. (2001). *Career paths for community college leaders.* Research Brief. Leadership Series, No. 3. Washington, D.C.: Community College Press. http://www.aacc.nche.edu/Template.cfm? Section=Research_Briefs&template=/ContentManagement/ContentDisplay.cfm&ContentID=9440&Interest CategoryID=221&Name=Research%20Brief&ComingFrom=InterestDisplay

Education Commission for the States. (2000). *State funding for community colleges: A 50-state survey.* Denver, CO: Author. http://www.communitycollegepolicy.org/pdf/CC%20Finance%20Survey.pdf

Getskow, V. (1996). *Women in community college leadership roles.* ERIC Digest. ED400025. Los Angeles, CA: ERIC Clearinghouse for Community Colleges. http://www.ericdigests.org/1997-2/women.htm

National Center for Education Statistics. (2002). *Enrollment in postsecondary institutions, fall 2001, and financial statistics, fiscal year 2001.* NCES 2004-155. Washington, DC: Author. http://nces.ed.gov/pubs2004/ 2004155.pdf

Plecha, M. (2003). *Community college tuition and financial aid: Current trends.* EDO-JC-03-010. http://www.gseis.ucla.edu/ccs/digests/digest0310.htm

Walker, K. L. (2001). *Facing challenges: Identifying the role of the community college dean. ERIC Digest.* ED441551. Los Angeles, CA: ERIC Clearinghouse for Community Colleges. http://www.ericdigests.org/2001-1/dean.html

Weisman, I. M., & Vaughan, G. B. (2001). *The community college presidency, 2001.* Research Brief. Leadership Series, No. 3 Washington, D.C.: Community College Press. http://www.aacc.nche.edu/Template.cfm?Section= Research_Briefs& template=/ContentManagement/Content Display. cfm&ContentID=8185&InterestCategoryID=221 &Name=Research%20Brief&ComingFrom=Interest Display

Part IV

CURRICULAR MISSIONS

INTRODUCTION

DEBRA D. BRAGG

As community colleges evolved over the past century they evidenced an increasingly comprehensive curricular mission. Beginning at the turn of the century with a primary focus on liberal arts and transfer, the curriculum of junior colleges continued to expand and diversify. Quite early, vocational education gained momentum and by mid-century assumed a prominent place in the curriculum of many two-year colleges (Brint & Karabel, 1989). While instruction in the liberal arts and sciences (also referred to as academics or academic education) and vocational education continued to be central to the evolutionary development of community college curricula, other foci emerged, including continuing education and remedial education. Credit as well as non-credit courses proliferated, utilizing various pedagogical approaches and instructional formats to address the learning needs of their increasingly diverse students. The developments have been so extensive that today's community colleges arguably offer the most expansive curriculum of any type of higher education institution in the United States today.

In looking at the community college, strong parallels exist between the way curriculum is categorized and described in the literature generally (see, for example, Cohen & Brawer, 2003) and what Dougherty has described in various writings (see particularly Dougherty, 1994) and again in this Reader as the functionalist perspective. Drawing on functionalist theory, Dougherty observes the mission of the community college is complimentary to other social and educational institutions, most importantly secondary schools, universities, and businesses. This complimentarity plays out in different ways with different implications. For example, universities benefit from community colleges offering the first two years of undergraduate curriculum and thus diverting students who are unfocused or unprepared for college. The effect is that universities institute selective admission policies to teach their high-achieving students while open-access community colleges offer an array of curricula to educate their highly diverse students. Though controversial, the historic and complimentary relationship between community colleges and universities allows each to develop its own unique agenda. The unique mix of students and stakeholders that community colleges serve and are accountable to shapes their curricular missions in important ways. By gaining a deeper and more nuanced understanding of curricular missions, scholars, policy makers and practitioners alike can come to understand that community colleges have their own legitimate place in higher education and that they can and should set their own course for the future, both complimentary to and independent of other forms of higher education.

The literature chosen for this section of the reader gives a sense of the distinctive curricular missions of modern-day community colleges. Much of the chosen literature examines curricular foci familiar to scholars and students of the community college, offering definitions and perspectives independent of the rest of higher education. Though there is a plethora of literature examining various aspects of curriculum, very little research examines curriculum in a systematic fashion. Several sources devote attention to different facets of community college curriculum, including Cohen and Brawer's (2003) *The American Community College,* Grubb and Associates' (1999) *Honored but Invisible,* and Townsend and Twomby's (2001) *Community Colleges: Policy in the Future Context.* Yet none of these texts claim to offer a comprehensive treatment of curriculum; they primarily explore policies and practices pertaining to transfer, vocational education and remediation. Further, several volumes of *New Directions for Community Colleges* provide insights into curricular missions, including recent texts on remedial education (Kozeracki, 2005), transfer (Townsend, 1999), the new vocationalism (Bragg, 2001), and Schuyler's (2000) volume on curriculum trends, including chapters on liberal arts and non-liberal arts. Extremely valuable, each of these texts provides useful descriptions of the curriculum as it exists today.

Nine publications comprise this section of the Reader on curricular missions. All publications selected for this section have relevance to the core curriculum, yet each offers new insights, poses new questions, and suggests new ways of thinking about community college curriculum than was evident only a few years ago. The first two writings focus on the curricular mission most aligned with traditional undergraduate education, focusing on preparing students to transfer to the university or continue at the community college in pursuit of the bachelor's degree. The next two articles offer new insights into vocational education and related forms of education and training offered to nontraditional students through non-credit courses. Two articles on remedial and developmental education follow, examining organization of remedial instruction and support services with respect to student learning, stigmatization and student marginalization. Finally three articles look deeper at curriculum, exploring courses, classrooms and alternative delivery modes as means of understanding what community colleges do to promote teaching and learning and enhance access to high quality learning experiences for students.

This section begins with an article by Barbara Townsend (2001) titled "Redefining the Community College Transfer Mission" (Chapter 18). Townsend's article reminds us that, at the beginning, community colleges—then junior colleges—cut their teeth on the transfer function. Recognizing that curriculum offered when junior colleges first formed was far narrower than today, Townsend introduces a comprehensive range of definitions of transfer that open our thinking to how students' aspirations to attend college translate into behavior. Understanding that transfer is more complex today than the "upwardly vertical" movement that defined it at the start, Townsend points out the fallacy in defining transfer in only one way: beginning at community colleges and culminating at universities. For some time and certainly today, college

students move between colleges and universities as they pursue their undergraduate education, sometimes beginning at community colleges but sometimes starting at universities and reversing direction (hence reverse transfer) to attend the community college. For a growing number of students the transfer process takes an entirely different form when students accumulate college credits before graduating from high school, sometimes before setting foot on a college campus (Waits, Setzer, & Lewis, 2005). Thinking as Townsend does of transfer as a diversified process involving multiple types of institutions at various points in students' college-going experiences captures the reality of what college is about for many students today.

Three additional readings are recommended on the curricular mission of transfer. Each offers additional insights into the complexity and importance of transfer to the community college, including Jan Ignash's article, co-authored by Townsend, on good practice to support state-level articulation (transfer) agreements; an article by Wassmer, Moore, and Shulock (2004) on racial/ethnic composition of students engaged in community college-to-university transfer; and Shaw and London's (2001) discussion of three community colleges deeply committed to transfer in the "Culture and Ideology in Keeping Transfer Commitment: Three Community Colleges," examining organizational concerns related to transfer.

The second article in this section is the introductory chapter to a book on the community college baccalaureate edited by Deborah Floyd, Michael Skolnik, and Kenneth Walker (2005). Titled "The Community College Baccalaureate in the U.S." (Chapter 19), this work by Floyd presents a valuable discussion of a logical progression of the transfer mission, essentially the integration of the community college's sub baccalaureate curriculum with the baccalaureate curriculum. Referred to as the community college baccalaureate, Floyd's chapter reexamines issues of access in relation to the organizational structure and purpose of higher education. She defines concepts useful to understanding emerging models and approaches associated with the community college baccalaureate, drawing lessons from history. She points out the logical progression and consequence of adoption of the baccalaureate degree by community colleges, cautioning that today's two-year colleges may transform into four-year colleges as their predecessors have done. A unique and important perspective of Floyd's chapter is her recognition of the community college baccalaureate in two North American countries: Canada and the United States. By capturing details of this contemporary development of community college curriculum, Floyd enlightens readers about ways community colleges struggle with their complementary missions with universities as they strive to fulfill their own open access agenda.

Two articles provide additional depth into this important development. The first recommended reading is John Levin's (2004) article on the community college as a baccalaureate-granting institution, examining organizational perspectives associated with globalization of community colleges, and the next is Ward's (2001) article on British polytechnics for American community colleges. Picking up on a prominent theme in Floyd's chapter, both of these writings offer a comparative dimension that is almost completely neglected in the community college literature, recognizing that two-year colleges are evolving throughout the world.

Two articles offer insights into the comprehensive mission of the community college in terms of offering insights into public policy linked to curriculum, increasingly blending vocational education with other curricula of the community college. Though some scholars distinguish vocational education as a separate curricular track, articles by Bragg (2001) and by Grubb, Badway and Bell (2003) illustrate how vocational education can be integrated with various aspects of community college curriculum, highlighting its importance to the growing diversity of students using the community college as an entry point to higher education. This important perspective on blending vocational curriculum with other curricular missions is further elaborated in an article by Dolores Perin (2001) on academic-occupational integration as a reform strategy for community colleges, a piece included in the recommended readings list.

With respect to vocational education, Bragg (2001), in "The Past, Present, and Future Role of Federal Vocational Legislation in U.S. Community Colleges" (Chapter 20), describes the evolution of vocational education, identifying its origins in federal legislation passed in the early 1900s. She specifically chose the term "vocational education" despite criticism of scholars (see, for example, Brint & Karabel, 1989), because this term has been the most enduring and encom-

passing to describe education for employment throughout the twentieth century. Her article sets current postsecondary vocational education in the context of the legacy of federal legislation, identifying the relative advantage secondary schools have had over community colleges because of their capturing the lion's share of federal funding. Though disadvantaged on funding, postsecondary vocational education has benefited by being less encumbered by federal mandates. Even so, Bragg's article discusses the evolution of new reform agendas endorsed by the federal government, including tech prep. Reporting on her own research and that of others, Bragg discusses the legislative intent of tech prep and the challenges faced by community colleges in attempting to transition more students from the secondary to the postsecondary level.

Two recommended readings offer useful background and perspectives on Bragg's article. First, a book chapter by Bragg (1995) is recommended because it defines various tech prep models and discusses their merits and limitations. Also recommended is an article by Margaret Terry Orr (1998), who discusses ways the school-to-work initiatives initiated by federal legislation in the 1990s have influenced the reform of secondary schools and community colleges.

Grubb, Badway and Bell's (2003) "Community Colleges and the Equity Agenda: The Potential of Noncredit Education" (Chapter 21) is about what they call the "equity agenda." This selection explores vocational education and other curriculum missions such as academic education and remedial education through non-credit courses. Recognizing the increasing use of non-credit curriculum, a phenomenon they suspect to be very extensive though not well documented, Grubb et al. propose the extended use of non-credit courses as a means of expanding access to college for the "neediest" (p. 219) of students, mentioning recent immigrants with language barriers, persons with family problems, welfare recipients and the long-term unemployed, recently individuals with criminal backgrounds, and students with physical and mental disabilities. It is the contention of Grubb et al. that, while community colleges have claimed to reach out to the most disenfranchised of all citizens, they have done a poor job of it. The existing curriculum of the community college, by and large, emphasizes a curriculum for the middle-income class, not those with the greatest social and educational needs. They argue that noncredit courses are expanding in a plethora of areas, in vocational education to prepare people for jobs but in other areas as well such as remedial education, and they contend these non-credit courses can open the doors of higher education even wider. They cite examples of community colleges utilizing non-credit courses to build bridges to credit-generating courses, including allowing students to move from the pre-collegiate level through the community college to the baccalaureate level. Grubb et al. acknowledge their "equity agenda" could result in further stratification of higher education, creating a lower tier to the community college directed not exclusively but certainly targeted at students who have heretofore not had access to higher education. They also acknowledge students with extensive social and educational need cannot be served by community colleges without systemic change to the entire higher education system.

A recommended reading offering further perspective on non-credit education offered by the community college is the article on contract training by Dougherty and Bakia (2000). Reporting on their national study, Dougherty and Bakia offer insights on how community colleges conceive of contract training as a delivery strategy to extend the curricular mission to meet the needs of more students and stakeholders, particularly business and industry.

Two selections are included that address aspects of remediation and developmental education, including issues strongly related to non-credit mentioned by Grubb et al. The first is an article by Regina Deil-Amen and James Rosenbaum (2002): "The Unintended Consequences of Stigma-Free Remediation," (Chapter 22). Deil-Amen and Rosenbaum tackle the enormously important issue of social stratification, in particular that open admissions provides access to college for students who are not academically prepared to enroll in college-level course work. Citing Clark's (1960) early work on the ways in which then junior colleges encouraged students to lower their expectations for the bachelor's degree, Deil-Amen and Rosenbaum report results from fieldwork over two years to understand how two community colleges engaged students in what they labeled "stigma-free remediation." A key feature of the approach was offering students "institutional credit" (p. 254) that did not transfer but counted toward financial aid and full-time student status, avoiding blaming

students by encouraging a nonjudgmental, supportive attitude among staff. Their interviews with students revealed the ways community college students experienced remedial education, demonstrating that many community college students lacked a full and complete understanding of how limitations of their prior preparation and academic performance impacted their ability to engage in college-level studies. Rather than deflate students' high expectations, community college staff worked with students in "ingenious ways" to engage them in remedial instruction without their feeling stigmatized. While this could be viewed as a positive occurrence, Deil-Amen and Rosenbaum worry that such circumstances simulate the "cooling out" principle that Clark (1960) hypothesized several decades earlier (see Chapter 5). In hopes of keeping students in college by encouraging their participation in courses offering "institutional credit," a form of credit not recognized outside the particular community college where it is awarded, community colleges may be obscuring the lines between what constitutes college-level study and what does not. The solution, according to the authors is full disclosure about remediation so that students can take informed steps to work cooperatively with college staff to reduce their chances of failure.

Perin's article, "The Location of Developmental Education in Community Colleges: A Discussion of the Merits of Mainstreaming vs. Centralization" (Chapter 23), considers the organizational context for delivery of remedial or developmental education. Choosing the term developmental education to avoid the negative stigma of remediation mentioned by Deil-Amen and Rosenbaum (2002), Perin examines whether mainstreaming, referring to dispersing development education through the institution, versus centralizing, offering it in a separate, dedicated unit, offers advantages in terms of quality of instruction and engaging experienced faculty and keeping them motivated. Addressing a debate that rages in the field, Perin asks a fundamental question about organizational arrangements associated with developmental education: Is mainstreaming or centralizing developmental education better? Roueche and Roueche (1999), Bolyan, Bliss, and Bonham (1997) and others have taken a strong stand in favor of a centralized approach, despite anecdotal evidence that the majority of community colleges use a mainstream approach. To complicate matters, very little high quality empirical data exist to examine questions about quality. Recognizing the limitations of her data, Perin makes a valuable contribution to the literature by laying out advantages and disadvantages for each approach. An advantage of mainstreaming is that it appears to stimulate higher quality instruction and give students a more favorable impression of developmental education, avoiding the stigma of a separate department. On the other hand, Perin concludes that centralized departments are associated with more extensive support services and higher levels of faculty motivation and experience. Her research provides the basis for further study because she provides a meaningful conceptual framework for additional systematic research.

Two articles are recommended on the remedial mission of the community college to give additional insights into its philosophy, purpose, and practice. These are Shaw's (1997) article, "Remedial Education as an Ideological Battleground: Emerging Remedial Education Policies in the Community College," and Curry's (2001) discussion, "Preparing to be Privatized: The Hidden Curriculum of a Community College ESL Writing Class."

Moving from a macro to a micro perspective in terms of how curriculum is delivered by community colleges and how student behavior relates to curriculum are three articles that complete this section. These three writings give an understanding of curriculum not so much on the policy or organizational level, but on the level of the course or classroom. First, the article by Maxwell et al. (2003), "Community and Diversity in Urban Community Colleges: Coursetaking Among Entering Students" (Chapter 24), focuses on community and diversity in urban community colleges and examines coursetaking among entering students. Arguing higher education scholars have ignored courses as a unit of analysis to the detriment of understanding community colleges as a unique and important higher education institution type, this study offers a valuable perspective on community college courses and the students who engage in them as active coursetakers. Maxwell et al. point out the limited evidence of postsecondary coursetaking behaviors, offering results that enlighten readers on unique features of the community college curriculum, including finding that new students are widely dispersed throughout the community college from the time they

enter the institutions, a pattern that is different from universities where new students concentrate in relatively few core courses. Maxwell et al. provide an important new window into the community college, identifying courses in the liberal arts and sciences, vocational education, remedial education, and English as a Second Language (ESL) that comprise the substance of student's actual educational experiences upon entry to the institution. Searching for patterns of participation in relationship to student background characteristics, Maxwell et al. show gender and race/ethnic patterns that are expected and that are surprising, the most important of which is their finding that race/ethnic participation is not differentiated by academic as opposed to vocational participation but by college-level versus remedial participation. Urging scholars to undertake more research of this type, Maxwell et al. provide a valuable description of the lived experiences of new community college students while refuting or reaffirming long-held beliefs about the community college.

Setting his research in a large, urban setting, Tinto (1997), in "Classrooms as Communities: Exploring the Educational Character of Student Persistence" (Chapter 25), used a learning community as the context for exploring how students' classroom learning experiences relate to their persistence. Arguing that classrooms are the center of students' educational experiences "where the social and academic meet" (p. 599), Tinto sought to learn whether students who participated in a learning community benefited in terms of educational outcomes, in particular persistence. Studying a question quite similar to a recommendation from Maxwell et al. about the need to not only study courses but classrooms, Tinto hypothesized that students' learning experiences in the context of the classroom could have a significant impact on their behaviors and outcomes. A fundamental question he posed was: "How do classrooms influence persistence by changing the way students and faculty interact?" His study of the learning community program at one college, Seattle Central Community College, offers readers new insights on his theory of academic and social integration by examining more closely how community college students, whom he characterizes as commuters, engage in learning. In addition to confirming "some of the basic tenets of learning communities and the collaborative pedagogy that underlies them," Tinto takes a critical look at theories of student persistence. He asks what social involvement and academic integration really mean in the context of the community college where students' participation is almost entirely tied to the classroom. He urges researchers to consider complexities heretofore neglected because the predominant lens for investigation of learning in the community colleges has been the university. Rather than viewing academic and social integration as two-dimensional, Tinto urges a nested visualization where academics are offered as part of a broader social context wherein students have a range of experiences that influence how they engage in learning, what they learn, and whether they decide to persist.

The final article in this section, "Internet-Based Learning in Postsecondary Career and Technical Education" (Chapter 26), by Johnson, Benson, Duncan, Shinkareva, Taylor, and Treat (2004) delves into an entirely different aspect of learning, that is the format of Internet-based learning. In this case, Johnson et al. examine the status and future of Internet-based learning in career-technical education (CTE) (a label applied presently to vocational education) offered by community colleges. This national study represents one of only a handful to investigate the focus and prevalence of Internet-based instruction, despite the fact community colleges have been fairly aggressive adopters of distance learning, including Internet-based learning technologies (National Center for Educational Statistics, 2000). Though not representative of the entire curriculum, this selection is valuable because it provides insights into what community colleges are doing and where they may be headed with distance technologies in the future. Specifically, Johnson et al. found the preponderance of community colleges are offering some Internet-based CTE courses, amounting to about one-fifth of the total credit and non-credit CTE courses offered. The Internet-based technologies used to deliver courses were mostly on low-bandwidth technologies such as e-mail, chat, and course management systems such as Blackboard and WebCT rather than high-bandwidth technologies such as desktop videoconferencing and streaming video. Partnerships with external providers such as commercial vendors were not uncommon, particular for smaller rural community colleges that had limited resources and capability to develop and deliver Internet-based learning. In the next three years, community colleges expected to offer more of both low- and high-bandwidth technologies, but this study suggests community colleges are not moving quickly to abandon low-bandwidth technologies. The authors speculate community colleges are cognizant of research that questions whether high-bandwidth technologies facilitate learning, and they are fully aware that many community college students do not possess the computer equipment needed to utilize it.

References

Boylan, H., Bliss, L., & Bonham, G. (1997). Program components and their relationship to students performance. *Journal of Developmental Education, 20*(3), 2–9.

Bragg, D. (1995). Linking high schools to postsecondary institutions: The role of tech prep. In W. Norton Grubb (Ed.), *Education through occupations in American high schools,* Volume II (pp. 191–211). New York: Teachers College Press.

Bragg, D. D. (2001, Fall). The past, present and future role of federal vocational legislation in U.S. community colleges. *Journal of Applied Research in the Community College, 9*(1), 57–76.

Brint, S., & Karabel, J. (1989). *The diverted dream: Community colleges and the promise of educational opportunity in America: 1990–1985.* New York: Oxford University Press.

Clark, B. (1960). *The open door college.* New York: McGraw-Hill.

Cohen, A., & Brawer, F. (2003). *The American community college* (4th ed.). San Francisco: Jossey-Bass.

Curry, M. J. (2001). Preparing to be privatized: The hidden curriculum of a community college ESL writing class. In E. Margolis (Ed.), *The hidden curriculum in higher education* (pp. 175–192). New York: Routledge.

Deil-Amen, R., & Rosenbaum, J. (2002, July). The unintended consequences of stigma-free remediation. *Sociology of Education, 75,* 249–268.

Dougherty, K., & Bakia, M. (2000, February). Community colleges and contract training. *Teachers College Record, 102,* 197–243.

Floyd, D. (2005). The community college baccalaureate in the U.S. In D. Floyd, M. Skolnik, & K. Walker (Eds.), *The community college baccalaureate* (pp. 25–47). Sterling, VA: Stylus Press.

Grubb, W. N., Badway, N., & Bell, D. (2003). Community colleges and the equity agenda: The potential of noncredit education. In K. Shaw & J. Jacobs (Eds.), Community colleges: New environments, new directions. *The Annals of the American Academy of Political and Social Science,* Vol. 586.

Ignash, J. & Townsend, B. K. (2000). Evaluating state-level articulation agreements according to good practice. *Community College Review, 28*(3), 1–12.

Johnson, S. D., Benson, A. D., Duncan, J., Shinkareva, O. N., Taylor, G. D., & Treat, T. (2004). Internet-based learning in postsecondary career and technical education. *Journal of Vocational Education Research, 29*(2), 101–119.

Levin, J. S. (2004, Fall). The community college as a baccalaureate-granting institution. *Review of Higher Education, 28*(1), 1–22.

Maxwell, W., Hagedorn, L. S., Cypers, S., Moon, H. S., Brocato, P., Wahl, K., & Prather, G. (2003). Community and diversity in urban community colleges: Coursetaking among entering students. *Community College Review, 30*(4), 21–46.

Orr, M. T. (1998). Integrating secondary schools and community colleges through school-to-work transition and education reform. *Journal of Vocational Education Research, 23*(2), 93–113.

Perin, D. (2001, April). Academic-occupational integration as a reform strategy for the community college: Classroom perspectives. *Teachers College Record, 103*(2), 303–335.

Perin, D. P. (2002). The location of developmental education in community colleges: A discussion of the merits of mainstreaming vs. centralization. *Community College Review, 30*(1), 27–44.

Roueche, J. E., & Roueche, S. D. (1999). *High stakes, high performance: Making remedial education work.* Washington, D.C.: Community College Press.

Schuyler , G., (2000). *Trends in community college curriculum.* New Directions for Community Colleges, No. 108. San Francisco: Jossey-Bass.

Shaw, K. (1997). Remedial education as an ideological battleground: Emerging remedial education policies in the community college. *Educational Evaluation and Policy Analysis, 19*(3), 284–296.

Shaw, K. M, & London, H. B. (2001). Culture and ideology in keeping transfer commitment: Three community colleges. *The Review of Higher Education, 25*(1), 91–114.

Tinto, V. (1997). Classrooms as communities: Exploring the educational character of student persistence. *Journal of Higher Education, 68*(6), 599–623.

Townsend, K. (2001). Redefining the community college transfer mission. *Community College Review, 29*(1), 29–42.

Waits, T., Setzer, J. C., & Lewis, L. (2005). *Dual credit and exam-based courses in U.S. public high schools: 2002–03* (NCES 2005009). Washington, D.C.: National Center for Educational Statistics, United States Department of Education.

Ward, C. (2001). A lesson from the British polytechnics for American community colleges. *Community College Review, 29*(2), 151–163.

Wassmer, R., Moore, C., & Shulock, N. (2004). Effect of racial/ethnic composition on transfer rates in community colleges: Implications for policy and practice. *Research in Higher Education, 45*(6), 651–672.

CHAPTER 18

REDEFINING THE COMMUNITY COLLEGE TRANSFER MISSION

BARBARA K. TOWNSEND

When the public junior college was initially created in 1901, its central mission was transfer education. Students would take the first two years of an undergraduate degree at the two-year college and transfer to a four-year institution to complete the baccalaureate. Completion of the first two years was certified by the Associate of Arts (A.A.) degree or the more specialized Associate of Science (A.S.) degree depending on the student's program of study. Underlying the junior college's transfer mission was the assumption that transfer would occur in one direction only: upwardly vertical. Students would transfer *from* the two-year college, not to it, and ideally transfer after having completed the A.A. degree. Universities determined the terms of the transfer by indicating which courses and programs would transfer and which ones would not (Cooley, 2000, p. 23). How well this two-year college mission was accomplished was determined by what percentage of an institution's students transferred to the four-year sector and what their academic performance was, once there.

In the ensuing century since the first public junior college was created, the institution has evolved into the comprehensive community college. Transfer education, defined as "the capacity of community . . . colleges to assist students in the transition to a four-year college or university" (National Center for Academic Achievement and Transfer, 1990), is still a central institutional mission. The importance of this mission is exemplified in California's public system of higher education. A leader in the development of community colleges, California has planned its public system so that California students can "begin their postsecondary education at a community college and transfer to a public university to complete a baccalaureate degree" (California Postsecondary Education Commisssion, 1998).

Not only state planners but also students see the community college as a vehicle for facilitating baccalaureate attainment. Data from the National Center for Education Statistics show that 42% of the students attending public two-year colleges in 1995–96 intended to earn a bachelor's degree (Phillippe, 2000). How many of these students actually do is unclear. Limited evidence is provided by national studies that examine the transfer rate of "[a]ll students entering [a community college] in a given year who have no prior college experience, and who complete at least twelve college credit units within four years of entry . . . [and] who take one or more classes at an in-state, public university within four years" (Cohen & Brawer, 1996, p. 58). From 21 to 24% of these students transfer (p. 60).

Some critics have argued that the community college's transfer mission does not serve well those students who begin at the institution in anticipation of completing a four-year degree (e.g., Bernstein,

1986; Brint & Karabel, 1989; Pincus & Archer, 1989). The research consistently shows that when students beginning at the community college are matched on entering characteristics with students beginning at a four-year college, the four-year college students are more likely to complete the baccalaureate (Pascarella and Terenzini, 1991). Because of this fact, critics contend that the community college has failed in its transfer mission because beginning one's postsecondary education at the community college may work against the likelihood of attaining a baccalaureate. Indeed, some suggest that the community college should no longer have a transfer mission but rather should concentrate on preparing a workforce necessary for the college's local community and the state (e.g., Clowes and Levin, 1989).

This criticism of the community college's transfer mission is an important one and should not be ignored. It is significant to note, however, that the criticism reflects the perspective that the transfer mission is simply providing the first two years of a baccalaureate for students who start at a community college and intend to transfer to a four-year college. If the definition of the transfer mission is expanded to reflect college students' current transfer patterns, it becomes readily apparent that the transfer mission is a vital, healthy component of the community college. Therefore, the current transfer patterns of students taking courses at the two-year college will be described and assessed for how they facilitate baccalaureate attainment. Implications of these patterns for research and practice will then be discussed.

Current Transfer Patterns

The traditional transfer pattern associated with the community college is students beginning at a community college and transferring to a four-year institution after completing the A.A. degree. However, today's college students demonstrate a variety of other transfer patterns unanticipated by the founders of community colleges. These patterns can be categorized in terms of two student groups: those students who begin their postsecondary attendance at the community college, and those who begin at the four-year college. Among students who begin at the community college, some (1) transfer to a four-year school before completing the A.A. or A.S. degree, some (2) transfer with a nontransfer

degree such as the Associate in Applied Science (A.A.S.) degree or with "nonliberal-arts courses" (Cohen & Ignash, 1994), and some (3) transfer from and to the community college in what de los Santos and Wright (1989) have described as a "swirling" attendance pattern of moving rapidly back and forth among two-year and four-year colleges.

Students who initially matriculate at a four-year college include those who (4) transfer dual credit courses offered by a community college to high school students, (5) transfer community college courses taken during the summer, and (6) transfer community college courses taken concurrently with four-year college courses. Each of these six patterns is described in detail below.

(1) *Transferring to a four-year school before completing the two-year college transfer degree.* The A.A., described as the first two years of a baccalaureate program, was created as the two-year college transfer degree. Two-year college founders and university supporters hoped that students would complete this degree before transferring to a four-year school. However, founders' hopes often collide with student desires. Using data from the Beginning Postsecondary Student Longitudinal Study, Berkner, Lorn, and Clune (2000) tracked for three years students who started their higher education in 1995–96. Twenty-four percent of the students who started their higher education at a public community college in 1995–96 indicated they intended to transfer to a four-year college *before completing an associate's degree* (italics added) (p. vi), and 12% of the students who began at a two-year college actually transferred (p. 8). The downside to transferring before completing an associate's degree is a decreased likelihood of success at the four-year institution. Studies show that students who complete an associate's degree before transferring are more apt to complete their four-year degree than individuals who transfer without the degree (Cohen & Brawer, 1996; Keeley & House, 1993).

(2) *Transferring with nonliberal arts courses or programs.* Another transfer pattern unanticipated by community college founders is students transferring nonliberal arts courses or even nontransfer degrees such as the A.A.S. degree to four-year colleges. The A.A.S. is considered to be a nontransfer degree and sometimes is labeled as such in state-level transfer and articulation agreements or state-level policies about community

colleges. As students in A.A.S. programs succeed in their programs, they become "heated up," or motivated to achieve more, rather than "cooled down," or discouraged academically, and decide to reframe their goals to work towards a bachelor's degree. Armed with the A.A.S. degree or considerable courses in such fields as nursing, business management, and office administration, these students seek transfer to four-year colleges.

The extent of this phenomenon has been noted by several authors (e.g., Bernstein, 1986; Cohen & Ignash, 1994; Striplin, 2000). Also noted have been the differences among four-year institutions in accepting nonliberal-arts courses. For example, Striplin (2000) examined the transferability of these courses from 26 California community colleges to the California State University (CSU) System and the University of California (UC) system. She found that "in 1998, 72.6% of the nonliberal arts courses transferred to the CSU System and 26.75% transferred to the UC System . . ." (p. 76).

(3) *Transferring in a "swirling" pattern.* Traditional views of college attendance assume that students will graduate from the college at which they first matriculate. This perspective is exemplified in the following statement by the Southern Educational Foundation (1995): "No student enters a four-year college or university expecting to dropout or leave without graduating" (p. 1). A similar view has been held concerning students who begin higher education at a community college and seek a bachelor's degree. It is assumed these students will transfer just once— to the four-year college from which they will graduate (Piland, 1995).

Yet the reality is that a significant percentage of college students attend more than one college. "[S]tudents have become increasingly mobile, progressing through colleges in nonlinear patterns, collecting several institutional imprimaturs before attaining degrees" (Matthews & Mellow, 1996). In their national study of students who began their college education in 1995–96, Berkner, Horn, and Clune (2000) found that 20% of the students who began at a four-year college transferred within three years (p. iv). Similarly, McCormick & Carroll (1997), in their examination of NCES data, concluded that more than 25% of students matriculating at a four-year college transfer (as cited in Porter, 2000). Using several national data bases, Adelman (1999) looked at students who began in the community college

as well as those who began in the four-year college and found that:

> [t]he proportion of undergraduate students attending more than one institution swelled from 40 percent to 54 percent (and among bachelor's degree recipients, from 49 to 58 percent) during the 1970s and 1980s, with even more dramatic increases in the proportion of students attending more than two institutions. Early data from the 1990s suggest that we will easily surpass a 60 percent multi-institutional attendance rate by the year 2000. (p. vii)

Other researchers have documented this multiple-transfer phenomenon at the institutional level (DesJardins, 1999; Kearney, Townsend, & Kearny, 1995; Townsend, 2000).

The increase in the percentage of students who attend more than one college has been labeled by de los Santos and Wright (1989) as "swirling." As part of this swirl, some two-year students transfer to *another* two-year school before transferring to a four-year college. Typically, students switch two-year schools because they have moved from one state to another or from one part of the state to another. Whatever their reason, they continue to attend the two-year school in pursuit of a baccalaureate. Another dimension of the swirl is four-year students who transfer to two-year colleges. Those who do so are known as reverse transfer students or "drop-downs" (Kintzer, 1983, p. 1). Their existence was first documented by Burton Clark (1960) in a single-institution study conducted in the 1950s. By the end of the twentieth century, about 13% of two-year college students nationally were estimated to be undergraduate reverse transfers, although the percentage varied greatly in individual institutions (Townsend & Dever, 1999). Some reverse transfers complete an associate's degree but do not seek transfer to a four-year college, while other reverse transfers later reenroll at a four-year college (e.g., DesJardins, 1999).

Additionally, some students are "double-reverse transfer students" (Cooley, 2000, p. 23). They start at a community college, transfer to a four-year college, and then transfer back to the community college. They may or may not complete an associate's degree or transfer to another four-year college.

(4) *Transferring high school dual credit courses offered by a commununity college.* To ensure a seamless transition between high school and college, high schools and colleges work together

to offer dual credit courses to high school students. A college or university offers specific courses, which are taught at the high school, often by a high school teacher. The courses count for both high school and college credit, or may be taken for college credit only. Some high school students take dual credit courses offered through a community college, never intending to enroll at that institution upon graduation. Rather, they transfer the credits to the four-year college at which they matriculate. For example, a study of dual credit programs in Missouri revealed that in 1995–96, "about 56% of students receiving dual credit delivered by community colleges transferred that credit to a different institution upon graduation from high school" (Girardi & Stein, 2000).

(5) *Transferring summer courses.* A variant of the undergraduate reverse transfer occurs when four-year college students attend a community college during the summer. Technically, these students are not true reverse transfer students because they do not transfer their four-year college credits into the community college. Labeled "summer sessioners" (Hagedorn & Castro, 1999), these students accrue community college credits during the summer and transfer them to their home institution in the fall. Four-year students who do attend community colleges during the summer do so to save on college tuition and accrue college credits more quickly as well as "to make up a course," "tighten their fall schedule," or "help improve their grades" (Reverse Transfer Project, 1999, p. 1).

The extent of this phenomenon nationally is not known. For community colleges that actively recruit summer sessioners, their enrollment can be significant. One such college is Moraine Valley Community College (IL), which has kept data on these students for several years. In the summer of 1999 almost 1,500 four-year students from over 150 schools took an average of 4.8 credit hours at Moraine Valley (Reverse Transfer Project, 1999, p. 1).

(6) *Transferring courses taken through concurrent enrollment.* Besides taking two-year college courses during the summer, four-year students may also enroll concurrently or simultaneously at a two-year college and their four-year school. At term's end, the two-year college credits are transferred into their four-year program. How extensive this enrollment pattern is at a national level is unknown to this researcher, but Adelman's (1999) examination of national data bases indi-

cating student enrollment provides some insight into the pattern's magnitude. Adelman found that "sixteen percent of postsecondary students (and 18 percent of bachelor's degree completers) engaged in alternating or simultaneous enrollment patterns" (p. viii). What percent of this group engaged in simultaneous enrollment only was not indicated. Single-institution evidence of this phenomenon is provided by the findings of a study conducted at an urban, public, Doctoral I institution in the Midsouth. Among the sample of 605 two-year college transfer students enrolling from fall 1994 through spring 1998, 8% of the students enrolled simultaneously at an area two-year college as well as at the university during at least one semester. More than 5 % of the students had been summer sessioners at a two-year college (Townsend, 2000).

How These Patterns Affect Baccalaureate Attainment

As these patterns of students' transfer behavior demonstrate, "many successful college graduates [will] have community college credits on their transcripts" (Cooley, 2000, p. 30) although not through the transfer pattern assumed by founders of the two-year college. The effect of these patterns on baccalaureate attainment needs to be examined. Possible criteria to use include time-to-degree, college costs, and quality of courses. In other words, does attending the community college make attaining the baccalaureate quicker, less expensive, and academically easier?

(1) *Time-to-degree.* For high school students who have the option of taking dual-credit courses offered by a community college and for four-year college students with the institutional and geographic options of summer or concurrent enrollment at a community college, transferring courses earned from a community college can indeed shorten the time it takes to complete a degree. Dual-credit enrollment is not an option at all high schools. Similarly, concurrent enrollment is not always possible since some four-year colleges may prohibit students taking courses elsewhere during the academic year. Also, not all four-year colleges have a community college in close enough proximity to make concurrent enrollment geographically feasible. Similarly, attending during the summer is primarily an option for four-year students who have a community college in their home community.

Time-to-degree completion for students who begin their postsecondary education at the community college and transfer to a four-year college depends on a number of factors. One factor is a student's plans upon entry to the community college. Does the entering student plan to transfer to a four-year college? If so, does the student know where he or she wants to transfer and into what major? Another important factor is whether there is an up-to-date articulation agreement (either interinstitutional or system-wide) between the community college and the four-year college. If the answer to these questions is yes and if the student follows the prescribed plan appropriate for transfer to the particular four-year college and planned major, then the student should be able to complete the baccalaureate in the same time as a student who initially matriculated at the four-year college—even if the two-year student transfers before completing an A.A. or A.S. degree. However, for someone transferring with nonliberal arts courses or with an A.A.S. degree, time-to-degree completion may be lengthened because many of the courses may be transferred only as electives or may not transfer at all. The other transfer pattern, swirling among two- and four-year colleges, may result in a more costly degree both financially and time-wise than degrees earned in more traditional ways.

(2) *College costs.* There is no question that attending a community college saves on college costs. Typically, the cost of one year at a community college is less than one half that of attending a public four-year college in the same state. In 1995–96, the average community college tuition was $1,518 as compared to an average tuition of $5,771 at four-year colleges (Phillippe, 1997). Indeed, the community college was created partly as a low-cost option for the first two years of the baccalaureate (Cohen & Brawer, 1996). The one caveat may be that community college courses serving as prerequisites for upper-level courses may not adequately prepare students for the upper-level course. If so, a student may have to repeat the upper-level course, thus increasing college costs.

(3) *Quality of two-year college courses.* It is this last point or concern—the academic quality of two-year college courses—that may hinder baccalaureate attainment for students who attend the community college. There is widespread,

long-standing evidence of transfer shock, a decrease in the first semester's grade point average (GPA), when community college students transfer to a four-year school (e.g., Keeley & House, 1993). Reasons for the drop in GPA may include "the normal problems inherent in becoming socially and academically settled in a new institutional setting" (Pascarella & Terenzini as cited in Pascarella et al). Alternatively, the drop in GPA may reflect institutional differences in standards or expectations for academic performance as well as insufficient preparation for upper-division courses.

To determine if a particular community college's lower-division courses adequately prepare students for upper-division courses in the same subject area, Quanty and Dixon (1995) developed a "course-based model of transfer success" (p. 1). A four-year college identifies courses requiring prerequisites that could be taken either at the four-year college or at the local community college. The academic records of students who take the courses requiring prerequisites are checked to determine how well they did in the course and where they took the prerequisite course. When this model was used at Christopher Newport University in Virginia, findings indicated that "students who completed course prerequisites at TNCC [Thomas Nelson Community College] did as well or better than students who completed the prerequisites" (p. 5) at the university. If this model were used nationwide, it could have two results: in some instances the myth of inadequate preparation in two-year colleges would be laid to rest, or in instances where the evidence indicated inadequate preparation, individual community colleges would need to strengthen their courses.

Some evidence of the quality of community college education is provided by studies that have examined the cognitive effects of attending two-year colleges. Pascarella, Bohr, Nora, and Terenzini (1995) studied the cognitive impacts of the freshman year at five two-year colleges and six four-year colleges drawn from a national sample. In general, there was "parity between 2-year and 4-year college students on end-of-freshman year reading comprehension, mathematics, critical thinking, and composite achievement" (p. 83) as measured by the Collegiate Assessment of Academic Proficiency. More studies of this type need to be done to provide greater insight into the comparative cognitive effects of two-year and four-year college attendance and to provide data to answer questions regarding the quality of a community college education.

Implications for Research and Practice

The community college's initial transfer mission—providing the first two years of a baccalaureate degree for students who begin postsecondary education at the community college—is still a primary function of the community college. This traditional transfer mission must continue to justify its existence through serving the students who follow this enrollment pattern well. However, students' use of the community college to include other patterns of transfer is a reality that cannot be ignored. Some of these patterns clearly facilitate baccalaureate attainment for four-year college students as well. By earning credits at a community college, they can attain the baccalaureate more quickly and less expensively than if they only studied at a four-year school. The extent to which patterns demonstrated by students who begin at a community college facilitate baccalaureate attainment is less clear. On the factors of time to degree and cost of degree, the effect of attending the community college en route to the baccalaureate seems fairly obvious; less obvious is the effect of community college attendance on the actual education received. It is this question that most bears studying and is a challenge for both two-year and four-year college faculty and proponents.

Another question for researchers is whether four-year college students' use of the community college to hasten their baccalaureate attainment helps or hinders students who begin at the community college. In four-year college students' desire to attain the bachelor's degree more quickly and less expensively, are they taking seats in courses with limited enrollments? If so, they are potentially displacing students for whom the community college was designed—students who couldn't afford to go to a four-year college and sometimes would not be admitted to a four-year college because of their high school academic record. Alternatively, the presence of four-year college students may serve to energize community college classrooms. The students can also serve as role models for two-year students and provide "insider" information about what it is like to attend a four-year college and how to get financial aid.

The presence of four-year college students in the community college also contributes to the necessity of two-year and four-year college faculty working together to develop course-by-course equivalency guides as well as articulation agreements for entire programs to ensure consistency in course content and quality. These efforts have been urged for decades to facilitate the upwardly vertical transfer pattern. Now there is additional incentive for these efforts. Four-year institutions have much to gain from attention to transfer and articulation because many of their native four-year college students may well become community college students, at least briefly, during their journey to the baccalaureate.

Additionally, policy makers need to revise their understanding of student attendance patterns and use this understanding when fashioning state-level policy agreements affecting transfer. Of the 33 statewide articulation agreements in effect in 1999, one third did not cover any pattern of transfer besides the upwardly vertical (Ignash & Townsend, 2000). Policy makers need to decide if they wish to facilitate other patterns.

With regard to the community college itself, what is indisputable is that transferring courses from and to the community college is a common occurrence for many students. These new patterns necessitate a redefinition of the community college transfer mission as a function that facilitates attainment of the baccalaureate degree for college students in general, not just for students who begin their undergraduate education in the two-year college.

References

Adelman, C. (1999). *Answers in the tool box: Academic integrity, attendance patterns, and bachelor's degree attainment.* Jessup, MD: Education Publications Center, U.S. Department of Education.

Berkner, L. Horn, L. & Clune, M. (2000). *Descriptive summary of 1995–96 beginning postsecondary students: Three years later, with an essay on students who started at less-than-4-year institutions.* Washington, DC: National Center for Education Statistics.

Bernstein, A. (1986). The devaluation of transfer: Current explanations and possible causes. In L. S. Zwerling (Ed.), *The community college and its critics* (pp. 31–40). *New Directions for Community Colleges,* No. 54. San Francisco: Jossey-Bass.

Brint, S., & Karabel, J. (1989). *The diverted dream: Community colleges and the promise of educational opportunity in America 1900–1985.* New York: Oxford University Press.

California Postsecondary Education Commission. (1998). *New community college transfer students at California's public universities.* Factsheet 98-3. Retrieved November 29, 1999, from the World Wide Web: *http://www.cpec.ca.gov/factshts/ fs1998/ fs98-3.htm.*

Clark, B. (1960). The "cooling out" function in higher education. *American Journal of Sociology, 65* (6), 569–576.

Clowes, D. A., & Levin, B. H. (1989). Community, technical, and junior colleges: Are they leaving higher education? *Journal of Higher Education, 60* (3), 349–355.

Cohen, A. M., & Brawer, F. (1996). *The American community college.* San Francisco: Jossey-Bass.

Cohen, A. M., & Ignash, J. (1994). An overview of the total credit curriculum. In A. M. Cohen (Ed.), *Relating curriculum and transfer* (pp. 13–29). *New Directions for Community Colleges,* No. 86. San Francisco: Jossey-Bass.

Cooley, R. J. (2000). *The American community college turns 100: A look at its students, programs, and prospects.* Princeton, NJ: Educational Testing Service.

de los Santos, A. G., & Wright, I. (1989). Community college and university student transfers. *Educational Record, 79* (3/4), 82–84.

DesJardins, S. L. (1999). Tracking institutional leavers: An application. *AIR Professional File,* No. 71.

Girardi, T., & Stein, R. (2000). State dual credit policy and its implications for community colleges: Lessons from Missouri for the 21st century. In B. Townsend & S. Twombly (Eds.), *Community colleges: Policy in the future context.* Westport, CT: Ablex Publishing Co.

Hagedorn, L., & Castro, C. R. (1999). Paradoxes: California's experience with reverse transfer students. In B. Townsend (Ed.), *Understanding the impact of reverse transfers on the community college* (pp. 15–26). *New Directions for Community Colleges,* No. 106. San Francisco: Jossey-Bass.

Ignash, J., & Townsend, B. (2000). Transfer and articulation policy issues in the 21st century. In B. Townsend & S. Twombly (Eds.), *Community colleges: Policy in the future context.* Westport, CT: Ablex Publishing Co.

Kearney, G., Townsend, B. K., & Kearney, T. (1995). Multiple-transfer students in a public urban university: Background characteristics and interinstitutional movements. *Research in Higher Education, 36* (3), 323–344.

Keeley, E. J., & House, D. J. (1993). *Transfer shock revisited: A longitudinal study of transfer academic performance.* Paper presented at the annual meeting of the Association for Institutional Research, Chicago, IL.

Kintzer, F. (1983). *The multidimensional problem of articulation and transfer.* ERIC Digest 28857. Los Angeles, CA: ERIC Clearinghouse for Junior Colleges.

Matthews, R., & Mellow, G. (1996). Transfer and the dilemma of our students. *Metropolitan Universities, 7*(2), 87–97.

McCromick, A. C., & Carroll, C. D. (1997). (Report No. NCES 97-266). Washington, DC: National Center for Education Statistics.

National Center for Academic Achievement and Transfer. (1990). Good practices in transfer education. *Working Papers, 1* (3). Washington, DC: American Council on Education.

Pascarella, E., Bohr, L., Nora, A., & Terenzini, P. (1995). Cognitive effects of 2-year and 4-year colleges: New evidence. *Educational Evaluation and Policy Analysis, 17*(1), 83–96.

Pascarella, E., Bohr, L., Nora, A., Ranganathan, S., Desler, M., & Bulakowski, C. (1994). Impacts of 2-year and 4-year colleges on learning orientations: A preliminary study. *Community College Journal of Research and Practice, 18* (6), 577–589.

Pascarella, E. T., & Terenzini, P. T. (1991). *How college affects students: Findings and insights from twenty years of research.* San Francisco: Jossey-Bass.

Pincus, F. L., & Archer, E. (1989). *Bridges to opportunity: Are community colleges meeting the transfer needs of minority students?* New York: Academy for Educational Development and College Entrance Examination Board.

Phillippe, K. (Ed.). (2000). *National profile of community colleges: Trends & statistics,* 3rd Ed. Washington, DC: American Association of Community Colleges.

Piland, W. (1995). Community college transfer students who earn bachelor's degrees. *Community College Review, 23* (3), 35–44.

Porter, S. R. (1999). *Including transfer-out behavior in retention models: Using the NSLC enrollment search data.* Paper presented at North East Association of Institutional Research annual conference, Newport, Rhode Island.

Quanty, M., & Dixon, R. (1995). *A new paradigm for examining transfer success.* Paper presented at annual meeting of American Educational Research Association, San Francisco, CA.

Reverse Transfer Project, Summer 1999. (November 1999). Moraine Valley Community College, IL: Office of Institutional Research.

Southern Educational Foundation. (1995). *Redeeming the American promise: Report of the panel on educational opportunity and postsecondary desegregation.* Atlanta, GA: Author.

Striplin, J. C. (2000). An examination of non-liberal arts course transferability in California. *Community College Review, 28* (1), 67–78.

Townsend, B. (2000). Institutional attendance patterns of two-year college transfers at an urban public university. *College and University, 76* (1), 21–24.

Townsend, B., & Dever, J. (1999). What do we know about reverse transfer students? In B. Townsend (Ed.), *Understanding the impact of reverse transfers on the community college* (pp. 5–14). *New Directions for Community Colleges,* No. 106. San Francisco: Jossey-Bass.

Barbara K. Townsend is a professor and associate dean for research and development at the University of Missouri-Columbia in Columbia, Missouri. *townsendb@missouri.edu*

Chapter 19

The Community College Baccalaureate in the U.S.

Models, Programs, and Issues

Deborah L. Floyd

This chapter has three purposes. First and foremost, it aims to identify and describe community college models for expanding access to the baccalaureate. Among these models are community colleges that confer these degrees and partner with others to provide the "net effect" of a baccalaureate degree experience for community college graduates. Much like the 1960s, this is an era of innovation: Community colleges are changing rapidly as an increasing number of them strive to "make good" on their promise of access by implementing diverse (and sometimes controversial) models of baccalaureate programming.

Second, this chapter seeks to encourage constructive dialogue on this topic, using pragmatic descriptors of current U.S. programming models. Third, it raises questions and issues that invite further exploration, especially in ways that will assist policy makers at the national, state, and local levels.

By way of fulfilling these three purposes, this chapter offers first a four-part typology of community colleges and baccalaureate degrees and then a look at how this emerging megatrend is shaping research, policy, and practice vis-à-vis community colleges.

To help illustrate these models consider the case of a fictitious student who embodies many of the characteristics of community college students that are relevant to the rationale for these baccalaureate models. Martha Jane Smith is a 32-year-old first-generation college student enrolled in Rolling Hills Community College, a small rural college in the southeastern United States.[1] Her husband, Bill, is a union laborer who has worked construction all his life, like his father. They had the first of their three children when Martha Jane was only 16, and she dropped out of high school to take care of her family, as did her husband. Now, 16 years later, Martha Jane is taking time to pick up where she left off educationally, and she is a sophomore at the local community college.

Monday through Friday her three children ride the bus to, rural public schools while she drops her husband off at his construction site and drives herself to classes at the community college, 22 miles away. When not in class, she spends most of her time in the college library using the computer and studying. Her goal is to earn an associate degree at the community college and eventually finish a bachelor's degree so that she can teach high school science and math classes in her hometown. "I want to be a teacher because I want to help kids learn," she said, "but I also know that a teaching job will bring me security and a good income." She is well on her way towards that goal and lacks only 15 semester hours to complete her associate of science degree.

Martha Jane is a determined woman who doesn't want to end up like her mother, who is completely dependent on her husband. So, three years ago, Martha Jane (who knew instinctively that an education would be a key to her independence) decided to earn her high school diploma by enrolling for GED classes at night in a local elementary school. Her oldest daughter babysat for the younger two children when her husband was busy with bowling or spent the evening "with the boys" at the union hall. As she continued her GED classes, Martha Jane's confidence in herself grew in tandem with her rising competence in math, science, communications, and other basic fields. In less than a year, she completed her GED and was on her way to fulfilling her dream of earning a college degree and becoming a high school teacher.

Thanks to advice and encouragement from her community college's GED professor, Martha Jane successfully maneuvered the bureaucracy of financial aid and received enough money to pay for her tuition and books. While she tested into a "pre college" English class, she enrolled for a full load of college-level general-education courses each term, and her grades have earned her a place on the college dean's list. Last semester she accepted an invitation to join the college's Phi Theta Kappa honor society, which has connected her with a network of new friends.

After completing courses next semester, Martha Jane Smith will be the first in her family to graduate from a college. But she knows that this associate degree is only one step towards the baccalaureate, another major hurdle before she will qualify to work in her chosen field. Private and public state universities have offered her scholarships, but she cannot accept those offers because the institutions are too far away from her home, and commuting would be prohibitively expensive and time-consuming. Rolling Hills Community College has several articulation agreements with area universities, and a few of them offer courses on its campus, but only occasionally and without consistency. For the first time in her college career, Martha Jane knows that the toughest step of her journey towards becoming a high school teacher lies ahead of her: How will she get access to the courses that she needs to complete a bachelor's degree?

Martha Jane, like so many place-bound community college students, is likely to become a victim of a system that promises access to a college degree but simply fails to deliver the necessary programs.[2] Fortunately, the GED program worked well for her as a seamless entry to college. Like so many community college students, Martha Jane feels comfortable at the community college and would like to conclude her education locally, without having to leave her family and travel to a university. But unless the barriers that are now restricting her continued enrollment are removed, Martha Jane will be become a sad statistic, a would-be-teacher denied access to the necessary credentials for the teaching profession.

U.S. community colleges are noted for being responsive to community needs and addressing issues of access. They are "people's colleges" and the "last chance" for many individuals. These "open-door" institutions rarely turn away students as a demonstration of their commitment to access, at least until transition at the baccalaureate level becomes restrictive. States such as Florida led the way in mandating transfer of all community college credits and their counting towards state universities baccalaureate requirements. Most state universities and community colleges have articulation agreements that govern transfer into entire programs, but access may necessitate major and unexpected sacrifices. As some universities aspire to become more selective and research oriented, their emphasis on undergraduate education, especially off campus, often diminishes. Where does that leave Martha Jane, and many like her, who want to matriculate at a four-year college or university, but simply may not do so, given the transfer models currently available?

The topic of the community college baccalaureate has become extremely controversial, partly because of the lack of clarity in defining models and the use of an inconsistent, even confusing terminology. For example, the term "community college baccalaureate" has been used interchangeably to describe delivery models in which community colleges and universities collaboratively offer programs leading to the baccalaureate, with the university conferring the actual degree. Elsewhere, university branch and extension campuses conferring only associate degrees have recently added community college baccalaureates. Some community colleges that have added the baccalaureate to their degree offerings (without having a university partner) also use this term. Clearly, community colleges are trying to address increased need for access to the baccalaureate. Simultaneously, they are seeking a terminology to accurately represent a fundamental expansion in community colleges' mission.

Without question, community college educators would strongly agree that Martha Jane should have access to a bachelor's degree so that she might fulfill her dream. But, as the old adage goes, "The devil is in the details." Who will offer the upper-level courses? Who should confer the degrees? Where will courses be offered? Who will accredit these programs? And how will these programs be funded? Such devilish details complicate any well-intended desire to expand access to the baccalaureate for the place-bound.

A Four-Part Typology: Community Colleges and Baccalaureate Programs

Historical Context

Providing access to the baccalaureate was an early and central role of the two-year college. The first transfer agreement, adopted in 1903 by the University of Chicago and the new public junior college in Gary, Indiana, permitted Gary's young people to remain in their community for an additional two years before relocating to Chicago's south side (Pedersen, 2000).

The transfer function is a key role of community colleges with deep historical roots. Some commentators have argued that early junior colleges were established to permit universities to focus on upper-division instruction (Cohen & Brawer, 2003; Zwerling, 1976); others have asserted that they allowed place-bound students to remain at home for an additional one or two years of study before relocating to a university campus, law school, or medical college (Pedersen, 2000). Yet junior colleges never secured a monopoly over lower-division college instruction. Four-year colleges and universities never relinquished this role (Cohen & Brawer, 2003). Having retained a sense of control over the entire undergraduate curriculum, four-year colleges and universities became the "gatekeepers" of American higher education and used their power to approve (or deny) credits for "junior college" transfer courses.

Perhaps part of the underlying reason for the contemporary friction about the community col-

lege baccalaureate is that U.S. universities have had the authority to control the baccalaureate and this role has not been effectively challenged, until now. Those community colleges now proposing broad access to the baccalaureate may seem to threaten the power of universities to determine the baccalaureate curriculum and to award these degrees. While many argue that community college baccalaureate programs are "all about bumping up access for nontraditional students and helping to meet shortages like those in nursing and teaching fields," others fear that this movement could be counterproductive and mark the end of traditional community colleges (Troumpoucis, 2004, p. 6).

According to Cohen and Brawer (2003), "the community colleges have suffered less from goal displacement than have most other higher education institutions. They had less to displace; their goals were to serve the people with whatever the people wanted. Standing outside the tradition [of universities], they offered access" (p. 29). Today, community colleges are implementing numerous programmatic models and governance structures to deliver "whatever the people want." Increasingly, what people want includes proximate access to the baccalaureate, regardless of who confers the degree.

The typology offered here posits four models—articulation, the university center, university extension, and the community college baccalaureate—and reflects the author's best efforts to assimilate information from various sources. This list of institutions and models is not comprehensive, but is offered as a schema, with examples, to help shape the debate over the proper mission of community colleges. This typology may be useful to practitioners, researchers, and policy makers to study, compare, and contrast "like" programs. A comparison of key features that differentiate these models from one another is described in Table 1.

Articulation Model

Articulation agreements that ensure acceptance of freshman and sophomore credits by senior colleges and universities are vital to community colleges' transfer mission. In some states, such as Florida, associate degree graduates who complete a prescribed general-education core are guaranteed acceptance of credits and junior status at their state university. States such as California, Illinois, New York, Oklahoma, Tennessee,

Texas, and Washington have transfer rates well above the norm because most of their community colleges participate in a collaborative project with a nearby four-year college or university, with procedures governing student transfer spelled out in an intrastate agreement applicable to both institutions. In fact, according to a recent study of state policies and the success of community college transfer students, " effective state policies are at the heart of baccalaureate success for students transferring from two-year to four-year institutions with the goal of achieving their degrees" (Wellman, 2004 p. 1). Cohen and Brawer (2003) assert the articulation agreements become more effective when community colleges and universities collaboratively develop two-plus-two agreements in such specific program areas as teacher education, health, engineering, and agriculture and farm management.

With respect to teacher education, for example, recent studies report that almost 80 percent of U.S. community colleges (approximately 900 institutions) are implementing articulation agreements that encourage students to earn the first two years of a four-year degree at their local community college and also guarantee the full transfer of credits to a state university (Floyd & Walker, 2003; Hudson, 2000).

The dynamics of a community college student's transfer to a university, including the programmatic pathways and matriculation outcomes, have been the focus of numerous studies. Arthur M. Cohen (2003) describes the many roles that community colleges assume in assisting students with transfer transitions. He recognizes that there are models other than traditional transfer, which require community colleges' students to travel to an often-distant university for upper-division course work. New models, beyond the traditional two-plus-two models whereby students complete two years of study at the community college and transfer to a four-year college or university to finalize baccalaureate studies, are emerging. Some of these models include universities' offering upper-division courses on community college campuses. It is important to note that within the framework of the articulation model, creative three-plus-one models are becoming more popular (especially with proprietary and private colleges) whereby students complete 90 hours with a community college and the four-year college provides the final year leading to a baccalaureate.

For many students, articulation models work well, but for others like Martha Jane Smith, a traditional articulation model is not feasible because she is unable to leave her family and travel to a university to continue her studies in a traditional on-campus format. While the community college and university may have perfectly articulated transfer agreements, she is "place-bound" and needs relevant junior- and senior-level courses offered locally.

University Center Model and Concurrent-Use Campuses

The university center model is becoming increasingly popular. Often these centers are located close to or on community college campuses. The university confers the degree in partnership with others, including community colleges and sometimes other universities.

Implementation of this model often involves consortia of colleges and universities that jointly use facilities for the delivery of upper-division courses and programs. In Michigan, for instance, the Northwestern Michigan College University Center includes 11 four-year universities with programming that allows seamless entry to junior- and senior-level course work from the community college. In Texas, North Harris Montgomery Community College's university center includes six public universities that offer over 21 unduplicated bachelor's degree programs and 24 master's degree programs (Windham, Perkins, & Rogers, 2001). In south Florida, Broward Community College's central campus is the home of the 4,500-student Florida Atlantic University campus that is part of a much larger higher-education complex. The Edison University Center, on Florida's Edison College[3]campus, is an alliance among a number of regionally accredited colleges and universities that houses several baccalaureate programs that articulate with Edison's associate degree programs. Arizona Western College, located in isolated areas of Yuma and La Paz Counties, created a Yuma Educational Consortium with all levels of education providers, and they also house buildings and programs provided by Northern Arizona University.

Private and proprietary colleges and universities are becoming increasingly active partners with community colleges in the delivery of baccalaureate degrees on community college campuses, via distance learning and with uni-

TABLE 1
Comparison of Different Baccalaureate Models

	Articulation Model	University Center Model	University Extension Model	Community College Baccalaureate Model
Sequential attendance at community college followed by university	YES	YES	NO	NO
University uses community college facilities	NO	YES	NO	NO
Students complete baccalaureate degree at a campus other than the conventional university campus	NO	YES	YES	YES
University controls baccalaureate degree requirements	YES	YES	YES	NO
Community college controls baccalaureate degree requirements	NO	NO	NO	YES

versity centers. For instance, through their bachelor degree granting partner, Charter Oak State College (COSC) Bridgepoint Education (formerly Charter Learning) accepts 90 hours of transfer credits and offers the final year of upper-division courses on community college campuses in Arizona and Washington State, with plans to expand to California and other states soon (Scott Turner e-mail communication April 27, 2004). COSC is accredited by the New England Association of Schools and Colleges and is a public college in the Connecticut state university system. Bridgepoint Education is a private for-profit organization founded in 1999, and has offered degree completion programs at corporate sites such as Boeing, BF Goodrich, and the National Guard. Their first community college agreement was with the Maricopa County Community College District colleges in 2001, and later with Arizona's Pima Community College and Washington's Skagit Valley College. Another example of the three-plus-one university center partnership is the relationship between Regis University and Colorado's community colleges through online and on-site delivery of courses. Regis University, accredited by the North Central Association (NCA), launched a new initiative called Associate's to Bachelor's™ and in January 2004, hired Joe D. May, a former community college president, as its executive director of partnerships.

These are just a few of the many examples of the university center approach to delivery of the baccalaureate. These centers often engage private, proprietary, and state institutions as partners and may include online and on-site course delivery.

This model of joint-use facilities has emerged since the 1960s as a popular approach embraced by a number of states. According to the findings of a 1999 survey of State Higher Education Executive Officers (SHEEOs) on joint-use facilities (Windham, Perkins, & Rogers, 2001), 20 states reported the utilization of joint use facilities.[4] The governance models vary and include joint boards, local college governance, private boards, and some that are led by individual directors and presidents.

While the university center and concurrent-use models are not new, they are gaining in momentum and becoming increasingly popular. In Chapter 5, Albert L. Lorenzo describes various university centers and frames the discussion with a typology of six models: co-location, enterprise, virtual, integrated, sponsorship, and hybrid. The hybrid model is just that, a hybrid of other models, with one major addition—the community college is authorized to confer certain baccalaureate degrees.

Various forms of the university center model have been quite effective for expanding access to the baccalaureate and beyond to thousands of students. In fact, for Martha Jane Smith, the university center model may help her to obtain her baccalaureate in teaching. She would be dependent, however, on the university's keeping a promise to offer the courses (even if they had small enrollments) and to do so on a schedule that would allow her to complete her degree requirements locally.

University Extension Model

Universities have long provided baccalaureate education through off-campus and extension centers. Indeed, this was the mandate of the land-grant institutions from their inception. More recently, private and proprietary, as well as public institutions have seen this as a viable means of furthering their mission.

The twenty-first-century definition of the university extension model has various interpretations. Some colleges use their university affiliation in their own name, despite their own independent accreditation. Diverse forms of state governance further blur distinctions. Hawaii, for example, has given three of the University of Hawaii's community colleges (Honolulu, Kapi'olani, and Maui) approval to award the baccalaureate (Patton, 2003). West Virginia's Parkersburg Community College became the University of West Virginia in Parkersburg in 1989 and received legislative authority to grant the baccalaureate four years later. Westark Community College, Arkansas's oldest community college, became the University of Arkansas at Fort Smith in 2002 after a few years of offering four-year degrees. All the above institutions are associated with a university title, but they are independently accredited.

Another example of a university extension model for baccalaureate programming is the Louisiana State University—Alexandra, which was granted legislative authorization to move toward four-year status and by 2003, had reorganized itself. Its plans include officially completing the conversion by fall 2004, along with a tuition increase (www.lsua.edu/community/

4year.htm). An interesting plan is the Pennsylvania State University plan that authorizes 14 of its 17 branch campuses to offer baccalaureate degrees to address unmet needs of place-bound students (University Colleges of Technology, 1997).

Oklahoma State University (OSU) is unique among land-grant institutions in possessing two independently accredited campuses that deliver certificate and associate degree education in technical areas. OSU's Okmulgee campus won state approval in 2004 to award baccalaureates in specialized areas that articulate with its associate degree programs.[5] This development seems to be congruent with the traditional focus of land-grant universities and the original federal mandate for "mechanical and practical arts."

The university extension model is similar to the university center model in that baccalaureate courses are offered at a campus other than the main or largest campus of a university, however, in the university extension model, the campus where these courses are offered is formally part of the university.

No doubt, these university extension programs have been very successful in expanding access to the baccalaureate, especially in workforce areas. In theory, for students like Martha Jane, these university extension programs could present seamless opportunities to earn the baccalaureate, if offered in a timely and accessible format in the areas that the student needs. In practice, however, programs such as teacher education are not commonly offered through the university extension model.

Community College Baccalaureate

The term "community college baccalaureate" describes various models of delivery, including those described in the models discussed previously. Most frequently, however, it denotes community colleges that now "confer" the baccalaureate, not just partner with others for baccalaureate programming. A possible definitional problem associated with the term "community college baccalaureate" is that in some classification systems, a community college might be reclassified when it begins to offer baccalaureate degrees—even a single baccalaureate degree. For example, it appears that the practice of some, but not all, accreditation associations is to classify institutions according to the highest degree the institution awards. In such a case, a two-year institution that gains approval to offer a few baccalaureate programs would be reclassified as a four-year institution, even if the institution's intention is to remain effectively a community college, but one that offers a few baccalaureate programs. In reality, what we find in the field is the emergence of a new institutional type that embodies characteristics of different existing institutional types. The choice for classification is somewhere between trying to fit this new institutional type (imperfectly) into existing classification systems and developing a new way of classifying and describing these hybrid institutions.

An example of such a new way of classifying these hybrid institutions is the approach taken by The Southern Regional Education Board (SREB).[6] The SREB identifies those as associate/baccalaureate institutions, community colleges that grant mostly associate degrees but also some baccalaureates; specifically, Dalton State College and Macon State College in Georgia, and West Virginia University at Parkersburg.[7] It also includes University of Arkansas at Fort Smith (formerly Westark College) and will soon add Florida's community colleges that are (or will be) offering four-year degrees: Chipola, Miami Dade, St. Petersburg, and Okloosa Walton.

Similarly, three community colleges in Texas (Brazosport College, Midland College, and South Texas Community College) were granted authorization by the Texas Coordinating Board to offer baccalaureates in certain applied technical and science fields in July 2003 (Larose, 2003; Wertheimer, 2003). In time, they will become SREB "hybrids," even though the Southern Association of Colleges and Schools (SACS), their regional accrediting association, will classify them as four-year institutions, not community colleges.

In 2001, a task force of the North Central Association's (NCA's) Higher Education Commission issued a report with recommendations for dealing with community colleges' requests to offer four-year programs.[8] The report explains the task force's deliberations; in each case, the NCA classifies community colleges offering and conferring four-year degrees as four-year colleges. In fact, according to NCA's executive director, Ron Baker, five colleges have "moved from associate institutions to baccalaureate institutions and received accreditation at the baccalaureate level while retaining accreditation at the associate level" (e-mail communication with Ron Baker, October 1, 2003).

In 1993, Utah Valley Community College's name and status changed to Utah Valley State College, as a part of its initial baccalaureate candidacy; in 1995, it received accreditation at the baccalaureate level in several areas. Similarly, Utah's Dixie College became Dixie State College of Utah in 2000, during the candidacy phase, and obtained final accreditation in 2002. NCA gave Montana's Salish Kootenai College candidacy in 1990 and accreditation for baccalaureate offerings as of 1993. NCA granted Great Basin College in Nevada candidacy in 1999, initial accreditation in 2003 with formal accreditation awarded retroactively to September 1, 2002 (Danny Gonzales, June 23, 2004 personal communications).

The University and Community College System of Nevada's elected Board of Trustees governs all state postsecondary institutions. Great Basin College, in an isolated northern area, received approval in 2002 to confer baccalaureates in elementary education, integrated and professional studies, electronic instrumentation, and management technology; nursing is currently in development (Gonzales, 2003).

Thus a community college that is adding a baccalaureate emphasis, but keeping associate degree programs, may still fit the model of the community college baccalaureate. This "hybrid" institution is the result of a strong push to offer baccalaureate opportunities in communities.

For Martha Jane Smith, the other models—articulation, university center, and university extension—may not meet her needs, since partnerships with four-year colleges do not always result in appropriate courses being taught locally and in a timely manner. It is reasonable to assume that Martha Jane may not achieve her dream of being a high school teacher . . . at least not without a new model that offers relevant upper-division courses locally. If denied access to the baccalaureate, she would be justified in voicing her frustrations to leaders of the local community college (and anyone else who would listen) in hopes that it will take the lead by gaining approval to grant the baccalaureate. If the systems of four-year colleges that control the upper-division course work of the baccalaureate are unresponsive to this woman, who is typical of many place-bound students who deserve a chance to succeed in college, the local institution may have to do the "right thing" and lead the way toward implementing a community college baccalaureate.

A Mega-trend: Research, Policy, and Practice

Keeping current with local and state developments in community colleges and other associate degree-granting institutions that are petitioning for legislative and governance approval to confer baccalaureates is a challenge for even the most competent journalist. For instance, a bill introduced in California in early 2003 (Sturrock, 2003) would allow community colleges to offer upper-division courses jointly with the California State University System, although the model is unclear in terms of which institutions would confer the degrees. Also, in 2003, a failed South Carolina bill (Grimsley, 2003) would have allowed Trident Technical College to add one bachelor's degree to its offerings—culinary arts.[9] In suburban Chicago, Harper College has been exploring four-year degree offerings (*Community College Times*, 2003; Granderson, 2003); an editorial cautioned local leaders to "go slowly on the four-year degree idea" and to look at states with four-year community colleges, such as Arkansas, Florida, Texas, and Utah (*Daily Herald Reports*, 2003). Unquestionably, news sources across the country will continue to cover these evolutionary changes in baccalaureate programming. But, in the absence of clear and consistent terms and concepts to describe these approaches, some reported information may not be accurate, at least to scholars studying technical details.

Recent Research

Surprisingly, there is little research published about the specifics of national and state policies and practices related to the community college baccalaureate. While models and partnerships abound, specific information consists of anecdotal news and stories, opinion-editorial articles, a few journal articles, and a handful of doctoral dissertations. Clearly, these new programming areas are ripe for publications and research. This section looks at two recent related documents.

Floyd and Walker Survey

As an ancillary focus, one recent study of state practices in teacher education programming may be of interest. In 2002–2003, Deborah L. Floyd and David A. Walker (2003) surveyed state directors of community colleges and asked if one or more colleges in their state were awarding bachelor's degrees in teacher education. Thirty-three responded to their survey, for a 64 percent response rate, which yielded a sample representative of U.S. community colleges. Only two states, Florida and Nevada, responded "yes" (community college baccalaureate model). Almost 20 percent responded "yes" but added that these degrees are being awarded through partnerships with universities (university center model). Further, almost 80 percent of U.S. community colleges are implementing articulation agreements for teacher education, suggesting the dominance of the articulation model. Community colleges in Florida and Nevada that may now confer the baccalaureate are four-year colleges to their regional accrediting associations, although clearly the state directors still view them as community colleges.

Community College Baccalaureate Survey

In mid-2003, the Community College Baccalaureate Association (CCBA) commissioned an independent study to ascertain interest among U.S. community college presidents in organizational and programmatic issues related to the delivery of baccalaureate programs, including the community college baccalaureate model.[10] Researchers sent surveys to 500 presidents selected randomly and received 101 responses, a response rate of slightly over 20 percent. Among the key findings, presidents would prefer to partner with a "mission complementary" four-year university in hopes of delivering baccalaureate degrees locally (CCBA, 2003).

Other major findings of this study of presidents are as follows:

- Many presidents indicated that their state legislatures have considered, or are planning to consider, expanding the baccalaureate through community colleges.
- Over half noted that community college-based baccalaureate programming is not completely understood by the state's higher-education community and policy makers.
- Not surprisingly, interest in baccalaureates is greatest in areas where students are place-bound, such as isolated rural communities.
- Colleges that have expanded the baccalaureate through one or more of these

models have done so in key academic areas such as business, computer science, criminal justice, education, elementary education, and nursing.
- Almost half of the colleges already offer some form of baccalaureate programming on their own or in partnership.
- Over a third of respondents indicated that four-year institutions in their area are not meeting baccalaureate demand.
- More than one-third affirmed that the majority of their students do not transfer to four-year colleges and universities because of geographical or financial barriers.
- Over two-thirds agreed that there are specific, high-demand career fields that require a baccalaureate and that currently the four-year institutions in their area are not meeting these demands.
- Approximately a fourth had received requests from area employers to offer the baccalaureate in certain fields.
- Over one-third affirmed that their faculty and staff have expressed interest in developing the capacity to offer baccalaureate programming on their campus.
- Approximately half noted that several of their academic programs are well positioned for transition to four-year offerings, including having the necessary faculty, infrastructure, and technology.
- Most have not completed a feasibility study or needs assessment or otherwise researched the impact of, or need for, a community college baccalaureate in their service area.
- Almost half affirmed personal interest in participating in a national association advocating community college-based baccalaureates.

Critics may argue that these findings represented the views of just slightly over 100 people and thus might not be representative of all U.S. community colleges. However, this survey of presidents offers the most current research about this topic and is useful for practitioners and policy makers. Further, and more important, its findings offer much food for thought regarding the need to frame and address issues of policy, research, and practice.

Issues for Policy and Research

The ramifications of what appears to be a mega-trend among community colleges focusing on baccalaureate programming are many and multidimensional. The mere fact that current research is woefully inadequate to addressing these trends is troubling and offers an opportunity well worth embracing. One must wonder why national policy groups and associations have not been placing more emphasis on this trend. Is it because this topic is controversial so people imagine that not talking about it will make it "go away"? Perhaps associations, groups, and individuals have not fully grasped the enormity of this movement and the increasing pressures community college leaders face from students and communities to provide better opportunities for baccalaureate access. Or does the lack of engagement merely reflect normal inertia and uncertainty in the face of new challenges? Do some people took at community colleges' baccalaureate programming negatively and as involving "status creep" (Pedersen, 2001) or "mission creep" (Mills, 2003), or do they believe that colleges should "stick to what they do best" (Wattenbarger, 2002) and not take on baccalaureate programming?

Regardless of the reason, the time is overdue for state, national, and local policy makers, organizations, and leaders to recognize that this trend is very real and is begging for attention and focus. It necessitates articulation of a common language (terminology), such as the typology proposed in this chapter, to facilitate meaningful and useful policy studies and research. Foundations and other funding agencies should encourage the Community College Baccalaureate Association (CCBA) to serve as a convener to discuss relevant issues and as a documenter of this movement. The CCBA has been playing this role with very limited fiscal resources while dealing with an area of enormous interest to community college presidents and leaders.

Policy Issues

This mega-trend poses a number of other questions, such as:

- Is there truly a community college baccalaureate degree, since most regional accrediting associations view community colleges that confer the baccalaureate as four-year colleges?

- Do the regional accrediting associations, the Carnegie classification system, and organizations such as the SREB and AACC need a new scheme that recognizes these "new" colleges that are shifting to baccalaureate programming? What are the projected ramifications of such a move and of doing nothing in this regard?

- Is this movement actually a natural evolution of the community colleges' mission and promise of access to educational opportunities for the masses?

- If four-year colleges and universities do not respond to the underserved, who will, if not community colleges?

- What are the ethical and moral responsibilities of community colleges in terms of access to relevant baccalaureate programs after completion of the associate degree? Should they ensure that students understand fully the ramifications of a baccalaureate from each of the models proposed in this chapter, including the reality that some universities might not accept these baccalaureates as entry for graduate study and beyond?

- What are the specific curricular areas of emphasis and are they primarily workforce related or "new baccalaureates" rather than more traditional programs?

- As more universities are closing their doors to transfer students and cutting back for financial reasons, what will happen to community college students who need and want a baccalaureate but are not served by universities? Will community colleges seek new ways of providing access to baccalaureate programs without depending on universities?

- When universities shift focus and emphasize research while downplaying undergraduate education, should community colleges alter their missions and concentrate on the baccalaureate?

- How will these programs be funded? If community colleges are taking on baccalaureate programming, will universities relinquish state-appropriated monies for those functions and corresponding curricular control?

- What role do faculty members assume in these models of baccalaureate programming? What policies and practices will best sustain morale, fairness, support for their work, and other factors?

Research Issues

- One must ask who is responsible for this research agenda? Who will ensure that a timely, relevant research agenda is implemented for the benefit of practitioners, policy makers, researchers, and students? Will policy decisions rely solely on emotion and political factors, or will a research agenda help drive policy decisions? One hopes that this movement will catch the eye of influential leaders and organizations so that meaningful research can become part of this history in the making.

- There is a critical need for research about this mega-trend. But useful research requires a common language. The models of articulation and two-plus-two programming, university center, university extension, and community college baccalaureate must serve as discrete models. Not all baccalaureate programming that involves community colleges comprises a community college baccalaureate. There are many effective models whereby community colleges are providing access to the baccalaureate, in meaningful ways, without conferring the degree.

Conclusion: A Pressing Need

For Martha Jane Smith, and thousands like her in the United States, the issue of *who* confers the baccalaureate is not as important as having the accessible and affordable courses leading to that degree. Like the place-bound community college student who recently won the CCBA essay contest (McKinney, 2003), Martha Jane also wants access to the baccalaureate immediately after graduation from the community college.

Community college leaders are justified in their concern about providing access for graduates, such as Martha Jane, when better and more secure jobs require a baccalaureate. When times are toughest, universities and other four-year colleges are likely to close doors of opportunity to people like Martha Jane Smith, and community colleges will once again be struggling to keep the name of "people's college" by demonstrating

their commitment to access in creative and new ways that make good on the promise of the "open door."

Notes

[1] This story is representative of many situations the author observed while serving as a president of a community college. Individual names, including people and the college, are fictitious.

[2] The Education Commission of the States (ECS) released a Study, October 1, 2003, entitled "Getting Ready to Pay for College," part of a larger study by ECS to assist policy makers with efforts to increase attendance rates in higher education. According to ECS's president, Ted Sanders, "America is at risk for losing a vital ingredient for success—an educated populace" (Gomstyn, October 2, 2003 [online]). Sandra Rupert, director of the report and study, stated that the United States once was first in the world in baccalaureate-degree participation rates but now ranks eleventh because its rates did not grow while other nations invested in higher education and training (Mollison, 2003). The Lumina Foundation for Education has funded college-access projects, including one with the American Association of Community Colleges to address ways to increase access to the baccalaureate degree. While the United States once led the world in attainment of higher degrees, recent reports indicate that it is "losing ground."

[3] Edison College was formerly Edison Community College. The College's name was changed by the Florida legislature in late April 2004, House Bill 1867.

[4] States reporting joint-use facilities include Arizona, Colorado, Florida, Hawaii, Idaho, Illinois, Kentucky, Mississippi, Nebraska, New Jersey, Ohio, Oklahoma, Oregon, South Carolina, South Dakota, Tennessee, Texas, Utah, Virginia, and Wisconsin. The Windham, Perkins, and Rogers (2001) article in the *Community College Review* includes a more thorough analysis.

[5] OSU's Okmulgee technical campus proposal to offer specific baccalaureate programs was approved by the OSU Board late in 2003. The Oklahoma Board of Regents unanimously approved the plan February 13, 2004.

[6] SREB comprises Alabama, Arkansas, Delaware, Florida, Georgia, Kentucky, Louisiana, Maryland, Mississippi, North Carolina, Oklahoma, South Carolina, Tennessee, Texas, Virginia, and West Virginia.

[7] Dalton State College began offering the baccalaureate in 1998 in three types of management studies: industrial operations, information systems, and

technology. Macon State College began offering these programs in 1997 in communications and information technology, health information, human services, health services administration, and BSN nursing. Parkersburg Community College (West Virginia University at Parkersburg) began offering these programs in 1993. The classifications listed are as of 2002.

[8] The North Central Association (NCA) includes Arizona, Arkansas, Colorado, Illinois, Indiana, Iowa, Kansas, Michigan, Mississippi, Nebraska, New Mexico, North Dakota, Ohio, Oklahoma, West Virginia, Wisconsin, and Wyoming.

[9] According to a March 17, 2004 press release posted to the college's Web site (http://www.tridenttech.edu/ttcnews/3-17-04-bill-dh.html), legislation was passed by the 2004 South Carolina Legislature (after overriding the governor's veto). Prior to offering this degree, approvals must be gained from the South Carolina State Board for Technical and Comprehensive Education and the Commission on Higher Education. According to May 3, 2004 electronic mail communications from Kaye Koonce, general counsel for Trident Technical College, the College plans to submit the program proposal paperwork to the State Tech Board and the Council for Higher Education by mid-Summer, 2004.

[10] The contractor for this study was The Education Alliance from Framington, Massachusetts and the Community College Baccalaureate Association owns these unpublished data.

References

Cohen, A. M. (2003). *The community colleges and the path to the baccalaureate.* University of California–Berkeley: Center for Studies of Higher Education. www.repositories/edlib/cshe/CSH4-03

Cohen, A. M., & Brawer, F. B. (2003). *The American community college* (4th ed.). San Francisco: Jossey Bass.

Community College Baccalaureate Association (CCBA). (2003). *Baccalaureate Needs Assessment Survey.* Unpublished survey results available from the CCBA offices at Edison College, Ft. Myers, FL.

Daily Herald Reports. Go slowly on four-year degree idea. *Daily Herald.* Retrieved September 8, 2003 from www.dailyherald.com/search/main_story.asp?intID=37872128

Floyd, D. L., & Walker, D. A. (2003). Community college teacher education: A typology, challenging issues, and state views. *Community College Journal of Research and Practice, 27*(8), 643–663.

Gomstyn, A. (October 2, 2003). Nation faces a college-access crisis, education policy group warns.

Chronicle of Higher Education. Retrieved October 2, 2003 from www.chronicle.com/prm/daily/2003/10

Gonzales, D. A. (2003). *Great Basin College.* Presentation delivered March 14–16, 2003, to the Community College Baccalaureate Association Conference, Phoenix, Arizona. Available from the author at dgon1@gwmail.gbcnv.

Granderson, K. (September 7, 2003). Four years at Harper? *Daily Herald.* Retrieved September 18, 2003, from www.dailyherald.com

Grimsley, J. A. (January 20, 2003). Letters to the editor: Culinary arts program. *Post and Courier.* Retrieved October 13, 2003, from www.charleston.net/stories/013003/let_30letters.shtml.

Hudson, M. (2000). *National study of community college career corridors for K–12 teacher recruitment.* Belmont, MA: Recruiting New Teachers, Inc.

Illinois College Considers Offering Baccalaureate. (September 29, 2003). *Community College Times, 16*(4), 10.

Larose, M. (July 8, 2003). Three Texas community colleges to offer bachelors. *Community College Times, 15*(15), 5.

McKinney, D. T. (April 14, 2003). We need a baccalaureate now. *Community College Week, 15*(18), 4.

Mills, K. (2003). Community college baccalaureates: Some critics decry the trends as "mission creep." *National CrossTalk.* Published by the National Center for Public Policy and Higher Education. www/highereducation.org/crosstalk/ct0103/news0103-community.html

Mollison, A. (October 2, 2003). Too few go to college, reports say. *Atlanta Journal Constitution.* Retrieved October 2, 2003, from www.ajc.com/paper/editions/Thursday/news_f3b71da411be913D00

Patton, M. (May 27, 2003). University of Hawaii reorganizes community colleges. *Community College Times, 15*(11), 10.

Pedersen, R. P. (2000). *The Early Public Junior College: 1900–1940.* Unpublished dissertation, Columbia University.

Pedersen. R. P. (July 23, 2001). You say you want an evolution? Read the fine print first. *Community College Week,* 4–5.

Sturrock, C. (February 10, 2003). Bill alters Community college role. *Contra Costa Times.* www.bayarea.com/mld.cctimes/5146642.htm

Troumpoucis, P. (April 12, 2004). The best of both worlds? *Community College Week, 16*(16), 6–8.

University Colleges of Technology Alfred-Canton-Cobleskill-Delhi-Morrisville. (1997). *Report on the applied baccalaureate: A new option in higher education in the United States. May 1997.* Available from the United States ERIC Clearinghouse. Document number JC 970–340.

Walker, K. P. (2001). *An open door to the bachelor's degree.* www.league.org/publication/abstracts/leadership/labs0401.html

Wattenbarger, J. (2002). Colleges should stick to what they do best. *Community College Week, 13*(18), 4–5.

Wellman, J. V. (2004). *Policy Alert.* Summary of *State Policy and Community College Baccalaureate Transfer.* San Jose, CA: The National Center of Public Policy and Higher Education. Available on line at www.highereducation.org

Wertheimer, L. K. (July 19, 2003). Three Texas community colleges to grant bachelor's degrees. *Dallas Morning News,* B1 & B5.

Windham, P., Perkins, G., & Rogers, J. (2001). Concurrent use: Part of the new definition of access. *Community College Review, 29*(3), 39–55.

Zwerling, L. S. (1976). *Second best: The crisis of the community college.* New York: McGraw Hill.

CHAPTER 20

THE PAST, PRESENT AND FUTURE ROLE OF FEDERAL VOCATIONAL LEGISLATION IN U.S. COMMUNITY COLLEGES

DEBRA D. BRAGG
UNIVERSITY OF ILLINOIS AT URBANA-CHAMPAIGN

Over the twentieth century, vocational education has played an increasingly prominent role in the United States. This article examines the historical development and current status of federal support for vocational education at the postsecondary level. It considers the role federal laws have played in creating today's postsecondary vocational education programs, particularly in emphasizing student transition from secondary to postsecondary education through initiatives such as Tech Prep and in ensuring greater accountability. Looking to the future, the article considers the federal government's potential for supporting enhanced growth and quality by examining three issues: 1) the funding split between the secondary and postsecondary levels, 2) the need for a new vision for postsecondary vocational education, and 3) the importance of an accountability system based on valid indicators and measures of performance.

The federal government has played an important role in advancing vocational education at the state and local levels in the United States. Beginning in the early twentieth century, federal legislation was passed to support vocational education at the secondary level. Since that time, vocational education has grown from its initial emphasis on the high-school level to a more comprehensive system that encompasses both secondary and postsecondary education. This evolution was not without criticism; yet vocational training has continued to play a prominent role. Guided by the Carl D. Perkins Vocational and Technical Education Act of 1998 (Perkins III), today's vocational programs are shaped, at least in part, by the federal agenda.

This article examines the status and future of federal support for vocational education in the U.S. It considers the role federal laws have played historically to lay a foundation for today's vocational education system, including examining the legislation's emphasis on postsecondary education. Looking to the future, the article examines the evolving postsecondary vocational education enterprise and considers the federal government's potential for supporting enhanced growth and quality. This discussion is important because reauthorization of the current federal vocational legislation is imminent. The time is right to reflect on the past, critically examine the present, and voice alternative perspectives to help shape the future.

The Federal Legislative Legacy

The Initial Years

The Smith-Hughes Act of 1917 was among the first pieces of federal legislation to focus on education in the United States. Centering on secondary education, this law supported the creation and delivery of high-school level programs in agriculture, trade and industry, and home economics (Calhoun & Finch, 1976). Though the law was quite limited in comparison to what is associated with vocational education and workforce development today, it is significant because it paid the salaries of teachers and administrators to prepare high-school graduates to enter jobs associated with agriculture, manufacturing, and labor, or to engage in homemaking (Lynch, 2000). Though the provisions of the law were narrow, the Smith-Hughes Act laid the groundwork for the federal government's future role. It had an undeniable impact on creating separate curricula for students who were deemed better suited for work than college. Indeed, tracking emerged as a result of Smith-Hughes through the federal government's influence on differentiation of secondary curricula.

Except through indirect and unanticipated means, schools were prohibited from spending Smith-Hughes dollars for programs instructing college-age students. Transfer curricula predominated two-year college curricula during these early years, and it was not until societal and economic crises such as the depression, World War II, and the Cold War precipitated growth in postsecondary vocational education (Cohen & Brawer, 1996).

"Total" Commitment, Beginning in the 1960s

Several laws, such as the George-Reed Act of 1929 and the George-Barden Act of 1946, followed Smith-Hughes, but none of these laws allowed direct expenditures for postsecondary vocational education. In fact, it was not until the decade of the 1960s that federal legislation was passed to support what was already a growing postsecondary vocational enterprise.

The Vocational Education Act of 1963, as described by Calhoun and Finch (1976), "represented the beginning of the federal government's *total* commitment to vocational education" (p. 37, emphasis added). Among other foci, this progressive federal law supported a wide array of occupational programs dedicated to workforce preparation below the bachelor's level, including courses offered by community, junior and technical colleges. Initially, federal funds for postsecondary vocational programs were meager, but they were not restricted to a particular student group. Rather, they were intended to serve all students, including persons disadvantaged academically, physically, and socioeconomicaly. Such a far-reaching goal set the stage for growth of the vocational system, including at the postsecondary level, and an increasing emphasis on special populations. It is important to remember, however, that federal funds provided a relatively limited financial investment—generally estimated at eight to ten percent—of the total federal, state and local allocation for vocational programs, and this fact remains true today (Gray, 2002).

The Vocational Education Amendments of 1968 and related federal legislation passed from the late 1960s to the mid 1970s expanded the federal government's role in supporting state and local vocational programs. At the postsecondary level, these programs were increasingly associated with employment in technical fields associated with business, health care, and engineering, adding to the original notion of what was considered "vocational" by including a strong "technical" focus. The legislation also continued to grow in purpose and scope by stressing greater state control over local programs; greater emphasis on youth unemployment, particularly pertaining to academically, socio-economically, and physically disabled youths; greater support for curriculum development to support curricula across levels; enhanced leadership and professional development for teachers and administrators; and more experimentation with programs and instructional innovations.

By the latter 1970s, issues surrounding the efficacy of vocational education for diverse student populations began to emerge. The federal Education Amendments of 1976, specifically the vocational education amendments, devoted attention to developing new programs geared toward overcoming gender discrimination and stereotyping, and increased assistance to finding solutions to youth unemployment. Support for postsecondary vocational education was uneven across the U.S., with some states supporting the concept (though few made it the primary delivery system) and others continuing to support secondary vocational education nearly exclusively.

Across the levels, national priority was placed on establishing vocational education for handicapped persons, other disadvantaged persons, and persons of limited English-speaking proficiency (Calhoun & Finch, 1976). With respect to postsecondary, greater attention was given to persons who had completed or left high school and were seeking credit toward an associate or other degree not leading to the baccalaureate or higher degree, and for persons who had entered the labor market, or who were unemployed.

The 1976 amendments also provided for the development of the national vocational education data system to enhance the ability of states to report student participation more accurately and consistently than in the past. Improving programs and enhancing quality was a high priority of the federal government, setting the stage for national debate about educational reform, academic standards, and the role of vocational education.

The Reform Agenda, Beginning in the 1980s

The 1980s were a turbulent time for all of education. Calls for reform of public education gained greater attention nationally, with increased encouragement and support from public officials and the USDoE under the Reagan Administration. Critical issues pertaining to the quality and academic rigor of curriculum were central to recommendations of A Nation at Risk (National Commission on Excellence in Education, 1983), and this report has had a lasting impact on elementary and secondary education nationally, including precipitating a dialogue concerning standards and accountability (Asche, 1991). Reform ideas emanating from the report encouraged states to increase high school graduation requirements, emphasize standardized tests of academic achievement, and ensure that all students had the opportunity to engage in core academic courses (that sometimes crowded vocational courses out of the secondary curriculum).

Ushered in on the wake of A Nation at Risk, the Carl D. Perkins Vocational Education and Applied Technology Act of 1984 (referred to as Perkins I and named after the late Senator from Kentucky who was an adamant supporter of

vocational education in the U.S. Congress) attempted to continue many vocational initiatives begun during the 1960s and 1970s, again primarily emphasizing secondary education. For example, education and training directed at meeting the occupational needs of students who faced gender stereotyping and various programs serving disadvantaged (special needs) populations were encouraged. Lynch (2000) characterized this era as follows:

> [I]n the late 1980s and early 1990s, vocational education experienced unprecedented enrollment percentage increases from special populations as an increasing number of general student groups opted out of vocational education to take more academic courses and as funding favored inclusion of special populations in vocational education programs. (p. 10)

Criticism swelled as secondary vocational education was increasingly viewed as a "dumping ground" for special needs learners (Boesel, Hudson, Deich, & Masten, 1994; Lynch, 2000), and inextricably intertwined with tracking students away from the core academic curriculum (see, for example, Oakes, 1985). The postsecondary level was not immune from these charges. For example, Pincus (1980, 1986) claimed postsecondary vocational education delivered false promises because it did not produce the benefits for students that it professed to offer. In a widely publicized book, The Diverted Dream, Brint & Karabel (1989) argued increased vocationalization tracked students into work rather than further education, hampering upward mobility because of the lack of a viable transfer option for those in terminal vocational programs.

Partly to address this concern, attention began to be paid to linkages between the secondary and postsecondary levels in support of the notion that secondary students taking vocational courses need not end their schooling with a high-school diploma and entry-level jobs. To this end, articulation agreements to facilitate student movement from high school to college, mostly to community colleges, were encouraged (Bragg, 1995). Encouraging students to transition from the secondary to the postsecondary level for vocational training also made sense from an economic standpoint. Changes in the U.S. economy increased demand for students to gain at least some college-level education, often in technical fields, to secure employment offering a family-living wage (Grubb, 1996). This is an important development because increasingly students who ended schooling at the high-school level were subjected to unstable, low-wage jobs or unemployment (Carnevale, 2000).

For the first time, Technical Preparation (Tech Prep) was mentioned in federal legislation as a programmatic approach to facilitating secondary-to-postsecondary articulation. Even though no federal funds were targeted specifically to Tech Prep at this time, states were allowed to use federal funds to support Tech Prep programs, and some elected to do so. It is noteworthy that the book authored by Dale Parnell (1985), titled *The Neglected Majority*, introduced Tech Prep to a national audience only one year after passage of federal legislation. As President of the American Association of Community Colleges (AACC), undoubtedly Parnell had access to policy makers during the drafting of federal legislation, facilitating the nationwide launching of Tech-Prep programs over the next decade.

Another feature of Perkins I that is important to mention, because it laid the groundwork for future legislation, is accountability. Consistent with the national appeal for greater accountability in all of education and building on earlier federal vocational legislation, Perkins I placed greater priority on measuring student outcomes. Recognizing that previous federal legislation emphasized inputs, teaching practices, and student participation (Navaratnam & Hillison, 1985), federal policies encouraged an expanded effort to document educational and economic outcomes. Assessing the costs and benefits of vocational education which heretofore had been assumed or simply ignored was challenging for the states. While the heightened emphasis on outcomes was not concentrated on vocational education alone, vocational programs were on the front line. States and localities struggled to document student outcomes beyond reporting enrollments and rudimentary results. Many of them failed, placing even higher priority on accountability in subsequent legislation.

The Federal Mandate of the 1990s

In 1990, the Carl D. Perkins Vocational Education and Applied Technology Act Amendments (Perkins II) and later, in 1998, the Carl D. Perkins Vocational and Technical Education Act Amend-

ments (Perkins III) were passed, ushering in additional changes. Both of these laws endorsed increased attention to academic and technical skill development for all segments of the student population, not exclusively for special populations. Lynch (2000) noted that, "for the first time in federal vocational legislation, emphasis was placed on academics and funds could be directed to 'all segments' of the population" (p. 10). Still, funding formulas under Perkins II and III have favored vocational programs located in secondary schools and community colleges serving disadvantaged students. These students were to be engaged in an integrated core of academic subjects (math, English/communications, and science) and vocational education, and institutions receiving federal funds were to be held accountable for student outcomes associated with the entire curriculum. Assessment of student academic achievement moved to the forefront, and this action precipitated even further controversy and change.

The federal vocational legislation's foray into comprehensive (academic and vocational) curricula via Perkins II was instrumental in encouraging the USDoE's Office of Vocational and Adult Education (OVAE) to enter into the nation's high school reform agenda. By advocating for Tech Prep as an educational reform and later launching New American High Schools, officials of OVAE urged schools to make significant curricular changes and link course-taking in academic and vocational subjects to academic achievement.

Other reforms emerged during this time that had comparable goals to Tech Prep. The best known is High Schools That Work of the Southern Regional Education Board (SREB). The SREB's efforts are notable because this organization has championed reform of high school education to include strong academic and vocational components, including utilizing the National Assessment of Education Progress (NAEP) to assess students' learning outcomes. The SREB utilized this approach because it recognized that evidence of academic achievement would be critical to giving legitimacy to the High Schools That Work reform (Bottoms, Presson & Johnson, 1992).

Reflecting the growing emphasis on high school reform, federal policies under Perkins II and III have continued to emphasize secondary vocational education over postsecondary. Though the federal government has encouraged states to invest at least one-third of federal dollars in postsecondary vocational programs, it has not mandated such a split, and many states have failed to do so. As a result, the vocational mission of community colleges has blossomed during the 1980s and 1990s largely without the direct support of federal funding.

Grubb, Badway, Bell, and Kraskoukas (1996) reported that community colleges are engaged in numerous initiatives dealing with workforce preparation and workforce development, only some of which are influenced by federal legislation. Their list of programs includes:

- Accountability measures, including performance measures required by federal legislation;

- Proposals to enhance the academic competencies and "higher order" skills of the workforce, including federal initiatives to integrate academic and occupational education;

- Tech-Prep programs linking secondary schools with community colleges;

- School-to-work programs adding work-based learning and connecting activities to educational programs;

- The expansion of short-term job training programs, for groups ranging from welfare recipients to displaced workers;

- Contract education provided by community colleges to specific employers to upgrade certain skills of their workforce;

- State-funded economic development programs, providing still other funds for firm-specific training, often with the intention of attracting business and industry to an area;

- Proposals to develop skills standards, specifying the skills required in certain occupations and industries. (p. viii)

Of particular note in the Perkins II and III legislation are two areas that do have significant impact on community colleges: Tech Prep and accountability. When Perkins was reauthorized in 1990, Tech Prep became a formal part of the federal vocational agenda. Charged with supporting a multitude of goals and learner needs, Tech Prep program designers have sought to establish formal articulation agreements that identify logical progressions of integrated and rigorous academic and vocational-technical

courses from the secondary to the postsecondary level. Through at least a 2+2 sequential curriculum (or additional years of education before and/or after the 2+2), Tech Prep programs are intended to prepare for college secondary students who might not otherwise pursue careers requiring postsecondary-level math, science, and technology studies, and to support these students to completion of their associate degrees and/or transfer to baccalaureate programs.

Under Perkins III, Tech Prep policy and funding continues and encourages the creation of integrated curricula, instructional innovations, and the work-based learning that has taken hold in secondary education. Departing from previous federal legislation, Perkins III also encourages articulation mechanisms for Tech Prep between two-year and four-year colleges so that students can complete a baccalaureate degree. Recognizing that previous laws had mandated a sub-baccalaureate focus for all vocational programs, this departure was important in addressing criticisms about tracking. Greater accountability in identifying, and monitoring student progress from secondary school to college and work is a requirement of Tech Prep under Perkins III.

Several national studies of Tech Prep implementation (Boesel, Rahn, & Deich, 1994; Bragg, Layton, & Hammons, 1994; Bragg & Reger, 2002; Hershey, Silverberg, Owens, & Hulsey, 1998) show advancement in Tech Prep implementation over the decade of the 1990s, with the vast majority of U.S. school districts, and nearly all two-year colleges, participating. These studies show development of strong partnerships facilitated by local consortium arrangements involving secondary schools, community colleges, businesses, and community organizations. Through these partnerships, collaboration occurs among academic and vocational instructors on behalf of curriculum alignment and professional development. An increasing number of instructors have engaged in contextual teaching by including work-related examples, problem- and project-based instruction, and peer-oriented strategies.

National studies have also revealed barriers to Tech Prep implementation. For example, local consortia struggle to find time for instructors to meet and create sequential secondary-to-postsecondary course work, including developing dual credit options. Whereas many community colleges have played a facilitative role, only some have accepted goals that support systemic reform from the Kindergarten to Grade

14 or beyond (Orr & Bragg, 2001). Some community colleges have seen Tech Prep as a student recruitment tool without committing to the foundational work necessary to make it successful, and these attempts have floundered or failed.

Taking the lead of previous federal legislation, both recent Perkins laws have emphasized accountability. The unique feature of Perkins III, however, is that performance measures are tied to vocational *and* academic education. In crafting the core indicator framework for Perkins III, Schray (2000) pointed out, core indicators and performance measures are required at both the secondary and postsecondary levels in: 1) student attainment in vocational and core academic education (math, science, and English/communications); 2) credential attainment in terms of high school diploma, certification and associate degree; and 3) transition from the secondary to postsecondary level, including retention and completion. Plus, Perkins III renewed an old theme when it mandated the reporting of student enrollment in vocational programs by gender to identify nontraditional program participation.

Through an ever-evolving system of performance measures and standards enforced through state-level planning and reporting, OVAE has required that states comply with higher accountability demands. In fact, a state's portion of federal funding is associated with its ability to meet specified targets, which reinforces the importance of state-level evaluation systems. Referred to as performance-based budgeting, this approach uses "financial incentives and the budgeting process to drive performance improvement on a core set of performance measures" (Sheets, 2002, p. 6). To make the accountability system functional, specific operational definitions are created for key concepts associated with vocational course-taking and learner outcomes (vocational concentrators and vocational specialists, for example). A great deal of professional development and technical assistance has been provided to state officials by OVAE and other federal-sponsored organizations such as the National Centers for Career and Technical Education and its predecessor, the National Center for Research in Vocational Education.

A Glimpse at Postsecondary Vocational Education Today

Due to its enormous diversity, the nation's postsecondary vocational education enterprise is nearly impossible to quantify, though it is clear that it accounts for a significant portion of sub-baccalaureate education today. Most public two-year colleges provide vocational education of some sort, typically enrolling from 40 to 60 percent of all students. With public two-year colleges enrolling well over 5 million full-time equivalent students nationwide (National Center for Education Statistics, 1999a, 1999b), an estimated 2.5 million students account for public postsecondary vocational enrollments annually. Offering similar results, Levesque, Lauen, Teitelbaum, Librera and Nelson (2000) noted that one-half of the students who engage in public for-credit collegiate studies below the bachelor's level major in a vocational or technical field. Of the remainder, about 23 percent enroll in an academic field and another 28 percent do not report a major, based on the 1995–96 National Postsecondary Student Aid Study.

Looking at the demographic characteristics of students in vocational programs, Levesque et al. confirmed historic enrollment patterns that suggest the likelihood of majoring in a vocational or technical field increases as family income declines. Enrollment by race-ethnic group is complex and difficult to generalize from one setting to another, undoubtedly due to the complex interactions of race/ethnicity with socioeconomic status (SES). For example, Levesque et al. showed African Americans were under-represented in postsecondary vocational education, but the National Assessment of Vocational Education (NAVE)—a federally mandated evaluation of the impact of federal vocational legislation—showed African Americans overrepresented in postsecondary vocational programs, mirroring secondary enrollments (Boesel, Hudson, Deich, & Masten, 1994). In fact, these apparently contradictory results may both be true. By looking at vocational programs in public and private institutions rather than looking solely at publicly funded institutions as Levesque et al. did, Boesel et al. showed low-income race-ethnic groups are more likely to attend costlier (including private) institutions (p. 143). By taking into account both public and private institutions, Boesel et al. found a higher proportion of race-ethnic groups engaged in vocational education than did Levesque et al. Regardless of setting, both studies concluded vocational programs are more likely than other college curricula to enroll students who are economically or educationally disadvantaged, disabled, or who are single parents.

NAVE also concluded that overall enrollments in postsecondary vocational education were stable or growing at about the same pace as general collegiate enrollments (Boesel & McFarland, 1994). Vocational programs were more structured than similar programs at the secondary level, and the added structure was beneficial to students. The NAVE study recognized that postsecondary vocational programs had emphasized academic course work historically even though faculty were slow to adopt new models of academic and vocational curriculum integration and new instructional strategies advocated by Perkins II and III. This conclusion has been corroborated by numerous studies in a variety of settings (for examples see, Badway & Grubb, 1997; Grubb, Badway, Bell, & Kraskouskas, 1996; and Perin, 2000).

An examination of the postsecondary vocational curricula in which students enroll currently suggests an increasingly diverse set of occupations offering a growing number of certificate and degree options. Postsecondary vocational programs supported by Perkins III provide students with certification and/or licensure in an occupational or technical field, and many of these programs culminate in an associate degree, usually an associate of applied science (AAS) degree (though there is variation in the type of associate degree awarded by state.) Programs in business, health care, engineering and related technologies, computer and information technologies, and human and social services, including education, enroll the preponderance of today's postsecondary students (Boesel & McFarland, 1994). Spurred on by Perkins, increasingly these postsecondary programs are aligned with the secondary level, giving high-school students the ability to secure college credits via Tech Prep and other dual enrollment options. Also, more vocational programs are incorporating a career pathway approach where students can enter a sequential program of study at either the secondary or postsecondary level and earn certificates, licenses and/or educational credentials as they move through the system and demonstrate mastery of key knowledge and skills. Increasingly, these career pathways do not culminate with a terminal associate degree, but an associate degree allowing them to continue to the baccalaureate level (Townsend, 2001).

In most community colleges today, traditional programs and transitional options supported by Perkins are offered alongside newer models geared toward workforce development (Bragg, 2001). Some workforce development programs are analogous to Perkins-funded programs, but others are separate and distinct. Federal policies such as the Workforce Investment Act (WIA) emphasize workforce development for adult learners, allowing community colleges to deliver vocational offerings not confined to the parameters of Perkins III. Even so, Perkins III requires a coordinated reporting structure designed to enhance the comparability of various federally funded initiatives dedicated to preparing students for a variety of entry points into the labor market. In addition to publicly supported initiatives, community colleges offer an increasing array of vocationally oriented courses that are funded by the private sector (Phillippe & Valiga, 2000). Sometimes these initiatives are disconnected from Perkins III-funded vocational programs to enhance the ability of colleges to respond quickly to the business community, thus giving these programs an entrepreneurial flavor (Grubb, Badway, Bell, Bragg & Russman, 1997).

Examining outcomes for diverse learners in such a broad set of educational programs is quite challenging. Scholars offer varied conclusions about the benefits of participation in postsecondary vocational education programs. While critics such as Brint and Karabel (1989) and Pincus (1980, 1986) find little merit in them, others, such as Grubb (1999a), suggest that, relative to high school graduates, attending a community college and persisting to completion in a vocational program confers advantages in the labor market. Based on a series of studies utilizing national data sets, Grubb concluded: "[C]ompleting Associate degrees enhances wages, employment, and earnings by significant amounts, in both conventional and statistical senses" (p. 10). Looking at results by gender, Grubb shows men with associate degrees earn 18 percent more, and women 23 percent more, than high school graduates. Findings from NAVE (Boesel & McFarland, 1994) conclude that while benefits are relatively equally distributed to all members of the student population, there may be even more benefit to enrolling and completing postsecondary vocational education for minority than for non-minority students.

Considering the Future

Currently, under the direction of Assistant Secretary Carol D'Amico, OVAE is soliciting input regarding future federal legislation dealing with vocational education. A series of papers has been commissioned by Dr. D'Amico to allow scholars, experts and practitioners to present alternative perspectives on the role of federal legislation in vocational education in the U.S. (The website for downloading these commissioned papers is http://www.ed.gov/offices/OVAE/HS/commisspap.html) In addition, the NAVE, which is intended to evaluate implementation and outcomes associated with Perkins III, is due to be released soon. Historically, results of this federally required study has played an important role in determining the direction new legislation will take.

Not knowing the results of NAVE, the commissioned papers of OVAE provide some insights into possible directions for new legislation. These papers do not substitute for the empirical results that will emanate from NAVE and other research and development groups, including the National Centers for Career and Technical Education, but they do provide a logical start for identifying critical issues and policy alternatives. Using several of the commissioned papers as a resource, along with my own experience, I conclude this article with three observations about the past, present, and future role of the federal government in vocational education.

First, recognizing that the federal government has supported vocational education's growth throughout the twentieth century, including expanding to the postsecondary level, it is clear that federal legislation has played a part in precipitating growth in the vocational system. Despite that, how deep and lasting are changes advocated by federal legislation? To what extent is state and local policy and practice shaped by federal law? For years, scholars and policy observers have noted that federal funds account for less than 10 percent of the total vocational enterprise, and questioned the impact of such a limited share of the pie (Gray, 2002). This fact is particularly disconcerting knowing that, of the total allocation of federal funds for vocational education, postsecondary education receives far fewer dollars than the secondary level (often one-third or less of the total), and this is a particularly salient issue for community colleges. Specifically, it suggests an imbalance in the value placed on postsecondary vocational education relative to the secondary level. Why should the federal government continue such a heavy investment in secondary vocational education when most jobs require postsecondary vocational preparation? Everett, Gershwin, Hays, Jacobs & Mundhen (2002), representing the National Council on Workforce Education (NCWE), argue that future federal legislation should not continue to favor secondary education at the expense of the postsecondary level. Recommending separate but complementary federal policy, Everett et al. urge OVAE to advocate for distinct vocational legislation to address the unique needs of community colleges. This recommendation is a dramatic one, but it needs to be given serious attention to ensure that the entire vocational system receives adequate resources to meet growing student needs.

Second, in order for the federal government to endorse a strengthened priority for postsecondary vocational education, it is imperative that a more compelling vision be articulated (Grubb, 1999b). Contrasting postsecondary vocational education with the secondary level, Grubb claims that secondary vocational education has been propelled in recent years by the emergence of the notion of a "new vocationalism" emphasizing a broadened notion of preparation for careers through academic and vocational integration and transition to college. Research shows that sometimes community colleges struggle to implement vocational programs with these new goals and features because they do not fit logically with other workforce development offerings (usually those not supported by Perkins III). Often these workforce programs attract adult students who seek alternative employment, retraining or job upgrading rather than traditional students preparing for entry-level employment. Among others, Grubb (1999b) has cautioned community colleges to provide more supportive services, including guidance and counseling, for students of all ages who want to engage in vocational studies. Under Perkins, models that are effective at serving the needs of such a diversity of students at the postsecondary level have not emerged. Ideas and approaches associated with the new vocationalism such as Tech Prep, dual credit/enrollment, and career pathways should not be abandoned, but it is important to recognize that these models do not meet the needs of all students seeking postsecondary vocational programs. What types of programs are needed to meet the needs of postsecondary students? The answer to this question—the new vision—is not clear. Flexible strategies that take into account full- and part-time learners, credit and noncredit options, and various types of credentials need to be conceptualized more clearly and disseminated more widely. Without this happening, it is unlikely new legislation dedicated to postsecondary vocational education will be successful. Equally as problematic is the likelihood that, without redirection, new federal legislation will continue its predominant emphasis on secondary education to the detriment of vocational programs at the postsecondary level.

Finally, there is no refuting that accountability has become the watchword of federal legislation dealing with vocational education under Perkins II and III. Unfortunately, accountability requirements under the Perkins laws have reflected the federal government's bias toward secondary education, and this partiality appears in the core indicators and performance measures developed by OVAE. Almost from the day Perkins III was enacted, postsecondary educators pointed to difficulties in implementing a valid accountability system because of an over-reliance on concepts more appropriate to secondary than postsecondary education. Notions of academic achievement, graduation, and transition to college that seem logical for secondary students do not translate easily to the postsecondary environment. Without an evaluation system that is sensitive to the particular goals and processes relevant to postsecondary programs and students, community colleges are at a distinct disadvantage relative to secondary schools in demonstrating their effectiveness.

Recognizing this dilemma, Sheets (2002) recommends that future federal efforts "should be coordinated with state and local efforts to develop comprehensive frameworks for postsecondary institutions that balance the multiple missions and customer requirements of community and technical colleges" (p. 8). He recommends separate academic attainment measures for postsecondary institutions, relying mostly on measures of vocational and technical skill attainment to reflect the heavy emphasis of postsecondary vocational programs on technical subject matter. Wellman (2001) suggests that attainment indicators be tied to student goal, rather than a fixed institutional standard, to more accurately capture student intent. Measures of student transition from two- to four-year college endorsed by Everett et al. (2002) and Sheets (2002) reflect increased movement of stu-

dents into bachelor's degree programs. They also recommend better measures of the quality of employment as measured by wages and earnings to fully capture program effectiveness. Everett et al. (2002) also request that the federal government incorporate credentialing rates among students according to licensure, certification, and other external standards (p. 16). Finally, questioning why the federal core indicators are specified by gender only, Sheets (2002) recommends that postsecondary programs, known for serving a highly diverse student population, report on core indicators according to numerous demographic categories, not only gender.

Little doubt exists that federal vocational legislation has expanded in scope to encompass the postsecondary level. Federal resources are appropriated to support programs offered at the secondary and postsecondary levels, and competencies associated with vocational as well as academic education are incorporated into the nation's comprehensive vocational system. By creating a new vision of postsecondary vocational education, along with valid indicators of student success, community colleges would be better positioned to enhance the quality of their offerings and demonstrate how students benefit. Indeed, the time has come to reexamine the federal role, and it is important that community college professionals advocate for changes that enhance vocational education in the future.

References

Asche, M. (1991). Educational reform and vocational education: Review with implications for research and development. *Journal of Vocational Education Research, 16*(3), 1–34.

Badway, N., & Grubb, W. N. (1997). *Curriculum integration and the multiple domains of career preparation. A handbook for reshaping the community college.* Berkeley, CA: National Center for Research in Vocational Education, University of California at Berkeley.

Boesel, D., & McFarland, L. (1994). *National assessment of vocational education, Final report to Congress, Volume I, Summary and conclusions.* Washington, DC: U.S. Department of Education, Office of Educational Research and Improvement.

Boesel, D., Rahn, M., & Deich, S. (1994). *National assessment of vocational education, Final report to Congress, Volume II, Program improvement: Education reform.* Washington, DC: U.S. Department of Education, Office of Educational Research and Improvement.

Boesel, D., Hudson, L., Deich, S., & Masten, C. (1994). *National assessment of vocational education, Final report to Congress, Volume II: Participation in and quality of vocational education.* Washington, D.C.: U.S. Department of Education, Office of Educational Research and Improvement.

Bottoms, G., Presson, A., & Johnson, M. (1992). *Making high schools work.* Atlanta, GA: Southern Regional Education Board.

Bragg, D. (1995). Linking high schools to postsecondary institutions: The role of tech prep. In W. Norton Grubb (Ed.), *Education through occupations in American high schools, Vol. II,* (pp. 191–211). New York: Teachers College Press.

Bragg, D. (2001). Opportunities and changes for the new vocationalism. In D. Bragg (Ed.), *New Directions for Community Colleges, no. 115. The new vocationalism in community colleges* (pp. 5–16), San Francisco: Jossey-Bass.

Bragg, D., Layton, J., & Hammons, F. (1994). *Tech Prep implementation in the United States: Promising trends and lingering challenges.* Berkeley, CA: National Center for Research in Vocational Education, University of California, Berkeley.

Bragg, D., & Reger, W. (2002). *New lessons about Tech Prep implementation: Changes in eight local consortia since reauthorization of the federal Tech Prep consortia in 1998.* St. Paul, MN: National Research Center for Career and Technical Education, University of Minnesota.

Brint, S., & Karabel, J. (1989). *The diverted dream.* New York: Oxford University Press.

Calhoun, C., & Finch, A. (1976). *Vocational education: Concepts and operations.* Belmont, CA: Wadsworth Publishing Company.

Carnevale, A. (2000). *Community colleges and career qualifications.* (Issues Paper No. 11). Washington, DC: American Association of Community Colleges.

Cohen, A., & Brawer, F. (1996). *The American community college.* (3rd ed.). San Francisco: Jossey-Bass.

Everett, J., Gershwin, M., Hayes, H., Jacobs, J., & Mundhenk, R. (2002). *How should "quality" technical education and training be defined.* Washington, D.C.: U.S. Department of Education, Office of Vocational and Adult Education. Retrieved July 13, 2002, from http://www.ed.gov/offices/OVAE/HS/everett.doc

Gray, K. (2002). *The role of career and technical education in American high schools: A student centered analysis.* Washington, D.C.: U.S. Department of Education, Office of Vocational and Adult Education. Retrieved July 13, 2002, from http://www.ed.gov/offices/OVAE/HS/gray.doc

Grubb, W. N. (1996). *Working in the middle: Strengthening education and training for the mid-skilled labor force.* San Francisco, CA: Jossey-Bass.

Grubb, W. N. (1999a). *Learning and earning in the middle: The economic benefits of sub-baccalaureate education.* New York: Columbia University Teachers College, Community College Research Center.

Grubb, W. N. (1999b). *Edging toward effectiveness: Examining postsecondary occupational education.* Washington, D.C.: U.S. Department of Education. Retrieved July 12, 2002 from http://www.ed.gov/offices/OUS/PES/NAVE/Grubb.html

Grubb, W. N., Badway, N., Bell, D., & Kraskouskas, E. (1996). *Community college innovations in workforce preparation: Curriculum integration and tech prep.* Mission Viejo, CA: A joint publication of the League for Innovation in the Community College, National Center for Research in Vocational Education, and National Council for Occupational Education.

Grubb, W. N., Badway, N., Bell, D., Bragg, D., & Russman, M. (1997). *Workforce, economic and community development: The changing landscape of the entrepreneurial community college.* Mission Viejo, CA: League for Innovation in the Community College.

Hershey, A. M., Silverberg, M. K., Owens, T., and Hulsey, L. K. (1998). *Focus for the future. The final report of the national tech prep evaluation.* Princeton, NJ: Mathematica Policy Research.

Levesque, K., Lauen, D., Teitelbaum, P., Alt, M., Librera, S., & Nelson, D. (2000). *Vocational education in the United States: Toward the year 2000.* Washington, DC: U.S. Department of Education, Office of Educational Research and Improvement.

Lynch, R. (2000). *New directions for high school career and technical education in the 21st century.* (Information Series No. 384.) Columbus, OH: ERIC Clearinghouse on Adult, Career and Technical Education, The Ohio State University.

National Center for Education Statistics. (1999a). *Integrated postsecondary education data system (IPEDS) fall enrollment survey.* Washington, D.C.: U.S. Department of Education.

National Center for Education Statistics. (1999b). *Integrated postsecondary education data system (IPEDS) institutional characteristics survey.* Washington, D.C.: U.S. Department of Education.

National Commission on Excellence in Education. (1983). *A nation at risk.* Washington, D.C.: United States Department of Education.

Navarantam, K., & Hillison, J. (1985). Determining economic outcomes of vocational education. *Journal of Vocational Education Research, 10*(4), 1–11.

Oakes, J. (1985). *Keeping track: How schools structure inequality.* New Haven, CT: Yale University Press.

Orr, M., and Bragg, D. (2001). Policy directions for K–14 education: Looking to the future. In B. Townsend & S. Twombly (Eds.), *Educational*

Policy in the 21st Century, Vol. 2, Community colleges: Policy in the future context (pp. 101–128). Westport, CT: Ablex Publishers.

Parnell, D. (1985). *The Neglected majority.* Washington, DC: American Association of Community Colleges.

Perin, D. (2000). *Curriculum and pedagogy to integrate occupational and academic instruction in the community college: implications for faculty development.* (Brief No. 8). New York: Columbia University Teachers College, Community College Research Center.

Phillippe, K., & Valiga, M. (2000). *Faces of the future: A portrait of American community college students.* Washington, D.C.: American Association of Community Colleges.

Pincus, F. (1980). The false promises of community colleges: Class conflict and vocational education. *Harvard Educational Review, 50*(3), 332–361.

Pincus, F. (1986). Vocational education: More false promises. In L. S. Zwerling (Ed.), *New Directions for Community Colleges, no. 54: The community college and its critics* (pp. 41–52). San Francisco: Jossey-Bass.

Schray, V. (2000). *Core indicator framework.* Washington, D.C.: United States Department of Education, Office of Vocational and Adult Education. Retrieved July 13, 2002, from http://www.ed.gov/offices/OVAE/CTE/jan2000frame.doc

Sheets, R. (2002). *Improving state accountability systems for postsecondary vocational education.* Washington, D.C.: United States Department of Education, Office of Vocational and Adult Education. Retrieved July 13, 2002 from http://www.ed.gov/offices/OVAE/HS/sheets.doc

Townsend, B. (2001). Blurring the lines: Transforming terminal education to transfer education. In D. Bragg (Ed.), *New Directions for Community Colleges, no. 115 The new vocationalism in community colleges* (pp. 63–72). San Francisco: Jossey-Bass.

Wellman, J. (2001, April). Assessing state accountability systems. *Change, 33*(2), 47–53.

Debra D. Bragg is a professor and director of the higher education program and director of the Office of Community College Research and Leadership at the University of Illinois at Urbana-Champaign.

CHAPTER 21

COMMUNITY COLLEGES AND THE EQUITY AGENDA: THE POTENTIAL OF NONCREDIT EDUCATION

W. NORTON GRUBB, NORENA BADWAY, AND DENISE BELL

While community colleges pride themselves on their inclusiveness, they tend not to enroll many of the lowest-performing students leaving high schools, most of the disconnected youth who have dropped out of high school, and many low-income adults. This article explores the possibility of using noncredit education as a bridging mechanism to allow such students to enter the community college. Noncredit programs have many advantages including lower cost; greater accessibility, flexibility, and responsiveness; and greater access to immigrants. Some noncredit centers have worked hard to develop smooth transitions to the credit programs of their colleges. While noncredit education has great promise as a mechanism for expanding access to community colleges, it also faces familiar problems: inadequate funding, low status, inadequate support services, and developing in adequate articulation mechanisms with credit programs. Finally, community colleges cannot by themselves resolve the problems of inadequate schooling and poverty, and a variety of complementary social and economic policies must also be developed.

Keywords: *community colleges; noncredit education; equity*

W. Norton Grubb is a professor and the David Gardner Chair in Higher Education at the School of Education, University of California, Berkeley, where he is also the faculty coordinator for the Principal Leadership Institute. He received his doctorate in economics from Harvard University in 1975. He has published extensively on various topics in the economics of education, public finance, education policy, community colleges and second chance programs, and social policy for children and youth. He also consults extensively with high schools, community colleges, and public policy groups about both institutional and policy reforms. He is the author most recently of Honored but Invisible: An Inside Look at Teaching in Community Colleges *(1999, Routledge),* DOI: 10.1177/0002716202250226

Community colleges have prided themselves on their inclusiveness. The rhetoric about the people's college and democracy's open door has signaled the willingness of these institutions to serve lower-income students, immigrants, students whose parents have never been to college, older students including women returning to the labor force, and other nontraditional students. This inclusiveness is part of an old and glorious tradition in American education dating from the nineteenth century, the tradition of the common school that extended public support of education to everyone—initially for political purposes and then for occupational reasons. At their best, community colleges and their faculty are committed to their varied students and are supportive of them in many ways. As an economics instructor described this mission,

I find [the community college] very rewarding, exciting, challenging. I tend to think it's
probably one of the most important parts of
higher education in that, as far as I'm concerned, it's the last real opportunity for many
people in our community. You can be a high
school dropout, you can have all sorts of
problems or issues of your past and as long
as the community college is there for you,
there's still that hope. (Grubb and Associates
1999, 4)

In practice, however, community colleges
have never reached the neediest individuals in
any great numbers. The younger students coming right out of high school have tended to come
from the middle of the distribution—with middling grades, middling income levels, middling
(and sometimes inchoate) aspirations for their
futures.[1] Many older students are experienced
workers seeking to upgrade their skills; some
have been sent by their employers, who tend to
support only the most promising workers; and
those seeking retraining, to find new occupations
because of dislocations in the economy, tend to
be experienced.

And so while community college students
are nontraditional compared to four-year college
students, they still tend not to include those who
need further education the most: low-income
individuals; those with no experience in the labor
market, or with employment in low-wage jobs
with marginal employers where upgrade training is unlikely to be provided; recent immigrants,
without workable English or much familiarity
with employment opportunities; those with serious family problems; welfare recipients and the
long-term unemployed, many of whom have

multiple barriers to employment; and those with
criminal records or with physical or mental disabilities. These are potential students who have
been served, if at all—and often, we will argue
in the What Is the Alternative? section, they are
ill-served—by adult education, welfare-to-work
programs, and short-term job training including
the Job Training Partnership Act and now the
Workforce Investment Act (WIA). For simplicity,
we will refer to them as low-income or low-wage
students, but it is important to remember that
they do not constitute a single group, and both
the personal and the social sources of their needs
vary substantially.

So the equity agenda would involve community colleges in a series of reforms to increase
access among these potential students, as well as
improving their progress through college, so that
they too could have the benefits of postsecondary
education. There are many different elements of
a fully developed equity agenda, particularly
since access without progress is an empty
promise—and so issues like the improvement of
developmental education, the reform of guidance and counseling and other student services,
and better approaches to the work-family-
schooling dilemma (which we explore in the
Limits of the Equity Agenda and Education
Reform section) would be necessary. For this article, however, we examine a form of education
that could expand access for many of these
poorly served students. Some colleges—not that
many, we suspect, but enough to clarify a pattern and suggest a model—have developed programs of noncredit education that are in every
way more welcoming of low-wage students and
more supportive of their short-run goals while

Learning to Work: The Case for Re-Integrating Education and Job Training (1996, Russell Sage), Working in the Middle: Strengthening the Education and Training of the Middle-Skilled Labor Force (1996, Jossey-Bass), and Education for Occupations in
American High Schools (1995, Teachers College Press), on the integration of academic and occupational education.

Norena Badway is the director of the Community College Cooperative at the Graduate School of Education, University of
California, Berkeley. She received her doctorate in education policy from Berkeley in 1998. Her research focuses on access to
higher education and aspects of community college organization, curriculum, and teaching. She conducts evaluations of
federal and state grant-funded programs and consults with secondary schools and community colleges about curriculum
reform, assessment, developmental education, accreditation, and integrated program design.

Denise Bell is the director of assessment at Worcester State College and the program effectiveness coordinator at the University of California, Berkeley. She is currently a Ph.D. candidate in the School of Education at University of California, Berkeley. She received her Ed.M. in administration, planning, and social policy from Harvard University in 1987. Her research
interests include performance funding in higher education, educational policy, community colleges, and assessment and planning in education. As a consultant, she has conducted numerous program evaluations for the Math, Engineering, Science
Achievement program; Lucent Technologies; the Massachusetts Cultural Council; the Winnick Foundation; and Florida
community colleges.

NOTE: This article has been supported with funds from the David Gardner Chair in Higher Education and with additional
funding from the Metlife Foundation to Jobs for the Future. Jim Jacobs and Bob Gabriner provided helpful comments on an
earlier draft.

maintaining their long-run hopes. These non-credit programs constitute a precollege or bridging mechanism, helping individuals who might not otherwise gain access to community colleges make the transition into mainstream education. These programs are more flexible, less impersonal and bureaucratic than the credit divisions of community colleges, and more likely to be in community-based facilities, closer to where low-income students live. And under the right circumstances, they may be able to distinguish carefully among different types of low-income students and tailor programs to their specific needs—for example, the issues of recent immigrants, welfare mothers, or high school dropouts. We outline the advantages of these noncredit programs in the Advantages of Noncredit Education section, the heart of this article, based on research in four states.

However, noncredit education cannot escape the dilemmas of community colleges generally—the inadequate funding, the overuse of adjunct faculty, the low respect. As we clarify in the Endless Differentiation of Postsecondary Education section, again based on evidence from four states, noncredit education in community colleges represents yet another form of stratification within postsecondary education, with elite universities at the top, various gradations of progressively less selective universities below them, the credit programs of community colleges above the noncredit divisions, and various short-term job training and adult education programs at the very bottom. This is what we might term a huge inequity structure. It means that improving noncredit programs and enhancing the equity agenda in large numbers of community colleges requires confronting and overcoming the fundamental inequalities of funding, of status, and of attention in all of higher education.

However, to us, there is no other choice than to improve these aspects of community colleges because the alternatives—the freestanding basic skills programs in adult education and the short-term job training efforts in welfare-to-work programs and WIA—are so ineffective, as we argue in the What Is the Alternative? section based on the evaluation evidence available. They are also poorly linked to the mainstream educational opportunities, including the community college, that provide the best chances of getting out of poverty. If we as a country are serious about providing equity through education for a range of low-wage individuals, then the community col-

lege is the place to do it, and improvements in college are necessary to do so.

Finally, it is crucial to remember that education cannot achieve equity by itself—that equality of opportunity through education has never become a reality and cannot possibly be realized when the overall economy sputters. We need to understand the limitations of equality of educational opportunity as well as its promise and to develop other social and economic policies complementary to education policies. In The Limits of the Equity Agenda and Education Reform section, therefore, we outline some noneducation policies that can strengthen the effectiveness of the equity agenda and of community colleges, in an attempt to go beyond the limits of education alone.

The Advantages of Noncredit Education

We first became aware of the potential power of noncredit education as part of a sixteen-college study being undertaken by the Community College Research Center at Teachers College, Columbia, wherein one of the sixteen has a particularly active noncredit division serving low-income groups. Unfortunately, the information about noncredit programs is sparse.[2] For this article, we have conducted additional research in four states—California, Florida, North Carolina, and Wisconsin—that have relatively large amounts of noncredit education. In each state, we selected three to four colleges that we knew, based either on reputations or on the basis of state data, to have relatively large noncredit enrollments. We then administered open-ended phone interviews with directors of noncredit education and institutional researchers in thirteen community colleges, asking about the types of noncredit offerings, the numbers and types of noncredit students, the differences between credit and noncredit students, the availability of data on the subsequent education and enrollment of noncredit students, and the role within these institutions of noncredit divisions. We also interviewed state officials in each state and reviewed both state and local publications and data where available. In addition to information from these thirteen colleges, we have also drawn on evidence collected in the sixteen Community College Research Center case studies. The Advantages of Noncredit Education and The Endless Differentiation of Postsecondary Education sections rely almost entirely on this research, while the What is the Alternative? and The Limits of the Equity Agenda and Education Reform sections use other kinds of evidence to interpret the potential as well as the limits of noncredit education as a bridging mechanism for low-income individuals.

> . . . the equity agenda would involve community colleges in a series of reforms to increase access among these potential students, as well as improving their progress through college, so that they too could have the benefits of postsecondary education.

Noncredit education in community colleges serves several different purposes. Some courses offered in noncredit divisions[3] are clearly intended for upgrade training, including many at highly sophisticated levels; some are for retraining, for individuals who want or need new careers; some are designed to prepare for licensing exams in areas such as real estate, accounting, and human resources; some are plainly avocational or hobby-related courses or other forms of community education; and some colleges include customized training for specific employers in their noncredit divisions. It is often difficult to perceive which noncredit offerings focus on the equity agenda rather than upgrade training or retraining, although basic skills courses, English as a second language (ESL) classes, and lower-level occupational courses are usually intended for low-wage students. For example, one large noncredit program includes occupational programs in appliance repair, catering, electronic assembly and cabling, school bus driving, sheet metal work, and the ubiquitous early childhood programs—all entry-level positions that can be achieved with relatively short programs. The ambiguity in the purposes of noncredit education reflects a basic problem categorizing students as well: a student in upgrade training may be an experienced technician needing to learn a recent electronics process or an M.B.A. needing a specific accounting course, but he or she might equally be stuck in a low-paid service or medical job and seeking upgrade training to work his or her way out of poverty. So noncredit programs can be quite extensive without serving an equity agenda. On the other hand, they may serve this role in and among other purposes.

For similar reasons, it is difficult to answer the apparently simple question of how much noncredit education there is and especially how much of it supports low-income individuals. There are no national data on noncredit students, and the state-level data vary enormously in their definitions and coverage. Wisconsin's figures illustrate the problems of learning about magnitudes: enrollment in "vocational-adult," which includes all noncredit courses, was 264,320 on a headcount basis in 1999–2000, out of a total of 453,668, therefore representing 58 percent of all students. But because noncredit students typically enroll for short periods of time, they accounted for only 4,225 out of 58,074 full-time equivalents (FTEs), or only 7.3 percent. Furthermore, from discussions with Wisconsin colleges, the vast majority of noncredit enrollments are for upgrade training, not the equity agenda. In North Carolina, which has much better data than most states, "extension" (noncredit) programs represent 74.5 percent of all students but only 5.8 percent of FTE students (for 1999–2000); this implies that noncredit students are crucial to the community-serving mandates of these colleges but trivial in terms of the resources they generate. Of the noncredit students, 29 percent of all enrollments (but 40 percent of noncredit FTEs) are in basic education and programs for the long-term unemployed, 48.3 percent in occupational courses at various levels, 8.3 percent in firm-based training, and 14.4 percent in community service and avocational courses. Therefore, a substantial chunk of these noncredit enrollments—but again, a trivial fraction of FTEs—serves the equity agenda. For the moment, then, the magnitude of noncredit education in the country remains elusive, although the pattern from the two states with decent data seems reasonable: noncredit enrollments are often quite large, but much smaller in FTE terms, with much of this coming from occupational courses that have more to do with upgrading than with equity.

When college administrators refer to their low-income, noncredit students, they describe students who are tentative, uncomfortable with big bureaucracies, perhaps unsuccessful in prior efforts to get back into school, and uncertain about their identities as students. Noncredit programs allow them to "get their feet wet" or provide a "first step into college"; there are "no grades, no pressures," reducing the anxieties these students have about college. Noncredit programs are the "last best hope for lots of students," as one director in California declared. Another in North Carolina noted the clear difference between credit and noncredit students:

It certainly is a different population we're serving. Curriculum [credit education] is serving those who want to pursue a degree. They have the academic ability to do that. Ours [noncredit students] have some gaps in their academic abilities, and we're trying to bring them up. Many do not have high school diplomas. The primary difference is education level already attained, and maybe even their objectives. Noncurriculum [noncredit] folks, many of them, it's a goal to read, or trying to retool and get a skill.

The major advantages of providing noncredit courses and programs for low-wage students comprise quite a long list—most of which, we should remember, have also been cited for community colleges as a whole.

Cost.   Noncredit programs cost nothing at all, or considerably less than credit courses. In some cases, certain types of courses—basic education, for example—are free, while others—hobby courses, usually—require students to pay the full costs. For low-income students, even the modest tuition costs of credit courses may be a serious deterrent, and so reduced tuition may be an important way of increasing access.

Open enrollment.   Noncredit enrollment usually involves a simple sign-up procedure, without the more complex enrollment process, mandatory placement tests, and counseling referrals that some colleges have instituted for their regular programs. The problem is that these matriculation procedures are intended to help students find the right courses and programs, although they also operate to discourage potential students who are uncomfortable with impersonal bureaucratic procedures.

Flexibility.   Noncredit courses very often start every week or two, rather than at the beginning of conventional semesters. They also tend to be provided at various times of the day and sometimes on weekends for working adults.

Responsiveness.   While community colleges think of themselves as being responsive to new trends and demands, compared to four-year colleges with their bureaucratic procedures, noncredit programs are much more responsive than the credit programs of community colleges. They typically do not have to go through faculty and Senate approval, state approval mechanisms, or

other delays that can take two years or more for credit courses. One noncredit director in North Carolina clarified the procedural differences between credit and noncredit approval process: "If it's something we haven't done before, we make it happen. If you ask one of my curriculum [credit] directors about approval, they moan and groan" because the approval process by the campus, the system office, and the state board takes from one year to eighteen months. The principal importance of flexibility is that noncredit division can put new programs into place when a specific community need arises or when a particular kind of occupational course becomes hot.

Location.   In colleges with large noncredit divisions, individual centers are located throughout a city, often in community centers, centers for the elderly, community-based organizations (CBOs), churches, and other places familiar to the populations they are trying to reach. Not only are these centers physically closer and thus more accessible to low-income adults, but they are widely described as being small scale and more comfortable than the large central campuses of urban community colleges. More to the point, they can take on distinctive identities: in one city, for example, there are distinctive centers in Latino, in Chinese, and in black neighborhoods, each with a bilingual director and many bilingual staff, with a variety of support services specific to each community. Under these conditions, noncredit centers become what some CBOs aspire to be, except that they are also part of a larger college and can therefore provide access to more advanced programs that CBOs cannot provide.

Under these circumstances, neighborhood centers can identify and serve precise needs that might not be identified in other centers. For example, in the Latino population, a substantial fraction of immigrants (about 20 percent, according to a center director) have had substantial education and were professionals in their home country; their problems are quite different from those of immigrants with little formal schooling, little or no literacy in their native language, and prior employment only in subsistence agriculture. And so neighborhood-based centers can understand their students in ways that would be much more difficult in the large, heterogeneous classroom of regular credit courses.

Access to immigrants.   One adult education program in a heavily Latino city noted that prospective students need only a U.S. address to enroll. They do not need to have a green card or to fill out other paperwork, and this is widely known in the Latino community that is nervous about its immigration status and contact with the Immigration and Naturalization Serivce.[4] In this way, the more informal procedures of noncredit programs reduce the barriers, real or perceived, to enrollment.

Support services. Many community colleges we examined allow their noncredit students full access to all the support services they provide, including child care, guidance and counseling, and tutoring. (Financial aid is unavailable because it is allowed only for students attending credit programs at least half time; however, since noncredit courses are either free or have reduced fees, this is not usually an issue.) To be sure, these support services are often available only on a main campus, not in every community-based center, so in practice, low-income adults may not be able to take advantage of these services. But at least the intention of such programs is to make a full array of support services available. In other cases, however—especially in Florida, with an emphasis on upgrade training—there appears to be very little access to support services, and in this sense, noncredit students seem to be second-class citizens.

The transition to credit programs. Perhaps the greatest advantage of locating noncredit programs for low-income students in community colleges is that after students have completed a relatively short course, they can take other related courses and, at the end of an appropriate sequence, transfer into credit courses of the community college. As their own desire, time, and life circumstances permit, they can continue with certificate and associate's programs, transfer to baccalaureate programs, and continue on to any form of graduate education. Indeed, there is a modern version of the rags-to-riches myth that sometimes emerges in welfare programs, of a woman who enrolls in noncredit developmental education and vocational courses to become a nursing assistant, continues to an associate's program in nursing, later transfers to a four-year college, graduates, and goes on to medical school! The point is not that this trajectory is likely; but it is possible within a well-articulated system of second-chance education.

The noncredit programs we reviewed vary substantially in their articulation with credit pro-grams at the same college. In Florida, a final exam in a certain noncredit course can be used to earn credit; the Maricopa colleges also have a mechanism whereby noncredit courses are converted to credits. One institution has set up articulation agreements, just like those articulating two- and four-year colleges, promising that students who complete a specified roster of noncredit courses can join a credit program and have some of their prior course work count. This institution runs field trips for students from the various noncredit centers to visit the main campus, to familiarize them with the campus and the various administrative hurdles they will have to leap there. Counselors develop education plans with students and help them with the transfer process and with enrollment in credit programs for the first time. The centers are now reorganizing their counseling to concentrate on particular types of noncredit students (e.g., new students, continuing students, occupational students), with counselors developing greater expertise about the conditions such students face. This institution is one of the very few to keep track of how many students transfer from noncredit to credit every year; during the past few years, about 20 percent of their new students have enrolled from noncredit courses. The number who transfer from noncredit to credit programs represent about 6 percent of all noncredit students, although a transfer rate devised with longitudinal data would be somewhat larger. In this particular college, transfers come largely among students in transitional studies, earning a high school diploma or a General Equivalency Diploma (GED); among ESL students moving into credit programs; and among business students.

Another college with an active transfer policy is similarly establishing a series of articulation agreements with credit programs in three colleges within the same community college district. The district has also begun to track the numbers of students who transfer: about 2,000 to 3,000 students transfer every year, out of enrollments of about 57,000 in noncredit courses (excluding those for older adults), a number that surprised district administrators who thought it was much lower. But articulation at this district is still relatively new, and it is possible that the transfer numbers will increase as greater understanding of the possibilities for moving into credit programs develop. A third college has credit instructors recruit noncredit students by speaking to their classes and demonstrating what students will do in subsequent courses; they also have support service including counseling, pushing students aggressively to continue their schooling. About 15 to 20 percent of their credit students originate in noncredit courses, so among other things, the noncredit program is a recruitment mechanism—an important consideration in an enrollment-driven institution.

The mechanisms facilitating transfer from noncredit to credit programs are all easy to identify and quite familiar to colleges: student awareness of credit opportunities, articulation agreements, faculty advice and advertising, guidance and counseling, individual education plans, and support for students in the application and transfer processes. But the majority of the colleges we interviewed provided very few of these services. In most colleges, it was clear that if noncredit students could find a counselor interested in them, they can get help) in the transfer process; but this is idiosyncratic rather than institutionalized and systematic. We could find no evidence of any sort—not even guesstimates—about the magnitude of transfers into credit programs in the colleges in Florida,[5] North Carolina, and Wisconsin. And so, as far as we can determine based on a limited sample, relatively few colleges use noncredit programs as a transitional stage into community college. This is especially the case where noncredit education focuses on upgrade training and retraining of the experienced workforce.

Several factors seem to account for colleges that have used their noncredit programs to serve low-income students. Most of them emerged from histories where the college (or a division of the college) had provided adult education in the region; as a result, a commitment to low-income students had developed, without competition from adult education programs run by K–12 districts. In addition, a couple of these programs have had strong individuals with clear and compelling visions to serve these students well. Finally, state policy has been permissive, if not particularly encouraging: these states fund noncredit education for equity-related purposes, albeit at lower rates than credit programs (in California, Florida, and North Carolina). As one local director noted, "What they fund is what drives what we offer." But in recessions—or, in Florida and California, where fiscal problems are pressuring programs to become self-sustaining—serving low-income students may become a lower priority.

From these few colleges, a model emerges of noncredit education as a way of addressing the equity agenda of community colleges. This model operates, in large part, by extending the advantages that community colleges already have over four-year colleges: these noncredit programs are lower in cost; more flexible in their schedules; physically closer to students; and more overtly community based, less bureaucratic, more open to immigrant students, and better able to respond quickly to emerging community and employment needs. Unfortunately, as we will see in the next section, noncredit programs are also heirs to many of the same problems that community colleges have suffered.

The Endless Differentiation of Postsecondary Education: The Dark Side of Noncredit Education

The community college represents one of many ways in which postsecondary education has been fragmented into institutions of different levels of selectivity and status, aimed at occupational preparation at different levels of the labor market. Based again on our interviews in four states, the development of noncredit programs focused on low-income students represents a further stratification within community colleges, and once again differences of funding, status, and pedagogy have emerged.

One obvious problem is that noncredit education is usually funded at substantially less than credit education. In California, for example, the funding per FTE student is $3,800 per course for credit students but $1,900 for noncredit students; in North Carolina, reimbursement for noncredit FTE is three-quarters of what it is for credit FTE. So funding, already low in community colleges, is even lower in noncredit programs.

One result is that noncredit programs use an even higher proportion of adjunct faculty than the credit divisions of community colleges do. While there is no systematic data, one of the noncredit programs we interviewed had 12 full-time instructors and 172 part-time or adjunct faculty. These are situations where the full-time faculty develop courses and hire part-timers, who are essentially treated as cogs in a big education machine; part-timers have little time for additional planning, office hours, or participation in staff development or governance committees.

These are familiar problems in credit education as well, but they are worse in noncredit divisions.

> This model [of noncredit education addressing the equity agenda] operates, in large part, by extending the advantages that community colleges already have over four-year colleges.

Under conditions where there is low funding and high proportions of adjunct faculty, the quality of teaching—a serious problem in many community colleges, despite their pride in being "teaching institutions" (Grubb and Associates 1999)—is likely to suffer. Adjunct faculty are usually hired off the street, with no preparation in teaching methods. They are unable to attend staff development; they have too little time to discuss teaching with their own colleagues or to reflect on and improve their own teaching. While we did not observe noncredit classes to examine the quality of teaching firsthand, the conditions necessary to improve teaching are absent in noncredit programs. As if to corroborate this, one institutional researcher referred to "shitty teachers, with lots of handicaps" in the college's noncredit program. In fact, it appeared that the noncredit ESL department had an active faculty, trying to develop a coherent departmental approach to ESL and regularly examining data about their success. The business department was trying to coordinate with other subjects. But the transitional studies department, designed to prepare students for transition to credit programs, was highly traditional, with older instructors not much interested in changing. This story indicates substantial variation within the noncredit division, which the college—whether through inattention, lack of resources, or lack of expertise—has been unable to improve. But it also implies that coherent programs and better teaching can be developed even with adjunct faculty and low resources, as long as there is sustained attention to the quality of teaching.

Furthermore, the large amount of developmental education in noncredit programs—a subject that is especially prone to dreary teaching—cannot possibly enhance the overall commitment to teaching. A great deal of developmental teaching follows the familiar pattern of skills and drills (or drill and kill), where complex competencies are broken into discrete, decontextualized skills on which students then drill. Another familiar pattern, one that we have directly observed in many developmental classes, is the practice of giving a great deal of emotional support to students to encourage their learning while not making any substantial cognitive demands on them lest that undermine their self-esteem—a pedagogy of loving students into failure that one often sees in adult education.[6] We have not directly observed teaching in noncredit programs and do not know whether these conditions in credit programs are also replicated in noncredit programs, but we fear that without substantial attention to the difficulties of teaching developmental education and ESL, the quality of teaching in noncredit programs is likely to be variable at best.

We also suspect that access to support services is less successful in practice than in theory. It is hard to imagine, given low budgets and lower enrollments in neighborhood centers, that noncredit programs can provide a full roster of services such as tutoring and child care. Guidance and counseling in most community colleges are inadequate in amount and dominated by academic counseling intended to provide students with information about requirements to complete credentials and transfer; the kind of career-oriented counseling that students unclear about their futures need is usually scant.[7] Support services are everywhere underfunded, in part because they do not generate revenues in enrollment-driven formulas. There is no reason to think that poorly funded noncredit centers can get around this problem.

Another systematic problem in noncredit programs is the issue of credentials. Noncredit programs tend to issue certificates of completion, but these certificates are not recognized by the states in the same way that one-year certificates, two-year associate's degrees, and baccalaureate degrees are. How local employers treat the certificates of completion issued by noncredit programs is anyone's guess. It is possible that certain local noncredit programs work closely with local employers, who then hire students completing these programs regardless of what credential they have, but it is equally possible that employers do not know much about local programs or that individuals move away, to areas where the college where they studied is not known. In general, certain kinds of certificates and most associate's degrees have substantial economic returns, compared to the earnings of high school completers, but the benefits for small amounts of course work are low and quite uncertain. The implication is that small amounts of noncredit education may not have much effect on employment and earnings.[8] If this is true, then the main benefit of completing noncredit education would be its value in gaining access to more advanced credit programs.

Particularly in North Carolina, a confusing discussion has taken place asserting that employers want "skills, not credentials"—that they value their employees for the skills they have and can demonstrate on the job, not for the pieces of paper they may have earned. Aside from the fact that this statement is based entirely on anecdotal evidence, it seems to justify teaching limited skills for entry-level jobs rather than coherent sequences of competencies that might prepare an individual for a career over a lifetime. In addition, the assertion that employers want "skills, not credentials" avoids the question of how an employer knows that a prospective hire has the skills necessary for the job. There are various indicators or signals of these skills including work experience, the recommendation of a prior employer, or the recommendation of a trusted instructor, but under normal circumstances, credentials are also one of the ways of signaling skills. (Otherwise, an employer would be forced to hire individuals at random and then let them go if they proved not to have the necessary skills—an inefficient and legally precarious hiring process requiring substantial turnover.) Without any direct evidence about the employment effects of noncredit education, it is likely that noncredit programs are effective only when individuals are completing courses directly related to their employment, which older students in upgrade training usually do, or when they give students access to widely recognized credentials. Many noncredit programs do so by providing GED preparation, high school equivalency programs, and courses preparing students for specific credentials such as Microsoft's MOUS or Comp TIA's A++ Computer Repair Technician credential or Network+ for networking applications.

Finally, there is the important issue of respect and status. Community colleges lack status relative to four-year colleges, of course; within them, the transfer programs have the greatest status, developmental programs have the least status, and noncredit programs have substantially less status than credit programs. As one administrator noted, "Credit education gets all the rah-rah"; many described noncredit education as the institution's "stepchild." Noncredit programs are often physically segregated from the rest of a college, in community-based centers or in a separate facility elsewhere in the community. They are then literally invisible as well as institutionally invisible; their faculties do not get a chance to meet faculty members teaching credit courses; and their students do not mingle either. Virtually every administrator noted the problem of low status, with noncredit programs being ignored in long-run planning, in facility allocations, and in the overall sense of the college's mission. The only possible exceptions are continuing education courses for professionals, which are especially important in Florida.

Many administrators predict that noncredit enrollments will keep growing faster than credit enrollments, and this may rescue noncredit education from oblivion. However, it is likely that much of this growth—in enrollment as well as status—will come from professional continuing education, upgrade training, and customized training, where colleges can boast they are serving the large, economically important employers of their communities. If an administrator operates a noncredit division that combines contract training and continuing education with developmental education and other programs for low-income students, then the institutional incentives will always be to enhance programs working with wealthy corporations, not with the voiceless, powerless poor and unemployed. This is true in every educational institution, of course, but it is re-created even in the community college that prides itself as being the people's college.

In the end, extending and improving noncredit education so that it can better serve the equity agenda requires confronting a series of systematic issues that plague the credit programs of community colleges too: underfunding, the low political power of the poor and of the equity agenda in general, multiple barriers and higher costs in institutions sensitive to the costs and the revenues generated by different students, the need for student support services, and the need for improved developmental education. In all too many colleges, the equity agenda is at the bottom of the list of their many missions. Fortunately, there have been many experiments around the country, and many states and colleges have made progress on the issues of funding inequities, the use of adjunct faculty, the improvement of teaching, and the development of internally cohesive colleges—true community colleges. It remains to extend these experiments to the other colleges in the land.

What Is the Alternative? Adult Education, Job Training, and Potential Hybrids

For the low-income adults who need access to education and training, but do not live near a community college with active noncredit programs or other outreach activities, what are the alternatives? In the past, these individuals have been served in a motley mixture of local programs including adult schools administered by K–12 districts, usually offering Adult Basic Education, Adult Secondary Education leading to a GED, ESL, citizenship training, and sometimes limited vocational courses leading to entry-level occupations. In some states, area vocational schools provide adult courses, usually in short programs (fifteen weeks or less) leading to poorly paid entry-level jobs. Job training programs have been available to welfare recipients under Welfare to Work and to others under WIA, the successor to the Job Training Partnership Act of the 1980s and 1990s. In most local communities, there has been a wide spectrum of education and training alternatives, in most cases poorly coordinated with offerings in the educational system but providing potential routes into employment for the working poor, for immigrants, for dislocated workers, and for welfare recipients (Grubb and McDonnell 1996).

However, the quality of these offerings has been quite mediocre. Job training programs for welfare recipients and the long-term unemployed have consistently been found to have trivial effects on employment and earnings, not large enough to help individuals work their way out of poverty or welfare; some of them even have negative effects, especially for youth. Even programs that have positive effects in the short run turn out to be ineffective over five or six years, when the initial benefits of increasing the amount of employment dissipate.[9] Furthermore, WIA legislation took a mediocre job training program and made it worse, in at least three distinct ways. First, individuals wanting training have to go through two stages of job search before getting access to training, a requirement that transformed WIA into a work-first program with training only as a last resort and only for individuals who cannot find any kind of job on their own. Second, those who are eligible for training are given Individual Training Accounts, a kind of voucher that they can exchange for training from a list of approved providers. But the implementation of WIA has been slow, and at this moment, there have been very few Individual Training Accounts granted (Javar and Wandner 2002; D'Amico, et al. 2002). As a result, WIA has ceased to provide any substantial amounts of training. Third, many community colleges want nothing to do with WIA because the work-first requirements send them only the most difficult students, because the paperwork required to participate is extremely burdensome, because the performance measures necessary to participate in WIA are difficult to collect and narrowly defined, and because under the best of circumstances, WIA would not send colleges many students—at a time when most colleges are besieged with "regular" students. So many community colleges are not participating as approved providers (Javar and Wandner, 2002; D'Amico et al., 2002), thereby preventing WIA clients from gaining access to mainstream education.

> If those of us within education stress the promises of education and equality of educational opportunity, we should also remember that other social and economic policies must change as well if our country is to be serious about the equity agenda.

Adult education is, by and large, in similarly miserable shape.[10] With the possible exception of ESL, where adult students are highly motivated, attendance in adult education programs is sporadic and usually too limited to make much progress. The teaching, often by part-time instructors hired off the street, is usually the most dreary kind of skills and drills. It is usually focused on getting students to pass the GED, a credential of dubious value in the labor market.[11] Even though adult education is often revered because of its saintly connection to literacy, there is virtually no evidence that any of its programs work. The few studies in the literature with positive results are seriously flawed,[12] and even these acknowledge that gains are small. For example, Diekhoff (1988) claimed that "there is little doubt that the average literacy program participant achieves a statistically significant improvement in reading skill" (p. 625), citing a 1974 study for the Office of Education that documented a half grade reading gain during a four-month period. But given the limited amount of time most adults spend in Adult Basic Education, with only 20 percent enrolling for longer than one year, most Adult Basic Education students improve by one year or less, and their gains—from a fifth- to a sixth-grade reading level, for example—are trivial in practical terms. As Diekhoff concluded,

> Adult literacy programs have failed to produce life-changing improvements in reading ability that are often suggested by published evaluations of these programs. It is true that a handful of adults do make substantial meaningful improvements, but the average participant gains only one or two reading grade levels and is still functionally illiterate by almost any standard when he or she leaves training. But published literacy program evaluations often ignore this fact. Instead of providing needed constructive criticism, these evaluations often read like funding proposals or public relations releases. (P. 629)

This literature confirms the information from our own analyses (Grubb and Kalman 1994)—of a large, unwieldy set of programs, lacking any systematic information about completion or progress, with virtually no evidence of success.

But the worst aspect of current adult education and job training programs is that they lead nowhere. Once an individual has completed a fifteen-week job training program, there is no natural next program—and since such short programs are inadequate to find meaningful employment (especially in a recession) the individual must begin the process of searching for training alternatives all over again. Individuals can stay for long periods of time in adult education, of course, and some of them do earn GEDs; but the effects on employment are small (Murnane, Willett, and Boudett 1995), and the benefits in gaining access to postsecondary education are similarly trivial (Quinn and Haberman 1986). So once again, the graduates of adult education and short-term job training programs are likely to be left behind in the low-skilled labor market, unable to earn enough to escape from poverty.

Given the failures of job training and adult education, the community college is the most obvious institution to serve low-wage workers. Then the precollege or bridging role of noncredit education becomes particularly important as a way of providing access for welfare recipients, the working poor, disconnected youth, and others who would not otherwise show up in community colleges. However, having described some of the problems of job training and adult education, it seems that there are at least three ways of creating bridging mechanisms:

- The first is for more colleges to create or extend their noncredit divisions to encompass the equity agenda. This requires, most obviously, providing an appropriate roster of developmental education, ESL, and entry-level occupational programs allowing individuals who must earn a living to get into employment quickly. Such programs must also create articulation agreements, guidance in developing educational plans, support in applying for credit programs, and the other linkages to credit education that we described in The Advantages of Noncredit Education section. This direction would locate the bridging mechanism entirely within the community college, strengthening the likelihood that transfer to mainstream credit offerings could take place smoothly.

- An alternative is for community colleges to articulate their credit programs with programs offered by CBOs and other providers within the job training system. Then the CBO would provide initial recruitment, counseling, advocacy, and support while the college would provide developmental and occupational preparation; each draws on its own strength. Indeed, a few such efforts have been developed, especially Project QUEST in San Antonio profiled by Osterman and Lautsch (1996). In this case, a CBO recruited clients and provided more intensive support services. The program targeted high-growth jobs, particularly health care and computer occupations, that are accessible to a population with relatively little education; the local community colleges provided remedial and occupational education in two-year programs, and participants earned credits so they could continue in other educational programs later. The division of labor between the CBO and the community college is instructive: the CBO provided a vision of the program, recruitment, various support services, and an advocacy role for its clients, while the colleges provided the educational components. Other examples of cooperation between colleges and CBOs have developed (Roberts 2002), although they clearly are not particularly common and WIA has made such partnerships more difficult to construct. But in some areas with strong CBOs, such partnerships may be more effective than noncredit divisions that may be created.

- Third, a similar form of articulation between publicly funded adult education programs (or area vocational schools) and community colleges seems possible. Students could then progress through adult education and then transfer to community colleges to work toward credentials with more value than the GED, again with articulation agreements and other bridging mechanisms to smooth the transition between the two. This approach might work in localities with especially strong adult schools or area vocational schools. Unfortunately, most community colleges that have approached local adult schools report being rebuffed, and we have never seen any examples where adult schools cooperate with community colleges to create ladders of educational opportunities.[13]

To develop any kind of precollege, several reforms should be started. The first step, as always, is to clarify to colleges the value of noncredit education—or of functional equivalents such as bridging programs in CBOs or adult schools—as an entry point. A second is to obtain funding, presumably from existing state and federal resources; in addition to clarifying the role of states in funding noncredit programs, existing funds for job training, for adult education, and for area vocational schools could be transferred to community colleges.[14] A third is to be sure that the quality of such programs is substantial, including the quality of the inevitable developmental education and ESL. Support services and articulation mechanisms with credit courses are also central. And the status of the equity agenda must be enhanced relative to the other, better-established missions of the community college. None of these is conceptually difficult, although efforts to put them in place would reveal the political complexities of the equity agenda.

The Limits of the Equity Agenda and Education Reform

The use of noncredit education specifically, or community colleges in general, to address the employment problems of low-income adults is part of an educational strategy that extends back at least a century. Around 1900, reformers tried to reduce high school dropouts and laggards (those falling behind in high school) as a way of reducing the likelihood that they would then go into dead-end, poorly paid jobs. Vocational education was part of the solution then, and it continues in the impulse to provide occupational forms of education and training whether in short-term training programs, traditional vocational education, nontraditional "education through occupations" in high schools (Grubb 1995), the occupational programs of community colleges, or the professional programs of four-year colleges and graduate schools. As formal schooling has become increasingly important for almost all employment—and especially for middle-level and professional employment—the centrality of equality of educational opportunity as a way of equalizing economic opportunities has grown.[15] Enhancing access to college through noncredit divisions and other bridging mechanisms is obviously one dimension of equalizing opportunities.

Unfortunately, equality of educational opportunity offers only changes in education as a solution to inequality, poverty, racial discrimination, and unequal opportunity. With the demise of other mechanisms of equalizing opportunities—the antipathy to welfare and the harsh measures of the 1996 welfare "reforms," the lackluster state of antidiscrimination policy, the inability to legislate serious revisions in health care, the lack of any coherent housing policy or urban development agenda, the demise of job training programs, and the weak state of unions—the improvement of education is almost the only antipoverty strategy that has much political power in this country.[16]

In their broadest claims, proponents of education reform sometimes claim that increases in education and changes in education policy can cure all ills, social and individual. Michael Bloomberg, the new mayor of New York, claimed recently that if schools are improved then "a lot of what Dr. [Martin Luther] King wanted to accomplish in our society will take care of itself."[17] But this is so clearly not true.

Most obviously, of course, Martin Luther King promoted racial equity, social justice, freedom from the constraints of racism and poverty, and a clear moral vision that are difficult to develop through schooling alone, particularly through a vocationalized form of schooling. Partly, this kind of claim is untrue because the equity agenda remains chronically underfunded and underdeveloped, as inadequacies in noncredit education attest. Furthermore, even under the best of circumstances, reducing inequality, poverty, and other social problems requires more than what education can do. In the case of unemployment, for example, which has motivated many countries to increase education and training, such supply-side policies can reduce unemployment due to a mismatch of demand and supply, where there are shortages of certain high-skilled workers while there are surpluses of low-skilled workers, but they can do nothing about cyclical unemployment due to variation in demand, periodic shocks to an economy (like the recent concern with terrorism), or structural unemployment caused by inadequate growth.

In still other cases, the realization of educational reforms requires changes in noneducational policies, in social and economic changes that are complementary to educational reforms. Within community colleges, for example, at least three studies based on interviews with community college students indicate that the primary cause of dropping out, or making real progress, is the work-family-school dilemma—the fact that most community college students have jobs to support themselves and families who demand their attention (especially for women), all while they are attending college (e.g., Gittell and Steffy 2000; Matus-Grossman and Gooden 2002; California Tomorrow 2002). While some of them are more committed to college than to work, and have stay-in-school jobs to support their schooling, others reverse these priorities, trying to fit college around a demanding work schedule. The work-family-school dilemma means that students develop precarious arrangements for meeting their different obligations, but then any small change—different work hours, a change in a class schedule, a car breaking down, a family incident, the loss of child care—may cause the arrangement to breakdown. Schooling, the least pressing of these obligations, is usually the first casualty.

But community colleges by themselves can do little to resolve the work-family-schooling

dilemma. Doing so requires income support policies—for example, expanded forms of student aid or support through Temporary Aid to Needy Families for extended education, something that has been missing under relentless work-first pressures. Solutions to the family component of this dilemma require expanding child care, but also coping with a range of other family problems including health issues and physical abuse—issues that might be addressed with a series of family support centers or comprehensive services centers in each community but that are broader than educational institutions can provide. And low-wage workers who want to enter noncredit programs need income support, sufficiently flexible hours of employment, or employment leave policies that allow them to attend school while they are working—again, policies that colleges by themselves cannot develop. And so the equity agenda requires educational reforms, to be sure, but it also requires a series of reforms in income support, child care, family policies, employment leave, and other employment policies—including the policies that Europeans call active labor market policies[18]—all of which are social goals in their own right but are also complementary to postsecondary education reforms.

Therefore, it is inadequate to emphasize education as the only solution to the problems of unemployment, low income, poverty, and integration into mainstream economic institutions. This is a good place to remember John Dewey and his opposition to framing debates in terms of polar opposites—in this case, reforming education rather than other social and economic policies, as equality of educational opportunity sometimes assumes, or conversely emphasizing greater economic equality without confronting educational inequities, as radical egalitarians sometimes propose. As Dewey (1938) said in his introduction to *Experience and Education*, "Mankind likes to think in terms of extreme opposites. It is given to formulating its beliefs in terms of Either-Ors, between which it recognizes no intermediate possibilities" (p. 17). In the context of discussing contrasting pedagogies, which he labeled traditional and progressive, he asserted that "the problems are not even recognized, to say nothing of being solved, when it is assumed that it suffices to reject the ideas and practices of the old education and then go to the opposite extreme" (p. 22). And so the equity agenda in this country surely requires educational reforms, but it also requires other social and economic reforms as well—a both-and strategy rather than an either-or approach. And if those of its within education stress the promises of education and equality of educational opportunity, we should also remember that other social and economic policies must change as well if our country is to be serious about the equity agenda.

Notes

1. See Grubb (1987) for these patterns based on the High School and Beyond study of 1980 high school graduates, results that are by now somewhat out of date. However, it is clear that these patterns still hold: Roughly 30 percent of high school graduates go to four-year colleges, 30 percent go to two-year colleges, and the remaining 40 percent tend not go to any form of postsecondary education—of course, high school dropouts also tend not to attend any longer.

2. There is no national information about noncredit education since federal statistics do not include noncredit courses. Some states collect their own data since they must know about enrollments for funding purposes at a minimum; but even then, it is difficult to understand even the magnitude of noncredit education since the statistics are not comparable among states. For a handful of recent citations, see "The Role of Non-Credit Courses in the Future of Community Colleges" (2001). See also Cohen and Brawer (1989, chap. 10).

3. There are endless terminology problems, and we cannot clarify them in this short article. Colleges sometimes have divisions of noncredit education; others label this continuing education or community education. The Chicago colleges have bridge programs that play the same role. In some states (including North Carolina), contract education for specific employers is located within contract and continuing education divisions, combining programs for very different populations. In addition, in some institutions, there are noncredit courses, not-for-credit courses, zero-credit components of other courses (e.g., workshops and labs), credit courses that count for community college credentials but not for four-year college transfer, and credit courses that count for everything. Straightening out these technical complexities is, as they say, beyond the scope of this article.

4. However, a center serving a Latino population in another city denied that the lack of a green card was a particular barrier, although it might be a financial barrier because students without green cards would have to pay high out-of-state tuition.

5. Even though Florida has an excellent student tracking system, FETPIP, it is focused on credit students; following noncredit students is virtually impossible, even for counselors.

6. See especially Grubb and Associates (1999, chapters 1 and 5).

7. These results come from research in progress on guidance and counseling in sixteen community colleges, carried out by the Community College Research Center, Teachers College, Columbia University. See also Grubb (2001).

8. See Grubb (1999), also forthcoming in the *Economics of Education Review*. In these and all other statistical results, only credit courses are included, so strictly speaking, there has been no analysis of the economic effects of noncredit education.

9. There is a virtual industry summarizing the meager effects of training (see Grubb 1996; LaLonde 1995; U.S. Department of Labor 1995; Fischer and Cordray 1996; O'Neill and O'Neill 1997; Strawn 1998).

10. Adult education is so decentralized and so varied that some interesting programs can be found. However, in our experience they are usually idiosyncratic efforts disconnected from the main body of adult education programs.

11. The evidence suggests that completion of a General Equivalency Diploma (GED) has at best a very small effect on subsequent earnings compared to dropouts who have not earned a GED (see Cameron and Heckman 1993; Murname, Willett, and Boudett 1995). Educators who have worked with the GED tend to report that it is the equivalent of an eighth- or ninth-grade education, not completion of a high school diploma—and this judgment is in effect confirmed by the evaluation results.

12. See, for example, Balmuth (1985, 1988), Darkenwald (1986), Kazemek (1988), and Sticht (1988). The exhaustive literature review by Solorzano, Stecher, and Perez (1989) included no outcome evaluations despite the authors' attempt to collect them. An evaluation of federally funded programs sponsored by the U.S. Department of Education has been undertaken by Development Associates, Arlington, Virginia, but it resulted in no outcome studies at all (see Young, Fitzgerald, and Morgan 1994). For it review with some positive findings, see Mahaffy (1983); however, most of the studies he cited have obvious validity problems because they depend on opinion surveys of Adult Basic Education administrators. Darkenwald (1986) cited a study by Kent examining pretests and posttests during a five-month period, with an average gain of 0.5 grade levels in reading and 0.3 grade levels in math (p. 7); another result, from an MDTA program, found increases

of 0.4 grade levels after fifty-four hours of instruction. Paltry as they are, these gains may be due to selection effects, regression to the mean, practice effects, and other artifacts.

13. This information comes from the sixteen-college study being undertaken by the Community College Research Center. Other sources that found no evidence of adult education collaborating with other education programs include Grubb and McDonnell (1996), who investigated the complex of education and training programs in eight local communities, and Grubb and Kalman (1994), who examined all possible remedial education in other communities.

14. Obviously, we ignore the politics of such transfer. A favorite recommendation of ours in California has been to eliminate the area vocational programs—called Regional Occupation Centers and Programs—and transfer their resources to community colleges, but Master Plan Commissions in 1988 and 2001 were unable to broach this possibility because of political opposition.

15. The rise of occupational purposes throughout the twentieth century and its implications for schooling including conceptions of equity is the subject of Grubb and Lazerson (2002).

16. On the demise of the welfare state as an ideal and a reality, see Katz (2001).

17. See Richard Rothstein's (2002) column, "Linking Infant Mortality to Schooling and Stress."

18. While conceptions of active labor market policies vary, they usually include fiscal and monetary policy to reduce unemployment; labor matching efforts including job banks, sometimes career information and counseling, and apprenticeship policies; unemployment insurance; income support for low-income individuals, including direct funding (like welfare policies) as well as tax credits; legislation covering organized labor, wages, and working conditions, including minimum wage laws and employment leaves; health and safety legislation; retirement policies; antidiscrimination policies for women and minority groups; some aspects of trade policy, including tariffs on goods assembled abroad and efforts to prevent the export of jobs; the use and potential creation of tripartite groups (including business, labor, and government) to plan policies; and manpower policy covering job training (but not education). See also Esping-Anderson's (1990) conception of welfare capitalism, which covers the elements of active labor market policies.

References

Balmuth, M. 1985. *Essential characteristics of effective adult literacy programs: A review and analysis of the research.* The Adult Beginning Reader Project. New York: State Department of Education.

———. 1988. Recruitment and retention in adult basic education: What does the research say? *Journal of Reading* 31 (7): 620–23.

California Tomorrow. (2002). A new look at California community colleges: Keeping the promise alive for students of color and immigrants. Unpublished manuscript, California Tomorrow, Oakland, CA.

Cameron, S., and J. Heckman. 1993. The nonequivalence of high school equivalents. *Journal of Labor Economics* 11 (1): 34–56.

Cohen, A. M., and F. B. Brawer. 1989. *The American community college.* 2d ed. San Francisco: Jossey-Bass.

D'Amico, R., A. Martinez, J. Salzman, and R. Wagner. 2002. *An evaluation of the Individual Training Account/Eligible Training Provider Demonstration.* Research and Evaluation Monograph series 02-A. Washington, DC: U.S. Department of Labor.

Darkenwald, G. G. 1986. *Effective approaches to teaching basic skills to adults: A research synthesis.* Washington. DC: U.S. Department of Education, Office of Educational Research and Improvement. (ERIC Document Reproduction Service no. ED 325 631).

Dewey, J. 1938. *Experience and education.* New York: Macmillan.

Diekhoff, G. M. 1988. An appraisal of adult literacy programs: Reading between the lines. *Journal of Reading* 31 (7) : 624–30.

Esping-Anderson, E. 1990. *The three worlds of welfare capitalism.* Princeton, NJ: Princeton University Press.

Fischer, R., and D. Cordray. 1996. *Job training and welfare reform: A policy-driven synthesis.* New York: Russell Sage.

Gittell, M., and T. Steffy. 2000. *Community colleges addressing students' needs: A case study of LaGuardia Community College.* New York: Howard Samuels State Management and Policy Center, City University of New York.

Grubb, W. N. 1987. *The postsecondary vocational education of 1980 seniors.* LSB-87-4-10. Washington, DC: MPR Associates for the Center for Education Statistics, U.S. Department of Education.

———. 1995. *Education through occupations in American high schools.* 2 volumes. New York: Teachers College Press.

———. 1999. *Learning and earning in the middle: The economic benefits of sub-baccalaureate education.* Occasional paper. New York: Community College Research Center, Teachers College, Columbia University.

———. 2001. *"Getting into the world": Career counseling in community colleges.* Occasional paper. New

York: Community College Research Center, Teachers College, Columbia University.

Grubb, W. N., and Associates. 1999. *Honored but invisible: An inside look at teaching in community colleges.* New York: Routledge.

Grubb, W. N., and J. Kalman. 1994. Relearning to earn: The role of remediation in vocational education and job training. *American Journal of Education* 103 (1): 54–93.

Grubb, W. N., and M. Lazerson. 2002. The vocational roles of American schooling: Believers, dissenters, and the education gospel. Unpublished manuscript.

Grubb, W. N., and L. McDonnell. 1996. Combating program fragmentation: Local systems of vocational education and job training. *Journal of Policy Analysis and Management* 15 (2): 252–70.

Javar, J., and S. Wandner. 2002. Use of intermediaries to provide training and employment services: Experience under WIA, JTPA, and Wagner-Peyser Programs. In *Job training in the United States: History, effectiveness, and prospects,* edited by C. O'Leary, R. Straits, and S. Wandner. Kalamazoo, MI: W. E. Upjohn Institute for Employment Research.

Katz, M. 2001. *The price of citizenship: Redefining the American welfare state.* New York: Henry Holt.

Kazemek, F. 1988. Necessary changes: Professional involvement in adult literacy programs. *Harvard Educational Review* 58 (4): 464–87.

LaLonde, R. 1995. The promise of public sector–sponsored training programs. *Journal of Economic Perspectives* 9 (2): 149–68.

Mahaffy, J. E. 1983. *Impact evaluation of adult basic education: Program outcomes.* Final report. Helena, MT: Office of Public Instruction.

Matus-Grossman, L., and S. Gooden. 2002. *Opening doors: Students' perspectives on juggling work, family, and college.* New York: MDRC.

Murnane, R., J. Willett, and K. P. Boudett. 1995. Do high school dropouts benefit from obtaining a GED? *Educational Evaluation and Policy Analysis* 17 (2): 133–48.

O'Neill, D., and J. O'Neill. 1997. *Lessons for welfare reform: An analysis of the AFDC caseload and past welfare-to-work programs.* Kalamazoo, MI: W. E. Upjohn Institute for Employment Research.

Osterman, P., and Lautsch, B. 1996. *Project QUEST: A report to the Ford Foundation.* Cambridge, MA: MIT Sloan School of Management.

Quinn, L., and M. Haberman. 1986. Are GED certificate holders ready for postsecondary education? *Metropolitan Education* 2: 72–82.

Roberts, B. 2002. *The best of both: Community colleges and community-based organizations partner to better serve low-income workers.* Philadelphia: Public/Private Ventures.

The role of non-credit courses in the future of community colleges. Information bulletin. 2001. Los Angeles: ERIC Clearinghouse for Community Colleges, University of California, Los Angeles.

Rothstein, Richard. 2002. Linking infant mortality to schooling and stress. *New York Times,* 6 February, p. A20.

Solorzano, R., B. Stecher, and M. Perez. 1989. *Reducing illiteracy in California: Review of effective practices in adult literacy programs.* Report for the California State Department of Education, Adult Education Division. Pasadena, CA: Educational Testing Service.

Sticht, T. 1988. Adult literacy education. In *Review of research in education,* Vol. 15, edited by E. Rothkopf, 59–96. Washington, DC: American Educational Research Association.

Strawn, J. 1998. *Beyond job search or basic education: Rethinking the role of skills in welfare reform.* Washington, DC: Center for Law and Social Policy.

U.S. Department of Labor. 1995. *What's working (and what's not): A summary of research on the economic impacts of employment and training programs.* Washington, DC: U.S. Department of Labor, Office of the Chief Economist.

Young, M., N. Fitzgerald, and M. Morgan. 1994. *National evaluation of adult education programs, fourth report. Learner outcomes and program results.* Arlington, VA: Development Associates for the U.S. Department of Education.

CHAPTER 22

THE UNINTENDED CONSEQUENCES OF STIGMA-FREE REMEDIATION

REGINA DEIL-AMEN
JAMES E. ROSENBAUM
NORTHWESTERN UNIVERSITY

Social stratification may emerge within efforts to reduce it. Although open admissions policies increase access to college, many students may not really be college students; they are taking noncredit remedial courses, which raises concerns about stigma and "cooled-out" aspirations. Studying two community colleges, this article describes a remedial approach that avoids stigma and cooling out but creates unintended consequences. Analyses of interviews with staff and students and of institutional procedures show how this approach arises. The analyses also indicate how this approach inhibits and delays students' awareness of their remedial status, causes them to misjudge their prospects, and prevents them from considering alternative options.

True to American ideology, individuals have a say in their attainments, but their goals and efforts usually depend on their perceptions. Systematic misperceptions lead to blocked opportunity just as surely as do concrete barriers, and they produce less social protest and more self-blame. Recent studies have examined how individuals perceive the stratification process. O'Connor (1999) described how low-income African American students' perceptions of the mobility process are influenced by societal factors, and Lareau and Horvat (1999) showed how African American parents' suspicion of schools reduces their compliance with school standards of teacher-parent interaction and compromises their ability to advocate for their children. In contrast, some studies have noted the tendency of individuals to have excessive expectations that are unlikely to be realized (Smith and Powell 1990). This tendency may not be limited to individuals; institutional practices may encourage these misperceptions through distorted or unclear information.

It is often difficult to see where social stratification is created in institutions, and the lack of clarity may be an important mechanism for increasing the stability of stratification systems. Stratifying processes may be obfuscated by processes between and within institutions, particularly the classes and symbols that signal distinct tracks and trajectories (Useem 1992). Lack of clarity can arise between institutions if prior "feeder" institutions do not provide key information that would help individuals anticipate the demands of later institutions and how they will be evaluated and stratified within them (Dougherty 1994). In addition, within a single institution, information can be controlled so that individuals may have difficulty seeing how and when they are being stratified.

As a result, institutional stratification processes that are not clearly seen are not easily confronted.

The study reported here examined the institutional management of individuals' perceptions inside community colleges. Prior institutional practices play a key role in determining the need for information management and the possibilities for how it can be done. Colleges must manage information if feeder institutions allow students to have unrealistic college plans and do not provide key information about the demands of college. Colleges develop institutional practices to manage students' plans through their methods of conveying information and the content of that information. These practices may provide the conditions for students' misperceptions about their position within the structure of higher education and their prospects for success. These institutional processes have been given little attention by researchers.

One manifestation of this phenomenon has been noted in community colleges. The term *cooling out* is used to describe the process by which community colleges urge students to recognize their academic deficiencies and lower their aspirations (Clark 1960; Karabel 1977). This study found the use of a "nonstigmatized" approach not noted by prior researchers that is kinder and gentler. Although the intent of this approach is to avoid communicating low expectations and limiting students' goals, it has some unintended consequences that are less benign, making it even *more* effective in managing students' perceptions and channeling students into lower-status positions.

Background

Although our image of community colleges is still based on research from the 1960s and 1970s, community colleges are dramatically different institutions today. One artifact of open admissions policies has been the enormous growth of remedial programs. In fact, 64 percent of high school students who enroll in community college take some remedial courses (Adelman 1995). These changes have raised new issues and force us to reconsider our conceptions.

One concept that must be reexamined is cooling out. Derived from Goffman's (1952) description of the way confidence men get their victims to come to terms with having been swindled, cooling out may also be used to describe the ways in which community colleges get stu-

dents to lower their unrealistically high expectations for obtaining bachelor's degrees and to aim for one- or two-year degrees in vocational or applied programs (Clark 1960). Colleges accomplish this cooling out by a combination of preentrance testing, counseling, orientation classes, notices of unsatisfactory work, further referrals for counseling, and probation. These steps serve to convince students who aspire to transfer to four-year colleges to "accept their limitations and strive for success in other worthwhile objectives that are within their grasp" (Clark 1973:367). Just as the confidence man convinces victims to accept their loss as being in their own best interests,[1] colleges convince students that lowered plans are in their own best interests.

Cooling out may still occur today in community colleges. Indeed, it may be happening more, but in addition to the process described by Clark (1960, 1973), the phenomenon has taken on new and multiple forms. These new processes may have important implications. As we suggest, the primary concerns of the older literature may have been somewhat reduced in recent decades, but there has been a concomitant increased concern about another element.

The cooling-out process has been criticized primarily for demoralizing students and lowering their plans. It forces students to lower their expectations by indicating that they cannot meet their aspirations. It does so by subtly and not so subtly stigmatizing students and forcing them to realize their inferiority on the basis of their performance within a "legitimate" framework of "objective" academic standards. Karabel (1977) criticized cooling out for guiding students—primarily those of working-class or lower middle-class origins—into lower-status tracks. He was especially critical of the role that cooling out plays in actively pressuring students to sort themselves out of the competition for transfer on the basis of their substandard performance. If students do not seek guidance, Karabel (1977:239) stated, "the counselor with the authority of the disciplinary apparatus behind him requests to see the student" to inform him that he "had his chance" and did not "measure up." Karabel (1977:240) further noted that "community colleges . . . developed cooling out as a means not only of allocating people to slots in the occupational structure, but also of legitimating the process [and causing] people to blame themselves rather than the system for their 'failure.'" By convincing students to see lower-track vocational courses as their best alternative, cooling out gets students to accept the college's assessment as serving their own self-interest (Erickson 1973).

In addition, Dougherty (1994) highlighted the prevalence of community college faculty's low expectations of students and the negative impact they have on students' performance. His analysis drew on research by London (1978) and Weis (1985), which suggested that community college instructors respond to students' low skill levels by concentrating on a few promising students and largely giving up on the rest. As Dougherty (1994:90–91) noted:

> The sad irony is that these low expectations feed a self-fulfilling prophecy. In a process well described by labeling theorists within the sociology of education, . . . low expectations tend to lead teachers to withdraw attention and praise from poorer students, which in turn reinforces the very poverty of the student performance that is being decried.

A second aspect of cooling out that has been less emphasized is that it delays students' recognition of their situation. As Goffman (1952) observed, after a swindle is completed, delayed recognition is important for giving the victims time to get adjusted to their circumstances. Clark (1973) and Karabel (1977) noted a similar delaying process, but they de-emphasized it because of their focus on the lowering of expectations. Although community college staff are aware of students' poor prospects from the outset, they delay telling students. The process is somewhat deceptive, and purposely so, but it is seen as tactful kindness, a way of giving students time to recognize and adjust to their lower prospects. Students ultimately come to the same negative decision, and it is the negative implication, not the timing, that is the primary concern of critics. After all, what difference does it make if students figure out their situation only a few months later? As Clark and Karabel described, by the end of the first term of college, when they get their first college grades, students have come to a full recognition of their situation.

However, several decades after Clark (1973) and Karabel (1977) wrote about the cooling-out process, we find important changes. First, more high-school students plan to attend college, and many enter who have little likelihood of completing their degrees. The proportion of high

school seniors who are planning to get college degrees has increased by almost two thirds over the past two decades (National Center for Education Statistics, NCES, 2000:41). By 1992, 84 percent of high school seniors in the National Education Longitudinal Study planned to get a college degree (AA or higher), and 68 percent expected to get a BA degree (Schneider and Stevenson 1999), but less than half these students were likely to complete any degree (Rosenbaum 2001). These high expectations arise, in part, because many students with college plans think that their school achievement has little effect on their educational attainment (Rosenbaum 1998; Steinberg 1996). Students know that open admissions will allow them access to college, and they report that they can wait to exert effort until they get to college (Steinberg 1996). Unfortunately, for these students, high school grades strongly affect the completion of college degrees. In the High School and Beyond study, most seniors with poor high school grades (Cs or lower) planned to get college degrees, yet such students have only a 14 percent chance of doing so by age 28, and almost one-third get no college credits (Rosenbaum 2001).

Second, guidance counselors' practices have changed in ways that may further increase the burden of cooling out in colleges. High schools have reduced the ratio of high school counselors to students (McDonough 1997), and guidance counselors' practices now favor an approach that does not interfere with students' college ambitions. Although high school counselors acted as gatekeepers several decades ago (Cicourel and Kitsuse 1964; Rosenbaum 1976), more recent research (Rosenbaum, Miller, and Krei 1996) found that high school counselors subscribe to a "college-for-all" philosophy and avoid giving students unpleasant news. They advise nearly all students to try out college, even if they expect them to fail. Some counselors confided that they had misgivings about not warning students who had little chance of success, but they reported that parents often complained when they conveyed such warnings, and principals supported the parents.

Third, community colleges have radically changed higher education—increasing access and offering extensive remediation. They have implemented open admissions policies that allow all students to enter, regardless of qualifications, yet they have constructed remedial programs to provide instruction to students who are not prepared for college-level courses. Beginning in the 1960s, colleges, particularly community colleges, devised remedial programs to help students who lacked high school-level skills. The best national estimate of the extent of remedial education came from a careful analysis of college transcripts of a national survey of students of the class of 1982. It found that when they enter college, about 46 percent of students are in remedial courses, and among those who enter community colleges, 64 percent are in remedial courses (Adelman 1995). Although these individuals seem to be "college students," since they are enrolled in a college, they are actually taking some high school-level (remedial) courses.

Fourth, students who take several remedial courses are not accumulating many college credits, and their chances of completing a degree are lower than are other students'. Yet students do not lower their educational plans. Two studies documented a pattern in which the percentage of students who completed degrees sharply decreased as the number of remedial courses increased (Adelman 1999; Grubb and Kalman 1994). Yet analyses of national data have found that students' educational plans do not decline with increasing remediation (Deil-Amen 2002). How do students understand their situation, and what institutional practices influence their perceptions?

The present study examined the ways in which community colleges handle the information management dilemmas implicit in the current situation. These four conditions—high school students' college aspirations, college-for-all counseling, the large number of students in remedial courses, and the association between the number of remedial courses and college dropout—create the need for community colleges to deal with students whose circumstances contradict their high expectations.[2] In contrast to the cooling-out processes noted in prior research, we found a process not envisioned by the earlier researchers that has reduced some concerns but made others more important. We discovered a "stigma-free" approach that is used effectively. Although open admissions has allowed students to enter with lower qualifications than in previous decades, community college staff have found ways to avoid conveying stigma, so students feel more self-confident. We were amazed and favorably impressed by the techniques they used to avoid conveying stigma.

However, our analyses suggest a downside. Although school staff may keep students from feeling demoralized or inferior, they may be preventing students from considering a wider range of options. Just as Goffman's (1952) swindler cools out a victim ("mark") by delaying recognition and preventing timely constructive activity, nonstigmatized cooling out delays students' recognition, which prevents them from making timely career decisions to pursue other options that may be more constructive for their occupational attainment. While Clark (1973) and Karabel (1977) found relatively brief delays of recognition that they considered of minor harm, we found lengthy delays over several terms of college, which may be more detrimental. Students who do poorly at school feel self-confident, but like the complacency of a swindler's victim, this feeling is misleading, and it may prevent them from making other choices. In Clark's analysis, students who are cooled out are directed toward an alternative (albeit lower) degree goal. In our research, we discovered that this new stigma-free form of cooling out not only delays recognition, but fails to encourage students to choose alternative educational and career paths. Easily produced information is not being given to students, and students are paying the price in confusion, delayed recognition, efforts that have a low probability of attaining their goal, and failure to take actions that may be more promising.

Data and Methods

Data were collected from multiple sources in two community colleges, here called Northwest and Central College, in a large Midwestern city to examine how students' perceptions are managed.[3] The first author conducted fieldwork at these colleges, and in the process, developed a strong in-depth knowledge of both institutions. Data were collected from five sources: interviews with students; interviews with faculty and administrators; observations of daily life (including classes, events, meetings, advising sessions, and registration), analyses of college catalogs, course schedules, and other archival data; and a survey of students. Over two years, the first author interviewed over 130 students and approximately 54 faculty and staff, observed classrooms and informal interactions, lead seven focus groups with students, and attended meetings and school events. She also analyzed the college catalogs and class schedules of these two colleges, with a particular focus on remedial offerings. Furthermore, she conducted primary research on the district's organizational structure and history.

In addition, we administered surveys to 804 students at the two colleges that included questions about students' goals, attitudes, experiences, course-taking patterns, and perceptions.[4] Data were collected with a primary focus on students in precredit or college credit-level degree-granting programs. Therefore, our research did not encompass the other offerings of these colleges, such as continuing education, special-interest classes, adult basic education, vocational skills training, English as a Second Language, and preparation for general equivalency diplomas (GEDs).

Institutional Context

Our research revealed a combination of institutional characteristics that create the groundwork for the type of stigma-free approach mentioned earlier. In this section, we detail this institutional context, which underpins the stigma-free approach, and in the next section, we discuss the approach itself. The main elements of this institutional context are a strong emphasis on transferring to four-year colleges, a developmental approach to remediation, and a strong social mission.

Strong Emphasis on Transfer

Both colleges are located in an urban multicampus district in Illinois, where the junior college system was founded not long after the turn of the 20th century through the efforts of and pressure from five university presidents who championed the "definition of the junior college role and function . . . as a place of higher education distinguished from the four year college or university only by the brevity not the content or quality of the curricula" (Dobberstein 1987:16). In the 1950s and 1960s, as community colleges expanded rapidly across the nation (Brint and Karabel 1989, 1991; Dougherty 1994), this district

> experienced an expansion of conventional liberal arts courses and expansion of faculty largely hired directly from graduate schools.
>
> These faculty members brought a sense of higher education which reinforced the traditional mission and replicated [the traditional] view of the junior college. As this faculty acquired tenure and developed a strong union, these professors would form the bulk of the instructional staff which is still

dominant in the system (Dobberstein 1987:20).

The prevalence of this transfer-oriented junior college model of the community college has persisted in this district, particularly in these two colleges.

Although the two community colleges offer more and larger occupational programs than they did in earlier decades, an emphasis on transferring students to four-year colleges remains central, especially among liberal arts faculty. These colleges may emphasize transfer somewhat more than most community colleges in the nation, but the difference is small: 25.8 percent of the students at these two colleges planned to get BA degrees, compared to 22.9 percent of a national sample of community college students (Deil-Amen, 2002). Thus, the transfer of students to four-year colleges is still a major part of the missions of most community colleges.

Maintaining "Standards": A Developmental Approach

Today, this strong emphasis on transferring students orients the faculty at these colleges toward preparing students to meet the standards and requirements of the senior colleges to which they intend to transfer. This orientation is reflected in the highly complex hierarchy of course levels that are intended to preserve standards and move remedial students into the college-level courses that are accepted for transfer credit by senior institutions. An English professor commented:

> I think almost everybody sees that there is a commitment and dedication to the same type of ideals of helping the students and holding certain standards so that the students are not just passed along. I know in English we talk about it all the time. We do the students no favor to pass them along to the next level when they're not really prepared for it. So there's a lot of that making sure the [students are] academically prepared for the next level even here at the college so that they will then be successful. Because you sort of program them for failure if you're going to let them go on and they don't have the skills necessary.

In our interviews, virtually all faculty members vigorously approved of this system because they saw it as giving students a clear and structured pathway into college and providing students with a *college* education, not a *less-than-college* education. As a department chair stated:

> We spend a lot of time talking about how you keep standards up because the last thing this population needs is further fraud perpetrated upon them where they've been told "OK you've passed" when, in fact, they haven't mastered what they're going to need to survive out there. And pretty soon someone's gonna throw them out there, and they're gonna sink. And I won't be part of that fraud, and I don't think many of my colleagues will.

A philosophical approach to remediation that is grounded in developmental (rather than behaviorist) theories of learning fits well with this institutional culture. Rather than the less expensive behaviorist approach, which assumes that students can master subject matter using self-paced, computer-assisted instruction and an open entry–open exit format, remedial courses at Northwest and Central College reflect developmental theories. Such an approach views learning as

> a process in which individuals move from one level of knowledge to another. . . . The instructor plays a vital role . . . by creating a supportive and encouraging environment that provides challenges at appropriate levels to stimulate learning. Obviously, such programs rely heavily on instructor involvement and ideally involve small classes, making them relatively expensive to offer (McMillan, Parke, and Lanning 1997: 26).

In short, faculty and counselors view their mission as helping remedial students slowly but surely achieve their educational aspirations by guiding them through a series of short-term improvements.

Social Mission

The overall culture at Northwest and Central Colleges stresses a mission of providing opportunities to disadvantaged students. The faculty we interviewed expressed strong commitments to this role, and many acknowledged that it was a central component of their professional identity. The awarding of "institutional credit" for remedial classes is part of that same social mission. Like 80 percent of community colleges nationwide, Central and Northwest Colleges offer institutional credit for remedial classes in reading, writing, and mathematics. Institutional

credit counts toward financial aid, campus housing, and full-time student status, but it does not count toward the completion of degrees (NCES 1996). This status allows remedial students to receive Title IV financial aid, and it was opposed by conservatives in Congress who sought to limit Title IV funds to "those students most able to benefit" (Day and McCabe 1997), which would have compelled remedial students to pay for their own remediation. Giving institutional credit for remedial courses represents a battle won by nonconservative forces in their attempt to maintain financial access for disadvantaged students. The faculty and administrators we interviewed expressed sentiments that agreed with the position of the American Association of Community Colleges that "promoting access to higher education, especially for economically and socially disadvantaged students, needs to continue to receive priority consideration, and the investment of public dollars to support this commitment is not only essential, but appropriate" (Day and McCabe 1997).[5]

The faculty and administrators at the community colleges we studied thought that blaming students for deficiencies in their skills or financially penalizing them in a way that may restrict their access to and hamper their success in college was not compatible with their social mission of opportunity. Similarly, judging, evaluating, or altering students' long-term aspirations is not part of how college staff define their role, especially if students aspire to transfer to four-year colleges. Rather, the counselors and faculty think that they should not underestimate the potential for students to turn around and achieve their goals of attaining college degrees despite their histories of poor academic performance. As one department chair noted when asked whether he makes judgments about students who may not complete their degrees, "Some people are late bloomers. Some people just take a long time to click and get into it. . . . So I don't make those kind of determinations." A counselor at Northwest articulated a similar philosophy:

> You could easily misjudge or judge too fast an academic history by the fact that they didn't do too well the first couple of times. You'd be surprised. I try to stay away from that. Students can blow you away, and then you fall into the trap of making judgment calls and decisions that are not in your judgment call to begin with—to tell [students]

whether or not they can become a doctor simply because they had a bad semester. . . . Although there is the time that you gotta be real with them and tell them, get real . . . I hate those times; that's when I hate my profession. But other than that, you know, some people have bad semesters, but then they come around and do a 4.0 and do so well. . . . It doesn't happen all the time, but it happens.

Consequences of the Non-Stigmatic Approach

The faculty's reluctance to make judgments about students' ability to obtain their goals and the desire to encourage all students to transfer to four-year colleges has led to new practices. Schools have often been criticized for stigmatizing students by placing them in remedial programs. In our interviews with community college staff, we were surprised to discover that they had developed innovative ways to avoid conveying stigma. However, in interviewing students, we discovered a serious disadvantage to this approach: Many students did not recognize their remedial status or realize the crucial implications of that status.

The two community colleges offer a large number of remedial classes that do not count as credit toward a degree or transfer. Yet students' own remedial placements and the place of remedial classes within the larger structure of the college are not always clearly stated to the students. The term *remedial* is rarely used in conversations between staff and students. Instead, the term *developmental* is usually used. This term accurately reflects the colleges' modes of instruction, yet students do not understand what the word really means. In this institutional context, the term *developmental* is merely a euphemism for *remedial*.

This euphemistic approach seems highly desirable. It is a form of information management that downplays the negative and highlights the positive aspects of students' placement. It avoids the tendency to blame students for their deficiencies. Realizing that students' low skills may be due to difficult life circumstances or low high school standards, college staff encourage students to try to achieve more in college than they have in the past. The term *developmental* is used to imply a temporary stage from which individuals will emerge with assistance.

Traditionally, colleges were candid about remedial courses, and they communicated clear

stigma. This is still true at many four-year colleges. Some students at the two community colleges we studied first attended four-year colleges, where they reported that they had negative experiences regarding their low performance on placement tests. They were made to feel bad about themselves because they were in remedial classes. Steve, for example, recalled his experience with a remedial English instructor at a four-year college who "discouraged" him through her words and attitude:

> I took the placement test, and they placed me in her class and she felt that . . . she had the right to say things, to say that we were below all the other students in [the college] because we were placed in her class. I felt that wasn't a good, positive thing to say about students that come to your class. You've got to teach them or help them go to the next class.

Steve dropped out of that college after one semester. His experience was stressful, and he found the college's atmosphere to be unsupportive.

In contrast, these community colleges de-emphasize failure and emphasize students' need to improve their skills. Their practices remove the stigma and negative labels of these courses. First, faculty and counselors try to communicate their high expectations of students to combat their students' tendency toward low academic self-confidence. An English professor at Northwest explained the logic:

> As your student population becomes less elite, you can't assume a common background . . . and if there's not a common background and you have so-so students who are not completely confident of themselves as students, then you're going to have to support them . . . We assume we're not getting all the A students [and we're getting students] who aren't confident, and you have to kind of keep them afloat, particularly when it gets to be hard.

Second, most faculty and counselors truly believe that remedial placement is preferable to the placement of students in classes for which they are underprepared and in which they are likely to get frustrated and give up. Attempts to improve remedial English classes tend to focus on moving students steadily through a sequence of remedial courses, giving them the opportunity to develop their skills and transition to college-level English. The faculty member in charge of remedial English at Central described the logic:

> We feel that they get much more out of their experience because it's so connected with what they did the prior semester. . . . What I'm hoping is that we'll . . . work on our curriculum, so that it goes all the way . . . up to English 102 with the same basic aims, the same basic abilities that are being developed at higher and higher levels as the student goes through the curriculum.

A counselor at Northwest commented on the importance of moving students too quickly into college-level courses that may be too difficult for them to handle:

> There are a number of [reasons] why students drop out. There's the frustration level. They just give up and walk away. . . . If students are given the kind of course work or the opportunities to improve certain skills that they are lacking, then we have a better chance.

Faculty, who view the testing and placement system as legitimate and in the students' own best interest, try to inform students "gently" of their remedial placement by construing it as a positive and necessary step toward the fulfillment of the student's ultimate goals. A faculty member who teaches remedial English said this about the way she tries to communicate her remedial program during registration: "We try to build in that it's a positive experience."

Apparently, the efforts of faculty and counselors work as intended: Students do not feel stigmatized or demoralized on learning of their remedial placements. In interviews, students explained their remedial placements by repeating the positive language they heard from college staff. Steve, for example, later enrolled at Central College, where he believes he was treated much more positively when the results of his placement test were explained to him:

> They told me I would need help in English classes—not saying that I wasn't capable of doing the work, but . . . I would need that help first before I could just jump into something like [English 101].

The following two comments are representative of the explanations echoed by many other students:

> When I came back up here to pick up my test scores, they told me that my test scores were pretty high, but I didn't test in the high end, which is [English] 101 [the lowest college-credit English course]. (Tomisha)

> Ms. Bartlett discussed my scores [on the placement test]. She said they weren't weak, but they weren't at the strongest point. (Latoya)

Community colleges convey a stigma-free message: This is a second chance to improve some minor weaknesses and enhance your skills. There is no need to feel bad.

This stigma-free technique seems to be an appropriate strategy, given the lack of confidence and fragile academic egos that many students have when they walk through the community college's open door. For instance, when Enrique started, he was concerned because he had been out of school for so long. He actually expected that he would do so poorly that he would get Ds and then have to take his classes over again. However, after getting his placement test scores, he was reassured by his instructor's comments that he was only one level below regular English. Enrique said, "I guess I'm not that bad." Because of his positive experience with his current English class, he feels more confident. As Enrique put it:

> I feel more tenacious. . . . I'm trying to find a word for it. I don't feel that I don't belong here. I feel like this is what I want to do and I'm going to do it. I'm looking forward to succeeding.

Traci contrasted her experience at Central College with the negative treatment she received while she was completing her GED:

> I hated it [the GED program]. It was like being inside a little jail or something. Even the teachers treated you like you were a nobody because you didn't finish school. . . . They thought everybody was all ignorant and everything. Even when I tried to show them that I'm not that ignorant person, they still treated me like I was nothing, and I didn't like that.

Traci felt she was treated differently at Central College, right from the start. Other students who did not do well on the placement exam agreed. As Sylvester put it:

> When I got here, it was like the staff was more helpful. . . . It was no problem going through what I had to go through to start. So the staff was very welcoming, . . . hope you stay here and good luck, etc.

The softer approach has clear advantages over a stigmatizing approach that discourages students by labeling them deficient, disregards their ability to improve, and reinforces their doubts about their potential. It is likely to improve morale and the institutional culture and may interrupt the negative cycle of low expectations that exacerbate students' poor academic performance and failure (Dougherty 1994; London 1978; Weis 1985). Counselors, advisers, and instructors at Central and Northwest Colleges had clearly taken steps to communicate high expectations and minimize negative labeling.

On the other hand, a reluctance to use language that may have negative connotations can prevent students from receiving clear information. The vague language used by faculty to soften or avoid the stigma of the students' remedial placements led to confusion, particularly for students who were not familiar with the college environment. Annette, for instance, was not familiar with the system or with test-taking strategies and did not realize that the placement test would determine the type of courses she could take:

> I wanted to get each [question] . . . right, so I took my time with them. So I ran out of time. . . . I really didn't care cause I didn't know that the . . . test was what was going to count for what courses I'd be able to take.

She said that the "adviser" who helped her pick her courses did not say much about the placement test except "you scored fair on your reading and your English test." This did not sound bad to Annette, and she went along when they told her what classes to take. "And they just gave those classes. They just said, 'This is what you have to take.'" Annette agreed with their selection, not even realizing that she was in remedial courses for which she would receive no college credits. It was only after her classes started meeting that her instructor informed her of her remedial status:

> She [my teacher] told me that I scored low on the placement test; that's why I had to get in this . . . program for some remedial classes, to better my reading and my math skills, my English skills, so I could move on and start taking college classes. I wouldn't be able to take any college classes until I passed, finished out of the . . . program. I was like, "Why didn't anyone tell me that?" I would have gone to another school and took the test.

> They had me registering and everything, and now I have to take these remedial classes. This is going to hold me back because none of this counts. So I still have two years to go 'cause none of these classes here even count. So I was a little upset about that because it was really misleading, Especially with me signing up for financial aid and . . . [finding out that my] aid has to pay for all of this.

Annette's misperceptions were cleared up soon after she began taking her classes. However, many students experience much longer delays of recognition, and their lack of awareness is fostered by the lack of clarity in verbal exchanges, as well as in the written documents available to students.

Analysis of Catalogs and Course Listings

The softer approach has even been built into the structure through which these courses are offered and the labels attached to them. The college catalog and course schedule guide students' decisions and strategies, but Central and Northwest's catalogs and course schedules are unclear and potentially misleading about which courses count and for what purposes. As one may readily assume, remedial classes fall at the bottom of a hierarchical system of community college courses. Furthermore, remedial instruction itself is arranged hierarchically, and students are allocated to a place within this hierarchy through their performance on a placement test.

However, the hierarchy is difficult to see, and students often fail to recognize their own position within this system. Indeed, the system is not clearly defined. Just as the word *remedial* is not used in verbal interactions, it also does not appear in catalogs, course descriptions, or class schedules. After extensive effort to analyze the course offerings and interviews with staff about the meaning of certain terms and descriptions, we discerned the main elements of the course hierarchy. For simplicity, we grouped the community colleges' course offerings into four general categories: (1) "precredit" remedial, (2) "college" remedial, (3) "ambiguous" college credit, and (4) "definite" college credit.[6] We can describe these categories succinctly, but such distinctions are not readily apparent to students. Ambiguity is a major attribute of some of these categories.

At the lowest end, there is no ambiguity. Precredit remedial courses are tuition-free and are described in Central's catalog as "noncredit." At Northwest, they are housed in a separate non-college credit division of the college. Students who score below a 10th-grade threshold on the reading, writing, or math placement test are placed in a precredit curriculum at either the 8th- or 9th-grade level. According to Northwest's assistant to the dean of instruction, these students' scores are "below the required level for college level." Northwest's catalog states that precredit students must pass a "progress test" to advance to the college's "collegiate programs" or "credit division."

On the other hand, at the next two levels, the distinction between remedial and nonremedial classes is much more blurred. At the second level, college remedial classes, though offered with credit classes and labeled similarly to them, offer credits that do not count toward a degree or transfer. Students who score above the 10th-grade level on the placement test but below a "college" skill threshold are placed in courses that are labeled "college credit," yet do not count toward *any* degree or transfer requirements. These courses appear in the class schedule along with all other college credit classes, with no indication that they differ in any way from other classes (except that lower-level courses are pre-requisites for higher-level classes). The terms *remedial* and *noncredit* never appear. On the contrary, next to the name of each course, is a notation in parentheses ("3 cr hrs," "4 cr hrs," or "6 cr hrs"), which seems to imply that credit is given—even for courses that do not supply college credit toward a degree. These courses count for "credit hours" just like the rest, yet these credits cannot be used toward a degree or transfer.

Giving remedial classes the status of "institutional credit" was intended to prevent barriers to access for underprepared students and prevent remedial students from being segregated from other students. Institutional credit allows students to acquire the skills they lack without requiring the additional financial hardship that would come from denying them federal aid to help pay for these courses. It also allows remedial classes to be included along with the other college credit courses, rather than be segregated into a separate and often stigmatized remedial program. Ironically, these well-intended policies have led to unforeseen consequences. The discrete incorporation of remedial classes into the colleges' "credit" offerings leaves students confused, and many students cannot distinguish

between remedial and nonremedial courses. For example, Raymond did not know how some remedial courses differ from other courses in terms of credit. During registration, when he found that a course he needed was closed, he chose to sign up for a reading class instead, not realizing that it was remedial and that he would be paying for a course that would not count toward a degree or transfer credit:

> I wanted a math class, but they said the math classes were too full. . . . I didn't really need the reading, though, because they said I scored high and I didn't need the reading. I just took it anyway because they didn't have math. So I took it.

Included in this "credit, but not really credit," college remedial category are Reading 099, 125, and 126 and English 098 and 100, which actually account for about 60 percent of all "English" sections offered at Central College. The math courses include Math 100 and 110.

Third, the ambiguous college-credit classes count as credit toward some degrees and majors, but not others, and they may or may not count toward transfer to some programs of study and some four-year colleges. Math 112, for instance, counts as credit only toward the associate in general studies degree but not toward an associate in applied science degree (AAS), AA, associate in science (AS) or associate in engineering science. Including Math 112, these "remedial" and ambiguous classes make up 55 percent of all "mathematics" sections at Central. Fourth, definite college credit courses count for both degree credit and transfer. Confusion is less likely to occur for classes at this level.

A perceptive observer looking over the course numbers may infer that numbers below 100 were below college level, and the others were not. This is a reasonable inference, but it is wrong. Indeed, numbers vary among departments, so that Math 112 is the first college-level course, yet Reading 126 is not a college-level course. To complicate matters further, all math courses below Math 204 do not count toward an AS degree, yet Math 118, 125, and 135 count toward an AA degree.

Actually, if students were to ask about credit, they would have to be pretty sophisticated to get adequate information. They would have to ask if a course gives credit for a particular certificate or degree and which degree. In addition, just because a particular course counts as credit toward a degree does not necessarily guarantee that it will be transferable to a four-year college or university. The transferability of particular courses varies by each four-year college and each type of program. At the time of the study, neither community college indicated in its catalog course descriptions which courses were transferable.[7] Furthermore, the catalogs' course descriptions do not specify whether a course is remedial or whether it does or does not count as credit toward any degree.

If one had seen this kind of misleading information in a for-profit school, one might have inferred a swindle, since it encourages students to enroll in courses without clearly informing them whether they will receive "real" credits and whether these credits will count toward their goals. The situation is like a con man selling a stranger a watch, the value of which will be subsequently discovered to be less than expected. In community colleges, the reason for this action may be face-saving or oversight, but it is likely to mislead students into believing they will get more for their course efforts (and tuition) than they ultimately receive.

Pitfalls of Guidance and Delayed Recognition

The lack of clarity just described leaves students with ambiguous and confused ideas about their remedial status, and they lack the structured guidance they need to make timely and informed decisions about their path through college. Although the ambiguity we have noted in the catalogs and in students' minds could be overcome by effective guidance, these colleges lack the structured guidance necessary to help students navigate the organizations' structure and procedures.

College staff usually assume that students will take it upon themselves to discover the degree, certification, and transfer requirements for their program of interest. Many students eventually do, but many wait too long, wasting time and money in the process. This problem is especially acute among students in college remedial classes, the second category. In our interviews, faculty and staff reported a hesitancy to highlight the negative implications of remedial courses, including the lack of "real" degree or transfer credits earned in such courses. They feared that such an approach would unduly discourage students.

However, students experience some difficulty from this delayed information. Ivette, who was in her second full-time semester and aiming for an AA degree, responded to the question about how long she thought it would take to complete her degree by saying, "I still haven't seen what credits I need for the classes." Darius was also starting his second semester, and although he had definite plans to transfer to a specific university, he had not found out anything about the requirements for transfer. He thought that he would transfer to a four-year college with junior status the following year. Unfortunately, he was not aware that his full year of "full-time" course work—which he thought gave him 24 credits— actually gave him only 9 transferable credits. Five of his eight courses were either remedial or too low to count toward transfer.

Students often go for several months, a full semester, or even a full year without knowing that their remedial courses are not counting toward a degree or their transfer goals. Donald, a former remedial student, was in his *fourth* semester at Northwest College, and he had not yet talked to a counselor to find out which classes would be accepted at the university to which he wanted to transfer. Students with low achievement in English or math might have needed to take three terms of remedial courses before they could begin to get actual college credits, but few of these students realized this timetable. In a focus group, a couple of students who were enrolled in a special program that combined several different classes along with their remedial English and reading courses complained that they were not informed about the credit status of their courses:

> John: We had five classes. For each class, we're supposed to get three credit hours. We came up with just four credit hours [instead of the 15 he was expecting].
>
> Vanessa: We didn't even know that they were college prep classes.
>
> John: We didn't know. Like, they told us that we were in [this program]. They didn't explain exactly like, "You're going to take this, but you're not going to be credited for this." So like at the end when [the counselor said we] . . . only get four [credits], everybody is like, "Wait. [We weren't aware of this]."

Marta said that she also did not find out this information until *after* she enrolled in English 101:

When I first came here, I was so happy to be in college. . . . Now I know I really wasn't [in college]. It kind of disappointed me to know that those classes, I'm not going to get no credit for. But although they helped me, it would help me a lot if I could get credit for them, too. So I know I'm in college now. I didn't know [I wasn't in college] then.

Some of this confusion stems from the diffuse, unorganized way that students tend to get information about what courses to take and how best to go about their plans. Visits with counselors are voluntary. Students' limited use of the counselors is built into the structure of the colleges. Central and Northwest College each have eight counselors for over 7,000 students in a given semester, or one counselor for 875 students. This ratio obviously limits the amount of access that students have to counselors. As one counselor at Central College stated:

Unlike high school, students will come to us voluntarily. We don't have a command performance. Obviously we couldn't have with just eight of us for over 6,000 students. So students do come to us when there's a problem, either personal, academic, or vocational.[8]

Although counselors are officially the main staff responsible for providing information, in practice, they are not the central resource through which students gain their information. During registration at the beginning of each semester, full-time faculty, counselors, and administrators sit at the registration tables to help students select their courses. All students must meet with one of these staff members to pick and approve their courses. Staff have information about prerequisites and basic degree requirements. However, this is often a rushed and chaotic period, and the particular staff person who advises a student is arbitrary. As a result, the provision of information and advice is a random process, with many faculty knowing little about remedial courses and their implications. In addition, students can get a faculty member to approve their courses before the chaotic registration period. This strategy may be more fruitful, particularly if the faculty member is familiar with the students and their programs. On the other hand, there is still the great risk that students will obtain advice in bits and pieces from faculty members who often have incomplete information about remedial courses. Like Ivette and Darius, many students float around with little knowledge about whether or not they are accurately following their degree requirements because they choose not to visit counselors until they are well on their way toward graduating or transferring.

The students expressed regret about their lack of awareness of their remedial status and its implications. David said that he might have decided to forgo college altogether if he had known that his credits were not going to count toward anything:

I think that a student should know in the beginning . . . that these classes, even though we think they're necessary and you would benefit from them, will not count toward graduation. The students should know what they're getting into in the very beginning. Like I said, I don't have a lot of time to spend in school. . . . The program has helped me. . . . But if I had known from the very beginning that I wasn't going to be getting full credit for these classes, I may have thought twice about them. . . . I would have just gone on and tried to find a job. . . . I would have probably said, "Hey I don't have time for this. I've got to go."

For this student with limited funds and little time to spend in school, the "protecting" of students' self-esteem is preventing realistic career decisions. Goffman (1952) described such delaying of information as an essential element of a scam. Although we do not believe that this is the community colleges' intention, this nonstigmatized approach necessarily prevents students from making informed decisions and anticipating negative outcomes.

Do Students Realize the Implications?

We administered surveys in many sections of six different remedial math, English, and reading courses and among students who had formerly been enrolled in remedial courses. Of the 804 students who were surveyed, 610 had taken or were currently taking remedial courses.[9] Of these 610 students, 38.7 percent believed that these classes would count toward their degree requirements, and an additional 34.6 percent were not sure whether the credits would count. In sum, over 73 percent of the students who had taken remedial courses were either unclear or wrong about the actual status of their remedial credits.

The results indicate that students' awareness increases over time, but only modestly. Comparing students in the first year with those in the second year and above, we found improved accuracy over time, with 23.2 percent of first-year students and 29.7 percent beyond their first year correctly reporting that their credits would not count (see Table 1). The greater awareness that remedial courses do not count was accompanied by a decline in the proportion of students who were "not sure," while the proportion who held the mistaken belief that these courses count remained constant (almost 39 percent). Despite students' improved accuracy after their first year, over 70 percent of the students beyond their first year were still not aware that their remedial courses did not count toward a degree or transfer.

In our interviews, students who were taking multiple remedial courses seemed more confused about their situation. They were making sacrifices, improving themselves, and aiming toward a degree, and no one was telling them any discouraging information, even though they were taking several "developmental" courses. The survey data clarify students' response to this situation—students who were taking remedial courses in more subjects were less likely to realize that their courses would not count (see Table 2). Even among advanced students, students who were taking three or four remedial course areas were less likely to be aware that remedial courses did not count than were students who were taking one remedial course area (21 percent versus 37 percent). While some correct perceivers may have dropped out (especially by the second year), these findings also support the observations in our interviews: Students who take remedial courses in multiple areas are more likely to misperceive the value of their remedial courses.

Our survey also asked the students to assess their chances of achieving their degree goals (on a 5-point scale, from very likely to very unlikely).

We found that students' perceived likelihood of attaining their degree goals did not decline as they took more remedial subjects (see Table 3). Moreover, the remedial students did not have lower degree goals. They were actually slightly more likely to indicate that they were aiming toward a bachelor's degree (versus an associate degree or a certificate) than were the nonremedial students—46.3 percent and 44.2 percent, respectively. Although national data indicate that the dropout rate for students with three or more remedial courses is much higher than for students with only one remedial course (Adelman 1996, 1999; Deil-Amen 2002), we found that students do not lower their perceived chances of completing their degrees as the number of their remedial courses increases.

Conclusion

When students enter college, they may not really be college students, they may be taking high school-level courses that provide no "real" college credit. This study found that students may not realize their situation and its implications. We described the several ways that community colleges create this circumstance, inadvertently and with good intentions.

Community colleges are faced with serving students who arrive at their doors underprepared for "college-level" courses, yet who fully anticipate that they will complete their college degrees. The colleges must deal with these students and their high expectations. As one community college English professor aptly noted, "You have to serve your community if you're a community college."

Unlike Clark's (1973) description of the cooling-out process, we found that community college staff have found ingenious ways to preserve students' aspirations and avoid conveying stigma to students who are placed in remedial

TABLE 1
Remedial Students' Perceptions of Remedial Credits

| Students' Status | Do Remedial Classes Count Toward a Degree? | | | |
	% No	% Yes	% Not Sure	n
First year	23.2	38.9	37.9	330
Second year +	29.7	38.5	31.8	280
All remedial students	26.7	38.7	34.6	610

TABLE 2
Remedial Students' Perception of Degree Credits, by Number of Remedial Subject Areas

Number of Remedial Subjects	Do Remedial Classes Count Toward a Degree?				
	No	Yes	Not Sure	Total	n
First Year					
One remedial	36.5	35.4	28.1	100	96
Two remedial	17.2	45.2	37.6	100	93
Three remedial	15.4	36.3	48.4	100	91
Second Year +					
One remedial	37.0	39.5	23.5	100	81
Two remedial	32.4	40.3	27.3	100	139
Three remedial	20.9	35.5	43.6	100	110
All Remedial Students	23.2	38.9	37.9		610

courses. Indeed, we were impressed with how these community colleges were able to avoid damaging students' self-confidence while encouraging them to improve their skills to qualify for college-level courses and pursue their goals of transferring to four-year colleges.

However, we discovered that this stigma-free approach has some critical unintended consequences. The avoidance of "remedial" labels; a hesitancy to highlight students' remedial placements; and the lack of an adequate, structured counseling/advising system led to confusion and misperceptions among the students. Even after two, three, or four semesters, some students were still unclear about whether the courses were giving them college credit and how long it would take them to get a degree. Some students had lost time taking courses they did not need and for which they did not get credit. For students with limited funds and a narrow window of time for college study, such missteps can be costly to their careers.

Just as the hallmark of a scam is the selling of objects of little value, some students reported investing time and tuition in remedial courses that failed to deliver the "value" in degree credits they had been expecting. This process looks a lot like the swindles that Goffman (1952) described. Students are being gently led into a long-term process without having any idea of how little progress they are making or how long it will take to attain their goal. They are expending money and efforts, and there is a real risk that many of them will not

get a degree and that some will get few or no college credits. The staff have good intentions when they create these misperceptions, but they are deceptive nonetheless.

Could this deception be in the students' best interest? Is keeping students in college "for their own good" similar to the way parents trick their children into eating vegetables that are good for them? There are several reasons to think that deception is inappropriate here. First, these students are not children; they are adults with adult responsibilities—rent payments, car payments, jobs, spouses, and children—and a strategy of deception is patronizing. Second, these remedial courses are not as costless as eating vegetables. We were astounded at the enormous sacrifices that the students were making to be in college. We interviewed students who had to work 40 hours a week, who had taken out loans, and who were supporting parents and siblings. Some were working parents, for whom their college courses and homework were added on to 60 hours of work and family obligations. Tricking these students into losing sleep, reducing their time with their children, and avoiding overtime assignments at work is certainly more costly than eating vegetables. Third, deception has other costs: it creates credibility problems. Students have implicit timetables. Many students have promised their families that they will get an associate's degree in two years, and when the time comes and goes, parents and spouses are understandably disappointed and angry at the time college has taken away from home and job.

TABLE 3
Perceived Chances of Achieving Degree Goals, by Number of Remedial Course Areas

Number of Remedial Subject Areas	% "Very Likely" or "Likely" to Earn a Degree	n
None	90.7	194
One	94.4	177
Two	96.6	232
Three	91.0	201
All students	93.3	804

Fourth, these students have other options, which they could choose if they were not deceived. Some college programs require fewer remedial courses. The AAS degree often has fewer academic prerequisites than the AA and AS degrees, so that some students would need fewer noncredit remedial courses. In the colleges we studied, if a student scores poorly on the remedial exam, say at the 10th-grade level, she or he must take three noncredit (remedial) math courses before being able to take one that gives credit for an AA degree. But that same student would only need to take one noncredit math course if she or he were pursuing an AAS degree. Since three remedial courses delays the completion of a degree and may increase the likelihood of dropout (compared to one course), students may choose the AAS to avoid these outcomes. This easier choice is unlikely to affect employment outcomes, since it is unlikely that employers understand the difference between the two degrees. Furthermore, research has shown that taking more applied occupational courses has clear economic benefits (Bishop 1992; Grubb 1996; Rosenbaum 1996). In many cases, the bulk of these AAS credits can also be transferred to a four-year college if students choose to continue their education. Deception prevents students from even considering these alternative options.

Community colleges and their promise of open access do give disadvantaged students a second chance to overcome obstacles, just as they were intended to do. Unfortunately, this second chance leads to a degree only for a small proportion of students in this situation. Our study highlighted the possibility that the stigma-free approach may represent a more subtle form of blocked opportunity. Rather than a cooling-out approach that limits opportunity by steering students toward the structural alternative of a lower degree, the delayed recognition caused by a stigma-free approach may be contributing to stu-

dents dropping out of college altogether and hence accumulating *no* credentials rather than a lesser degree.

The institutional context we described fosters the type of misperceptions that inhibits students' ability to plan their long-term educational and occupational future effectively. At the least, it seems that students are being shortchanged in their chances to consider realistic backup options, like taking advantage of on-the-job training, short-term certificates, AAS degrees, or skill training at another kind of school in addition to their college studies.

It is appropriate to be concerned that informing students of their lower probabilities of success will be discouraging. However, withholding this information prevents students from taking steps to address the situation. College staff must find ways to convey full information while they encourage students' efforts. In addition, practitioners must find ways to support programs that reduce failure for at-risk remedial students. This is not an easy balance, but it is necessary to find ways to provide both information and encouragement.

We conclude that nonstigmatized counseling may solve the old complaints about cooling out but may raise additional concerns about candor and deception. Reduced stigma and improved self-confidence may have come at the cost of deception and delay, prolonging the time it takes for students to realize their situation. Students are not getting easily produced information, and they are paying the price in delayed recognition, efforts that have a low probability of attaining their goal, and failure to take actions that may be more promising.

Notes

1. The movie, *The Sting*, provides a clear example of Goffman's model. In the movie, the character

played by Robert Redford gets revenge on a powerful enemy by a confidence scheme but then creates a situation in which the enemy must decide that it is futile and risky to try to recover his lost money.

2. Although other postsecondary institutions were not included in this study, the impact of remedial programs can and should be explored at four-year colleges as well. *All* community colleges offer remedial courses, and they are the only institutions that have experienced an increase in remedial enrollments. However, 81 percent of four-year public and 63 percent of four-year private colleges offer remedial courses, and the consequences of these programs on their students is an important area of study (NCES 1996). Nearly two-thirds of students who attended only a community college or a community college and a four-year college took at least one remedial course, whereas 40 percent of those who attended only a four-year college took at least one remedial course. (NCES 2000:52).

3. Northwest College enrolled about 11,000 students during 1995 in its credit and precredit courses. Of the students in these courses, 61 percent were female and 39 percent were male; 50 percent were white, 27 percent were Latino, 12 percent were Asian, and 9 percent were African American; their average age was 26; 70 percent were enrolled part time; and 38 percent were employed full time. Central college enrolled about 13,000 students in its precredit and credit courses in 1995. Of the students in these courses, 63 percent were female and 37 percent were male, 47 percent were African American, 23 percent were white, 14 percent were Latino, and 11 percent were Asian; their average age was 30; 77 percent were enrolled part time; and 45 percent were employed full time. In-district tuition was $47.50 per credit hour.

4. Surveys were administered to students in class, so the response rate approached 100 percent. Classes were selected to target strategically a cross section of students in remedial courses and particular programs.

5. Since local funding is partially based on head-count enrollments, the awarding of institutional credit also conveniently allows community colleges to maintain enrollments by giving credit status to students who may otherwise not pay tuition if they were enrolled in noncredit remedial classes. This is a chicken-and-egg situation, however. Often, the more remedial classes a college offers, the fewer sophomore-level courses it offers. However, in Illinois, as in most states, community colleges did not actively seek to increase their remedial enrollments. They were forced to accommodate to the will of political decision makers, who, in the Board of Higher Education Act, designated community

colleges as the place where remediation efforts should be undertaken (Ignash 1997:7). In fact, many faculty and administrators oppose the increase in remedial classes and would prefer to offer (and teach) more higher-level courses. In any case, the financial incentives do not seem a prominent concern. In the district we studied, remedial credits are actually allocated funds at a rate that is 13 percent lower than baccalaureate transfer credits, 36 percent lower than technical credits, and 63 percent lower than health credits. Moreover, if financial concerns were primary, we would expect all remedial courses to be staffed with less-costly part-time faculty, which was not the case. Indeed, we were impressed to find that about half the credit-level remedial reading and writing courses at Northwest and 80 percent of them at Central were staffed with full-time faculty, who expressed an idealistic desire to provide opportunities to students from disadvantaged backgrounds. The relationship between structures of funding and remedial approaches in community colleges is a topic that is worthy of extensive research, but is beyond the scope of this article.

6. We created these classifications. Such concrete distinctions are not specified by the colleges themselves, nor are they presented to students.

7. A few years ago, students usually had to consult with a four-year college directly or get a "transfer guide" from the counseling office for their college and program of interest. These guides were constantly being revised and updated and therefore were often outdated. Many four-year colleges have recently participated in a broad-based articulation agreement that helps to create a consensus between two- and four-year colleges regarding the "approved" curricula. As a result, these two community colleges now have a list of transferable courses for schools that participate in the Illinois Articulation Agreement in their catalogs. However, confusion still abounds, since some "ambiguous" credit courses count for transfer to some schools but not to others and not for some AS degrees.

8. The counselor's estimates regarding student enrollments differ from the figure in the preceding paragraph, which was obtained from the district's Office of Planning and Research. The number of students enrolled changes from semester to semester as well as over the course of one semester, due to student withdrawals from the college.

9. The number of remedial course areas is based on students' reports of the titles of the courses they had taken, which is probably a better indicator than their own count of the number of remedial course areas because students do not always realize that a course is remedial.

References

Adelman, Clifford C. 1995. *The New College Course Map and Transcript Files.* Washington, DC: U.S. Department of Education.

———. 1996, October 4. "The Truth About Remedial Work: It's More Complex than Windy Rhetoric and Simple Solutions Suggest." *Chronicle of Higher Education,* p. A35.

———. 1999. *Answers in the Tool Box: Academic Intensity, Attendance Patterns, and Bachelor's Degree Attainment.* Washington, DC: U.S. Department of Education.

Bishop, John. 1992. "Workforce Preparedness" (Working Paper, 92–03). Ithaca, NY: School of Industrial and Labor Relations, Cornell University.

Brint, Steven, and Jerome Karabel. 1989. *The Diverted Dream: Community Colleges and the Promise of Educational Opportunity in America, 1900–1985.* New York: Oxford University Press.

———. 1991. "Institutional Origins and Transformations: The Case of American Community Colleges." Pp 337–60 in The New Institutionalism in Organizational Analysis, edited by Walter W. Powell and Paul J. DiMaggio. Chicago: University of Chicago Press.

Cicourel, Aaron, and John Kitsuse. 1964. *The Educational Decision-Makers.* Indianapolis, IN: Bobbs-Merrill.

Clark, Burton. 1960. *The Open Door College.* New York: McGraw-Hill.

———. 1973. "The Cooling Out Function in Higher Education." Pp. 362–71 in *The Sociology of Education,* edited by Robert R. Bell and Holger R. Stub. Homewood, IL: Dorsey Press.

Day, Phillip R., Jr., and Robert H. McCabe. 1997. "Remedial Education: A Social and Economic Imperative" (Executive issue paper). Available on-line at http://www.aacc.nche.edu

Deil-Amen, Regina. 2002. "From Dreams to Degrees: Social Processes of Opportunity and Blocked Opportunity in Community Colleges." Unpublished doctoral dissertation, Northwestern University, Department of Sociology.

Dobberstein, Keith. 1987. "On the Occasion of the 75th" *City: A Journal of the City Colleges of Chicago.*

Dougherty, Kevin J. 1994. *The Contradictory College: The Conflicting Origins, Impacts, and Futures of the Community College.* Albany: State University of New York Press.

Erickson, Fred. 1973. "Gatekeeping the Melting Pot." *Harvard Educational Review* 45:44–70.

Goffman, Erving. 1952. "Cooling the Mark Out: Some Aspects of Adaptation to Failure." *Psychiatry* 15:451–63.

Grubb, Norton W. 1996. *Working in the Middle: Strengthening Education and Training for the Mid-Skilled Labor Force.* San Francisco: Jossey-Bass.

Grubb, Norton W., and Judy Kalman. 1994. "Relearning to Earn: The Role of Remediation in Vocational Education and Job Training." *American Journal of Education* 103:54–93.

Ignash, Jan M. 1997. "Who Should Provide Postsecondary Remedial/Developmental Education?" Pp. 5–20 in *Implementing Effective Policies for Remedial and Developmental Education: New Directions for Community Colleges,* edited by Ian M. Ignash. San Francisco: Jossey-Bass.

Karabel, Jerome. 1977. "Community Colleges and Social Stratification: Submerged Class Conflict in American Higher Education." Pp. 232–53 in *Power and Ideology in Education,* edited by Jerome Karabel and A. H. Halsey. New York: Oxford University Press.

Lareau, Annette, and Erin M. Horvat 1999 "Moments of Social Inclusion and Exclusion: Race, Class and Cultural Capital in Family-School Relationships." *Sociology of Education* 72:37–53.

London, Howard B. 1978. *The Culture of a Community College.* New York: Praeger.

McDonough, Patricia. 1997. *Choosing Colleges: How Social Class and Schools Structure Opportunity.* Albany: State University of New York Press.

McMillan, Virginia K., Scott J. Parke, and Carol A. Lanning. 1997. "Remedial/Developmental Education Approaches for the Current Community College Environment." Pp. 21–32 in *Implementing Effective Policies for Remedial and Developmental Education: New Directions for Community Colleges,* edited by Ian N. Ignash. San Francisco: Jossey-Bass.

National Center for Education Statistics. 1996. *Remedial Education in Higher Education in Fall 1995* (NCES 97–584). Washington, DC: U.S. Government Printing Office.

———. 1998. *The Condition of Education: 1998* (NCES 98–013). Washington, DC: U.S. Government Printing Office.

———. 2000. *Digest of Education Statistics.* Washington, DC: Author.

O'Connor, Carla. 1999 "Race, Class, and Gender in America: Narratives of Opportunity Among Low-Income African-American Youths." *Sociology of Education* 72:137–57.

Rosenbaum, James E. 1976. *Making Inequality: The Hidden Curriculum of High School Tracking.* New York: John Wiley & Sons.

———. 1996. "Policy Uses of Research on the High School to Work Transition." *Sociology of Education* 69:102–22.

———. 1998. College-for-All: Do Students Understand What College Demands? *Social Psychology of Education* 2:55–80.

———. 2001. *Beyond College for All: Career Paths of The Forgotten Half.* New York: Russell Sage Foundation.

Rosenbaum, James E., Shazia Rafiullah Miller, and Melinda Scott Krei. 1996. "Gatekeeping in an Era of More Open Gates: High School Counselors' Views of Their Influence on Students' College Plans." *American Journal of Education* 104:257–79.

Schneider, Barbara, and David Stevenson. 1999. *The Ambitious Generation: America's Teenagers, Motivated but Directionless.* New Haven, CT: Yale University Press.

Smith, Herbert, and Brian Powell, 1990. "Great Expectations: Variations in Income Expectations Among College Seniors" *Sociology of Education* 63:194–207.

Steinberg, Lawrence. 1996. *Beyond the Classroom.* New York: Simon & Schuster.

Useem, Elizabeth L. 1992. "Middle Schools and Math Groups: Parents' Involvement in Children's Placement." *Sociology of Education* 65:263–79.

Weis, Lois. 1985. *Between Two Worlds: Black Students in an Urban Community College.* Boston: Routledge & Kegan Paul.

Regina Deil-Amen, Ph.D., is Research Project Director, Institute for Policy Research, Northwestern University, Evanston, Illinois. Her main fields of interest ore higher education, inequality, institutions, and culture. Dr. Deil-Amen completed her Ph.D. in sociology at Northwestern University and will begin her appointment as an assistant professor in the Department of Education Policy Studies at Pennsylvania State University in August. She is currently working on a project that explores institutional differences between public and private colleges in how they prepare students for jobs in the subbaccalaureate labor market.

James E. Rosenbaum, Ph.D., is Professor of Sociology, Education, and Social Policy, Institute for Policy Research, Northwestern University, Evanston, Illinois. His main fields of interest are education, work, careers and the life course, and stratification. After completing a book in the Rose Monograph Series on the high school-to-work transition, he is now conducting studies on the transition between community colleges and work.

The authors thank the Spencer Foundation for a major grant that supported the student survey and analysis and the Institute for Policy Research at Northwestern University for supporting portions of the work. They also thank the Ford Foundation for its support of the research project that initiated the qualitative data collection and Kathleen Show and Howard London for their guidance and direction during that phase of the research process. In addition, they thank Tom Cook, Stefanie DeLuca, Adam Gamoran, Maureen Hallinan, John Meyer, Marc Ventresca, and James Witte for their thoughtful comments and suggestions. Address all correspondence to Dr. Regina Deil-Amen, Educational Theory and Policy, Penn State University, 300 Rackley Building, University Park, PA 16802, e-mail: reggie@northwestern.edu, or Dr James E. Rosenbaum, Institute for Policy Research, Northwestern University, 2040 Sheridan Road, Evanston, IL 60208; e-mail: j-rosenbaum@northwestern.edu.

CHAPTER 23

THE LOCATION OF DEVELOPMENTAL EDUCATION IN COLLEGES: A DISCUSSION OF MERITS OF MAINSTREAMING VS. CENTRALIZATION

DOLORES PERIN

Ineffective high school education and increasing ethnic and linguistic diversity are combining to make developmental education critically important for individuals who wish to participate in post-secondary education. Developmental education has become an integral part of the community college mission (Carnevale & Desrochers, 2001; Levin, 2001). With their open admissions policy and commitment to serving a wide range of students in local communities, community colleges have historically played an important role in higher education by offering instruction in basic reading, writing, and math skills to enable academically underprepared students to master the college curriculum. As Levin (2001) stated,

> For many students in either large or small communities, the community college is the only public educational institution that will accept them for college-level studies given their high school academic performance. Furthermore, of the many types of postsecondary institutions facing students who are unprepared for college-level studies, the community college is the only institution whose legal and social mandate is remedial education. (p. xii)

Community college students display a number of academic and personal risk factors that are associated with low rates of persistence and achievement (McClenney, undated). In response, the colleges attempt to increase student preparedness for the college curriculum in a variety of ways including precollege level reading, writing, and math courses (variously termed "developmental education" and "remediation"); academic tutoring in learning assistance centers while students are enrolled in college-level courses; and instructional modifications such as writing-across-the-curriculum in discipline classrooms. Content-area remediation is also provided in some institutions in the form of supplemental instruction, a peer-tutoring model where students who have earned high grades in discipline courses (e.g. biology and history) lead study groups for students who are failing in those classes. However, among this complex array, developmental education courses are the most visible form of remediation in community colleges because these courses are clear catalog offerings in which basic skills instruction is formalized.

Organizational Approaches: Mainstreaming and Centralization

Given the importance of developmental education courses, the question has arisen as to whether they should be integrated into regular departments, here called *mainstreaming*, or housed in separate organizational units, referred to as *centralization*. The distinction between mainstreaming and centralization is an important issue for college policy because the organization of developmental education may have direct impact on its quality (Boylan, Bliss, & Bonham, 1997). When developmental education is mainstreamed, precollege level remedial courses are offered in academic departments, such as English or mathematics, whose main purpose is to offer college-level courses applicable to associate's degrees or certificates. Courses are numbered as part of a sequence that begins with noncredit, remedial level instruction and continues through advanced associate-level preparation. Instructors are all considered faculty of the department in question and are paid through its budget. Working in close proximity in a departmental context permits developmental education instructors to mingle with colleagues who teach college-level courses. In fact, some faculty teach both developmental and credit-bearing courses simultaneously. On the other hand, when remediation is centralized, the remedial courses are offered in a separate department whose sole function is to offer precollege-level courses. Course numbers reflect the separateness of the department, and the faculty may communicate more often with each other than with instructors from academic departments. In addition to courses, the centralized department may offer ancillary support services such as counseling and tutoring. Most of the instructors will be paid from the centralized department's budget although some may have joint appointments with academic departments and teach courses in both (see McKay et al., 1998).

The term "mainstreaming" is used here in the context of stand-alone developmental education courses. The current question is whether such stand-alone courses should be offered in a regular college department or in a separate remedial department. Arendale (1998, cit. Damashek, 1999) uses the term to refer to the replacement of stand-alone courses with a comprehensive system of support available to all students via a learning assistance center. Boylan et al. (1997) use

the term "decentralized" for what we are calling mainstreamed developmental education.

Although there have been strong statements in favor of centralization (e.g., Roueche & Roueche, 1999), there is little direct evidence to support this policy. The purpose of this article is to consider the relative merits of each approach. Because there is a shortage of empirical evidence in the previous literature, the discussion is speculative, relying on practitioners' views and relevant data reported in the existing literature. Sources of information for this discussion were journal articles, book chapters, and technical reports on community college developmental education identified in a search of the ERIC and Educational Abstracts electronic data bases, as well as bibliographies, conference presentations, and personal communications with experts in developmental education. Some of the studies relate specifically to two-year colleges and others to four-year institutions but the organizational issues in both settings are identical.

Current Practices

Roueche and Roueche (1999) have reported that the majority of community colleges across the country mainstream their developmental education programs. Some community colleges have a separate remedial division that teaches their lower level developmental courses, with an academic department teaching the higher level courses. In other colleges, a mixed model may be used, for example, mainstreaming writing and math in their respective content departments, while offering reading courses in a separate developmental education department. According to NCES (1996, Table 10), 54% of community colleges mainstream remedial reading, 59% mainstream remedial writing, and 62% mainstream remedial math courses.

A study of 15 states by the Southern Regional Education Board (Abraham, 1992) found that in community and four-year colleges combined, most developmental education was mainstreamed: 41% of institutions delivered reading remediation in an academic department, (57% in writing, 58% in math) while only about one-third centralized remedial education. Since separate percentages were not provided for community colleges, it is difficult to compare these figures with the NCES data.

Similarly, Boylan, Bliss, and Bonham (1997) examined the organization of developmental education in two- and four-year colleges combined. In a national sample, they found that 52% centralized developmental education. In contrast, the findings of a national survey conducted by the American Association of Community Colleges (Shults, 2000) indicated that only 25% of community colleges centralized their remedial courses, while 15% mainstreamed these courses within academic departments. Although a further 61% of institutions surveyed offered their courses "within their respective subject areas," a term not defined, it is notable that Shults' (2000) findings differ from the NCES (1996) data in finding a low incidence of mainstreaming. Similarly, Grubb and Associates (1999) reported that remediation tended to be centralized, stating, "Within community colleges, remediation is usually organized as an activity separate from the core purposes, isolated in a jigsaw puzzle of developmental reading and writing departments and tutorial programs" (p. 171). Taking into consideration all of these studies, it is not clear whether the trend is for colleges to mainstream or centralize remediation.

Drawing on NCES (1996), Roueche and Roueche (1999) note that community colleges with high proportions of minority students are more likely than are low-minority institutions to centralize rather than mainstream their developmental courses. People from ethnic and racial minority groups may predominate among the segment of students who are academically underprepared. In a national study of students who completed remedial programs, McCabe (2000) found that among individuals whose skills were, "seriously deficient" (i.e., students who tested into reading, writing, and math remediation, including at least one lower level course), minority groups were overrepresented (56%). In particular, 51% of all students in this category were women from minority groups. McCabe found that only 20% of the seriously deficient students in his sample completed remediation, compared to 43% for higher functioning students. The tendency of minority-dominated institutions to provide centralized rather than mainstreamed developmental education suggests that this approach may be particularly helpful for lower achieving remedial students.

Beyond the prevalence of the two approaches, Boylan et al. (1997) studied the relation between organizational structure and student outcomes. Based on an analysis of academic data on a random sample of 6,000 developmental education students attending 300 community and four-year colleges, it was found that students attending institutions where developmental education was centralized had significantly higher first-term grade point averages, cumulative grade point averages, retention rates, and math and English grades, compared with students in colleges where remediation was mainstreamed. Unfortunately, the means were not reported so that it cannot be ascertained whether the group differences were in fact educationally meaningful or only an artifact of statistical power associated with large sample size.

Because other empirical evidence is lacking, the remainder of this discussion relies on descriptive studies and practitioner commentary that, although not providing direct evidence, help weigh the advantages and disadvantages of the two approaches. We frame the discussion in terms of a number of educational components that are frequently mentioned in discussions of remedial education: quality of instruction; availability of ancillary support services; teacher motivation and experience; students' reactions; and the reputation of developmental education in the larger college structure. How do the two models compare in those areas?

This discussion considers the organizational structure of remediation from the perspective of student learning. The issue could also be considered from philosophical, political, or budgetary perspectives. For example, Klicka (1998) claims that centralization protects program philosophy, makes remediation more visible, and ensures budget allocation and administrative representation in the college. The issue of student learning is considered here in terms of transfer of skill from the remedial context to college classrooms. However, whatever measure of learning is considered important, there are no empirical studies in the literature that determine the impact on student learning through direct comparison of mainstreamed and centralized developmental education.

Comparison of Mainstreamed and Centralized Developmental Education In Terms of Critical Educational Components

Quality of instruction. The main purpose of remedial education is to prepare students for the college-level academic demands. Therefore, the quality of remedial instruction can be considered in terms of its alignment with the college curriculum. Specifically, the skills and content taught in developmental reading, writing, and math classrooms should be related to those that students will later encounter in their subject-matter classrooms. From a cognitive perspective, close alignment of developmental and college-level instruction should promote students' generalization of learning beyond remediation to the college-level classroom. Transfer from learning to application is one of three major types of cognitive generalization (Simons, 1999) and is a central goal of education (Bereiter, 1995). An important factor in the transfer of learning is the reinforcement of students' original learning through the use of multiple examples in numerous contexts. As Haskell (2001) states, "Teaching that promotes transfer . . . involves returning again and again to an idea or procedure but on different levels in different contexts, with apparently 'different' examples." (pp. 26–27). The remedial classroom is where academic skills are learned and the various college-level classrooms that the student attends as he or she moves through the discipline program are the settings in which these skills are applied. Transfer of skill is more likely if learning and application occur close in time.

Remedial programs described as exemplary include the "integration of coursework within and beyond the developmental program" (McCabe & Day, 1998, p. 25). There are several ways to accomplish the integration of remediation and higher-level instruction, for example, through paired courses that create formal links between precollege developmental and college-level courses in discipline areas (Badway & Grubb, 1997). These pairings provide immediate opportunities for the application of newly learned reading, writing, and math skills. The alignment of remedial with occupational courses seems useful, since many remedial students plan to pursue career-related degree programs (McCabe, 2000). However, most alignment between developmental and college level curriculum involves general education courses such as freshman composition, history, and psychology, rather than specialized technical courses (Perin, 2001).

Irrespective of students' interests, course pairing may be ruled out when state or institutional policy mandates remedial completion prior to enrollment in college-level courses. That is, if students are prohibited from enrolling in college-level courses before they complete their remedial requirements, they are necessarily barred from participating in a paired-course model since one of the courses bears college credit.

In situations where policy allows formal connections between remedial and college-level classes, is this innovation more likely when developmental education is mainstreamed or centralized? Instructional reform requiring the interdisciplinary collaboration necessary for course linking depends on positive working relationships among instructors (Perin, 2000). Centralizing developmental education may serve to marginalize it within the college, reducing the likelihood of regular interaction between developmental and college-course instructors. If this is the case, curricular alignment in the form of paired courses may be more likely to occur when developmental education is mainstreamed.

Apart from course pairing, instruction can also be aligned by matching exit levels of developmental education to entry levels of the college-level courses. Lining up these levels, at least for college composition and mathematics courses, seems more feasible when developmental education is mainstreamed, because in principle, at least some instructors who teach college-credit classes would also have as part of their teaching load some developmental-level classes.

In practice, as discussed below, discipline area instructors may decline developmental teaching assignments, and when taught in academic departments, the instruction of remedial courses may be left to part-time, adjunct faculty who may or may not also be teaching college-level courses. If this problem can be overcome administratively, mainstreamed developmental education may have better potential than centralized departments to align curriculum, at least in the subject areas of English and mathematics, thus facilitating the generalization of student learning.

The benefits of the greater use of full-time instructors in centralized rather than mainstreamed developmental education programs may be undermined by the lack of awareness of the academic demands and content of college-level study that such instructors may have as a result of isolation from the academic departments. The danger in this case is that even at the highest level remedial courses, students considered ready to exit remediation may actually remain underprepared for academic study in the content areas (Perin et al., in press).

Availability of ancillary support services. Overall, community colleges have a strong reputation for providing assistance to support learning and are perceived by students as more nurturing than four-year colleges (Carlan & Byxbe, 2001). A report by the Institute for Higher Education Policy (1998) suggested that the effectiveness of remediation in higher education could be improved by including "support services that rely on multiple intervention strategies" (p. 23). Roueche, Ely, and Roueche (2001) linked community colleges' effectiveness in educating remedial students to the provision of supplementary tutoring, mandatory participation in learning labs, and "case management models" (p. 33) that permit individualized attention. Programs described as exemplary by McCabe and Day (1998) provide support services including tutoring, academic and career advisement, and workshops in areas such as time management and study skills (Moriarty et al., 1998).

These ancillary services may be necessary to increase the persistence and performance of academically low functioning students, many of whom experience not only the family and financial difficulties typical of community college students in general but may also suffer from low self-esteem related to academic difficulties. Remedial students can feel lost in a college environment that they may perceive as impersonal. Support services seem especially important for students at the lower remedial levels who test into three or more remedial courses. In particular, students who enter the college with reading difficulties are at severe academic risk (Adelman, 1998; Roueche & Roueche, 1999).

Centralized developmental education departments may be more likely to recognize the need for support services for at-risk students. Since the sole purpose of a centralized department is remediation, chairs may be more willing than heads of regular academic departments to allocate funds to provision of support services. Further, because their teaching staff may be more attuned and sympathetic to the needs of academically low performing students, centralized departments may be more likely to implement an "early alert" system (Hebel, 1999) that identifies and refers at-risk students for counseling or other support services. However, taking into consideration both the need for curricular alignment and provision of support services, one can speculate that the lower level remedial student, marked by the need for reading instruction, is best served in a centralized department while the higher functioning student may benefit most from developmental courses in a mainstreamed department.

Teacher motivation and experience. Faculty in centralized developmental education departments see the teaching of remedial students as a primary task, while academic discipline instructors may view developmental teaching as a low status assignment and even a punishment. Developmental teachers seem more likely to be able to identify both strengths and weaknesses, rather than only deficiencies, in remedial students. Additionally, hiring criteria in centralized departments are more likely to include commitment to teaching remedial reading, writing or math. Professional development activities are more likely to focus expressly on remedial issues in a centralized than in a mainstreamed department. Thus, on the dimension of teacher motivation and experience, centralized departments seem superior to mainstreamed developmental education.

Students' reactions. Developmental education courses have been criticized as causing feelings of discouragement by reinforcing students' sense that they are at risk and forcing them to take longer to finish their degrees (McCusker, 1999). Alternatives to traditional remedial courses include tutoring and adjunct courses directly connected with regular college-level courses (Commander & Smith, 1995; Maxwell, 1997, both cited by McCusker, 1999). These options provide opportunities for academically underprepared students to interact with their higher achieving peers and participate more fully in college life. Locating remedial education in a regular academic department may hold similar promise. Course numberings indicating that remedial reading, writing, and math courses are part of a larger departmental sequence including college-level English and math may also have positive effects on students' feelings about education. In terms of student reactions to developmental education, mainstreaming appears to be superior to centralization.

In fact, when the mandate to attend remedial classes is weak, students may take it upon themselves to mainstream their remediation within their own programs of study by taking developmental education and credit-bearing courses simultaneously, even where remediation is centralized administratively within the college. Since developmental education courses are intended as preparation for postsecondary-level study, it is surprising that students are rarely required to complete remediation prior to matriculating in college-level programs. NCES (1996) reported that only 2% of higher education institutions (community and four-year colleges combined) prohibited simultaneous enrollment in remedial and credit courses of any type. Among the other 98% of institutions, practices varied across the remedial areas of reading, writing, and math. Between 29% and 35% of institutions placed no restrictions on simultaneous course taking in any area, and between 64% and 69% of situations imposed some restrictions in one or more remedial areas (NCES, 1996, Figure 4).

While NCES provides some information at the institutional level, little has been reported about state policy regarding completion of remediation prior to matriculation, although at the time of writing this report, the Education Commission of the States was in the process of surveying states on this among other issues (Boswell, 2001, personal communication). That state policy tends to be weak or nonexistent on this topic is suggested by findings of Boylan et al. (undated) that only one half of all states require remedial placement based on initial assessment. Where remedial placement itself is not mandatory, it seems unlikely that completion of remediation would be required for entry to college-level courses. In contrast, within institutions and states where remediation must be completed prior to program matriculation,

developmental education serves as a vestibule that must be exited in order for credit-bearing college work to begin. Students may react to the long wait by simply dropping out. The mainstreaming of remedial courses either organizationally within the college or programmatically within students' own course selections seems more likely than centralization models to create positive student reactions.

Reputation of developmental education in the larger college structure.   Centralizing developmental education in effect segregates it from the rest of the college (Eaton, 1994), which may make it difficult for remedial faculty to engage in discussion about curriculum and pedagogy that may occur in the rest of the college (Grubb & Associates, 1999, p. 206). Despite the sometimes unfavorable view of developmental education within academic departments, centralizing remediation may be worse by stigmatizing remediation in the whole college.

Summary.   The following table summarizes the relative potential effectiveness of the centralized and mainstreamed structures in the five areas discussed above. Relative superiority is indicated as "+" and inferiority as "-."

Conclusions and Recommendations

Both centralized and mainstreamed developmental education models show advantages and disadvantages. Among five critical features considered, mainstreaming appears to have the potential for higher quality instruction and more positive student reactions. Centralized

TABLE 1
Relative Potential Effectiveness of Centralized and Mainstreamed Structures

Educational Component	Centralized Model	Mainstreamed Model
Quality of instruction	--	+
Ancillary support services	+	--
Teacher motivation and experience	+	--
Student reactions	--	+
Reputation of developmental education	--	--

departments seem superior regarding ancillary support services and teacher motivation and experience. Both models seem to suffer from the low reputation of developmental education in higher education.

One issue that emerged in this discussion is that lower level remedial students may benefit from a centralized department while students closer to the college level of academic performance may be better served in a mainstreamed department. The tendency of institutions with higher proportions of minority students to centralize developmental education provides indirect support for this speculation, since minority students show greater academic risk than do nonminority students. However, at-risk students are also particularly prone to drop out of community college altogether. One wants to prevent remedial education from driving them away. Any evaluation of the relative merits of centralized versus mainstreamed developmental education should include data from both successful completers and drop-outs.

Pending the availability of comparative evaluation studies, colleges in the process of selecting between centralized and mainstreamed approaches must weigh the severity of each disadvantage. On a more positive note, it is possible to incorporate the beneficial features of both models in either a centralized or mainstreamed setting. The following recommendations could be implemented within either model given the necessary level of administrative commitment and financial resources.

Whether mainstreamed or centralized, developmental reading, writing, and math curricula should be aligned with content and skills found in college-level courses. Remedial literacy and math practices should be authentic, utilizing actual material and examples from the college curriculum rather than drilling in skills that fragment the literacy process (Grubb & Associates, 1999; Levin, 1999). While alignment of remedial reading, writing, and math curricula may be easier when developmental education is mainstreamed in English and mathematics departments, there is no reason in principle why teachers in centralized departments could not incorporate meaningful, content-based, college-level reading, writing, and math material. Ideally, whether centralized or mainstreamed, the content of remedial reading, writing, and math instruction should be closely connected to the subject matter students will later study in degree programs. Many would benefit

from being exposed to specific technical and career-related knowledge in the context of reading, writing, and math remediation.

Individualized attention and supplementary tutoring are important sources of support for academically underprepared students. Borrowing practices characteristic of centralized departments, colleges that mainstream developmental education should ensure that appropriate support services are available to students who need them. This may require setting up the early-warning system referred to above. A major challenge concerns the allocation of funds for these services in departments that are also committed to a wide range of college-level activities, as well as the administrative attention of program heads whose primary commitment may be to degree preparation. To overcome these challenges senior administrators need to work with relevant academic program chairs to ensure that remedial students are adequately supported and monitored. Whether developmental education is centralized or mainstreamed, it should "create conditions for learning," and provide the advisement and support needed to help students overcome the fear of failure (McClenney, undated).

Crowe (1998) asked, "Do colleges train and support developmental instructors or just throw them in the breach?" (p. 15). Professional development, with appropriate incentives for participation and application, would help improve teaching ability and motivation in both mainstreamed and centralized developmental education. In the mainstreamed model, collaborations between remedial and college-level instructors may help the latter develop the passion that the former feel for helping students who have failed in the past. Further, mainstreamed developmental faculty need to learn systematic techniques for teaching reading, writing, and math typical of the learning disabilities field, with which centralized faculty are often highly familiar. On the other hand, instructors in centralized departments may not be adequately familiar with the literacy requirements and content of the college-level, subject-matter curriculum. Contact with college-level English and math instructors would give them an opportunity to examine discipline curricula in order to identify content and skills that could improve the effectiveness of developmental courses in preparing students for college-level work.

There may be a trade-off between instructional quality and teacher motivation across the two models of developmental education. In the mainstreaming approach, instructors may dislike the assignment of teaching remedial courses, but within this same model there may be greater opportunities to link remedial instruction to college-level material. The challenge for institutions would be to raise instructor motivation within the mainstreaming model or to provide incentives for linking remedial and college-level content within the centralized model. Possible mechanisms for accomplishing this aim include incentive pay, caps on class size, and reduction in teaching load.

Whether in mainstreamed or centralized departments, developmental education students should be encouraged to participate in college activities, especially related to the majors and professions to which they aspire, to reduce their feelings of discouragement and self-perceptions as academic failures. Although their skill levels may preclude enrollment in college-level courses, developmental instructors could find ways to provide contact between developmental and college-level students that could raise the motivation of developmental students to persist in what may be a multiyear remedial endeavor. For example, developmental educational students could visit selected credit-level courses as guests, or peer-tutoring programs could be mounted in which students in credit courses work with developmental education students on basic academic skills needed in the degrees to which the latter aspire.

Learning experience is enhanced when students feel that they are connected with an endeavor that is respected in the college. Efforts should be made by academic departments and college administrators to integrate developmental education with the rest of the college program, rather than marginalizing it within departments or within the college. Colleges will have different ways of accomplishing this integration. Doing so seems appropriate given the extent of remedial need in the student body and the growing centrality of developmental education to the community college mission.

Although centralized models have been recommended by experts in the field, Boylan and his colleagues (Boylan et al., 1997; Boylan, 1999) suggest that it is not the centralization itself that might be responsible for superior outcomes but the fact that this structure makes it easier to coordinate services and promote communication among staff. Coordination and communication

may come more easily in a centralized model but are, of course, entirely possible in a situation where remedial education is incorporated in a larger department. In conclusion, both mainstreamed and centralized models have good potential to prepare students for postsecondary academic work, as long as the college demonstrates commitment to the ongoing improvement of developmental education in whatever form is institutionally appropriate.

References

Abraham, A. A. (1992). College remedial studies: Institutional practices in the SREB states. Atlanta, GA: Southern Regional Education Board.

Adelman, C. (1998). The kiss of death: An alternative view of college remediation [Online]. Available: *www.highereducation.org/crosstalk/ct0798/ voices0798-adelman.html*

Arendale, D. (1998). Trends in developmental education [Online]. Available: *http://umkc.edu/cad/nade/ nadedocs/trends.htm*

Badway, N.; & Grubb, W. N. (1997). A sourcebook for reshaping the community college: Curriculum integration and the multiple domains of career preparation, Vols. I and II. Berkeley, CA: National Center for Research in Vocational Education.

Bereiter, C. (1995). A dispositional view of transfer. In A. McKeough, J. Lupart, & A. Marini (Eds.). *Teaching for transfer: Fostering generalization of learning* (pp. 21–34). Mahwah, NJ: Erlbaum.

Boswell, K. (2001, July 5). Education Commission on the States [personal communication].

Boylan, H. R. (1999). Developmental education: Demographics, outcomes and activities [Online]. Available: *www.ncde.appstate.edu.*

Boylan, H., Bliss, L., & Bonham, B. (1997). Program components and their relationship to student performance. *Journal of Developmental Education, 20* (3), 2–9.

Boylan, H., Saxon, P., & Boylan, H. M. (undated). State policies on remediation at public colleges and universities. Paper prepared for the League for Innovation in the Community College. Boone, NC: National Center for Developmental Education, Appalachian State University.

Carlan, P. E., & Byxbe, F. R. (2000). Community colleges under the microscope: An analysis of performance predictors for native and transfer students. *Community College Review, 28* (2), 27–43.

Carnevale, A. P., & Desrochers, D. M. (2001). *Help wanted, credentials required: Community colleges in the knowledge economy.* Princeton, NJ: Educational Testing Service.

Commander, N. E., & Smith, B. C. (1995). Development adjunct reading and learning courses that work. *Journal of Reading, 38*, 352–360.

Crowe, E. (1998, September). *Statewide remedial education policies: State strategies that support successful student transitions from secondary to postsecondary education.* Denver, CO: State Higher Education Executive Officers.

Damashek, R. (1999, fall). Reflections on the future of developmental education. *Journal of Developmental Education, 23* (1), 18–20, 22.

Eaton, J. (1994). *Strengthening collegiate education in community colleges.* San Francisco: Jossey Bass.

Grubb, W. N., & Associates (1999). *Honored but invisible: An inside look at teaching in community colleges.* New York: Routledge.

Haskell, R. E. (2001). *Transfer of learning: Cognition, instruction and reasoning.* San Diego: Academic Press.

Hebel, S. (1999, May 7). Community College of Denver wins fans with ability to tackle tough issues. *Chronicle of Higher Education,* A37.

Institute for Higher Education Policy (1998). College remediation: What it is, what it costs, what's at stake. Washington, DC: Author.

Klicka, M. A. (1998). Developmental education services at Bucks County Community College. In R. H. McCabe & P. R. Day, Jr. (Eds.). *Developmental education: A twenty-first century social and economic imperative* (pp. 37–52). Mission Viejo, CA: League for Innovation in the Community College.

Levin, H. (1999). Improving remedial education. Paper prepared for the Social Science Research Council, New York.

Levin, J. S. (2001). *Globalizing the community college: Strategies for change in the 21st century.* New York: Palgrave.

Maxwell, M. (1997). What are the functions of a college learning assistance center? (ERIC Document Reproduction Service No. ED413031)

McCabe, R. H. (2000). *No one to waste: A report to public decision-makers and community college leaders.* Washington, DC: Community College Press.

McCabe, R. H., & Day, P. R., Jr. (1998). *Developmental education: A twenty-first century social and economic imperative* [Online]. Mission Viejo, CA: League for Innovation in the Community College. Available: *www.league.org*

McClenney, K. M. (undated). Teaching in a future that ain't what it used to be. [Online]. In Celebrations: An Occasional Publication of the National Institute for Staff and Organizational Development (NISOD). Austin, TX: University of Texas at Austin. Retrieved May 24, 2001, from: *www.nisod.com*

McCusker, M. (1999). ERIC review: Effective elements of developmental reading and writing programs. *Community College Review, 27* (2), 93–105.

McKay, S. E., Red Shirt, E. M., and Hickey, M. C. (1998). The Guilford Technical Community College Developmental Education Program. In R. H. McCabe & P. R. Day, Jr. (Eds.), *Developmental education: A twenty-first century social and economic imperative* [Online]. (pp 67–72). Mission Viejo, CA: League for Innovation in the Community College. Available: *www.league.org*

Moriarty, D. F., with Naigus, N., Wyckoff-Byers, N., Greenfield, T., & Mulligan, D. (1998). In R. H. McCabe & P. R. Day, Jr. (Eds.), *Developmental education: A twenty-first century social and economic imperative* [Online]. (pp. 73–77). Mission Viejo, CA: League for Innovation in the Community College. Available: *www.league.org*

National Center for Education Statistics, Statistical Analysis Report (1996, October). Remedial education at higher education institutions in Fall 1995. Postsecondary education quick information system (PEQis). (NCES No. 97-584). Washington, DC: Author.

Perin, D. (2001). Academic-occupational integration as a reform strategy for the community college: Classroom perspectives. *Teachers College Record, 103*, 303–335.

Perin, D., Keselman, A., & Monopoli, M. (in press). The academic writing of community college remedial students: Text and learner variables. To appear in *Higher Education.*

Roueche, J. E., & Roueche, S. D. (1999). *High stakes, high performance: Making remedial education work.* Washington, DC: Community College Press.

Roueche, J. E., Ely, E. E., & Roueche, S. D. (2001). Challenges of the heart: Pursuing excellence at the Community College of Denver. *Community College Journal, 71* (3), 30–34.

Shults, C. (2000). Remedial education: Practices and policies in community colleges. AACC Report No. RB-00-2. [Online]. Washington, DC: American Association of Community Colleges. Available: *http://www.aacc.nche.edu/initiatives/issues/Remedial.pdf*

Simons, P. R. J. (1999). Transfer of learning: Paradoxes for learners. *International Journal of Educational Research, 31*, 577–589.

Dolores Perin is an associate professor of psychology and education in the Health and Behavior Studies Department and senior research associate in the Community College Research Center, Teachers College, Columbia University in New York.

CHAPTER 24

COMMUNITY AND DIVERSITY IN URBAN COMMUNITY COLLEGES: COURSETAKING AMONG ENTERING STUDENTS

WILLIAM MAXWELL
LINDA SERRA HAGEDORN
SCOTT CYPERS
HYE S. MOON
PHILLIP BROCATO
KELLY WAHL
GEORGE PRATHER

Classrooms and curriculum are increasingly recognized as uniquely significant for student success. Due to high attrition rates, especially in urban community colleges, the first semester of study has garnered particular concern. Our limited knowledge about the student mix and coursetaking behaviors severely limits our ability to suggest policy and develop procedures to aid student success during the critical first semester. Surprisingly, there is virtually no research examining where first-semester, first-time students are concentrated or dispersed in the curriculum, or which courses nontraditional and other students take as their entry points of study.

Our lack of understanding of such matters is a result of ignoring courses as a unit of analysis in curriculum research. While curriculum research has analyzed the proportions of courses or enrollments, using the college as the unit of analysis, it has not looked at courses or the individual students that populate the classrooms. Academic success has been analyzed in terms of student characteristics but not in relation to coursetaking. This paper proposes to link student characteristics and courses through transcript research using courses as a unit of analysis.

Questions about such issues offer a fundamentally new direction in transcript analysis that builds on, and yet departs from, previous studies of curriculum trends (Cohen & Ignash, 1994; Grubb, 1989) and student demographics (Adelman, 1992). An understanding of the success of individual students presupposes basic research regarding which courses specific types of students enter, their subsequent paths through the curriculum, and the conditions affecting their success in particular courses. This study will address the first of these issues, while the others will require extensive investigations beyond the boundaries of this or any single report.

To explore the initial coursetaking patterns of students, this study will examine the general question: In the first semester of study at an urban community college, what types of students enter which sectors of the curriculum? Specifically, what kinds of first-time students—with regard to gender, age, ethnicity, and full- or part-time status—enroll in which specific types of courses? The principal findings of this study provide important implications concerning the dispersal, concentration, possibility of community among students, and the access of racial minorities to various tracks in the curriculum.

The broader question driving this study is exploratory in nature and tests the usefulness of using courses as a unit of analysis in curriculum research. While we did not focus on one or a few specific hypotheses drawn deductively from existing conceptual traditions, we will indicate some of the theoretical implications for current ideas and controversies in the conceptual literature. Our goal is to identify whether or not student patterns emerge when using transcripts and courses as a unit of analysis.

In addition to the value of this question for fundamental knowledge about students, this topic is important for college efforts in supporting first-time students. Recent research has identified classrooms as a key area of focus for colleges seeking to promote the success of their new students (Maxwell, 1998). When the college does not know which classrooms at-risk students are entering, students may be in classes without sufficient support. Thus, colleges need information as to which kinds of entering students are attending what kinds of courses.

Changing Community College Roles

The role of community colleges has expanded from strictly "university parallel programs" to full-service colleges (Cohen & Brawer, 1996; Gleazer, 1994), adding components such as occupational curriculums (Zwerling, 1976; Brint & Karabel, 1989), remedial and developmental courses (McGrath & Spear, 1994; Spann, 2003), ESL education (Ignash, 2000; Striplin, 2000), and other types of courses.

Though researchers continue to debate the relative importance of these new functions and their effects on student outcomes (Clark, 1980; Brint & Karabel; 1989), the expanded community college mission has encouraged the enrollment of diverse types of students. The curriculums have increased considerably, but knowledge is lacking about the types of students enrolled in the various types of courses provided by the comprehensive community college.

Changing Coursetaking Patterns

Recent reviews of the curriculum (Cohen & Ignash, 1994; Schuyler, 1999; Striplin, 2000) highlight the changing numbers of students within various types of courses. Cohen and Ignash (1994) found that enrollment patterns in the humanities changed little between 1978 and 1991, while at the same time enrollments in some science subjects doubled, and enrollments in ESL courses tripled. A more recent review by Striplin (2000) noted that between 1991 and 1998, computer science courses showed the greatest increase in enrollments. Examinations of types of course offerings provide another form of evidence that coursetaking patterns are changing (Striplin, 2000).

The present study combines and elaborates analytic schemes that have been previously used to examine trends in the curriculum. First, we borrow from Cohen and Ignash's (1994) distinction between remedial and standard types of academic courses, in which remedial courses are defined as below college-level proficiency and without transferability to four-year degree programs (Hagedorn, Chavez, & Perrakis, 2001). Cohen and Ignash observe that the "standard" level include courses which are applicable to the A.A. degree but not to transfer, and also courses which carry both A.A. graduation and transfer credit. The analysis in this study incorporates this distinction between these two levels of standard courses, "A.A. applicable/not transferable" and "A.A. applicable/transferable," because it is useful in identifying demographic patterns among first-time students. Secondly, some analyses have paid particular attention to two academic subjects with very large numbers of enrollments: English and mathematics courses. Third, adapting Grubb's (1987) conceptualization of occupational courses, Cohen and Ignash (1994) found that most occupational enrollments fall within four areas: business and office, health, technical education, and trade and industry. Along with these four occupational areas we add Grubb's category of education, because distinctive types of students enroll in large numbers in programs concerning the development and care of children. And fourth, the recent growth of ESL merits a separate category.

Based upon the work of these foregoing authors and recent trends, we suggest in Table I a refined classification of courses which identifies two main dimensions: 1) the level of the courses—remedial, A.A. applicable/not transferable, and A.A. applicable/transferable and 2) the subjects of study. (As examples of the categories, Table 1 lists the courses that will be analyzed in this study.)

Changing Student Demographics

The community college literature has consistently noted demographic changes through both individual institutional accounts (e.g., Angle, Dennis-Rounds, Fillpot, & Gaik, 1992; Spicer, Karp, & Amba, 1999) and national accounts of community colleges (Adelman, 1992; Phillippe & Patton, 2000).

National accounts document changes within community colleges, such as the finding that female enrollments have increased to a majority, about 58%, of the population of community college students. While 50% of the students in community colleges are less than 25 years of age, those aged 40 and above represent about 16% of the enrollments. Nearly two-thirds (63%) of community college students attend less than full time (as compared to 22% of four-year college students). Minority enrollments increased 5% from 1992 to 1997 due primarily to increasing numbers of students of Hispanic and Asian origins (Phillippe & Patton, 2000). As indicated earlier, these demographic reports ignore any relationships with curriculum.

One of the few studies to examine the link between the curriculum and ethnicity was Hirose's (1994) analysis of the proportions of liberal arts and minority enrollments. Finding that the community college's proportion of liberal arts course offerings was unrelated to the college's proportion of non-White students, this evidence was interpreted as refuting the contentions of Pincus (1980) and Brint and Karabel (1989) that the community college curriculum was tracking ethnic minority students into vocational rather than baccalaureate education. This interpretation was in fact not supported by Hirose's data because her unit of analysis was college (instead of course) enrollments, resulting in what Robinson (1950) coined as an "ecological fallacy." We contend that ethnic tracking remains an open question.

Method

Student Population.   This study focused on an entering cohort of students in their first semester of study. (Data about continuing cohorts is also included in Table 2 for purposes of comparison.) Although future research on the sequence of subsequent course enrollments for a continuing cohort would be valuable, the importance and complexity of the course selections of the entering students is sufficient to require the full attention of this present study.

The study's population consisted of the first-time students among the 155,361 students who registered for courses in the Los Angeles Community College District (LACCD) in the spring of 2001. The district has great student diversity across its nine campuses, representing 8% of the state's community college enrollment and 6% of the public undergraduate enrollment in California (LACCD, 2001). Compared to the rest of the state and to national norms, the residents of the Los Angeles district have significantly higher proportions of persons below the poverty level and with less than a ninth grade education and of nonnative speakers of English.

Students were defined as enrolled in a course if they remained in the course past the first census date and thus earned either a favorable (A,B,C,D, Pass) or unfavorable (F, Withdrawal, Incomplete, No Pass) grade. Using this definition of enrollment, 18,825 of the first-time students were dropped from the analysis because they had not enrolled in any course in LACCD for the spring of 2001. From the remaining 136,536 students, first-time entering college students were identified by having marked on their admission form that they were a "first-time college student." This yielded a group of 13,108 first-time students.

Drawing on the experience of several institutional researchers, we note that delimitation of the sample of first-time college students in studies of this kind may involve discrepancies of as much as 5–10%. Some of the students report themselves as a "first-time college student" when in fact they 1) previously have attended their college or another college in the district (frequency is estimated as ≤5%) or 2) previously have attended another college outside the district (≤5%). Discrepancies in the opposite direction occur when students, or the college data systems, report continuing status when in fact 1) they are first time college students with previous college

TABLE 1
Classification of Sources

Academic

Level	English	Mathematics	Other
A.A. applicable/ transferable	*English 101*--College Reading and Composition	*Math 245*--College Algebra *Math 240*--Trigonometry *Math 225*--Introduction to Statistics	*Psychology 001*--General Psychology I
A.A. applicable/ not transferable	*English 064*--Intermediate Reading and Composition *English 031*--Composition and Critical Reading *English 028*--Intermediate Reading and Composition	*Math 125*--Intermediate Algebra *Math 120*--Plane Geometry *Math 115*--Elementary Algebra	
Remedial	*English 021*--English Fundamentals *English 073*--Beginning College Reading and Writing	*Math 112*--Prealgebra *Math 105*--Arithmetic for College Students	

Occupational

Level	Business and Office	Health	Technical	Trade and Industry	Education
A.A. applicable/ transferable	*Bus 001*--Introduction to Business *OFF ADM 001*--Typewriting/ Keyboarding	*Chem 051*--Fundamentals of Chemistry I *Chem 055*--Chemistry for Health Sciences	*CO SCI 001*--Introduction to Computers and Their Users *ADM 001*--Introduction to Administration of Justice	*AST 001*--Automotive Engines *AUTO TEK 113*--Automotive Principles *AUTO TEK 001*--Drive Train Components Principles and Practices	*CH DEV 001*--Child Growth and Development
A.A. applicable/ not transferable					
Remedial					

ESL

Level					
A.A. applicable/ transferable					
A.A. applicable/ not transferable					
Remedial	*ESL 001*--Beginning College ESL				

course(s) acquired as part of their high school curriculum (5–10%) or 2) previous college experience involved merely registering and attending no or very few class sessions (≤5%). To some extent these several types of distortions cancel each other's effects, and in the experience of institutional researchers these sampling distortions appear to have only small effects on the measures of demographic differences between courses.

Of the first-time students, 6,196 (47.27%) were identified through analysis of enrollment records as enrolling in at least one of the courses selected for this study (see below). Since students could enroll in more than one of these courses, the total enrollment number for first timers (8530 enrollments) exceeded the number of first-time students in the selected courses.

Measures. Computerized files of section enrollments were used to determine the courses in which each student was enrolled. Given the careful processes involved in assembling these files

TABLE 2
Percent of First-Time Students in Various Introductory Courses, Spring 2001

Course	All enrollments	% First timers (n)
Remedial English	4589	24.1% (1108)
A.A. applicable/not transferable English	6429	14.8% (953)
A.A. applicable/transferable English	5988	7.5% (447)
Remedial mathematics	5856	24.1% (1410)
A.A. applicable/not transferable mathematics	10411	9.8% (1018)
A.A. applicable/transferable mathematics	2393	8.1% (193)
Psychology	5790	14.9% (865)
ESL	540	55.6% (300)
Business	1929	18.7% (361)
Office administration	1501	22.3% (334)
Chemistry	628	7.3% (46)
Computer science	3436	18.4% (632)
Automotive technology	124	33.9% (42)
Administration of justice	793	24.3% (193)
Child development	3087	20.3% (628)
Total enrollments in these courses	53496	15.9% (8530)

(which are the basis for course transcripts), these data provide a much higher degree of reliability and validity than do student survey reports of course enrollments. Adelman (1995) has called for greater reliance in research on transcripts because, as he observes, they do not "lie, . . . exaggerate, [or] . . . forget" (p. vii). The demographic variables were measured with student responses on their college admission forms.

Sample.   As this study's goal was to understand variability of enrollment patterns by first-time students entering the college curriculum, a list of introductory courses was sought that would identify both representative courses with large enrollments and probable entry points into the curriculum by specific groups. The search was conducted through discussions with college counselors, institutional researchers, and by

exploratory examination of the district datasets. From these efforts, the following list of courses was generated (for the specific course titles, please refer to Table 1):

- remedial, A.A. applicable/not transferable, and A.A. applicable/transferable levels of English
- remedial, A.A. applicable/not transferable, and A.A. applicable/transferable levels of mathematics
- psychology
- English as a second language (ESL)
- business
- office administration
- chemistry (a prehealth sciences course)
- computer science
- automotive technology

- administration of justice
- child development

The selected courses are only a fraction of the large number of courses in which first-time students enter. However, these courses include the courses in both the academic and occupational sectors which have the largest enrollments, courses with demonstrated variability, and smaller occupational courses.

Demographic variables. Four student demographic characteristics were examined in relation to the above courses: gender, ethnicity, age, and full-time or part-time enrollment.

Females comprised 59% of the sample.

Ethnicity was measured with an item from the admission form. Southeast Asians (6% of the sample) were defined as those who selected any of the following categories: Laotian, Cambodian, Vietnamese, Indian Sub-Continent, Filipino, or other Asian. East Asians (6%) were defined as those who selected any of the following: Chinese, Japanese, or Korean. Hispanics (48%) were defined as those who selected any of the following: Mexican, Chicano, Mexican American, Central American, South American, or other Hispanic. Pacific Islanders (1%) were defined as those who selected any of the following: Pacific Islander (Guamanian), Pacific Islander (Hawaiian), Pacific Islander (Samoan), or other Pacific Islander. The remaining general ethnic categories included: African American (19%), Caucasian (16%), American Indian (1%), or other Non-White (2%). (These figures corresponded to the distributions, within 2% or less, in each of the ethnic categories in the district population of all first-time students.) Those first-time students who did not identify their ethnicity were labeled as Unknown.

The variable of age was classified in five categories: less than 20 (18%), 20–24 (38%), 25–34 (26%), 35–44 (12%), and over 44 (6%). A full-time student was defined as being enrolled in four or more classes during the present semester (33%). The students enrolled in three or fewer courses were designated as part time (67%).

Results

The transcript data show a remarkable dispersal of the first-time students among courses. The evidence in Table 2 indicates that the students entered the colleges through a wide range of courses comprised mainly of continuing students. First-time students comprised a minority of the enrollments in various introductory courses across the curriculum, generally ranging between 7.3% to 24.3% of the enrollments. First timers were broadly distributed among these courses, not concentrated in any one sector of the curriculum. In striking contrast to many four-year colleges, entering students apparently were not clustered with each other in designated introductory courses. The contrast is particularly dramatic for courses such as A.A. applicable/transferable English. At the four-year campus such a course exists as a classic freshman classroom, but in these urban community college courses, less than 10% of the students were first timers. Only the introductory ESL course was dominated by first-time students, comprising 55.6% of the enrollments, and these ESL courses enrolled only a small minority of the total number of first timers.

At all three entry levels in the academic track—remedial, A.A. applicable/not transferable, and A.A. applicable/transferable—and in both English and mathematics courses, first timers filled only about one-fourth or less of the enrollments in these courses. Each of these levels of academic track courses was comprised mainly of students from continuing cohorts. An examination of the several levels of English and mathematics courses revealed that at the higher levels there were smaller proportions of first-time students, with first-time students accounting for no more than between 7% to 8% of the population in these A.A. applicable/transferable level English and mathematics courses.

Historically introductory English courses have been a primary point of concentration for community college freshmen. Such courses continue to enroll the largest number of students, but they do not enroll many of the entering students who register for occupational courses. Table 3 indicates that only about 7% to 20% of the first-timers enrolled in occupational courses were also enrolled in any of the several levels of introductory English courses. Overall, only 16% of the first-time students in the occupational courses examined here were concurrently enrolled in an introductory English course. Some of the first-time students enrolled in English courses undoubtedly have occupational rather than academic educational goals, yet these findings suggest that the general education courses such as English do not enroll a large portion of

TABLE 3
Percent of First-Time Students in Various Vocational Courses Also Enrolled in
English Courses, Spring 2001

Vocational courses	Concurrent English
Business	17.7%
Office administration	19.2%
Computer science	16.3%
Automotive technology	7.1%
Administration of justice	10.9%
Child development	15.5%
Total	16.1%

Note: remedial, A.A. applicable/not transferable, or A.A. applicable/transferable
English courses

first-time students with primarily occupational purposes. (Though not reported here in the data tables, our analyses found a similar low level of overlapping enrollments across introductory mathematics and vocational courses.) Among entering students there is limited overlap across different sectors of the curriculum.

A gender analysis of first-time students in various introductory courses (Table 4) indicates different coursetaking patterns between the sexes. Females accounted for over 85% of the first-time enrollments in child development, and over 70% of office administration, and prehealth sciences such as chemistry (a result of a largely female nursing program). In contrast, males dominated enrollment in automotive technology, accounting for 98% of the enrollment, and were slightly over 50% of the first-time enrollments in business, computer science, and administration of justice. The percentage distributions did not vary by much for either women or men between the several levels of the English and mathematics courses.

Important coursetaking differences occurred among the various ethnic groups (Table 5). There was a high concentration of first-time Hispanic students in the introductory automotive technology courses (69%), remedial math (58%), remedial English (59%), and introductory child development (60%). Less frequent choices for Hispanics included business and computer science courses. A high proportion of first timers

(52%) in the ESL course identified themselves as White, many of whom were Russian or Armenian immigrants (Prather, 1995). Whites were more likely to enroll in office administration and less likely to enroll in administration of justice and child development. Compared to other courses, African Americans were more likely to enroll in business, office administration, and computer science courses, and noticeably less likely to be enrolled in the automotive technology and A.A. applicable/transferable mathematics courses. Asian Americans were more likely to enroll in computer science and A.A. applicable/transferable mathematics courses, and less likely to enter courses in the administration of justice, auto technology, and child development. Notwithstanding these ethnic differences in coursetaking, in general there was great ethnic diversity among first timers in many of the introductory courses.

The distinction earlier proposed in the conceptualization of remedial, A.A. applicable/not transferable, and A.A. applicable/transferable courses was particularly relevant for the ethnic differences among students. These findings have important implications for transfer to four-year colleges and the attainment of the bachelor's degree. Among the several levels of English, there was a decline in the proportion of Hispanic students at the higher levels, similar proportions of Asian Americans, and increases in the proportions of African-American and White students.

TABLE 4
Gender Among First-Time Students in Various Courses, Spring 2001

Course	Men	Women	Total (n)
Remedial English	42.0%	58.0%	100% (1108)
A.A. applicable/not transferable English	42.0%	58.0%	100% (953)
A.A. applicable/transferable English	40.0%	60.0%	100% (447)
Remedial mathematics	41.2%	58.8%	100% (1410)
A.A. applicable/not transferable mathematics	45.1%	54.9%	100% (1018)
A.A. applicable/transferable mathematics	46.6%	53.4%	100% (193)
Psychology	34.3%	65.7%	100% (865)
ESL	34.3%	65.7%	100% (300)
Business	54.0%	46.0%	100% (361)
Office administration	26.6%	73.4%	100% (334)
Chemistry	23.9%	76.1%	100% (46)
Computer science	54.7%	45.3%	100% (632)
Automotive technology	97.6%	2.4%	100% (42)
Administration of justice	52.3%	47.7%	100% (193)
Child development	12.4%	87.6%	100% (628)
Totals	40.3%	59.7%	100% (8530)

Note: Percentages are computed as the ratio between the number of first timers of the target gender in the course to the total number of first timers enrolled in the course.

The contrasts between the levels of mathematics were quite different, with increases in the proportions of Asian Americans and Whites, and decreases in the proportions of African Americans and Hispanics. In the remedial mathematics courses Hispanic students comprised 58% of the first-timer enrollments, but only 33% of the enrollments in the A.A. applicable/transferable course. The increases between the levels of mathematics were dramatic for East Asians, involving a proportion at A.A. applicable/transferable levels that was double that of the A.A. applicable/not transferable level and 10 times that of the remedial level.

An examination of first-time students' coursetaking patterns by age (Table 6) demonstrates that older and younger students had some different course interests, and yet there was also a broad range of age categories in most of the courses. In most of the introductory academic track courses, such as English, mathematics, and psychology, the majority of first timers were less than 25 years of age. By contrast, in ESL and occupational subjects such as computer science, office administration, and child development courses, the majority of new students were 25 years or older. However, in some of the occupational courses such as administration of justice, auto technology, and business, the majority of the first-time students were younger. Moreover, computer science, office administration, and child development display a diverse mix of age ranges by first-time students. Thirty percent or more of the first-timer occupational course enrollments in areas such as prehealth sciences, chemistry, and office administration were com-

TABLE 5
Ethnic Origins Among First-Time Students in Various Courses, Spring 2001

Course	East Asian	Southeast Asian	African American	Hispanic	White
Remedial English	5.6%	5.9%	15.5%	58.6%	8.5%
A.A. applicable/not transferable English	4.5%	5.8%	19.5%	48.8%	13.3%
A.A. applicable/ transferable English	5.4%	6.7%	19.7%	35.6%	22.4%
Remedial mathematics	1.9%	4.0%	21.1%	58.4%	8.9%
A.A. applicable/ not transferable mathematics	9.6%	8.4%	14.2%	43.2%	17.5%
A.A. applicable/ transferable mathematics	22.3%	8.8%	11.4%	32.6%	18.1%
Psychology	4.7%	6.2%	20.0%	45.0%	17.3%
ESL	7.0%	2.0%	0.0%	34.7%	52.3%
Business	4.7%	5.5%	24.9%	39.6%	17.5%
Office administration	1.8%	5.1%	25.1%	42.5%	20.1%
Chemistry	2.2%	4.3%	17.4%	45.7%	23.9%
Computer science	10.8%	9.8%	23.3%	31.8%	16.1%
Automotive technology	0.0%	2.4%	4.8%	69.0%	19.0%
Administration of justice	1.6%	0.0%	20.2%	50.3%	8.8%
Child development	1.9%	4.9%	17.8%	59.7%	10.0%
Totals	5.5%	5.9%	18.3%	48.1%	15.2%

Note: Percentages are computed as the ratio between the number of first timers of the specified ethnicity who are enrolled in the course to the total number of first timers enrolled in the course.

prised of students in the age range of 25 to 34. Interestingly, the ESL course manifested a distinctive pattern, such that ages 45 and up accounted for the largest proportion of the enrollment.

The distribution of full and part timers varied across the curriculum. A breakdown of coursetaking patterns by enrollment status, full or part time (Table 7), reveals that the majority of first-time students enrolled in these various introductory courses were enrolled part time, taking three or fewer classes. The only exception to this pattern was the administration of justice course, for which the majority of its students were enrolled full time (four or more courses). In several of the classes—administration of justice, prehealth sciences, chemistry, both levels of A.A. applicable English, A.A. applicable/

TABLE 5 (*Continued*)
Ethnic Origins Among First-Time Students in Various Courses, Spring 2001

Native American	Pacific Islander	Non-White Other	Unknown data	Total (n)
.5%	.4%	2.1%	3.0%	100% (1108)
.9%	.2%	2.0%	4.9%	100% (953)
.9%	0%	2.7%	6.7%	100% (447)
.4%	.4%	1.8%	3.1%	100% (1410)
.5%	0%	2.6%	3.9%	100% (1018)
.5%	.5%	2.1%	3.6%	100% (193)
.5%	.3%	2.2%	3.7%	100% (865)
0%	.3%	2.7%	1.0%	100% (300)
0%	.8%	2.2%	4.7%	100% (361)
.6%	.3%	1.2%	3.3%	100% (334)
0%	0%	2.2%	4.3%	100% (46)
0%	.3%	3.2%	4.7%	100% (632)
0%	0%	2.4%	2.4%	100% (42)
1.0%	1.0%	1.0%	16.1%	100% (193)
.5%	.2%	1.8%	3.2%	100% (628)
.5%	.3%	2.1%	4.1%	100% (8530)

Note: Percentages are computed as the ratio between the number of first timers of the specified ethnicity who are enrolled in the course to the total number of first timers enrolled in the course.

transferable mathematics, office administration, and psychology—more than 43% of the students were taking four or more courses. In all of the courses, except ESL and auto technology, at least one-third of the students were enrolled in four or more courses. This was the case even for the students enrolled in remedial English or mathematics courses where over one-third of the students were taking four or more courses. Note that these courses represented both academic and occupational areas of the curriculum. In none of the courses did the proportion of first-timers enrolled in only one course exceed 30%. However, 28% of the first-timers in child development were enrolled in only that one course. In contrast with the other courses, very few of the first-time students in ESL were enrolled in more than two courses. Auto technology was also distinctive in that one-half of its new students were enrolled in only one or two courses (this is

TABLE 6
Age Groups Among First-Time Students in Various Courses, Spring 2001

Course	<20	20-24	25-34	35-44	45+	Total (n)
Remedial English	23.3%	40.3%	23.7%	9.4%	3.2%	100% (1101)
A.A. applicable/not transferable English	21.2%	39.3%	25.8%	9.6%	4.1%	100% (945)
A.A. applicable/transferable English	20.0%	38.6%	27.6%	9.4%	4.5%	100% (446)
Remedial mathematics	17.1%	40.3%	27.2%	11.4%	4.0%	100% (1398)
A.A. applicable/not transferable mathematics	26.3%	43.9%	20.0%	7.5%	2.3%	100% (1006)
A.A. applicable/transferable mathematics	16.6%	46.6%	25.9%	8.8%	2.1%	100% (193)
Psychology	23.3%	44.3%	20.7%	8.2%	3.5%	100% (857)
ESL	2.1%	8.2%	20.3%	32.6%	36.8%	100% (291)
Business	22.8%	40.3%	25.6%	8.9%	2.5%	100% (360)
Office administration	14.8%	26.9%	30.5%	18.4%	9.4%	100% (331)
Chemistry	15.2%	41.3%	32.6%	10.9%	0%	100% (46)
Computer science	14.2%	33.0%	24.6%	17.1%	11.0%	100% (625)
Automotive technology	24.4%	39.0%	29.3%	4.9%	2.4%	100% (41)
Administration of justice	18.4%	49.5%	27.9%	3.2%	1.1%	100% (190)
Child development	13.8%	30.7%	27.3%	17.2%	11.1%	100% (623)
Totals	19.5%	38.4%	24.7%	11.5%	5.9%	100% (8453)

Note: Percentages are computed as the ratio between the number of first timers of the target age in the course to the total number of first timers enrolled in the course.

TABLE 7
Full-Time vs. Part-Time Students Among First-Time Students in Various Courses, Spring 2001

	Total number of courses enrolled in spring 1999				
Course	1	2	3	4+	Total % (n)
Remedial English	12.6%	26.7%	22.8%	37.8%	100% (1108)
A.A. applicable/not transferable English	11.3%	24.1%	20.5%	44.1%	100% (953)
A.A. applicable/ transferable English	10.1%	22.4%	20.4%	47.2%	100% (447)
Remedial mathematics	13.3%	28.4%	21.5%	36.7%	100% (1410)
A.A. applicable/ not transferable mathematics	10.3%	22.5%	29.0%	38.2%	100% (1018)
A.A. applicable/ transferable mathematics	15.5%	17.6%	21.8%	45.1%	100% (193)
Psychology	12.3%	21.8%	22.1%	43.8%	100% (865)
ESL	21.7%	66.0%	10.3%	2.0%	100% (300)
Business	13.3%	24.4%	24.4%	38.0%	100% (361)
Office administration	18.6%	22.8%	15.0%	43.7%	100% (334)
Chemistry	13.0%	13.0%	26.1%	47.8%	100% (46)
Computer science	21.4%	22.5%	18.5%	37.7%	100% (632)
Automotive technology	23.8%	26.2%	21.4%	28.6%	100% (42)
Administration of justice	17.1%	14.5%	17.1%	51.3%	100% (193)
Child development	27.9%	24.0%	12.7%	35.4%	100% (628)
Totals	14.7%	25.5%	21.0%	38.7%	100% (8530)

Note: Percentages are computed as the ratio between the number of first timers enrolled in the course by the number of other concurrent course enrollments to the total number of first timers enrolled in the course.

explained in part by the fact that these auto technology courses involve more hours of meeting time than do other courses, usually about eight hours per week for each auto technology course).

Though there were these variations among the courses in the proportion of full-time students, with the exception of the ESL course, there was also great variation within each of the courses. In general, most of these courses had within them a broad range of students differing in the numbers of courses in which they were enrolled.

Discussion

The dispersal of the entering students is a dramatic feature of the colleges. First-time students are not concentrated in a few main introductory courses. They are a minority in the introductory English and mathematics courses. Moreover, even though English is the largest area in the curriculum, most first-time students in occupational courses are not enrolled in an English course. The first-time students enter the curriculum as minorities in most courses and are broadly distributed across a range of introductory courses. Based on a spring semester sample, the course concentrations of these entering students were smaller than students who enter the colleges in the fall, but not by much.

Dispersal of first-time students is one of the distinguishing, but often unnoted, characteristics of the community college and possibly one of several reasons why there is so little community among the students. There is no broad common first year, or even first semester, experience for the new students. Though the colleges are not perceived as unfriendly, there are relatively few social bonds between the students, few participate together in campus organizations, and little leisure time is spent with each other on campus (Maxwell, 2000). This situation potentially poses major dilemmas for faculty attempting to relate to the distinctive needs of entering students.

It must be recognized that a finding of dispersal among courses may imply but does not demonstrate that first-time students are scattered among classrooms. Because the unit of analysis in this study is courses rather than classrooms, the findings are not conclusive regarding the classroom densities of entering students. For example, even though the percentage of first-time students may be low for a course title, it is possible in specific sections of this course that the percentage of first timers might be high. Further research that takes the classroom as the unit of analysis is necessary to determine if first-time students are concentrated in or dispersed among specific classrooms.

If it is found that first-time students are dispersed among classes, such a finding might have large implications for college administrators and counselors as they consider using class schedules as a strategy for reducing the high attrition rates among entering students. Social and academic integration have been posited as central in promoting student persistence (Braxton, Sullivan, & Johnson, 1997; Tinto, 1993). A growing body of research suggests that classrooms organized as learning communities promote both integration and increased persistence for entering students (MacGregor, 2000; Tinto, 1997). Scheduling courses to mandate learning com-

munities for entering students is a feasible, relatively low-cost policy that could address the dispersion of first timers.

The classification of courses as academic, occupational, or ESL, and as remedial, A.A. applicable/not transferable, or A.A. applicable/transferable levels, was found to be to useful for identifying relationships with the student characteristics of gender, ethnicity, age, and full-time or part-time enrollment.

Not surprisingly, gender is related to course-taking in ways that parallel the labor market. However, the enrollments do not simply mirror the gender distributions in the job structure. The segregation in the curriculum appears to be less than in the labor market (Hagedorn, Nora, & Pascarella, 1996). The most gender-segregated courses are auto technology and child development; the former course's population of males is 98%, and women comprise 88% of the latter. Other courses such as the administration of justice, formerly an almost exclusive male preserve, are now comprised of almost equal distributions of men and women. Although gender continues to be related to coursetaking, in general, most of the courses have substantial numbers of both women and men.

Ethnic distributions varied among courses. These patterns appear to be related to local systems of culture, opportunities, and social relations. In a few of the courses some ethnic groups appeared to be nearly absent. However, this was not a feature common to most of the college-level curriculum. There was little sense of segregation by race. There was great ethnic diversity in most college-level courses. There was not a clear pattern of tracking and exclusion in vocational and academic courses along a White/non-White divide. White students were interested in most of the vocational courses examined here. East Asians were the most likely of all ethnic groups to tend to avoid several specific vocational areas, and yet, they were the most likely to enroll in a vocational area such as computer science.

There are large differences among ethnic groups in entry into the colleges at remedial or A.A. applicable/transferable levels of English and mathematics. It is here that evidence for a hypothesis of some partial degree of tracking is implied for some but not all minorities. White and, to a lesser degree, African-American students have an advantage in English courses. East Asian students have an overwhelmingly greater level of advantage in mathematics courses, and

Southeast Asian and White students have a moderate level of advantage here. Some members of all racial and ethnic categories enter the colleges at privileged levels. Indeed, due to their large numbers in the college population, in the A.A. applicable/transferable levels of both English and mathematics courses, Hispanic students outnumber members of any other ethnic group. However, Hispanic students are at a great proportional disadvantage in the English courses, and in mathematics courses both Hispanic and African-American students are entering remedial levels at an even greater rate of proportional disadvantage. The "tracks" are operating thus not along a simple White/non-White divide, but in a complex fashion with many tracks and an uneven mix of advantages for the groups.

There was much variation in age among the first-time students and some relationship between age and types of courses. Students under the age of 25 were more likely, than were students 25 or older, to be enrolled in academic courses. In contrast to the younger students, students over the age of 24 were more likely to enroll in occupational courses. Despite these differences between age groups, for both the younger and older students, the courses with the largest enrollments were English and mathematics.

In most of the introductory courses examined here, the majority of the entering students were enrolled in three or fewer courses. Full-time and part-time students were generally distributed broadly among almost all of the courses examined. Both full-time students and nontraditional part timers did not appear to be concentrated at particular points of entry into the curriculum. They were scattered across a broad range of courses. There were a few areas, ESL and some occupational courses, in which the majority of the students were enrolled in only one or two courses.

Counselors and curriculum administrators may be concerned that large proportions of the students in the remedial English or mathematics courses are taking four or more courses, and that well over one half are enrolled in three or more courses.

Lack of language skills creates one of the great divides in the community college. Thus, in the beginning ESL courses that were examined, the students displayed very different features from the other first-time students. It was only in these ESL courses that first timers were in the majority. The majority of the students were Whites despite their being a minority in the general student population. Ninety percent of these students were over the age of 24, and one-third were over 44. Given this distribution of age it is possible that many of these students had major responsibilities outside college, such as work and families, and thus, almost all of these students were enrolled in only one or two courses. It is likely that at higher levels of the ESL courses there is a different distribution of student demographic characteristics. Further research is necessary on the characteristics of students at other levels of the ESL curriculum. We know too little about "tracks" or successes that may follow ESL enrollments.

In summary, our main conclusion is that this new direction in research is fruitful for finding many distinctive patterns when courses are examined as the unit of analysis. We have touched on the relevance of the findings for campus community and for ethnic tracking. There are potentially many other theoretical and policy issues that could be raised in relation to the gender, ethnic, age, and part-time study patterns reported above.

The results of this study lead to many possibilities for future investigation. The units of analysis in further curriculum research must include not only the individual but also the classroom. Given the problem of high first semester attrition rates, it has been useful in this study to examine only one semester of coursetaking patterns. However, several limitations of the current study emanate from a sample of one semester. The use of only one semester's data precludes our knowing whether the observed findings are reliably representative or an anomaly. Additionally, weaknesses in the method for identifying first-time students within the curriculum may have slightly distorted or hidden patterns. Thus, future research can deepen our understanding of the students by refining the measure of first-time and continuing enrollments, and by examining the enrollments of continuing cohorts in addition to first-timers, and by studying fall and summer terms in addition to the spring term. Coursetaking research is needed to understand the patterns of shopping and dropping of courses that leads to repetition and high enrollments of continuing students in introductory courses. Research is needed on various kinds of students on their entry points and pathways through the curriculum that are linked with success in subsequent education and occupations.

Future research can continue to build on the examination of student enrollments by examining the academic outcomes in these courses and success and failures along various subsequent course pathways. New conceptual schemes are needed which capture the full complexity of the relationships between students and curriculum. Findings from these types of inquiries will aid both researchers and community college leaders in locating and helping students within the curriculum.

References

Adelman, C. (1992). *The way we are: The community college as American thermometer.* Washington, DC: U.S. Department of Education.

Adelman, C. (1995). *The new college course map and transcript files.* Washington, DC: U.S. Department of Education.

Angle, N., Dennis-Rounds, J., Fillpot, J., & Gaik, F. (1992). *The changing student demography of Cerritos College.* Norwalk, CA: Cerritos College Topical Paper Series (ERIC Document Reproduction Service No. ED354976)

Braxton, J. M., Sullivan, A. V. S., & Johnson, R. M. (1997). Appraising Tinto's theory of college student departure. In J. C. Smart (Ed.), *Higher education: Handbook of theory and research, 12.* (pp.107–164). Edison, N.J.: Agathon.

Brint, S. & Karbabel, J. (1989). *The diverted dream: Community colleges and the promise of educational opportunity in America, 1900–1985.* New York: Oxford University Press.

Clark, B. (1980). The 'cooling out' function revisited (pp. 67–78). In J. Ratcliff, S. Schwarz, & L. Ebbers (Eds.), *Community Colleges (2nd ed.).* Needam Heights, MA: Simon & Schuster Custom Publishing.

Cohen, A. M., & Brawer, F. B. (1996). *The American community college (3rd ed).* San Francisco, CA: Josey-Bass.

Cohen, A. M., & Ignash J. M. (1994). An overview of the total credit curriculum. In A. M. Cohen (Ed.), *Relating curriculum and transfer* (pp.13–29). *New Directions for Community Colleges,* no. 86. San Francisco: Jossey-Bass.

Gleazer, E. J. (1994). Evolution of junior colleges into community colleges. In G. Baker III (Ed.), *A handbook on the community college in America: Its history, mission, and management.* (pp. 17–27). Westport, CT: Greenwood Publishing Group, Inc.

Grubb, W. N. (1989). The effects of differentiation on educational attainment: The case of community

colleges. *The Review of Higher Education, 12(4),* 349–374.

Grubb, N. (1987). *The postsecondary education of 1972 seniors completing vocational A.A. degrees and certificates.* Washington, DC: U.S. Department of Education.

Hagedorn, L. S., Chavez, C., & Perrakis, A. (2002). Remedial education. In J. J. K. Forest & K. Kinser (Eds.), *Higher education in the United States: An encyclopedia.* (pp. 518–512) Santa Barbara, CA: ABC-CLIO.

Hagedorn, L.S., Nora, A., & Pascarella, E. T. (1996). Pre-occupational segregation among first-year college students: An application of the Duncan Dissimilarity Index. *Journal of College Student Development, 37(4),* 425–437.

Hirose, S. M. (1994). Curriculum and minority students. In A. M. Cohen (Ed.), *Relating curriculum and transfer* (pp. 93–100). *New Directions for Community Colleges,* no. 86. San Francisco: Jossey-Bass.

Ignash, J. M. (2000). *ESL population and program patterns in community colleges.* Los Angeles, CA: ERIC Clearinghouse for Junior Colleges (ERIC Document Reproduction Service No. ED353022)

Los Angeles Community College District (2001). [Online] Retrieved from http://research.laccd.edu/research

MacGregor, J. (2000). Restructuring large classes to create communities of learners. In J. MacGregor, J. Cooper, K. Smith, & P. Robinson (Eds.), *Strategies for energizing large classes: From small groups to learning communities* (pp. 47–61). *New Directions for Teaching and Learning,* no. 81. San Francisco, CA: Jossey-Bass.

Maxwell, W. E. (1998). Supplemental instruction, learning communities, and studying together. *Community College Review, 26(2),* 1–18.

Maxwell, W. E. (2000). Student peer relations at a community college. *Community College Journal of Research and Practice, 24(3),* 207–217.

McGrath, D. & Spear, M. (1994). The remedialization of the community college. In J. Ratcliff, S. Schwarz, & L. Ebbers (Eds.), *Community Colleges (2nd ed.).* (pp. 217–228). Needam Heights, MA: Simon & Schuster Custom Publishing.

Phillippe, K., & Patton, M. (Eds.). (2000). *National profile of community colleges: Trends and statistics (3rd ed.).* Washington, DC: American Association of Community Colleges. (ERIC Document Reproduction Service No. ED440671)

Pincus, F. (1980). The false promises of community colleges: Class conflict and vocational education. *Harvard Educational Review, 50 (3),* 332–361.

Prather, G. (1995). *Educating a generation of immigrants: Dispatches from the front.* Paper presented at the meeting of the Association for Institutional Research Forum, Boston, MA.

Robinson, W. S. (1950). Ecological correlation and the behavior of individuals. *American Sociological Review, 15,* 351–357.

Schuyler, G. E. (1999). A historical and contemporary view of the community college curriculum. In G. E. Schuyler (Ed.), *Trends in community college curriculum* (pp. 3–16). *New Directions for Community Colleges,* no. 108. San Francisco, CA.: Jossey-Bass.

Spann, M. G., Jr. (2000). *Remediation: A must for the 21st century learning society* (Rep. No. CC-00-4). Denver, CO: Center for Community College Policy. (ERIC Document Reproduction Service No. ED439771)

Spicer, S., Karp, E., & Amba, C. (1999). *Glendale community college campus profile '99.* Glendale, CA: Planning and Research Office. (ERIC Document Reproduction Service No. ED437082)

Striplin, J. C. (2000). A *review of community college curriculum trends.* Los Angeles, CA: ERIC Clearinghouse for Community Colleges. (ERIC Document Reproduction Service No. ED438011)

Tinto, V. (1993). *Leaving college: Rethinking the causes and cures of student attrition.* Chicago: University of Chicago Press.

Tinto, V. (1997). Classrooms as communities: Exploring the educational character of student persistence. *Journal of Higher Education, 68*(6), 599–623.

Zwerling, L. (1976). *Second best: The crisis of the community college.* New York: McGraw-Hill Book Company.

The research reported in this paper is drawn from the Transfer and Retention of Urban Community College (TRUCCS) research project, a collaborative project between the University of Southern California, the University of California, Los Angeles, and the Los Angeles Community College District. This project is supported by a U.S. Department of Education, Office of Education Research grant no. R305T000154. The authors are grateful for this support, and acknowledge that the opinions expressed in this paper are their own.

William Maxwell, Associate Professor, Center for Higher Education Policy Analysis, Rossier School of Education, University of Southern California, and Co-Principal Investigator on the TRUCCS Project.

Linda Serra Hagedorn, Associate Professor and Associate Director of the Center for Higher Education Policy Analysis; also Chair of the Community College Leadership Program, and Program Director on the TRUCCS Project, Rossier School of Education, University of Southern California.

Scott Cypers, Research Assistant, TRUCCS Project, Rossier School of Education, University of Southern California.

Hye S. Moon, Senior Research Associate, TRUCCS Project, and College Persistence, Transfer, and Success of Kamehameha Students Project, Center for Higher Education Policy Analysis, Rossier School of Education, University of Southern California.

Phillip Brocato, Project Coordinator, TRUCCS Project, Rossier School of Education, University of Southern California.

Kelly Wahl, Director of Assessment and Data Analysis, Loyola Marymount University.

George Prather, Chief, Office of Institutional Research, Los Angeles Community College District.

CHAPTER 25

CLASSROOMS AS COMMUNITIES EXPLORING THE EDUCATIONAL CHARACTER OF STUDENT PERSISTENCE

VINCENT TINTO

Introduction

The college classroom lies at the center of the educational activity structure of institutions of higher education; the educational encounters that occur therein are a major feature of student educational experience. Indeed, for students who commute to college, especially those who have multiple obligations outside the college, the classroom may be the only place where students and faculty meet, where education in the formal sense is experienced. For those students, in particular, the classroom is the crossroads where the social and the academic meet. If academic and social involvement or integration is to occur, it must occur in the classroom.

Seen in this light, it is surprising that the classroom has not played a more central role in current theories of student persistence (e.g., Bean, 1983; Cabrera, Castañeda, Nora, & Hengstler, 1992; Tinto, 1987). Though it is evident that classrooms matter, especially as they may shape academic integration, little has been done to explore *how* the experience of the classroom matters, how it comes, over time, to shape student persistence.[1] The same may be said of institutions of higher education. Though they have certainly not ignored the classroom, most have not seen it as the centerpiece of their efforts to promote student persistence, preferring instead to locate those efforts outside the classroom in the domain of student affairs. Therefore while it is the case that student experience outside classrooms have changed, their experience within them has not.

This article presents the results of a multimethod, quantitative and qualitative, study of the efforts of one college, Seattle Central Community College, to alter student classroom experience through the use of learning communities and the adoption of collaborative learning strategies. The study seeks to ascertain to what degree such strategies enhance student learning and persistence and, if so, how they do so. Beyond its obvious policy implications, the study provides the context for a series

The author wishes to thank Pat Russo for her contributions to the research project from which this study is drawn and three anonymous reviewers for their helpful comments.

Vincent Tinto is Distinguished University Professor in the School of Education at Syracuse University.

Journal of Higher Education, Vol. 68, No. 6 (November/December 1997) Copyright 1997 by the Ohio State University Press of reflections on the ways in which current theories of student persistence might be modified to account more directly for the role of classroom experience in the process of both student learning and persistence.

Literature Review

We know that involvement matters. As numerous researchers have pointed out (e.g., Astin, 1984; Mallette & Cabrera, 1991; Nora, 1987; Pascarella & Terenzini, 1980; Terenzini & Pascarella, 1977) the greater students' involvement or integration in the life of the college the greater the likelihood that they will persist. We also know that involvement influences learning (e.g., Astin, 1984, 1993; Friedlander, 1980; Parker & Schmidt, 1982; Ory & Braskamp, 1988; Pascarella & Terenzini, 1991). Generally speaking, the greater students' involvement in the life of the college, especially its academic life, the greater their acquisition of knowledge and development of skills. This is particularly true of student contact with faculty. That engagement, both inside and outside the classroom, appears to be especially important to student development (Endo & Harpel, 1982; Astin, 1993). Even among those who persist, students who report higher levels of contact with peers and faculty also demonstrate higher levels of learning gain over the course of their stay in college (Endo & Harpel, 1982). In other words, high levels of involvement prove to be an independent predictor of learning gain. The same conclusion follows from the growing body of research on the quality of student effort; namely, that there is a direct relationship between the quality of student effort and the extent of student learning (e.g., Pace, 1984; Ory & Braskamp, 1988; Kaufman & Creamer, 1991). Quite simply, the more students invest in learning activities, that is, the higher their level of effort, the more students learn.[2]

What we do not yet know, or at least have not yet adequately documented, is *how* involvement is shaped within the context of differing institutions of higher education by student educational experiences. And though we have a sense of why involvement or integration should matter (e.g., that it comes to shape individual commitments), we have yet to explore the critical linkages between involvement in classrooms, student learning, and persistence. In effect, we have yet to fully understand the educational character of persistence in higher education.

This is not to say that researchers have ignored the classroom experience. Quite the opposite is the case. In their reviews of the research on college teaching and student learning, for instance, McKeachie (1970, 1994) and Smith (1980, 1983) document the many studies that have sought to disentangle the multiple relationships between teacher behaviors and student participation in classroom discussion and learning. But those and other studies aside, the case remains that there is little empirical data on the impact of faculty members' behavior on student participation (Auster & MacRone, 1994). What we do know is that students' participation in college classrooms is relatively passive, that "learning appears to be a 'spectator sport' in which faculty talk dominates" (Fischer & Grant, 1983) and where there are few active student participants (Smith, 1983; Karp & Yoels, 1976; Nunn, 1996). Interestingly, both Fassinger (1995) and Nunn (1996) find that classroom traits, specifically a supportive atmosphere, is as important to student participation as are student and faculty traits.

The recognition of the importance of classroom environment is part of another area of inquiry, namely the role of classroom context, its educational activities and normative orientations, in student learning. Rather than focus on the behaviors of faculty, a number of researchers have focused on the role of pedagogy (e.g., Karplus, 1974; Lawson & Snitgen, 1982; McMillan, 1987) and, in turn, curriculum (e.g., Dressel & Mayhew, 1954; Forrest, 1982) and classroom activities (e.g., Volkwein, King, & Terenzini, 1986) as predictors of student learning. Generally speaking, these have led to a growing recognition that student learning is enhanced when students are actively involved in learning and when they are placed in situations in which they have to share learning in some positive, connected manner (Astin, 1987).

The issue, then, is not that researchers have ignored the classroom. Clearly they have not. Rather it is that the work they have done has yet to be connected to that in the field of student persistence. The two fields of inquiry have gone on in parallel without crossing. This study represents a beginning effort to bridge that gap.

Background

Though it is apparent that the college classroom is, for many if not most students, the only place where involvement may arise, it remains the case that most college classrooms are less than involving. At the same time, students continue to take courses as detached, individual units, one course separated from another in both content and peer group, one set of understandings unrelated in any intentional fashion, to what is learned in another setting. There are however a growing number of exceptions. A range of institutions, both two- and four-year, have sought to redefine students' learning experience by restructuring the classroom, altering faculty practice, and linking courses one to another so that students encounter learning as a shared rather than isolated experience. One of these institutions, Seattle Central Community College, and its Coordinated Studies Program is the object of this study.

Coordinated Studies Programs at Seattle Central Community College

The Coordinated Studies Program (CSP) provides students the opportunity to share the curriculum and learn together.[3] Rather than enroll in separate stand alone courses, students in the CSP enroll together in several courses that are tied together by a unifying theme. The theme of the CSP, defined by its title (e.g., Ways of Knowing, Of Body and Mind), crosses disciplinary areas usually in the Humanities Division, but may extend to the Math-Science or Professional-Technical Divisions. During a quarter, CSPs meet for a total of 11 to 18 hours each week in four- to six-hour blocks over two to four days. Generally all instructors are present and active in all class meetings. In addition to sharing the curriculum, students are required to share the experience of learning. They participate in cooperative learning activities that call for them to be interdependent learners (e.g., the learning of the group depends on the learning of each member of the group). In this way, students experience a form of interdisciplinary learning that requires active involvement with their peers.

Methodology

The research project sought to answer two basic questions regarding the program. First, does the program make a difference? Second, if it does, how does it do so? To answer these questions, we used two forms of inquiry, survey (longitudinal panel) and qualitative case study, to study the experiences of a sample of first-year students. Though conducted separately, the two forms of inquiry were linked by a common concern, namely to understand not only what students experienced, but also how those experiences were associated over time with their behaviors and changing views of learning and their subsequent persistence. In this very important manner, the methods were complementary to one another, each yielding information that together provided a richer sense of the impact of program participation than any one method could provide on its own.

In this regard it is important for the reader to understand that as a collaborative research team we sought to uncover those findings that overlapped, that together provided deeper insight into the impacts of the program we studied. Therefore, although it is possible to see and report the study as two separate studies, one qualitative, one quantitative, we did not view, nor will we report, our collaborative work in that manner. Though we will describe our work in separate sections, the reader should understand our work as representing two dimensions of a larger, multidimensional study. Given space limitations, this will lead us to provide less information about each method than some readers might prefer. Readers are therefore urged to read the larger research reports from which this article is drawn for more complete details about our methods, sample, and analyses (Tinto & Russo, 1993).

Longitudinal Panel Study

Sampling. We sampled first-year students in both the Coordinated Studies Program and in the traditional curriculum. We did so by first selecting a sample of CSP and comparison classes and then sampling all students in those classes. We did so not only because classrooms served as logical units of analysis, but also because that procedure greatly simplified the task of reaching students.

We selected a total of four CSP classes in the Liberal Arts Division of the College and eleven comparison classes that, in the view of the program staff, best captured a representative sampling of first-year students enrolled in similar subjects but not enrolled in the CSP. Our selection of CSP classes was such that it captured a range of students, some of whom chose to enroll in the program because they had few other options or enrolled in the program for reasons that had little to do with the pedagogical character of the course. The significance of this fact is that it enables us to test for possible self-selection artifacts.[4]

Data collection. Questionnaires were administered in the beginning of the fall quarter and later at the end of that quarter. The first questionnaire collected information on a range of student attributes, prior education, current life situations (e.g., family and work responsibilities), educational intentions, learning preferences, perceptions of ability, and attitudes regarding education. The second questionnaire collected information on current life situations, a range of classroom and out-of-classroom activities, estimates of learning gains, perceptions of the institution, and expectations regarding subsequent enrollment.

Measures of student engagement in classroom and out-of-classroom behaviors were derived from Pace's (1984) Quality of Student Effort Scales. Rather than being adopted in its entirety, Pace's items were modified to suit the specific context of the institution and program being studied. While ruling out comparisons with prior research, the modifications allowed us to better capture both the intent and impact of program participation upon student behaviors.

The first questionnaire was administered during the second week of the fall quarter by the faculty of the selected classes. Only beginning students were included in the survey administration. We obtained a total of 517 usable questionnaires, 210 and 307 from the CSP and the comparison classes respectively. The second, follow-up, questionnaire was administered during the last two weeks of the fall quarter. Again the questionnaires were distributed in class by the respective faculty. In this instance, students

who returned completed questionnaires became eligible for a drawing for a gift certificate to be used in the bookstore. A total of two $50 gift certificates were awarded by blind drawing. Of the 517 students who responded to the first questionnaire, we obtained a total of 287 usable responses (55.5 percent) to the second questionnaire; 121 from program students (57.6 percent) and 166 (53.5 percent) from students in the comparison group.[5]

In the following fall, information was obtained from institutional records about students' earned credits, grade point averages, and quarter to quarter enrollments (winter, spring, and fall of the following academic year). These data, together with students' estimates of learning gains, formed the outcome variable set. Estimates of learning gains, grade point averages and subsequent persistence, in that order, were seen to represent temporarily ordered outcomes that followed from college activities.

The final panel utilized in this study consisted of only those persons who responded to both questionnaires. The resulting panel therefore consisted of 121 program and 166 comparison group students for a total panel sample of 287 students. Comparisons of the attributes of program and comparison group students is provided below in Table 1. All analyses were carried out on this panel of students.[6]

Data Analysis. Several forms of quantitative analysis were carried out. First, descriptive statistics were employed to describe and compare the attributes, experiences, and outcomes of students in the program and comparison panels. Z-tests of difference between proportions were used to assess the presence of statistical significance. Second, regression analyses were used to ascertain how attributes and experiences were related, over time, to behaviors and, in turn, to outcomes over the course of the year. Since persistence was

TABLE 1
Characteristics of Program and Comparison Group Students

Characteristics	Program Group	Comparison Group
Age (mean years)	20.5	21.7
Gender (% female)	52.6	51.1
Marital status (% married)	2.5	11.5
Employment status (% working)	74.2	67.7
Parental education (% some college or more)	73.1	69.8
High-School GPA (A = 4.0; B = 3.0; etc.)	3.2	3.5

measured by a simple dichotomous variable, we used logit regression analysis in the study of persistence into the second year. Stepwise procedures were employed with variables added to the analysis according to a conceptual ordering system that places variables in order of their time occurrence.[7] In all instances, SAS, a statistical package for the mainframe, was employed in the statistical analyses.

Qualitative Case Study

The intent of the qualitative component of the study was to understand, from the students' point of view, how participation in a collaborative learning program influenced students' learning experiences and how those learning experiences fit in with their broader experiences as first-year students. In this case, we focused exclusively on the views of students in the CSP classes. In those classes, students were selected to be interviewed using a purposeful sampling (Bogdan & Biklen, 1992). Our sampling plan included talking to students who were diverse in many ways—age, gender, race, and attitude about the program.

Data collection. We visited each site for three one-week periods during the academic year. The first site visit took place during the early part of the fall quarter. It allowed us to become familiar with the institution. In addition we were able to see how the collaborative learning program was functioning at an early stage. The second site visit took place during the late part of the fall quarter. The program was ending, and the students were able to tell us about their experiences during the quarter. The third site visit was made during the middle of the spring quarter. At that time students were able to reflect upon experiences with and without the program.

Data collection consisted of participant observation, interviews, and document review. Participant observation was conducted in and around classrooms, and on campus and in the surrounding community, wherever possible. Interviews consisted of numerous informal conversations with students, faculty, and staff; over forty-five scheduled open-ended interviews with students and staff; approximately twenty informal telephone interviews with key informants; and thirty-six scheduled interviews with students which followed a semistructured protocol. These latter interviews lasted an average of forty minutes.

Document review consisted of gathering school publications and class materials, course syllabi, and schedules.

Data analysis. Data analysis was conducted in an ongoing process that enabled us to explore themes as they emerged and to pursue unexpected leads during the second and third site visits. Data were analyzed by reading and rereading field notes and interview transcripts to familiarize ourselves with them, assigning codes to portions of the data, identifying emerging themes in the data, and generating working hypotheses based on these themes. The working hypotheses were checked against the data and modified, as necessary, before being presented as findings. This process of incorporating emerging themes from the data with hypotheses constructed during the study is characteristic of inductive analysis used in qualitative research (Bogdan & Biklen, 1992). The strength of inductive analysis is that it facilitates the "grounding" of new models or theories (Glaser & Strauss, 1967). To make the mechanical aspects of data analysis more manageable (retrieving and sorting the coded data), we used QUALOG, a qualitative data analysis program for the computer (Shelly & Sibert, 1987).

Results

Longitudinal Panel Study

Patterns of activity and perceptions. In response to survey questions that probed the range and extent of student activities, CSP students reported greater involvement in a range of academic and social activities and greater perceived developmental gains over the course of the year than did students in the comparison classes of the regular curriculum. These differences are reported in factor form in Table 2. Noticeably, the two largest differences between program and nonprogram students are in course and student activities (3.05% and 3.12% versus 2.46% and 2.85%). In both cases, students in the CSPs reported being substantially more involved in course (academic) activities and activities involving other students than did students in comparison non-CSP classes.

It is noteworthy that in response to a series of semantic differential questions on college and classroom environment, students in the CSPs also reported significantly more positive views

TABLE 2

Activity Factor Scores for First-Year Students in CSP and Comparison Classes

Factor Score	CSP	Comparison
Course	3.05*	2.46
Library	2.15*	1.94
Faculty	2.25*	1.99
Students	2.81*	2.25
Writing	3.12*	2.85
Clubs	1.70	1.57
Arts	1.91*	1.60
Perceived gain	2.68*	2.46

NOTE: Variables are measured on a four-point scale from 1 to 4. For activity scores these range from 1 = Never to 4 = Very Often. For perceived gains, they range from 1 = very little to 4 = very much.
* Indicates a significant difference between groups at the 0.05 level.

of the college, its students and faculty, its classes and climate, and of their own involvement in the college (Table 3). This was particularly noticeable with student perceptions of their classes (6.03% versus 5.16%) and their own sense of involvement in learning (5.80% versus 5.01%). As we shall see, these differences were reflected in the way students talked about their classroom experiences.

Given these data, it is not surprising that students in the CSPs persisted to the following spring and fall quarters at a significantly higher rate than did similar students in the regular classes (Table 4). Interestingly, differences in persistence in the following fall quarter (66.7% versus 52.0% percent) were considerably greater than those for the spring quarter of that academic year (83.8% versus 80.9%). They were greater still when transfer to four-year institutions was included in our measure of persistence, that is, when we took account of the total rate of educational continuation of students.[8]

Multivariate analysis.   Though informative, the above descriptive analysis does not demonstrate

that participation in the CSP classes is independently associated with enhanced persistence. It merely suggests an association that is univariate in character. To test the question of independent association we carried out a step-wise logit regression analysis that sought to predict second-year persistence as a function of the independent and treatment variables. Table 5 indicates the variables used in each of the multivariate analyses. Logit regression was utilized because the dependent variable, persistence, is a categorical variable (1,0). One interprets parameters in a logistic regression as specifying how changes in an independent variable increases or decreases the likelihood of persisting onto the second year. The results of these analyses are presented in Table 6. Only those variables are shown that are significant at the 0.10 level.

Five variables proved to be significant predictors of persistence among students at Seattle Central Community College. These are participation in the CSP, college grade point average, hours studied per week, perceptions of faculty, and the factor score on involvement with other students. Again, being a member of a CSP

TABLE 3

Perceptions of College Environment of CSP and Comparison Class Students

Perceptions of:	CSP	Comparison
Classes	6.03*	5.16
Other students	5.64*	5.19
Faculty	6.00*	5.62
Administrators	4.86*	4.54
Campus climate	5.31*	5.17
Yourself	5.80*	5.01

NOTE: Variables are scored on a scale from 1 to 7, where higher scores indicate a more positive view of college environment. In each case a score of 4 represents a neutral response.
*Indicates a significant difference between groups at the 0.05 level.

TABLE 4
Spring and Fall Re-Enrollment Among First-Year CSP
and Comparison Class Students

Student Population	Spring Persistence	Fall Persistence
Coordinated studies program (N = 121)	83.8*	66.7*
Comparison classes (N = 166)	80.9	52.0

*Indicates a significant difference at the 0.05 level.

proves, even after controlling for performance and other attributes and behaviors of students, an independent predictor of persistence into the second year of college. It should be noted that similar and even more powerful results were obtained when the rate of total educational continuation was taken as the dependent variable.

Qualitative Case Study

While the quantitative analyses yielded evidence of the impact of learning communities on student persistence and suggested some possible ways of understanding that impact, the qualitative analysis provided direct insight in the ways in which those communities influenced persistence. The results of this analysis can best be summarized under three headings, each of which reveals something about the underlying forces that link classroom experiences to persistence. These are Building Supportive Peer Groups, Shared Learning-Bridging the Academic-Social Divide, and Gaining a Voice in the Construction of Knowledge.

Building supportive peer groups. Participation in a first-year learning community enabled students to develop a network of supportive peers that helped students make the transition to college and integrate them into a community of peers. This community of peers, formed in their learning communities, provided students with a

TABLE 5
Variables in a Multivariate Analysis of Persistence at
Seattle Central Community College

AGE	= age.
MAR	= marital status.
HSGPA	= high-school grade point average.
WORK	= working while attending college.
AID	= receiving financial aid.
MED	= mother's educational level.
FED	= father's educational level.
HDEG	= degree aspiration.
HSTUDY	= hours per week studying.
COURSE	= course activity factor score.
FACULTY	= faculty activity factor score.
STUDENT	= student activity factor score.
WRITING	= writing activity factor score.
LIBRARY	= library activity factor score.
CLUBS	= involvement in clubs activity factor score.
ARTS	= involvement in arts activity score.
ENVIRON1	= perceptions of other students.
ENVIRON2	= perceptions of faculty.
ENVIRON3	= perceptions of administrators.
ENVIRON4	= perceptions of classes.
ENVIRON5	= perceptions of campus climate.
ENVIRON6	= perceptions of oneself.
GAIN	= perceptions of intellectual gain.
GPA	= college grade point average.

TABLE 6
Logistic Regression Analysis on Persistence Among CSP
and Comparison Class Students

Variable	Parameter Estimate	Standard Error	Wald Chi-Square	P > Chi-Square
CSP	1.557	0.539	8.331	0.004
GPA	0.753	0.361	6.482	0.038
HSTUDY	0.279	0.167	2.802	0.094
STUDENT	0.957	0.345	7.681	0.006
ENVIRON1	0.472	0.239	3.869	0.050

NOTE: CSP   = participation in CSP
GPA   = mean grade point average in college.
HSTUDY   = hours studying per week.
STUDENT = student activities factor score.
ENVIRON1 = perceptions of students.

small, knowable group of fellow students with whom early friendships were formed. Some friendships lasted; others faded. But in all cases students saw those associations as an important and valued part of their first-year experience.

Meeting people and making friends during the first year of college is a major preoccupation of student life, especially among younger students who have yet to establish families or acquire significant work obligations. Whereas making friends in smaller, more intimate residential colleges may be a relatively easy task, it is far more difficult in commuter institutions and in very large institutions. It is not surprising then that so many students talked of their learning communities as a place to meet new people and make new friendships; a way to make the large college a smaller, more knowable place. A student in the program put it this way: "That's why the cluster is really great, because right now I've made a lot of friends. In another school if I had different classmates, it would have been harder. I've made a lot of friends that I didn't know before, so that's good."

Not surprisingly, many students saw participation in the learning community as an important part of being able to manage the many struggles they faced in getting to and participating in class (see Russo, 1995). Through seminars, group projects, class discussions, and self-evaluation reports, the CSPs contributed not only to a high level of student participation in learning, but also to the development of supportive peer groups that helped students balance the many struggles they faced in attending college. The groups, which developed within the classroom, extended beyond it providing support that students saw as influencing their desire

to continue college despite the many challenges they faced. One student, looking back on her experience in the prior fall's program, put it this way:

> In the cluster we knew each other, we were friends, we discussed and studied everything from all the classes. We knew things very, very well because we discussed it all so much. We had a discussion about everything. Now it's more difficult because there are different people in each class. There's not so much—oh, I don't know how to say it. It's not so much togetherness. In the cluster if we needed help or if we had questions, we could help each other.

It is important to note that students in the CSP often made friends who fell outside their prior social networks. In these settings, where students came from a great diversity of backgrounds and traditions, students spoke not only of making new friends, but also of the diversity of views and experiences they came to know through those friendships.

Shared learning: Bridging the academic-social divide. The shared learning experience of learning communities did more than simply cement new friendships; it served to bridge the academic-social divide that typically plagues student life. Often, social and academic concerns compete, causing students to feel torn between the two worlds so that students have to choose one over the other. Learning communities helped students draw these two worlds together.

The development of these interpersonal relationships was important, because it was against this backdrop of a supportive network of peers that academic engagement arose. And it did so both inside and outside the classroom. Groups that formed within the classroom often extended beyond the classroom in informal meetings and study groups. Once these were in operation, students were able to turn toward the material presented in class and their assignments. A common perception among program students was captured in the following comment:

> You know, the more I talk to other people about our class stuff, the homework, the tests, the more I'm actually learning, . . . and the more I learn not only about other people but also about the subject, because my brain is getting more, because I'm getting more involved with the students. I'm getting more involved with the class even after class.

In this and other ways, participation in a shared learning experience enabled new college students to bridge the academic-social divide that typically confronts students in these settings. It allowed them to meet two needs, social and academic, without having to sacrifice one in order to meet the other. But more than simply allowing the social and academic worlds to exist side by side, the learning communities provided a vehicle for each to enhance the other. Students spoke of a learning experience that was different and richer than that with which they were typically acquainted. As one student noted "not only do we learn more, we learn better."

Little surprise then that in our quantitative data, students in the CSP had higher peer and learning activity scores. Their engagement with their peers in and outside the classroom served to involve them more fully in the academic matters of the classroom. They spent more time with their peers and more time with their peers on class matters. As a result, they spent more time studying. Not surprisingly, they also saw themselves as having gained more from participation in the CSPs.

Gaining a voice in the construction of knowledge. Learning communities at Seattle Central Community College met as one large class, and the faculty worked together as a collaborative team in the classroom. They consciously sought to model learning for the students and include students as active participants in the construction of classroom knowledge. Equally important, they sought to challenge student assumptions about how knowledge is constructed and have students take personal ownership over the learning process. It was an experience that required students to rethink what they knew and become personally involved in deciding what they knew and how they knew it. In that way, they sought to have students take ownership over the learning process. The result was not only a sense of personal involvement in learning that students saw as very different from past educational experiences, but also a type of learning that students saw as richer and, for some, empowering. As one student observed:

> So you're constantly having to think, rethink, and even re-rethink what's going on in light of all the feedback you're getting from all these different points of view, and what it does is shape and mold your own point of view to a much finer degree. . . . We not only learn more, we learn better.

Students appreciated the contrasting, though complementary, ideas from different instructors. They saw instructors grapple with and analyze their own content and synthesize it with the content from other disciplines into a course with one main theme. The continuity of course activities and assignments provided students with opportunities for guided practice in their own thinking across disciplines, in-depth exploration of key concepts, and relating course materials with their lived experiences. The result was high levels of discussion and activity within the CSP and a sense of personal involvement in learning that students saw as very different from past educational experiences.

The multidisciplinary approach also provided a model of learning that encouraged students to express the diversity of their experiences and world views. In doing so, it allowed age, ethnic, and life experience differences among students to emerge and become part of class content. Many students commented on the range of diversity as a way to learn more than just *about each other*. They saw student (and faculty) diversity as an important factor in their learning *about the content*. They appreciated the multiple perspectives that a diverse population provided in the CSP process and, in turn, felt comfortable expressing their own ideas and questions.

> I think more people should be educated in this form of education. I mean, because it's good. We learn how to interact not only with ourselves, but with other people of different races, different sizes, different colors,

different everything. I mean it just makes learning a lot better.

The innovative approach of the CSP encouraged students consciously to address issues of their own learning. The diversity of learning experiences challenged students' understandings of what it means to attend college and to learn and their assumptions about how knowledge is constructed. The process of collaboration between students and faculty and with the course content provided a new model of learning that encouraged students to embrace an expanded picture of the learning process. The students reported that they learned concepts better by seeing them presented from perspectives that crossed content areas and found deeper appreciation of the many ways in which knowledge is created.

Before turning to the conclusions, it should be noted that these findings, both quantitative and qualitative, were the same regardless of when students enrolled in the CSP classes. Students who enrolled late in the CSP, that is to say for whom it was the only available option—indeed some were not aware of the program prior to enrolling—showed similar outcomes and expressed similar views of their experience. Clearly, one could not dismiss the outcome of program participation as merely the result of the program having allowed particular types of students to self-select themselves into a program that permitted them to engage in behaviors they would have otherwise carried out elsewhere.

Conclusions

These results provide insight into two distinct, yet interrelated, issues: what impact learning communities have on student learning and persistence and what role classroom experience plays in the process of student persistence.

Learning Communities, Learning, and Persistence

The results of our studies lend support to some of the basic tenets of learning communities and the collaborative pedagogy that underlies them. First, it is evident that participation in a collaborative or shared learning group enables students to develop a network of support—a small supportive community of peers—that helps bond students to the broader social communities of the college while also engaging them

more fully in the academic life of the institution. This community of classroom-based peers, formed in the CSP, served to support students and encourage their continued attendance and class participation. It did so both inside and outside the classroom. Groups that formed within the classroom often extended beyond the classroom in informal meetings and study groups—or as one student put it, "we are more involved with class after class." In this manner, collaborative learning settings enabled new students to bridge the academic-social divide that typically confronts students in these settings. They were able to meet two needs, social and academic, without having to sacrifice one in order to meet the other. In effect, these classrooms served as the academic and social crossroads out of which "seamless" educational activities are constructed.[9]

Second, it is apparent that students are influenced by participating in a setting in which sources of learning come from a variety of perspectives beyond that of one faculty member. The sharing of a curriculum and the use of collaborative pedagogy that brought students and faculty together to teach added an intellectual richness to student experience that the traditional pedagogy did not. Course activities allowed students to connect their personal experiences to class content and recognize the diversity of views and experiences that marked differing members of the classroom. In opening up the conversation about what is known to many voices, student and faculty, the program led many students to discover, or better yet uncover, abilities they had not appreciated until then.

Third, though we did not obtain information about "learning" as measured by tests either of content or skills (e.g., critical thinking, etc.), we know that student perceptions of intellectual gain as well as academic performance as measured by GPA were greater in the learning community setting than in the more traditional learning settings and that these "gains" were independent of student attributes.[10] Just as important, we know from student comments that the quality of learning was seen to be different, indeed deeper and richer, in the collaborative learning settings. Again as one student told us; "we not only learn more, we learn better."

Finally, our findings reveal that it is possible to promote student involvement and achievement in settings where such involvement is not easily attained. Unlike many "involving" colleges that are small, private, and residential, the setting we studied was nonresidential. More importantly, the students we studied, unlike students in residential settings who typically devote most, if not all, of their time, in one form or another, to the life of the college, students in non-residential settings, such as Seattle Central Community College, have to attend to a multiplicity of obligations outside of college. For them, going to college is but one of a number of tasks to be completed during the course of a day. Yet even in that setting, collaborative learning "works." Indeed, it may be the only viable path to greater student involvement (Tinto & Russo, 1993; Tinto, Russo, & Kadel, 1994).

In this manner, our research fills a critical gap in the work of Astin (1993), Tinto (1987, 1993) and others who have explored the importance of student involvement to student attainment. While reaffirming the fact that involvement matters, our research provides empirical documentation of at least one way in which it is possible to make involvement matter in an urban community college setting. In doing so, it moves our conversation about involvement beyond the recognition of its importance to the practical issue of how involvement can be generated in settings where involvement is not easily obtained, in this case by restructuring the student educational experience of the classroom.

Classrooms as Communities and Theories of Student Persistence

Our research also provides insight into the ways in which classroom experience shapes student persistence and, in turn, the manner in which current theories of student persistence might be modified to better reflect the educational character of college life. Specifically, it suggests important relationships, on one hand, between the educational activity structure of the classroom, student involvement, and the quality of student effort and, on the other, between quality of student effort, learning, and persistence. And, again, it suggests that these relationships are likely to be especially important for those students and in those collegiate settings where involvement is not easy to achieve, namely, for commuting and working students and on non-residential campuses, in particular those in urban settings.

Student social involvement in the educational life of the college, in this instance through the educational activity structure of the curriculum and classroom, provides a mechanism through which both academic and social involvement arises and student effort is engaged. The more students are involved, academically and socially, in shared learning experiences that link them as learners with their peers, the more likely they are to become more involved in their own learning and invest the time and energy needed to learn (Tinto, Goodsell, & Russo, 1993). The social affiliations that those activities provide serve as a vehicle through which academic involvement is engaged. Both forms of involvement lead to enhanced quality of effort. Students put more effort into that form of educational activity that enables them to bridge the academic-social divide so that they are able to make friends and learn at the same time. That increased effort leads to enhanced learning in ways that heighten persistence (Endo & Harpel, 1982; Tinto & Froh, 1992). Figure 1 graphically represents how a modified theory of student persistence, which links classrooms to effort and persistence, might appear.

It does not follow, however, that the linkage between involvement and learning, on one hand, and between learning and persistence, on the other, is simple or symmetrical. As to the impact of involvement upon learning, one has to ask about the specific nature of student involvement. Not all involvements lead to learning in the same fashion. Much depends on the degree to which student involvement is a meaningful and valued part of the classroom experience. Having a voice without being heard is often worse than having no voice at all. As to the linkage between learning and persistence, though learning is in general positively associated with persistence, it is not the case that learning guarantees persistence or that failure to learn, beyond the obvious case of academic failure ensures departure. Although for most, if not all, institutions academic involvement does matter more than social involvement, it is also true that both social and academic involvement influence persistence. For some students, even high levels of academic involvement and its consequent learning may not be enough to offset the effect of social isolation; for others, sufficient social integration or involvement may counterbalance the absence of academic involvement. These students stay because of the friendships they have developed. Of course, the absence of any academic involvement typically leads to academic failure and thus forced departure.

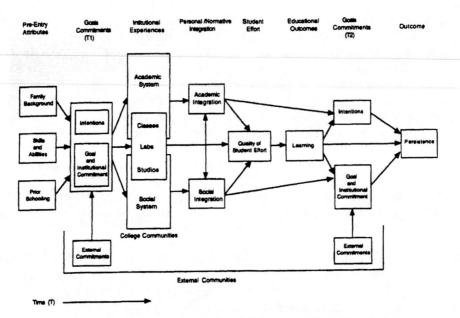

FIG. 1. Suggested Model Linking Classrooms, Learning, and Persistence

The informed observers might argue, at this point, that there has been little research to support this claim. Indeed they might note that measures of academic integration have not always been found to be associated with persistence. True enough. But issues of specification aside—that is, of the ways we have measured, or perhaps better yet, mismeasured the concept "academic integration"—it is very likely that what we have measured reflects the fact that most classrooms are not involving and therefore not a factor in student persistence. This does not mean that they *could not* play a role in persistence, only that they have typically *not yet* played that role. This research shows that they can.

Classrooms as learning communities.   The results of our research lead us to speak, then, of classrooms as smaller communities of learning which are located at the very heart of the broader academic community of the college. Classrooms serve as smaller academic and social meeting places or crossroads that intersect the diverse faculty and student communities that mark the college generally. Membership in the community of the classroom provides important linkages to membership in communities external to the classroom. For new students in particular, engagement in the community of the classroom becomes a gateway for subsequent student involvement in the academic and social communities of the college generally (Tinto, Goodsell, & Russo, 1993).

Colleges can be seen as consisting not merely of multiple communities, but of overlapping and sometimes nested academic and social communities, each influencing the other in important ways. By extension, the broader process of academic and social integration (involvement) can be understood as *emerging from* student involvement with faculty and student peers in the communities of the classrooms. It is a complex multidimensional process, which links classroom engagement with faculty and student peers to subsequent involvement in the larger academic and social communities of the college. Thus the likely link exists between this research and that of Attinasi (1989), Kuh (1993, 1995), Kuh, Schuh, Whitt, & Associates (1991), and Rendon (1994) on the role of out-of-class experiences to student learning and persistence.

This view of the role of classrooms in student academic and social involvement leads us to the recognition of the centrality of the classroom experience and the importance of faculty, curriculum, and pedagogy to student development and persistence (see Pascarella & Terenzini, 1991). This is true not only because contact with the faculty inside and outside the classroom serves directly to shape learning and persistence, but also because their actions, framed by pedagogical assumptions, shape the nature of classroom communities and influence the degree and manner in which students become involved in learning in and beyond those settings. Faculty do matter and not only because of their out-of-classroom activities.

Thinking about the temporal process of learning and persistence. If we take seriously the notion argued above of the dynamic interplay between involvement, quality of effort, learning, and persistence, we can then postulate a more complex view of the longitudinal process of student persistence as it occurs over the course of the first year of college, if not the entire student career, than has thus far been described in the literature on student persistence (Tinto, 1989). Specifically, our preceding conversation suggests that the manner in which social and academic involvements (integration) shape learning and persistence will vary over the course of the college career and do so in differing ways for different students inside and outside the classroom.

During the first several weeks of the first-year of college, the work of Attinasi (1989) and, very recently, Tinto and Goodsell (1994) suggests that issues of social membership may be somewhat more important than those of academic membership, at least for younger students who leave home after high school to attend residential four-year institutions. Attinasi (1989) notes that new students—in this case Mexican American students entering a large public university—talk about the need to attach themselves to relevant social groups as a way to cope with the difficulties of "getting in" to college. More importantly, this attachment and the social support it provides may be a necessary precondition for subsequent involvements.

The same observation can be made about the first-year experiences of students attending a large public university on the West Coast (Tinto & Goodsell, 1994). At first, new student attention is focused on the need to make social connections with their student peers. Though classes matter, students' concern regarding academic involvement appears to be played out against a broader backdrop of social issues and concerns they have over social membership. As students progress through the first year and toward their degree, their concerns appear to shift toward a greater emphasis on academic issues. Once social membership has been achieved, or at least once concerns over it have been addressed, student attention appears increasingly to center on academic involvements.

It is noteworthy, in this regard, that Neumann and Neumann's (1989) study of junior and senior persistence at a northeastern university indicates that students' progress from freshman to senior years is increasingly shaped by educational rather than social concerns and by their educational experiences in the institution. Their study emphasized what they refer to as a "Quality of Learning Experience" approach, wherein persistence is conceptually linked to student perceptions of the quality of their learning environments and their interaction with faculty about learning issues. The significant predictors of junior and senior persistence proved to be student involvement in learning activities, students' views of the quality of teaching, advising, and course work, and their contact with faculty.

The likelihood that persistence is marked over time by a changing balance of academic and social involvements leads us to consider the parallels between the longitudinal process of persistence we have just described and those that describe moral and intellectual development. Could it be that the process of persistence in being linked to that of learning is, like Chickering's (1969) or Perry's (1970) model of student development, also shaped by a shifting need in students for differing forms of social and intellectual engagements? Might it be that fulfilling one need, the social, is, for many students, a developmental precondition for addressing the need for intellectual engagement? We should, of course, be very cautious about pushing these parallels too far. By noting the possible parallel between our view of the temporal process of persistence and that of student development, we are forced to ask whether our impressions are merely a reflection of the types of students who have thus far been studied, namely youthful students attending four-year institutions. Would the same results apply equally well to older students or to students in two-year institutions who are immersed in external communities of work, family, and friends? For older students who commute to school, for instance, early academic involvements may be more important, especially as they shape the person's sense of their own ability to cope with the academic demands of college or, to borrow Rendon's term, "validate" a student's presence on campus (Rendon, 1994). Clearly there is a much research to be done.

Closing Comment

What does all this mean for our existing models of student persistence? First it means that we need to remind ourselves that our current two-dimensional graphic representations of interaction, which depict social and academic systems of colleges as two separate boxes, mask the fuller relationship between these two spheres of activity. A more accurate representation would have academic and social systems appear as two nested spheres, where the academic occurs *within* the broader social system that pervades the campus. Such a depiction would more accurately capture the ways, noted here, in which social and academic life are interwoven and the ways in which social communities *emerge* out of academic activities that take place within the more limited academic sphere of the classroom, a sphere of activities that is necessarily also social in character.

As a methodological aside, this research reminds us that we would be well served by supplementing our use of path analysis to study the process of persistence with network analysis and/or social mapping of student interaction patterns. These will better illuminate the complexity of student involvements and the linkages that arise over time between classroom and out-of-class experiences. More importantly, they will shed important light on how interactions across the academic and social geography of a campus shape the educational opportunity structure of campus life and, in turn, both student learning and persistence.[11]

We have too long overlooked the essentially educational and developmental character of persistence as it occurs in most college settings. There is a rich line of inquiry of the linkage between learning and persistence that has yet to be pursued. Here is where we need to invest our time and energies in a fuller exploration of the complex ways in which the experience of the classroom comes to shape both student learning and persistence. Among other things, we need to pursue Braxton's (1995) lead and ask about the role of faculty teaching in persistence and more carefully consider the notion, as we have here, that choices of curriculum structure (e.g., learning communities) and pedagogy invariably shape both learning and persistence on campus (e.g., cooperative teaching), because they serve to alter both the degree to which and manner in which students become involved in the academic and social life of the institution. As we do so, we will discover what many educators have been trying to tell us for years, namely, that at its core college is an educational experience and that conversations about persistence that ignore important questions of educational practice are conversations that are at best shallow.

Notes

[1]Perhaps this arises from the institutional lenses through which most researchers have looked at student persistence. We see the issue as it is conditioned by the settings in which we work, that is, large residential universities with relatively privileged students who have the luxury of being able to spend time on campus.

[2]It is perhaps telling that current versions of Quality of Student Effort Scales are relatively insensitive to the range and degree of educational experiences that arise within the classroom. For the most part, these scales tend to emphasize activities that arise outside the classroom.

[3]For a fuller description of the program at Seattle Central Community College the reader should refer to Tinto and Russo (1993).

[4]For the purposes of this study we took first-year college students as representing those persons who enrolled in the institution in question for the first time, regardless of prior enrollment.

[5]We compared student attributes and persistence outcomes for the initial response group as a way to testing whether the results of the study might have been shaped by the character of those who responded to the follow-up questionnaire. We found nothing to suggest that our results would not have applied to all students, had they all responded to the follow-up questionnaire.

[6]For a more complete discussion of the data (e.g., variables, measures, etc.) the reader is again urged to see Tinto and Russo (1993).

[7]In this case, variables were entered in a logical order as determined by the temporal sequence of events that describe the students' movement from entry through to the start of the second year of college, namely, from preentry attributes to experiences within the time frame of the study to outcomes as measured first by learning and second by persistence over subsequent time periods.

[8]We also developed a measure of educational continuation to capture the fact that a number of students in the CSP transferred to the nearby university after having participated in the CSP. Though subject to some error, logit regression analysis on continuation yielded similar but even stronger results.

[9]The term "seamless" is Kuh's (1995). It refers to that type of collegiate setting where the boundaries between the academic and social are blurred, where there is an integration of the academic and social. In this case, we argue that such seamless settings, from the students' perspective, can be constructed from the classroom experience. Indeed, in the case of nonresidential institutions, the great bulk of institutions of higher education, it may be the only viable mechanism through which seamless institutions are "constructed."

[10]At some point, the researchers run the risk of being excessively intrusive and placing themselves in the position of studying people who are very aware of being studied. We sought to avoid that situation.

[11]Much like the concept "opportunity structure," which sociologists have employed to study the dynamic aspects of social stratification, the term "educational opportunity structure" can be seen as describing the interconnected chains of relationships and interactions out of which personal affiliations are wrought and contextual learning arises.

References

Astin, A. (1984). Student involvement: A developmental theory for higher education. *Journal of College Student Personnel, 25,* 297–308.

Astin, A. (1987). *Achieving educational excellence.* San Francisco: Jossey-Bass.

Astin, A. (1993). *What matters in college: Four critical years revisited.* San Francisco: Jossey-Bass.

Attinasi, L. C., Jr. (1989). Getting in: Mexican Americans' perceptions of university attendance and the implications for freshman year persistence. *Journal of Higher Education, 60,* 247–277.

Auster, C. J., & MacRone, M. (1994). The classroom as a negotiated social setting: An empirical study of the effects of faculty members' behavior on students' participation. *Teaching Sociology, 22,* 289–300.

Bean, J. (1983). The application of a model of turnover in work organizations to the student attrition process. *Review of Higher Education, 6,* 129–148.

Bogdan, R. C., & Biklen, S. K. (1992). *Qualitative research in education: An introduction to theory and methods* (2nd ed.). Boston: Allyn and Bacon.

Braxton, J. (1995). *Faculty classroom behaviors and their influence on academic and social integration and student departure decisions.* Paper presented at the annual meeting of the Association for the Study of Higher Education.

Cabrera, A. F., Castañeda, M., Nora, A., & Hengstler, D. (1992). The convergence between two theories of college persistence. *Journal of Higher Education, 63,* 143–164.

Chickering, A. W. (1969). *Education and identity.* San Francisco: Jossey-Bass.

Dressel, P., & Mayhew, L. (1971). *General education: Explorations in evaluation.* Westport, CT: Greenwood Publishing Group. Originally published in 1954, Washington, DC: American Council on Education.

Endo, J. J., & Harpel, R. L. (1982). The effect of student-faculty interaction on students' educational outcomes. *Research in Higher Education, 16,* 115–135.

Fassinger, P. A. (1995). Understanding classroom interaction: Students' and professors' contribution to students' silence. *Journal of Higher Education, 66,* 82–96.

Fischer, C. G., & Grant, G. E. (1983). Intellectual levels in college classrooms. In C. L. Ellner & C. P. Barnes (Eds.), *Studies of college teaching* (pp. 47–60). Lexington, MA: D.C. Heath.

Forrest, A. (1982). *Increasing student competence and persistence: The best case for general education.* Iowa City: American College Testing Program.

Friedlander, J. (1980). *The importance of quality of effort in predicting college student attainment.* Unpublished doctoral dissertation, The University of California-Los Angeles.

Glaser, R., & Strauss, R. (1967). *The discovery of grounded theory: Strategies for qualitative research.* Chicago: Aldine.

Karp, D., & Yoels, W. (1976). The college classroom: Some observations on the meaning of student participation. *Sociology and Social Research, 60,* 421–439.

Karplus, R. (1974). *Science curriculum improvement study. Teacher's handbook.* Berkeley, CA: Lawrence Hall of Science.

Kaufman, M., & Creamer, D. (1991). Influences of student goals for college on freshman year quality of effect and growth. *Journal of College Student Development, 32,* 197–206.

Kuh, G. (1993). In their own words: What students learn outside the classroom. *American Educational Research Journal, 30,* 277–304.

Kuh, G. (1995). The other curriculum: Out-of-class experiences associated with student learning and personal development. *Journal of Higher Education, 66,* 123–155.

Kuh, G., Schuh, J., Whitt, E., & Associates. (1991). *Involving colleges.* San Francisco: Jossey-Bass.

Lawson, A., & Snitgen, D. (1982). Teaching formal reasoning in a college biology course for preservice teachers. *Journal of Research in Science Education, 19,* 233–248.

Mallette, B. I., & Cabrera, A. (1991). Determinants of withdrawal behavior: An exploratory study. *Research in Higher Education, 32,* 179–194.

McKeachie, W. (1970). *Research on college teaching: A review.* Washington DC: ERIC Clearinghouse on Higher Education.

McKeachie, W. (1994). *Teaching tips: Strategies, research, and theory for college teaching* (8th ed.). Boston: D.C. Heath.

McMillan, J. (1987). Enhancing college students' critical thinking: A review of studies. *Research in Higher Education, 26,* 3–29.

Neumann, Y., & Neumann, E. F. (1989). Predicting juniors' and seniors' persistence and attrition: A quality of learning experience approach. *Journal of Experimental Education, 57,* 129–140.

Nora, A. (1987). Determinants of retention among Chicano college students. *Research in Higher Education, 26*(1), 31–59.

Nunn, C. E. (1996). Discussion in the college classroom. *Journal of Higher Education, 67,* 243–266.

Ory, J. C., & Braskamp, L. A. (1988). Involvement and growth of students in three academic programs. *Research in Higher Education, 28,* 116–129.

Pace, C. R. (1984). *Measuring the quality of college student experiences.* Los Angeles: University of California, Higher Education Research Institute.

Parker, J., & Schmidt, J. (1982). Effects of college experience. In H. Mitzel (Ed.), *Encyclopedia of Educational Research* (5th ed.). New York: Free Press.

Pascarella, E. T., & Terenzini, P. (1980). Predicting persistence and voluntary dropout decisions from a theoretical model. *Journal of Higher Education, 51,* 60–75.

Pascarella, E. T., & Terenzini, P. (1991). *How college affects students.* San Francisco: Jossey-Bass.

Perry, W. G. (1970). *Forms of intellectual and ethical development in the college years.* New York: Holt, Rinehart & Winston.

Rendon, L. (1994). Validating culturally diverse students: Toward a new model of learning and student development. *Innovative Higher Education, 19,* 33–52.

Russo, P. (1995). Struggling for knowledge: Students, coordinated studies, and collaborative learning. Unpublished doctoral dissertation, Syracuse University.

Shelly, A., & Sibert, E. (1987). *The QUALOG user's manual.* Syracuse, NY: Syracuse University.

Smith, D. G. (1980). *College instruction: Four empirical views.* Paper presented at the annual meeting of the American Educational Research Association, Boston (ERIC Document Reproduction Service No. ED 192 676).

Smith, D. G. (1983). Instruction and outcomes in an undergraduate setting. In C. L. Ellner & C. P. Barnes (Eds.), *Studies in college teaching* (pp. 83–116). Lexington, MA: D.C. Heath.

Terenzini, P. T., & Pascarella, E. T. (1977). Voluntary freshman attrition and patterns of social and academic integration in a university: A test of a conceptual model. *Research in Higher Education, 6,* 25–43.

Tinto, V. (1987). *Leaving college: Rethinking the causes and cures of student attrition.* Chicago: The University of Chicago Press.

Tinto, V. (1989). Stages of student departure: Reflections on the longitudinal character of student leaving. *Journal of Higher Education, 59,* 438–455.

Tinto, V. (1993). *Leaving college: Rethinking the causes and cures of student attrition* (2nd. ed.). Chicago: The University of Chicago Press.

Tinto, V., & Froh, R. (1992). *Translating research on student persistence into institutional policy.* Paper presented at the annual meeting of the Association for the Study of Higher Education, Chicago.

Tinto, V., & Goodsell, A. (1994). Freshman interest groups and the first year experience: Constructing student communities in a large university. *Journal of the Freshman Year Experience, 6,* 7–28.

Tinto, V., Goodsell, A., & Russo, P. (1993). *Gaining a voice: The impact of collaborative learning on student experience in the first year of college.* Unpublished manuscript, Syracuse University.

Tinto, V., & Russo, P. (1993). *A longitudinal study of the Coordinated Studies Program at Seattle Central Community College.* A study by the National Center for Postsecondary Teaching, Learning, and Assessment, Syracuse University.

Tinto, V., Russo, P., & Kadel, S. (1994). Constructing educational communities: Increasing retention in challenging circumstances. *Community College Journal, 64,* 26–30.

Volkwein, J., King, M., & Terenzini, P. (1986). Student-faculty relationships and intellectual growth among transfer students. *Journal of Higher Education, 57,* 413–430.

CHAPTER 26

INTERNET-BASED LEARNING IN POSTSECONDARY CAREER AND TECHNICAL EDUCATION

SCOTT D. JOHNSON
ANGELA D. BENSON
JOHN DUNCAN
OLGA N. SHINKAREVA
GAIL DIANE TAYLOR
TOD TREAT
UNIVERSITY OF ILLINOIS AT URBANA-CHAMPAIGN

Abstract

This article presents the results of a national study of distance learning in postsecondary career and technical education (CTE). The main purpose of this study was to identify the current status and future trends associated with distance learning in postsecondary CTE. The results show that community colleges are actively involved in the delivery of CTE via distance learning. Internet-based courses are the most prominent form of distance learning in community college CTE programs, especially for credit courses. While some colleges are creating their own online programs, many are partnering with external providers (e.g., commercial vendors) and other colleges and universities to make credit and noncredit CTE courses available to students. It was noted that the community colleges are relying heavily on low-bandwidth technologies, although significant growth in all forms of Internet-based CTE courses and technologies is expected within the next three years.

Introduction

The Internet and web-based computer technologies that support online learning have changed the education landscape considerably. Internet technologies now provide easy to use, powerful, and economically sound media for educational purposes. As a result, large numbers of public higher education institutions are offering courses online and they expect growth in this type of education in the near future (Allen & Seaman, 2003). According to the same source, the majority of public higher education institutions indicated that online courses attract growing number of students when compared to traditional education, and achieve the same or even higher learning outcomes. Also, faculty involvement and acceptance of online education is increasing. This growth has come, in part, because of the increase in access to computers, broadband Internet, and software packages, such as course management software, that are designed to make Internet-based learning more user-friendly (Phipps & Merisotis, 2000). In addition, the changing demographics of college students support the need of a flexible postsecondary educational delivery system. Students today are older, employed, married and/or have dependents; this creates a need for flexibility of course delivery, both in terms of time and place (National Center for Education Statistics [NCES], 2000). Finally, traditional students (i.e., those entering higher education immediately following high school) are Internet-literate and have come to expect a high level of technology use in their coursework, making them more receptive to Internet-based courses (Synergy Plus, 2002).

The growth of Internet-based courses has been accompanied by the development of benchmarks of quality based on best practices in institutional support, course structure, instructor student interactions and support, and assessment (Phipps & Merisotis, 2000). In addition, numerous studies have found no significant differences in learning outcomes or student satisfaction between traditional courses and Internet-based courses. Criticisms of these comparison studies have focused on the lack of theoretical frameworks, rigorous controls, or researcher objectivity. However, rather than discrediting the "no significant difference phenomenon," these criticisms have led to the understanding that "it is irrelevant to speak of the effects of using the Web without understanding how it is entwined with instructional design and especially faculty choices about instructional design" (Meyer, 2002, p. 19).

Career and technical education (CTE) means many things to many people. To some people, it refers to a single course that provides specific skill training for job employment or advancement, while to others, it refers to a lifelong learning pathway that is used to obtain, update, and extend the knowledge, skills, and attitudes required to pursue a career successfully. Career and technical education imparts both specific occupational skills to those students wishing to enter employment directly and the academic skills they need for advancement and further postsecondary education (NCES, 2000).

According to the Association for Career and Technical Education (2003), CTE ". . . is about helping students, workers and lifelong learners of all ages fulfill their working potential" (p. 1). Although community colleges are known for providing high school and college students with relevant application of academic subject matter, employability skills, and career education, it also provides second-chance education and training for the unemployed and those seeking to upgrade their employability skills as well as professional development for career advancement through corporate training and continuing education. While CTE continues to be offered at the high school level, a more significant role is now being played by community colleges, technical institutes, and private, for-profit organizations. CTE programs offered by community colleges include health professions, office careers, computer science, agriculture, construction, and automotive A.A.S. degrees and certificates.

Community colleges have played a key role in connecting high school tech prep, industry training, and baccalaureate education.[1] As an institution of higher education known for its adaptability and willingness to provide customized training, the community college has been influenced by industry (Dougherty & Bakia, 1999; Grubb, 1996) and federal policy, such as the Workforce Investment Act (WIA) and the Carl D. Perkins Vocational and Technical Education Act. Federal policy has generally acted to increase the workforce preparation role played by the community college. In fact, community colleges are becoming the designated provider of customized training in many states (Villadsen & Gennett, 1997).

Community colleges have not only played a major role in the delivery of CTE courses, but have also rapidly expanded their Internet-based programs (NCES, 2000; Reese, 2002). The number of nontraditional postsecondary CTE programs offered through distance learning is increasing—"a trend that should benefit both the students and the workplace of tomorrow" (Reese, 2002, p. 24). Lever-Duffy, Lemke, and

Johnson (1996) compiled examples of model community college distance learning programs and concluded that distance learning, while "once a fringe methodology, is fast becoming a fundamental methodology for the Information Age institution" (p. vii). In a 3-year trend study of the 700 member colleges of the League for Innovation in the Community College, Milliron and Miles (2000) identified expected trends for instructional technologies and distance learning in community colleges. Most of the participating schools agreed that the trend towards the use of information technology in instruction would increase over the next 3 to 5 years while fewer than 15% expected that the trend towards distance learning would decrease. According to the Campus Computing Survey, 74% of community colleges now offer online courses to students (Green, 2000). In the early stages however, courses were developed that were oriented to the delivery of general education, liberal arts, and business and management courses (Synergy Plus, 2002). Colleges now offer online technical and vocational courses to students as well.

Statement of the Problem

As community colleges expand their role as a CTE provider, they are exploring the potential of distance learning through Internet-based CTE courses and programs. Internet-based CTE courses and programs, however, provide a particular challenge because of the need to develop skills at a distance. As with any new area of emphasis in education, there is limited understanding of the scope of distance learning in CTE and its impact on distance learning on postsecondary CTE. Hence, the primary purpose of this study was to determine the current status and future trends associated with Internet-based learning in postsecondary CTE. The study was designed to address the full breadth of postsecondary CTE rather than a specific subset of the field. To accomplish this purpose, a national study was conducted to answer the following research questions:

1. How prominent is Internet-based learning in postsecondary CTE?

2. What strategies do community colleges use to provide and coordinate Internet-based CTE?

3. What types of technologies are used to deliver postsecondary Internet-based CTE

courses and what technologies are expected to be used in the future?

Method

This study involved a descriptive analysis of the status of Internet-based learning in postsecondary CTE programs. A nationally representative sample of community colleges was asked to participate in the research to answer questions addressing the prevalence of Internet-based learning in postsecondary CTE.

Participants

The target population for this study was defined as postsecondary colleges and technical institutes that are members of the American Association of Community Colleges (AACC). The sampling frame containing 1,015 member institutions was obtained from AACC. This list provided a national representation of institutions, and included all types, sizes, geographic locations, and settings (i.e., urban, suburban or large town, rural).

Based on discussions with AACC researchers, it was determined that their membership, in terms of institutional characteristics, was heterogeneous across states and homogenous within states. Therefore, a proportionally representative sample was obtained using a stratified random sampling technique. A total of 552 member institutions were randomly selected from the AACC membership database with the number selected proportional to the number of community colleges in each state.

Instrumentation

The development of the questionnaire for this study involved working closely with contacts at several professional associations that are closely connected to community college research, including studies of distance learning. The associations were contacted to gain insight into related studies they have completed, to seek their advice on increasing response rates, and to identify the critical questions that needed to be included in the questionnaire. In addition to involving these professional associations in the development and validation of the questionnaire, the instrument was pilot-tested with two community college leaders whose institutions were not included in the national sample. Only minor changes were in the questionnaire were suggested.

The questionnaire employed the definition of distance learning used by the National Center for Education Statistics in their studies of distance learning in postsecondary education institutions (NCES, 2000, 2003). This definition highlighted education or training courses that are delivered to off-campus locations using both synchronous and asynchronous delivery modes of instruction. As with the NCES surveys, courses offered exclusively on-campus, those offered via written correspondence, and those where the instructor travels to a remote site to deliver instruction in person were not included in this definition of distance courses. Data from all CTE courses and programs at the institution were to be included in the responses.

The questionnaire contained 14 items that asked for specific data regarding courses, programs, enrollments, and technologies used in distance CTE. The estimated amount of time needed to complete the questionnaire was 1–2 hours. The anticipated length of the questionnaire and projections of respondent burden were determined based on estimates used by NCES in their national study of postsecondary institutions (NCES, 2002).

Data Collection Procedures

This study involved mailing a questionnaire to the executive officers of each of the postsecondary institutions identified in the sample. A four-round data collection process was used to obtain responses to the survey that included sending questionnaires to the institutions in the sample and using several follow up techniques to increase the response rate.

The procedure used for response rate calculation was based on the guidelines established by the Council of American Survey Research Organizations (CASRO) and used by the American Association for Public Opinion Research (2000). Forty entries were removed from the originally selected sample because of incomplete contact information, leaving an accessible sample of 512. Using the CASRO RR_2 formula, a final response rate of 53.3% was achieved, which compared quite favorably with a study conducted by AACC. AACC obtained a 19% response rate for their study that involved chief academic officers at more than 1,100 community colleges, and 205 colleges responded (Nock & Shults, 2001).

An important consideration in survey research is the degree to which the survey respondents are representative of the target population. To verify the representativeness of the respondents to the population, several statistical comparisons were performed, including demographic comparisons, respondent versus nonrespondent comparisons, and early versus late respondent comparisons. Because no apparent differences were found between the groups, one may conclude that the respondents are representative of the nonrespondents within the sample and the target population in general. Overall, the usable responses represent 26.6% of the target population.

Data Coding and Analysis

The current status of Internet-based CTE was determined by describing the characteristics of a nationally representative sample of community colleges at one point in time. In accordance with the research questions, the examined variables reflect the extent of colleges' participation in Internet-based CTE, types of courses offered, technologies used, and future trends in technology usage.

The current status and future trends of CTE distance teaming was determined by measuring the characteristics of the nationally representative sample of community colleges at one point in time. Pre-specified variables and several types of groupings were used (i.e., urban, suburban or large town, and rural; East, Midwest, West) to organize the data and to calculate frequencies and trends associated with Internet-based CTE. Groupings were based on the categorizations used by AACC. Version 11 of SPSS was used to complete the analysis.

Results

Institutional Participation in Distance CTE

Overall, the majority of community colleges provide some form of CTE courses and programs through distance learning. Of the responding community colleges, 76.3% offered CTE courses via distance learning in 2001–2002 (Table 1). CTE distance learning courses were more likely to be offered by community colleges in urban (82.8%) and suburban/large towns (80.5%) than in rural (66.3%) areas. Large community colleges were

TABLE 1
Distribution of Community Colleges Offering CTE Courses

Institutional Characteristic	N	Institutions Offering Distance CTE (%)	Institutions Not Offering Distance CTE (%)
All respondents	270	76.3	23.7
Regions			
East	114	76.3	23.7
Midwest	81	76.5	23.5
West	75	76.0	24.0
Institution Locale			
Urban	93	82.8	17.2
Suburban or Large Town	82	80.5	19.5
Rural	95	66.3	33.7
Institution Size			
1,000 or fewer	23	52.2	47.8
1,001–3,000	90	70.0	30.0
3,001–10,000	114	81.6	18.4
More than 10,000	43	88.4	11.6

Note. Percentages are computed within each classification variable; *n* represents the actual number of responding institutions.

also more likely to offer CTE via distance learning than were small community colleges. About 82% of the colleges with 3,001–10,000 students, which represents 42% of the respondents, offered CTE courses via distance learning. In comparison, 70% of the colleges with 1,001–3,000 students and about 52% of the colleges with fewer than 1,000 students offered CTE courses via distance learning. No substantial differences in offering CTE courses via distance learning were found among the responding community colleges located in East, Midwest, and West regions of the country.

Internet-Based Courses and Programs in Postsecondary CTE

The community colleges that offered CTE distance learning courses were asked to report the number of credit and noncredit Internet-based CTE courses. Table 2 shows that an average of 36 Internet-based CTE courses are offered for credit and 67 noncredit Internet-based CTE courses per academic year. The average number of Internet courses offered for credit was higher in urban colleges (47.6) than in community colleges located in suburban areas or large towns (33.9) and rural areas (24.0). The average number of noncredit courses for colleges located in suburban areas or large towns (57.8) was higher than for colleges located in urban (25.6)

and rural areas (16.9). Overall, larger community colleges offered more credit and noncredit Internet-based courses.

Table 3 shows that, on average, community colleges offered 74.8% of their credit CTE courses and 46.6% of their noncredit distance CTE courses via the Internet. These credit and noncredit percentages remained fairly constant across locale. Although larger community colleges tend to offer more courses, there was no significant correlation between institution size and the percentage of credit ($r = -.0046$) and noncredit ($r = -0.05$) Internet-based CTE courses offered.

Table 4 shows the percentage distribution of community colleges offering credit and noncredit CTE courses via the Internet according to the total number of Internet-based courses offered. As a group, 95.1% of community colleges offer credit courses and 41.1% offer noncredit courses. Of the responding community colleges, 52.4% offered 1–25 Internet-based courses for credit, 22.2% offered 26–50, 20.5% offered more than 50 courses, and 4.9% offered no credit CTE Internet courses. Similar numbers were reported for noncredit Internet-based courses. Of the responding colleges, 58.9% offered no noncredit Internet-based courses; while 21.9% offered 1–25 courses and only 19.2% reported offering more than 25 Internet-based courses.

TABLE 2
Average Number of Internet-Based CTE Courses

Institutional Characteristic	Internet-Based CTE CTE Credit Courses		Internet-Based CTE Noncredit Courses	
	n	M	n	M
All Institutions	185	36.0	150	67.0
Region				
East	76	32.2	62	25.5
Midwest	57	41.4	47	57.5
West	52	35.5	41	13.5
Institution Locale				
Urban	69	47.6	61	25.6
Suburban or Large Town	58	33.9	44	57.8
Rural	58	24.0	45	16.9
Institution Size				
1,000 or fewer	11	12.6	9	15.3
1,001–3,000	60	35.9	43	41.6
3,001–10,000	79	32.2	69	14.6
More than 10,000	35	51.6	29	65.7

Note. Of the 206 responding institutions that offer distance CTE, 185 provided CTE credit enrollment numbers, and 151 provided CTE noncredit enrollments for Internet courses.

TABLE 3
Number and Percentage of Community College Distance CTE Courses Offered via Internet

Institutional Characteristic	Internet-Based CTE Credit Courses		Internet-Based CTE Noncredit Courses	
	n	%	n	%
All Institutions	131	74.8	77	46.6
Region				
East	61	70.6	33	58.1
Midwest	39	75.8	27	41.2
West	31	81.8	17	32.8
Institution Locale				
Urban	48	74.3	36	43.7
Suburban or Large Town	39	78.7	19	50.0
Rural	44	71.9	22	48.4
Institution Size				
1,000 or fewer	7	76.3	5	66.0
1,001–3,000	50	75.5	20	35.5
3,001–10,000	50	73.5	40	53.6
More than 10,000	24	74.9	12	33.4

Note. Of the 206 responding institutions that offer distance CTE, 131 provided the total number of distance and Internet CTE credit courses, and 77 provided the total number of distance and Internet CTE courses.

Strategies for Providing Internet-Based CTE

Community colleges were asked for the number of Internet-based CTE courses they offered through external providers or partnerships with colleges and universities. The term "partnership" connotes a sharing of resources for mutual benefit. Community colleges are uniquely positioned to partner with a wide variety of educational, professional, and commercial entities. The obvious focus of such partnerships is to provide enhanced learning opportunities, maximize use of costly infrastructure, and deliver courses to

TABLE 4
Percentage of Internet-Based CTE Credit and Noncredit Courses

Credit Internet Courses	n	None	1–25	26–50	51–100	>100
All Institutions	185	4.9	52.4	22.2	13.5	7.0
Region						
East	76	7.9	50.0	23.7	11.8	6.6
Midwest	57	1.8	54.4	21.1	17.5	5.3
West	52	3.8	53.8	21.2	11.5	9.6
Institution Locale						
Urban	69	5.8	42.0	23.2	18.8	10.1
Suburban or Large Town	58	3.4	46.6	29.3	15.5	5.2
Rural	58	5.2	70.7	13.8	5.2	5.2
Institution Size						
1,000 or fewer	11	0	81.8	18.2	0	0
1,001–3000	16	6.3	62.5	12.5	0	18.8
3,001–10,000	79	5.1	54.4	22.8	12.7	5.1
More than 10,000	35	2.9	28.6	25.7	28.6	14.3

Noncredit Internet Courses	n	None	1–25	26–50	51–100	>100
All Institutions	151	58.9	21.9	6.6	5.3	7.3
Region						
East	62	56.5	21.0	11.3	8.1	3.2
Midwest	47	51.1	31.9	4.3	0	12.8
West	42	71.4	11.9	2.4	7.1	7.1
Institution Locale						
Urban	61	63.9	18.0	3.3	6.6	8.2
Suburban or Large Town	45	55.6	20.0	11.1	2.2	11.1
Rural	45	55.6	28.9	6.7	6.7	2.2
Institution Size						
1,000 or fewer	9	44.4	33.3	11.1	11.1	0
1,001–3,000	9	66.7	11.1	0	0	22.2
3,001–10,000	69	56.5	27.5	5.8	7.2	2.9
More than 10,000	30	66.7	10.0	6.7	0	16.7

Note. Of the 206 responding institutions that offer distance CTE, 185 provided CTE credit enrollment numbers, and 151 provided CTE noncredit enrollments for Internet courses. Row percentages may not add to 100 due to rounding.

under-served populations. Partnerships typically include the community college and entities such as other community colleges, businesses, universities, regional organizations, professional organizations, technical suppliers, high schools, and publishers. One example of a community college partnership is the Illinois Virtual Campus (http://www.ivc.illinois.edu), which consists of 68 institutions delivering 3,500 courses in 115 programs while providing comprehensive support services at a lower cost. Another partnership example is the "Direct Path" program instituted by Rutgers University and three community colleges in order to improve transfer rates by providing increased access to online courses along with support for students and faculty.

Table 5 shows that the responding community colleges offered 16.2% of their Internet-based courses through external providers and 18.9% through external partnerships with colleges and universities. The external provider percentages were fairly consistent across institution locale, while rural colleges (23.2%) outpaced urban (18.6%) and suburban (15.2%) colleges in college/university partnerships. Both external providers and partnerships were related to institution size. Smaller colleges (3,000 or fewer students) tended to provide a higher percentage of their Internet-based courses through external providers and partnerships than did larger colleges (more than 3,000 students). These data suggest that exciting new connections are being made as these participants in education find new ways of partnering to provide services for niche markets.

Table 6 shows the percentage distribution of community colleges providing Internet-based

TABLE 5
Percentage of Internet-Based CTE Courses Provided Through External
Providers and Partnerships

Institutional Characteristic	External Providers		College/University Partnerships	
	n	(%)	*n*	(%)
All Institutions	172	16.2	185	18.9
Region				
East	71	17.6	77	20.3
Midwest	51	14.6	59	20.0
West	50	16.0	49	15.4
Institution Locale				
Urban	68	14.9	70	18.6
Suburban or Large Town	56	16.3	60	15.2
Rural	48	17.9	55	23.2
Institution Size				
1,000 or fewer	9	23.4	12	37.3
1,001–3,000	48	22.0	57	27.4
3,001–10,000	81	14.3	82	11.8
More than 10,000	34	10.8	34	15.2

CTE through external providers and partnerships. Of the responding community colleges that offered CTE distance learning courses, 69.2% offered no Internet-based courses through external partnerships. The distributions were fairly similar across institution locale (urban, 70.6%; suburban, 67.9%; rural, 68.8%) for institutions that offer no Internet-based courses through external providers. Over half of the responding community colleges (53.5%) offered no Internet-based courses through partnerships with colleges and universities. The distributions were fairly similar across institution locale (urban, 60%; suburban, 51.7%; rural, 47.3%), with most institutions using no partnerships for their Internet-based CTE courses.

Internet Technologies Used in Postsecondary CTE

Current technologies in use. The community colleges that offered CTE distance learning courses were asked about the technologies they used in their CTE Internet-based courses. As shown in Table 7, the most frequently used technologies were e-mail (94.3%), course management systems such as Blackboard® and WebCT® (84.2%), and asynchronous discussion lists (64.2%). The least frequently used technologies included high-bandwidth technologies such as desktop videoconferencing (16.1%), voice chat (13.7%), streaming video (37.7%), streaming audio (44.5%), and streaming PowerPoint® (47.3%). Accordingly, a high percentage of community colleges reported no use of high-bandwidth technologies such as desktop videoconferencing (83.9%), voice chat (86.3%), streaming video (62.2%), streaming audio (55.6%), and streaming PowerPoint® (52.7%).

Anticipated utilization of technology. The community colleges that offered CTE distance learning courses were also asked about the technologies they planned to use in their distance CTE courses within the next 3 years. Table 8 and Figure 1 show that the responding community colleges anticipate an increased use of both high-bandwidth and low-bandwidth technologies. Increases in the high-bandwidth technologies include streaming audio/video (87%) and streaming media synchronized with PowerPoint® slides (80.8%), while the low-bandwidth technologies include Internet courses with asynchronous interaction (79.3%), CD-ROM/DVD (77.2%), and asynchronous discussion lists or bulletin boards (72.5%). Most of the responding institutions (81.5%) reported that the use of course management systems is expected to increase.

TABLE 6
Percentage of Internet-Based CTE Courses Provided Through External
Providers and Partnerships

| External Providers | n | None | Number of Courses | | |
			1–25	26–50	51–100
All Institutions	172	69.2	11.0	5.2	14.5
Region					
East	71	64.8	14.1	4.2	16.9
Midwest	51	76.5	3.9	5.9	13.7
West	50	68.0	14.0	6.0	12.0
Institution Locale					
Urban	68	70.6	11.8	5.9	11.8
Suburban or Large Town	56	67.9	14.3	1.8	16.1
Rural	48	68.8	6.3	8.3	16.7
Institution Size					
1,000 or fewer	9	66.7	0	0	33.3
1,001–3,000	48	68.8	4.2	6.3	20.8
3,001–10,000	81	66.7	17.3	3.7	12.3
More than 10,000	34	76.5	8.8	8.8	5.9
Partnerships	n	None	1–25	26–50	51–100
All Institutions	185	53.5	27.0	3.8	15.7
Region					
East	77	54.5	24.7	2.6	18.2
Midwest	59	45.8	35.6	1.7	16.9
West	49	61.2	20.4	8.2	10.2
Institution Locale					
Urban	70	60.0	21.4	2.9	15.7
Suburban or Large Town	60	51.7	33.3	3.3	11.7
Rural	55	47.3	27.3	5.5	20.0
Institution Size					
1,000 or fewer	12	41.7	8.3	16.7	33.3
1,001–3,000	57	43.9	29.8	1.8	24.6
3,001–10,000	82	59.8	29.3	2.4	8.5
More than 10,000	34	58.8	23.5	5.9	11.8

Conclusions and Discussion

Internet-based courses are the most prominent form of distance learning in community college CTE programs, especially in credit courses. It may be useful for benchmarking purposes to know that community colleges teach an average of 36 credit and 67 noncredit CTE courses via the Internet. However, the important finding is the large proportion of the CTE courses taught via distance learning being delivered using the Internet. The Internet courses represent nearly three-fourths of all of their distance credit courses and nearly half of their noncredit courses. Given that the feasibility of using the Internet is a fairly recent

phenomenon, these data show that the community colleges have made significant progress in developing Internet-based courses in a short amount of time. These data also imply that other forms of distance learning delivery (e.g., correspondence courses, interactive television) are being replaced by Internet-based courses.

The findings from this study also show that the use of the Internet for course delivery has increased dramatically in recent years, particularly in CTE programs. This study found that 95.1% of community colleges offer CTE credit courses via the Internet and 41.1% offer noncredit CTE courses via the Internet. In contrast, Green (2000) found that 74% of community

TABLE 7
Percentage of Technology Use in Internet-Based CTE Courses

Distance Learning Technology	n	Ranges of Technology Use				
		0%	1–25%	26–50%	51–75%	76–100%
Low-Bandwidth Technologies						
E-mail	174	2.9	1.7	1.1	0	94.3
Course Management Systems	190	4.2	2.1	4.2	5.3	84.2
Asynchronous Discussion	162	8.0	5.6	6.8	15.4	64.2
Text Chat	136	26.5	38.2	12.5	3.7	19.1
CD-ROM	142	22.5	58.5	8.5	2.8	7.7
High-Bandwidth Technologies						
Streaming Video	127	62.2	29.9	4.7	0	3.1
Streaming Audio	126	55.6	38.1	2.4	1.6	2.4
Streaming PowerPoint®	131	52.7	35.1	9.9	0	2.3
Voice Chat	117	86.3	7.7	2.6	1.7	1.7
Desktop Videoconferencing	118	83.9	15.3	0	0	.8

Note. Table indicates the percentage of responding institutions within ranges of use of a specific technology.

TABLE 8
Future Use of Technologies by Colleges that Currently Offer Distance CTE Courses

Technologies for Distance Learning in CTE	n	Decreased Use	No Change	Increased Use
Low-Bandwidth Technologies				
Course Management Systems (e.g., WebCT®)	200	2.5	16.0	81.5
Internet Courses with Asynchronous Interaction	198	1.5	19.2	79.3
CD-ROM/DVD	184	2.2	20.7	77.2
Asynchronous Discussion Lists or Bulletin Boards	193	2.6	24.9	72.5
E-Mail	191	1.6	29.3	69.1
Synchronous Text Chat	164	6.7	37.8	55.5
Video/Audio Tapes	169	23.1	47.9	29.0
Fax	160	17.5	61.3	21.3
High-Bandwidth Technologies				
Streaming Media (Audio and/or Video)	177	1.7	11.3	87.0
Streaming Media Synchronized with PowerPoint®	172	2.3	16.9	80.8
Internet Courses with Synchronous Interaction	185	8.1	30.3	61.6
Desktop Videoconferencing	166	3.6	37.3	59.0
Two-Way Audio/Two-Way Video	168	6.0	41.4	53.0
One-Way Prerecorded Audio	146	15.8	42.5	41.8
One-Way Prerecorded Video	153	15.7	43.8	40.5
One-Way Live Video	140	17.1	50.0	32.9
Instructional Television	162	20.4	48.1	31.5
Two-Way Audio	144	10.4	61.1	28.5
One-Way Live Audio	140	15.0	58.6	26.4

Note. Table indicates the percentage of responding institutions that projected the use of a specific technology will decrease, increase, or remain the same.

colleges were using the Internet for course delivery. It is important to note that Green's study focused on community college programs and courses in general, while this study focused solely on CTE courses and programs.

Many colleges that offer CTE courses through distance learning are not using the Internet as *a delivery vehicle for non-credit courses.* In spite of the fact that the majority of colleges are using the Internet for the delivery of CTE courses, there are still a number of institutions that offer no CTE courses via the Internet, especially in noncredit CTE courses. Over half of the institutions that offer some form of distance CTE had no Internet-based noncredit courses. It is

Figure 1. Anticipated increases/decreases in the use of technologies for CTE courses offered at a distance.

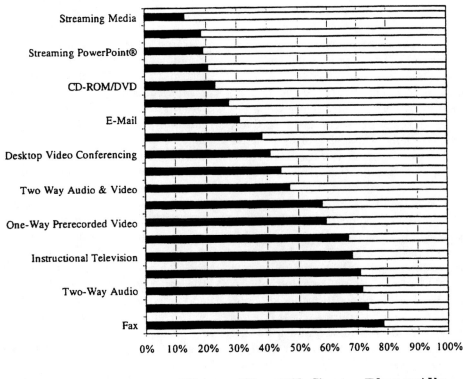

unclear why the community colleges use the Internet for the majority of their credit courses (74.8%) but fewer than half use it for their noncredit courses (46.6%). The data clearly show that the lack of Internet-based noncredit courses is neither a function of institution size or locale. The differentiation between credit and noncredit courses might be the result of having more noncredit courses (67 per institution) than credit courses (36 per institution) already developed for "traditional" distance delivery, and it could be too costly in terms of time and money to redesign courses for the Internet when they are already effective in their current format. It could also be that many of the noncredit courses are standardized for certification purposes (e.g., Microsoft or Cisco training) and modification of the courses is outside the authority of the college faculty. If part-time faculty are the ones most likely to teach the noncredit courses, then it is possible that they have neither the time, the expertise, nor the authority to redesign courses for Internet delivery. It is also possible that the noncredit courses are more skill-based than the credit courses, which may make them less feasible to offer online. More research is needed to determine why the noncredit CTE courses are less prevalent in distance learning.

Community colleges are partnering with external providers (eg., commercial vendors) and other colleges and universities to make credit and noncredit CTE courses available to students. According to the survey findings, nearly one third of all credit and noncredit courses were made available to students via external providers and more than half of the colleges had established partnerships with other colleges and universities. Smaller community colleges (those with 3,000 or fewer students) used this service more than the larger institutions.

Faced with competitive markets, businesses frequently form joint ventures as a way to share strengths and pool resources (Pocorobba, 1999). Community colleges are forming partnerships with external providers and other colleges and universities for similar reasons. They may enter into a simple partnership with a software provider to develop a set of courses (Rinear, 2002) or they may enter into a complex partnership by becoming members of a multi-institution consortium that may be regional, national, or international in scope. According to the NCES (2003), 60% of 2-year institutions that offered distance learning courses in 2000–2001 participated in some type of distance learning consortium (state, system, regional, national, or international).

Internet-based CTE courses in the community college currently rely on low-bandwidth technologies. Although community colleges are actively involved in the delivery of CTE courses using the Internet, they are using what can be classified as "low-bandwidth" technologies. The most common technologies being used in Internet-based CTE courses are course management systems, e-mail, text chat, and asynchronous discussion. What is lacking in these technologies is the ability to incorporate multimedia and real-time exchange of information among individuals or groups within a course. Very few of the colleges are using the high-bandwidth technologies in their Internet-based CTE courses. These types of technologies include streaming audio and video that may be synchronized with presentations (e.g., PowerPoint®), real-time voice chat, and desktop videoconferencing. By taking advantage of fast connection speeds, these technologies make it possible to include multimedia and real-time exchanges of voice and images.

Why aren't the community colleges taking advantage of the cutting edge technologies in their CTE Internet-based courses? There are likely a variety of reasons for this. First, numerous studies comparing traditional classroom-based instruction with technology-supported instruction have found no significant differences on critical educational variables such as learning outcomes and student satisfaction (Russell, 1999). Those involved in the field of instructional technology now conclude that the technology used in an online program is not as important as other instructional factors, such as pedagogy and course design (Phipps & Merisotis, 1999). Just because a technology is not "cutting-edge" does not mean that it is not an effective tool for education. The colleges may also have purposely selected low-bandwidth technologies with the end user in mind. High-bandwidth technologies demand a fast connection speed for the end user as well as a computer that has a fast processor and lots of memory and file storage space. Incorporating high-bandwidth technologies into CTE courses may prevent students from participating because they do not have access to the computers or Internet connections needed to support these more advanced technologies. Since the colleges are using distance learning to attract nontraditional students, their decision to design their distance learning courses around the lowest common denominator is probably an appropriate choice.

Growth is expected in virtually all forms of Internet-based CTE courses and technologies within the next 3 years. Most community colleges expect to see continued growth in the development and delivery of Internet-based CTE courses. These future courses will see expanded use of course management systems, asynchronous discussion technologies, CD-ROM/DVD for the delivery of course content, and streaming media for delivery of live or recorded audio and video. It can be expected that the CTE courses taught via distance learning in the future will rely less on the exchange of audio and video tapes, fax machines, instructional television, and one-way live audio or video.

A significant portion of community college CTE courses is offered via distance learning. Distance courses, on average, comprised nearly one fifth of the total credit and one fifth of the noncredit CTE courses offered at community colleges. These numbers suggest that both credit and noncredit programs have made inroads in the development of distance CTE courses. Since current and previous NCES distance learning studies focused solely on credit-granting courses, the data from this study become the first to illuminate the extent to which the noncredit offerings on the community college campus are provided through distance learning. More research needs to be directed towards this understudied area.

Notes

[1]For the sake of brevity, the term "community college" will be used generically to include not only community colleges, but also technical institutes and junior colleges.

References

Allen, I. E., & Seaman, J. (2003). *Sizing the opportunity: The quality and extent of online education in the United States, 2002, 2003.* Needham, MA: SCOLE. Retrieved May 10, 2004 from http://www.sloac.-c.org

American Association for Public Opinion Research. (2000). *Standard definitions: Final dispositions of case codes and outcome rates for surveys.* Retrieved on December 5, 2002, from http://www.aapor.org/pdfs/newstandarddefinitions.pdf

Association for Career and Technical Education. (2003). *What's career and technical education?* Retrieved October 1, 2003, from http://www.acteonline.org/career_tech/

Dougherty, K. J., & Bakia, M. F. (1999, November). *The new economic development role of the community college.* New York: Columbia University, Community College Research Center.

Green, K. C. (2000). *The 2000 national survey of information technology in U.S. higher education.* Encino, CA: The Campus Computing Project.

Grubb, W. N. (1996). *Working in the middle.* San Francisco: Jossey-Bass.

Lever-Duffy, J., Lemke, R., & Johnson, L. (1996). *Learning without limits: Model distance education programs in community colleges.* Mission Viejo, CA: League for Innovation in the Community College.

Meyer, K. A. (2002). Quality in Distance Education: Focus on On-Line Learning. *ASHE-ERIC Higher Education Report, 29*(4), 1–121.

Milliron, M., & Miles, C. (Eds.). (2000). *Taking a big picture look @ technology, learning, and the community college.* Mission Viejo, CA: League for Innovation in the Community College and the Miami-Dade (FL) Community College District.

National Center for Education Statistics. (2000). *Distance education at postsecondary education institutions: 1997–1998* (NCES Publication No. 2000-013). Washington, DC: U.S. Government Printing Office.

National Center for Education Statistics. (2002). *A profile of participation in distance education: 1999–2000* (NCES Publication No. 2003–154). Washington, DC: U.S. Government Printing Office.

National Center for Education Statistics. (2003). *Distance education at degree-granting postsecondary institutions: 2000–2001* (NCES Publication No. 2003–017). Washington, DC: U.S. Government Printing Office.

Nock, M., & Shults, C. (2001). Hot programs at community colleges. *AACC Research Brief* (AACC-RB-01-4). (ERIC Document Reproduction Service E*Subscribe, ERIC No. ED456883)

Phipps, R., & Merisotis, J. (1999, April). *What's the difference? A review of contemporary research on the effectiveness of distance learning in higher education.* Washington, DC: The Institute for Higher Education Policy. Retrieved October 1, 2003, from http://www.ihep.com/Pubs/PDF/Difference.pdf

Phipps, R., & Merisotis, J. (2000). Quality on the line: Benchmarks for success in internet-based distance education. Institute for Higher Education Policy [Online]. Retrieved May 13, 2004, from http://www.ihep.com/quality.pdf

Pocorobba, J. S. (1999). Schools team up for technology. *American School & University, 72*(3), 309–311.

Reese, S. (2002). Breaking the stereotype. *Techniques, 77*(1), 24–25.

Rinear, K. (2002). Different kinds of partnerships: One size doesn't fit all. *Distance Education Report, 6*(13), 3.

Russell, T. (1999). *The no significant difference phenomenon.* Montgomery, AL: International Distance Education Certification Center.

Synergy Plus. (2002). *The role of distance learning in vocational education.* Retrieved April 10, 2003, from http://www.itcnetwork.org/DuboisVocEdFeb2002.pdf

Villadsen, A., & Gennett, N. (1997). Providing short-term educational programs: Welfare reform and one-stop centers. *Leadership Abstracts, 10*(10). Retrieved December 18, 2002, from http://www.league.org/publication/abstracts/leadership/labs1097.htm

Author Note

The work reported herein was supported under the National Research Center for Career and Technical Education, PR/Award (No. VO51A990006), as administered by the Office of Vocational and Adult Education, U.S. Department of Education. The contents do not necessarily represent the positions or policies of the Office of Vocational and Adult Education or the U.S. Department of Education, and you should not assume endorsement by the Federal Government.

Scott D. Johnson is Professor and Head, Department of Human Resource Education, University of Illinois, 1310 South Sixth Street, Champaign, IL 61820. Johnson may be reached by phone at (217) 333-0807 or by e-mail at sjohnson@uiuc.edu.

Angela Benson is Assistant Professor, Department of Human Resource Education, University of Illinois, 1310 South Sixth Street, Champaign, IL 61820. Benson may be reached by phone at (217) 333-0807 or by e-mail at abenson@uiuc.edu.

John Duncan, Olga N. Shinkareva, Gail Diane Taylor, and **Tod Treat** are Ph.D. candidates and graduate research assistants in the Department of Human Resource Education, University of Illinois, 1310 South Sixth Street, Champaign, IL 61820. They can be reached by phone at (217) 333-0807.

CHAPTER 27

RECOMMENDED READINGS AND WEB-BASED RESOURCES

Recommended Readings

Ignash, J. & Townsend, B. K. (2000). Evaluating state-level articulation agreements according to good practice. *Community College Review, 28*(3), 1–12.

Wassmer, R., Moore, C., & Shulock, N. (2004). Effect of racial/ethnic composition on transfer rates in community colleges: Implications for policy and practice. *Research in Higher Education, 45*(6), 651–672.

Shaw, K. M., & London, H. B. (2001). Culture and ideology in keeping transfer commitment: Three community colleges. *The Review of Higher Education, 25*(1), 91–114.

Levin, J. S. (2004, Fall). The community college as a baccalaureate-granting institution. *Review of Higher Education, 28*(1), 1–22.

Ward, C. (2001). A lesson from the British polytechnics for American community colleges. *Community College Review, 29*(2), 151–163.

Perin, D. (2001, April). Academic-occupational integration as a reform strategy for the community college: Classroom perspectives. *Teachers College Record, 103*(2), 303–335.

Bragg, D. (1995). Linking high schools to postsecondary institutions: The role of tech prep. In W. Norton Grubb (Ed.), *Education through occupations in American high schools,* Volume II (pp. 191–211). New York: Teachers College Press.

Orr, T. (1998). Integrating secondary schools and community colleges through school-to-work transition and education reform. *Journal of Vocational Education Research, 23*(2), 93–113.

Dougherty, K., & Bakia, M. (2000, February). Community colleges and contract training. *Teachers College Record, 102,* 197–243.

Shaw, K. (1997). Remedial education as an ideological battleground: Emerging remedial education policies in the community colleges. *Educational Evaluation and Policy Analysis, 19*(3), 284–296.

Curry, M. J. (2001). Preparing to be privatized: The hidden curriculum of a community college ESL writing class. In E. Margolis (Ed.), *The hidden curriculum in higher education* (pp. 175–192). New York: Routledge.

Web-Based Resources

Adelman, C. (1999). *Answers in the Toolbox: Academic Intensity, Attendance Patterns, and Bachelor's Degree Attainment.* U.S. Department of Education, Office of Educational Research and Improvement. Washington, DC: U.S. Government Printing Office. *http://www.ed.gov/pubs/Toolbox/index.html*

U. S. Government Accountability Office. (2004, October). *Public community colleges and technical schools: Most schools use both credit and noncredit programs for workforce development* [GAO-05-4]. Washington, DC: Author. *http://www.gao.gov/new.items/d054.pdf*

Jenkins, D., & Boswell, K. (2002). *State policies on community college remedial education: Findings from a national survey.* Boulder, CO: Education Commission of the States. *http://www.communitycollegepolicy.org/pdf/html/top.asp?page=/html/publications_main.asp*

Karp, M. M., Bailey, T., Hughes, K., & Fermin, B. J. (2004, September). *State dual enrollment policies: Addressing access and quality.* Washington DC: U.S. Department of Education, Office of Vocational and Adult Education. *http://www.tc.columbia.edu/Publications.asp?UID=323*

Part V

FACULTY

INTRODUCTION

BARBARA K. TOWNSEND

Two-year college faculty constitute over 40% of all postsecondary faculty (NCES, 2001). One reason this group is so large is because it contains many part-time faculty. Over two-thirds of community college faculty are part-time (Cohen & Brawer, 2003); in 1998 these part-time faculty constituted 44% of all part-time faculty nationally (NCES, 2001). That same year full-time community college faculty were 18% of all full-time faculty (NCES, 2001).

For a faculty so large, relatively little is known about them because they are understudied as a group. Most studies of faculty, such as Bowen and Schuster's (1986) *Academic Professors* and Finkelstein, Seal, and Schuster's (1998) *The New Academic Generation*, focus on four-year college and university faculty. When community college faculty are included in faculty studies, they may be treated as different and even deficient because they are not like four-year faculty. For example, Clark (1987) in *Academic Life: Small Worlds, Different Worlds* asked about teaching at a community college: "Could there be a separate academic occupation here, one not far from schoolteaching in its general character?" (p. 21).

A few scholars have authored books focusing only on community college faculty. In the 1970s Cohen and Brawer examined them in two national studies: *Confronting Identity: The Community College Instructor* (1972) and *The Two-Year College Instructor Today* (1977). In the 1980s Seidman (1985) wrote up a series of interviews with community college faculty in his book *In the Words of the Faculty*. The next major study of community college faculty was Grubb and Associates' (1999) *Honored but Invisible: An Inside Look at Teaching in Community Colleges*, a qualitative study that examined the teaching of both arts and sciences faculty and occupational-technical faculty. Outcalt (2002), partially replicating Cohen and Brawer's 1977 study, surveyed faculty for his *Profile of the Community College Professorate*.

Grubb and Associates' (1999) book, as well as Seidman's (1985), were national qualitative studies of two-year college faculty. Occasionally an ethnography has included a close look at a particular institution's faculty as part of examining how a community college's culture affects its students. The most well known are London's (1978) *Culture of a Community College* and Weis's (1985) *Between Two Worlds: Black Students in an Urban Community College*.

With the development of government-sponsored national surveys of faculty, such as the National Study of Postsecondary Faculty (NSOPF), two-year college faculty have been included in national surveys. Thus a number of journal articles about community college faculty rely on government-collected survey data. Several of the chapters and recommended works in this part of the Reader use NSOPF data. Data from NSOPF:93 are used in Chapter 30, where Perna (2003), in "The Status of Women and Minorities Among Community College Faculty," examines certain employment experiences of women and minority full- and part-time faculty, and in the recommended article, "Dimensions of the Community College Faculty Labor Market," by Gahn and Twombly (2001), where they examine the community college faculty labor market. In the selection "Internet Access and Use of the Web for Instruction: A National Study of Full-Time and Part-Time Community College Faculty"

(Chapter 32), Akroyd, Jaeger, Jackowski, and Jones (2004) use NSOPF:99 data to focus on how much access full- and part-time faculty have to the Internet and how this access, or lack thereof, may affect their instructional use of the web. Palmer's (2002) study, "Disciplinary Variations in the Work of Full-time Faculty Members," listed in Chapter 33, Recommended Readings, also uses NSOPF:99 data to look at disciplinary variations among full-time faculty in such areas as employment histories, instructional methods, and assessment of students.

The U.S. Department of Education's National Center for Education Statistics is not the only group to sponsor national surveys of faculty. So also has the U. S. Department of Education grant-funded National Center for Postsecondary Improvement, which conducted a survey of community college faculty in 1997 to determine their attitudes and trends. The findings from this survey are available on the web in a report by Huber (1998), "Community College Faculty Attitudes and Trends, 1997," listed in Chapter 33.

Individual researchers have also conducted their own national surveys of community college faculty to study a variety of issues. Included in this part are two studies: the already mentioned study by Akroyd et al. (2004) about the extent of Internet access and instructional use of the web, and a study by Roueche, Roueche, & Milliron (1996) about practices surrounding part-time faculty. Their study is "In the Company of Strangers: Addressing the Utilization and Integration of Part-time Faculty in American Community Colleges" (Chapter 31). Two recommended readings that used national surveys are Murray's (2001) "Faculty Development in Publicly Supported 2-Year Colleges," which is about the nature and extent of faculty development activities, and Olson, Jensrud, & McCann's (2001) study about state-level requirements for preparation and credentialing of technical faculty. This last study, "Preparation and Credentialing Requirements of Two-Year College Technical Instructors: A National Study," is available on the web (see Chapter 33).

Occasionally a qualitative study published in article form has looked closely at community college faculty. Two such studies are included here. Twombly (2004), in "Looking for Signs of Community College Arts and Science Faculty Professionalization in Searches: An Alternative Approach to a Vexing Question," conducted a case study of three community colleges in one region of the country to examine the concept of faculty professionalization as seen in these colleges' search process for arts and sciences faculty. Twombly's study (Chapter 28) continues the dialogue about the professionalization of community college faculty that was prominent in Cohen and Brawer's books on community college faculty and updated in Outcalt's (2002) more recent work. The qualitative study conducted by Wolfe and Strange (2004), "Academic Life at the Franchise: Faculty Culture in a Rural Two-Year Branch Campus" (Chapter 29), had a broader focus—faculty culture—but in a particular kind of two-year college: a rural branch campus of a university. This study is included for several reasons: its recent examination of faculty culture, its focus on a rural two-year school, and its setting of a branch campus, an understudied subset of two-year colleges.

The chapters included in this part of the Reader illustrate several key points about community college faculty. First of all, since a significant percentage is part-time, this group merits being studied in its own right, as Roueche, Roueche, & Milliron (1996) do in Chapter 31. Community college faculty also merit being included in studies about women and minority faculty (see Perna's (2003) Chapter 30), in studies about faculty use of technology (see Akroyd et al.'s (2004) Chapter 32), and in studies about faculty culture at a particular campus (see Wolfe & Strange's (2004) Chapter 29). Community college faculty's demographic diversity is also made apparent through Perna's study, as is their disciplinary diversity through her distinction between career and academic faculty. This distinction is indirectly apparent through Twombly's (2004) focus only on arts and science faculty in her examination of the concept of professionalization. Wolfe and Strange are more direct about this distinction, as they describe disciplinary differences, particularly as they relate to job responsibilities. Finally, the dominance of the teaching role shines forth in all the works, including those listed in Chapter 33, Recommended Readings and Web-Based Resources.

Community college faculty—whether full- or part-time, female or male, white or non-white—are teachers above all else. Educating almost half of all entering undergraduates and almost 40 percent of all undergraduates, they have a significant and sometimes unappreciated effect upon all of higher education. They also merit greater attention and research.

References

Akroyd, D., Jaeger, A., Jackowski, M., & Jones, L. C. (2004). Internet access and the use of the web for instruction: A national study of full-time and part-time community college faculty. *Community College Review, 32*(1), 40–51.

Bowen, H. R., & Schuster, J. H. (1986). *American professors: A national resource imperiled.* New York: Oxford University Press.

Clark, B. R. (1987). *The academic life: Small worlds, different worlds.* Princeton, NJ: Carnegie Foundation for the Advancement of Teaching.

Cohen, A. M., & Brawer, F. B. (1972). *Confronting identity: The community college instructor.* Englewood Cliffs, NJ: Prentice Hall.

Cohen, A. M., & Brawer, F. B. (1977). *The two-year college instructor today.* New York: Praeger.

Cohen, A. M., & Brawer, F. B. (2003). *The American community college* (4th ed.). San Francisco: Jossey-Bass.

Finkelstein, M. J., Seal, R. K., & Schuster, J. H. (1998). *The new academic generation: A profession in transformation.* Baltimore: Johns Hopkins University Press.

Gahn, S., & Twombly, S. B. (2001). Dimensions of the community college faculty labor market. *The Review of Higher Education, 24*(3), 259–282.

Grubb, N., & Associates (1999). *Honored but invisible: An inside look at teaching in the community college.* New York: Routledge.

Huber, M. T. (1998). Community college faculty attitudes and trends, 1997. Stanford, CA: National Center for Postsecondary Improvement, Stanford University.

London, H. B. (1978). *The culture of a community college.* New York: Praeger.

Murray, J. P. (2001). Faculty development in publicly supported 2-year colleges. *Community College Journal of Research and Practice, 25*, 487–502.

National Center for Education Statistics (September 2001). *Institutional policies and practices: Results from the 1999 National Study of Postsecondary Faculty, Institutional Study.* U.S. Department of Education: Office of Educational Research and Improvement. NCES 2001-201.

Olson, S. J., Jensrud, Q., & McCann, P. L. (2001). Preparation and credentialing requirements of two-year college technical instructors: A national study. *Journal of Industrial Teacher Education, 38*(2). http://scholar.lib.vt.edu/ejournals/JITE/v38n2/olson.html

Outcalt, C. L. (2002). *A profile of the community college professorate.* New York: Routledge Falmer.

Palmer, J. C. (2002). Disciplinary variations in the work of full-time faculty members. In C. Outcalt (Ed.), *Community college faculty: Characteristics, practices, and challenges* (pp. 9–19). New Directions for Community Colleges, No. 118. San Francisco: Jossey-Bass.

Perna, L. (2003, April). The status of women and minorities among community college faculty. *Research in Higher Education, 44*(2), 205–240.

Roueche, J. E., Roueche, S. D., & Milliron, M. D. (1996). In the company of strangers: Addressing the utilization and integration of part-time faculty in American community colleges. *Community College Journal of Research and Practice, 20*(2), 105–118.

Seidman, E. (1985). *In the words of the faculty.* San Francisco: Jossey-Bass.

Twombly, S. B. (2004). Looking for signs of community college arts and science faculty professionalization in searches: An alternative approach to a vexing question. *Community College Review, 32*(1), 21–39.

Weis, L. (1985). *Between two worlds: Black students in an urban community college.* Boston: Routledge & Kegan Paul.

Wolfe, J. R., & Strange, C. C. (2002). Academic life at the franchise: Faculty culture in a rural two-year branch campus. *The Review of Higher Education, 26*(3), 343–362.

CHAPTER 28

LOOKING FOR SIGNS OF COMMUNITY COLLEGE ARTS AND SCIENCES FACULTY PROFESSIONALIZATION IN SEARCHES: AN ALTERNATIVE APPROACH TO A VEXING QUESTION

SUSAN B. TWOMBLY

Several recent studies have addressed the question of whether and to what extent community college faculty are professionalized or constitute a separate or unique profession (Braxton & Bayer 1998; Outcalt, 2002; Palmer, 1992). On the one hand, authors such as Palmer (1992) seek to establish that community college teaching has achieved the necessary characteristics to constitute a unique profession, while others such as Clark (1987) view college teaching as an academic profession with different degrees of professionalization depending on institutional type. Definitions of professionalism as applied to community college faculty have varied and have included such elements as control over the type and number of students taught, access to professional development opportunities, availability of professional colleagues (Garrison, 1967), self-management, independence, self-evaluation, provision of discrete services (Cohen & Brawer, 1991), engagement in scholarly activities (Palmer, 1992), and norms (Braxton & Bayer, 1998). Even though authors agree that some markers of professionalization, such as norms surrounding teaching practices, exist, most are unwilling to conclude that community college teaching constitutes a unique profession. In fact, Outcalt (2002) argues that the community college faculty is more fragmented than ever. That is, he does not see the existence of a common identity among community college faculty. Likewise, Grubb (1999) argues that community colleges claim to be teaching colleges while doing little to encourage the profession of teaching.

In this study the researcher argues that much can be learned about where community college teaching stands as a profession by examining faculty searches. The search process serves as the window through which to examine the rules guiding the hiring process, the critical process in a labor market through which prospective faculty are linked with jobs (Granovetter, 1974). In the process of opening a faculty position, creating a job description, determining mechanisms for recruiting, identifying and applying criteria for screening candidates, and making a final selection, an institution reveals both how it acts on its values and the values of the profession. By examining faculty searches, crucial elements of the academic profession in community colleges can be identified. This study is limited to faculty in arts and sciences fields, as professionalization issues may be different for faculty in occupational fields.

Conceptual Framework

The conceptual framework guiding this study comes from Burton Clark's seminal *The Academic Life: Small Worlds, Different Worlds* (1987). Clark believes several dimensions of the academic profession along which faculty work in various types of institutions can be analyzed. First, Clark makes the argument that research is the defining component of the academic profession because conducting research gives professors power to determine important parameters of their work environment, such as what subjects are taught, whom they teach, and what they research. The alternative is control by administrators. Second, he argues that the academic profession is built on a disciplinary base that exerts a strong influence over the work life of faculty. Third, professionalization in higher education is driven by difference and hierarchy. Clark argues that commonness, similarity, and equality work against professionalization. He says, "In the schools, the professionals were 'teachers,' similar and equal. In higher education, they were 'professors,' dissimilar and—not to worry—unequal" (p. 54). Fourth, the nature of academic work varies widely depending on disciplinary and institutional affiliation, with some institutions emphasizing teaching and others emphasizing research. Fifth, belief, commitment, and interest are important aspects of faculty culture that help define the academic profession. Do faculty identify with their institutions or with their disciplines? Further, there are specific ideologies of the academic profession, such as the constant search for knowledge, the norm of academic honesty, and the importance of academic freedom. Do these norms obtain among community college faculty? If not, what anchoring ideologies define teaching in community colleges? Sixth, the degree of authority held by the faculty to control their work lives is an important dimension of professionalism. Seventh, the academic profession offers the promise of a career. That is, faculty begin to see themselves as neophyte disciplinary experts in graduate school where they become initiated into the norms and expectations of a discipline and an academic career. The academic career involves choice of an institutional setting that, in turn, shapes the career. And eighth, disciplinary associations play an important role in professionalism.

Not surprisingly, community college faculty did not fare very well in Clark's (1987) study of the academic profession based on the ideal of the research university. In fact, Clark describes community college faculty as "positioned at the extreme" (p. 203) and as being closer to public school teachers than to their university counterparts. With respect to academic work, he finds institutional mandates diminishing the role of disciplines. For example, community colleges do not hire PhDs with narrow disciplinary interests. Faculty are heavily involved in serving nonpermanent and nonelite clienteles in lower division courses, and they are heavily involved in remedial work and serving the community. Moreover, Clark argues that faculty control over work conditions in community colleges is substantially diminished, and the role of bureaucracy and unions are more prevalent. He concludes, "Astute observers have argued cogently that community college faculty are not in a position to follow the cosmopolitan road to professionalism so heavily traveled by university professors: The community college faculty disciplinary affiliation is weak, the institutions' demands for scholarship are practically nonexistent, and the teaching loads are too heavy for that form of professionalism to occur" (p. 243). In fact, Clark suggests that community college teachers will either become more like public school teachers, a status he considers to be less professional than university teaching, or they will find a way to become more like faculty in research universities. Paradoxically, Clark finds more commitment to an anchoring ideology—belief in open access and success for all students—among community college faculty than he finds in other types of colleges, such as comprehensive colleges and universities. That is, community college faculty know, and are committed to, the open-access mission of the community college, whereas the mission of some other types of colleges may be less clear, therefore resulting in less commitment on the part of faculty to one clearly identified value.

This researcher is by no means an apologist for Clark's negative depiction of community college faculty. In using his work to frame this study, his specific conclusions about community college faculty are less important than are the eight elements of the academic profession he identified, which provide a comprehensive framework for examining professionalization in higher education.

Using Clark's conception of the academic profession as a beginning point, this study addresses the question: What can faculty searches tell us about professionalization of community college faculty, particularly about those dimensions of the academic profession identified by Clark?

Methods

A case study of the values, policies, and practices guiding the search process for full-time arts and sciences faculty in three community colleges served as the source of data for this study. As Lofland and Lofland (1995) note, a case study provides a means to study a phenomenon holistically, taking into account institutional context. The three community colleges included in this study were selected based on size, location, and accessibility to the researcher. One college was chosen from a large suburban area, one from a medium-sized town, and one from a rural area. Location and size were key variables in choosing sites because of the potential effect of proximity to labor pools and because of the size of faculty. Each study site also had to have hired more than five full-time instructors in the last 5 years. One of the colleges chosen was a charter member of the League for Innovation in the Community Colleges, which is the closest to a group of "elite" community colleges as there is in the community college world.

Within each site, purposive sampling was utilized to select interviewees. Interviewees included the president, the personnel director, deans of hiring units, and chairs of hiring committees for recent searches in transfer programs at each college. The researcher also interviewed some recently hired full-time arts and sciences faculty members (two at Rural Community College, two at Oil County Community College and six at Suburban County Community College). Following Burke's (1988) interview protocol, the researcher asked questions about where and how positions were advertised, what qualifications were listed as required and preferred, and what factors distinguished selected candidates from those not selected. To analyze data, the researcher first conducted within-case analyses of data using the constant comparative method (Merriam, 1998) looking for themes within major topics, for example, recruiting and interviewing. These data were then used to construct a narrative description of each campus. Cases were compared to identify common themes and emerging patterns inductively. This paper pre-sents the results of the cross-case analyses identifying common patterns among institutions regarding hiring of faculty in transfer programs.

Several limitations of the study must be mentioned. First, the study was based on three community colleges in one particular region of the country resulting in findings that may be particular to this region. Second, this study focuses only on those aspects of the profession that can be assessed through the search process. And importantly, this study was based on participants' recollections and perceptions of searches as they remembered them. Multiple sources of data were used to establish the consistency of perceptions and behaviors, but the researcher neither participated in nor observed searches in process. No follow up was done to ascertain whether hired faculty were in fact effective teachers.

The Colleges

Rural Community College. Rural Community College (RCC) is located in the small community of Rural, Midwest State, population 850. It sits in the northeast corner of the state about 30 miles from the nearest city of any size. It offers courses at 32 sites in eight counties and a major service center halfway between the state capital and State University. The total approximate population of the service area in 2000 was 106,721 (U.S. Census Bureau, 2004). In 1999 RCC enrolled 789 full-time and 1920 part-time students (National Center for Education Statistics, 2001). RCC offers primarily transfer programs and does not have a comprehensive array of technical and occupational programs. As of February 2001, RCC had 34 full-time and 204 part-time faculty members. Since it is small, RCC is centrally organized. At the time of this researcher's visit, the organizational structure included the president (who subsequently left the college), a dean of instruction (vacant when this researcher visited), an assistant dean of instruction, and various program coordinators. The administrative assistant to the president handled human resource functions. The president made the final hiring decisions with final approval from the board of trustees. RCC usually conducts one or two searches per year to fill full-time positions.

Oil County Community College. Oil County Community College (OCCC) is located in a small city about 20 miles northeast of a major city. Just off the Midwest State Turnpike, OCCC is easily accessible. OCCC serves a five-county area in the south central part of the state with a total population of 90,000 (U.S. Census Bureau, 2001). OCCC offers courses at five major centers and other smaller locations in the five-county area, and it works in conjunction with two nearby universities to provide services to two other counties on request. In 2001, OCCC had 137 full-time faculty members and 433 part-time or adjunct faculty. OCCC enrolled 2,263 full-time and 4,903 part-time students in the fall of 1999 (National Center for Education Statistics, 2001). As a medium-sized community college, OCCC's administrative structure and resulting authority for faculty hiring is relatively decentralized. A vice president for academic affairs and five deans oversee the college's transfer and occupational academic units. The office of human resources handles faculty searches and reports to the vice president for finance. During the past 5 years, OCCC had conducted approximately 40 searches to fill full-time faculty positions. Deans make the final hiring decisions with approval from the vice president of academic affairs and consent of board of trustees.

Suburban County Community College. The third college in this study, Suburban County Community College (SCCC), is somewhat different from the other community colleges in the state. A member of the League for Innovation, it is twice the size of OCCC and 10 times the size of RCC. It is located in an affluent suburb of a major metropolitan area. The host county is home to several national white-collar service industries. The population of the county is approximately 451,000—a 27% increase since 1990 (U.S. Census Bureau, 2001).

Like OCCC, Suburban County Community College offers a full complement of transfer and technical programs and enrolled 4,500 full-time students and 11,000 part-time students in 1999 (National Center for Education Statistics, 2001). In fall 2001, SCCC employed 291 full-time teaching faculty members and approximately 460 part-time faculty. Due to its size, SCCC has a more elaborate organizational structure than the other two colleges. For example, the organizational chart includes the president, executive vice president for academic affairs, vice president for administrative affairs, vice president for student affairs, vice president for instruction, deans, and academic directors. Deans oversee the academic

divisions and make the final hiring decisions with approval of the vice president for instruction and consent of the board of trustees. Estimates of the number of yearly searches for full-time faculty varied from a high of 10 % of all full-time positions, or about 29 individual searches, to a low of 6 or 9 searches per year.

Results

The findings are organized around the eight elements of professionalism identified by Clark, although there clearly is overlap among several elements, namely research orientation, disciplinary affiliation, and academic work.

Research

Community colleges are weak on research almost by definition. Their mission as teaching colleges is well known and trumpeted, if not supported, by the research (see, for example, Grubb, 1999). Conversely, research is not emphasized, a point that is discussed more fully in relation to academic work. A dean at OCCC summarized the value placed on teaching: "Teaching is what we are all about. Our people do research, but someone could come here or any other community college and never do research. If they're an excellent teacher, we're going to keep them because that's what we do." Thus, search and selection criteria emphasize teaching and downplay research. For example, despite an excess of individuals with PhDs in certain fields, the community colleges in this study list the master's degree, or in some cases 18 graduate hours in the teaching field, as the required qualification. Only one of the three colleges even lists the PhD, the quintessential degree signaling research competence, as preferred. The master's degree is recognized as an appropriate degree for the demands of the community college because faculty are expected to be generalists who are able to teach lower division courses as well as occasionally teach outside their specific discipline and because they are not expected to do research.

SCCC lists the PhD as a preferred qualification but seemingly more for symbolic reasons than for reasons related to the nature of the job. As one administrator said, "That [PhD] puts a certain stamp of acceptance on you. And, community colleges have, I think, throughout their history felt like they were perceived as high schools with ashtrays. And one of the ways you get around that . . . is to say we have quite a few PhDs here." Thus, while community colleges may support scholarly activities, such as conference presentations, the colleges in this study do not seek research skills in the search process. In fact, as one faculty association president noted, "We've not been impressed frankly with lots of people who've done lots of publishing, who've done a lot of journal writing and who've done lots of grant writing and . . . we need people here who are real teachers." Despite an excess of PhDs in some fields and a popular belief that community colleges would hire PhDs if they could, only 2 of the 10 recently hired faculty interviewed for this study held a PhD although a couple were ABD.

In summary, the community colleges in this study do not emphasize research and do not seek faculty who are researchers.

Disciplinary Base

Clark argues that the academic profession is built on a disciplinary base. Faculty work and norms for scholarship are based on close affiliation with a group of scholars outside the institution. Outcalt (2002) has argued that community college faculty have become more discipline oriented through establishment of community college branches of disciplinary associations. As one might expect, discipline plays a major organizing role in the search process for full-time faculty. That is, faculty search committees are organized around discipline, although this is difficult at small colleges, and candidates are typically expected to have a master's degree with 18 graduate hours in the teaching field or discipline. Moreover, they are expected to be committed to that discipline; as one dean stated, "We're looking for somebody who has a true love for their discipline and who is excited about it. Sometimes you can see that in their cover letters."

Beyond these expectations, there is little evidence that strength of disciplinary affiliation matters in the search process. In fact, there seems to be a "soft" approach to discipline, as faculty are often expected to teach introductory courses in subjects outside but related to their discipline. RCC's president explained, "For example, our physics instructors will also teach astronomy and maybe geology. The chemistry person might teach earth sciences." This more flexible approach to discipline seems to apply also to the largest, wealthiest community college in the study as

well as to the smaller ones. An SCCC faculty member who does have a PhD in English admitted that he likes the more general approach at the community college. He can now be a humanist and teach English, history, and Western Civilization, whereas he believes he would be more boxed in at a four-year university.

Another factor that potentially weakens disciplinary emphasis in community colleges is that, at least for the three colleges in this study, the master's or doctoral degree can be in another field, such as education, as long as one has the requisite number of graduate hours in the discipline. Membership or involvement in disciplinary associations is not a major concern of search committees, but that is not to say that such participation is unimportant in faculty work. Its role may be weaker than in other sectors, however.

Difference and Hierarchy

According to Clark, one of the reasons K-12 teaching is considered less of a profession than university teaching is because there is little difference in status among teachers, whereas there is a great deal of difference among professors at research universities. There are a couple of ways of assessing this aspect of professionalism through the faculty search process. First, there is a great deal of commonness to the search process itself. Each college uses a template for advertising positions, and the process is tightly controlled by the human resources offices, which follow Equal Employment Opportunity guidelines carefully. At RCC, search committees are expected to ask all candidates in a given search exactly the same interview questions. The other two colleges interpret the need to provide the same interview for all candidates somewhat more flexibly.

Second, there is a great deal of equality in starting salaries. In all three colleges, salary schedules result from negotiations between the faculty association (union) and college officials. As the faculty association president at SCCC reported, "What we have now is truly just a hiring, an entry point where we could say on there if you have a master's degree and this is a 9-month instructional position, they'll give you up to 15 years experience. You will start at this amount. And then after that, it's just a matter of everybody gets the same percent raise." The number of years of experience that can count toward the salary schedule is the only point at which hiring units have degrees of freedom to offer higher salaries. Otherwise, all faculty start at the same salary, regardless of field or accomplishments.

There is also apparent similarity among candidates. Search committees typically interview at least three and up to seven candidates for a position, suggesting that multiple candidates are deemed acceptable. In research universities, disciplinary departments vie with their counterparts around the country to secure the best and brightest rising star in a discipline as measured by research products or potential (where they earned their degree, whom they studied with, and such). How do community colleges differentiate among candidates? The factors used to differentiate candidates center around commitment to teaching, past teaching experience, and demonstrated teaching ability as measured by a short teaching demonstration. Additionally, according to one of the presidents, "Equally important [in the hiring process] is the answer to the question of whether the people we are about to hire will embrace the culture of the organization." For RCC geographic fit is an important selection criterion. As a faculty member explained, "If we had two candidates that were otherwise equal and one came from Midwest [state] and one came from Connecticut, we would choose the one from this area. Just because they know the area, they are going to be more comfortable."

Performance in the teaching demonstration plays a critical role in the decision process. As one president said, "It [teaching demonstration] gives us a chance to evaluate not just what we see in the classroom, but if they really did go to the trouble to prepare something and how creative they were in that process." Another administrator added, "They're looking for comfort in front of a group, ability to communicate, organization." Yet another administrator explained how the demonstration helps differentiate among candidates, "But there's a difference with someone who, when given all the same instructions, gives us a lecture on photosynthesis and one guy who gets up and talks and another guy gets up and uses charts, and another guy reaches in his pockets and comes up with demonstration models and breaks it all down and makes it very clear."

Factors that were *not* considered are almost as revealing as those that were. Neither the interview nor the demonstration was used to assess differences among candidates relative to knowledge of field. In fact, an administrator noted, "As a committee we're not qualified to say 'yeah, they should have that in a biology demonstration.' . . . We don't know that." As long as candidates held the requisite degrees or number of graduate hours, they were assumed to have adequate command of the subject. Additionally, the status of the institution where the candidates earned degrees plays no role in the screening process. An individual with a master's degree from a regional comprehensive university is considered on the same footing as an individual with a master's degree from Harvard. In fact, RCC might question why an individual with a degree from an elite school would even apply for a job there. Thus, two of the factors commonly used in other settings to distinguish among candidates—differences in command of the field and the status of degree-granting institution—played no role in community college faculty searches at the colleges in this study.

Differentiating among candidates based on teaching is complicated in part because teaching involves a relationship between students and teacher that is difficult to assess in an interview but also because there is no simple way of comparing candidates on teaching, such as a national ranking of departments or faculty based on teaching. In evaluation of teaching, common indicators of differentiation such as status of degree-granting institution and graduate mentor matter little. Because community college faculty are selected for their ability to teach, there is little need to (and no way to) search for the hottest young star in a discipline. Also, although it may be more difficult to differentiate among good teachers, it may be also easier to substitute one candidate for another. This is less the case at a research university, where continued reputation of a department or university depends on ability to hire the best scholar in a particular field in order to compete with other like universities (Clark, 1987).

Another way of assessing difference and hierarchy is to examine the competition for faculty. Were some colleges deemed more acceptable than others? And, were some candidates highly sought by multiple colleges? Colleges did not seem to complain that they were losing their first choices to other colleges, perhaps because there were multiple equally qualified candidates; therefore, getting one's first choice is not viewed as critical. There did not seem to be a great deal of competition for the candidates. Most of the recently hired faculty talked about applying for other positions but usually took the first job offered or did not receive a response from other colleges. For example, a recently hired chemistry instructor at SCCC had been working in Washington, DC, but had wanted, in his words, "to teach at a community college in the Midwest." He applied for nine positions and interviewed at two schools, SCCC and one other. He interviewed at the other school first but was offered the SCCC job first after deciding he would turn down the other school even if they did make an offer.

When offered other positions, differences such as quality of facilities, interpersonal relationships and, to a lesser extent, salary seemed to be the most significant factors in the decision regarding which job to accept. Status or the perceived reputation of the college was not a factor. A recently hired faculty member at OCCC applied for four jobs. One other college offered him a job on the spot (for more money), but he said, "It was a no-brainer to come here. . . . It was between two schools. . . . I looked at the people who I'd be working with and, I don't know if you met Dean [Jones], but . . . I instantly said, 'I can work with this woman. This a woman that is going to let me work' and then my lead instructor, I just clicked with him." He was one of the few who talked about having multiple offers.

Academic Work

Academic work varies widely among institutional types. In community colleges, faculty teach up to five lower division courses per week to a wide range of students each semester. In addition, faculty typically maintain a set number of office hours per week. They are not expected to do research and get no released time for this purpose. A dean at OCCC explained, "We tell them [candidates] when we interview, and even when I have people inquiring, I say, 'We are not a research institution. Our primary purpose here is to teach. To teach, that's our objective, that's our major goal.' If a person wants to do some research, that's fine, but they have to be in the classroom teaching. We don't give you reassign time or something so you can do a research project and not spend any time in class." Although colleges such as SCCC may give rewards for research, faculty are under no pressure to do research.

Ideology of the Profession

The ideology guiding the faculty profession in community colleges is that of commitment to learning and success for all students. This was noted by Clark (1987) and was evident in the criteria used by the colleges in this study to select faculty. Faculty and administrators (former faculty) clearly identified with the community college mission. They were unanimous in defining characteristics they sought in faculty: an understanding of the community college mission, a concern for student success, and a devotion to teaching. The new faculty members themselves often expressed a commitment to teaching, if not a direct commitment to the community college. For example, one new chemistry instructor explained:

> It took me 6 months [in my former job] to realize what I already knew and that other people knew—which was I wanted to teach. I finally admitted to myself that I specifically wanted to teach. . . . I wanted to teach at a community college because in so many words, I think this is what I am supposed to be doing. I think this is my calling, if you will, and therefore I want to be judged on my teaching. I didn't want to be at a four-year school . . . because I didn't want any of the publish or perish environment that goes with that or the necessity to do research. I wanted an institution where I could teach and be evaluated by my supervisor and peers based on my teaching and spend my time figuring out how to teach. And high school was not exactly my cup of tea, so community college fit exactly the bill that I was looking for.

While the other candidates displayed less missionary fervor about their positions, it was evident that they all wanted to teach. What is not entirely clear is whether their commitment is to teaching or more specifically to teaching in a community college. Several made it clear that they thought the community college to be a good match because they did not want to do research. On the other hand, individuals with a master's degree may recognize that for them the community college is the best option. Other newly hired faculty interviewed for this study seemed more interested in teaching and less committed to the specific ideology of the community college. These faculty had applied for teaching positions at different types of colleges.

Authority

With respect to authority, community college faculty seemingly have more authority for hiring colleagues than do teachers in public K-12 schools (Rebore, 1995) but have less authority than do faculty in research universities. Human resources offices play a significant role in determining the guidelines for job descriptions and application forms, receiving applications, and even screening out applicants who do not meet minimum required qualifications. In all cases, faculty committees review applications of candidates meeting minimum qualifications, select those to be interviewed, participate in interviews, and play a role in identifying the top choices. However, an administrator usually serves on each search committee as well, somewhat lessening the degree of authority of faculty for choosing their colleagues. The degree of authority for hiring decisions held by faculty search committees varies from little at RCC to considerable at SCCC and OCCC. In the case of RCC, an administrator frequently chairs the search committee and the president always interviews the finalists and makes the final decision. At OCCC, deans frequently participate, often as chair of the search committee, check references and make recommendations (based on faculty input) to the vice president for academic affairs. A similar process is followed at SCCC. The executive vice president at SCCC is clear that he can exert moral persuasion in the hiring process, but the main decisions are made at the division level where division directors may or may not sit on search committees. All full-time faculty appointments are approved by the board of trustees at each college.

One additional area in which faculty have some authority is in the setting of the salary schedule. Each of the three colleges is unionized and the salary schedule at each is negotiated between the union (faculty association), administrators, and board of trustees. The faculty association also typically determines how salary increases will be allocated: as raises to continuing faculty, to boost starting salaries on the schedule, to improve health insurance, and such. Although Clark (1987) sees unions as working against professionalism of faculty, it is clear that the faculty associations at community colleges can give faculty some authority in determining salaries and benefits.

Promise of an Academic Career

If community college teaching were a unique profession, we might expect faculty to train for a position in a community college, get a job in one, and either build a career in that college or move to positions in other community colleges. On this dimension, the evidence from the colleges in this study is mixed. Although some of the recently hired faculty thought about the community college when it came time to look for a teaching position, none spoke about planning and preparing specifically for such a career—or of even being aware that such a career possibility existed. Furthermore, community colleges are more concerned about good teaching when they hire new faculty than they are about where a person has previously worked. Only 1 of the 10 arts and sciences faculty members who were interviewed came from a full-time position at another community college (although several had taught part-time in community colleges). An administrator at SCCC estimated that about 20% of new hires come from positions in other community colleges. For the recently hired faculty in this study, coming directly from graduate school or directly from a community college position is not the typical mobility pattern either. These findings suggest that a well-defined labor market, in which many faculty move from one community college to another, does not exist. Several of the new faculty interviewed for this study had worked in business before deciding they wanted to teach.

Due to the high numbers of adjunct faculty employed by community colleges, one might expect a tight internal labor market to exist. That is, community colleges would fill their full-time positions with individuals in adjunct positions who are already trained and evaluated. This did not appear to be the case in this study. Administrators involved in hiring at each of the three colleges indicated that being an adjunct could help, but it could also hurt one's chances of being hired into a full-time position. Although some administrators said they hired adjuncts with an eye toward their becoming full-time faculty members, judging by the fact that only 1 of the 10 recently hired faculty had served in an adjunct capacity at the same college, adjuncts did not seem to have an advantage.

Disciplinary Associations

As discussed earlier, disciplinary associations may be playing a larger role for community college faculty work as disciplinary associations establish branches specifically devoted to community college faculty. However, this particular aspect of professionalization identified by Clark (1987) was not evident in the search process itself. It is left to other researchers to investigate disciplinary associations as an aspect of professionalization.

Conclusion

This study confirms what other studies have shown: Applying traditional conceptions of academic professionalism to community college faculty produces mixed results. On some measures community college faculty are seemingly more like faculty in four-year colleges, and on other measures they are more like K-12 teachers. Community college faculty have less control over their work lives than do professors at research universities but have more control than do K-12 teachers. They are not expected to do research and usually are not rewarded for doing so. They are expected to teach five lower division courses per week, resulting in an emphasis on teaching skills in searches. Discipline is important to some extent in the search process in that search committees are typically discipline based; however, the nature of the work of community colleges dictates that they search for generalists who can teach lower division courses and who can teach outside their disciplines.

The community colleges in this study fall down on the "difference and hierarchy" criterion. The nature of the primary task—teaching—coupled with the fact that community colleges are judged by their service area and not by national reputation leads to a de-emphasis in faculty searches on factors contributing to status and hierarchy such as the status of the degree-granting institution, research agenda, and prominence of a graduate mentor. The focus is rather on teaching ability. The trappings of hierarchy and prestige are not used by the colleges included in this study as evidence of teaching ability. The author did not verify whether, in fact, measures used in searches resulted in hiring faculty with excellent teaching ability. Other aspects of hierarchy and prestige may figure into the actual workings of community colleges through teaching awards, granting tenure, and such, that were not examined in this study. Faculty do have authority in the sense that they have the opportunity to, and are expected to, participate in the search and screening process to hire their colleagues, along with administrators; however, administrators play a greater role than is typical of research universities. And although Clark (1987) sees unionization as detracting from professionalization to the extent that it encourages sameness and lack of control, unionization does give faculty power to participate in setting salaries and determining how salaries will be implemented.

Finally, community colleges offer the prospects of a career for faculty, albeit one that may develop differently from a faculty career in other sectors. Tenure is granted after a relatively short probationary period, and community college faculty tend to stay in their positions (Huber, 1998). But unlike other sectors such as research universities and K-12 schools, faculty have not specifically prepared for positions in the community college sector. The evidence from this study suggests that teaching is the professional commitment and the community college the setting where teaching is practiced. Unlike research, where the university is one of the few places to practice, teaching can be practiced in many settings. The nature of the organization and its mission shape how the professional teaching career develops. Community colleges are interested in identifying good teaching and will hire individuals who provide evidence of this regardless of whether they have taught in community colleges or not (Gahn & Twombly, 2001). And, because teaching is a more generalized skill than research in a specific discipline, community colleges can hire good teachers with varying backgrounds; the doctoral degree can be earned later. Thus, the path to membership in the profession of community college teaching may not follow the traditional path depicted by Clark (1987) and established as the academic norm—disciplinary apprenticeship in a doctoral program followed by a faculty position.

The results of this study are not surprising. If one conceptualizes formal education in the United States along a continuum with elite research universities at one end and K-12 schools at the other, community colleges fit somewhere in the middle, sharing some characteristics with each and often serving as a conduit between K-12 and four-year institutions. Particularly with respect to the transfer mission, community colleges are in the middle in every sense, sending their students on to four-year colleges and universities. Applying Clark's conceptualization of academic professionalism to faculty searches is useful in helping to describe further the nature of this professional middle ground.

For community college faculty, the profession seems to be college teaching that is practiced within a specific setting. Should community colleges and their faculty be happy with this status or should they seek status as a unique profession with specific norms, values, career entry points, and such? Community college faculty may not be in a "position to follow the cosmopolitan road to professionalism so heavily traveled by university professors" (Clark, 1987, p. 243), but that does not mean they are not professionals. Although some might like to argue for the existence of a unique profession of community college teaching, it seems that community colleges are well-served by their increasingly important place between high schools and four-year colleges and universities. As a result of their place, community colleges can, and may be advantaged by, their ability to hire faculty with a wide range of backgrounds and prior professional commitments. From the search perspective, the existence of a highly specialized profession might actually limit the community college's ability to fill its full-time faculty positions.

If one accepts the argument that all college professors belong to a larger profession of teaching that has varying dimensions depending on the sector in which it is practiced, then the question becomes not *whether* but *how* community college faculty are professionals. The pressing question facing community colleges and their faculty seems to be how they can take individuals with teaching potential from diverse professional backgrounds and orient them to the specific history, mission, and culture of the community college. That is, what does it mean to be a professional within the community college, and how is a sense of professional identity necessary for effective mission fulfillment developed? The more general interest in teaching, as opposed to teaching in a community college specifically on the part of new faculty, may make it all the more important for community colleges to pay attention to developing faculty according to important dimensions of the academic profession such as the norms of teaching described by Braxton and Bayer (1998). The alternative is to work toward establishing a labor market in which only faculty members trained specifically for community colleges or who have had previous positions in community colleges are hired for faculty positions. The research reported in this article suggests that faculty need not be trained specifically for community college teaching in order to be professionals. In fact, the current approach allows community colleges to draw their faculty from a wide variety of backgrounds, which may be of benefit to community colleges. However, this approach to hiring faculty places more responsibility on individual colleges and the community college sector as a whole to socialize faculty to what it means to be a professional within the context of the community college.

References

Braxton, J., & Bayer, A. (1998). The normative structure of community college teaching: A marker of professionalism. *Journal of Higher Education, 69,* 187–205.

Burke, D. (1988). *A new academic marketplace.* Westport, CT: Greenwood.

Cohen, A., & Brawer, F. (1991). *The American community college,* (2nd ed.). San Francisco: Jossey-Bass.

Clark, B. (1987). *The academic life: Small worlds, different worlds.* Princeton, NJ: Carnegie Foundation for the Advancement of Teaching.

Gahn, S., & Twombly, S. (2001). Dimensions of the community college faculty labor market. *Review of Higher Education, 24,* 359–282.

Garrison, R. H. (1967). *Junior college faculty: Issues and problems.* Washington, DC: American Association of Community and Junior Colleges.

Granovetter, M. (1974). *Getting a job.* Boston: Harvard University Press.

Grubb, W. N. (1999). *Honored but invisible: An inside look at teaching in community colleges.* New York: Routledge.

Huber, M. T. (1998). *Community college faculty attitudes and trends, 1997.* Stanford, CA: Stanford University, National Center for Post-secondary Improvement.

National Center for Education Statistics. (2001). *Integrated Postsecondary Education Data System.* Retrieved August 20, 2001, from http://NCES.ed.gov/ipeds

Lofland, J., & Lofland, L. (1995). *Analyzing social settings.* Boston: Wadsworth.

Merriam, S. (1998). *Qualitative research and case study applications in education.* San Francisco: Jossey-Bass.

Outcalt, C. (2002). A *profile of the community college professoriate, 1975–2000.* New York: Routledge Falmer.

Palmer, J. (1992). Faculty professionalism reconsidered. In K. Kroll, (Ed.), *Maintaining faculty excellence* (pp. 29–38). *New Directions for Community Colleges,* no. 79. San Francisco: Jossey-Bass.

Rebore, R. (1995). *Personnel administration in education: A management approach,* (4th ed.). Boston: Allyn & Bacon.

U.S. Census Bureau. (2001). *Quickfacts.* Retrieved August, 15, 2001, from http://quickfacts. census.gov

U.S. Census Bureau. (2004). *Quickfacts.* Retrieved May 30, 2004, from http://quickfacts.census.gov/qfd/states/

Susan B. Twombly is professor of higher education at the University of Kansas. *stwombly@ku.edu*

CHAPTER 29

ACADEMIC LIFE AT THE FRANCHISE: FACULTY CULTURE IN A RURAL TWO-YEAR BRANCH CAMPUS

JOHN R. WOLFE AND C. CARNEY STRANGE

The university branch campus has emerged as a relatively recent but significant addition to the landscape of American higher education, fulfilling the goals of a growing number of institutions to extend postsecondary learning to a broader public. Structuring themselves in a typical array of associate degrees, transfer programs, and even a smattering of graduate courses, while borrowing from a range of local faculty talents and main-campus consultants and instructors, these institutions—mostly two year and community based—quickly distinguished themselves by developing flexible practices and responsive programs to meet a wider range of learning needs at a reasonably low cost. The scope of this outreach can be appreciated in the efforts of several states that have invested in such developments. For example, Ohio enrolls 37,265 students in mostly associate of arts programs at 23 branch campuses, sponsored by 8 different institutions. Pennsylvania enrolls 40,197 students at 25 branches which offer primarily baccalaureate degrees. Indiana has established 8 different campuses enrolling approximately 46,845 students; and South Carolina sponsors 7 branch campuses, offering mostly associate programs for 11,430 students. On average, these 63 branch campuses enroll just over 2,150 students each, serving 135,737 students in all (Rodenhouse, 1998).

In spite of the significant, if not acclaimed, contributions these colleges make to the education of citizens, relatively little research has examined their role or the experiences of those who serve in them, in particular, their faculty. Much of our understanding of academic life, both the good (e.g., Boice, 1992) and the bad (e.g., Anderson, 1992) of it, has long been dominated by selective observations of faculty in research-oriented flagship universities and highly competitive liberal arts colleges. However, in the absence of data on emerging nonelite sites, such understandings are certainly incomplete. Becher (1987) concluded that among the number of "under-researched areas . . . in the study of the distinctive way of life of teachers and learners . . . [are] the cultures in non-elite institutions." This is a potentially

JOHN R. WOLFE is Director of Academic and Instructional Services at Wright State University Lake Campus (Celina, Ohio), where for the past 16 years he has developed programs targeted at student success and directed institutional efforts on behalf of part-time faculty.

C. CARNEY STRANGE is Professor of Higher Education and Student Affairs at Bowling Green State University (Bowling Green, Ohio), where he has taught for 24 years. He is senior coauthor with James Banning of *Educating by Design: Creating Campus Learning Environments That Work* (San Francisco: Jossey-Bass, 2000). Address queries to Strange at Bowling Green State University, Higher Education and Student Affairs, 330 Education, Bowling Green, OH 43403; telephone: (419) 372-7388; fax: (419) 372-9382; e-mail: strange@bgnet.bgsu.edu.

important area, since faculty at these institutions "promise a very different perspective on the findings derived from elite cultures" (pp. 194–195). This study illuminates the nature of faculty life and culture at one small, rural, nonelite, two-year branch campus of a large state university, local information and understandings about faculty members' roles and working conditions, their socialization and attitudes towards one another, their values and expectations, and their sources of work satisfaction.

Research Site and Context

The site for this study was "Metro University—Park Campus," a pseudonym for a two-year branch campus located between two rural communities in a populous Midwestern state. As Metro's only branch, Park provides prebaccalaureate and technical education at the associate degree level for approximately 900 enrolled students from a three-county area. The faculty consists of 25 full-time and 28 part-time members, with occasional participation from 3 Metro University faculty members who teach graduate classes part-time. Although Park Campus is considered part of Metro University, it has its own mission statement that reflects its identity in a rural environment. Park's parent institution serves over 16,000 students in more than a hundred undergraduate majors, 27 master's degree programs, and programs of study for the M.D., Psy.D., Ed.S., and Ph.D. degrees.

Park is set in rich farmland dotted by a number of small towns (population a few hundred to 12,000) that are each host to one or two major manufacturers and a number of smaller business enterprises employing mostly blue-collar workers, typically White and of German-Catholic ancestry. Local community leaders established Park's first facility in 1962 by affiliating with a private university in a nearby rural location that enabled the "educational board" (as the community leaders then referred to themselves) to offer classes in an older building of one of the local communities. After several years, that relationship yielded to a new affiliation with Metro, the major public institution located approximately 75 miles away. From this arrangement evolved a new branch campus facility ("Park Campus"), built just outside a small town, a location designed to make a broader appeal for students from surrounding communities than the original site.

Although Park's present physical facilities include only three buildings, the campus is beautifully situated in serene surroundings, including a lake and campgrounds. Today, Park Campus provides two-year associate and technical degree programs in many of Metro University's majors. It also offers programs in a number of engineering and business technology fields. In addition, Metro faculty teach a few master's degree program courses, while a number of certificate programs, most often a business-related field, are offered on Saturdays for local community residents who desire advanced certification.

During its early years, Park Campus was nearly independent, with financial structures, institutional supports, and policies varying dramatically from the university with which it had since become affiliated. Over time, especially during the mid-1980s when a new university president was hired, changes were instituted that brought Park Campus more in line as one of Metro University's colleges within a university system rather than as a separate entity. For example, the branch campus dean began reporting to the main campus's Vice-President of Academic Affairs, Park Campus's budget was incorporated into Metro's allocation process, and the hiring and promotion policies and practices were streamlined within the larger university system. Along with these important substantive and procedural organizational changes came a key symbolic change. The name of the university was incorporated within the branch campus title to clarify the new relationship.

In more recent years, this relationship has evolved into a marriage of convenience for Park Campus faculty, generating the increased esteem associated with the new label of "university," insulating them from the kind of demands an expanded community college mission might have made on their resources, and at the same time freeing them from the usual layers of bureaucracy, as well as the trappings and pressures associated with other kinds of university settings. Thus, Park Campus has evolved over its recent history into an academic hybrid in which faculty are finding that the "rules of the game" are changing rapidly and that the challenges are increasing significantly as complex needs are met with diminishing resources.

Participant Selection and Data Collection

We used both reputational and purposive sampling methods to select faculty participants for this study. First, a sociometric questionnaire generated an initial list of informants, yielding a relatively high degree of consensus among faculty about peers perceived to be "influential, knowledgeable, and perceptive regarding campus issues and concerns" at this particular institution. Purposive sampling then permitted the researchers to identify those from the list whose experiences included teaching in different disciplines for varying lengths of tenure with varying characteristics and employment statuses. The original informants also identified an additional part-time faculty member who taught only in the evenings and who was considered a valuable resource person for his "real world" perspective in the classroom.

We thus derived a sample of seven faculty participants with a variety of experiences and backgrounds. Four of the participants taught full-time and three part-time. Among them were five men and two women, whose institutional experience base ranged from 3 to 22 years, with an average of slightly over 10 years. Five faculty members taught in the Humanities Division and two in Technologies. One participant had completed the doctorate, four the master's degree, and two held bachelor's degrees. Only three had achieved full tenure status at this particular institution. Two individuals had come to Park Campus from out of state, while the other five members were from various locations throughout the state. Two of the four full-time participants were from the local Park Campus community, having left to acquire their degrees before returning to teach. In fact, one participant was an earlier graduate of the institution. Three of the seven participants came directly from high school teaching appointments, two came directly from graduate school, one came from the business sector, and one had relocated due to the spouse's employment at the institution.

Like other examinations of faculty culture (e.g., McCart, 1991; Whitt, 1991), this study employed techniques of naturalistic, qualitative research—interviews, observations, and document analysis—to construct the experiences and meaning of this select group of faculty members. In 1995 we recorded two semi-structured interviews with each participating faculty member, focusing on questions designed to elicit constructions about various artifacts of faculty culture. In addition to transcribing the interviews, we also made summary notes of dialogues, as well as observations of participants' demeanor and nonverbal responses. All prescriptions for informed consent were met; and as the need arose, we solicited additional documents (e.g., participants' resumes, minutes of meetings, college catalogue) as a means of collecting further background data on the institution and verifying points raised in the inquiry process. We used a case study format to solicit, organize, and present the data.

The primary data collector also held a faculty-staff appointment at Park. As an insider, he was in a unique position to inform the process, having observed for several years the dynamics of this particular faculty group. The peer debriefer, a faculty member at a different campus who has taught course work in qualitative research for ten years, monitored and participated in the data collection and analysis process. We assured the quality of the data by applying appropriate procedures of trustworthiness (Lincoln & Guba, 1985) and authenticity (Guba & Lincoln, 1989), including prolonged engagement at the site, member checks of emergent constructions, and an audit trail sufficient to determine the credibility and dependability of the research process.

Themes of Faculty Life at Parks

Four themes related to the daily aspects of faculty life at this campus emerged from the data: (a) the conservative and provincial culture of the institution, (b) its diminutive size, (c) faculty role perspectives, and (d) influences on faculty role implementation. These themes not only illuminated the uniqueness of this campus but also figured prominently in understanding the ways in which these faculty fulfilled their roles.

Conservative and Provincial

The geographic isolation of Park Campus has nurtured over the years a homogeneous, conventional, conservative, and provincial student body. Such features have supported a historically male-dominated institutional culture which is less than supportive for female faculty and students. With only two full-time female faculty, a gender disparity has often manifested itself in the form of mixed perceptions about the quality of interactions between males and females. One participant explained:

> I would say that until recent years there has been somewhat . . . of an antagonistic relationship between male and female faculty, due in part to the fact that there are not very many [female faculty]. . . . There was a resentment on the part of a few individual female faculty. . . . They felt that due to the fact that there [were] just a few of them that they were being dominated by a male establishment.

Although most acknowledged the problems of the limited presence of female faculty, one male faculty member simply viewed it as a function of the types of programs offered. Accordingly, since there were few "traditional female departments," he asserted strongly the patronizing belief that a female presence was not missed on campus.

> The areas that you would normally have (pause) female/male type positions is pretty well balanced out. . . . For example, if you had [a] cosmetology program . . . [or] if you had a nursing program, those would definitely be female oriented programs. So you would definitely look for women to teach those probably, so you would have more of a balance. In our campus here, the disciplines we have don't really require—or it's usually not staffed by—females. So it's not like we're missing females. It's just that the positions we have (pause)—the men just have them, I guess.

Interestingly, although the female faculty participants dismissed gender as a factor in their usual interaction with male counterparts, one woman interviewee reported that she witnessed a patronizing attitude from some of her male colleagues. Both female participants commented on the definite lack of female role models for students. In fact, one believed that a few male faculty seemed to prefer interacting with other male colleagues instead of her, perhaps viewing her as less competent. This, in her view, accounted for their patronizing perspective.

> As one of only two females on [the] faculty at this point in time, I have found that most of the people, most of the male faculty, are open to what I have to say and willing to work with me and so forth. There are a few people who simply do not interact with me; and in some situations, I do believe it's

because of the male-female thing. They would really rather converse with a male whom they see as more competent. . . . I think it spills over into the classroom too. . . . I hear that same kind of thing coming from female students relative to those faculty people—you know, that they feel that they're not really listened to or taken seriously and so forth.

In a retrospective manner, another female faculty member revealed that her main concern is that there were so few women role models for female students:

> Well, since there are so few female faculty out here, (laugh) it's really hard to tell. I've never sensed that I was not being given consideration just because I was female. . . . [But] the fact that there aren't very many women teaching out here is pretty—pretty blatant. I don't know if that was deliberate procedure on the part of the administration or not. . . . I think the only thing that it affects is that there isn't much in the way of [a] role model here for young women students. . . .

The essence of the male-dominated culture at Park is perhaps reflected most clearly by one faculty member who articulated his philosophy in dealing with students on an individual basis, albeit with a paternal but genuine concern for students.

> Hey, we're an educational family unit—right here, and I'm the dad. When you've got problems with what's going on here, I'm the one you come to. When you have a question about your classes, I'm the one you come to. You guys are in the . . . program, and that means that I am going to run a lot of the things that you do here, and if you're having problems with whatever is going on here, then yeah, come to me.

This masculine hegemony, in turn, is reinforced by the conservatism of surrounding small communities, which poses additional challenges to the success of female faculty and students. With effortless consistency, one female faculty member shared her thoughts on the naivete and unwitting victimization of women students on campus:

> Very frankly, female students are sometimes their own worst enemy because they don't understand when or how they are being discriminated against. . . . The nature of this community has been so conservative that many things—and I'm not just talking femi-

nist here—but many things that women in a large community or certainly in a larger university setting would see and object to are accepted here as the way things are, and no one questions whether it ought to be changed or not. I think that for the most part the male faculty are very willing to give all women an equal chance; but if the women don't ask for it, they are not necessarily going to push it on them; and since the average female student in this university does not ask for it, they don't get it. They don't get equal treatment. They don't get equal consideration of a project input, work, and consideration.

Following this observation, she elaborated insightfully on the reluctance of many of these students to assert themselves.

I still have young women who come into my office and ask if I'll fill out scholarship papers or something because their dad doesn't think girls will need a college education, so they have to make it on their own. Their dad will put their brothers through school, but . . . not them, because they're females and they don't need it. And there's a lot of that attitude in this area.

These conventional mores among students present a special challenge for faculty too. For instance, one participant found such a necessity for students to explore their own perceptions and attitudes toward the world that these discussions have become an integral part of her class instruction.

I do the same thing in my teacher education courses. We spend a lot more time talking with the students about themselves in terms of how they feel and what they think and how that's going to impact on their teaching than I do talking about specific teaching methods or theory.

Diminutive Size

A second category of themes addressed the diminutive size of Park Campus. While allowing a more personalized atmosphere to flourish, this feature also necessitated a reliance on "one-person" departments to carry out the institution's educational mission, contributing to: (a) greater job complexity, (b) generalist role expectations, (c) professional isolation and (d) limited collegiality.

Greater Job Complexity.   The many "hats" faculty at Park Campus must wear provide a variety of opportunities that enrich their experience, but this factor also becomes a major source of stress for them as they try to accomplish all of their duties. As one faculty member recalled his socialization to a one-person department on campus, the complexity factor became clear:

I know when I was hired, they told me, "Well, one thing you'll have to be aware of is that everybody around here wears a lot of hats," and that's how they put it, and that's basically true. You do have a lot of one-person departments, which does create stress. You have one person here doing what three or four people would be doing at Metro.

These one-person departments promote an inevitably high level of job complexity which is both fulfilling and challenging. In an introspective manner, one faculty member described the nature and consequence of these competing demands:

We are called upon to do many more things . . . things of such a diverse nature that it ends up taking a whole lot more time. If I were in the department at a much larger university, I wouldn't have to be concerned about things other than teaching in that area and activities that were very closely related. . . . Although I enjoy the variety, it does create a lot more work and stress and so forth, and so that's a disadvantage and that's not true just for me. . . . It's true for lots and lots of people and I think that's a disadvantage.

Nevertheless, faculty often cite the opportunity to gain a broad-based experience while serving in multiple roles as a benefit of this arrangement. In fact, one faculty member shared his appreciation for

. . . the broadness of the experiences that I can get. . . . Here, I get involved in a variety of different committees. It's been a really nice place to get started in teaching college because it's kind of like we're our own little microcosm and everything, you know. You get to see what's going on in the English Department, the Math Department, and the secretarial program, and electronics and my department, and it's just been a real broad-based experience. So, I think that's probably what I value most about being here.

A colleague concurred:

It is true that you're able to get a broader range of experiences than down on the Metro

campus. . . . It does make for a more interesting job and hopefully something that
would look better on a resume later on than
one single job on another campus.

Course scheduling, student recruitment and
advisement, ordering books, orientation of part-
time faculty members, evaluation of programs,
maintenance of equipment and supplies, teaching, service commitments, and research projects
offer a rich array of tasks and opportunities with
potential for enhancing career choices. However,
the demands of time and energy required to "do
it all" exact a price in terms of stress, an often-
strained veil of collegiality, and a sense of never
completing the job.

Generalist Roles.   The preponderance of one-
person departments at Park has nurtured the
development of individuals rather than a team
orientation among faculty. As one participant
noted, "There's only so many faculty members
here. There's only so much expertise that this few
of people can have. When I've got a question I
can't just go to someone and say, 'How do you
do that?'" Acknowledged one faculty member,
"Doing your own thing as long as it's within the
guidelines" has become the organizational *modus
operandi* at Park, a fact that many faculty cherish.
Another participant observed, "You control the
class. . . . Each person's a department. . . . You
pretty much do as you please. . . . You are kind
of on your own."

The press toward autonomous functioning
at Park has led to faculty being valued as generalists rather than as specialists in their respective fields of instruction, whether that was their
original desire or not when they joined the campus. As a result, they are often unable to devote
sufficient time and effort in their specific disciplines for any in-depth study since they have
multiple duties to perform and are expected to
share an overall knowledge of their particular
discipline with others, including students, individuals in the community, business people, and
local industry officers. Also contributing to a
generalist orientation is the fact that faculty
spend most, if not all, of their time teaching introductory courses. While one participant found
meaning in teaching basic courses, she nevertheless yearned for a more specialized class.

I get a lot of satisfaction out of dealing with
the introductory courses and I know that's
not true for everybody, but it happens to be

true for me. . . . There are times . . . I wish I
could teach just Shakespearean tragedy for
a quarter (laugh), and we would have maybe
three students who'd be interested in doing
that.

Another participant revealed a similar desire
to develop a more concentrated focus but realized it would not be possible on this campus: "It
would be nice to move on to a larger campus at
some point because I feel like I would get more
of the opportunities to specialize in something."

Professional Isolation.   In addition to greater job
complexity and generalist role expectations, Park
also contributes to a sense of professional isolation among faculty. While this isolation assured
a degree of autonomy that these participants
appreciated, it also exacted a professional toll.
As one faculty member reflected, "You miss the
camaraderie with other faculty members in your
area," a concern echoed by another participant:
"With no one else around here on campus that
does the things that I do, I sometimes miss being
able to consort with other people who are
directly involved in the same types of programs." For some, that's a price worth paying:

The fact that we don't have a lot of colleagues
in our same discipline to discuss things with
and . . . talk about new advances and so
forth . . . I feel alienated, isolated, whatever
term you want to use, but I like it that
way. . . . I've always figured I can do anything I want until someone absolutely says,
"No, you can't do that!"

Others find the limited feedback troublesome at
times:

No one knows your area enough to give you
guidance, so, when you have an idea, they
don't know how to react to it. . . . Here [at
Park] you're the department, so you kind of
work for yourself and [set] your own goals.

The cumulative effect of this dynamic ultimately
fragments the experience of faculty at Park, as
one observed:

We don't work well together to tie all of our
programs together, to make them feed off
each other. It's like you do your own program. We're not going to require our students to take your classes, but we'd like for
your students to take our classes.

Some faculty compensate for this isolation
by involvement in professional organizations.

Such affiliations also enhance credential-building for promotion and tenure; they present an avenue for networking and ultimately become a sign of the administration's support. Yet, at the same time, Park faculty also find professional associations too overwhelming for any individual impact. As one participant acknowledged, "It's given me something to put down for professional activities and so forth," while another added more cynically, "There's no question it helped me get my full professorship . . . and to me, that's almost like playing a game."

In spite of the benefits of affiliation, faculty at this campus find more value and focus more energy instead on local and regional community relationships. In so doing they enjoy a greater impact in being the "generalist" in their particular discipline rather than trying to perfect a "specialist" role within any national organization. This dynamic again underscores the importance of a local community commitment as a measure of career success and satisfaction.

Congeniality vs. Collegiality. Interestingly, many of the faculty participants noted that the small, informal, and relaxed atmosphere of one-person departments at Park had produced a more collegial faculty even though specific instructional ideas were only infrequently offered or exchanged. Perhaps due to competition for limited resources or the inability to find a common language and set of concerns around which to focus, reservations about working together on joint ventures involving different disciplines were plentiful among these faculty. In fact, Park's confederation of one-person departments seemed to promote relationships that are best described as congenial (i.e., friendly) rather than collegial (i.e., collaborative).

Overall, the diminutive size of Park includes a mix of positive and negative factors that contributes to its current status. From these faculty members' perspectives, the positive characteristics of being associated with a small institution include: a personable environment, individualized interactions, a cooperative atmosphere, the ease of initiating change, opportunities for broad-based experiences, and high personal and professional autonomy. On the other hand, negative aspects include a reliance on one-person departments, a resultant high degree of job complexity, high stress, greater demands on faculty time and energy, professional isolation, and a limited value placed on professional affiliations for academic revitalization.

Faculty Role Perspectives

Park faculty were cognizant of the traditional missions of faculty life (i.e., teaching, research, and service) and understood that Park emphasized teaching first. One participant concluded, "I would probably rate it teaching, service, and then research in that order, with the primary focus on teaching." His comment is congruent with another participant's thoughts that faculty at Park need a "definite aspiration to teach," followed by service to the community and then research.

Although service and research are integral aspects of faculty life on many college campuses, faculty noted that teaching and encouraging students to achieve academically and personally was their premier motive at Park Campus. In fact, the heart and soul of this commitment to teaching, particularly given the nature of the students served, was reflected best by one faculty member who noted that she cherished the

> . . . opportunity to help people reach their potential, achieve some of their dreams . . . offer encouragement, . . . [have] a real impact on their lives. . . . My perspective has never been to turn any of our students into scholars . . . rather . . . convincing them that they are capable, and showing them where they succeed, and helping them to have successes so that they are willing to reach forward and do more.

She added that "the most important thing we do" is to "give . . . confidence."

Teaching to inspire and encourage requires effort and creativity, a fact appreciated by another faculty member who commented:

> First of all, I really like the classroom work. I enjoy it. A good classroom teacher is part actor, and I have done a fair amount of acting—both for money and for fun—and there's a satisfaction in just doing it. I love the sudden look of understanding that appears on a student's face when [it's] something they hadn't thought about. . . . Hell, it's fun! You're getting paid for something that you like to do. I mean, what could be better?

Faculty at Park unanimously agreed that their main source of enjoyment was teaching, interacting with, and helping students "succeed, when they thought they couldn't," as one participant noted. Such interactions with students inspire, motivate, and give meaning to their roles as faculty members. Consequently, these faculty reported a strong satisfaction in their careers, shaped primarily by dedication to their teaching and service roles, a motivation expressed in terms of the enjoyment found in encouraging students with limited opportunities to achieve their potential, and a desire, for some, to give back to the local community that which was offered to them. As one revealed:

> Having lived around here and knowing what it was like as I was growing up, and even when I first came back as a faculty member, and having seen the changes that have come about in the community . . . I've been really proud and pleased to be a part of it.

In addition, faculty at this campus generally have not found the institution restrictive with regard to their careers, but rather supportive and fulfilling. As one participant explained,

> I've been very happy with my career, and I don't feel I've been inhibited at all, simply because this is a branch campus . . . located in the middle of a cornfield, or whatever. I think we've had more opportunity here to make a difference and to have impact simply because we are the first, you know, to touch so many people's lives in this area.

The positive interactions among faculty and students at Park also extend to members of the community in the form of professional service. In fact, most of these faculty believed that service to the community played a major role for themselves and the institution. For instance, one member indicated that individuals in the community look toward faculty members to provide leadership by serving on various committees like a North Central Evaluation team, speaking to classes, or being a judge for some type of event. The importance of service within the community is most noticeable among Park Campus faculty and representatives of local business and industry. Although such relationships create their own challenges at times for Park faculty (such as when business and industry leaders attempt to dictate curriculum or take attention away from meeting the needs of students), they seem sustained by the understanding that such links are vital to the continued growth and welfare of the institution. Among many benefits, these partnerships help to raise money, attract students, and advertise services for the institution. In addition, they modify the curriculum, keeping it current with the needs of society. In turn, the faculty at Park Campus play a critical role in meeting the social and educational needs of the community.

While teaching and service contribute greatly to faculty life at Park, research plays a more subsidiary role for most. In fact, as one faculty member claimed, most individuals at this campus really do not conduct research. With stark honesty, another noted:

> Sometimes I feel like a fraud, in the sense that I don't consider myself a scholar. I consider myself a teacher, and at the university level, I know that that's not what we're supposed to do, or at least that's not what we hear all the time.

Similarly, another colleague revealed, "I probably am not as academically oriented as some, as far as the desire to pursue advanced degrees, write articles, and do research—that sort of thing." Finally, perhaps out of resignation, another participant summarized his assessment of faculty research at Park:

> I don't think we put enough emphasis on it or . . . we get so ingrained in teaching and service that we don't have enough time maybe to do that because I think at this campus teaching and service are just almost mandated to you by the students and the community.

In terms of faculty role perspectives, the bottom line for faculty at Park is maintaining a commitment to students and nurturing an active service involvement with the local community.

Faculty Role Implementation

Success as a faculty member at Park is a function of differences in a distinctive hierarchy of disciplines, faculty preparation and credentials, and employment status. The effect of these factors also varies depending upon whether the faculty member is in the humanities or in the technical fields.

Disciplinary Differences. A faculty member's particular discipline at Park (e.g., humanities, business, technologies) significantly shapes the nature of his or her faculty life and culture in several ways. Faculty often described varying conditions of job complexity, with those in the technical fields having to assume broader tasks and responsibilities than those in the humanities.

Representing the technical faculty, two interviewees underscored the necessary, yet cumbersome, role of recruiting for their respective fields of instruction. Both were swift to point out that this is not something the humanities faculty have to be concerned about, since all students are required to take general education courses. The advantage from the humanities' side of the fence was quickly acknowledged by one faculty member:

> Recruitment has never been a factor in whether or not my classes are going to go, because they've either been courses they have to take or that are written into other programs that they still have to get them, and I haven't been responsible for going out there and dragging people in.

The technical faculty also added lab upkeep, development of promotional materials, and working with advisory boards to the number of tasks that they have had to contend with on a regular basis, leaving some overwhelmed by the sheer number of activities required of them.

Opportunities to conduct research also seem to be heavily dependent on discipline, with those in the technical fields being at a distinct disadvantage due to the equipment-intensive nature of their scholarship. Sensitive to the difference, one faculty member reflected on this issue:

> The whole issue is: How will research be carried out in such a small facility as this? Especially for the sciences there's simply no place to do research here. For the humanities, it's a little bit easier because we have access to the library through interlibrary loans and that kind of thing, so it's not impossible, but in biology or chemistry it would be almost impossible, except by computer, to do real research projects.

The few opportunities to do so are often precluded, once again, by competing tasks and responsibilities associated with their broader job roles. As another faculty member suggested, it may take an extraordinary commitment to be successful at this aspect of the faculty role at Park:

> In my opinion, I don't care what discipline you come from. . . . You have to go out and make an effort to do [research]. . . . Distance and the time are factors. . . . You have to work

through that. . . . You have to make an effort and you have to take the time to do it. But I think the biggest thing is, the teaching and the service take so much time that you don't want to do the others—you get tired—and you simply, you just say, "Well, I'm not going to do that. I don't have time to do that. " And then I can use an excuse. It is tough—it is. No question about that.

Distinctive differences among disciplines at Park also seem to account for variations in movement through formal faculty career ladders at the institution. In fact, those succeeding recently in the promotion and tenure system have been primarily humanities faculty with terminal degrees, who were rewarded for prior experiences before becoming associated with this campus. As one participant noted,

> In the past couple of years those people who have gotten tenure pretty readily have been those people who have had a long list of publications, even though ironically these things haven't been published while they were here. They mostly [had] gotten tenure on the basis of their past performances somewhere else.

In contrast, faculty members who have not been successful in the promotion and tenure process recently have typically come from technical fields of instruction. However, increasing the ante for faculty in all departments at Park have been the changing standards in the promotion and tenure process due primarily to the influence of its parent university system, where emphasis on research activity has gained stronger currency in peer reviews. Reflecting on this trend, one participant revealed:

> Quite a long time ago . . . teaching was considered much more important and community service [was] . . . considered differently. Credit at that point was given to things like participating in local clubs and that sort of thing. Whereas now, I think they would regard community service more in the light of . . . going out and giving lectures to the community or establishing ties between the community and the university.

Subsequently, an uneasy alliance between past expectations and current practices compounds the role of faculty at Park. Regardless though, faculty at Park seem to focus their energy on what they have always found to be of value—concern for the students enrolled on campus.

Professional Credentials.   In addition to the above disciplinary distinctions, differences in the academic preparation and credentials of faculty, including type of education and degrees earned, is another aspect which contributes to the implementation of their roles at Park. The type of education and whether an individual has earned a terminal degree presents a distinctive certification of status among faculty there. For some, this distinction contributes to feelings of inferiority to on-site colleagues or to a world evenly divided between an "ivory tower" versus "vo-tech" mentality. For others such a distinction contributes to an "elitist attitude" among faculty, where some view Park Campus as a "second-rate" appointment, in contrast to others who find satisfaction in their long-term commitment to the institution. As one participant reflected:

> I think they feel they're a little too good to be here—that this is somehow a second-class place, and they just got stuck here somehow instead of choosing to be here. . . . I'll be real honest. When I came here, I had no desire to ever go on anywhere else. I saw my opportunities here as fulfilling exactly what I wanted to do, and I had no burning desire to go somewhere else. My only concern was making sure that I maintained the credentials, qualifications, and so forth to be qualified to be here. I think a lot of the people . . . who feel differently about this . . . looked at this as somehow a starting, a stepping stone, a starting position where they could use it as a jumping off point to go on to better, bigger things.

Differences of education and credential also seemed to contribute further to collegial disengagement among some faculty, again adding to their self-imposed isolation and to an individual rather than a team orientation in fulfilling their roles and responsibilities.

Employment Status.   Employment status, that is full- versus part-time, also shaped the functioning of faculty at Park. The small core of full-time faculty who directed and staffed these one-person departments was supplemented by the services of a cadre of permanent and temporary part-time faculty appointments from the surrounding area. In fact, the numbers of part-time faculty at this campus accounted for more than half of the total number of faculty. However, of the 12 (out of 29) part-time faculty whom peers identified in the initial sampling questionnaire,

none was listed more than a few times, reflecting, not surprisingly, a certain degree of disenfranchisement on this campus. Yet while all of the participants in this study unanimously acknowledged that part-time faculty were not integrated fully into the institution, all agreed that they were effective and productive in their roles.

Although full-time faculty figured most prominently in the character of faculty culture at Park, part-time faculty, depending on whether they taught during the day or only at night, also contributed in significant ways. For instance, those part-time faculty who taught during the daytime hours typically had more visibility among and subsequently more contact with their full-time counterparts, which may have strengthened their belief that they were more integrated than those part-time faculty who were only on campus during the evening. According to one faculty member's observation,

> If they're a day adjunct, they might [be integrated] because they come here and they might linger a little. They might have lunch before they go home or they might come a little early. Definitely not the night. I think they just come and teach their class basically and then leave so they're not really integrated . . . with the other faculty. Some of . . . the students have responded better to them than a full-time faculty member.

One "day-timer" among the interviewees corroborated:

> Well, in my case, the relationship is very cooperative. . . . As far as I'm concerned, people treat me like a colleague completely. . . . I think maybe other adjuncts might feel more of a distance because they're not here all the time or maybe just here in the evening, you know, this kind of thing. . . . I'm here most days and into, say, the earlier evening.

Although evening part-timers may not be as integrated as those who teach during the day, they all have office space, secretarial assistance, computer access, and library privileges at Park, as one part-timer gratefully acknowledged:

> I also value the fact that I can come out here and use an office full-time, (laugh) and I have access to the library and interlibrary loans, and do my own kinds of research which would be rather difficult if I were doing adjunct work at a larger university, because I just wouldn't have the kind of space.

Interestingly, while part-time status seemed to relegate some faculty to a distant point from Park campus culture, for others, especially in the technologies and business fields, coming from professional positions in area industries seemed to elevate their status among Park faculty as prized resource people who represented "real world" authorities in various teaching specialties. In fact, as one full-time faculty member believed, part-time faculty brought a different dimension from the outside world that was valuable for students, even though he suggested caution in their utilization:

> I find the part-timers being very cooperative, very helpful, and they want to do it, and I think they bring a different dimension on campus. . . . I think basically the students identify with them quite well because they know they're coming from the outside world, and I think they like to hear some of the experiences and some of their philosophies . . . a definite value. I think we can overdo. . . . I think they can bring some current information on . . . the do's and the don'ts and how it really is. . . . Besides, they can add the practical things along with the theory from the textbooks, and I think that's a positive.

"Real world" or not, faculty members at Park who are able to follow students through to the completion of their total education are given the highest honor and most respect among peers.

In conclusion, it is clear that Park campus is searching for its institutional identity as a one-time local community effort, now turned branch campus of a large state university. Although there appears to be a consensus as to what some of the issues are in regard to the evolution of this institution, it remains unclear as to how the campus is yet to respond to them. As one faculty member acknowledged reflectively:

> We haven't decided what we want our branch campuses to do, how we want them to function. . . . I think the community itself hasn't decided whether they . . . really wanted a community college here or they wanted a branch campus of a university with its own priorities and that sort of thing. . . . I mean, we really haven't decided . . . what we want the faculty to be. . . . Do we want them to be primarily teachers? Do we want them also to be doing research, writing, you know, this kind of thing? It just strikes me that there's been a real lack of forethought in any of this.

Discussion and Conclusion

Although the transferability of these data is left to the reader to determine, some aspects of our foray into Park Campus faculty culture speak clearly to some of the key issues facing American higher education in general and its professoriat in particular. Any number of recent reform reports (e.g., AAHE, 1987; Kellogg Commission, 1997; Wingspread Group, 1993) have raised serious questions about the ability of our postsecondary system to deliver on its promises. Among a list of troublesome issues are the fragmentation and presumed irrelevance of curriculum, poor student advising, the disengagement of faculty and students, institutional bureaucracy and inflexibility, unresponsiveness to consumer interests and needs, and failure to develop the most basic learning skills necessary for success in a changing world of work. Faculty have even been characterized as "impostors" (Anderson, 1992) who squander taxpayers' money, professional shirkers who relegate teaching responsibilities to graduate lackeys (Sykes, 1988), and unproductive sluggards who must be held more accountable for the use of a rapidly shrinking pool of resources (Huber, 1992). Above all, more recent demands have spoken forcefully for the restoration of student learning as a premier goal of any academic enterprise (ACPA, 1994).

In contrast to the images purveyed by these popular analyses, this picture of faculty life at the Park Campus franchise reflects much of the *best* of what higher education has to offer—responsive programs and a dedicated faculty who genuinely care about students. However, for anyone contemplating an academic career at such a place, there are troubling themes here, consistent with challenges observed by other recent inquiries into faculty life.

Park Campus-like institutions may demand of faculty a commendable, dedicated focus on the whole student; after all, teaching is its preeminent activity, and nurturing the educational community as a "caring family" (Bowen & Schuster, 1986, p. 134) is an ever-present goal. At such institutions the transformative power of learning is perhaps most apparent as faculty engage in the kind of integrated and personal experiences most fulfilling to those motivated by service to students. However, the price exacted by such involvement may be too costly in the long run for those who expect a progressive academic career ladder. The stress of job complexity and service demands may all but preclude development of the kind of active scholarship likely to lead from one rung to the next. Letting scholarship take second place, especially when standards of research productivity are on the rise in the academic community, may seal the fate of any faculty member who begins a career, expecting to move "up and out" from such an institution. This foreclosed future is particularly poignant at a time when many colleges and universities are delivering mixed signals about faculty expectations. As Clark (1987) has observed, "The greatest paradox of academic work in modern America is that most professors teach most of the time, and large proportions of them teach all of the time, but teaching is not the activity most rewarded by the academic profession nor most valued by the system at large. Trustees and administrators in one sector after another praise teaching and reward research" (pp. 98–99). A few probationary years at a place like Park may significantly disadvantage any faculty member who wishes to succeed in this rapidly changing reward system. On the other hand, for those who find "that students are nearly everything, the source of daily satisfaction, the basis for a successful career" (Clark, 1987, p. 264), a Park Campus may provide all that is needed.

One of the ironies here is that the institutional sector represented by those with a two-year focus, including branches like Park, is presently the fastest growing sector in American higher education and one that serves a disproportionate number of first-generation students. Yet this is also the institutional sector with the greatest potential for faculty vacancies over the coming decades. If the core dynamics of faculty life at Park are indicative of conditions at similar institutions, the next generation of academics, especially those from underrepresented populations, may be in for a challenge of Herculean dimension in succeeding at such a career. The larger picture is framed by the competing missions of a Park Campus; to serve both a community-based constituency and to comply with the standards of a comprehensive, doctoral-granting university may be more than can be met, and perhaps is ill advised in the first place. The strengths of one seem to detract from the strengths of the other, ultimately risking the status of those most committed to the campus.

If these data imply policies and practices, it seems vital to pay more careful attention to the orientation and development of new faculty

under these circumstances. Differentiation and clarity of roles may be especially important for the successful matriculation of these personnel in the early stages of their careers. Gappa and Leslie (1993) have alerted educators to the integral roles played by part-time faculty, in particular at places like Park, suggesting further that this segment may warrant special focus in determining the best use of resources to support their efforts. Among them, perhaps female faculty especially could benefit from a more careful assessment of their status.

Questions raised by this study indicate a need for further inquiry into the lives of faculty at other institutions not usually examined from a cultural perspective. It is all the more important that these kinds of campuses, which are really on the leading edge of accessibility and service to students, be seriously examined and further studied. Hopefully, a sense of the isolated but dedicated path these faculty embrace and travel has illuminated the unique place a small branch campus faculty can have within the hierarchy of higher education. In conclusion, as Clark (1987) noted,

> The expansion of nominal universities, state colleges, and especially community colleges during the last quarter-century has notably put the majority of academics in locales far from the fellowships of the old-time colleges and the special worlds of the top private universities. Organizationally, those academics may have a champagne taste, but what they get is bottled beer. (pp. 260–261)

While a branch campus may not have the sophistication of champagne, neither is the flavor that of common beer. Rather, the taste might be more in line with a good table wine, reasonable in price, yet attractive in body and spirit. In many respects, the niche these faculty at Park have carved for themselves by engaging in teaching and service in a community context, while still viewing themselves as university colleagues, at least for now has placed them in the best of both, albeit demanding, academic worlds.

References

AAHE. American Association for Higher Education (1987). *Seven principles for good practice in undergraduate education.* Washington, DC: AAHE.

ACPA. American College Personnel Association (1994). *The student learning imperative: Implications for student affairs.* Washington, DC: ACPA.

Anderson, M. (1992). *Impostors in the temple.* New York: Simon and Schuster.

Becher, T. (1987). The cultural view. In B. R. Clark (Ed.), *Perspectives on higher education: Eight disciplinary and comparative views* (pp. 165–198). Berkeley: University of California Press.

Boice, R. (1992). *The new faculty member.* San Francisco: Jossey-Bass.

Bowen, H. R., & Schuster, J. H. (1986). *American professors: A national resource imperiled.* New York: Oxford University Press.

Clark, B. R. (1987). *The academic life: Small worlds, different worlds.* Lawrenceville, NJ: Princeton University Press.

Gappa, J., & Leslie, D. (1993). *The invisible faculty: improving the status of part-timers in higher education.* San Francisco: Jossey-Bass.

Guba, E., & Lincoln, Y. (1989). *Fourth generation evaluation.* Newbury Park, CA: Sage.

Huber, R. M. (1992). *How professors play the cat guarding the cream: Why we're paying more and getting less in higher education.* Fairfax, VA: George Mason University Press.

Kellogg Commission on the Future of State and Land-Grant Universities (1997). *Returning to our roots: The student experience.* Battle Creek, MI: Kellog Commission.

Lincoln, Y. S., & Guba, E. G. (1985). *Naturalistic inquiry.* Beverly Hills, CA: Sage.

McCart, C. L. (1991). *Using a cultural lens to explore faculty perceptions of academic freedom.* Unpublished doctoral dissertation, Pennsylvania State University.

Rodenhouse, M. P. (Ed.) (1998). *1999 Higher education directory.* Falls Church, VA: Higher Education Publications.

Sykes, C. J. (1988). *Profscam: Professors and the demise of higher education.* Washington, DC: Regnery Gateway.

Whitt, E. J. (1991). "Hit the ground running": Experiences of new faculty in a school of education. *Review of Higher Education, 14,* 177–197.

Wingspread Group on Higher Education (1993). *An American imperative: Higher expectations for higher education.* Racine, WI: Johnson Foundation.

CHAPTER 30

THE STATUS OF WOMEN AND MINORITIES AMONG COMMUNITY COLLEGE FACULTY

LAURA W. PERNA*,**

This article uses data from the 1993 National Study of Postsecondary Faculty to examine the status of women and minorities among faculty employed at public 2-year colleges nationwide. A variety of outcomes are considered including: employment status, salary, rank, and tenure status. The analyses show that human capital, structural, and market characteristics appear to explain the observed differences in the employment experiences of women and men faculty at public 2-year colleges and some, but not all, of the observed racial/ethnic group differences. When compared with the results of other research, this study suggests fundamental differences in the reward structures for faculty at public 2- and 4- year institutions. Implications of the analyses are discussed.

Key Words: *faculty; community colleges; salary; rank; tenure; equity.*

Although more than one fourth of the nation's faculty work at community colleges (National Center for Educations Statistics [NCES], 2001), a limited amount of rigorous research has focused on the status and experiences of community college faculty in general (Cohen and Brawer, 1996; Gahn and Twombly, 2001) or differences in the status and experiences of women and minority faculty at these institutions in particular (Clark, 1998; Townsend, 1995; Twombly, 1993). For example, of the 75 tables included in a recent NCES report on the "differences between subgroups of faculty and staff within the public 2-year sector" (Palmer, 2000, p. v), only two describe differences between women and men and two describe differences between "minorities" (as a group) and whites. Consequently, sex and racial/ethnic group differences in the employment experiences of community college faculty are poorly understood.

Researchers should focus on understanding sex and racial/ethnic group differences in the status and experiences of faculty at public 2-year institutions for several reasons. First, the observed underrepresentation of women, African Americans, and Hispanics is smaller among faculty at public 2-year institutions than at 4-year institutions. Analyses of the Integrated Postsecondary Education Data System 1997 Fall Staff Survey show that women represented 48% of full-time faculty employed at public 2-year colleges but only 34% of full-time faculty employed at 4-year colleges and universities. African

---

*Laura W. Perna, Department of Education Policy & Leadership, College of Education.

**Address correspondence to: Laura W. Perna, Assistant Professor, 2200 Benjamin Building, College Park, MD 20742. E-mail: lperna@wam.umd.edu

Americans and Hispanics also represented a higher share of full-time faculty at public 2-year colleges than of full-time faculty at 4-year colleges and universities (6.5% vs. 4.5% and 3.8% vs. 3.5%, respectively). Despite their relatively high representation at public 2-year colleges, some researchers (Townsend, 1995) have observed that average salaries and ranks are lower for women than for men at these institutions. Other researchers (Carter, 1994) have used descriptive statistics to suggest that, while African American and Hispanic faculty at community colleges may be more likely than white faculty to hold tenured positions, they also may be more likely than white faculty to be lecturers and instructors. Multivariate analyses are required to understand the extent to which these observed differences are explained by variables that are legitimately related to such employment outcomes.

A second reason for conducting research on sex and racial/ethnic group differences in the employment experiences of faculty at public 2-year colleges pertains to differences between the public 2- and 4-year college sectors in tenure and promotion practices. Unlike at 4-year institutions, tenure is typically awarded at community colleges after only 1–3 years of employment (Cohen and Brawer, 1996), and promotion to associate or full professor is based largely on the number of years of experience and holding a doctorate (Townsend, 1995). Perna (2001b) found that, while more than 70% of full-time faculty at both public 2- and 4-year colleges and universities were tenured, the share of tenured faculty who held the rank of full professor was smaller at public 2-year institutions than at 4-year institutions (31% vs. 57%). Although these differences suggest that the criteria used to determine faculty rewards vary between the two sectors, most research on faculty reward systems has been focused on faculty employed at 4-year colleges and universities.

Researchers have consistently shown that women faculty receive lower salaries (Barbezat, 1988; Bellas, 1993; Nettles, Perna, and Bradburn, 2000; Perna, 2001a; Toutkoushian, 1998a, 1998b; Weiler, 1990) and hold lower academic ranks (Smart, 1991; Toutkoushian, 1999; Weiler, 1990) than their male counterparts after controlling for differences in such characteristics as education, experience, productivity, institutional characteristics, and academic discipline. Nonetheless, with only a few exceptions (Lassiter, 1983; Perna, 2001b), most research on the employment expe-

riences of women has been limited to faculty employed at 4-year colleges and universities (Barbezat, 1988; Perna, 2001a; Smart, 1991; Toutkoushian, 1998a, 1998b; Weiler, 1990). While a few researchers (e.g., Nettles et al., 2000) have examined sex and race equity issues among a sample of faculty employed at both 4- and public 2-year institutions, merely including a dichotomous variable for employment at a public 2-year institution ignores the likely possibility that, because of differences in mission and structure, the process for determining such rewards as salary and rank is different for faculty employed at public 2-year colleges than for faculty employed at 4-year colleges and universities. Perna (2001b) concluded that the predictors of tenure and promotion to full professor are different for faculty at public 2-year institutions than for faculty at 4-year institutions and that tenure and promotion decisions are less predictable for faculty at public 2-year institutions than at 4-year institutions. Conducting separate equity analyses for faculty at community colleges seems to be appropriate given Clark's (1987) conclusion that faculty work is "qualitatively different" at community colleges, particularly with regard to the relative pull of institutional and disciplinary ties.

Therefore, this research explores sex and racial/ethnic group differences among faculty employed at public 2-year colleges nationwide in terms of several employment outcomes. This research contributes to our knowledge not only by identifying explained and unexplained sex and racial/ethnic group differences among public 2-year college faculty in employment outcomes but also by developing and testing a conceptual framework for examining the employment experiences of these faculty.

Theoretical Framework

Theoretical approaches to the academic labor market generally assume that the market forces of supply and demand determine faculty rewards (Perna, in press). For example, an excess supply of labor relative to demand is expected to depress faculty salaries, while a shortage of labor relative to demand is expected to raise salaries. While variations in supply and demand across academic fields may explain a portion of the observed differences in the employment experiences of women and men faculty and faculty of different racial/ethnic groups (Bellas, 1994), two other theoretical perspectives have been used to examine sources of observed differences: human capital and structural (Perna, in press). The neoclassical economic theory of human capital focuses on variations in the supply of labor, particularly the characteristics of individual workers, whereas structural approaches emphasize variations in the demand for labor, particularly the attributes of the organizations with which individuals are connected.

According to human capital theory, differences in employment experiences are determined by differences in individual productivity. Productivity differences are expected to reflect the investments that individuals have made in their personal development, such as the quantity and quality of their education, the amount of their on-the-job training, their geographic mobility, and their emotional and physical health (Becker, 1962; Schultz, 1961).

Despite the popularity of the traditional economic theory of human capital for explaining labor market experiences, some economists and sociologists have noted the theory's limitations (DeYoung, 1989; Dreijmanis, 1991; England, 1982; England, Farkas, Kilbourne, and Dou, 1988; Kalleberg and Sorenson, 1979). Critics have argued that, "focusing on the supply of human skills to explain economic inequality and lack of productivity is a theoretical mistake" (DeYoung, 1989, p. 155) and that, "human capital theory has not generated an explanation of occupational sex segregation that fits the evidence" (p. 358). Among the limitations of human capital theory is its failure to adequately explain the lower returns to educational investments for women and minorities (DeYoung, 1989) and the segregation of women into lower paying occupations (England et al., 1988).

Social scientists interested in issues of social inequality and poverty have responded to the inadequacies of human capital theory by developing structural or institutional approaches to labor markets (Youn, 1988). During the 1950s, institutional economists developed theories positing that institutions establish internal labor markets that are defined by administrative rules and procedures (Kalleberg and Sorenson, 1979; Youn, 1988). These rules, established by unions, government, and employers, define the job market and influence supply and demand (Kerr, 1950). In higher education institutions, such rules and procedures may include a tenure system and a policy of equitable wages across disciplines. In effect, internal labor markets constrain market

forces by institutionalizing nonmarket organizational factors (Bridges and Nelson, 1989). The internal labor market controls the distribution of jobs and an individual's progression within and between jobs, while the external labor market controls competition among institutions for jobs and labor via enrollment changes, fluctuations in research expenditures, production or supply of new doctorates, and faculty retirements (Youn, 1988).

Structural approaches to academic labor markets focus on the influence of the characteristics of the colleges and universities in which faculty were trained and work, including student enrollment, the tenure system, and collective bargaining agreements. According to such approaches, labor market inequalities are attributable to organizational attributes, including the tendency of organizations to structure positions, sort employees, and institutionalize rewards (Youn, 1992). Youn identified three forms of segmentation in the academic labor market: segmentation by academic discipline, institutionalized job task (e.g., primarily research, primarily teaching), and job status (e.g., full time or part time). Movement across segments (e.g., from mathematics to English, from a 2-year institution to a research university, from part time to full time) is restricted. Because competition among faculty in different segments is limited, inequities among faculty in different segments may persist.

Structural models also posit that sex and racial/ethnic group differences in salaries are attributable to the segregation of women and minorities in the types of institutions, academic fields, and work roles that have lower prestige and value (Smart, 1991; Verdugo and Schneider, 1994). In higher education, the average salaries of faculty in institutions and disciplines with higher proportions of women have been found to be lower than the average salaries of faculty in institutions and disciplines with smaller proportions of women (Bellas, 1994, 1997; Perna, 2001a; Smart, 1991), although some (Barbezat, 1988) have concluded that the relationship is small in magnitude. Tolbert (1986) concluded that when the minority group is smaller in size and relatively segregated within an organization, average differences in salaries are greater.

Research Method

This study draws on human capital, structural, and market perspectives to develop a conceptual model for exploring sex and racial/ethnic group differences in several employment outcomes among faculty who are employed at public 2-year colleges nationwide. Although this study does not explore sex and racial/ethnic group differences in all types of employment outcomes, this analysis is designed to provide a comprehensive picture of the status of women and minorities among the nation's community college faculty in terms of the most visible employment outcomes. The analyses also explore the status of women and minorities among community college faculty by limiting the sample in ways that reflect the outcome that is being considered. Specifically, this study examines the extent to which sex and race/ethnicity are related to the following employment outcomes after controlling for human capital, structural, and market explanations for the observed relationships:

1. type of institution of employment among faculty at 4-year and public 2-year institutions;

2. employment status (full time vs. part time) and appointment type (temporary or adjunct vs. regular) among public 2-year college faculty;

3. salaries among full- and part-time public 2-year college faculty with regular appointments;

4. academic rank among faculty with regular appointments at public two-year colleges; and

5. employment status (full time vs. part time) and tenure status (tenured, tenure track, nontenure track) among regular faculty employed at public 2-year colleges that have tenure systems.

Data and Sample

Data from the 1993 National Study of Postsecondary Faculty (NSOPF:93) are used to address the research questions. Sponsored by the U.S. Department of Education's National Center for Education Statistics, the NSOPF:93 is a nationally representative sample of college and university faculty and instructional staff who were employed by public and private nonproprietary higher education institutions in fall 1992. The NSOPF:93 includes data from 25,870 responding faculty (87% response rate) and 872 institutions (91% response rate) (Selfa et al., 1997).

Table 1 shows the criteria that are used to select the sample for each of the research questions and the resulting number of cases in the analyses. For each set of analyses, the data are weighted by the NCES WEIGHT divided by the average weight for the sample. This procedure corrects for the oversampling of some groups, while minimizing the effects of large sample sizes on standard errors and t statistics (Thomas and Heck, 2001). To correct for the design effects of the NSOPF:93 that are associated with the nested nature of the data (i.e., faculty selected from within selected institutions), a rigorous threshold of statistical significance ($p < .001$) is

TABLE 1
Criteria that Are Used to Select the Sample for Each Research Question

Criteria	RQ # 1 Institution Type	RQ # 2 Appoint. Status	RQ # 3 Base Salary	RQ # 4 Academic Rank	RQ # 5 Tenure Status
Faculty status	x	x	x	x	x
4-year institution	x				
Public 2-year institution	x	x	x	x	x
Some instructional duties	x	x	x	x	x
Primary activity teaching	x	x	x	x	x
At least 9-month appointment	x	x	x	x	x
Regular appointment			x	x	x
Full-time employment				x	
Tenure system					x
Number of cases in the analyses	15,499	5,262	4,073	3,372	2,819

Source: Analyses of NSOPF: 93.

used to interpret the results of the statistical analyses (Thomas and Heck, 2001).

Analyses and Definitions of Dependent Variables

Several types of analyses and dependent variables are used to address the research questions. At the descriptive level, ANOVA and cross tabulations are used to compare the characteristics of women and men faculty and faculty of different racial/ethnic groups.

For the first research question, the dependent variable is defined as employed at a public 2-year institution (yes or no). Because the dependent variable is dichotomous, logistic regression is used to isolate the relationships between sex and race/ethnicity and the probability of holding a faculty position at a public 2-year college rather than at a 4-year college or university after controlling for human capital, structural, and market explanations for the observed relationships.

For the second research question, the dependent variable has the following four categories: full-time regular appointment, full-time temporary appointment, part-time regular appointment, and part-time temporary appointment. Because of the categorical nature of this variable, multinomial logit, a special case of the general log-linear model, is used to examine the relationships between sex and race/ethnicity and the dependent variable (employment status and appointment type) after controlling for human capital, structural, and market characteristics.

For the third research question, the dependent variable is defined as the base salary that is received from the institution. Ordinary least squares (OLS) regression is used to isolate the relationships between sex and race/ethnicity and this continuous dependent variable after controlling for measures of human capital, structural characteristics, and market forces. Preliminary analyses showed that employment status (i.e., full time vs. part time) interacted with 18 of the other independent variables, including sex and race/ethnicity. These interactions indicate that the salary determination process is different for full-time than for part-time faculty. To reduce the complexity of the interpretations, separate analyses of the relationships between sex and race/ethnicity and base salary are conducted for full-time and part-time faculty.

For the fourth research question, the dependent variable has four categories: full professor, associate professor, assistant professor, and instructor or lecturer. Instructors and lecturers are combined since only 0.3% ($n = 12$) of faculty with some instructional duties, whose principal activity is teaching and who hold at least a 9-month, regular, full-time appointment at a public 2-year college are lecturers. Faculty with no ($n = 370$) or other ($n = 57$) rank are excluded from the analyses. Multinomial logit is used to examine the relationships between sex and race/ethnicity and this categorical dependent variable after controlling for differences in human capital, structural characteristics, and market forces.

For the fifth research question, the dependent variable has three categories: full-time tenured, full-time tenure track, and part-time, nontenure track. Only 2.7% ($n = 76$) of regular faculty at public 2-year colleges hold part-time tenured or tenure-track positions, and only 3.9% ($n = 111$) hold full-time nontenure-track positions. Faculty who hold these two types of positions are excluded from the analyses rather than combined with another category since these faculty appear to be different from faculty in other groups. Most importantly, men are observed to represent a higher share of faculty with part-time tenured or tenure-track positions than part-time nontenure-track positions (65% vs. 55%) and a smaller share of faculty with full-time nontenure-track positions than part-time nontenure-track positions (46% vs. 55%). Because of the categorical nature of this variable, multinomial logit is used to examine the effects of sex and race/ethnicity on employment and tenure status after controlling for human capital, structural, and market explanations.

Logistic and multinomial logit models estimate the log-odds of one outcome occurring relative to the baseline category. If the baseline category is j, the model for the ith category is:

$$Log(P_i/P_j) = B_{i0} + B_{i1}X_1 + B_{i2}X_2 + \ldots + B_{ip}X_p$$

The logistic coefficients that result from this equation may be interpreted as the change in log odds associated with a one-unit change in the independent variable. The interpretation of the coefficients is facilitated by the use of odds ratios, as described by the following equation:

$$(P_i/P_j) = e^{B_{i0} + B_{i1}X_1 + \ldots + B_{ip}X_p} = e^{B_{i0}B_{i1}X_i} \ldots e^{B_{ip}X_p}$$

The odds ratio represents the change in the odds of a particular outcome relative to the reference outcome that is associated with a one-unit change in a particular independent variable. An odds ratio greater than one represents an increase in the likelihood of a particular outcome relative to the reference outcome, whereas an odds ratio less than I represents a decrease in the likelihood of the particular outcome.

The test of whether a coefficient is different from zero is based on the Wald statistic, which is calculated as the coefficient divided by its standard error, squared. A pseudo-R^2 reported to provide an indication of the strength of the relationship between the outcome variable and the independent variables. The percentage of cases that is classified correctly provides an additional indicator of model fit.

Independent Variables

Because research suggests that both human capital and structural theories play a role in explaining observed differences in such faculty rewards as salaries (Perna, 2001a, in press; Smart, 1991; Verdugo and Schneider, 1994), this examination

of sex and racial/ethnic group differences in employment experiences uses a conceptual model that incorporates both human capital and structural approaches to academic labor markets as well as the market forces of supply and demand. Table 2 shows the particular variables that are included in the analyses for each research question.

Human capital is accumulated via educational attainment, on-the-job training and experience (Becker, 1962). Educational attainment is measured by a categorical variable that indicates whether the highest degree is a doctoral, first-professional, or master's degree relative to no more than a bachelor's degree. Depending on the outcome (see Table 2), experience is measured by the continuous variables, number of years since the highest degree was earned and/or number of years in the current position. In the analysis of faculty salaries, measures of experienced squared are also included to control for the observed decline over time in the return to investments in education and training (Fairweather, 1995; Perna, 2001a; Weiler, 1990).

Productivity is also a reflection of an individual's human capital (Becker, 1962). Teaching

TABLE 2
Variables Included in the Analysis for Each Research Question

Variables included	RQ #1 Institution type	RQ #2 Appointment type	RQ #3 Base salary	RQ #4 Academic rank	RQ #5 Tenure status
Sex	x	x	x	x	x
Race/ethnicity	x	x	x	x	x
Human capital					
Educational attainment	x	x	x	x	x
Years since highest degree	x	x	x	x	x
Years in current position			x	x	x
Time on teaching			x	x	
Teaching load			x	x	
Number presentations			x	x	
Engaged in research			x	x	
Time on research			x	x	
Time on service			x	x	
Time on administration			x	x	
Department chair			x		
Structural characteristics					
Appointment length			x		
Undergraduate enrollment		x	x	x	x
Tenure system		x	x	x	
Unionization		x	x	x	x
Geographic region			x		
Structural & market forces					
Academic field	x	x	x	x	x

productivity is measured by the percentage of time that is spent on teaching and teaching-related activities and the total number of classes taught. The percentage of time spent on teaching and teaching-related activities is recoded into a categorical variable to correct the non-normal distribution. For example, analyses of the NSOPF:93 show that two thirds of faculty with regular appointments at public 2-year colleges spend at least 70% of their time on teaching and teaching-related activities. For the percentage of time that is spent on teaching, the categories are: 0%–25%, 26%–50%, 51%–70%, 71%–80%, 81%–90%, 91%–99%, and 100% (reference category). Research productivity is measured by the number of conference presentations during the past 2 years, whether the faculty member engages in externally funded or nonfunded research, and the percentage of time spent on research and research-related activities. Because of the skewed distribution, the number of conference presentations in the past 2 years is treated as a categorical variable: 0 (reference category), 1–3, 4–9, and 10 or more. Because teaching is the predominant activity of faculty employed at public 2-year colleges, the percentage of time spent on research is treated as a dichotomous variable: spend more than 5% of time on research (yes/no). Similarly, service productivity is measured by the dummy variable, spend more than 5% of time on service activities (yes/no), and administrative productivity is measured by the dummy variable, spend more than 10% of time on administration (yes/no). In the analysis of faculty salaries, administrative productivity is also measured by whether the individual is the chairperson of the department.

Structural attributes describe the characteristics of the institution in which a faculty member works and the faculty member's job status (Youn, 1992). One institutional characteristic is size as measured by undergraduate enrollment. Undergraduate enrollment is measured in quartiles, with the highest quartile serving as the reference group. A second institutional characteristic is a dichotomous variable reflecting whether the individual works at an institution with a tenure system (yes or no). Job status is measured by the length of the individual's annual appointment (i.e., 9 or 10 months rather than 11 or 12 months) and whether the individual is a member of the union. Union status is measured by whether an individual works at a unionized institution and is a member (reference category), whether the individual works at a unionized institution but is not a member, and whether the individual works at a nonunionized institution. Geographic region of the institution is included in the analyses of salaries to control for cost of living differences and other market forces. The following regions are considered: Northeast, Midwest, Southeast, Southwest, and West (reference category).

In this research, academic field is included as a proxy for the segregation of women and minorities in particular fields, a structural characteristic, as well as for differences in the supply of and demand for faculty across disciplines, the primary indicator of market forces. Academic field is measured by 16 categories. Analyses of NSOPF:93 reveal that these 16 categories can be organized by the percentage of women in the field, ranging from fields with less than 20% women (economics and political science, engineering, and occupational programs), to fields with 20%–55% women (history and philosophy, physical sciences, computer science, mathematics, biological sciences, other or unknown field, fine arts, other social science, and business), to fields with more than 55% women (English, education, foreign language, and health sciences). Occupational programs are the reference category for two reasons. First, Lassiter (1983) found that whether a faculty member worked in a discipline related to the transfer function rather than the technical-vocational function of the institution was a significant predictor of salaries at 2 of 10 community colleges in Tennessee. Occupational programs are assumed to be related to the technical-vocational function rather than the transfer function of the institution. Second, along with economics and political science as well as engineering, occupational programs is one of three academic field groupings in which women represent less than 20% of the faculty.

Limitations

The NSOPF:93 has such strengths as a reasonably large, nationally representative sample size and high response rates. But, like all secondary data analyses, use of this database results in several limitations. One limitation pertains to the availability of appropriate proxies for potentially important constructs. Although the occupational program category is assumed to be related to the technical-vocational function rather than the transfer function of a public 2-year institution, the extent to which faculty in other disciplines are teaching courses that are related to the transfer function cannot be determined using the NSOPF:93. Other structural characteristics that Gahn and Twombly (2001) observed to be potentially important but that are omitted from these analyses include such characteristics of the institutional mission as the types of programs offered and whether the institution has traditionally served as a continuation of high school or the first 2 years of a 4-year degree.

A second limitation pertains to the examination of the employment experiences of American Indian/Alaskan Native faculty and faculty who are not U.S. citizens. Because of their small sample sizes, including separate categories for these groups in the multinomial logit analyses would result in problems with zero cells and unstable estimates of coefficients and standard errors (Menard, 1995). Therefore, the multinomial logit analyses are limited to four racial/ethnic groups: Asians, Blacks, Hispanics, and Whites.

A third limitation is the use of a cross-sectional database to examine employment experiences. In the absence of longitudinal data describing the experiences of faculty over time, conclusions about causality are limited. As a result, this research focuses on exploring relationships among sex and race/ethnicity and various employment outcomes, not the effects of sex and race/ethnicity on these outcomes.

Findings

Employment at a Public 2-Year Institution Rather Than a 4-Year Institution

Descriptive analyses show that women represent a substantially higher share of faculty employed at public 2-year institutions than at 4-year institutions (45% vs. 34%). Although the representation of faculty of color is small regardless of institutional type, Table 3 suggests that the representation of blacks (5.5% vs. 5.1%), Hispanics (4.6% vs. 2.3%), and American Indians (0.9% vs. 0.3%) is somewhat higher at public 2-year colleges than at 4-year institutions.

Because of the difficulty that is associated with determining the direction of causality in this cross-sectional database (as described previously), this exploratory analysis of sex and racial/ethnic group differences in the probability of employment at a public 2-year rather than a 4-year institution includes a limited number of control variables. Table 4 shows that the observed greater likelihood of employment at a public 2-year institution than a 4-year institution for women is eliminated when differences in human capital are taken into account. Controlling only for sex shows that American Indians and Hispanics are more likely, and Asians are less likely, than whites to be employed at a public 2- than a 4-year institution. When differences in human capital are taken into account (Model 2), Asians are as likely, but American Indians and Hispanics continue to be more likely than whites to be employed at public 2-year institutions. Also controlling for academic field, a measure of both structural and market forces, reduces the magnitude but does not eliminate the relationship between Hispanic and institutional type. Even after taking into account differences in human capital and academic field, Hispanic faculty continue to be more likely than other faculty to be employed at a public 2-year college than at a 4-year institution. The relationship between institutional type and American Indian is not significant at the $p < .001$ level.

An examination of the block X^2 in Table 4 suggests that differences in institutional type of employment are due primarily to differences in human capital and only secondarily to differences in academic field. The probability of employment at a public 2-year institution relative to employment at a 4-year institution declines as educational attainment increases. Although teachers of mathematics, biological sciences, and English are as likely as teachers of occupational programs to be employed at public 2-year colleges, individuals working in other fields (history and philosophy, physical science, computer science, other/unknown field, fine arts, other social science, business, education, foreign language, and health science) are less likely to be employed at public 2-year colleges than their counterparts in occupational programs.

Employment Status and Appointment Type

Regardless of sex or race/ethnicity, about one half of all community college faculty hold full-time regular appointments, one fifth hold part-time temporary appointments, and one fifth hold part-time regular appointments. Only about 7%

TABLE 3
Observed Representation of Faculty by Institutional Type,
Sex, and Race/Ethnicity: Fall 1992

Characteristic		Total	4-Year	Public 2-Year
%		100.0%	69.0%	31.0%
n		15,499	10,691	4,808
Sex	p < .001			
Total		100.0	100.0	100.0
Men		22.7	66.3	54.7
Women		37.3	33.7	45.3
Race/ethnicity	p < .001			
Total		100.0	100.0	100.0
American Indian		0.5	0.3	0.9
Asian		4.5	5.2	3.1
Black		5.2	5.1	5.5
Hispanic		3.0	2.3	4.6
White		86.7	87.1	85.8

Notes: Sample is limited to faculty with at least some instructional duties, who were employed at 4-year and public 2-year institutions, whose primary responsibility was teaching and who held at least a 9-month appointment.

Tests of statistical significance for the crosstabs are based on chi-square.

Source: Analyses of NSOPF: 93.

of faculty at public 2-year institutions hold full-time temporary appointments.

Both the descriptive (Table 5) and multinomial logit (Table 6) analyses show that sex and race/ethnicity are unrelated to employment and appointment status among faculty at public 2-year institutions. The analyses suggest that the odds of holding a part-time regular or temporary appointment rather than a full-time appointment are lower for those who have attained a doctoral, professional, or master's degree than for those who have attained no more than a bachelor's degree. Structural characteristics also play a role, as the odds of holding a part-time regular or temporary appointment are lower for those who work at institutions in the lowest quartile of size (measured by undergraduate enrollment), lower for those who work at institutions with a tenure system, and lower for individuals who are members of their institution's union.

Institutional Base Salary

Women are observed to average lower institutional base salaries than men among full-time public 2-year college faculty ($35,413 vs. $40,210). Table 7 shows that observed salaries are statistically equivalent among full-time faculty of different racial/ethnic groups. Table 8 shows that controlling for differences in education and expe-

rience reduces from 13% to 6% the male–female differential full-time faculty salaries. The observed lower salary for women full-time faculty than for men full-time faculty is eliminated when differences in productivity are taken into account. Academic field, a proxy for structural characteristics and market forces, is unrelated to the salaries of full-time faculty at public 2-year colleges after taking into account other variables.

Examining the results of the OLS regression analyses and additional descriptive statistics (available from the author on request) suggests that the observed differences in the salaries of women and men full-time faculty are primarily explained by sex differences in two measures of human capital: educational attainment and years of experience in the current position. The OLS regression analyses (Table 8) show that, on average, salaries are 20% higher for full-time faculty who hold a doctoral degree than for their counterparts who hold no more than a bachelor's degree. But, fewer women than men full-time faculty hold a doctoral degree (12% vs. 20%). Similarly, while average salaries increase with the number of years employed in the current position net of other variables, women have worked fewer years at their current position than men (10.1 years vs. 13.5 years).

In contrast to full-time faculty, descriptive analyses suggest that average institutional base

TABLE 4
Predictors of Faculty Employment in a Public 2-Year College Rather than in a 4-Year College or University: Fall 1992

Independent Variable	Model 1 Sex and Race			Model 2 Human Capital			Model 3 Structural/Market			
	B	S.E.	Exp(B)	B	S.E.	Exp(b)	B	S.E.	Exp(B)	Delta-p
Female	0.503	0.036	1.654***	0.001	0.043	1.001	0.067	0.048	1.069	
American Indian	1.106	0.229	3.021***	0.971	0.270	2.642***	0.935	0.274	2.547	0.224**
Asian	-0.445	0.095	0.641***	-0.136	0.110	0.873	-0.173	0.113	0.841	
Black	0.062	0.078	1.064	-0.011	0.089	0.989	0.002	0.092	1.002	
Hispanic	0.748	0.095	2.113***	0.643	0.113	1.902***	0.685	0.118	1.983	0.161***
Doctoral degree				-3.320	0.074	0.036***	-3.608	0.081	0.027	-0.298***
Professional degree				-3.344	0.113	0.035***	-3.236	0.118	0.039	-0.293***
Master's degree				-1.099	0.065	0.333***	-1.210	0.069	0.298	-0.192***
Years since highest degree				-0.007	0.002	0.993**	-0.007	0.002	0.993	-0.002**
Economics & political science							-0.607	0.170	0.545	-0.113***
Engineering							-1.117	0.162	0.327	-0.182***
History or philosophy							-0.651	0.159	0.521	-0.120***
Physical sciences							-0.544	0.160	0.580	-0.103**
Computer science							-0.473	0.161	0.623	-0.091**
Mathematics							0.090	0.141	1.094	
Biological sciences							-0.043	0.156	0.957	

	Model 1			Model 2			Model 3			
	B	SE	Exp(B)	B	SE	Exp(B)	B	SE	Exp(B)	Delta-p
Other or unknown field							-1.292	0.133	0.275	-0.200***
Fine arts							-1.886	0.136	0.152	-0.246***
Other social science							-0.565	0.142	0.568	-0.107***
Business							-0.819	0.134	0.441	-0.145***
English							-0.142	0.134	0.867	
Education							-0.940	0.141	0.390	-0.161***
Foreign language							-1.146	0.173	0.318	-0.185***
Health sciences							-1.237	0.134	0.290	-0.195***
Constant	-1.032	0.024	0.356***	1.124	0.075	3.079***	2.025	0.129	7.579	***
Number of cases in analyses	15,329			15,329			15,329			
χ^2, df	307.2	5***		4,174.1	9***		4,895.0	24***		
Block χ^2, df	307.2	5***		3,866.8	4***		720.9	15***		
G^2/df	1.21			0.96			0.92			
Pseudo R^2	0.020			0.214			0.242			
Percentage correctly classified	60%			72%			75%			
% 4-year correctly classified	66%			68%			73%			
% public 2-year correctly classified	48%			83%			80%			
Baseline P	0.310			0.310			0.310			

Notes: Sample is limited to faculty with at least some instructional duties, employed at 4-year and public 2-year institutions, whose primary responsibility was teaching and who held at least a 9-month appointment. Delta-p represents the change in the probability of employment in a public 2-year college associated with a one-unit change in each independent variable. Pseudo $R^2 = \chi^2/(N + \chi^2)$; Delta-$p = \exp(L_1)/[1 + \exp(L_1)] - P_0$ (Cabrera, 1994). Percentage of cases correctly classified corrected for non-50/50 distribution.

Source: Analyses of NSOPF: 93.

***$p < .001$, **$p < .01$, *$p < .05$.

TABLE 5
Observed Distribution of Faculty at Public 2-Year Colleges
by Appointment Status, Sex, and Race/Ethnicity: Fall 1992

Characteristic	Total	Full-Time Temporary	Part-Time Regular	Part-Time Temporary	Full-Time Regular
n	5,262	391	1,074	1,163	2,635
Sex	*p* = .40				
Total	100.0	7.4	20.4	22.1	50.1
Men	100.0	7.6	19.7	21.6	51.2
Women	100.0	7.2	21.3	22.7	48.7
Race/ethnicity	*p* = .24				
Total	100.0	7.4	20.4	22.1	50.1
American Indian	100.0	12.2	18.4	20.4	49.0
Asian	100.0	8.6	20.2	19.0	52.1
Black	100.0	6.5	17.5	21.9	54.1
Hispanic	100.0	4.5	25.4	24.2	45.9
White	100.0	7.5	20.4	22.1	50.0

Notes: Sample is limited to faculty with at least some instructional duties, who were employed at public 2-year institutions, whose primary responsibility was teaching and who held at least a 9-month appointment.
Tests of statistical significance for the crosstabs are based on chi-square.
Source: Analyses of NSOPF: 93.

salaries are higher for women than for men part-time faculty at the $p < .01$ level but not at the more stringent $p < .001$ ($10,882 vs. $8,736). The OLS regression analyses show that, after controlling for human capital, structural, and market characteristics, average salaries are about 25% higher for women than for men. As with full-time faculty, race/ethnicity is unrelated to salaries among part-time faculty.

Unlike for full-time faculty, such measures of productivity as course load appear to explain the largest portion of the variance in part-time faculty salaries. Table 9 shows that, on average, the salaries of part-time faculty increase by about 25% with each additional course that is taught. This premium appears to benefit women more than men, since descriptive analyses (available from the author on request) show that women average a higher number of courses than men (2.4 vs. 2.0).

As among full-time faculty, educational attainment is also an important predictor of salaries for part-time faculty. Although part-time faculty with doctorates earn substantially higher salaries than part-time faculty with lower levels of educational attainment, only about 6% of women and men part-time faculty at public 2-year colleges hold this credential. While spending more than 10% of time on administration is associated with lower salaries, comparable proportions of women and men allocate this amount

of time to administration (about 9%). Part-time faculty in education average lower salaries than faculty in other academic fields. Women are disproportionately affected by this difference, since 15% of women, but only 4% of men, teach in education.

Academic Rank

The most common academic rank among faculty at public 2-year colleges is instructor. Approximately 84% of regular part-time faculty hold the rank of instructor, compared with about 42% of regular full-time faculty. In contrast, only 7% of part-time faculty hold the rank of full, associate, or assistant professor, compared with 45% of full-time faculty. Because of the smaller variance in the distribution of faculty by rank among part-time faculty, the examination of sex and racial/ethnic group differences in rank is limited to full-time faculty.

While comparable shares of full-time women and men faculty are observed to hold the most common rank of instructor (about 42%), Table 10 suggests that a smaller portion of women than men hold the highest rank of full professor (15% vs. 23%). Table 10 also shows that the distribution of faculty across academic ranks varies by race/ethnicity. A smaller share of Hispanics (7%) than of faculty overall (14%) appear to hold the rank of associate professor, while a

TABLE 6

Predictors of Employment and Appointment Status Among Faculty Employed at Public 2-Year Institutions: Fall 1992

Independent Variables	Part-Time Regular			Part-Time Temporary			Full-Time Regular		
	B	Std. Error	Exp(B)	B	Std. Error	Exp(B)	B	Std. Error	Exp(B)
Female	-0.018	0.142	0.983	-0.104	0.140	0.902	0.081	0.126	1.085
Asian	-0.016	0.345	0.984	-0.218	0.353	0.804	-0.161	0.301	0.851
Black	-0.101	0.290	0.904	0.107	0.282	1.113	0.166	0.253	1.180
Hispanic	0.484	0.346	1.622	0.253	0.351	1.288	0.457	0.325	1.580
Doctoral degree	-1.767	0.263	0.171***	-1.170	0.254	0.310***	0.517	0.222	1.676*
Professional or master's	-1.090	0.170	0.336***	-0.673	0.173	0.510***	0.228	0.158	1.257
Years since highest degree	-0.006	0.007	0.994	0.003	0.007	1.003	0.022	0.006	1.022***
UG enrollment—1st quartile	-0.976	0.183	0.377***	-1.417	0.183	0.242***	-0.310	0.161	0.733
UG enrollment—2nd quartile	-0.346	0.192	0.707	-0.477	0.188	0.621*	0.068	0.172	1.070
UG enrollment—3rd quartile	-0.086	0.184	0.917	-0.420	0.182	0.657*	-0.207	0.167	0.813
Tenure system	-1.219	0.139	0.296***	-1.396	0.138	0.248***	0.116	0.129	1.123
Unionized/not member	1.319	0.168	3.740***	1.760	0.171	5.815***	-0.174	0.156	0.840
Nonunionized institution	0.354	0.153	1.424*	1.085	0.154	2.960***	-0.040	0.130	0.961
Econ & political science	1.129	0.589	3.093	1.800	0.587	6.048**	0.547	0.522	1.728
Engineering	0.178	0.392	1.194	-0.189	0.474	0.828	-0.143	0.335	0.866

TABLE 6 (Continued)
Predictors of Employment and Appointment Status Among Faculty Employed at Public 2-Year Institutions: Fall 1992

Independent Variables	Part-Time Regular			Part-Time Temporary			Full-Time Regular		
	B	Std. Error	Exp(B)	B	Std. Error	Exp(B)	B	Std. Error	Exp(B)
Engineering	0.178	0.392	1.194	−0.189	0.474	0.828	−0.143	0.335	0.866
History or philosophy	0.048	0.449	1.050	1.548	0.412	4.700***	−0.626	0.347	0.535
Physical sciences	0.598	0.410	1.819	0.644	0.453	1.904	−0.440	0.345	0.644
Computer science	0.369	0.365	1.447	1.285	0.377	3.616**	−0.196	0.322	0.822
Mathematics	1.125	0.323	3.080***	2.163	0.339	8.696***	−0.135	0.290	0.874
Biological sciences	0.543	0.385	1.721	1.096	0.397	2.991**	−0.596	0.324	0.551
Other field	0.806	0.316	2.239*	1.219	0.342	3.384***	−0.027	0.282	0.973
Fine arts	0.843	0.338	2.323***	1.855	0.353	6.391***	−0.814	0.307	0.443**
Other social science	1.905	0.427	6.722***	2.784	0.437	16.184***	0.613	0.391	1.846
Business	0.516	0.308	1.675	1.067	0.330	2.907**	−0.269	0.269	0.764
English	0.787	0.308	2.197*	1.853	0.324	6.380***	−0.264	0.267	0.768
Education	1.173	0.339	3.231**	1.494	0.364	4.454***	−0.515	0.306	0.598
Foreign language	2.232	0.585	9.316***	2.598	0.602	13.443***	−0.132	0.567	0.877
Health sciences	0.078	0.314	1.081	0.330	0.348	1.391	0.181	0.268	1.198
Intercept	1.761	0.307	***	0.665	0.329	*	1.563	0.276	***
Number of cases in the analyses			1,002			1,137			2,580
Pseudo R^2 (Cox and Snell)	0.315								
Percentage classified correctly	59.3%		23.5%			45.5%			88.0%

Notes: Sample is limited to faculty with at least some instructional duties, who were employed at public 2-year institutions, whose primary responsibility was teaching and who held at least a 9-month appointment. Odds ratios are relative to holding a full-time temporary position.
Source: Analyses of NSOPF: 93.
***$p < .001$; **$p < .01$; *$p < .05$.

TABLE 7
Observed Differences in Salaries by Sex and Race/Ethnicity
Among Regular Full-Time and Part-Time Faculty Employed at
Public 2-Year Colleges: Fall 1992

Characteristic	Total		Full Time		Part Time	
	Mean	Std. Dev.	Mean	Std. Dev.	Mean	Std. Dev.
Total	$30,239	17,455	$38,090	11,509	$9,742	13,162
Sex	$p < .001$		$p < .001$		$p < .01$	
Men	31,803	18,045	40,210	11,704	8,736	10,821
Women	28,323	16,508	35,413	10,677	10,882	15,320
Race/ethnicity	$p = .50$		$p = .50$		$p = .83$	
American Indian	30,820	17,022	38,831	11,945	8,552	3,159
Asian	31,790	18,090	39,941	12,516	7,214	5,733
Black	31,483	16,837	38,170	11,236	10,535	14,070
Hispanic	28,862	17,602	38,870	11,061	10,141	11,032
White	30,171	17,469	37,967	11,506	9,765	13,486

Notes: Sample is limited to faculty with at least some instructional duties, who were employed at public 2-year institutions, whose primary responsibility was teaching and who held at least a 9-month, regular appointment.

Salaries exclude "extreme" salaries, defined as greater than $200,000 ($n = 34$) or equal to $0 ($n = 76$).

Test of statistical significance for women is based on a t test. Test of statistical significance for race/ethnicity is based on an F test.

Source: Analyses of NSOPF: 93.

higher share of Hispanics than of faculty overall appear to hold the rank of assistant professor (17% vs. 12%).

Table 11 shows that the observed sex differences in academic rank are eliminated when human capital, structural, and market characteristics are controlled. Although a smaller share of women than men are observed to hold the rank of full professor, this difference is eliminated when differences in human capital are taken into account. (The coefficients for the blocked entry of variables are available from the author on request.)

Racial/ethnic group differences in academic rank also appear to be eliminated after taking into account differences in human capital, structural, and market characteristics. Table 11 shows that the odds of holding the rank of associate professor rather than the rank of assistant professor are lower for Hispanics than for faculty of other racial/ethnic groups at the $p < .01$ level, but not at the more stringent $p < .001$ level.

Measures of human capital are important predictors of academic rank. Attaining a doctoral degree is associated with higher odds of holding the rank of full professor but lower odds of holding the rank of instructor or lecturer relative to holding the rank of assistant professor. Experience also matters, as the odds of holding the rank of full or associate professor increase with the number of years since the highest degree was earned and the number of years in the current position.

Structural characteristics are also related to academic rank among public 2-year college faculty. Working at an institution in the lowest quartile of undergraduate enrollment reduces the odds of holding the highest rank of full professor, while working at an institution with a tenure system reduces the odds of holding the rank of instructor. Faculty in economics and political science and health sciences—fields with among the lowest and highest representation of women—are less likely than faculty in occupational programs to hold the rank of instructor after controlling for other variables.

Employment and Tenure Status

The descriptive statistics show that a smaller share of women than men faculty with regular appointments at institutions with a tenure system hold full-time tenured positions (54% vs. 65%), and a higher share of women than men hold full-time tenure-track positions (22% vs. 14%). Table 12 shows that the distribution of faculty of different racial/ethnic groups does not vary by employment and tenure status.

The multinomial logit analyses show that women are less likely than men to hold a full-time

TABLE 8
Predictors of Institutional Base Salary Among Faculty Employed at Public 2-Year Institutions: Fall 1992
(unstandardized regression coefficients)

Independent Variables	Sex and Race		Human Capital		Productivity		Structural		Market	
	B	Std. Error	B	Std. Error	B	Std. Error	B	Std. Error	B	Std. Error
Female	-0.130	0.020***	-0.056	0.020**	-0.039	0.021	-0.030	0.021	-0.028	0.023
American Indian	-0.005	0.105	0.005	0.101	-0.033	0.101	-0.048	0.100	-0.062	0.100
Asian	0.011	0.057	0.045	0.054	0.056	0.054	0.003	0.054	0.001	0.054
Black	0.021	0.043	0.034	0.041	0.031	0.041	0.004	0.041	0.002	0.042
Hispanic	0.047	0.050	0.081	0.048	0.080	0.048	0.068	0.048	0.073	0.048
Doctoral degree			0.142	0.034***	0.155	0.035***	0.165	0.035***	0.204	0.039***
Professional or master's			0.059	0.027*	0.062	0.027*	0.066	0.027*	0.096	0.030**
Years since degree			0.002	0.003	0.002	0.003	0.001	0.003	0.003	0.003
Years since degree, squared			0.000	0.000	0.000	0.000	0.000	0.000	0.000	0.000
Years current position			0.020	0.004***	0.020	0.004***	0.020	0.004***	0.019	0.004***
Years position, squared			0.000	0.000	0.000	0.000	0.000	0.000	0.000	0.000
Number courses taught					0.015	0.006*	0.016	0.006**	0.019	0.006**
25% or less time teaching					-0.053	0.072	-0.057	0.071	-0.053	0.072
26%–50% time teaching					0.119	0.048*	0.120	0.047*	0.108	0.048*
51%–70% time teaching					0.083	0.043	0.082	0.043	0.069	0.043
71%–80% time teaching					0.042	0.038	0.041	0.038	0.030	0.038
81%–90% time teaching					0.040	0.037	0.047	0.037	0.045	0.037
91%–99% time teaching					-0.027	0.043	-0.021	0.042	-0.021	0.042
1–3 presentations past 2 yrs					-0.040	0.029	-0.043	0.028	-0.042	0.028
4–9 presentations past 2 yrs					-0.041	0.031	-0.037	0.030	-0.034	0.031
10 + presentations past 2 yrs					0.022	0.028	0.009	0.028	0.011	0.028
Funded research					0.056	0.046	0.032	0.045	0.046	0.045
Nonfunded research					-0.050	0.024*	-0.063	0.023**	-0.057	0.024*
More 5% time research					-0.020	0.027	-0.023	0.026	-0.015	0.026
More 5% time service					-0.064	0.026*	-0.053	0.026*	-0.051	0.026*
More 10% time admin.					0.020	0.030	0.028	0.030	0.034	0.030
Chair of department					0.050	0.030	0.061	0.030*	0.058	0.031

Variable	Model 1 b	Model 1 SE	Model 2 b	Model 2 SE	Model 3 b	Model 3 SE	Model 4 b	Model 4 SE	Model 5 b	Model 5 SE
11–12 month appointment							0.066	0.023***	0.062	0.023**
UG enrollment							0.030	0.009***	0.031	0.009**
Tenure system							0.016	0.024	0.020	0.024
Unionized instn/not member							-0.058	0.029*	-0.058	0.029*
Nonunionized instn							-0.136	0.028***	-0.137	0.028***
Northeast							-0.053	0.032	-0.060	0.032
Midwest							-0.022	0.030	-0.026	0.030
Southeast							-0.056	0.036	-0.059	0.036
Southwest							-0.102	0.036**	-0.105	0.036**
Econ/political science									-0.033	0.068
Engineering									0.053	0.059
History or philosophy									-0.035	0.066
Physical sciences									-0.071	0.062
Computer science									0.035	0.059
Mathematics									-0.107	0.050*
Biological sciences									-0.097	0.061
Other programs									-0.115	0.048*
Fine arts									-0.119	0.063
Psych/social science									-0.061	0.054
Business									-0.043	0.048
English									-0.081	0.047
Education									-0.045	0.056
Foreign languages									-0.059	0.087
Health sciences									0.005	0.046
Constant	10.525	0.014***	10.176	0.038***	10.084	0.054***	10.092	0.065***	10.089	0.071***
Number cases in analyses	2,831		2,831		2,831		2,831		2,831	
R^2 change	0.015***		0.086***		0.016***		0.030***		0.007	
R^2	0.015***		0.101***		0.117***		0.147***		0.154***	
Adjusted R^2	0.013***		0.098***		0.108***		0.136***		0.138***	

Note: Sample limited to faculty with at least some instructional duties, who were employed at public 2-year institutions, whose primary responsibility was teaching and who held at least a 9-month, regular, full-time appointment.

Source: Analyses of NSOPF: 93.

$***p < .001, **p < .01, *p < .05.$

TABLE 9
Predictors of Institutional Base Salary Among Part-Time Faculty Employed at Public 2-Year Colleges: Fall 1992 (unstandardized regression coefficients)

Independent Variables	Sex and Race		Human Capital		Productivity		Structural		Market	
	B	Std. Error	B	Std. Error	B	Std. Error	B	Std. Error	B	Std. Error
Female	0.154	0.066*	0.210	0.065**	0.144	0.063*	0.156	0.064*	0.252	0.069***
American Indian	0.312	0.340	0.340	0.335	0.407	0.315	0.426	0.314	0.468	0.314
Asian	-0.152	0.192	-0.160	0.188	-0.066	0.177	-0.159	0.177	-0.207	0.177
Black	0.143	0.152	0.089	0.149	0.100	0.141	0.088	0.140	0.183	0.140
Hispanic	0.068	0.137	0.092	0.135	0.142	0.129	0.135	0.130	0.211	0.131
Doctoral degree			0.646	0.144***	0.637	0.143***	0.673	0.142***	0.648	0.152***
Prof. or master's degree			0.169	0.068*	0.201	0.067***	0.204	0.066**	0.225	0.072***
Years since degree			0.012	0.010	0.018	0.009	0.016	0.009	0.008	0.009
Years since degree, squared			0.000	0.000	0.000	0.000	0.000	0.000	0.000	0.000
Years current position			0.038	0.011***	0.031	0.010**	0.024	0.010*	0.028	0.010**
Years position, squared			-0.001	0.000	0.000	0.000	0.000	0.000	0.000	0.000
Number courses taught					0.228	0.022***	0.231	0.022***	0.249	0.022***
25% or less time teaching					-0.054	0.107	-0.061	0.107	-0.061	0.110
26%–50% time teaching					0.245	0.113*	0.266	0.114*	0.203	0.117
51%–70% time teaching					0.146	0.126	0.151	0.125	0.154	0.125
71%–80% time teaching					0.311	0.115**	0.274	0.115*	0.278	0.114*
81%–90% time teaching					0.142	0.106	0.108	0.106	0.082	0.105
91%–99% time teaching					0.215	0.127	0.205	0.127	0.270	0.126*
1–3 presentations past 2 yrs					-0.072	0.103	-0.121	0.103	-0.129	0.103
4–9 presentations past 2 yrs					-0.155	0.120	-0.180	0.120	-0.146	0.120
10 + presentations past 2 yrs					-0.099	0.099	-0.099	0.098	-0.051	0.099

Funded research	0.085	0.153	0.043	0.154	0.052	0.160
Nonfunded research	0.101	0.081	0.026	0.083	-0.036	0.088
More 5% time research	0.037	0.089	0.064	0.089	0.076	0.089
More 5% time service	0.277	0.084**	0.264	0.083**	0.269	0.084**
More 10% time admin.	-0.489	0.119***	-0.488	0.118***	-0.467	0.121***
Chair of department	0.328	0.243	0.371	0.243	0.313	0.241
11–12 month appointment			0.098	0.074	0.099	0.075
UG enrollment			-0.051	0.029	-0.064	0.029*
Tenure system			0.125	0.061*	0.141	0.061*
Unionized instn/not member			-0.172	0.077*	-0.136	0.077
Nonunionized instn			-0.282	0.093**	-0.261	0.094**
Northeast			-0.204	0.103*	-0.230	0.105*
Midwest			-0.178	0.084*	-0.213	0.085*
Southeast			-0.207	0.108	-0.282	0.112*
Southwest			0.144	0.108	0.082	0.109
Econ. or political science					-0.270	0.261
Engineering					0.473	0.193*
History or philosophy					-0.004	0.270
Physical sciences					0.427	0.243
Computer science					0.104	0.174
Mathematics					0.115	0.144
Biological sciences					0.082	0.216
Other programs					-0.134	0.146
Fine arts					0.079	0.168
Other social science					-0.103	0.176
Business					-0.164	0.150
English					-0.038	0.149
Education					-0.563	0.149***

TABLE 9 (Continued)

Independent Variables	Sex and Race		Human Capital		Productivity		Structural		Market	
	B	Std. Error	B	Std. Error	B	Std. Error	B	Std. Error	B	Std. Error
Foreign languages									-0.068	0.215
Health sciences									-0.018	0.159
Constant	8.585	0.048***	8.161	0.098***	7.496	0.116***	7.853	0.174***	7.870	0.196***
Number cases in analyses	1,033		1,033		1,033		1,033		1,033	
R^2 change	0.007		0.050***		0.150***		0.026***		0.038***	
R^2	0.007		0.058***		0.207***		0.233***		0.271***	
Adjusted R^2	0.003		0.048***		0.186***		0.206***		0.233***	

Note: Sample is limited to faculty with at least some instructional duties, who were employed at public 2-year institutions, whose primary responsibility was teaching and who held at least a 9-month, regular, part-time appointment.
Source: Analyses of NSOPF: 93.
***$p < .001$, **$p < .01$, *$p < .05$.

TABLE 10
Observed Distribution of Regular, Full-Time Faculty at Public 2-Year
Colleges by Academic Rank, Sex, and Race/Ethnicity: Fall 1992

Characteristic	Total	Full Professor	Associate Professor	Assistant Professor	Instructor or Lecturer	Other or No Rank
n	3,372	654	471	397	1,423	427
Sex	*p* < .001					
Total	100.0	19.4	14.0	11.8	42.2	12.7
Men	100.0	22.8	13.7	9.7	42.0	11.8
Women	100.0	15.1	14.2	14.4	42.5	13.8
Race/ethnicity	*p* < .001					
Total	100.0	19.4	14.0	11.8	42.2	12.7
American Indian	100.0	12.5	6.3	3.1	53.1	25.0
Asian	100.0	16.5	13.8	14.7	46.8	8.3
Black	100.0	19.8	16.8	10.4	47.5	5.4
Hispanic	100.0	19.0	7.0	16.9	48.6	8.5
White	100.0	19.5	14.2	11.6	41.2	13.4

Notes: Sample is limited to faculty with at least some instructional duties, who were employed at public 2-year institutions, whose primary responsibility was teaching and who held at least a 9-month, regular, full-time appointment.
Tests of statistical significance for the crosstabs are based on chi-square.
Source: Analyses of NSOPF: 93.

tenured position than a full-time tenure-track position after controlling only for race/ethnicity. (The coefficients that are associated with blocked entry of variables are available on request.) After also controlling for such measures of human capital as education and experience, women are still less likely than men to hold a full-time tenured position, but the relationship is only marginally statistically significant ($p < .01$). Table 13 shows that when structural characteristics and academic field are also added to the model, the negative relationship is significant only at the $p < .05$ level. The odds of a woman holding a part-time non-tenure-track position rather than a full-time tenure-track position are lower for women than for men at the p .01 level, but not the more stringent p .001 level, after controlling for measures of human capital, structural characteristics, and market forces.

The odds of holding a full-time tenured position are higher for those who have attained a master's or professional degree and for those with more years since their highest degree and more years in the current position. Being a nonunion member at a unionized institution increases the odds of holding a part-time non-tenure-track position, while working at a nonunionized institution reduces the odds of holding a full-time tenured position. The prob-

ability of holding a part-time nontenure-track position rather than a full-time tenure-track position varies by academic field, with a greater likelihood of holding a part-time nontenure-track position for faculty in foreign languages, education, English, business, and other social sciences—among the fields in which women comprise the highest proportions of faculty.

Conclusions

This research provides a comprehensive exploration of the employment experiences of women and minorities among the nation's public 2-year college faculty. Several conclusions may be drawn from this research.

First, sex differences in human capital, structural, and market characteristics appear to explain the observed differences in the employment experiences of women and men faculty at public 2-year colleges. The observed overrepresentation of women among faculty at public 2-year colleges, the relative underrepresentation of women among full professors, and the lower salaries of women than men full-time faculty are all eliminated when differences in other variables are taken into account. Although women are observed to hold a smaller share of full-time tenured positions than men, this difference is

TABLE 11
Predictors of Academic Rank Among Full-Time Regular Faculty Employed at Public 2-Year College: Fall 1992

TABLE 11. Predictors of Academic Rank Among Full-Time Regular Faculty Employed At Public 2-Year Colleges: Fall 1992

Independent Variables	Instructor			Full Professor			Associate Professor		
	B	Std. Error	Exp(B)	B	Std. Error	Exp(B)	B	Std. Error	Exp(B)
Female	-0.255	0.142	0.775	-0.136	0.165	0.873	0.052	0.168	1.053
Asian	0.190	0.318	1.210	-0.032	0.390	0.969	-0.184	0.385	0.832
Black	0.382	0.268	1.465	0.358	0.305	1.430	0.253	0.306	1.288
Hispanic	-0.112	0.269	0.894	-0.197	0.328	0.821	-1.096	0.404	0.334**
Doctoral degree	-1.272	0.258	0.280***	1.188	0.318	3.282***	0.921	0.338	2.511**
Prof. or master's degree	-0.552	0.195	0.576**	0.631	0.263	1.879*	0.967	0.281	2.629***
Years since degree	-0.015	0.008	0.985	0.040	0.010	1.041***	0.041	0.010	1.042***
Years in position	0.013	0.009	1.013	0.114	0.010	1.121***	0.051	0.010	1.052***
Number courses taught	0.001	0.041	1.001	0.120	0.048	1.128*	-0.046	0.050	0.955
0–25% time teaching	-0.276	0.480	0.759	0.568	0.528	1.765	0.818	0.553	2.265
26%–50% time teaching	-0.646	0.330	0.524	0.229	0.373	1.257	0.559	0.386	1.748
51%–70% time teaching	-0.230	0.305	0.794	-0.043	0.350	0.958	0.547	0.359	1.728
71%–80% time teaching	-0.508	0.275	0.602	-0.260	0.315	0.771	0.239	0.328	1.270
81%–90% time teaching	-0.720	0.269	0.487**	-0.318	0.307	0.727	-0.094	0.323	0.910
91%–99% time teaching	-0.405	0.295	0.667	-0.321	0.343	0.726	-0.588	0.374	0.555
No presentations last 2 yrs	0.455	0.176	1.576*	-0.270	0.195	0.763	-0.161	0.197	0.852
1–3 presentations	0.136	0.214	1.145	-0.258	0.243	0.773	-0.049	0.243	0.952
4–9 presentations	-0.106	0.221	0.900	-0.294	0.243	0.745	-0.424	0.253	0.655
More than 5% time research	-0.192	0.160	0.826	-0.252	0.184	0.777	-0.212	0.185	0.809
More than 5% time service	-0.222	0.155	0.801	-0.028	0.181	0.973	-0.552	0.186	0.576**
More than 10% time admin.	-0.526	0.179	0.591**	-0.159	0.204	0.853	-0.384	0.205	0.681
UG enrollment—lowest quartile	-0.438	0.184	0.645*	-0.859	0.217	0.424***	-0.606	0.221	0.546**
UG enrollment—2nd quartile	-0.359	0.185	0.698	-0.364	0.208	0.695	-0.556	0.219	0.574*
UG enrollment—3rd quartile	-0.363	0.191	0.696	-0.460	0.211	0.631*	-0.077	0.214	0.926

	B	SE	Exp(B)	B	SE	Exp(B)	B	SE	Exp(B)
Tenure system	-1.086	0.172	0.338***	-0.290	0.215	0.749	-0.339	0.216	0.712
Unionized/not member	-0.234	0.174	0.791	-0.538	0.211	0.584*	-0.403	0.214	0.668
Nonunionized institution	-0.255	0.142	0.775	-0.399	0.166	0.671*	-0.117	0.166	0.889
Econ & political science	-1.853	0.531	0.157***	-1.289	0.578	0.276*	-0.214	0.578	0.807
Engineering	-1.020	0.479	0.361*	0.189	0.539	1.208	-0.284	0.575	0.753
History or philosophy	-1.473	0.483	0.229**	-1.505	0.535	0.222**	-1.499	0.586	0.223*
Physical sciences	-1.019	0.505	0.361*	-0.881	0.560	0.414	-0.322	0.572	0.725
Computer science	-1.157	0.450	0.314*	-0.854	0.541	0.426	-0.954	0.567	0.385
Mathematics	-1.234	0.412	0.291**	-1.001	0.473	0.368*	-0.688	0.491	0.502
Biological sciences	-0.792	0.481	0.453	-0.553	0.534	0.575	-0.964	0.580	0.381
Other field	-1.246	0.395	0.288***	-1.369	0.462	0.254**	-1.250	0.488	0.286*
Fine arts	-1.254	0.503	0.285*	-0.652	0.549	0.521	-0.661	0.577	0.516
Other social science	-2.077	0.421	0.125***	-1.742	0.471	0.175***	-1.377	0.498	0.252**
Business	-0.922	0.414	0.398*	-0.655	0.466	0.519	-0.486	0.489	0.615
English	-1.292	0.396	0.275**	-1.233	0.449	0.292**	-1.074	0.473	0.342*
Education	-0.887	0.454	0.412	-1.240	0.530	0.289*	-0.354	0.529	0.702
Foreign language	-1.711	0.620	0.181**	-1.172	0.649	0.310	-0.839	0.675	0.432
Health sciences	-1.693	0.385	0.184***	-0.844	0.446	0.430	-0.934	0.467	0.393*
Intercept	4.918	0.548	***	-0.550	0.646		0.048	0.671	
Number of cases in the analyses			1,382			646			469
Pseudo R^2 (Cox and Snell)	0.354								
Percentage classified correctly	58.9%		85.9%			60.8%			14.8%

Notes: Sample is limited to faculty with at least some instructional duties, who were employed at public 2-year institutions, whose primary responsibility was teaching and who held at least a 9-month, regular, full-time appointment. Odds ratios are relative to holding an assistant professor position.

Source: Analyses of NSOPF: 93

***$p < .001$; **$p < .01$; *$p < .05$.

TABLE 12
Distribution of Regular Faculty at Public 2-Year Colleges
with a Tenure System by Employment and Tenure Status, Sex,
and Race/Ethnicity: Fall 1992

Characteristic	Total	Full-Time Tenured	Full-Time Tenure Track	Part-Time Tenured or Tenure Track	Full-Time Nontenure Track	Part-Time Nontenure Track
n	2,819	1,696	479	76	111	456
Sex	*p* < .001					
Total	100.0	60.2	17.0	2.7	3.9	16.2
Men	100.0	65.0	13.5	3.0	3.1	15.3
Women	100.0	53.6	21.8	2.3	5.0	17.3
Race/ethnicity	*p* = .28					
Total	100.0	60.1	17.0	2.7	3.9	16.2
American Indian	100.0	75.0	5.0	—	—	20.0
Asian	100.0	56.8	16.1	0.8	3.4	22.9
Black	100.0	59.8	16.2	5.6	4.5	14.0
Hispanic	100.0	53.7	21.8	2.7	4.8	17.0
White	100.0	60.6	16.9	2.6	3.9	16.0

Notes: Sample is limited to faculty with at least some instructional duties, who were employed at a public 2-year institution with a tenure system, whose primary responsibility was teaching and who held at least a 9-month, regular appointment.
"—" indicates sample size too small for reliable estimate.
Tests of statistical significance for the crosstabs are based on chi-square.
Source: Analyses of NSOPF: 93.

eliminated at the *p* < .001 when other variables are taken into account. Moreover, women are observed to fare better than men on one outcome: average institutional base salaries of part-time faculty. Even after controlling for human capital, structural, and market explanations, average salaries are higher for women part-time faculty than for men part-time faculty.

Second, the analyses reveal a few unexplained racial/ethnic group differences in the employment experiences of faculty working at public 2-year colleges. The analyses reveal no observed differences across the four racial/ethnic groups in terms of appointment type, salary, or tenure and employment status. But, Hispanics appear to be more likely than white faculty to be employed at a public 2-year institution rather than a 4-year institution, even after controlling for differences in education, experience, and academic field. The lower observed promotion rate for Hispanics from assistant to associate professor is eliminated at the *p* < .001 level, but not at the *p* < .01 level, when differences in other variables are taken into account. These findings suggest that differences in human capital, structural characteristics, and market forces

may not completely explain some of the employment experiences of Hispanic faculty at public 2-year colleges.

Third, although, as noted by Galin and Twombly (2001), researchers have generally assumed that labor markets at 2- and 4-year institutions function similarly, the results of this research suggest several fundamental differences in the reward structures for faculty at public 2- and 4-year institutions. In contrast to faculty reward structures at 4-year colleges and universities, measures of productivity appear to play a very limited role for faculty at public 2-year institutions. Only in the analyses of salaries for part-time faculty do productivity measures play a role. As expected, part-time faculty who teach more courses earn higher salaries. Faculty who spend at least 10% of their time on administration receive lower salaries. Confirming the conclusions of others (Cohen and Brawer, 1996; Townsend, 1995), this research shows that educational attainment and experience are the primary determinants of employment outcomes for faculty employed at public 2-year colleges. Unlike prior research, such structural characteristics as unionization, institutional size, and the

TABLE 13
Predictors of Employment and Tenure Status of Faculty
at Public 2-Year Colleges: Fall 1992

Independent Variable	Part-Time Nontenure track			Full-Time Tenured		
	B	Std. Error	Exp(B)	B	Std. Error	Exp(B)
Female	−0.518	0.172	0.596**	−0.397	0.155	0.672*
Asian	0.605	0.347	1.831	0.397	0.317	1.487
Black	−0.203	0.320	0.817	0.211	0.275	1.235
Hispanic	−0.498	0.317	0.608	−0.185	0.283	0.831
Doctoral degree	−2.668	0.319	0.069***	0.258	0.264	1.294
Prof. or master's degree	−1.190	0.200	0.304***	0.712	0.202	2.038***
Years since highest degree	0.021	0.010	1.021*	0.048	0.009	1.049***
Years in position	0.138	0.018	1.148***	0.282	0.017	1.326***
UG enrollment—lowest quartile	−0.071	0.216	0.932	0.155	0.193	1.168
UG enrollment—2nd quartile	−0.418	0.216	0.658	−0.072	0.186	0.930
UG enrollment—3rd quartile	0.527	0.217	1.694*	0.331	0.197	1.393
Unionized/not member	1.827	0.199	6.216***	−0.114	0.185	0.892
Nonunionized institution	0.535	0.183	1.707**	−1.022	0.158	0.360***
Econ & political science	0.867	0.564	2.379	−1.030	0.507	0.357*
Engineering	−0.225	0.485	0.798	−0.930	0.414	0.394*
History or philosophy	1.195	0.692	3.302	−0.070	0.551	0.933
Physical sciences	0.343	0.584	1.409	−0.442	0.449	0.643
Computer science	0.523	0.463	1.688	−0.088	0.395	0.916
Mathematics	1.285	0.400	3.613**	−0.267	0.360	0.766
Biological sciences	0.367	0.591	1.444	−0.816	0.461	0.442
Other field	0.916	0.377	2.500*	−0.440	0.343	0.644
Fine arts	1.469	0.502	4.347**	−0.242	0.466	0.785
Other social science	1.663	0.432	5.277***	−0.574	0.403	0.563
Business	1.799	0.419	6.043***	0.295	0.378	1.343
English	1.528	0.404	4.608***	−0.142	0.356	0.867
Education	2.106	0.438	8.218***	−0.237	0.407	0.789
Foreign language	3.031	0.659	20.713***	0.245	0.624	1.277
Health sciences	0.671	0.382	1.955	−0.230	0.342	0.794
Intercept	−1.602	0.362	***	−1.510	0.317	***
Number of cases in the analyses		427			1,673	
Pseudo R^2 (Cox and Snell)	0.463					
Percentage classified correctly	77.1%		40.4%			91.2%

Note: Sample is limited to faculty with at least some instructional duties, who were employed at public 2-year institutions, whose primary responsibility was teaching. Part-time tenure-track and full-time nontenure track are excluded from the analyses because of small sample sizes. Odds ratios are relative to full-time tenure-track employment.
Source: Analyses of NSOPF: 93.
***$p < .001$; **$p < .01$; *$p < .05$.

existence of a tenure system also appear to play a role in faculty reward systems at public 2-year colleges. The presence of a tenure system appears to reduce the odds of holding a part-time regular or temporary position and the rank of instructor. Working at a nonunionized institution is associated with lower salaries among full-time faculty and lower probability of holding a full-time tenured position, net of other variables. Being a member of a union, not just working at a unionized institution, is associated with lower

likelihood of holding a part-time nontenure-track position and lower likelihood of holding a part-time regular or temporary position. These relationships are likely not surprising given that union membership at many public 2-year institutions may be restricted to full-time faculty.

Implications

This study has several implications. First, although this study provides a comprehensive picture of the employment status of women and minorities among community college faculty, the conclusions are based on analyses of data that were collected in fall 1992. The conclusions should be tested using more recent national data to identify any changes in the relationships that were identified in this research.

Second, because the research uses a nationally representative sample, the findings provide a critical frame of reference for administrators, institutional researchers, and faculty who are interested in examining the status of women and minority faculty on individual community college campuses. Officials at public 2-year institutions are encouraged to use the findings from this research as a guide for examining the extent of sex and racial/ethnic group equity on their own campuses.

Third, this research contributes to the understanding of the most appropriate conceptual model for examining the employment experiences of faculty employed at public 2-year colleges. While some evidence suggests that both faculty and administrators at community colleges support the inclusion of "scholarship" in the criteria for promotion and tenure decisions (Padovan and Whittington, 1998), before the current study few researchers had examined the extent to which aspects of productivity other than teaching are being considered in faculty reward systems at community colleges. The results of this research suggest that such human capital measures as education and experience play an important role in determining the employment experiences of faculty at public 2-year colleges but that measures of productivity play a minimal role. However, the relatively low percentage of variance that is explained by the model for full-time (14%) and part-time (23%) faculty salaries and the relatively low share of correct classifications for appointment status (59%) and rank (59%) suggests that these measures of human capital, structural characteristics, and market forces are insufficient and that much about the predictors of these outcomes is not predictable and/or well understood. The models developed in this research explain a smaller share of variance in salaries for full-time faculty than is typically explained by analyses of faculty salaries of full-time faculty at 4-year institutions. For example, using the same database, Perna (2001a) found that a model drawing from human capital and structural perspectives explained 53% of the variance in salaries for full-time faculty at 4-year institutions.

Developing an appropriate conceptual model is a first step toward identifying and addressing the variables that limit the status, compensation, and advancement of women faculty and faculty of color at the nation's public 2-year colleges. With the possible exceptions of attainment of a full-time tenured position for women, promotion to associate professor for Hispanics, and attainment of a position at a 4-year rather than a 2-year institution for Hispanics and American Indians, this research suggests the barriers that limit access to high status and high paying positions for women and minority faculty at public 2-year colleges. Identifying the variables that are related to these outcomes is clearly a first step toward developing the interventions necessary to ensure that women and racial/ethnic minorities have access to the highest status and highest paying faculty positions.

Although the general absence of observed racial/ethnic group differences in several types of employment experiences for faculty at public 2-year colleges suggests an absence of racial/ethnic inequity, greater attention must be devoted to identifying ways to correct the continued underrepresentation of faculty of color at these institutions. As others (Opp and Smith, 1994) have noted, undergraduate enrollments are more racially/ethnically diverse at community colleges than at 4-year institutions. Nonetheless, the representation of minorities among community college faculty continues to be substantially less than their representation among community college students. Analyses of data from the Fall Enrollment Survey of the Integrated Postsecondary Education Data System show that African Americans represented 12.7%, and Hispanics represented 9.6%, of first-time, full-time freshmen at public 2-year colleges in fall 1997. As others (e.g., Opp and Smith, 1994) have argued, increasing the racial/ethnic diversity of community college faculties may help public 2-year colleges more successfully recruit and retain minority students by providing minority students with positive role models.

Acknowledgments

This article is based on a paper presented at the annual meeting of the Association for Institutional Research, Toronto, June 2002. This research was supported by a grant from the Association for Institutional Research Improving Institutional Research in Postsecondary Educational Institutions Program. Opinions reflect those of the author and do not necessarily reflect those of the granting agencies.

References

Barbezat, D. A. (1988). Gender differences in the academic reward system. In: Breneman, D. W., and Youn, T. I. K. (eds.), *Academic Labor Markets and Careers,* Falmer Press, New York, pp. 138–164.

Becker, G. S. (1962). Investment in human capital: A theoretical analysis. *J. Polit. Econ.* 70(Suppl. 5): 9–49.

Bellas, M. L. (1993). Faculty salaries: Still a cost of being female? Soc. *Sci. Q.* 74: 62–75.

Bellas, M. L. (1994). Comparable worth in academia: The effects on faculty salaries of the sex composition and labor-market conditions of academic disciplines. *Am. Sociol. Rev.* 59: 807–821.

Bellas, M. L. (1997). Disciplinary differences in faculty salaries: Does gender bias play a role? J. *Higher Educ.* 68: 299–321.

Bridges, W. P., and Nelson, R. P. (1989). Markets in hierarchies: Organizational and market influences on gender inequality on a state pay system. *Am. J. Sociol.* 95: 616–658.

Cabrera, A. F. (1994). Logistic regression analysis in higher education: An applied perspective. In: Smart, J. C. (ed.), *Higher Education: Handbook of Theory and Research* (Vol. 10), Agathon Press, New York, pp. 225–256.

Carter, D. J. (1994). The status of faculty in community colleges: What do we know? In: Harvey, W. B., and Valadez, J. (eds.), *Creating and Maintaining a Diverse Faculty* (New Directions for Community Colleges, 87), Jossey-Bass, San Francisco, pp. 3–17.

Clark, B. R. (1987). *The Academic Life: Small Worlds, Different Worlds,* Carnegie Foundation for the Advancement of Teaching, Princeton, NJ.

Clark, S. L. (1998). Women faculty in community colleges: Investigating the mystery. *Commun. Coll. Rev. 26:* 77–88.

Cohen, A. M., and Brawer, F. B. (1996). *The American Community College* (3rd Ed.), Jossey-Bass, San Francisco.

DeYoung, A. J. (1989). *Economics and American Education: A Historical and Critical Overview of the Impact of Economic Theories on Schooling in the United States,* Longman Inc., White Plains, NY.

Dreijmanis, J. (1991). Higher education and employment: Is professional employment a right? *Higher Education Review* 23(3): 7–18.

England, P. (1982). The failure of human capital theory to explain occupational sex segregation. *J. Hum. Resour.* 17: 358–370.

England, P., Farkas, G., Kilbourne, B. S., and Dou, T. (1988). Explaining occupational sex segregation and wages: Findings from a model with fixed effects. *Am. Social. Rev.* 53: 544–558.

Fairweather, J. S. (1995). Myths and realities of academic labor markets. *Econ. Educ. Rev.* 14: 179–192.

Gahn, S., and Twombly, S. B. (2001). Dimensions of the community college labor market. *Rev. Higher Educ.* 24: 259–282.

Kalleberg, A. L., and Sorenson, A. B. (1979). The sociology of labor markets. *Annu. Rev. Sociol.* 5: 351–379.

Kerr, C. (1950). Labor markets: Their character and consequences. *Am. Econ. Rev.* 40: 278–291.

Lassiter, R. L., Jr. (1983). The development and use of a faculty salary model for a higher education system. *Res. Higher Educ.* 18: 333–358.

Menard, S. (1995). *Applied Logistic Regression Analysis,* Sage Publications, Thousand Oaks, CA.

National Center for Education Statistics (2001). *Digest of Education Statistics: 2000* (Report No. NCES 2001–034). U.S. Department of Education, Office of Educational Research and Improvement, Washington, DC.

Nettles, M. T., Perna, L. W., and Bradburn, E. M. (2000). *Salary, Promotion, and Tenure Status of Minority and Women Faculty in U.S. Colleges and Universities* (Report No. NCES 2000–173), U.S. Department of Education, Office of Educational Research and Improvement, Washington, DC.

Opp, R. D., and Smith, A. B. (1994). Effective strategies for enhancing minority faculty recruitment and retention. In: Harvey, W. B., and Valadez, J. (eds.), *Creating and Maintaining a Diverse Faculty* (New Directions for Community Colleges, 87), Jossey-Bass, San Francisco, pp. 43–55.

Padovan, P., and Whittington, D. (1998). Rewarding faculty scholarship at two-year colleges: Incentive for change or perceived threat? *Commun. Coll. J. Res. Pract.* 22: 213–228.

Palmer, J. C. (2000). *Instructional Faculty and Staff in Public 2-year Colleges* (Report No. NCES 2000–192), U.S. Department of Education, Office of Educational Research and Improvement, Washington, DC.

Perna, L. W. (2001a). Sex differences in faculty salaries: A cohort analysis. *Rev. Higher Educ.* 24: 283–307.

Perna, L. W. (2001b). Sex and race differences in faculty tenure and promotion. *Res. Higher Educ.* 42: 541–567.

Perna, L. W. (in press). Studying faculty salary equity: A review of theoretical and methodological approaches. In: Smart, J. C. (ed.), *Higher Education: Handbook of Theory and Research.*

Schultz, T. W. (1961). Investment in human capital. *Am. Econ. Rev.* 51: 1–17.

Selfa, L. A., Suter, N., Myers, S., Koch, S., Johnson, R. A., Zahs, D. A., et al. (1997). *1993 National Study of Postsecondary Faculty: Data File User's Manual Public-Use* (Report No. NCES 97–466), U.S. Department of Education, Office of Educational Research and Improvement, Washington, DC.

Smart, J. C. (1991). Gender equity in academic rank and salary. *Rev. Higher Educ.* 14: 511–526.

Thomas, S. L., and Heck, R. H. (2001). Analysis of large-scale secondary data in higher education research: Potential perils associated with complex sampling designs. *Res. Higher Educ.* 42: 517–540.

Tolbert, P. S. (1986). Organizations and inequality: Sources of earnings differences between male and female faculty. *Sociol. Educ.* 59: 227–235.

Toutkoushian, R. K. (1998a). Racial and marital status differences in faculty pay. *J. Higher Educ.* 69: 513–54 1.

Toutkoushian, R. K. (1998b). Sex matters less for younger faculty: Evidence of disaggregate pay disparities from the 1988 and 1993 NCES surveys. *Econ. Educ. Rev.* 17: 55–7 .

Toutkoushian, R. K. (1999). The status of academic women in the 1990s: No longer outsiders, but not yet equals. Q. *Rev. Econ. Finance 39*(special issue): 679–698.

Townsend, B. K. (1995). Women community college faculty: On the margins or in the mainstream? In: Townsend, B. K. (ed.), *Gender and Power in the Community College* (Vol. 89), Jossey-Bass, San Francisco, pp. 39–46.

Twombly, S. B. (1993). What we know about women in community colleges: An examination of the literature using feminist phase theory. *J. Higher Educ.* 64: 186–210.

Verdugo, R. R., and Schneider, J. M. (1994). Gender inequality in female-dominated occupation: The earnings of male and female teachers. *Econ. Educ. Rev.* 13: 251–264.

Weiler, W. C. (1990). Integrating rank differences into a model of male-female faculty salary discrimination. *Q. Rev. Econ. Bus.* 30: 3–15.

Youn, T. I. K. (1988). Studies of academic markets and careers: An historical review. In: Breneman, D. W. and Youn, T. I. K. (eds.), *Academic Labor Markets and Careers*, Palmer Press, New York, pp. 8–27.

Youn, T. I. K. (1992). The sociology of academic careers and academic labor markets. *Research in Labor Markets* 13: 101–130.

CHAPTER 31

IN THE COMPANY OF STRANGERS: ADDRESSING THE UTILIZATION AND INTEGRATION OF PART-TIME FACULTY IN AMERICAN COMMUNITY COLLEGES

JOHN E. ROUECHE
COMMUNITY COLLEGE LEADERSHIP PROGRAM, THE UNIVERSITY OF TEXAS
AT AUSTIN, AUSTIN, TEXAS, USA

SUANNE D. ROUECHE
NATIONAL INSTITUTE FOR STAFF AND ORGANIZATIONAL DEVELOPMENT,
THE UNIVERSITY OF TEXAS AT AUSTIN, AUSTIN, TEXAS, USA

MARK D. MILLIRON
MAYLAND COMMUNITY COLLEGE, SPRUCE PINE, NORTH CAROLINA, USA

From a national survey of selected community colleges and a review of research and debate, the authors identify issues, implications, and directions for college administrators addressing their colleges' use of part-time faculty. The key recommendation is that colleges take serious steps toward improving the utilization and integration of part-time faculty. The authors then identify strategies for improving community college part-time faculty use. Recommended strategies include (a) recruiting, selecting, and hiring part-time faculty with clear purpose and direction; (b) requiring part-time faculty participation in substantial orientation activities and providing faculty support structures; (c) requiring part-time faculty participation in professional development, (d) integrating part-time faculty into the life of the institution; (e) evaluating part-time faculty performance; and (f) providing equitable pay schedules, Study results indicate that these strategies improve the relationship between part-time faculty and the institution and part-time faculty performance.

There is no longer any point in arguing over the place of part-time faculty in American colleges and universities. (Gappa & Leslie, 1993, p. 3)

It is time for cooperation and making a common cause. That common cause is academic excellence, which can only be ensured when the best faculty members, both full- and part-time, are working together. (Gappa & Leslie, 1993, p. 285).

Address correspondence to John E. Roueche, University of Texas, College of Education, Austin, TX 78712, USA.

> Because adjuncts' numbers are increasing so rapidly and because they are such positive ambassadors, community colleges must give them strong and increased attention. (Campion, 1994, p. 172)

It is time for community colleges to aggressively address their utilization and integration of part-time faculty. These faculty have long been a part of community college faculty cadres (Eells, 1931) and more recently have been integral in meeting a rapidly increasing demand for services and extraordinary economic contingencies (H. R. Bowen & Schuster, 1986; W. G. Bowen & Sosa, 1989). Without part-time faculty, community colleges would have been hard pressed to serve the expanding cohort of part-time students in the 1970s and 1980s and to survive the recession of the late 1980s and early 1990s. It is during the past 20 years that the use of part-time faculty increased significantly. From 1973 to 1991, part-time faculty ranks tripled, whereas full-time faculty increased by only 15% (American Association of Community Colleges [AACC], 1991). The National Center for Education Statistics (1990) reported that somewhere between 30 to 40% of all the full-time equivalent contact hours in American community colleges are taught by part-time faculty, and the AACC (1992) reported that somewhere between 55 and 65% of all community college faculty are teaching part-time. In the future, as institutions of higher education face increasing demands, decreasing funds, and waves of full-time faculty retirements, the staffing of part-timers will have a significant impact on the way community colleges serve students.

In addition to this expanding utilization, part-time faculty in the community college are asked to play the vital role of instructing underprepared students. Recent reports to the Florida State Board of Community Colleges and to the Illinois Community College Board (Armstrong, 1993) have documented that part-time faculty are increasingly used in the instruction of general education and remedial courses. Research has demonstrated that faculty selected to teach the underprepared are the key to the success of at-risk students. Faculty must provide support and direction, and they must use a wide variety of instructional strategies to be successful in reaching this growing contingent of students

(Roueche & Roueche, 1993). Yet Astin (1985) noted that teaching poorly prepared students is "considered a low-level enterprise, often left to part-time faculty members hired specifically for this purpose" (p. 104). Moreover, Gappa and Leslie (1993) found that developmental or general education courses were not only staffed heavily by part-timers, but were often the only classes part-time faculty were allowed to teach.

These ever-present, expanding, and important roles notwithstanding, research and experience have indicated that institutions of higher education nationwide treat part-time faculty less like valuable organizational players and more like "invisible faculty" (Gappa &Leslie, 1993), "expendable, interchangeable components of a 'Tinker Toy' system of staffing" (Richardson, 1992, p. 29), "a[n] academic underclass" (Smith, 1990, p. 7), or strangers in their own land (Roueche, Roueche, & Milliron, 1995). *Underpaid, overworked,* and *left in the shadows* are but some of the descriptors part-time faculty use to describe their situation (Roueche et al., 1995). Furthermore, research has shown that typical use of part-time faculty by a community college involves haphazard selection, poor orientation, and weak or nonexistent organizational support (Erwin & Andrews, 1993; Gappa & Leslie, 1993; Parsons, 1980; Richardson, 1992). Gappa and Leslie demonstrated that a part-time faculty member's relationship with the organization will depend largely on one contact—the department chair, who tends to be "underprepared and administratively overwhelmed in trying to deal responsibly with part-time faculty issues" (p. 12). Considering these trends in part-time faculty use in community colleges, even the most cursory assessment of this situation should generate concern. Furthermore, it is ironic that these "invisible faculty" trends exist in community colleges—those institutions that claim (a) to be of and about building *community,* (b) to promote egalitarian and inclusive values, and (c) to provide access while simultaneously achieving excellence in higher education.

Studying Strangers in Their Own Land

In *Strangers in Their Own Land: Part-Time Faculty in the American Community College* (Roueche et al., 1995), we sought to move beyond the polarizing arguments around the place of part-time faculty in American colleges and universities and beyond descriptions of the current state of affairs in part-time faculty use. Put simply, part-time faculty are here, have been here for decades, and are likely to be more common in future community college faculty cohorts. There is little evidence to implicate part-time faculty as culprits in any instructional crimes; in fact, there is an abundance of evidence to suggest that the manner in which part-time faculty are used by the community college is the key factor influencing the quality of part-time faculty instruction.

Given this current situation, our aim was to explore how community colleges can effectively use part-time faculty and bring them into the fold. Although we addressed the major issues and controversies in the use of part-time faculty and provided a state-of-the-art survey of current trends in the use of part-time faculty, our primary purpose was to profile and explore selected colleges' part-time faculty utilization and integration strategies and thereby provide community colleges with useful models for improving their use of part-time faculty.

The Study

We designed the study as a multistage quantitative and qualitative descriptive analysis. In Stage 1, we developed a general trends survey and mailed it to a stratified random sample of community college districts and colleges. This survey gathered such data as the numbers of part-time and full-time faculty, faculty salaries, faculty teaching loads, and availability of benefits. Although these data were of interest to us, the real intent was to have this broad, national cross-section of community colleges respond to the final question, which asked the respondents to note any college or district they considered exceptional in the use of part-time faculty. From these references and from reports in current literature on part-time faculty, we developed a purposive sample of community colleges for analysis in Stage 2 of the study. In essence, Stage 2 was qualitative best-practice study of community college part-time faculty utilization and integration processes. We scheduled and conducted interviews with a variety of administrators (e.g., presidents, vice presidents, deans, continuing education directors, staff development directors, and department chairs) from the selected institutions. The interviews followed a guided interview format that led the respondents through the college's or department's recruiting, selection, orientation, development, evaluation, and integration processes for part-time faculty. In addition to the interviews, we requested documentation of process and college specifics to inform the descriptions further. Interview transcripts were then coded into an ACCESS database and combined with submitted documentation to develop profiles of each college and each specific utilization process.

Stage 1: The State-of-the-Art Survey

The results of the general trends survey of part-time faculty utilization support the contention that part-time faculty are playing a significant and increasing role in American community colleges. Data demonstrate that approximately 58% of the faculty teaching in the average AACC community college are teaching part-time, with significantly greater percentages of part-timers in district-related colleges (63%) and nondistrict-related colleges with more than 8,000 students (68%). Furthermore, results show that, on average, part-time faculty are responsible for delivering more than one third of the credit-hour instruction in AACC-member colleges and that they receive between $1,000 to $1,200 per course in compensation. Both the amount of credit hours and amount of salary varied by type of institution, with larger institutions relying more heavily on part-time faculty (up to 43% of credit-hour instruction) and paying larger salaries. In addition, although some colleges had a system in place, standard fringe benefits (e.g., medical insurance, retirement plans) for part-time faculty were extremely rare. Survey data supported the contention that part-time faculty have a large role in the instruction of underprepared students. Finally, survey data showed that community college administrators almost unanimously saw the use of part-time faculty by community colleges as an important issue; most agreed that their use of part-time faculty would increase in the future.

Stage 2: Best-Practice Part-Time Faculty Utilization Process Descriptions

Arguably, one of the most disturbing findings of this study was the relative dearth of focused and systemic programs for the utilization and integration of part-time faculty in American community colleges. Representatives from slightly more than 20% of the community colleges in the

TABLE 1
Recruiting and Selecting Clustered Summary Table

Process	Recruiting	Selecting/Hiring
Exemplar colleges	Cowley County Community College (KS) Greenville Technical College (SC) Hagerstown Junior College (MD) Valencia Community College (FL) Rio Salado Community College (AZ) Triton College (IL) Tarrant County Junior College (TX)	College of the Canyons (CA) Rio Salado Community College (AZ) Community College of Allegheny County, English Department (PA)
Utilization and integration strategies: illustrative examples	Proactively develop a complete database using business and industry contacts and advisory committees so college can be more selective. Focus on applicants with "real world" experience who specifically want to teach part-time. Make the database easily accessible and useful for department chairs in the hiring process. Use job fairs to begin initial connection to college: preview college culture for potential part-timers.	Train interviewer(s)—specifically department chairs—to select the type of person most likely to be successful with the college while teaching part-time. Use hiring process to pre-socialize part-timer to important college values (e.g., teaching). Require a teaching demonstration. Involve part-timers and full-timers in the selection/hiring process (e.g., search committees); vest them in the success of their colleagues Adhere to affirmative action guidelines and goals.

country provided fewer than 40 references to colleges they considered to be exceptional in their use of part-time faculty. Moreover, of the colleges identified, fewer than 10 had more than three processes, of the six we explored, that *they themselves* considered exceptional. The trend in the data was more toward what one respondent called "pockets of excellence," where "personal champions" (e.g., devoted or interested administrators, task forces, or committees) had created programs or strategies specifically for part-time faculty.

Nonetheless, we were encouraged by the innovative and thoughtful strategies that our profiled colleges used. The cross-college and cross-process analyses of these colleges were replete with examples of interesting and innovative strategies for the utilization and integration of part-time faculty. The following clustered summary tables (influenced by Miles & Huberman, 1994) provide a synthesis of some of the exemplar colleges and their identified utilization

strategies. Tables 1–3 read vertically (beginning with the analyzed utilization process, then the listing of some colleges we considered exemplars in that process, followed by illustrative examples of utilization and integration strategies).

Discussion and Recommendations

Our research shows that, although it may not be happening on a grand scale, part-time faculty can make significant contributions to and be effectively included in fulfilling the community college mission. Indeed, the college part-time faculty utilization processes described here offer interesting and useful models for any college. However, responses to our interview questions and the written descriptions of successful programs more specifically point to the following recommendations as important components in the design of any part-time faculty utilization and integration plan.

TABLE 2
Orientation and Staff Development Clustered Summary Table

Process	Orientation	Staff development
Exemplar colleges	Rio Salado Community College (AZ) Santa Fe Community College (FL) Richland College (TX) Ocean County College (NJ) Lakeland Community College (OH) Kirkwood Community College (IA) Cuesta College (CA) Cowley County Community College (KS) St. Petersburg Junior College (FL)	Triton College (IL) Lakeland Community College (OH) Cowley County Community College (KS) Valencia Community College (FL) Community College of Aurora (CO)
Utilization and integration strategies: illustrative examples	Create flexible high-quality, and mandatory orientations to socialize part-timers (e.g., SPJC video series). Move beyond general information-giving to imparting important organizational values; make orientation "inspirational." Use large group sessions to bring college community together, making it an all-part-timer or all-college event. Combine with breakout groups to create departmental or individual communicative connections. Involve part-time faculty in planning and delivering orientation. Have upper administration communicate the value of part-time faculty during orientation.	Communicate the organizational value of instructional excellence by creating rank distinctions for part-time faculty. Link staff development attendance to this ranking system. Garner the support of upper administration for staff development—involve them in delivery. Involve part-time faculty in coordinating and delivering staff development. Move beyond one-shot workshops to ongoing staff development programs to build part-time/full-time faculty relationships (e.g., mentoring relationships).

Overarching Recommendation: Colleges Must Take Serious Steps Toward Improving the Utilization and Integration of Part-Time Faculty

Colleges should begin taking these steps by analyzing their current utilization and integration processes and identifying areas for improvement. This procedure can be initiated by using task forces, roundtables, committees, faculty senates, or other college-sponsored groups. However, the support of the college's leadership is the most essential component; it must be present from the onset of the initiative. A collegewide, systemic approach to part-time faculty utilization rarely develops in the isolation of single departments or divisions. In addition, the following implementation strategies, each of which

emerged in our analysis of exemplar colleges, should be included.

All Part-Time Faculty Should Be Recruited, Selected, and Hired with Clear Purpose and Direction

The intake of part-time faculty should be part of a proactive plan, not a reactive response to budget constraints or random enrollment fluctuations. To this end, a number of colleges in our study aggressively recruited and developed pools of potential part-timers, even as they were flooded with unsolicited applications. These colleges moved beyond hiring individuals who could teach part time to trying to identify individuals who would be *best* to teach part time with the college (e.g., higher credentials,

TABLE 3
Evaluation and Integration Clustered Summary Table

Process	Evaluation	Integration
Exemplar colleges	County College of Morris (NJ) Cuesta Community College (CA) Rio Salado Community College (AZ) Santa Barbara City College (CA) Tarrant County Junior College (TX) Community College of Allegheny County, English Dept. (PA)	Greenville Technical College (SC) Community College of Aurora (CO) Lakeland Community College (OH) Westchester Community College (NY) Kirkwood Community College (IA) Central Piedmont Community College (NC) Richland College (TX) Vista College (CA) Cuesta Community College (CA) Cowley County Community College (KS)
Utilization and integration strategies: illustrative examples	Use evaluation to communicate organizational values—specifically, type and quality of instruction. Use a variety of evaluation methodologies (e.g., portfolios, student surveys, self-evaluations, and in-class observations). Use identical systems for full- and part-time evaluation. Link evaluation to rank advancement. Further involve part-timers in the process of evaluation to create a sense of ownership of the goals of evaluation and organizational improvement.	Utilize a part-time faculty committee, focus group, roundtable, or task force to explore part-time faculty issues on the campus. Increase opportunities for participation in college life (e.g., committee work, advising students, graduations, and social functions). Create opportunities for formal and informal interaction between and among part-timers and full-timers (e.g., mentoring, teaching/learning teams, retreats, newsletters). Create a part-time faculty support center to balance organizational support across departments. Recognize part-time faculty for years of service and teaching excellence.

real-world experience, or a specific desire to teach part time). In like vein, colleges must pay close attention to affirmative action guidelines while recruiting and selecting part-timers. A commitment to diversity cannot be neglected during the part-time faculty hiring process. In addition, colleges should gather data about their current part-time faculty use, question the roles they are asking part-timers to play, and explore whether the additional students brought to the college through part-time instruction can be served effectively with the college's existing infrastructure (e.g., advising, counseling, financial aid). The answers to these questions will better inform decisions regarding part-time faculty staffing. Next, those involved in the hiring of part-time faculty—particularly department chairs—need to develop their interviewing skills and to guarantee that hiring protocols are followed. A specific hiring protocol used by a number of colleges, and one that we strongly support, is teaching demonstrations. Community colleges need to ensure that the students part-time faculty serve—especially under-prepared students—encounter effective classroom instructors. Finally, we encourage broadening the involvement of upper administration and full-time and part-time faculty in the part-time faculty hiring process. This type of broad-based inclusion will involve and will make more of the college community responsible for the success of new part-time faculty.

All Part-Time Faculty Should Be Required to Participate in Substantial Orientation Activities and Provided with Faculty Support Structures

No part-time faculty member should enter a community college classroom without (a) being socialized to the community college environment (e.g., community college mission, diversity of students), (b) understanding institutional priorities (e.g., focus on instruction), and (c) being exposed to faculty and student support services (e.g., part-time faculty support centers, student advising centers). The college should make a strong attempt to provide this service to part-time faculty before the first class, throughout the first semester, and beyond. Orientation should also be connected to the college's ongoing professional development program and to the part-time faculty member's teaching discipline. Efforts should be made to encourage part-time faculty to stay current in subject content and to develop their instructional skills. Within-department mentoring efforts are often the most useful strategies to achieve these ends, provided that mentors serve voluntarily and are well trained. Finally, a comprehensive, all-faculty handbook—one that can serve as a guide to the college, its students, and its services and that can be used as an instructional strategy resource—should be developed and provided to all new part-time instructors.

All Part-Time Faculty Should Be Required to Participate in Professional Development Activities

Teaching and learning is at the heart of the community college enterprise. Given that part-time faculty compose the largest faculty cohort in today's community college, and that for many students—particularly evening students—part-time faculty will serve as their primary or only instructors, institutions must make every effort to develop well-informed and instructionally accomplished part-time faculty. Part-time faculty should be invited to all full-time faculty development activities and have alternative activities scheduled specifically for their needs (e.g., on weekends or evenings). We further recommend that all part-time faculty be provided with a mentor for at least their first full term with the college. Colleges that encourage the development of full- and part-time faculty relationships

through professional development activities and that compensate part-time faculty for their participation in this development reported improved part-time faculty teaching performance and increased full- and part-time faculty collaboration.

All Part-Time Faculty Should Be Integrated into the Life of the Institution

Put simply, the subtle—and at times not so subtle—neglect of part-time faculty should end. Part-time faculty are a vital resource that can and should be integrated into the college's community of learners. This can be accomplished by focusing on (a) socializing part-time faculty into the college's organizational culture; (b) creating communication connections between part-time faculty, full-time faculty, and other college employees (social as well as work-related communication connections); and (c) encouraging participation in college activities. In the colleges we profiled, part-time faculty were actively involved in faculty senates, professional development activities, and a wide variety of college committees. Part-time faculty should be invited to college celebrations (e.g., graduations), recognized for their contributions (e.g., teaching awards), and supported with college services (e.g., part-time faculty support centers). Part-time faculty organizations should be developed to explore part-time faculty issues, provide avenues for interaction, and identify venues for contribution to the academic community.

The Performance of All Part-Time Faculty Should Be Evaluated

Part-time faculty should be evaluated as fully as full-time faculty. This evaluation should focus on both the assessment of current instruction and professional development. More important, this evaluation process should be tied to the instructional issues emphasized during orientation and the college's professional development activities. The college and department need to send a consistent and focused message to the part-timer regarding the importance and elements of effective instruction. Finally, part-tame faculty should be included in any teaching recognition program, their contributions to excellent instruction merit recognition commensurate with the contributions of the full-time faculty.

All Part-Time Faculty Should Be Provided Equitable Pay Schedules

We encourage colleges to assess their current pay schedules for part-time faculty to determine if they are based on the idea of "equitable compensation for work performed" (Gappa & Leslie, 1993, p. 256). Clearly, in the majority of colleges, part-time faculty are not expected to contribute equally or as broadly to a college or department as, are full-time faculty (e.g., with committee assignments, service activities, curriculum development). Therefore, using such a strategy as dividing full-time faculty salaries by the number of classes taught to determine equitable compensation for part-time faculty makes little sense. We encourage colleges to follow Gappa and Leslie's recommendation that colleges assess whether part-time faculty pay schedules are "rational, clear, and based on the traditions and practices the institution has established for setting salary policy for other employees" (p. 256). For example, any benefits available for full-time faculty (e.g., merit pay system, cost-of-living adjustments, and pay scale advancement) should also be available to part-time faculty. Finally, a compensation system should be developed for activities outside of instruction in which part-time faculty are encouraged to participate (e.g., advising, serving on committees, and developing curricula) to reward this increased involvement fairly. The value of this system—measured in terms of faculty commitment, college esprit de corps, committee contributions, and increased college student service—should justify any increase in budget allocations that such a program might require.

Conclusion

We contend that the cohort of part-time faculty in American community colleges is a sleeping giant. The untapped and often ignored contributions these faculty can and do make to institutions are marked. The numbers of part-time faculty account for ever-larger percentages of the total number of community college faculty. Furthermore, the roles these faculty play are essential to college and student success. In good conscience, and certainly in light of current educational demands and their associated economic realities, community colleges cannot ignore these strangers in their own land. The intent of this research was to serve those colleges poised to address the current demands for improved part-time faculty utilization and integration. It is here, in the company of strangers, that this admonition is particularly compelling:

> Unless the priority of the future is placed on people—the people who staff the peoples' college—the community college we know now may cease to exist and the community college we dream of may never come to be. (O'Banion, 1972, p. 40)

References

American Association of Community Colleges Annual Fall Survey. (1991). Washington, DC; American Association of Community Colleges.

American Association of Community Colleges. (1992). *Statistical yearbook of community, technical, and junior colleges.* Washington, DC: Author.

Armstrong, D. (1993). *Information on part-time full-time faculty* (Report to Florida State Board of Community Colleges, September 30, 1993; memo to State Board of Community Colleges, Tallahassee, FL).

Astin, A. W. (1985). *Achieving educational excellence.* San Francisco: Jossey-Bass.

Bowen, H. R., & Schuster, J. H. (1986). *American professors: A national resource imperiled.* New York: Oxford University Press.

Bowen, W. G., & Sosa, J. A. (1989). *Prospects for faculty in the arts and sciences.* Princeton, NJ: Princeton University Press.

Campion, W. J. (1994). Providing avenues for renewal. *Community College Journal of Research and Practice, 18,* 165–176.

Eells, W. C. (1931). *The junior college.* Boston: Houghton Mifflin.

Erwin, J., & Andrews, H. A. (1993). State of part-time faculty services at community colleges in a nineteen-state region. *Community College Journal Of Research and Practice, 17,* 555–562.

Gappa, J. M., & Leslie, D. W. (1993). *The invisible faculty: Improving the status of part-timers in higher education.* San Francisco: Jossey-Bass.

Miles, M. B., & Huberman, M. A. (1994). *Qualitative data analysis: An expanded sourcebook.* London: Sage.

National Center for Education Statistics. (1990). *Staff and faculty in higher education institutions (1988).* Washington, DC: U.S. Department of Education.

O'Banion, T. (1972). *Teachers for tomorrow: Staff development in the community-junior college.* Tucson: University of Arizona Press.

Parsons, M. H. (Ed.). (1980). *New directions for community colleges: Using part-time faculty effectively.* San Francisco: Jossey-Bass.

Richardson, R. C. (1992). The associate program: Teaching improvement for adjunct faculty. *Community College Review, 20*(1), 29–34.

Roueche, J. E., & Roueche, S. D. (1993). *Between a rock and a hard place: The at-risk student in the open-door college.* Washington, DC: Community College Press.

Roueche, J. E., Roueche, S. D., & Milliron, M. D. (1995). *Strangers in their own land: Part-time faculty in the American community college.* Washington, DC: Community College Press.

Smith, P. (1990). *Killing the spirit: Higher education in America.* New York: Viking.

CHAPTER 32

INTERNET ACCESS AND USE OF THE WEB FOR INSTRUCTION: A NATIONAL STUDY OF FULL-TIME AND PART-TIME COMMUNITY COLLEGE FACULTY

DUANE AKROYD
AUDREY JAEGER
MELISSA JACKOWSKI
LOGAN C. JONES

Introduction

The increased use of part-time faculty in community colleges has generated considerable debate and discussion. The National Center for Educational Statistics (NCES, 1997a) estimated that, in 1988, 52% of all community college faculty were part time. In 1993 that number increased to 64% (NCES, 2001a). Furthermore, between 1991 and 1992, 37% of all postsecondary faculty who left their institution did so because of retirement. Specifically at community colleges during that period, 50% of exiting faculty had retired (NCES, 1997b). The increased rate of retirement at two-year colleges creates a situation where future percentages of part-time faculty may be even higher, depending in large part on the policies that community colleges adopt in the future.

In addition to an increase in the use of part-time faculty, community colleges also have the greatest number of enrollments in distance education courses with 48% (1,472,000 students), while public four-year institution enroll 31% (NCES, 2003). Nine percent of all students at community colleges participate in distance education; of the community college students participating in distance education, approximately 60% are taking internet-based courses (NCES, 2002a). It is projected that the number of students taking on-line courses will reach 2.2 million by 2004 (Green, 2000; Moe, 2002). Projections indicate that by the year 2025, forty-five million people worldwide could be learning through online higher education opportunities (Moe, 2002). These data support the notion that a greater percentage of community college faculty are involved in distance education, particularly on-line education, than faculty at four-year institutions (NCES, 2002b). While the data are not available, it may be assumed that even more faculty use Web sites to provide some type of course information to enhance traditional courses, even though the course may not be an actual distance education course. It is important that the large cadre of part-time community college-faculty have the same access to the Internet and opportunity to develop web-enhanced courses as do their full-time counterparts. It is also important to determine if part-time faculty are as engaged in the use of computer technology for instruction as are full-time faculty.

The purpose of this study is to compare access to the Internet and use of the web for instructional purposes between full-time and part-time community college faculty using data from the National Study of Post Secondary Faculty (NCES, 2002a). The specific research questions for this study are the following:

1. Is there a relationship between the availability of Internet access and faculty status (full time or part time)?

2. Is there a relationship between the use of Web sites to provide instructional information and faculty status?

3. Do the two faculty groups vary in their use of Web sites to provide instructional information by discipline area?

4. Is there a relationship between how Web sites are used and faculty status?

5. Is there a relationship between use of e-mail to communicate with students and faculty status?

Methods

Sample and Data

Data for this study are from the 1999 National Study of Postsecondary Faculty (NSOPF:99), a survey project funded by the National Center for Educational Statistics (NCES, 2001b). The data are collected every 5 years, and NSOPF:99 is the most current version of the data at the time of publication. A two-stage stratified clustered probability design was used to select the sample for NSOPF:99. The first stage consisted of sampling postsecondary institutions, and the second stage consisted of sampling faculty from first-stage institutions. The final data set consisted of responses from a representative sample of 17,600 faculty working either full time or part time at a variety of postsecondary educational institutions ($N = 960$). There were 4,392 public two-year college faculty respondents from 298 public two-year colleges. For analysis in this study, only two-year faculty at public institutions who met the following criteria were included: teaching was their primary responsibility, they taught credit courses, and they were not administrators.

Applying this criteria resulted in 3,195 respondents (1,524 part-time faculty and 1,671 full-time faculty). Some totals will not be 3,195, since some respondents did not respond to all questions or else the questions were not applicable to some respondents.

Variables and Analysis

For the first research question, respondents indicated if they had had Internet access during the fall 1998 term (at home and work, at work only, at home only, or no Internet access). These responses were cross tabulated with faculty status (full time or part time), and chi-square was used to determine if a significant relationship exists between Internet access and faculty status.

The second research question responses were examined by cross tabulation between respondents' answers to a question on the use of Web sites for class information (yes or no) and faculty status (full time or part time). Chi-square was used to detect significance.

Since the use of part-time faculty varies considerably by discipline at community colleges, the third research question examined the use of Web sites for course information for faculty status (full time and part time) by discipline area. The NSOPF:99 data were subset to create the following five discipline groups: humanities, natural-physical-mathematical sciences, social sciences, business, and occupational programs. Chi-square was used to detect relationships between Web site use for courses and faculty status by discipline area.

The variables for the fourth research question (of whether both groups use class Web sites in the same way) were measured by respondents' answers to five separate questions. Each respondent indicated yes or no for whether they used the class Web site for each of the following options: to post syllabus and office hours, to post homework assignment and readings, to post exams and exercises for immediate scoring, to post exam results, and to provide links to other information. To answer this question, several techniques were used. First, the uses of Web sites were rank ordered by types of usage by full-time and part-time faculty groups. Next, a chi-square analysis was done to determine if significant differences existed between full-time and part-time faculty groups for each type of Web site use.

The final research question was answered by comparing respondents' answers to whether they used electronic mail (e-mail) to communicate with students in their class (yes or no) by faculty status (full time or part time). Chi-square was used to detect differences between full-time and part-time faculty groups. All analyses used $p < .05$ for hypothesis testing.

Results

While the results for the first research question indicate that the majority of both full-time (93%) and part-time faculty (84%) have some type of Internet access, 40% of part-time faculty do not have access to the Internet at their college (compared to 14% for full-time faculty). Chi-square $X^2(3, N = 3153) = 294, p < .0001$ indicates that there is a significant relationship between faculty status and availability of Internet access (Table 1). More specifically, a greater percentage of full-time faculty (86%) have Internet access at work and at work and home than do part-time faculty (60%). A greater percentage of part-time faculty (40%) have Internet access only at home or no

Internet access compared to full-time faculty (14%). This finding may impact some of the other findings in this study, since Internet access is one critical factor in using web-based instruction.

The results of research question number two, $X^2(1, N = 3244)$ 8.4, $p = .004$, indicate that there is a significant relationship between full-time and part-time faculty status and the use of Web sites for instructional information (Table 2). While the majority of faculty did not use Web sites to convey class information (72% for full-time faculty and 77% for part-time faculty), there was a significant, albeit slight, difference. More full-time faculty (28%) used Web sites to convey a variety of class information than did part-time faculty (23%).

The percentage of full-time faculty varied considerably by discipline area: business had 55% full-time faculty (45% part time), humanities had 45% full-time faculty (55% part time), the natural-physical-mathematical sciences had 57% full-time faculty (43% part time), occupational programs had 66% full-time faculty (34%

TABLE 1
Internet Access by Employment Status

Frequency (Row Pct) (Col Pct)	Employed P/T or F/T		Total
	Part time	Full time	
Both at home and at work	601	854	1455
	(41.3)	(58.7)	
	(39.6)	(52.3)	(46.2)
At work only	308	550	858
	(35.9)	(64.1)	
	(20.3)	(33.7)	(27.2)
At home only	377	118	495
	(76.2)	(23.8)	
	(24.8)	(7.2)	(15.7)
No access to the Internet	233	112	345
	(67.5)	(32.5)	
	(15.3)	(6.9)	(10.9)
Total	1519	1634	3153
	(48.2)	(51.8)	(100.0)

TABLE 2
Use of Web Sites for Class Information

Frequency (Row Pct) (Col Pct)	Employed P/T or F/T		Total
	Part time	Full time	
Yes	360	478	838
	(43.3)	(56.7)	
	(23.6)	(28.1)	(26)
No	1184	1222	2406
	(49.1)	(50.9)	
	(76.4)	(71.9)	(74)
Total	1544	1700	3244
	(47.6)	(52.4)	(100.0)

TABLE 3
Use of Web Sites for Classes by Discipline

	Discipline									
	Business*		Humanities		Natural/ Physical Sciences*		Occupational Education		Social Sciences*	
	PT	FT	PT	FT	PT	FT	PT	FT	PT	FT
Yes	26	35	25	28	18	26	23	22	21	27
No	74	65	75	72	82	74	77	78	79	73

Note. All numbers are column percentages.
* $p \leq .05$.

part time), and the social science had 44% full-time faculty (56% part time). Results of the third research question indicate that a significantly greater percentage of full-time faculty in three of five discipline areas (business, natural-physical-mathematical sciences, and social sciences) used Web sites to provide class information for students compared to part-time faculty (Table 3). Even for full-time faculty in the social sciences, while the chi-square test was not significant ($p > .05$), the percentage trends indicated that more full-time faculty used Web sites for student information than did part-time faculty. For faculty in occupational programs (the largest group), the distribution of Web site use for class information was almost identical for both full-time and part-time faculty (77%–78% do not use

Web sites and 22%–23% use Web sites). With the exception of faculty in occupational programs and the social sciences, a greater percentage of full-time faculty use Web sites for dissemination of class information than do part-time faculty.

The NSOPF:99 questionnaire had five separate questions that asked respondents if they used course Web sites for specific purposes (yes or no). Identified in Table 4 is a rank order, by faculty status, of the percentage responses for the following specific uses of class Web sites: (1) provide links to other information, (2) class syllabus and general information, (3) homework, assignments and readings, (4) practice exams that need scoring, (5) post exams or exam results.

Table 4 demonstrates that full-time and part-time faculty rankings for uses of class Web sites

TABLE 4
How Faculty Used Web Sites

Specific Uses of Class Website	Employed P/T or F/T	
	Part time	Full time
(1) Provide links to other information	81	81
(2) Class syllabus and general information	73	77
(3) Homework, assignments and readings	62	65
(4) Practice exams that need scoring	27	29
(5) Post exams or exam results	23	23

Note. All cell numbers are percentages of faculty that use the Web in the stated way.

are very similar. While more full-time faculty may use Web sites for class information, the reasons both groups use the web are very similar.

The final research question (Table 5) sought to determine if there was a difference between e-mail use for the two faculty groups. A question on the NSOPF:99 questionnaire asked respondents to indicate (yes or no) if they use e-mail to communicate with students in their classes. Results of the chi-square $X^2(1, N = 3293) = 64$, $p < .001$ indicated that a significantly greater percentage of full-time faculty (48%) use e-mail to communicate with students in their class than do part-time faculty (34%).

Discussion

Nontraditional course-delivery methods are increasing at all institutions (Lewis, Snow, Farris, & Levin, 1999), and a greater percentage of community college faculty are involved in nontraditional courses am faculty at other types of institutions (NCES, 2002a). These nontraditional methods are slowly becoming the traditional method of delivery. PowerPoint presentations take the place of overheads, references to Web sites take the place of handouts, and online webcams take the place of face-to-face contact.

TABLE 5
Use of E-Mail to Communicate with Students

Frequency (Row Pct) (Col Pct)	Employed P/T or F/T		Total
	Part time	Full time	
Yes	542	825	1367
	(39.7)	(60.3)	
	(34.4)	(48.1)	(41.5)
No	1036	890	1926
	(53.8)	(46.2)	
	(65.7)	(51.9)	(58.5)
Total	1578	1715	3293
	(47.9)	(52.1)	(100.0)

The findings of this study—that 40% of part-time faculty do not have Internet access at work—would seem to indicate that part-time faculty are poorly integrated into the instructional infrastructure of the institution, at least from an instructional-technology standpoint. Not having access to the Internet may be one factor that accounts for less utilization by part-time faculty of Web sites to provide course information and of e-mail to communicate with students in their classes. The NSOPF:99 data were collected in the fall of 1998 (released in the fall of 2002), and it may be that conditions have changed since then. A follow-up study should be done with the next release of NSOPF to determine if access to the Internet and use of web-based instruction have improved for part-time faculty.

The Internet has become a vital tool in course development and teaching. Internet access is not only important for faculty—it is also important for students. The Internet gives students easier access to faculty and information. This aspect may be important for community colleges since the vast majority of their students are nonresidential.

Thus, the use of web-based technology is critical for meeting the needs of diverse learners at community colleges. Two examples illustrate this point.

One example involves the growing student population who work full time and are pursuing degrees on a part-time basis. When faculty have Internet access and Web pages for their courses, this technology gives the working student much more flexibility in meeting the requirements of the course. Assignments may be submitted through e-mail rather than in person. Questions may be asked and answered by e-mail rather than having to make an appointment with the faculty member during office hours. In short, when faculty have Internet access, it gives students greater flexibility in meeting their educational goals.

Students with disabilities rely on various types of assistive technology (any device that enables people with disabilities to function better in their environment) to function successfully in the classroom. The number of students with disabilities enrolled in higher education is growing rapidly, with the largest enrollments at community colleges (Buggey, 2000).

Faculty need to use web-based and other technologies to accommodate diverse learners. It is interesting to note that the data in NSOPF:99 indicate a significant percentage of part-time faculty at these institutions are not using institutional funds to improve instruction $X^2(1, N = 3244) = 463, p < .001$ (Table 6). Only 10% of part-time faculty used institutional funds to improve instruction, while 44% of full-time faculty used such funds (NCES, 2001). This lack of institutional support for improvement of instruction may have some impact on part-time faculty's use of Web-enhanced courses.

With the exception of faculty in occupational programs, part-time faculty in other disciplines

TABLE 6
Use of Institutional Funds to Improve Teaching

Frequency (Row Pct) (Col Pct)	Employed P/T or F/T		Total
	Part time	Full time	
Yes	155	747	902
	(17.2)	(82.8)	
	(10.0)	(43.9)	(27.8)
No	1389	953	2342
	(59.3)	(40.7)	
	(90.0)	(56.1)	(72.2)
Total	1544	1700	3244
	(47.6)	(52.4)	(100.0)

generally use Web sites less than do full-time faculty to provide student information. While less availability to Internet access may be one factor that impacts Web utilization, another may be that the greatest percentage of part-time faculty is generally in mathematics, English, and some sciences. If semester enrollments increase, the immediate demand for part-time faculty to cover general education areas will be more immediate and last minute. It may be difficult on short notice for newly hired part-time faculty to develop and design a Web site for student information. The NSOPF:99 data indicate that part-time faculty with longer tenure at an institution use Web sites more than those who are recently hired. Unexpected enrollment increases may create situations where new part-time faculty need to be hired on very short notice, and thus instructional design time will be minimal.

Simply put, this situation, calls for greater administrative vision on the part of educational institutions. Resources need to be available to meet the changing educational needs of students. The more that community colleges integrate computer access into their curricula, the more flexibility will be available to students.

Conclusion

Community, colleges are leaders in providing distance education, yet the data in NSOPF:99 indicate a significant percentage of part-time faculty at these institutions do not have access to the Internet and are not using institutional funds to improve instruction. Part-time faculty play an indispensable role in meeting the needs of students and should be better integrated into the structures of colleges.

Further, it is imperative that avenues be provided for part-time faculty members to use technology in their courses. The diversity of learners at community colleges, particularly disabled and part-time students, will be severely disadvantaged by the lack of web-based technology in the classroom. Students who work full time will find pursuing an education more available, obtainable, and practical if both full-time and part-time faculty have access to the Internet and use the web to meet the needs of diverse learners.

References

Akroyd, D. (1999, April). *Satisfaction and institutional support of full-time and part-time community college faculty: A national perspective.* Paper presented at the annual meeting of the American Educational Research Association (Division J), Montreal, Canada.

Avakian, A. N. (1995). Conflicting demands for adjunct faculty. *Community College Journal, 65,* 34–36.

Buggey, T. I. (2000). Accommodating students with special needs in the on-line classroom. In R. E. Weiss, D. S. Knowlton, & B. W. Speck (Eds.), *Principles of effective teaching in the on-line classroom* (pp. 41–46). *New Directions for Teaching and Learning,* no. 84. San Francisco: Jossey-Bass.

Gappa, J. M., & Leslie, D. W. (1993). *The invisible faculty: Improving the status of part-timers in higher education.* San Francisco: Jossey-Bass.

Green, J. (2000, October 23). The online education bubble. *The American Prospect, 11.* Retrieved August 4, 2003, from http://www.prospect.org/print/V11/22/green-j.html

Lewis, L., Snow, K., Farris, E., and Levin, D. (1999). *Distance education at postsecondary educational institutions: 1997–98* (NCES Publication No. 2000–013). Retrieved July 1, 2004, from http://nces.ed.gov/pubs2000/2000013.pdf

Moe, M. T. (2002). *Emerging trends in post secondary education: The view to 2012.* Paper presented at the Education Industry Finance and Investment Summit "Driving Post-Secondary Education" conference, Washington, DC. Retrieved August 4, 2003, from http://www.usdla.org/html/whatsNew/newsAlerts.htm

Monroe, C., & Denman, S. (1991). Assimilating adjunct faculty: Problems and opportunities. *ACA Bulletin, 77,* 56–62.

National Center for Educational Statistics (1997a). *1993 National Study of Postsecondary Faculty (NSOPF-93). Instructional faculty and staff in higher education institutions: Fall 1987 and fall 1992* (NCES Publication No. 97–470). Retrieved July 1, 2004, from http://nces.ed.gov/pubs97/97470.pdf

National Center for Educational Statistics. (1997b). *1993 National Study of Postsecondary Faculty (NSOPF-93). Retirement and other departure plans of instructional faculty and staff in higher education* (NCES Publication No. 98–254). Retrieved July 1, 2004, from http://nces.ed.gov/pubs98/98254.pdf

National Center for Educational Statistics. (2001a). *1999 National Study of Postsecondary Faculty (NSOPF:99). Background characteristics, work activities, and compensation of faculty and instructional staff in postsecondary institutions: Fall 1998* (NCES Publication No. 2001–152). Retrieved July 1, 2004, from http://nces.ed.gov/pubs2001/2001152.pdf

National Center for Educational Statistics. (2001b). *National Study of Postsecondary Faculty NSOPF:99 public access data analysis system (DAS)* [Data file on CD-ROM]. (NCES Publication No. 2001–203).

Available from http://nces.ed.gov/pubsearch/pubsinfo.asp?pubid=2001203

National Center for Educational Statistics. (2002a). *1999 National Study of Postsecondary Faculty (NSOPF:99). Methodology report* (NCES Publication No. 2002–154). Retrieved July 1, 2004, from http://nces.ed.gov/pubs2OO2/2002154.pdf

National Center for Educational Statistics. (2002b). *Distance education instruction by postsecondary faculty: Fall 1998.* (NCES Publication No. 2002–155). Retrieved July 1, 2004, from http://nces.ed.gov/pubs2002/2002155.pdf

National Center for Educational Statistics. (2002c). *The condition of education 2002. Indicator 38: Student participation in distance education* (NCES Publication No. 2002–025). Retrieved October 1, 2003, from http://nces.ed.gov//programs/coe/2002/pdf/38_2002.pdf

National Center for Educational Statistics. (2003). *Distance education at degree-granting postsecondary institutions: 2000–2001* (NCES Publication No. 2003–017). Retrieved July 1, 2004, from http://nces.ed.gov/pubs2003/2003017.pdf

Roueche, J., Roueche, S., & Milliron, M. (1995). *Strangers in their own land: Part-time facully in American community colleges.* Washington, DC: Community College Press.

Duane Akroyd is an associate professor of Higher Education and Director of Graduate Programs in the Department of Adult and Community College Education at North Carolina State Universi ty. *duane_akroyd@ncsu.edu*

Audrey Jaeger is an assistant professor of Higher Education in the Department of Adult and Community College Education at North Carolina State University. *audreyjaeger@ncsu.edu*

Melissa Jackowski is a doctoral candidate in the Department of Adult and Community College Education at North Carolina State University. *mjackowski@wakemed.org*

Logan C. Jones is a doctoral student in the Department of Adult and Community College Education at North Carolina State University. *loganjones@earthlink.net*

CHAPTER 33

RECOMMENDED READINGS AND WEB-BASED RESOURCES

Recommended Readings

Cejda, B. D., & Rhoades, J. H. (2004). Through the pipeline: The role of faculty in promoting associate degree completion among Hispanic students. *Community College Journal of Research and Practice, 28*(3): 249–262.

Gahn, S., & Twombly, S. B. (2001). Dimensions of the community college faculty labor market. *The Review of Higher Education, 24*(3), 259–282.

Murray, J. P. (2001). Faculty development in publicly supported 2-year colleges. *Community College Journal of Research and Practice, 25*, 487–502.

Palmer, J. C., (2002). Disciplinary variations in the work of full-time faculty members. In C. Outcalt (Ed.), *Community college faculty: Characteristics, practices, and challenges* (pp. 9–19). New Directions for Community Colleges, No. 118. San Francisco: Jossey-Bass.

Thaxter, L. P., & Graham, S.W. (1999). Community college faculty involvement in decision making. *Community College Journal of Research and Leadership, 23*: 655–674.

Web-Based Resources

Huber, M. T. (1998). Community college faculty attitudes and trends, 1997. Stanford, CA: National Center for Postsecondary Improvement, Stanford University. *http://www.stanford.edu/group/ncpi/documents/pdfs/4–03_ccfacultyattitudes.pdf*

Olson, S.J., Jensrud, Q, & McCann, P. L. (2001). Preparation and credentialing requirements of two-year college technical instructors: A national study. *Journal of Industrial Teacher Education, 38*(2). *http://scholar.lib.vt.edu/ejournals/JITE/v38n2/olson.html*

Part VI

Students and the Impact of Community College Attendance

INTRODUCTION

FRANKIE SANTOS LAANAN AND DEBRA BRAGG

Students who enroll in community colleges today represent a generation of individuals who are diverse in every aspect. With over 11 million students enrolled in credit and non-credit courses (Phillippe & Patton, 2000), these individuals come to community colleges to pursue different educational and vocational interests. Known for their comprehensive mission, these institutions provide numerous educational opportunities for individuals interested in pursuing career and technical education, transfer education, adult basic education, or life-long learning (Cohen & Brawer, 2003).

Unlike any other higher education institution in the U.S., community colleges pride themselves uponwith serving a diverse student body. Today, there are more ethnic minority students, more English learners, more first-generation college students, more adult students, and more students from low-income families (Boswell & Wilson, 2004) than in other higher education institutions. In fact, a significant number of community college students can be identified as a "nontraditional students," defined as students one who have one or more of these characteristics: are financially independent, attend part-time, work full-time, delay enrollment after high school, have dependents, are single parents, or do not have a high school diploma (National Center for Education Statistics, 2002). Today, almost two-thirds of community college students are enrolled part-time, compared to about a quarter of students in baccalaureate institutions (Voorhees, 2000). Over half of community college students work full-time, over one-third have dependents and about 16 percent are single parents (CCSSE, 2003). Notably, slightly less than half are first-generation college students and 25 years of age or older.

The impact of community college attendance on individuals has been documented by numerous scholars (e.g., Bailey et al., 2004; Grubb, 1996). Economists have argued consistently that there is a positive relationship between education and earnings. That is, the more education completed the higher the earnings. For community college students, completing a vocational certificate or an associate's degree has direct benefit to an individual's ability to secure employment in the world of work. More importantly, these credentials are viewed positively in the employment arena and can be used to meet the "certification" or "screening" process during the application process. Today's community colleges have developed career and technical education (CTE) programs that are closely tied to business and industry. Specifically, these CTE programs prepare individuals to have a skill-set that will prepare them for high-wage, high-demand, and high-technology positions in the workforce.

The chapters in this section of the Reader represent research that describes community college students and the impact of community college attendance on students' educational, personal, economic, and intellectual development. Although the majority of the research has tended to focus on college students enrolled in four-year institutions, these chapters provide an introduction to the current issues and policy and research implications for a significantly growing population.

In Chapter 34, Clif Adelman draws upon data collected by the U.S. Department of Education in its NELS88 longitudinal study to demonstrate that there are three distinct clusters of community college students who were high school seniors in 1992. His point is that there are increasing numbers of traditional-age college students who start their postsecondary education in the community college and thus the perception that the average age of community students is 29 is erroneous.

The next two chapters focus on socialization of minority students into the community college. In Chapter 35, Berta Vigil Laden examines a suburban and urban community college and the socialization process of a culturally diverse student body. Specifically, she uses an ecological model to examine community college students' lives in a cultural context. In the two case studies, Laden uncovers the interactions and experiences of students involved in a culturally-specific academic and support service. In her chapter, Laden offers examples of models of culturally-responsive institutions using the two colleges. For example, she argues that the two colleges have in common several aspects of presidential leadership, resource allocation, and faculty commitment. Other models included curriculum and programs and student services and activities. In her conclusion, Laden argues that it is crucial for community colleges that enroll high numbers of ethnically diverse students to design culturally sensitive academic and support programs and activities that provide a sense of welcome and belonging, motivate and empower, and make knowledge meaningful and accessible. In Chapter 36, Rendón examines the extent to which the concept of validation (Rendón, 1994) has a positive impact on the academic and personal growth of community college students in the Community College Puente program. In her conclusion, she maintains that Community College Puente has implications in the area of promoting access and academic success for Latino students. Finally, she presents implications for access, involvement theory, and teaching and learning theory.

In the next three chapters, the authors investigate the economic benefits of a community college education. In Chapter 37, Sanchez, Laanan, and Wiseley investigate a sample of students from California community colleges. The authors sought to answer the questions: what is the economic value of obtaining a vocational certificate or an associate degree; how do students' post-college earnings differ from last year in college, first year out of college, and third year out of college by educational attainment; and what is the relationship between educational attainment and

earnings for special populations? The authors conclude that there is empirical evidence to suggest a positive relationship between educational attainment and earnings. However, several methodological issues were raised when studying this line of inquiry. In the study conducted by Averett and Dalessandro (Chapter 38), the authors utilize a national database to examine racial and gender differences in the return to 2-year and 4-year degrees. The authors concluded that for women and black men, attending a two-year college is a viable option due to the low-cost.

The next chapters focus on the effects of attending community colleges on students' educational plans, cognitive outcomes and student performance and growth, with the three selected studies examining these variables relative to student attending 4-year colleges and universities. In Chapter 39, Pascarella et al. (1998) tested a hypothesis that community college attendance lowers students' precollege plan to obtain a bachelor of arts degree. A second study by Pascarella et al. (1996), conducted a few years earlier, investigated the cognitive impact of college for freshmen attending 2- and 4-year colleges drawn from throughout the United States (Chapter 40). Results showed a general parity between 2-year and 4-year college students on end-of-freshman year reading comprehension, mathematics, critical thinking, and composite achievement after controlling for background characteristics. Differences in cognitive outcomes were found, however, by gender and ethnicity with men and non-whites realizing greater cognitive returns at the 2-year level, and women and whites receiving greater returns from 4-year colleges. In Chapter 41 Strauss and Volkwein (2002) compared the organizational characteristics of 51 2- and 4-year higher education institutions on students' performance and growth. Results confirm differences in mission, size, wealth, complexity and selectivity between the institutional types and show that these factors exert difference influences on students' grade point average and self-reported intellectual growth. The authors conclude that students attending 2-year colleges receive higher grades, and 4-year college students experience more growth.

The chapters included in this section are not an exhaustive list of the extant literature on community college students. The research on these students and the impact of community colleges on individuals is a growing body of knowledge.

With the development of new national survey instruments, researchers and policy makers are beginning to scratch the surface of understanding the demographic characteristics of students, educational objectives as well as their level of engagement. Also, with the increasing understanding and proficiency of large national datasets maintained by the National Center for Education Statistics, researchers are publishing more empirical work on the topics such as the transfer behavior patterns, nontraditional students, impact of financial aid on persistence, and a whole host of other topics. In less than ten years, the literature has been filled with some of the most comprehensive and methodologically rigorous studies. Although the majority of the empirical research is quantitatively based, there is a growth of qualitative inquiries about community college students. These studies, as well as research that employs a mixed-method design, will continue to broaden our understanding of students and the impact of the complex community college environment on students' personal, intellectual, economic, and human development.

Like the rest of higher education, community colleges are faced with greater expectations to demonstrate their effectiveness as educational institutions (Laanan, 2001). In other words, community college have to be accountable to state and federal stakeholders with respect to their impact on individuals and society. Therefore, more research is likely to emerge that responds to external forces. Critical to demonstrating the effectiveness of community colleges is fully understanding the complexity of the students, differentiating missions and functions, institutional cultures and context, political forces, and structural characteristics. Community colleges are unique and so are their students, locations, and contexts. Maintaining this understanding will be critical to the success of painting an accurate profile of the community college context.

References

Bailey, T., Alfonso, M., Scott, M., & Leinbach, T. (2004). *Educational outcomes of postsecondary occupational students.* CCRC Brief No 22, Teachers College, Community College Research Center.

Boswell, K., & Wilson, C. D. (2004). *Keeping America's promise: A report on the future of the community college.* Denver, CO: Education Commission of the States.

Cohen, A. M., & Brawer, F. B. (2003). *The American community college* (4th ed.). San Francisco: Jossey-Bass.

Community College Survey of Student Engagement. (2003). *Engaging community colleges: National benchmarks of quality.* Austin, TX: Author.

Grubb, W. N. (1996). *Working in the middle: Strengthening education and training for the mid-skilled labor force.* San Francisco: Jossey-Bass.

Laanan, F. S. (2001). Accountability in community colleges: Looking toward the 21st century. In B. K. Townsend and S. B. Twombly (eds.), *Community colleges: Policy in the future context.* Westport, Connecticut: Ablex Publishing.

National Center for Education Statistics. (2002). *Nontraditional undergraduates. Findings from the Condition of Education, 2002.* U.S. Department of Education, NCES 2002–012

Pascarella, E., Bohr, L., Nora, A., & Terenzini, P. (1995). Cognitive effects of 2-year and 4-year colleges: New evidence. *Educational Evaluation and Policy Analysis, 17*(1), 83–96.

Phillippe, K. A., & Patton, M. (2000). *National profile of community colleges: Trends and statistics* (3rd ed.). Washington, D.C.: Community College Press, American Association of Community Colleges. (ED 440 671).

Strauss, L. C., & Volkwein, J.F. (2002). Comparing student performance and growth in 2- and 4-year institutions. *Research in Higher Education, 43* (2), 133–161.

Voorhees, R. (2000). Financing community college for a new century. In M. Paulsen & J. Smart (eds.), *The finance of higher education: Theory, research, policy and practice.* Edison, NJ: Agathon Press.

CHAPTER 34

A GROWING PLURALITY: THE "TRADITIONAL AGE COMMUNITY COLLEGE DOMINANT" STUDENT

CLIFFORD ADELMAN

Among the principal assumptions that have governed enrollment management in community colleges for the past two decades is that the community college sector serves a distinctly older population than do other sectors of our postsecondary system. When the noted community college researcher, Arthur Cohen of the University of California–Los Angeles, proclaimed that the average age of community college students was 29, the number became a threshold benchmark and set a tone for program development, student services, and community outreach. For enrollment management, this tone drives one toward tasks of recruiting working adult populations with specialized curricula, ensuring adequate delivery sites and modes, and maintaining enrollment volume in targeted programs.

While the community college sector was busy serving these older populations, something else was happening in the demographics of U.S. education. After a trough in the early 1990s, the size of the high school graduating classes began to grow, the result of what is popularly known as the "baby-boom echo." Even if the community college sector simply maintained its 1989/1990 share of first-time students who entered directly from high school at 36.4 percent, the number and proportion of traditional-age students was bound to increase (Data Analysis System, 1989–1994).

Judging from data submitted by community colleges to the Integrated Postsecondary Education Data System (IPEDS) during the 1990s, increase it did. Table 1 reflects this change among students enrolled for credit (the only type of enrollments reported to IPEDS).

This trend suggests that community colleges might look more carefully at their traditional age students, the ways in which they are attending school, who is most likely to spend the bulk of their undergraduate careers in the community college sector, and, among the latter group, what they study. Greater attention to this group, the "community college dominant" student, may make a considerable difference in the traditional measures by which community colleges are held accountable.

What the Age-Cohort Studies Tell Us

The U.S. Department of Education has sponsored a series of longitudinal studies that shed considerable light on these features of the growing plurality. The most recently completed of the age-cohort studies, the NELS88, began with a national sample of eighth graders in 1988, and followed them for 12 years until age 26/27. At the end of that period, the transcripts from all the postsecondary institutions they told us they attended were collected and coded so as to produce a very accurate file of student postsecondary histories. (The file also contains high school transcripts, test scores, regular surveys of the students, and surveys of parents and teachers.)

TABLE 1
Age Distribution of community College Credit Enrollments,
1991–1999 (Snyder, 2001)

IPEDS Reporting Year	% Enrollments Under 22 Years Old	Median Age
1999	42%	23.5
1997	39	24.0
1993	35	24.5
1991	32	26.5

Here are some basic background markers from the NELS88 postsecondary file covering the period 1992–2000:

- 40 percent of those who continued their education after high school started in a community college; 60 percent attended a community college at some time

- 72 percent entered postsecondary education in the modal year of their high school graduation, 1992; 59 percent of those who started in community colleges entered that year

- 47 percent of those who started in community colleges ultimately attended more than one institution as undergraduates; 20 percent attended more than one community college

In a way, these are very traditional data categories, but the NELS88 transcript data also allow us to elaborate on student mobility in the 1990s:

- One out of 10 four-year college students used the community college for incidental course work, principally in summer terms

- 7 percent of all postsecondary students were engaged in alternating or simultaneous enrollment involving community colleges and four-year institutions; another 4 percent were true (prebaccalureate) reverse transfers

- One-third of the students who began in a community college also attended a four-year college at some time, and 26 percent formally transferred

- 16 percent of those who earned bachelor's degrees started at a community college and one-third attended a community college at some time

The theme here is inter-sectoral behavior: the volume is substantial, takes many forms, and, among beginning community college students, traditional age students are nearly three times as likely to attend more than one school as are older students. Thirty-six percent of those under the age of 22 when they started attended more than one school in their first three years of enrollment, versus 13 percent of students who were 22 and older. (Data Analysis System, 1995–2001) The challenges of this mobility to enrollment management and student academic advisement are considerable, especially if students don't tell you where else they have attended school and what they have studied.

Customary Accountability Questions

As the community college presidents participating in the National Community College Working Group of the U.S. Department of Education have pointed out in discussions of these data, community colleges are often placed in a difficult position when it comes to the kinds of program completion questions asked by the public. We know that students who first come to community colleges at age 29—or 39—are on completely different life trajectories than traditional age students (Horn, 1996), and that their other commitments (families, jobs) influence enrollment intensity and persistence (Berkner, et. 1996). Yet data reporting puts them in the same bin with dependent, single 19 year-olds.

But the longitudinal studies teach us that, even among traditional-age students, there is a very important sub-population that affects reporting for all program completions—bachelor's degree completions as well as associate degree and certificate completions—namely, incidental students. As defined in all three of the age cohort longitudinal studies completed to date, incidental postsecondary students are those who earned 10 or fewer additive credits—less than an adjusted semester's worth of credits—in their entire postsecondary careers. When one looks carefully at this group, one finds students engaged in fragmentary continuing education, GED-level adult education, or students who took only one course and then disappeared. If one

TABLE 2

Highest Degree Earned by 1992 12th Graders Who Started Out in Community Colleges and Earned More Than 10 Credits by Dec. 2000

None	53.4
Certificate	7.4
Associates	17.9
Bachelor's	21.4

removes the incidental students from the equation, this is what an 8.5 year program completion rate looks like for the NELS88 students who started out in community colleges:

TABLE 3

Highest Degree Earned by 1992 12th Graders Who Started Out in Community Colleges and Transferred to a 4-Year College After at Least 10 Community College Credits, by Dec. 2000

None	26.4
Certificate	0.2
Associates	14.6
Bachelor's	58.8

Now, within this population, if we isolated those who transferred after at least 10 community college credits and asked after their degree completion rates, here's what we would see:

For comparative purposes, consider: among the NELS88 students who started in four-year colleges and earned more than 10 credits, the 8.5-year bachelor's degree attainment rate was 66.5 percent. In the previous two age cohort longitudinal studies, one stretching for 12 years (1972–1984) and the other for 11 years (1982–1993), the bachelor's degree attainment rate for community col-

lege transfer students was 71 percent—5 points higher than that for nonincidental students who started out in four-year colleges.

The overall completion rates for traditional age students who start out in community colleges and earn more than an adjusted semester's worth of credits, then, are higher than they normally appear when combined with those of older beginning students.

Dominant and Sub-Dominant

In light of these background markers, let us use the NELS88 transcript-based history to think about the growing plurality of traditional age community college students in a different configuration. While no one can predict whether students will continue to behave in the same way that they did between 1992 and 2000, three clusters of community college attendance histories emerge:

- The first type is that of a community college dominant student. These students started in a community college, earned more than 29 credits from community colleges, and earned at least 60 percent of all their undergraduate credits from community colleges. These are the students who stay with you. They constituted 33 percent of all traditional age students for whom the community college was the first institution of attendance.

- For convenience of labeling, I call the second type sub-dominant. They look exactly like the community college dominant student, with one important exception: less than 60 percent of their undergraduate credits came from community colleges. The sub-dominant group are students who stay with you for at least a year or its equivalent in credits. It consists overwhelmingly of transfer students, and constituted 15 percent of all traditional age students for whom the community college was the first institution of attendance.

- The third group is a large residual (52 percent of the traditional age students who start out in community colleges). They earned between 0 and 29 credits from community colleges, and, as it turns out, most of them earned credits elsewhere.

TABLE 4
Selected Characteristics and History of Three Groups of 1992 12th Graders for Whom Community College was the First Institution of Attendance, 1992–2000

	Dominant 33%	Sub-Dominant 15%	Residual 52%
Institutional Combinations			
Transferred to 4-Year	18.7%	81.0%	11.5%
Alternating Community College/4-Year Enrollment	8.8	12.4	3.6
Community College Only	70.1*	2.1	78.6*
Other Combinations	2.4	4.5*	6.3*
Highest Degree Earned			
None	46.7	16.5	90.0
Certificate	10.1	2.2*	4.0*
Associates	36.8	5.0	1.2
Bachelor's	6.3*	76.3	4.8*
Continuity of Enrollment			
Continuously Enrolled	63.0	83.0	29.8
Continuous for At Least 3 Years before Stop-Out	5.9*	5.2*	1.8
Non-Continuous	27.8	11.8	31.5
Enrolled for Less than 1 Year	3.3	0.0	36.9
Earned Credits by Dual-Enrollment in High School	14.2*	18.9	13.9*
Earned Credits in Summer Terms	61.3	82.5	24.8
Mean Credits Earned in Introductory College-Level Mathematics[†]	2.7	5.1	0.6
Percent Who Took More than One Remedial Course	39.7	29.9	45.8
Mean Credits Earned from Community Colleges	64.4*	56.6*	21.0
Mean GPA in Community Colleges	2.72*	2.84*	2.12

[†]The course cluster category includes College Algebra, Finite Mathematics, Statistics, Pre-Calculus, and technical mathematics grounded in any of these.
Note: All comparisons of estimates are significant at $p \leq .05$ except those pairs marked by asterisks.

Table 4 compares these three groups in terms of post-matriculation behavior and long-term (8.5 year) attainment. The students of the sub-dominant population are a community college success story. Thirty percent took more than one remedial course, and yet over 80 percent acquired the momentum to transfer, and with a 77 percent bachelor's degree completion rate. The determination of these students (and, one has to assume, solid advisement) is reflected in a very high rate of continuous enrollment, no summer vacation, and attainment in college-level mathematics that is essential to degree completion at any level.

These are students who spent an average of 57 credits with you, almost enough for an associate degree in many community colleges. Indeed, 40 percent of them earned associates degrees, and 75 percent of those who earned associates degrees did so in general studies, science/math, or fine and applied arts. All of these features of their success are guidelines for effective enrollment management of traditional-age students.

These guidelines are reinforced when one turns to the larger community college dominant population, who, it appears, are less interested in transfer than in a full community college experience with a credential at the end of it. Some 70 percent never attended any other kind of institution, and, on average, they earned 64 credits from community colleges. With that volume of credits, program completion rates could be higher. How do we get there? Take some lessons from the sub-dominant group.

1. First, by encouraging continuous enrollment, even if it's for only one course in a term for which the student would otherwise stop-out.

2. Second, by making sure that key degree-qualifying courses are offered during summer terms (in late afternoon and evening hours) and assuring students that one course in a summer term does more good than harm.

3. Third, by creative approaches to remediation in mathematics involving sequences that culminate in one term of college-level work. These steps require continuous monitoring of students and contact by e-mail or phone. They show that you care.

The comparison of sub-dominant and dominant populations suggests a quasi-experimental design to accompany initiatives involving bringing the three behaviors of the former group to bear on the latter. Institutional research officers can determine which combinations of these behaviors (continuous enrollment, summer school, and mathematics sequence) and at what levels of intensity, result in higher program completion rates for students who fit the profile of the community college dominant student. The experiment will take time, of course; the value of a strong evaluation component is worth the added effort.

Not surprisingly, the NELS88 community college dominant students were more oriented toward occupational curricula than general studies, with their major fields of concentration in business/financial services (19 percent), health services (12 percent), and engineering/technology/computer-related (11 percent). These will differ by institution, of course, but what the data suggest is that program completion rates can be enhanced by focusing resources and advisement on the larger occupational program areas and avoiding fragmentation. In economic terms, would be called rationalization enrollment management. Traditional age students have time later on in their labor market life to seek training, in more specialized niches. Get the students already spending the bulk of their time and effort at community colleges to a certificate or degree now, and community colleges will see them again.

References

Beginning Postsecondary Students Longitudinal Study, 1996–2001, Data Analysis System, National Center for Education Statistics.

Berkner, L., Cuccaro-Alamiri, S., and McCormick, A.C. *Descriptive Summary of 1989–90 Beginning Postsecondary Students: 5 Years Later.* Washington, DC: National Center for Education Statistics, 1996.

Horn, L. J. *Nontraditional Undergraduates.* Washington, DC: National Center for Education Statistics, 1996.

Snyder, T. D., *Digest of Education Statics, 2001* Washington, DC: National Center for Education Statistics, 200 table 176, page 210, and parallel tables in previous annual editions of the *Digest*. The "age unknown" figures are subtracted from totals to produce the denominator.

Clifford Adelman is a Senior Research Analyst with the Institution of Education Sciences of the U.S. Department of Education, which has supported the in-process research project from which this material is drawn. He thanks the community college presidents participating in the National Community College Working Group of the Department's Office Vocational and Adult Education for their feedback in discussions of this material at Working Group meetings during the winter of 2003. The observations and judgments expressed are his own, and do not reflect any observations or judgments of the U.S. Department of Education.

CHAPTER 35

CELEBRATORY SOCIALIZATION OF CULTURALLY DIVERSE STUDENTS THROUGH ACADEMIC PROGRAMS AND SUPPORT SERVICES

BERTA VIGIL LADEN

Introduction

Culture exists in every context and plays a role in the way people function. It is a social sharing of cognitive codes and maps, norms of appropriate behavior, and assumptions about values and beliefs which profoundly influence our thoughts and actions (Delgado-Gaitan and Trueba, 1991). Observing, understanding and interpreting the cultural behavior and needs of ethnically and linguistically diverse students is critically important, yet remains problematic in community colleges. Students once labeled "nontraditional"—namely, those from low socioeconomic backgrounds, who are first-generation college-going, 25 years and older, from diverse racial or ethnic and cultural backgrounds, with limited English and linguistically diverse, recent immigrants, academically underprepared, full-time workers and parttime enrollees, reentry women, and learning- and physically-challenged—have become the majority students in most community colleges in the 1990s (Cohen & Brawer, 1996).

Going to college is an eventful point in all students' lives, one that both prompts and hastens movement into a culture that differs from the one they have known all their lives. When this transition occurs, powerful social and personal dramas are played out, for cultural membership helps define who we are in the eyes of others as well as ourselves (London, 1992). What happens, however, is that all too often, students of diverse backgrounds are forced to live between two worlds (Weis, 1985). These students must either maintain separate identities, behavioral patterns, and peer associations, or they are forced to leave one cultural world behind and uneasily accept the dominant culture. Frequently, they become uncomfortable in both cultures, resulting in a profound sense of isolation or loss.

Crossing these cultural borders is an integral part of the community college experience for many students. Hence, the question of how community colleges can help students to make a successful transition into the academic world while retaining their own sense of cultural identity is a critical one, Those who possess border knowledge—knowledge that resides outside the canon, outside of the cultural mainstream (Rhoads and Valadez, 1996, p. 7)—must be incorporated into a learning community that recognizes distinct groups, builds on their socialization experiences, and provides culturally appropriate academic and student support programs. While ambitious, these goals can no

411

longer be ignored by educators today if a learned, informed democratic citizenry is to be realized that can also function competently and competitively in the economic and technological spheres of the twenty-first century. How then do community colleges provide for such diverse groups and meet their multicultural, multilingual, and complex needs without violating their cultural identities?

Van Maanen's (1984) concept of celebratory socialization refers to creating an institutional culture in which students not only celebrate their own cultural knowledge, values, skills, and histories, but also take an active role in their learning process, transforming the organization's culture through their participation and contributions (Giroux, 1992; Tierney, 1992; Van Maanen, 1984). By accepting the cultural knowledge that diverse students bring to the institution and building an educational experience on its foundation, community colleges can help to break down the difficulties inherent in border crossings.

This chapter utilizes the notion of celebratory socialization to assess how the critical cultural Knowledge and values which ethnically diverse students bring with them to the community college can become positive influences on their motivation and academic achievement. More specifically, I illustrate the ways in which a community college can help students learn the new organizational Culture of the community college while it simultaneously embraces students' diverse experiences and multiple ways of knowing. In doing so, I utilize Rhoads and Valadez's (1996) notion of organizational socialization, in which the organization specifically seeks to create conditions of celebration and affirmation that embrace students' border knowledge. Acknowledging border knowledge allows diverse students to take an active role in participating in their own education along with classroom teachers and other college personnel (Giroux, 1992; Rhoads and Valadez, 1996).

As an example of the way in which community colleges can utilize celebratory socialization to empower culturally diverse students, I examine academic and support programs in two community colleges. These programs are specifically designed to motivate and encourage Hispanics and others to excel academically. The first is a suburban community college with a low but rising enrollment of these students; and the second is an urban community college with a majority population of ethnically diverse students. In both institutions, students are provided with opportunities to become powerful learners while the schooling process is transformed at the same time (Hull, 1993).

Creating a Web of Empowerment

How students who are distinct from the mainstream, dominant, college-going group experience college continues to be the subject of much research attention (Astin, 1988; Attinasi, 1989; Pascarella and Terenzini, 1991; Tinto, 1975, 1987, 1988; Olivas, 1979; Rendon, 1982; Rendon, Justiz, and Resta, 1988; Nora, 1987). Some researchers (Nora, Attinasi, and Matonak, 1990; Pavel, 1991; Tierney, 1992; Cabrera and Nora, 1994) have sought to understand how the constructs of academic and social integration leading to persistence or departure as conceptualized by Tinto (1975; 1989, 1993) are applicable to different institutional types and student populations. Tinto's (1987, 1988) process model of separation, transition, and incorporation leading to integration and embedded in the concept of rites of passage (Van Gennep, 1960) dominates the literature. However, several researchers (Tierney, 1992; Attinasi, 1994; Nora and Cabrera, 1994), have explored its applicability for students of racial or ethnic backgrounds, and found it to be culturally inappropriate.

Tierney (1992), for example, argues that the underlying assumptions of acculturation embedded in Tinto's model ignore cultural differences of ethnic groups. Moreover, he suggests that Tinto's use of the term integration is perhaps a veiled synonym for assimilation. Attinasi (1994) posits that Van Gennep's (1960) theory of rites of passage is actually a series of "nested passages" (p. 5) leading to passage-within-passages stages that occur over a longer period of time than just during the freshman year, as Tinto asserts. Nora and Cabrera (1994) found that individuals from various cultures and segments of society can and do undergo successful passages of initiation into the college community. However, they found that encouragement and support for ethnic students from significant others was critical for these students to adjust to their academic and social environments.

As noted above, culture exists in every social context and plays a role in the way that people can function and make sense of their world. Individuals within a cultural group share a common language, norms and patterns of appropriate behavior, beliefs, values, world views, and similar lifestyles (Delgado-Gaitan and Trueba, 1991). Within the context of community colleges, students' cultural differences can be an advantage if conditions are provided which enable the students to empower themselves by understanding their place in the world, and changing the relationships that constrain and silence them (Tierney, 1992). In particular, the curriculum, part of which remains largely hidden to those on the borders outside of the dominant group, can be explored and examined for its multiple meanings and interpretations by ethnically diverse students.

Tierney (1992) suggests that educational organizations can examine how "to transform power relations so that all the participants within are encouraged to reconstruct and transform the organization's culture" (p. 41). Seeking a metaphor to explain this process, Tierney and others reject the image of students floating—somewhat powerlessly—through an educational pipeline. Instead, the metaphor of the web (Geertz, 1973) is seen as the symbol of greater equalization and empowerment for all participants, in that each individual is both inside the web as a participant in all the activities and outside the web as a constructor of new layers. That is, each is "at the center of the web," (Helgesen, 1990b, F 13, cited in DiCroce, 1995) while also acting as a spinner producing the web itself. Moreover, if one thinks of the rites of passage as distinct intersections where distinct processes come together, all that passes through becomes a part of the web that is interwoven and crossed with a multiplicity of voices (Tierney, 1992, p. 53–4). These rites of passage, in turn, can be transformed to empower students to find their own voices and manage their own lives, and thus become powerful, independent learners in their own right. Using this concept of student empowerment, it is important to understand how the community college can transform itself into a webbed organizational structure which will empower ethnic students in the process.

Methodology

This chapter is drawn from a larger study which focused on first-year students of color enrolled in community college with the goal of transferring to four-year institutions (Laden, 1994). Two community colleges in northern California offer examples of how two-year institutions can promote culturally-sensitive and culturally-specific programs in academic and student services to increase ethnic student motivation and commitment to college while also changing the institution as a result of the commitment to the students. The outcomes resulted in improved student persistence and academic achievement, a sense of belonging within the institution, and the transforming of these students into powerful learners. The programs examined here were selected because of their efforts to improve academic and support services and increase the transfer rates for students of color who had enrolled with the goal of transferring to a four-year institution.

This study utilizes an ecological model which considers the cultural context of students' lives. Students are connected to families and communities and function within cultural, economic and geographical boundaries. An ethnographic case study methodology was adopted for this study. The two cases provide rich, descriptive analysis of events, interactions, and experiences of students involved in culturally specific academic and support services programs as seen through the lenses of the organization, that is, individuals involved with the transfer function in various ways, and as observed by this writer over the period of an academic year.

The Colleges

Suburban College has an enrollment of 14,016 students with a majority population of white students, reflective of its affluent, predominantly white suburban area. Suburban College is well regarded in its community and as evidence has historically offered a comprehensive day and evening curriculum, with most students attending fulltime. Moreover it enjoys high transfer rates to a variety of public and private four-year institutions for its majority students. However, in 1989 the college began to experience a shift in student demographics, drawing an increasing number of students from diverse racial, ethnic, and socioeconomic backgrounds in the greater metropolitan community. In 1988 Suburban College enrolled 89 percent white students; by 1991 this percentage had dropped to 73 percent.

In contrast, Urban College has an enrollment of 11,341 students, with 59 percent of its student population coming from very diverse racial and ethnic backgrounds, many of whom are first-generation college-going, nearly 30 percent enrolled in English as a Second Language, attending on a parttime basis, mainly in the evening, and often selecting vocational programs as the most expedient for providing faster career mobility. A much younger college still trying to build more needed physical facilities on its campus, Urban College is located in a rapidly developing urban area of electronic and computer technology firms, with more high-tech firms moving in each year and surrounding the campus. Moreover, Urban College is shifting its curricular emphasis from being primarily a vocationally-oriented institution to increasing its academic and transfer programs, especially during the day. This shift has attracted younger, fulltime students, and raised the transfer rates of its students of color in particular. Table 35.1 provides more detailed demographic information on each college.

Thirty-eight administrators, faculty, and support staff involved with transfer were interviewed to get an organizational perspective on how the two colleges were developing programmatic efforts to increase the transfer rates for students of color. Table 35.2 lists the respondents who were interviewed. In-depth interviews using semistructured questions with probes for expanding on individuals' responses, yielded context-specific data, insights, and anecdotes. Interviews were audio taped and verbatim transcripts obtained. Observation and a collection of archival data (e.g., college catalogs, governing board agendas and minutes, reports, and other varied campus literature for students) provided additional descriptive data. Observations occurred at different times of both day and evening throughout the academic year and in a variety of settings (e.g., classrooms, transfer center, cafeteria, student center, library) on each campus.

Pattern matching prototypes and relational matrices of merging and repeated themes (Yin, 1984; Miles and Huberman, 1984) were used to code and analyze the data. The data were separated out by academic and student services programs and activities. The emergent themes provide the framework for the analysis. Themes were triangulated in order to enhance validity of findings and alternative explanations were sought and compared to initial findings in Lin attempt to disconfirm the hypotheses (Lincoln and Guba, 1985).

Models of Culturally-Responsive Institutions

The efforts undertaken by Suburban College and Urban College to meet the needs of its ethnically diverse students offer models for how an organization can develop a process for responding to and empowering racially and ethnically different groups through culturally-specific offerings. While different in many ways, these community colleges have in common several aspects of presidential leadership, resource allocation, and faculty commitment which facilitates changes in the curriculum, programs, and student services. The influence of leadership and commitment are discussed first, followed by descriptions of some of the programmatic offerings specific to each college.

TABLE 35.1
Demographic Information by Community College

	Suburban College	Urban College
Enrollment	14,016	11,341
Race/Ethnicity:		
African American	2.0	5.0
Asian American	11.0	28.0
Filipino	1.0	10.0
Hispanic	10.0	13.0
Middle Eastern	2.0	2.0
Native American	1.0	1.0
White	73.0	41.0
Gender:		
Women	60.0	48.0
Men	40.0	52.0

TABLE 35.2
Community College Respondents Interviewed

N=31	Suburban College	Urban College
Administrators	4	6
Faculty	9	7
Support Staff	3	2
Total Interviewed	16	15

Leadership, Commitment, and Resources

An organizational commitment to any goal must be publicly articulated and embraced by the institution's leadership so that all participants are aware of and understand it. Leadership and commitment come from both the president and the faculty in Suburban College. The president's commitment to addressing issues of diversity is fundamental in this college. As a new president and a Latino himself, early in his tenure he "publicly embraced and articulated a vision for the college which included increasing the transfer offerings and transfer rates of students traditionally underrepresented in the institution, namely, Hispanics, African Americans, Asian Americans, and Native Americans. He remarked, "We have put the emphasis on transfer for Hispanic and other ethnic students. There is no reason why we cannot put our resources to work to help these students succeed. It is up to us to make that happen." He added, "While transfer has always been a priority at this college, now the focus is on special groups. It's put center-stage."

With the support of the governing board, the president has also allocated financial resources to address the needs of these groups. Use of these funds include hiring new faculty from more ethnically diverse backgrounds, creating a center which combined all career and transfer information and activities, having more active on-campus and outreach and recruitment efforts in high schools in the greater community, and supporting the development of innovative curriculum and programs. From the very beginning, these changes were expected to have a positive and direct effect on ethnic students and in transforming the college. One of the counselors remarked on the president's and the faculty's commitment to focusing human and capital resources on minority students by stating, "It's always been in place, the philosophy of "Let's get everyone transferred," but never really dis-

tinctly to given [special] populations until now. That's a big difference."

The hiring of faculty from different racial or ethnic backgrounds in particular has had a galvanizing effect on changing the composition of the faculty. For example, in a period of growth between 1989 and 1991, 14 new faculty were hired which included three Hispanics, one African American, and three Asian Americans. Faculty comment on the hirings as an affirmative action commitment to diversity and the beginning of a "critical mass" of students and staff representative of the society at large. As an academic dean notes:

> It is well documented that if students connect with the institution, they are more likely to stay, and they are more likely to connect with people who look like them, or talk like them, or dress like them. When students come on campus and find no reflection of themselves or their culture, then the alienation is just multiplied and the likelihood of their remaining is less.

The president noted that the new faculty of color had an immediate effect on the college in terms of curriculum and programs. He gave credit to "the new hires who are promoting and increasing equal educational opportunities for students not traditionally attracted to higher education in significant numbers." Faculty and administrators commented on the contributions of the new faculty in creating new programs, supporting innovative changes, and displaying a willingness to assume responsibilities even when not explicitly stated as part of their responsibilities. A new Hispanic counselor stated, for example, "No one put the in charge of being the transfer counselor for students [of color]. I put myself in charge."

The faculty's commitment to improving the environment for students of color was expressed initially in two documents: the college master plan and a minority task force report. In the college master plan, armed with empirical data and national reports, the faculty acknowledged the changing demographics of the state, the community, and the college, and cited the need to reach out into the community and expand outreach efforts to the new majority students. This report was approved overwhelming by the faculty as its master plan for leading Suburban College into the next century.

The minority task force report was based on an assessment of the college regarding (1) how to respond to the changing ethnic patterns of the communities the college now serves; (2) flow to focus campus attention on the "new majority" students emerging in California; and (3) how to focus on minority students' transition into four-year institutions and into the job market. The task force made recommendations to the governing board, the administration, and to the faculty accordingly. These recommendations included one stating that Suburban College make efforts to develop an improved image and campus climate to meet the needs of the increasing number of students of color matriculating at Suburban College, undertake appropriate curriculum changes that addressed the needs of this new population, and offer more culturally-oriented and culturally-sensitive student services.

At Urban College, leadership comes primarily from the academic and student-services vice-presidents and faculty with the backing of the president. The president commented that he thought the "process ought to be more proactive in trying to get students of color interested who have never thought of going to a four-year college. We need to work more closely with the faculty in the various disciplines and programs to incorporate changes that attract and keep these students in college."

Faculty at Urban College, however, credit the two vice-presidents directly for finally giving prominence to the transfer function by making a commitment to develop new transfer courses and upgrade existing ones, raising aspirations of current students and recruiting new minority students interested in transfer, and creating a transfer center. With the support of the president, the vice presidents allocated fiscal and human resources to develop a strong transfer program in Urban College—which has hitherto been relatively weak due to the institution's primary emphasis on vocational programs that had historically generated larger enrollments but were now declining sharply in some areas. For example, interested faculty have not only developed

and strengthened transfer core courses, but they formed a special core transfer program for young, daytime students who were attending in increasing numbers. The new transfer program focuses on this younger, rapidly growing population at Urban College. A core of general education transfer requirements is offered in convenient time slots so that day transfer students can easily take a full load, yet still have time to study and go work—a necessity for more than 50 percent of these students, who express a need to work at least parttime while in college. Faculty who teach transferable general education courses in the evening have been offered incentives to also teach in the day.

Counselors have also formalized recruitment activities at high schools with large minority populations beyond the local feeder schools, and meet with parents as well as students, faculty, and administrators in their efforts to publicize Urban College as a transfer institution with a diverse student body. As part of the overall effort, college literature was revamped and revised to highlight the new curriculum and transfer offerings. Moreover, the strength of Urban College, which is its highly diverse student population, is prominently profiled in all its new literature and publicity.

Curriculum and Programs

The goal of creating powerful learners can be achieved in a number of ways; however, the most powerful approach is by transforming the curriculum and supporting programs. Both Suburban College and Urban College have undertaken various efforts to promote curricular and programmatic changes which affirm students' border knowledge and cultural heritage.

Curriculum, the fiercely protected prerogative of the faculty, has received attention at Suburban College in response to ethnic students' call for courses reflecting their own heritage. Integrated into the general education offerings are new transfer credit courses which are culturally specific, such as African American Literature, Mexican American History, Culture and the Humanities, and Cross Cultural Counseling. An ethnic studies requirement was added to the associate degree to give salience to the courses. The student services dean acknowledged, "We are very excited about the degree requirement and all of these courses, including the cross counseling course which was developed and is team taught by Hispanic and African American counseling faculty."

In addition, a cross disciplinary honors program has been developed which recruits high-achieving students, according to the program coordinator, "from every socioeconomic and racial or ethnic group because we don't want this to be an elitist group of white privileged students, but a program for everyone who excels academically and wants to be even more intellectually challenged and stimulated. Five of our first ten honors students to transfer are Latinos [or Latinas] and African Americans, for example."

The Urban College faculty, on the other hand, has taken an across-the-curriculum approach that incorporates a multicultural perspective with new and revised courses whenever possible. A faculty member commented, "We want everyone to be exposed to multiple perspectives and students will not get that if we restrict the curriculum to just a few courses not everyone will take." New and revised courses such as Cross-Cultural Communication, Southeast Asian and American Literature, and Math Across Cultures have emerged as a result of the institutional decision. To further encourage transformation of the curriculum, faculty development workshops are offered at the beginning of each semester for new and other interested faculty to orient them to multiculturalism and to demonstrate ways they can incorporate cultural perspectives into their curriculum.

At Suburban College, a powerful and distinctive program specifically for Hispanic students, the Puente Project, has been instituted. The Puente Project integrates students' culture, academic preparation, and college orientation through the curriculum. Fittingly, the Puente Project[1] was initially developed by a local community college in 1981 with the goal of increasing the number of Hispanic students transferring to a four-year institution. It met with immediate success and by 1985 the University of California was a collaborative partner with the California Community Colleges in financing and expanding the Puente Project to interested community colleges. As of summer 1997, at least 38 other community colleges were participating in the Puente Project (Laden, in press).

Of special emphasis in the Puente Project are the threefold goals, which include: (1) two semesters of intensive English instruction focusing on writing and reading about the students' Hispanic cultural experiences and identity; (2) Hispanic counselors who have first-hand knowledge of the challenges the students face; and (3) mentors from the Latino and Latina, professional and academic community (McGrath and Galaviz, 1996).

The Puente Project is a practical, cost-effective model for Hispanic Students that addresses their unique needs by not only being sensitive to but also affirming their ethnic identity by building on their cultural strengths—much along the lines of the celebratory socialization advocated by some researchers (Van Maanen, 1984; Rhoads and Valadez, 1996; Tierney, 1997; Laden, in press). In effect, the students' border knowledge is validated and incorporated into the curriculum rather than ignored or dismissed. The Puente Project cultural model offers a tri-bridge approach that leads to successful academic outcomes, increased self-esteem, and greater self-confidence for Hispanic students.

The writing component of the project is based on a two-semester sequence of accelerated writing instruction with approximately 30 Hispanic students. In the fall semester, students take a pretransfer developmental English course and read Hispanic literature and write compositions based on their own cultural and community experiences. The rationale is that students are able to write about what they know best, that is, drawing from their own Latin American life experiences, their families and friends, their neighborhoods, and all that is most intimately familiar to them. In the second semester, students enroll in a transfer-level English composition class with the same Puente faculty. Hispanic literature and personal cultural experiences continue to be integrated into the curriculum. Oral and written mentor activities in the classroom are incorporated during this semester. Additionally, guest Hispanic writers and artists share their work and experiences with the Puentistas, stressing the ways they are able to remain true to their own cultural identities while functioning successfully in the mainstream society.

The academic counseling component strives to provide daily close contact between the counselor and the students, thus placing the counselor in a proactive a position to address student needs whenever necessary. The counselor also takes an active role in the courses, offering practical academic advice, teaching study skills, and assisting in the English course work. The counselor offers not only typical academic and career guidance and advice about degree requirements, transfer eligibility, financial aid information and assistance, and the college application process, but provides the necessary day-to-day understanding, encouragement, motivation, and psychological support to persist and succeed in what for many is still an alien environment.

Working closely with parents also is critical to the success of the program by helping them to understand and become involved with their children's pursuit of higher education. Hence, a variety of activities are held in the evenings or weekends that include the parents of the students. Parents are also invited to attend off-campus trips with the class and any Puente Project regional and state events. An added bonus is that some parents have enrolled in college themselves and some have become students in the Puente Project as well.

The program is funded by the respective colleges, Therefore, it is an expensive one for community colleges to undertake, as the Puente Project faculty team of two must attend an intensive two-week summer institute at the University of California, Berkeley, participate in followup conferences and workshops throughout the year, attend a number of evening and weekend events, and dedicate 50 percent of their faculty load exclusively to the program.

Another hallmark of the program is that the two faculty members' commitment to the program and the student transcends the typical expectation of faculty involvement. They must contend with students' academic and personal in-class and out of class concerns. These students are typically the first in their families to attend college, and as Zwerling, London and associates (1992) point out, regardless of race and ethnicity, first-generation college students need special understanding and support to make the cultural and academic socialization experiences positive. They also frequently have financial concerns, often work at least parttime, and usually have other competing interests and demands in their lives. The Puente counselor's remarks about her relationship specific to the Hispanic students can be applied to all students: "You have to go after them. You have to establish personal relationships with them. They want to know you because you have been referred by someone they know and trust, so they then trust you. It is all very culturally specific what we do with them."

Throughout the year-long process, due to the combined efforts of the facility, the mentors, and the culturally enriched curricular activities, the students gain it sense of empowerment and academic success. An administrator commented, "It is one of the best things we do on this campus. We validate the students, respect who they are as Latinos, and what they bring with them to college. They connect with role models in the community, their mentors, who encourage them and support them, too. Is it any wonder these Latinos succeed and do its well as they do?" The dean of student services added, "The retention and success rates of these students far exceed the normal rates for Hispanic students. One of the best things is that Puente deals with the issue of self-worth and valuing who the students are. It does not try to change them."

In talking about the Puente Project's success on campus, the president of Suburban College echoed the concepts embedded in celebratory socialization. He stated:

> The Puente Project is the most successful program in the state for helping Hispanics succeed. Students get a strong sense of self-esteem and develop good coping skills in an environment that tells them they are okay just the way they are. But at the same time, it raises their aspirations by showing them that education can offer them a whole lot more without losing a sense of who they are. I think every college, whether it be a community college or a university, should have Puente programs for their students. It is a model we should be emulating in higher education to help *all* low income and minority students succeed.

Urban College has created a similar program modeled on the Puente Project called *La Mision*,[2] but because of the high cost of training, implementing, and maintaining the program, it does not affiliate directly with the Puente Project or participate in any of the Puente Project state and regional activities. Nonetheless, an English instructor and an Hispanic counselor have formed a teaching partnership to offer a developmental English composition class together using some of the Puente Project's culturally-specific curricular strategies. The two faculty members also work with La Mision students collaboratively in and out of the classroom with a selected cohort of first-year Hispanic students for the full academic year. As a team akin to the Puente Project faculty, drawing from their respective areas of expertise, the faculty provide in-depth instruction in English composition, career and college orientation, culturally-specific readings and guest speakers, and an understanding of the "hidden curriculum" of college.

From the very beginning, the students are encouraged in the English class to use their own voices, thus, they write about what they know intimately—their own personal and family cultural experiences. As in the Puente classes, the students learn the formal mechanics of grammar and syntax through the context of their culturally-specific writings. Integrated into the English course is explicit information regarding how to understand and use the organizational structure to the students' own advantage. The La Mision students receive specific guidance in transfer preparation, and obtain information and role models through guest speakers and off-campus college visits. Unlike the Puente Project, however, La Mision does not incorporate the use of mentors. The counseling faculty member commented:

> I knew we could make a difference for Latino students and get more of them to not only do well in English, but get them to start thinking about at least a B.A. degree, and helping them prepare academically for transferring to a university. La Mision is working just as I knew it would. We are attracting more Latinos to [Urban College] and many of them are interested in transferring; They like the personal approach we offer through La Mision. College does not seem so alien to them and they do not feel isolated in their new setting. La Mision is definitely a successful program!

At the beginning of the third year of the program, the dean with program oversight commented, "It is really what we needed for our Hispanic students. The faculty are committed to making it work and we are having a huge success with it. We have students transferring to some selective universities when they had never even thought of going to college before we recruited them." He added that he thought including a mentoring component would be especially beneficial to La Mision students and was encouraging the La Mision faculty to consider it for the next cohort of students. He concluded by stating:

> Ideally, the most desirable for our college and for our students would be to affiliate with the statewide Puente Project, but with the financial retrenchment that the college is in, we are fortunate to have La Mision at all. For-

tunately, the program is a huge success, one I wish we could offer it to every student of color, if not to every student who comes to [Urban College].

Thus, La Mision at Urban College—much like the Puente Project at Suburban College—offers Hispanic students an opportunity to develop their writing and oral proficiency in English in a classroom setting that validates and daily honors their cultural heritage through the curriculum, increases their self-esteem and self-confidence, and raises their commitment to persist in college, while preparing them to transfer to a four-year institution in pursuit of the bachelor's degree.

Also at Suburban College is a summer bridge program called the Summer Leadership Institute for high school graduates with the express goal of giving these incoming freshman students of color a "head-start" preparation for the fall. The six-week summer program offers six one-unit credit courses in English fundamentals, effective reading, career exploration, study skills, and computer literacy. The director of the program and the faculty work closely with the students on a daily basis to ensure the students feel welcomed and connected to Suburban College. Among the many activities are a variety of guest speakers, field trips, cultural events, and meetings with parents about the benefits of college and financial aid availability are part of the six-week experience. For example, the summer bridge students also visit several nearby universities and meet with campus representatives and students of color who spend the day with them showing them the campus and talking about the four-year college experience. These students get priority registration as well an opportunity to meet with some of the faculty they will have in fall classes before they leave the summer program.

Student Services and Activities

How else can students be affirmed in their cultural heritage while still instilling a sense of belonging and achieving? A prospective student's first contact with a college is often with student services staff, frequently during off-campus or on-campus recruitment activities. Student services staff are typically responsible in one way or another for most activities held outside of the classroom. The transformation of the organization frequently begins in this area of the college community because administrators, counselors, and support staff typically deal with a variety of student issues and concerns first. Often they are able to recognize and respond to the need for changes first. Even small changes can have an unexpected impact.

For example, transforming traditional activities such as College Day or Transfer Day can produce surprising results. College Day or Transfer Day is a typical, large scale fall event held in community colleges that brings four-year college recruiters to campus to provide students with information about postsecondary choices and opportunities. In keeping with the concept of celebratory socialization, Suburban College offers an additional fall college information day specifically for Hispanics and other students of color. Started by the Puente Project counselor at Suburban College, the event is called Raza Day.[3] It features ethnic four-year college and university representatives who offer a more personalized presentation of the academic and social aspects of their institutions, including information about special campus programs offered for students of color. They also offer workshops on academic majors, student affairs programs, financial assistance and scholarships, extracurricular and social programs, and a myriad of activities of special interest for racial or ethnic students. In keeping with their own outreach efforts in the community, Suburban College invites ethnic students from surrounding high schools to attend Raza Day. According to the student affairs dean:

> The event has become very popular with our students of color here and in the high schools. They all like the special day just for them. It gives them an opportunity to talk with college representatives they feet comfortable with and who can understand a little bit better who they are and how their needs may be different from our mainstream students. In fact, this event has been so successful that we are thinking of changing the name to Minority Transfer Day to be more inclusive for all races and ethnic groups even though they are all invited.

In keeping with its commitment to provide alternative experiences for its students, Urban College offers a second transfer-day event at night time to address the needs of the evening students, many who are older, working fulltime, often the first in their families to attend college, and from diverse racial and ethnic backgrounds. Known as College Night, the event is held in the late afternoon and early evening to capture working students arriving for evening classes between 4:00 p.m. and 7:00 p.m. The transfer counselor explained:

> We wanted to inform our evening, working students about four-year college opportunities and about the variety of evening and accelerated programs oriented to this special population, especially for our minority students, that can make it possible for them to get a bachelor's degree in a reasonable amount of time. We keep finding that so many of our first-generation students just are not aware that there are a variety of transfer options open to them after they complete their requirements here. We're one of the few community colleges that actually puts on College Night—and I know this event makes a difference for so many of our evening students.

Recruitment and outreach activities are common in every postsecondary institution. However, both Suburban College and Urban College have increased their recruitment into the larger community where large ethnically and socio-economically diverse populations reside. Both colleges hire buses to bring in junior and senior students from high schools every fall and spring for High School Days, and for Raza Day in the case of Suburban College, and tailor their on-campus events to the groups invited.

At Suburban College, students spend the entire day going to class with peer mentors and attending a variety of academic, culturally-specific, and social activities. Already a favorite series of events are the buffet luncheon followed by a fashion show featuring the elaborate work of students in the state awarding-winning Fashion Design program, and a cultural program featuring considerable student talent. During the spring visit, for example, I observed a group of Aztec dancers with elaborate feather headdresses who swayed to rhythmic chants and drumbeats while faculty, administrators, students, and visiting high school students along with their peer college guides watched, smiling and clapping along with the drummers. "Everyone—faculty, administrators, the president, staff, and of course, students—gets involved in High School Days. It is a major event on our campus and we are all very committed to having it be a success each and every time," remarked one faculty member.

At Urban College, high school students attend a half-day of activities coordinated by the counselors and members of the student body association. The visit culminates with a lunch which features speakers and entertainment by college faculty and students. On the day I visited, the entertainment included a group of Vietnamese students who read poetry, and a band who sang in Vietnamese several recognizable rock songs, and several Latin American students who performed folkloric dances. In speaking about the high school visits, a dean explained, "We have such a highly diverse student population already that when our high school visitors see our mix of students and faculty as people they can identity with racially and ethnically, this image sells our college to them."

Emphasis on Transfer

Access to knowledge pertinent to meeting one's goals and meeting people whom one can identify with have a great deal to do with becoming self-empowered. Both community colleges have developed transfer centers which integrate career and academic information and make its dissemination and utilization accessible. At Suburban College, the new transfer center has gone from "being nearly in a closet" to being located in the counseling building in a high traffic area, and staffed with a counselor, a career specialist, and a counselor aide. All community college information is consolidated with information on four-year institutions so that students go to only one site for all academic information. Four-year college representatives regularly meet with transfer students there and also present motivational, application, and financial aid workshops. Specific ethnic recruiters from different universities are invited often to speak with and meet students of color on the campus. An administrator commented, "When minority students see people who look like them, they are more likely to want to talk with them. It is an important connection we try to provide and one students seem to appreciate."

A unique component to the transfer center at Suburban College is the addition of a counselor aide. The position of counselor aide is still uncommon in most California community college counseling departments. In those few instances where the position does exist, it is used not only as a way to add staff in budget crunch times, but to create greater diversity within the counseling department. In the case of Suburban College, an Asian American was hired while she

was enrolled in a counseling master's-degree program to assist the transfer counselor and the career specialist. Her presence was credited in part to attracting students of color to the transfer center. A counselor not directly affiliated with the transfer center commented that he saw students using the transfer center whom he had not seen there before the counselor aide was hired. The counselor added:

> I cannot say for sure that it because of [the counselor aide] that more minority students are using the transfer center, but it certainly looks like that to me. I think students who are not too familiar with college, who may be the first in their family to go to college, tend to feel more comfortable asking for information from someone who is more like them, who may understand something about how they feel being there.

The creation of a transfer center at Urban College was considered long overdue by some faculty. Bringing the transfer center to fruition is attributed to the efforts of several counselors and the vice president of student services. While "a career center of sorts had existed off and on for several years," according to one of the counselors, "we were working out of cardboard boxes that held our catalogs and transfer materials." With the remodeling of the student services area, a transfer center was created next to the counseling center and a full-time coordinator and career specialist were hired. The career specialist noted that being located next door to counseling and across from the bookstore and the cafeteria "gave us an ideal location for students to find us." Credit for attracting students of color to the transfer center in increasing numbers is attributed to the hiring of student workers from diverse racial and ethnic backgrounds "because students know that there is someone here who can speak their language if they need to ask questions and can understand some of their cultural needs or situations more readily."

The transfer counselor noted that students of color are using the transfer center with increasing frequency. She attributed that to "making the students feel welcomed, especially when they see the student workers and meet with our diverse counseling faculty. The transfer counselor added:

> It is terrific having diverse student workers because they attract students who are like them—students who might not come in here otherwise. The student workers can relate to these students in a way we cannot. They also

tell us what students are thinking or need and we can try to address their needs. It really makes such a difference to have them, such that I don't know how we could serve our diverse students in the same way without them.

Toward A More Empowering Organizational Culture

Culturally sensitive academic and support programs and activities especially designed to provide a sense of welcome and belonging, to motivate and empower, and to make knowledge meaningful and accessible to ethnically diverse students remain crucial in community colleges that enroll high numbers of these students. As Tierney (1992), Rhoads and Valadez (1996), and others (London, 1992; Rendon, 1993; Rendon and Nora, 1992; Turner, 1988; Laden, 1994, in press) remind us, empowering students involves helping them to understand and make sense of their relationship to the world and to the complex organizations, that is, the community colleges, they inhabit. In the environment of the community college, the process of empowerment is one that individuals take on themselves as they come to an understanding of their place in the world, and are then able to transform themselves in light of their new knowledge in an organizational context that welcomes and affirms their presence.

The task for educators is to create conditions for change. Educators must transform organizational practices and policies in ways that acknowledge the range and diversity of' the contextual experiences students bring to higher education institutions. The programmatic efforts described here suggest how two community colleges initiated efforts that addressed some of the cultural and academic needs of diverse students. The interactions occurring among the various elements—academic offerings, cultural identity, motivation, and student support services—have the potential for creating a web effect that leads to student empowerment and success. Such programs and activities, however, cannot occur without the dedicated commitment and leadership of all members of the organization—that is, the president, administrators and faculty—to transform the college community in ways that celebrate and emphasize differences positively.

Moreover, it is the allocation of critical human and financial resources that also enable the structural and psychological changes to occur. Individuals at Suburban College and Urban College take active roles in using the available resources to promote the recruitment, retention, and academic achievement of Hispanics and other racial and ethnic students by creating environments on their campuses which welcome them, give them a sense of belonging, and value them for who they are. The resources allocated are used to create or strengthen programmatic efforts and to develop culturally-specific offerings and services encouraging student acceptance and empowering them toward the goals of personal and academic accomplishment. A comment by the president of Suburban College may best sum up the critical necessity of allocating resources and transforming the institution for populations who are currently under served and under represented in higher education in general. He exclaimed:

> For years, the biggest flaw in the educational system is that we took students from different backgrounds and said, 'if you want to succeed, you have to adopt our values, our mores, our culture, or you die'—die meaning drop out. Well, now that the numbers are changing in our colleges and universities, they have to change or they will shrivel up and die from lack of traditional students. So, the question is what new things do we do to accommodate the new majority, the diverse population? There is something that Hispanics have, that blacks have, that Asians have, that's good and that's unique to being Hispanic, black, or Asian. The challenge for us is to not have those groups become like us, but rather have the institutions become like them. There are a lot of things that need to occur in terms of what we call reverse acculturation. We need to change the institutions now. We need to stop having the institution change us. To me, education is simply as set of options—*a set of keys* which just open up more doors, Whatever we do with our students, we need to give them as many keys on that key ring as possible so that they have options in their own lives.

It is only by first understanding the culture of the students that the process of organizational and individual transformation can yield significant outcomes for these students or the community college as a whole. Students of different cultural groups, no less than those of the dominant group, who "come to college believing that they may be unsuccessful . . . can be transformed into powerful learners" (Rendon and Jalomo, 1993, p. 1), and powerful participants in the institution. This can be accomplished through the institution's efforts to transform the students' experiences into meaningful in and out-of-class experiences which facilitate their psychological growth, cognitive development, and learning experiences while recognizing and valuing their cultural distinctiveness-and transforming themselves as institutions at the same time.

Notes

1. The term *puente* has several meanings. *Puente* is Spanish for "bridge." A student who participates in the Puente Project also is referred to as a *puentista*. In this form, the word also refers to someone who crosses a bridge or someone who works on a bridge, hence all individuals who are affiliated with the Puente Project can also be referred to as *puentistas*.

2. *La mision* is Spanish for "the mission."

3. *Raza* is Spanish for "race." It is also an inclusive term often used by Latinos and Latinas to refer to themselves as *la Raza*, meaning "our people."

References

Astin, A. W. (1988). *Minorities in American higher education.* San Francisco: Jossey-Bass.

Attinasi, L. C., Jr. (1989). Mexican Americans' perceptions of university attendance and the implications for freshman year persistence. *Journal of Higher Education,* (60) 3.

————. (1994). "Is going to college a rite of passage?" Paper presented at the annual meeting of the American Educational Research Association, New Orleans, April.

Cabrera, A. F. & Nora, A. (1994). "The role of perceptions of prejudice and discrimination on the adjustment of minority students to college." Paper presented at the annual meeting of the Association for the Student of Higher Education, Tucson, November.

Cohen, A. M., & Brawer, F. B. (1996) *The American community college.* (3rd Ed.) San Francisco: Jossey-Bass.

Delgado-Gaitan, C., & Trueba, H. (1991). *Crossing cultural borders: Education for immigrant families in America.* London: Falmer Press.

DiCroce, D. M. (1995). "Women and the community college presidency: Challenges and possibilities," in B. K. Townsend (Ed.), *Gender and power in the community college. New Directions in Community Colleges, 89.* San Francisco: Jossey-Bass.

Geertz, C. (1973). *Local knowledge.* New York: Basic Books.

Giroux, H. A. (1992). *Border crossings.* New York: Routledge, Chapman and Hill.

Helgesen, S. (1990b). The pyramid and the web. *New York Times Forum,* May 27, 1990, p. F13, cited in DiCroce, Deborah M. (1995) "Women and the community college presidency: Challenges and possibilities," in B. K. Townsend (Ed.), *Gender and power in the community college. New Directions in Community Colleges, 89.* San Francisco: Jossey-Bass.

Hull, G. (1993). Critical literacy and beyond: Lessons learned from students and workers in a vocational program on the job. *Anthropology and Education Quarterly, 24* (3), 373–96.

Laden, B. V. (1994). "The educational pipeline: Organizational and protective factoring influencing the academic progress of Hispanic community college students with potential at risk characteristics." Unpublished Ph.D. dissertation. Stanford University.

————. (In press). "An organizational response to welcoming students of color," in Levin, John S. (Ed.), *Organizational change in the community college: A ripple or a sea of change? New Directions in Community Colleges.* San Francisco: Jossey-Bass.

Lincoln, Y. S., & Guba, E. G. (1985). *Naturalistic inquiry.* Newbury Park: Sage.

London, H. B. (1992). "Transformations: Cultural challenges faced by first–generation students," in S. L. Zwerling & H. B. Howard London (Eds.), *First–generation students: Confronting the cultural issues. New Directions for Community Colleges, 80.* San Francisco: Jossey-Bass.

McGrath, P., & Galaviz, F. (1996). "Message from the co–directors." *Puente News,* (Fall), 1. Oakland: University of California Office of the President.

Miles, M. B., & Huberman, A. M. (1984). *Qualitative data analysis.* Beverly Hills: Sage.

Nora, A.; Attinasi, L. C.; & Matonark, A. (1990). "Testing qualitative indicators of precollege factors in Tinto's attrition model: A community college student population." *The Review of Higher Education,* 23 (4), 351–73.

Olivas, M. A. (1979). *The dilemma of access.* Washington, D. C: Howard University Press.

Pascarella, E. T., & Terenzini, P. T. (1991). *How college affects students.* San Francisco: Jossey-Bass.

Pavel, M. (1991). *Assessing Tinto's model of institutional departure using American Indian and Alaskan Native longitudinal data.* Paper presented at the annual meeting of the Association for the Study of Higher Education, Boston, November.

Rendón, L. I. (1982). "Chicanos in south Texas community colleges: A study of student institutional-related determinants of educational outcomes." Unpublished Ph.D. Dissertation. University of Michigan.

Rendon, L. I.; Justiz, M. J.; & Restas, P. (1988). *Transfer education on southwest border community colleges.* New York: The Ford Foundation.

Rendon, L. I., & Nora, A. (1992). "A synthesis and application of research on Hispanic students on community colleges." *Community College Review,* 17 (1), 17–24.

Rendon, L. I., & Jalomo, R. (1993). *The in- and out-of-class experiences of first-year community college students.* Paper presented at the annual meeting of the Association for the Study of Higher Education, Pittsburgh, November.

Rhoads, R. A., & Valadez, J. R. (1996). *Democracy, multiculturalism, and the community college.* New York: Garland.

Tierney, W. G. (1992). *Official encouragement, institutional discouragement: Minorities in academe—the Native American experience.* Norwood: Ablex.

Tinto, V. (1975). "Dropout from higher education: A theoretical synthesis of recent research." *Review of Educational Research,* 45 (1), 89–125.

———. (1987). *Leaving college.* Chicago: The University of Chicago Press.

———. (1988). "Stages of student departure: Reflections on the longitudinal character of students leaving." *Journal of Higher Education,* 59 (July/August), 438–55.

———. (1993). *Leaving College.* (2nd Ed.) Chicago: The University of Chicago Press.

Turner, C. S. V. (1988). "Organizational determinants of the transfer of Hispanic students from two- to four-year colleges." Unpublished Ph.D. dissertation. Stanford University.

Van Gennep, A. (1960). *The rites of passage.* (N. Vizedon and G. Caffee, translators). Chicago: University of Chicago Press.

Weis, L. (1985). *Between two worlds: Black students in an urban community college.* Boston: Routledge & Kegan Paul.

Yin, R. K. (1984) *Case study research.* Beverly Hills: Sage.

CHAPTER 36

COMMUNITY COLLEGE PUENTE: A VALIDATING MODEL OF EDUCATION

LAURA I. RENDÓN

Employing Rendón's theory of validation, the validating elements in Community College Puente are identified. Implications for promoting access, use of involvement and validation theory, and employment of learning theory for nontraditional student populations are presented.

Although Latino students have made important gains relative to high school graduation and access to college, this cohort continues to be underrepresented in terms of college participation and degree attainment (Harvey, 2001). In 1999, about 60% of all Latino college students were enrolled in the 2-year college sector, where retention and transfer rates to 4-year institutions remain low ("Almanac Issue, 2001–2", 2001). The past 25 years have witnessed a proliferation of early outreach programs designed to expand the pool of college-ready students, such as MESA (Mathematics, Engineering, Science Achievement), AVID (Advancement via Individual Determination), Project GRAD (Graduation Really Achieves Dreams), GEAR UP (Gaining Early Awareness and Readiness for Undergraduate Programs), and High School Puente, among others. These programs work with middle and high school students and their families to get students ready for college and to ensure they enroll in college. But gearing students up for college is only a part of what it takes to promote access to college. Once students enroll in college, they need progressive and sustained assistance to ensure that they stay enrolled and graduate from college. Institutions of higher education have responded to the need to enhance student retention, transfer, and college completion rates with academic and student support programs of their own, such as Freshman Year Experience initiatives, bridge programs, mentoring, and tutoring. Community College Puente is one such program.

In 1981, the Puente Project was initiated as a Latino-specific program at Chabot College in Hayward, California, and is now in place at some 38 two-year colleges in California. The original emphasis of Community College Puente was to enlarge the pool of Latino students who transferred from 2- to 4-year colleges and universities in California. In the fall of 1993, Puente began a high school pilot program which grew to 18 schools in 11 districts by 1995 (Gándara et al., 1998). Thus, High School Puente evolved from Community College Puente, and the high school program imported key components from its 2-year college counterpart, such as writing, counseling, and mentoring. However, High School Puente aims to send students directly to 4-year colleges and universities, though some students will enroll in community colleges. Like its high school counterpart, Community College Puente has a team of three individuals working with students: an English faculty member, a counselor, and a mentor. In the community college, students are asked to commit to a year-long writing program which includes both a pre-English 100 (Freshman English) and the standard transferable English course. The role of the English faculty member is to enhance the writing and reading skills of the students. Counselors work with students to provide them with the information they need to transfer and become successful college students. Mentors represent the community and work with students to expose them to professional opportunities.

What accounts for the success of Community College Puente, a 1998 national winner of Innovations in American Government? This is a program that touts impressive results. Roughly 48% of Puente Program completers successfully transfer to a 4-year college or university. Higher-than-average passing rates in developmental writing have been noted for Puente students. These students are enthusiastic about Puente. In a 1996 survey, about 95% of all Puente students would have recommended the program to their friends. Some 90% of transfer students believed Puente prepared them for university-level reading and writing, and about 82% believed their Puente counselor did a "great job" in preparing them for transfer (Puente Project, 1997). Interestingly, High School Puente has been evaluated with more rigor than Community College Puente (Gándara et al., 1998). In this study, I attempt to address this research gap by analyzing how validation (Rendón, 1994), a concept that has been found to have a positive impact on the academic and personal growth of nontraditional students, is employed in Community College Puente.

Theory and Literature Review

Research indicates that validating experiences such as encouragement, affirmation, and support have a significant impact on student development in and out of college (Belenky, Clinchy, Goldberger, & Tarule, 1986; California Tomorrow, in press; Rendón, 1994; Terenzini et al., 1994). In- and out-of-class validating experiences are especially important with nontraditional student populations such as returning adults, low-income students, first-generation students, and many women and minority students from working-class backgrounds. Many nontraditional students come to college needing a sense of direction and wanting guidance but not in a patronizing way. They do not succeed well in an invalidating, sterile, fiercely competitive context for learning that is still present in many college classrooms today. For example, some faculty and staff view certain kinds of students as incapable

of learning, assault students with information and/or withhold information, instill doubt and fear in students, distance themselves from students, silence and oppress students, and/or create fiercely competitive learning environments that pit students against each other. This kind of "no pain, no gain" learning context greatly disadvantages nontraditional student populations such as working-class women and minorities (Rendón, 1994; Belenky et al., 1986). Some of these students may also be experiencing invalidation from their friends and families, such as being told they are not going to amount to anything or being teased for attending college. Some students have a memory of being invalidated in the past and yearn for acceptance and confirmation, especially in the first semester of college (Jalomo, 1995).

Validation Theory

The theory of validation (Rendón, 1994) has six elements that lend themselves well to the study of Latino students in community colleges. "Validation is an enabling, confirming and supportive process initiated by in- and out-of-class agents that fosters academic and interpersonal development" (Rendón, 1994, p. 44). This first element is important because it places the responsibility for initiating contact with students on institutional agents such as faculty and counselors. Many times, low-income students are reluctant to ask questions because they have been treated as incompetent in the past and because they are unfamiliar with how the higher education system works. They cannot ask what they do not know. Second is the notion that when validation is present, students feel capable of learning as well as a sense of self worth. This is absolutely essential for students who lack self-confidence in their ability to be successful college students. Third is that, like involvement theory (Astin, 1985), validation is a prerequisite to student development. In other words, students are more likely to get involved and feel confident after they experience academic and/or interpersonal validation on a consistent basis. Fourth is that validation can occur in and out of class with multiple agents such as faculty, classmates, family members, spouses, children, partners, tutors, teaching assistants, coaches, advisers, and so on actively affirming and supporting students and/or designing activities that promote academic excellence and personal growth. Fifth is that validation is a developmental process as opposed to an end in itself. Numerous instances of validation throughout the college over the course of time can result in a richer academic and personal experience. Finally, validation is especially needed early in the student's college experience, especially the first year of college and the first few weeks of class (Rendón, 1994).

There are two types of validation. Academic validation occurs when in- and out-of-class agents take action to assist students to "trust their innate capacity to learn and to acquire confidence in being a college student" (Rendón, 1994, p. 40). Interpersonal validation occurs when in- and out-of-class agents take action to foster students' personal development and social adjustment (Rendón, 1994). It should be noted that there are some qualitative differences between validation and involvement theory. Astin's (1985) theory of involvement poses that highly involved students are likely to devote considerable energy to studying, working on campus, participating in student organizations, and interacting with faculty and peers. Although getting involved in the social and academic life of the college is important for persistence and academic growth, students from low-income backgrounds and who are the first in their family to attend college usually find it difficult to get involved on their own. These students want to get involved but often do not know what questions to ask and may be reluctant to ask questions that make them appear stupid or lazy. Validation theory (Rendón, 1994) recognizes the limitations of expecting all students, regardless of backgrounds, to get involved in institutional life. In a validation model, institutional agents, not students, are expected to take the first step to not only promote involvement but to affirm students as knowers and valuable members of the college learning community. Validation theory poses that college faculty, counselors, and administrative staff take a proactive role in reaching out to students to affirm them as being capable of doing academic work and to support them in their academic endeavors and social adjustment. Because there are stark differences between traditional and nontraditional students, it is important to distinguish between the two groups.

Profile of Traditional Students

Most traditional students come from middle- and upper-class backgrounds and are predominantly white, though some minority students fit this category. Many traditional students have experienced a significant amount of academic and personal validation in their lives and have had early access to cultural and social capital (Bourdieu, 1986), such as being taken on trips to museums, art galleries, trips abroad, and so on. They come from families in which one or more of their parents and siblings have attended college. Many of these students are supported and encouraged to attend college, and view college attendance as a normal and expected part of their family traditions. Traditional students have several privileges and academic advantages that nontraditional students do not have. These students normally do not have to work to help with family finances. Many have attended resource-rich schools and have been taught by well-educated teachers who have validated them as college-eligible students. Parents, siblings, and teachers see these students as smart and on their way to being the next generation of leaders.

For many traditional students, the transition to college is not a disjunctive process but a normal rite of passage. Once in college, the curriculum and social structures validate and privilege the backgrounds of most traditional students. Most of these students are more likely to understand and manipulate the values, traditions, and practices of college academic and social life because these college aspects reflect them. College social life, such as fraternities and sororities, tends to reflect middle- and upper-class values and traditions. In many cases, faculty and administrators are predominantly White. When the college world reflects and affirms the world of the student, it is easier for students to get involved in the academic and social life of the institution (Rendón, Jalomo, & Nora, 2000).

Profile of Nontraditional Students

Nontraditional students come from low-income, working-class backgrounds and are often the first in their family to attend college. Many are students of color, although a high number of white students can be considered nontraditional. Although teachers and families have validated some of these students, many of them have doubts about their ability to succeed in college and have experienced invalidation. Some have never made an *A* in their lives. Others have a history of dropout behavior and trauma in their home life. Some have been told they will never amount to anything. Clark (1960) has argued that community colleges actually "cool out" nontraditional students, lowering their aspirations to obtain a bachelor's degree. For example, counselors might subject students to counseling and testing that force students toward other alternatives, such as taking courses that lead to dead ends and considering more "realistic" occupational choices. For nontraditional students, college is not a natural process. Even when they manage to enroll in college, nontraditional students find the transition to be a disjunctive process. When nontraditional students step onto a college campus, they find a brand new world with little that validates their backgrounds and ways of knowing. They rarely see themselves in the curriculum and are unfamiliar with the traditions of college clubs and organizations. On predominantly White campuses, they have few faculty and staff role models they can turn to for assistance. When the college world is in stark opposition to the world of the student, it is difficult for students to get involved and take full advantage of all academic and student support services. Nontraditional students have little, if any, of the traditional students' privileges and advantages. They normally have to work to help their family survive. They grow up in communities such as the barrio, ghetto, and reservation, where oftentimes no one they know has ever attended college. They have typically attended resource-poor schools, getting the least of the best that the K-12 system has to offer. Because they are first-generation students, no one in their family can help them to understand and take full advantage of the world of college. These students are often labeled "remedial" or "poor college material" (Rendón, 1994; Jalomo, 1995; Orfield & Ashkinaze, 1991).

Learning Theories

What considerations do educators give when designing teaching and learning environments for nontraditional student populations? Learning theories developed by critical feminist researchers such as Gilligan (1982), Belenky et al. (1986), hooks (1994), and Hurtado (1996) offer some important insights about how race, gender, class, and culture are related to the construction of knowledge and the dynamics of teaching and learning in the classroom. Educators setting up teaching and learning programs for low-income

minority students must consider epistemological issues such as who can teach, what gets taught, how content gets taught, and how students are assessed, keeping in mind that being poor and of color results in a systematically different relationship to producing, understanding, and using knowledge (Hurtado, 1996). Like Freire (2000), feminist researchers argue that traditional teaching and learning paradigms that place professors in power and authority, situate students in passive learning activities, exclude diverse perspectives, and privilege detachment and objectivity result in oppressive learning conditions. For example, the authors of *Women's Ways of Knowing* (Belenky et al., 1986) point out that knowledge identified as historically feminine, such as intuition and personal experience (subjective knowing) has been devalued and discouraged in American higher education. What is privileged is what feminists call "separate knowing," stressing impartiality and detachment. Goldberg (1996) notes that separate knowing "effectively ignores (renders invisible) the self-evaluations and ways of knowing of people of color, many of whom have assertive voices and positive self-regard and do not accommodate white norms and white sex role stereotypes" (p. 9).

Several learning theories offer alternatives to traditional paradigms that silence and ignore the ways of knowing of low-income students, women, and people of color. These include Friere's (2000) libratory pedagogy, which poses that the teaching and learning process can be democratic, participatory and relational, allowing both teachers and students to be holders and beneficiaries of knowledge. Freire asks educators to transform oppressive structures to liberate oppressed students. This is opposed to what Freire calls the "banking model," in which the teacher's role is merely to "deposit" information in the students' minds. A key starting point for change is knowing and reflecting the aspirations of the students. Belenky et al. (1986) describe "connected teaching" as providing a space for growth, allowing the expression of uncertainty, fostering community, honoring diversity of perspectives, and viewing teaching as simultaneously objective and personal. Other theories stress the development of the whole person. For example, hooks (1994) speaks to "engaged pedagogy," in which teaching and learning emphasize a union of mind, body, and spirit; the inner life of students and teachers; a connection between learning in the classroom and life experiences; and the empowerment of teachers and students. Similarly, Palmer (1998) advocates that good teaching delves into three important paths that address the development of the whole person: intellectual, emotional and spiritual. If nontraditional students are to find academic success in higher education, it is important to advance teaching and learning theories to assist educators with models that are effective for working with these kinds of students. Because Puente works primarily with Latino students who have a history of oppression and who have been the victims of negative stereotypes (i.e., viewed as having limited intelligence and potential for college), it becomes important to learn how Puente's teaching and learning component is designed to validate these students as fully capable of engaging in college-level work.

Purpose and Method

Employing Rendón's (1994) theory of validation, the purpose of the study was to identify the validating elements in Community College Puente. Who are the validating agents in Puente? What are examples of in- and out-of-class academic and interpersonal validation? How is validation employed in the Puente English classroom? What is the impact of validation on Latino students and on Puente faculty and staff? To conduct this analysis, I spent roughly 6 hours doing face-to-face interviews with the Puente Project's staff in the main office located in Oakland, California. Interviews were conducted with Puente's codirectors, Patricia McGrath and Felix Galaviz; Sallie Brown, English instructor and trainer; Ramon Parada, director of counselor training; Jane Pieri, high school training coordinator; and Luis Chavez, director of mentoring training. I also conducted a focus group interview with 15 high school and community college Puente Project counselors. In addition, I spent a half day visiting a Puente Project English class as a participant/observer at El Camino College in Torrance, California. Moreover, I reviewed 22 written El Camino College student narratives about what the Puente Project meant to them.

Interviews followed a narrative approach, which has the following features: (a) The questions, agenda and structure are open to development and change. (b) Narrative studies are conducted with small groups of individuals, as opposed to large sample sizes, knowing that a single case study yields extremely rich data. (c) The interaction of the interviewer and interviewee influence the data, as do additional contextual factors. (d) There are usually no a priori hypotheses. (e) The research work is interpretive, a process that is personal, partial, and dynamic. (f) The work requires dialogical listening, and individuals are treated as storytellers rather than as respondents. (g) The research does not require replication of results as a criterion for its evaluation but does require self-awareness and self-discipline in the overall data analysis and interpretation (Holloway & Jefferson, 2000; Lieblich, Tuval-Mashiach, & Zilber, 1998).

All interview sessions, as well as the class visit, were tape-recorded. Audio recordings and written narratives were analyzed and sorted into themes such as academic validation, interpersonal validation, validating agents, impact of validation, and reciprocal nature of validation. Exemplars for each theme were identified and categorized. Findings were compared with validation theory as a means to assess the extent and nature of validation present in Puente, as well as the impact of validation. Member checking (Guba & Lincoln, 1985) was employed by sharing earlier drafts of the study narrative with Puente's codirectors, as well as with El Camino College English instructor Barbara Jaffe and counselor Stephanie Rodriguez. These individuals were asked to review the drafts for validity—to ascertain whether or not the explanation and description of the study were credible. The study is limited in the sense that only one Puente English classroom (El Camino College) was analyzed. Interviews were conducted with only a small sample of Puente faculty and staff. Although generalizations beyond the sample cannot be made, it is possible to use the findings to provide depth of understanding about how Puente works in community colleges and to use the study as a guide for future research and better practice in 2-year college settings.

I include a first-person, subjective experience as an explicit and active component of the analysis of the diverse body of information I acquired about the Puente Project. I found this approach useful and necessary, given my positionality in relationship to Puente. At one level, researching and writing about Puente is like writing about myself. To write authentically about Puente, I find I must connect to my own history as a low-income, first-generation, Chicana student. My path to college began in resource-poor schools in the predominantly Mexican American community of Laredo, Texas. I attended two community colleges in Laredo and San Antonio, Texas, before transferring to the University of Houston to earn a bachelor's degree. Consequently, my sociocultural history and educational path are much like that of Puente students. Thus, I chose to reject a positivist approach that is based in part on what critical theorists, as well as feminist scholars and first-person methodologists (Held, 1980; Lather, 1991; Varela & Shear, 1999), would consider questionable, erroneous assumptions of objectivity and detachment. Thus, my analyses include personal experience, which in itself is a valuable source of "narrative truth" (Spence, 1982; 1986).

Validation in a Puente English Classroom

A great deal of academic and interpersonal validation takes place in Puente's English class with faculty, counselors, and students acting as validating agents. The following case study illuminates how validation is employed in the classroom.

I walk into the Puente English classroom led by Professor Barbara Jaffe and Counselor Stephanie Rodriguez at El Camino College in Torrance, California. I am joined by my California State University–Long Beach graduate student research assistant, Renita, and my mentee, Gabby. Renita is African American, born in the deep South, has three children, and is making ends meet while she completes her master's degree in student development in higher education. Gabby is a Latina first-year student from a migrant family background. She is enrolled in the Educational Opportunity and College Assistance Migrant programs, both designed for working class, first-generation college students. I too have a similar background. I was born to parents who completed only the second and third grades, grew up in poverty in a barrio where no one I knew had attended college, attended schools with few resources, and received little encouragement to get a college degree. The three of us form quite the triangle, one just starting her college career, another nearly finished with her advanced degree, and the third being what could be considered the highly successful role model—a Latina professor who has successfully navigated the elemen-

tary through graduate school educational system. Instead of focusing on our obvious differences, we became a unified whole, connected by similar sociocultural histories and kept alive by our passion to grow and keep learning.

I look around the classroom and see some 20 students. When these students see us, their life experiences are instantly affirmed. The first half of this class is structured to focus on the inner worlds of these students. To do so, students have been assigned to read my essays, "From the Barrio to the Academy: Revelations of a Mexican American Scholarship Girl" (Rendón, 1992) and "Life on the Border" (Rendón, 1996). Students are eager to share their reflections about these essays, which basically capture my experiences as I made the transition to a community college and wound up at the University of Michigan to earn my doctorate. The students and I know that much of my story is basically their story. I cannot help but be very moved by what these students say about my work.

Around the classroom, students connect to the notions of adjusting to college, not being prepared for college, feeling lost and needing a sense of direction, and separating from their culture to find success in college. One student says:

> For me it was very hard to relate to school . . . because of my background and culture, it is very different. I want to adjust to the academic world. . . . It's hard to let go of my culture. . . . It feels like you're leaving your culture behind . . . like family, that's where culture begins. When you start to be successful, something isn't meshing. Something is out of place. Family constantly asks questions: Why are you going out of town? Why are you leaving for the weekend?

Family issues surface repeatedly with these students. They talk about how they can't have a normal dinner with their family because they have to do schoolwork, how family members think college is only for rich people, how difficult it is to explain what they are doing in college to their family members. Some family members worry about their children becoming different. One woman expresses this by saying: "My mom has always told me that education should not change me. Bringing up college work, you can't have a normal conversation with your family." Students also connect to their memories of being invalidated, and to the notion that many educators do not expect students like them to succeed. A woman says,

To me it's so true. Educators look at you and judge you for how you look. And I've had that a lot. Teachers pick on me or they try to make me look dumb in front of the rest of the class. But I prove them wrong. I pass their class with As.

The second half of the class is when students present their "I-Search" papers. English professor Barbara Jaffe explains that an I-Search paper is different from a research paper. In a research paper, students search for what someone else has already researched, mostly in the library. An I-Search paper is an original search that tells the story of a student's quest for information about a topic they (not the teacher) care about. This kind of paper includes both information about the student's chosen topic and how the student conducted the search for information—interviews, phone conversations, feelings as student searched, and so on.

The I-Search paper requirements are academically rigorous. The paper must include primary resources such as observation, personal interview, or letters. The paper also includes secondary sources such as a nonfiction book, a chapter in a longer book, and two magazine articles related to the topic. Each report also must have a form of the following creative sources: short story, poem, movie, play, work of art, or musical composition related to the topic. Besides a written paper, students are responsible for a 5- to 10-minute oral presentation using a visual aid. Students have been given an extensive set of guidelines to be used in conducting their I-Search papers, including how to select a topic, how to cluster ideas, how to develop paragraphs, how to write a letter of intent to interview someone, steps to conduct the I-Search process, timeline, interviewing tips, note taking techniques, and how to document sources.

Today, four students are presenting their I-Search papers to the Puente English class. They look excited, eager to share what they have found. The instructor hands out forms for students to provide feedback on the papers to be presented. The first presenter begins by putting up a poster about his I-Search and talking about his investigation into drugs and the juvenile justice system. A second student discusses the information he got about one of his joys, snowboarding, and brings a film on this topic for the class to watch. The third student puts up another poster to discuss teen pregnancy with candor, explaining some of the reasons teens get preg-

nant and the myths about sexual activity that get teens into trouble. A fourth student explains her poster on immigration research. She relates a poignant story about a woman who fled from El Salvador only to be raped by the very soldiers who were supposed to help her come into this country. She explains that she is interested in this topic because her parents also fled Central America and took dangerous risks so that their children could have a better life in America. After each presentation, the class has an opportunity to ask questions and to engage in a critical dialogue about the information students have presented.

Professor Jaffe asks, "What was this process like for you?" The students respond by articulating how it is difficult to research topics that are painful to them. At the same time, caring passionately about a topic makes it easier to find information. They explain that they found the process of researching to be educational. Other students relate how proud they are of their colleagues and the work that they have presented. These are students who, according to Professor Jaffe, did not want to talk when the class first began. Now these students are doing critical thinking, they feel comfortable doing research and presenting in front of class. As students get ready to leave, Professor Jaffe reminds them that if they need help with their assignment, they can call her, and she gives students her pager number.

Analysis of Academic Validation in the English Classroom

This brief case study provides ample examples of academic validation. It should be noted that the role of the instructor is critical, for it is the teacher who sets up the classroom in a way in which validation can take place. Below are examples of academic validation.

Affirming the real possibility that students can be successful college students. When the English instructor invites Latino role models and experts to the classroom, Puente students are exposed to individuals who come from similar backgrounds. These individuals make it possible for students to see that they too can be successful college students and community leaders. As one student noted, speakers who come to class "inspire us to continue toward our goals. They, like us, grew up in humble homes and families that require them to never lose their roots." When my students and I visit the classroom, we help to affirm students' life experiences, and we serve as examples of individuals who overcame formidable odds to attain academic success.

Validating the notion that Latinos can be valuable contributors to the body of knowledge that is studied in the classroom. In this class, the English instructor gave students the opportunity to read and discuss essays reflecting the experiences of a Latina's journey in higher education. Indeed, all Puente English classrooms are infused with Latino literature, including writers such as Sandra Cisneros and Richard Rodriguez, among others. Puente staff understand that students need to see themselves in what they are reading. Many students are awed that there is a large base of Latino literature.

Providing the opportunity for students to witness themselves as capable learners. The requirements of the I-Search paper call for high levels of critical thinking skills and writing abilities. Students engage in synthesis, analysis, research, writing, and speaking. The fact that students are able to meet these requirements by presenting their papers to class confirms that they are able to engage in college-level academic work.

Affirming the value of students' personal voice. In this class, the English instructor allows students to bring who they are and what they represent to the classroom's discussions. The personal voice of the students is invited and given an equal privilege with the voice of the writers they are studying. For example, students express the angst related to making the transition to college (i.e., leaving their culture behind, negotiating tensions with their family, being stereotyped as dumb, etc.). Giving students personal and intellectual voice in the classroom allows students to know that the knowledge and experiences that they bring to the college classroom are just as important as what others represent and know. Moreover, in this class the faculty member communicates that knowledge can initiate from the students' personal experience. In the I-Search paper, students are allowed to select topics of interest to them, which often translates into selecting a topic rooted in a student's personal history. Here, what a student knows, understands, and cares about are validated and privileged as valuable knowing.

Actively reaching out to students to offer academic assistance. At the end of the class, the professor does not wait for students to ask her for academic help. Instead, she takes the initiative to assist students with their assignments, offering her pager number. This is a critical validating action with nontraditional students who often feel unentitled to request academic assistance.

Providing opportunities for students to validate each other. After students present their I-Search paper, the professor gives students an opportunity to communicate how they feel about the academic work that their peers have presented in class. Students provide encouraging comments that validate the work of their peers.

Honoring and validating subjective forms of knowledge. The I-Search paper does something many other kinds of research assignments do not do. It connects an intellectual process (rigorous research) with emotions and feelings (use of art, poetry, music, etc.) and discussion of personal feelings as students engaged in their research.

Affirming the culture of the students. Students learn to read and write while developing cultural pride and examining the purpose and meaning of getting a college education. Students are given time to openly talk about their experiences as learners and what going to college means for them, their families, and the Latino community.

It is noteworthy to point out that my interviews with Puente's codirectors, Patricia McGrath and Felix Galaviz; Jane Pieri, English instructor and trainer; Barbara Jaffe, English instructor; and Stephanie Rodriguez, counselor, revealed additional examples of in-class academic validation that are used throughout Puente programs in different community colleges. These included the following.

Stressing academic strengths to build self-confidence. Puente treats its English class as "accelerated writing" and avoids working with students using a deficit model. In fact, many Puente students read and write more than students in a regular English class. Puente faculty and counselors understand that their students have been underserved and invalidated in the past. These types of students have not had the opportunity to have someone believe in them. They are missing self-confidence about expressing their ideas, asking questions, and engaging in class. For many, Puente is the first time they are allowed to experience their voice, thinking, and ideas. This builds self-esteem and confidence, which transfer to other classrooms.

Affirming the value of personal experience as a reservoir of knowledge that can be used in the classroom. Students initially enroll in a college-level writing class based on the Bay Area Writing Project that begins with a personal narrative. This is intended to give students confidence that they can write. Patricia McGrath explains how Puente works with students:

> In the beginning all students were remedial. We created a community of writers. Students wrote about what was relevant and important to them. They wrote about their community experiences. They were writing for each other, not for me. I would not let them see their writing [mistakes] at first. There were too many mistakes. But if they read their paper to someone at first, it would sound good. The more they read to each other and got positive feedback, the more they wanted to learn to write correctly. I tried to facilitate the class so when students want to get it right, they ask. When they cared about what they were writing, then they were ready to learn the writing skill.

Providing positive feedback. The initial feedback students get about their writing is not about whether they used a good verb or pronoun. Students are asked to say more about the person they are writing. Patricia McGrath explained that she had used yellow sticker paper to write comments such as, "Can you say more about your grandmother? Is she a *Virgen de Guadalupe* type?" "Tell me a little bit about your brother. How old is he? He sounds like a very interesting guy." McGrath elaborated:

> Their papers have always been marked up. I'm not going to do that. If they want to take the sticker off to save face, they can do that. They've had marks all their lives. They don't know the kind of instruction that comes from the other way, from something positive.

Students also get feedback regarding their progress through journal writing, ongoing meetings with students in and out of class, and Puente team meetings with students. Portfolios are used to assess writing progress over the course of one academic year. An anthology of student writing is created at the end of the semester.

Allowing students to work, in teams to validate each other's work. Writing is a community experience, not one that pits students against each other. In Puente, an authentic learning community is one in which students care about each other and assist each other to learn. Counselor Stephanie Rodriguez elaborates: "Teamwork is critical. Students need to know how to work with each other. This is a skill that is needed in the workplace . . . how to work with others, share information."

Creating a familia *learning atmosphere.* Puente staff recognize that the family is one of the most validating elements of the Latino community. Students are not told they are going to study English. Instead, they are told they are going to write about *"la familia."* Students organize into familias in class for essay or topic discussions. These evolve into study groups outside the classroom. The importance of familia is captured by a student who wrote, "Puente was not only a class, but a second family. Our familias helped students to be more expressive on essays as well as to feel comfortable when speaking in class."

Validating the students' personal journeys to discover meaning and purpose. Built into writing activities is journal writing, a contemplative practice activity that is designed for students to reflect on the larger meaning and purpose of what they are learning. Professor Jaffe elaborates:

> Students write in their journals to both [the counselor] and me. We read their notes to us and each of us responds to them. They often disclose very essential information within these journals that helps us to understand what is going on with them, thus allowing us to be more aware of their academic and personal needs. This activity is absolutely essential to their development both in and out of the classroom.

Providing a safe, affirming academic environment. Puente students benefit from teaching and learning environments where they feel comfortable expressing and recognizing themselves as knowers. One student commented: "With the help and support of my professor through the last year I have been provided with a safe environment in which to speak and be heard."

Analysis of Interpersonal Validation in the English Classroom

The English classroom I observed also exhibited examples of interpersonal validation. Examples include the following.

Affirming students as persons, not just students. The English classroom combines the expertise of two important validating agents, the faculty member and the counselor. Both are present in class and provide academic assistance as well as encouragement and support. One student expresses,

> I find Barbara and Stephanie not only to be my teachers, but I consider them more like close friends or almost family due to their warm love and affection expressed throughout the year. Barbara would always spare her time in order to go over a paper for me and Stephanie never hesitated in helping me to plan my academics or sign my overload petition. . . . They encouraged me to give my best in all my classes even while going through struggles outside school such as work, girlfriend, church, and personal issues.

Allowing students to validate each other and build a social network. Two students commented on the sense of caring and support fostered in the Puente learning community: "Not only did we form study groups, but we went out as friends and had great times." "We all have each other's phone numbers so we always have someone to counsel us."

Impact of Validation

A key finding is that validation helps students to gain confidence in their academic ability and to know that their newly acquired skills can transfer to other classes. The following student statements substantiate the impact of validation.

> My new skills have simultaneously merged into my other classes, and for the first time I feel confident in the pursuit of my future educational goals in any classroom environment.
>
> I know that if I survived Puente, I can survive any other class that I take here [at the community college] or at the university.
>
> My writing skills have gone up tremendously. I remember coming from high school hating English class. It was never my best subject. . . . In fact, my English teacher in high

school told me I was never going to do well in English. I guess I proved her wrong.

> We do a tremendous amount of writing and it really helps us improve with grammar and the organization of our work. I especially like that we get to be in the class for the whole year; this way we get to develop better relationships with our classmates and our teachers.
>
> I have learned both academically and personally. . . . I believe in this because I created inner motivation. . . . I have improved my writing skills; I also learned to take notes when it wasn't required to do so. I learned to seek help from instructors . . . I have developed the skill of listening.

Counselors as Validating Agents

Traditionally, a counselor's role has been confined to being in an office, taking appointments, and meeting with students to assist them with course scheduling and issues that affect their education. Felix Galaviz explains this traditional role:

> Counselors wait for students to come see them. They ask for their name and major. They don't spend time trying to get behind the student. Where are you from? What are you doing in this community? They never ask personal questions. They cooled students out. That was the worst thing they could have done. This was the student's first attempt to make a connection.

Traditional counseling practices do not work well with nontraditional students. "Cooling students out" is inherently invalidating and harmful. Many Puente students are students who feel lost and need a sense of direction. They do not understand higher education—its traditions, terminology, or offerings. Their parents, many who have never attended college, are not sure that college is good for their children, and they are unable to help their children to navigate the world of college. Parents have concerns about the costs of college and often believe that higher education is only for affluent families. The following students elaborate on these points:

> Before Puente I did not know how my life was going. I had no sense of direction.
>
> Before Puente I took one class my first semester and four classes my second semester at El Camino. The reason was that I did not know who to go for help.

I came to college as a lost puppy. I had no one to turn to with my questions and no direction with my life. I was very scared when I came straight from my high school into a completely new environment.

To assist these kinds of students, Puente Project counselors engage in both academic and interpersonal validation.

Academic and Interpersonal Validation From Counselors

Puente counselors affirm the importance of academics to all students and become their cheerleaders. Counselors become actively involved in the students' academic growth. As noted earlier, a team of three people supports students: an English instructor, a counselor, and a mentor. Counselors work very closely with the English instructor to validate students as capable learners. They attend English classes and monitor academic progress. Counselors and instructors always strive to make students feel important enough to understand they can return to Puente even when they succumb to the temptation to drop out of college. They tell students, "If you leave, please know you can always come back."

Counselors consistently affirm that transferring to a 4-year college is a real possibility. They guide students with an education plan. This plan details the courses students need to get degrees and to be able to transfer. Counselors explain the academic system and its terminology, including the different (a) types of college degrees and what it takes to earn them, (b) range of institutions and their admissions requirements, (c) kinds of college programs of study, and (d) types of financial aid. Students go on field trips to visit potential 4-year colleges and universities. Counselors constantly remind students that they will be transferring. They help make college a natural process, as opposed to one that is disjunctive in nature. Counselors educate admissions officers about the issues related to nontraditional students, which can help student affairs personnel to design interventions that will facilitate the transition to college. Counselors validate students as capable of setting and meeting high expectations. Counselors help shape high aspirations to go beyond study at the community college. They arrange for students to attend the Puente Motivational/ Transfer Student Conference held each fall in the north and south at a University of California campus. Counselors also let students see the difference between long-term and short-term gratifications and inform students that they need to be ready to make some sacrifices.

Counselors also engage in interpersonal validation, providing encouragement and support to students and their families. Counselors establish a supportive relationship with parents. They facilitate parent-to-parent family discussions about their children going to college. Counselors explain the world of college and help parents through their children's transition to college. Counselors establish a personal, caring relationship with students. Puente counselors are trained to work with nontraditional student populations. Rather than developing an impersonal connection, counselors hook students on a personal level by sharing their own stories. They build a sense of pride in students. Felix Galaviz explains what counselors are trained to tell students: "You know what, you're going to be the first in your family to go to college and you are going to share this with your little sister. . . . You are going to make so many people proud." Galaviz explains that it is this validating, personal connection that builds a relationship between students and Puente staff. The end result is a commitment on the part of the student to stay in college. Once students make the commitment, it is harder for them to break their pledge.

Impact of Validation From Counselors

Engaging in academic and interpersonal validation makes Puente counselors different from counselors who employ traditional counseling approaches. In the Puente counseling model, counselors frequently interact with faculty and students in and out of class, know every student's grades, keep teachers informed, stay in touch with parents, and provide students with baseline information to get them ready to transfer to a 4-year institution. A Puente student sums up the impact of this kind of validation:

> These caring and knowledgeable educators really and genuinely care about their students. The caring shows in everything they have done for us on a daily basis. They have provided me with information, advice, one-on-one help, emotional support, understanding, jobs, etc., that I would have otherwise found it difficult, if not impossible, to gather on my own.

Mentors as Validating Agents

Mentoring in Community College Puente is not simply about connecting a student with a personal guide to careers and future possibilities. Puente's mentors actively engage in academic and interpersonal validation.

Academic and Interpersonal Validation from Mentors

Mentors validate the notion that academic achievement is an individual as well as a collective success for the Latino community. Mentors represent the community and tell students that education is more than getting a degree. Mentors emphasize that students are expected to give something back to their communities because someone helped them to succeed. Mentors also affirm the notion that students can be a part of a successful professional class. As such, mentors provide professional role modeling. They take students to their work sites and visit students in their classrooms.

Luis Chavez, director of mentor training, explained that mentoring is the way to involve parents, family, and community in a student's educational progress. These are the groups that will make students accountable and fulfill the promise to return as mentors and leaders in the community. Mentoring is also interfaced with Puente's teaching and counseling component. Sallie Brown explained:

> Success in fostering and sustaining community links with students and staff depend upon both the Puente counselor and instructor recruiting, training, and maintaining a mentoring component. This process requires constant communication with the community: asking mentors to come to the classroom to talk to a class, sponsoring social events for students to meet mentors and pair off one-on-one, monitoring mentor-student relationships, presenting at community-based organizations, and keeping a high profile of the mentoring component.

Mentors also engage in interpersonal validation, providing care, support, and encouragement both in and out of class. Mentors assist students in making career choices and take students to community activities such as ball games and barbeques. Mentors also talk with students about issues such as handling parents, leaving home, and feeling isolated in college.

Impact of Validation From Mentors

Many students speak highly of their Puente mentors as role models and encouragement agents:

> It never crossed my mind that I would have a mentor. My mentor . . . is an excellent example of a person that has pursued many goals in life. . . . I look up to her because . . . she has demonstrated that there's nothing stopping her to reach her goals.
>
> My mentor . . . has encouraged me to follow my dreams and not to stop until I get to where I want to be.

Implications

Community College Puente has much to offer in terms of what it takes to promote access and academic success for Latino students.

Implications for Access

Access is not merely getting students to graduate from high school and enroll in college. It is well substantiated that even when Latino students enroll in college, their retention rates and transfer rates from 2- to 4-year colleges and universities leave much to be desired (Garza, 1997; Rendón, Jalomo, & Nora, 2000). Getting into college does not guarantee that a student will stay enrolled long enough to earn a college degree. Educators wishing to promote access for Latinos and nontraditional students should know that once a student enrolls in college, active and sustained intervention is needed to ensure that students do not leave. To this end, Puente's validating team of instructors, counselors, and mentors plays a very important role in promoting college access. In a sense, these validating agents may also be viewed as an access team, because together these individuals take on the responsibility for moving students through the educational pathway, finding, as Cooper (2002 [this issue]) suggests, *el buen camino.*

This validating team provides students with (a) information and all education plan about what it takes to transfer and earn a degree from 4-year institutions—addressed through the counseling component; (b) a solid academic preparation, especially literacy skills—addressed through the writing component; and (c) knowledge about the pay-offs of getting a college education, including knowing what it takes to secure a high-income career, as well as how to put student talents to work in their communities to nurture the next generation of leaders—addressed through the mentoring component. In Community College Puente, promoting access is a comprehensive undertaking that includes Puente faculty, counselors, and mentors taking an active role in providing validation-rich in- and out-of-class experiences, demystifying the college participation and degree attainment process, and providing ample experiences for students to witness themselves and other Latinos as capable of academic success. Students are also assisted in developing a sense of professional identity and in understanding that being a college student is not just about taking courses, it is about developing a professional orientation to life and work. This comprehensive approach can ensure greater opportunities for Latinos to persist beyond the 1st year of college, make satisfactory progress toward transferring and earning bachelor's degrees, and assume leadership roles in their communities.

Implications for Validation and Involvement Theory

No one can deny the importance of getting students engaged in the social and academic life of a college. However, Rendón, Jalomo, and Nora (2000) indicate that practioners have tended to concentrate on having students (regardless of background and preparation for college) take the primary responsibility for getting involved in institutional life. Yet Rendón (1994) argues: "It appears that nontraditional students do not perceive involvement as *them* taking the initiative. They perceive it when someone takes an active role in assisting them" (p. 44). This is a critical point that is often missed or disregarded by student retention theorists as well as faculty and staff who erroneously assume that traditional and nontraditional students have similar ways of getting engaged and that all the institution has to do to promote involvement is to offer the opportunity to get involved. This study shows that Puente students benefit substantially from direct, sustained, and genuinely supportive (not patronizing) academic and interpersonal validation. Puente staff have internalized the notion that they must take an active role to reach out to students and to help these students to believe that they can be valuable members of the college community of knowers. Rather than "cooling out" (Clark, 1960) students by diverting them away from high aspirations, Puente faculty and staff encourage and guide students toward furthering their education and setting their goals higher than what they think they should be. English instructor and trainer Sallie Brown summarizes a Puente guiding principle: "Teachers and counselors need to believe in students more than students believe in themselves."

A good example of this is how Puente counselors work with students. Puente counselors do not wait for students to ask for help. They get to know the stories of their students, their family background, and their goals and aspirations. Similarly, the Puente English teacher takes the initiative to validate students academically, socially, and emotionally. She actively affirms the personal experience of the students, communicates that they are capable learners, and allows students to validate each other's work. The lesson learned here is that validation should be intentional, proactive, and systematic, not an afterthought or byproduct of whatever program is developed for these students. Puente staff verify that creating personal, caring relationships is central to building a commitment from students to stay in college. The effect of validation does not appear to coddle students or make them weak. Rather, student narratives indicate a transformative effect of validation. As one student indicates, "Puente has changed this student into a butterfly." Validation also offers real hope for working with students who are often viewed as "noncollege material." An analysis of Community College Puente provides ample evidence that academic and interpersonal validation can be a powerful mechanism that can turn even some of the most at-risk students into capable learners who can become involved in college-level learning. Consequently, validation theory (Rendón, 1994) should be considered side by side with involvement theory (Astin, 1985) when working with nontraditional student populations. Moreover, future research should explore the extent that validation is a prerequisite to student involvement in college.

Implications for Teaching and Learning Theory

In both high school and college, Puente has learned that low-income, first-generation students simply do not fare well in highly competitive, invalidating learning contexts. In essence, a model that distances teachers and learners, excludes the culture of the student, views students as deficient, is invalidating in nature, and designates teachers as the sole experts in the classroom will simply not work for students like those in the Puente program. The authors who address the components of High School Puente in this issue, notably Cazden (2002), González and Moll (2002), Pradl (2002), and Grubb, Lara, and Valdez (2002), point to many of the key elements that contribute to student learning and personal development. These include creating validating learning environments and family-like learning atmospheres, linking instruction to student lives, incorporating the students' culture into what they are learning, linking faculty and counselors in the classroom, and viewing students as competent learners who bring a foundation of knowledge to the classroom.

My analysis of Community College Puente verifies these high school findings and substantiates the perspectives taken by feminist teaching and learning theorists such as Belenky et al. (1986), Gilligan (1982) and hooks (1994). Moreover, although this study did not delve into holistic learning theory, it is apparent that Puente employed strategies that went beyond intellectual development to attend to social, emotional, and inner life skills. These included attention to personal development (i.e., giving students voice, honoring diverse perspectives, etc.) and social and emotional development (i.e., building student self-confidence, creating a social network of support, etc.).

Moreover, engaging students in contemplative practice such as journaling and personal reflection allowed students to engage in the larger questions of what it means to get a college education for them, their families, and their communities. Current research is addressing the development of the whole person in the classroom and includes the work of Palmer (1998), Burgis (2000) and Rendón (2000), among others. These holistic learning perspectives, which merit further study, offer complimentary insights to feminist learning theories and hold promise for the education of both traditional and nontraditional students.

Conclusion

High School and Community College Puente have much to offer the school and college reform movement in terms of what it takes to promote access, transform nontraditional students into powerful learners, promote learning communities, and create validating in- and out-of-class learning environments that foster academic success and personal growth. In its quiet yet powerful way, Puente continues to overturn years of educational neglect and to eradicate exclusionary practices and policies that have restricted access for working-class students. For all who

seek examples of equity and liberation in education, the Puente Project is an example of the mantra that many Puentistas refer to: "¡Si se Puede!" Yes, it can be done.

References

Almanac Issue 2001–2 [Special issue]. (2001). *Chronicle of Higher Education*, August 31.

Astin, A. (1985). *Achieving educational excellence: A critical assessment of priorities and practices in higher education*. San Francisco: Jossey-Bass.

Belenky, M., Clinchy, B., Goldberger. N., & Tarule, J. (1986). *Women's ways of knowing: The development of self, voice, and mind*. New York: Basic Books.

Bourdieu, P. (1986). The forms of capital. In J. G. Richardson (Ed.). *Handbook of theory and research in the sociology of education* (pp. 241–258). New York: Greenwood Press.

Burgis, L. (2000). *How learning communities foster intellectual, social and spiritual growth in students*. Unpublished doctoral dissertation, Arizona State University, Tempe.

California Tomorrow (in press). *A new look at the California community colleges: Keeping the promise alive for students of color and immigrants*. Oakland, CA: Author.

Cazden, C. B. (2002). A descriptive study of six High School Puente classrooms. *Educational Policy, 16*, 496–521.

Clark, B. R. (1960). *The open door college: A case study*. New York: McGraw Hill.

Cooper, C. R. (2002). Five bridges along students' pathways to college: A developmental blueprint of families, teachers, counselors, mentors, and peers in the Puente project. *Educational Policy, 16*, 607–622.

Freire, P. (2000). *Pedagogy of the oppressed*. (30th-anniversary ed.). New York: Continuum.

Gándara, P., Mejorado, M., Gutiérrez, D., &Molina, M. (1998). *Final report of the evaluation of High School Puente, 1994–1998*. Unpublished manuscript. University of California, Davis.

Garza, H. (1997). *An examination of institution-related factors and their effect on student transfer*. Unpublished doctoral dissertation, University of Michigan, Ann Arbor.

Gilligan, C. (1982). *In a different voice*. Cambridge. MA: Harvard University Press.

Goldberg, N. R. (1996). Looking, backward, looking forward. In N. Goldberger, J. Tarule, C. Blythe, & M. Belenky (Eds.), *Knowledge, difference and power* (pp. 1–21). New York: Basics Books.

González, N., & Moll, L. (2002). *Cruzando el Puente: Building bridges to funds of knowledge*. *Educational Policy, 16*, 623–641.

Grubb, W. N., Lara, C. M., & Valdez, S. (2002). Counselor, coordinator, monitor, mom: The roles of counselors in the Puente program. *Educational Policy, 16,* 547–571.

Harvey, W. (2001). *Minorities in higher education, 2000–2001.* Washington. DC: American Council on Education.

Held, D. (1980). *Introduction to critical theory.* Berkeley/Los Angeles: University of California Press.

Holloway, W., & Jefferson, T. (2000). *Doing qualtiative research differently.* Thousand Oaks, CA: Sage.

hooks, b. (1994). *Teaching to transgress.* New York: Routledge.

Hurtado, A. (1996). Strategic suspensions: Feminists of color theorize the production of knowledge. In N. Goldberger, J. Tarule, C. Blythe, & M. Belenky (Eds.), *Knowledge, difference and power* (pp. 372–388). New York: Basic Books.

Jalomo, R. E. (1995). *Latino students in transition: An analysis of the first-year experience in community college.* Unpublished doctoral dissertation, Arizona State University. Tempe.

Lather, P. (1991). *Getting smart: Feminist research and pedagogy with/in the postmodern.* New York: Routledge.

Lieblich, A., Tuval-Mashiach, R., & Zilber, T. (1998). *Narrative research* (Applied Social Research Methods Series, Vol. 47), Thousand Oaks, CA: Sage.

Guba, E. G., & Lincoln, Y. S. (1985). *Naturalistic inquiry.* Beverly Hills. CA: Sage.

Orfield, G., & Ashkinaze, C. (1991). *The closing door: Conservative policy and Black opportunity.* Chicago: University of Chicago Press.

Palmer, P. J. (1998). *The courage to teach: Exploring the inner landscape of a teacher's life.* San Francisco: Jossey-Bass.

Pradl, G. M. (2002). Linking instructional intervention and professional development: Using the ideas behind Puente high school English to inform educational policy. *Educational Policy, 16,* 522–546.

Puente Project (1997). *Puente community college program by the numbers.* Oakland, CA: Author.

Rendón, L. I. (1992). From the barrio to the academy: Revelations of a Mexican American scholarship girl. In S. Zwerling & H. London (Eds.), First-generation students: Confronting the cultural issues. *New Directions for Community Colleges, 80,* 55–64.

Rendón, L. I. (1994). Validating culturally diverse students: Toward a new model of learning and student development. *Innovative Higher Education, 19*(1), 33–50.

Rendón, L. I. (1996, November/December). Life on the border. *About Campus, 1,* 14–19.

Rendón, L. I. (2000). Academics of the heart. *About Campus, 5*(3), 3–5.

Rendón, L. I., Jalomo, R. E., & Nora. A. (2000). Theoretical considerations in the study of minority student retention. In J. Braxton (Ed.), *Rethinking the departure puzzle: New theory and research on college student retention* (pp. 127–156). Nashville: Vanderbilt University Press.

Spence, D. P. (1982). *Narrative truth and historical truth: Meaning and interpretation in psychoanalysis.* New York: Norton.

Spence, D. P. (1986). Narrative smoothing and clinical wisdom. In T. R. Sarbin (Ed.), *Narrative psychology: The storied nature of human conduct* (pp. 211–232). New York: Praeger.

Terenzini. P., Rendón. L. I., Upcraft, L., Millar, S., Allison, K., Gregg. P., et al. (1994). The transition to college: Diverse students, diverse stories. *Research in Higher Education, 35*(1), 57–73.

Varela, F., & Shear, J. (Eds.). (1999). *The view from within. First-person approaches to the study of consciousness.* Bowling Green, OH: Imprint Academic Philosophy Documentation Center.

CHAPTER 37

POSTCOLLEGE EARNINGS OF FORMER STUDENTS OF CALIFORNIA COMMUNITY COLLEGES: METHODS, ANALYSIS, AND IMPLICATIONS

JORGE R. SANCHEZ, FRANKIE SANTOS LAANAN, AND W. CHARLES WISELEY

In the wake of new federal and state mandates, community colleges are faced with demands to provide accountability reports on student outcomes. With the use of the Employment Development Department Unemployment Insurance (EDD-UI) wage record data, along with the California Community Colleges Chancellor's Office Management Information System administrative database, this study sought to investigate the extent to which completing an associate degree and vocational certificate impacts the postcollege earnings of students. Based on information from 700,564 students from California community colleges during the 1992–93 academic year, the findings suggest that students' gains from first year out of college to third year out will differ by age group. Among economically disadvantaged students, a strong positive relationship exists between educational attainment and postcollege gains. An important finding among vocational students is that as women complete more education, the earnings gap closes between men and women. Finally, this study raises several policy implications and presents suggestions for future research.

There are many reasons why individuals attend college. One popular argument found in the literature is the notion that obtaining an education beyond high school will yield not only higher-paying salaries but higher-level jobs (Elam, 1983; Grubb, 1996; Pascarella and Terenzini, 1991). Numerous studies suggest that individuals are motivated to attend college because of the economic returns, and that there is a strong positive relationship between formal education and earnings (Grubb, 1996; Pascarella and Terenzini, 1991). In other words, workers who have the most education have the highest average annual earnings and the lowest unemployment rates (*Occupational Outlook Quarterly*, 1992).

Although most of the research has focused on the comparison between high school graduates and four-year college graduates in relation to earnings (Adams and Jaffe, 1971; Haller, 1982; Henderson and Ottinger, 1985; Pace, 1979), very little is known about the economic value of an associate degree or vocational certificate from community colleges. In fact, most reports and studies show what the economic payoffs are if you obtain a baccalaureate degree on an individual's average earnings. Data provided by federal agencies such as the U.S. Bureau of the Census tend to aggregate educational attainment level from the spectrum of not a high school graduate, high school graduate, some college, baccalaureate, master, doctorate, to professional. The "some college" category usually includes associate degree completers and as a result remains ambiguous and vague. Attributing the ultimate contribution to community colleges in terms of the economic benefit to individuals' postcollege earnings is difficult and often impossible.

For community colleges, a popular outcome measure is assessing the economic impact of the community college on the local economy (Head, 1994; Katsinas, 1994; McIntyre, 1996; Stout, 1996; Weitzman, 1991; Winter and Fadale, 1991). Many studies in this area specifically examine the direct impact of the college in terms of the total expenditures in supplies and services, college budgetary expenditures, employee expenditures, employee training, and new business development in their respective communities. These studies focus on the college or system, its resources (e.g., fiscal and facilities), and its economic impact on the local community. Although these studies are important, the economic impact on students as measured by individual earnings is rarely discussed. In studying the economic benefit of a community college education on students' earnings, the unit of analysis moves from the college as an institution to the student as the unit. That is, investigating multiple outcomes by examining students provides the opportunity to attribute the impact of a community college education on an individual's economic worth in the world of work.

Purpose

This study examines data from California Community Colleges and the Employment Development Department's Unemployment Insurance (EDD-UI) wage record data. Specifically, a cohort of *leavers* and *completers*, which is comprised of over 700,000 students during the 1992–93 academic year, is examined. The purpose of this study is to address the questions: What is the economic value of obtaining a vocational certificate or an associate degree from California community colleges? How do students' postcollege earnings from last year in college, first year out of college, and third year out of college differ by educational attainment for all students and vocational students? What is the relationship between educational attainment and earnings for students under 25 and for students 25 and over? Are there differences by racial/ethnic background, economic status, gender, and age group among vocational students? Finally, this study raises policy implications and offers suggestions for future research in this area.

Review of Related Research

In researching the economic benefits of a college education, a generalization is made that formal education has a strong positive association with earnings (Blaug, 1970, 1972; Grubb, 1996; Psacharopoulos, 1973, 1985) even when factors such as age, gender, and occupational category are held constant. Much of the research examining the net effects of college on students' earnings has focused primarily on the influence of different levels of formal education. According to Jencks et al. (1979), when you control for work experience, measures of intelligence, and socioeconomic background, a high school diploma provides a 15% to 25% earnings advantage over an eighth-grade education. Although most of the comparisons tend to focus on differences between high school graduates and baccalaureate-degree recipients, little is known about the value of an associate degree or vocational certificate from community colleges in relation to earnings advantage over a high school diploma.

Theoretical and Conceptual Perspectives

Several theoretical and conceptual perspectives are synonymous in studying the economic benefits of postsecondary education. The human capital theory (Becker, 1964, 1975, 1992, 1993), which derives from the economics paradigm, is one of the most popular frameworks scholars have employed. Becker defined human capital as the economic effects of investment in education on employment and earnings. The concept of human capital is in all respects analogous to the economist's traditional concept of physical capital. In the lexicon of economists, physical capital includes all useful physical assets (e.g., currency, property, precious metals, jewelry). In education that would be analogous to acquiring energy, motivation, skills, and knowledge possessed by human beings, which can be harnessed over a period of time to the task of producing goods and services. In essence, the human capital theory measures the return on investment in oneself.

The aim of Becker's work was to convey to the public the importance and magnitude of investment in human capital. He postulated that the major factor influencing the level of human capital is the degree of investment in education and training. By referring to a simple model, he assessed the costs and benefits of such investment. He cautioned that care must be taken to distinguish between the social rate of return and the private rate of return.

Becker postulated that the skills and knowledge embodied in an individual could be defined as human capital. All individuals attain a certain stock of human capital and this level is primarily influenced by education and training. Further, that investment in human capital increases productivity. He analyzed this investment in human capital by comparing the costs and benefits of an educational investment. He was able to arrive at some conclusions as to the profitability of investing in education.

The human capital model has been criticized by some economists on a number of points. For example, the model assumes that all expenditures on education are investments. Blaug (1972) refutes this by saying that "a year's schooling for someone, invariably shares both consumption and investment aspects." By ignoring these consumption aspects, Becker's (1964) research underestimated the rate of return on educational investments.

Another conceptual framework used in the literature to explain the effects of formal education on earnings is the socialization hypothesis (Pascarella and Terenzini, 1991). Most of these studies have applied these perspectives to individuals who have completed a four-year college education. According to the hypothesis, those with baccalaureate degrees earn more than high school graduates because students who obtain a four-year education develop the cognitive skills and/or personal traits that make them more productive employees (Pascarella and Terenzini, 1991). For students who attend a two-year institution, the socialization perspective could also be applicable. That is, students who complete formal programs and complete the certificate or associate degree are likely to be socialized in the respective environments of their discipline. Therefore, students completing extensive programs in a vocational area will be required to develop the skills, knowledge, and abilities to be an employable candidate in the workforce.

Another hypothesis advanced in the literature is the notion of certification or screening. That is, employers can use college education as a way to screen the applicant pool or can require a bachelor's degree as a way of certifying prospective employees (Jencks et al., 1979). That is, by virtue of possessing the bachelor's degree, individuals are perceived as meeting a certification, which distinguishes them from nondegree recipients, and they are thus awarded with higher-paying jobs or career paths.

Net Effects of Community College Education

The between-college effects of two-year and four-year institutions on economic benefits have been examined. Specifically, there is a small body of literature that has addressed the net impact of initially attending a two-year rather than a four-year institution on earnings. The evidence suggests that when controlling for background traits and educational attainment, any direct earnings penalties for attending a two-year college are quite small early in the career but may increase slightly with longer work experience (Pascarella and Terenzini, 1991). However, students who begin at a two-year institution may experience a negative impact on earnings since they are less likely to complete a bachelor's degree than their four-year counterparts (Astin, 1985).

Recently, Grubb (1996) reported the latest findings using the Survey of Income and Program Participation (SIPP) in his book entitled *Working in the Middle*. According to Grubb, while individuals with baccalaureate degrees dominate managerial and professional jobs, those who earn an associate degree double their chances of becoming a professional or manager compared to the chances for someone with a high school diploma. Further, he maintains that the chances of obtaining a job, which requires technical skills, are highly increased with an associate degree or vocational certificate, and the likelihood of becoming a laborer or having an unskilled position is reduced. That is, having a subbaccalaureate credential as well as postsecondary coursework without credentials helps individuals move from the bottom levels of the labor force into mid-skilled positions.

State Efforts Using Unemployment Insurance Wage Records

Questions of the contributions that community colleges make to an individual's economic worth have been quantified in terms of income enhancement. States including California, Florida, North Carolina, Texas, and Washington and a few others have conducted statewide studies using the Unemployment Insurance (UI) wage record data to develop a methodology to measure students' postcollege earnings. Most of the studies have followed program completers or graduates into the workplace to estimate average annual earnings or placement. Collaborative efforts with the Department of Labor unemployment records offices have yielded information from the quarterly wage/earnings files for those students identified as program completers or graduates. Since matching with the student's social security number is required in order to access not only earnings but also educational data, the concern surrounding confidentiality and privacy issues has been in the forefront of researchers, policymakers, and state agencies.

Florida is considered to be the pioneer in developing a follow-up strategy using the UI Wage Record data. As a result of a legislative directive and a joint agreement between the State Department of Education and the Department of Labor and Employment, the Florida Education and Training Placement Information Program (FETPIP) was developed. In a recent study (Pfeiffer, 1990), 200,000 vocational education graduates during the 1988–89 academic year were tracked. Of these students, 64% of program completers were found employed in Florida businesses, an additional 20% continued their education within the state's higher education system, and 2% were federal employees or in the military.

In the state of Washington, over 12,269 postsecondary vocational education program completers during the 1990–91 academic year were tracked (Seppanen, 1993, 1994). The Washington State Board for Community and Technical Colleges (WSBCTC) compiles data on educational and job-related outcomes for students leaving vocational preparation programs. Using an automated data matching procedure, this method examines state unemployment insurance and benefit records, public postsecondary enrollments, U.S. Armed Forces enlistments, and state community college enrollments. Specifically, data are compiled on employment status, estimated annual wages, hours worked per week, the relation of employment to training, postsecondary or military status, and a host of others. Based on a nine-month analysis for the 12,269 graduates of vocational programs, the study revealed the overall job placement rate of 85%, with 27% of the graduates going into health-related fields, 23% going into trades, 13% entering the service industry, and 12% in administrative support. To

account for out-of-state employment of Washington program completers, efforts were made to collaborate with neighboring states such as Alaska, California, Idaho, and Oregon.

During the spring of 1990, the Indiana Commission on Vocational and Technical Education completed a pilot study of 1,497 student program completers from the 1988–89 school year. Other than social security identification, no student demographic information was analyzed. Overall, 71% of the completers were found in either the state's unemployment insurance, the Department of Defense military personnel, or the Indiana Commission for Higher Education databases. Specifically, 66% were found in state wage records, 16% were in higher education, and 3% were in the military (Piper, 1990).

In Illinois (Merano, 1990), a pilot study was conducted of the 1988–89 cohort of students who completed an occupational program. Of the 15,485 occupational education program completers, 70% matched in the subsequent quarter following their education/training. Of these students, 84% were still employed for one year. Average quarterly earnings increased from $4,207 to $4,621 for the first two quarters following program completion; no student demographic data were analyzed.

In 1993, the adoption of a new legislation and goals statement for the North Carolina Community College System reemphasized the efforts by community colleges on workforce preparedness (Vanderheyden, 1994). In response to this policy, efforts were put forth to account for two outcome measures of successful workforce training: employment rates and median salary of program completers. In a study examining 15,817 who completed a program during 1990–91, the findings revealed that 92% of students were employed during the third quarter of 1991 and their median earnings were $3,830. One year later, 97% of former students were employed and had an increase in their median earnings of $4,279.

More recently, Yang and Brown (1998) investigated the employment status and earnings of North Carolina Community College System curriculum students. These students specifically were enrolled in credit programs that either grant associate degrees, certificates, or diplomas (e.g., college transfer, general education, technical and vocational programs). Specifically, the study compared students' employment status and mean quarterly and annual earnings among completers who did not reenroll in any of the colleges in the following year (i.e., exit completers), completers who did reenroll in the following year (i.e., comeback completers), noncompleters who did not reenroll in the following year (i.e., exit noncompleters), and noncompleters who did reenroll in the following year (i.e., comeback noncompleters). The merging of three separate databases was conducted to answer the research questions: the Common Follow-Up System (CFS), the community college system curriculum registration file, and the community college system Curriculum Student Progress Information System (CSPIS). Based on this study, the authors highlighted several findings. First, exit noncompleters had the highest annual earnings. However, the mean quarterly earnings of exit completers increased at a faster rate from quarter 1 to quarter 4 than the other groups. Second, older students had higher annual earnings than younger students for all groups. Third, completers who had earned an AAS degree, certificate, or diploma had higher annual earnings than those who had earned an associate degree. Finally, the mean annual and quarterly earnings for exit noncompleters were not necessarily increased by simply completing more credit hours.

In Texas, Froeschle (1991) examined 8,162 completers and nonreturning postsecondary vocational-technical education students from four institutions. Approximately 85% of the former students were found in the UI wage records file during the five quarters subsequent to the graduation. In Colorado, Smith (1989) reviewed 3,797 associate-degree and certificate completers in 1985–86. The longitudinal student tracking system contained data from three sources: (1) Colorado Commission of Higher Education, (2) Colorado Department of Labor and Employment, and (3) Colorado Community College and Occupational Education System. Of the award and program completers, 20% were enrolled in higher education, 58% were in the UI wage records file one year after graduation, and 12% of those found in the UI wage records were also enrolled in higher education.

Alaska, Florida, Indiana, and Washington have accessed additional employment-related databases (i.e., federal personnel records, postal service employment, and military/defense records) in order to account for a greater proportion of their students. Only Alaska and Washington have arranged to retrieve employment earnings from neighboring states. Conversely, California and Texas have examined students who did not complete their program and left training, compared with students who completed their program. Generally, the results for California and Texas reveal that students who do not complete a certificate or degree have substantially lower quarterly earnings compared with program completers. This information suggests that in order to maximize quarterly earnings, students would be best served by completing their program. Although a few of the studies have addressed the need to account for those students who entered the ranks of the self-employed, efforts to examine earnings of those students have not been undertaken by these states. Estimates of how much of the workforce is self-employed vary greatly from as little as 3% to 5% (Stevens et al., 1992) to a high of 10% to 15% and rising (U.S. Department of Commerce, 1996).

California's Efforts Using UI Wage Record Data

Jack Friedlander (1993a, 1993b, 1996) has been credited with being the pioneer in examining the postcollege employment rates and wages of California community college students. A pilot study was conducted in 1992–93 in coordination with the California Community Colleges Chancellor's Office (CCCCO), California Economic Development Department (EDD), Santa Barbara City College, and Grossmont College. This feasibility study was used to develop the Post-Education Employment Tracking System (PEETS) to track the postcollege employment rates and earnings of community college program completers and leavers over an extended period of time. The methodology used social security numbers to match EDD quarterly wage data with student records maintained by the State Chancellor's Office. The study confirmed that PEETS can be used to answer questions regarding employment patterns of former students, employment rates by major and type of degree, comparative earnings of associate-degree graduates and those who did not complete the degree, and earnings and employment rates in different student population groups (Friedlander, 1993a). Friedlander concluded that PEETS is an inexpensive method for tracking the success of former students, and can be used to meet accreditation requirements and respond to consumer inquiries.

Another study by Friedlander (1993b) examined students who attended Santa Barbara City College (SBCC) from 1986–87 to 1989–90 to determine the earnings made by students while they were enrolled and the first and third years after leaving SBCC. Using the same methodology of matching students' social security numbers with income data collected from employers by the California EDD, the study compared employment status and earnings by occupational field, and outcomes for associate-degree completers and those earning 12 or more credits at SBCC. In general, Friedlander found that students who completed associate degrees experienced an increase in annual wages of 41% compared with students completing only 12 units or more (28%). Among students who completed an associate degree, postcollege earnings were highest among nursing graduates.

To refine the use of PEETS, Friedlander (1996) conducted a follow-up study that included a sample of 173,523 students from 18 California community colleges who either completed a certificate or degree or stopped attending in 1991 or 1992. The study found that UI records were available for the majority of the sample and that wages of students who received a certificate or degree from an occupational program were higher than both those who left occupational programs without a degree or certificate and those who completed nonoccupational programs. Moreover, occupational students with a degree or certificate made a 47% gain in wages from the last year in college to the third year out of college.

Data Sources and Methodology

There are three main sources that were used to derive a data set to respond to questions about the postcollege earnings of students. The process involves electronically matching the social security number in the UI wage record data files maintained by EDD and the California State University (CSU) Chancellor's Office with the student record files stored in the Chancellor's Office MIS. Specifically, the three sources are: (1) the Unemployment Insurance (UI) wage record data collected by the California Employment Development Department (EDD); (2) the student records maintained by the CSU Chancellor's Office; and (3) the demographic and educational data for all California community college students maintained by the Chancellor's Office Management Information System (MIS).

The California EDD collects and maintains UI wage records, which are used to determine employment and earnings of individuals in the labor market. Employers are required to comply with the state's UI compensation law by submitting UI quarterly reports of earnings for their employees. For each employee covered, an employer is required to report the employee's social security number and the total amount of earnings received during the quarter. Additional information about the employer is also reported, such as the unique employer identification number, the county in which the business is located, and the industry affiliation of the business.

The Chancellor's Office MIS database contains demographic and educational data of all students who attended California community colleges since fall 1990. As the state's official repository of community college student data, the MIS contains demographic data such as age, gender, ethnicity, financial aid status, English-language proficiency, and disability status. Furthermore, educational data maintained include precollegiate basic skills courses, occupational and nonoccupational courses completed, grades, and degrees and certificates awarded.

For this analysis, the target population includes students who were either *completers* or *leavers* during the 1992–93 academic year. A *completer* is defined as a student who received a certificate or degree, whereas a *leaver* is defined as a student who did not receive a certificate or degree but may have completed some units. The data analyses conducted for this study are based on information from 700,564 students enrolled in 103 of the 106 California community colleges. The reporting domain of the cohort included students with a social security number, students who met the Full-Term Reporting Criteria (FTR) and were enrolled in a least one-half unit or eight hours of positive attendance during the academic year. Excluded from the reporting domain were students enrolled in K-12 during the cohort year, students enrolled in any California state university during the two years following the cohort year, and students enrolled in one year following the end of the cohort year at any college in the California community colleges system. Individuals who were employed by the military or federal government, self-employed, unemployed, or not in the workforce were also not part of the data set.

Analytic Approach

In order to make comparisons of earnings from the last year in college to the third year out of college and the first year out to the third year out, the California Consumer Price Index for Urban (CPI-U) Consumers was used to adjust earnings for changes in inflation. Thus, all earnings were adjusted to 1996 dollars. For this study, only students who worked all four quarters were examined. These students were found in the labor market beginning July 1 during their last year in college and third year out of college. Further, the median annual earnings were used instead of the mean earnings because this is how the data were made available to colleges from the Chancellor's Office. The median annual earnings represent the middle value in the distribution of the annual income. The annual income is derived by summing earnings for those working all four quarters. The purpose of using the median annual earnings is to have a more stable statistic. Compared to the mean, the median is more robust and less likely to be influenced by extreme outliers.

Results

Figure 1 illustrates the different typology of students from California community colleges in 1992–93 by enrollment concentration. The data produced by the Chancellor's Office have been disaggregated into five concentrations: (1) all stu-dents (no vocational courses); (2) vocationally exposed; (3) skills upgrade; (4) vocational students; and (5) vocational students' major. Each typology is defined by the number of vocational courses and the Student Accountability Model (SAM) codes found in the *Chancellor's Office Data Element Dictionary.* The SAM coding scheme (i.e., A, B, C, D, and E)[1] is used to indicate the degree to which a course is occupational and to assist in identifying course sequence in occupational pro-grams. It is important to note that the "vocational major" category is not based on student decla-ration but rather based on degrees and certifi-cates received or course-taking patterns as assessed by the MIS office.

For this study, the focus of the analysis is on all students and vocational majors. Students identified as vocational majors have taken 12 or more units in the same four-digit Taxonomy of Program (TOP) code or program area (e.g., accounting, nursing, engineering technology).

All Students

Table 1 shows the median annual earnings of all students ($N = 700,564$) from California commu-nity colleges in the 1992–93 academic year by educational attainment. The table presents descriptive information such as educational attainment level, total students, median annual earnings of students' first year out and third year out of college, and percent change. The educa-tional attainment spectrum ranges from .01 to

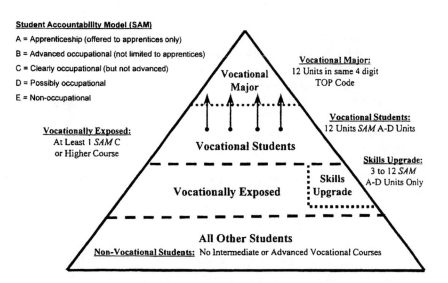

FIG. 1. Typology of California community college students by enrollment concentration (1992–93 cohort).

TABLE 1
Percent Change in Median Annual Earnings of *All Students* from California Community Colleges in the 1992–1993 Academic Year by Educational Attainment Level (1996 Dollars)

Education Attainment Level	Total Students	First Year Out of College"	Third Year Out of College	Percent Change (%)
		Median Annual Earnings Worked Four Quarters		
All Students	700,564*	$23,539	$25,341	7.7
.01–11.99 Units	265,266	$26,255	$27,847	6.1
12–23.99 Units	80,225	$22,722	$24,970	9.9
24 + Units	124,060	$23,320	$25,584	9.7
Certificate	6,674	$25,033	$28,403	13.5
A.A. or A.S. Degree	13,745	$23,824	$26,790	12.5

*Excluded from this table is the 0 units or noncredit category (*n* = 210,594).

"In order to make comparisons of earnings from First Year Out of College to Third Year Out of College, the California Consumer Price Index for Urban Consumers was used to adjust earnings for changes in inflation. For the purpose of this study, all earnings were adjusted to 1996.

Source: California Community Colleges Chancellor's Office Management Information System.

11.99 units to associate-degree completers. The results show that gains are evident across all levels; however, the largest gains are among certificate and associate-degree completers. Although positive gains are evident among .01–11.99 to 24+ unit completers, they are not substantial. Certificate completers experienced a 14% gain from first year out to third year out; associate-degree completers experienced a 13% gain, respectively. For the other educational attainment levels, the percent gain from first to third year out ranged from 6% to 10%.

In examining the data by age (see Table 2), students under 25 (*n* = 222,818) experienced substantial gains across educational attainment levels from their first year out to third year out of college. Students who completed 24 or more units experienced a 29% gain from first year out to third year out of college, a 29% gain among certificate holders, and a 33% gain among associate-degree recipients. Students who completed the certificate had higher median annual earnings during their first year out and third year out of college compared with the others. For students under 25, their third-year median earnings ranged from $18,000 to $22,000. Figure 2 illustrates the data for students under 25 for the three time periods (i.e., last year in college, first year out of college, and third year out of college).

Table 3 presents the findings for students 25 and over (*n* = 473,171). The results and patterns are very different compared with younger students. As a group, younger students had a 26% gain compared to 5% for older students from first

year to third year out of college. For this group, the percent gains are very small across the educational attainment levels. However, if students completed a certificate (+ 9%) or associate degree (+ 9%), they were more likely to experience slightly higher gains three years out. Older students had higher earnings for both time periods (first year out of college and third year out of college). In other words, students 25 and over were already making more money and were likely to be in the workforce much longer compared with their counterparts. Compared with younger students, students 25 and over had median third-year earnings that ranged from $30,000 to $33,000, which is substantially higher than their counterparts. Figure 3 illustrates the data for students 25 and over for the three time periods (i.e., last year in college, first year out of college, and third year out of college).

Vocational Students' Major

For students who comprised the vocational students major category (see Table 4), they were identified to have had a "major" because they completed at least 12 units in the same program area or four-digit TOP code. Overall, the 37,434 vocational majors experienced a 16% gain from first year out to third year out in terms of postcollege earnings. An interesting pattern is evident among vocational majors. In terms of first-year-out to third-year-out earnings, students who completed 24 or more units experienced a 17% gain, while certificate holders had slightly

TABLE 2

Percent Change in Median Annual Earnings of *All Students Under 25* from California Community Colleges in the 1992–1993 Academic Year by Educational Attainment Level (1996 Dollars)

| Education Attainment Level | Total Students | Median Annual Earnings Worked Four Quarters | | Percent Change (%) |
		First Year Out of College*	Third Year Out of College	
All Students	222,818*	$14,303	$18,075	26.4
.01–11.99 Units	77,670	$14,659	$18,468	26.0
12–23.99 Units	27,711	$14,408	$18,198	26.3
24 + Units	40,738	$14,810	$19,157	29.4
Certificate	1,487	$17,531	$22,539	28.6
A.A. or A.S. Degree	5,428	$15,101	$20,007	32.5

*Excluded from this table is the 0 units or noncredit category (n = 69,784).

*In order to make comparisons of earnings from First Year Out of College to Third Year Out of College, the California Consumer Price Index for Urban Consumers was used to adjust earnings for changes in inflation. For the purpose of this study, all earnings were adjusted to 1996.

Source: California Community Colleges Chancellor's Office Management Information System.

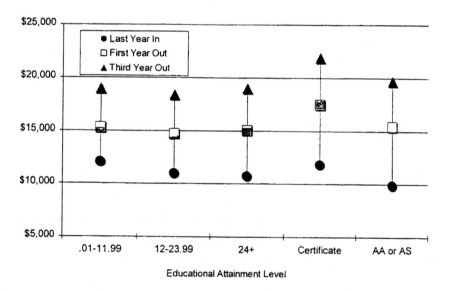

FIG. 2. Median earnings of students under 25 from California community colleges by educational attainment (n = 222,818).

lower gains (+ 14%) and 15% for associate-degree completers. Three years out, students with certificates or associate degrees had higher earnings that ranged between $28,000 and $30,000 compared with the other groups.

About 13% of vocational majors were identified as economically disadvantaged students. To be identified as economically disadvantaged (see Figure 4), a student had to meet one of the following criteria: (1) awarded a Board of Governor's grant; (2) awarded a Pell grant; (3) identified as a GAIN participant; or (4) identified as a participant in the Job Training Partnership Program. According to Figure 4, there is a positive relationship between earnings and level of education. This trend is evident for students' first year out and third year out of college earnings. Overall, economically disadvantaged students

TABLE 3
Percent Change in Median Annual Earnings of *All Students 25 and Over* from California Community Colleges in the 1992–1993 Academic Year by Educational Attainment Level (1996 Dollars)

Education Attainment Level	Total Students	Median Annual Earnings Worked Four Quarters		Percent Change (%)
		First Year Out of College[a]	Third Year Out of College	
All Students	473,171*	$29,122	$30,505	4.7
.01–11.99 Units	186,816	$31,728	$33,227	4.7
12–23.99 Units	52,389	$28,999	$30,483	5.1
24 + Units	83,157	$28,361	$30,118	6.2
Certificate	5,163	$28,087	$30,684	9.2
A.A. or A.S. Degree	8,299	$29,709	$32,408	9.1

*Excluded from this table is the 0 units or noncredit category ($n = 137,297$).

[a]In order to make comparisons of earnings from First Year Out of College to Third Year Out of College, the California Consumer Price Index for Urban Consumers was used to adjust earnings for changes in inflation. For the purpose of this study, all earnings were adjusted to 1996.

Source: California Community Colleges Chancellor's Office Management Information System.

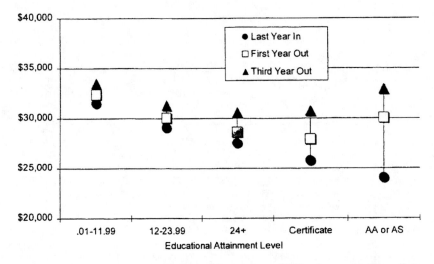

FIG. 3. Median earnings of students 25 and over from California community colleges by educational attainment ($n = 473,171$).

experienced a 29% gain from first year to third year out. As students complete more education, they experience higher earnings. For students' gains from last year to third year, certificate completers experienced a 147% gain, while associate-degree completers experienced a 145% gain, respectively. In examining their first year out to third year out, certificate holders had a 33% gain and 25% gain for A.A. or A.S. degree completers.

Figure 5 depicts the median annual earnings of vocational students who earned an associate degree by racial/ethnic background. All students experienced positive gains in their postcollege

earnings. In terms of students' first-year-out to third-year-out gains, African-Americans ($n = 424$) experienced + 13%, Hispanic/Latinos ($n = 757$) + 10%, and Asian/Pacific Islanders ($n = 688$) + 15%. White ($n = 4,715$) students had a 15% gain in their postcollege earnings from first to third year out. In terms of actual earnings, students in the African-American (or black) category had the highest third-year earnings ($32,700) followed by white students ($31,321).

Figure 6 depicts the median annual earnings of vocational students who earned a certificate by racial/ethnic background. Across all groups, students experienced positive gains in their post-

TABLE 4

Percent Change in Median Annual Earnings of *Vocational Students* from California Community Colleges in the 1992–1993 Academic Year by Educational Attainment Level (1996 Dollars)

| Education Attainment Level | Total Students | Median Annual Earnings Worked Four Quarters | | Percent Change (%) |
		First Year Out of College°	Third Year Out of College	
All Students	37,434*	$23,835	$27,533	15.5
.01–11.99 Units	631	$20,492	$25,188	22.9
12–23.99 Units	7,451	$22,378	$25,937	15.9
24 + Units	14,169	$20,785	$24,284	16.8
Certificate	6,368	$24,563	$28,069	14.3
A.A. or A.S. Degree	7,225	$26,550	$30,420	14.6

*Excluded from this table is the 0 units or noncredit category (n = 1,590).

°In order to make comparisons of earnings from First Year Out of College to Third Year Out of College, the California Consumer Price Index for Urban Consumers was used to adjust earnings for changes in inflation. For the purpose of this study, all earnings were adjusted to 1996.

Source: California Community Colleges Chancellor's Office Management Information System.

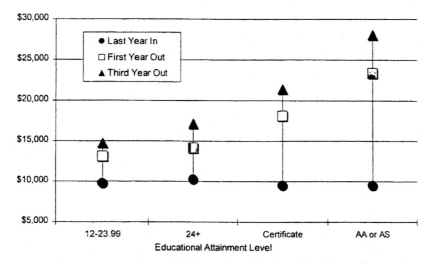

FIG. 4. Median earnings of economically disadvantaged students (1992–93 cohort) from California community colleges by educational attainment (n = 4,925).

college earnings. In terms of students' first-year-out to third-year-out gains, African-Americans (n = 385) experienced - 3%, Hispanic/Latinos (n = 862) + 14%, and Asian/Pacific Islanders (n = 601) + 24%. White (n = 3,871) students had a 14% gain in their postcollege earnings from first year out to third year out. In terms of actual earnings, white students had the highest third-year median earnings ($28,613) followed by Asian/Pacific Islanders ($29,906).

For the 1992–93 cohort, female vocational students (major) included 19,128 students, compared to 18,257 of men. In examining within the group, female students (see Table 5) experienced

substantial gains as they completed more education. Further, female students were more likely to have higher actual median annual earnings if they completed the certificate or associate degree. This is evident when examining female students' last year in college to third year out. A 41% gain among certificates and 87% among A.A. or A.S. degree completers was realized. The third-year median earnings among female vocational students ranged from $20,000 to $30,000. Conversely, male vocational students (see Table 6) had slightly higher gains from first year out to third year out compared to women. Certificate holders had a 14% gain while the A.A. or

TABLE 5

Percent Change in Median Annual Earnings of *Female Vocational Students* from California Community Colleges in the 1992–1993 Academic Year by Educational Attainment Level (1996 Dollars)

Education Attainment Level	Total Students	Median Annual Earnings Worked Four Quarters		Percent Change (%)
		First Year Out of College*	Third Year Out of College	
All Female	19,128*	$21,473	$24,086	12.2
.01–11.99 Units	318	$16,554	$21,716	31.2
12–23.99 Units	3,261	$18,415	$20,004	8.6
24 + Units	6,894	$18,569	$21,015	13.2
Certificate	3,465	$22,323	$25,288	13.3
A.A. or A.S. Degree	4,685	$26,063	$29,694	13.9

*Excluded from this table is the 0 units or noncredit category (*n* = 505).

ⁱIn order to make comparisons of earnings from First Year Out of College to Third Year Out of College, the California Consumer Price Index for Urban Consumers was used to adjust earnings for changes in inflation. For the purpose of this study, all earnings were adjusted to 1996.

Source: California Community Colleges Chancellor's Office Management Information System.

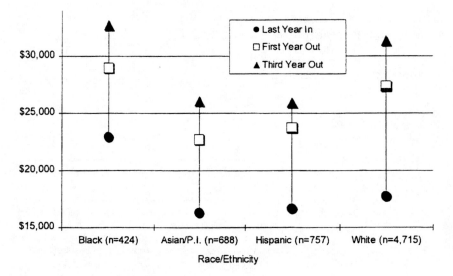

FIG. 5. Median earnings of vocational students from California community colleges with associate degree by racial/ethnic background (*n* = 6,584).

A.S. degree recipients among men experienced a 15% gain.

Figure 7 presents the third-year-out median earnings for male and female vocational students (major). These are students who either completed a vocational program or earned 12 or more units in the same program area and were coded as vocational by the Chancellor's Office MIS. Figure 3 shows the closing of the earnings gap between men and women. The results reveal that as women complete more education, the gap closes. That is, completing the certificate or associate degree positively impacts the earnings among women and thus closes the gap. Although men tend to have higher third-year earnings across all levels, women catch up and close the gap when they complete a formalized program, namely the certificate or associate degree.

The aggregate data were also made available for vocational students (major) by age group. The

TABLE 6

Percent Change in Median Annual Earnings of *Male Vocational Students* from California Community Colleges in the 1992–1993 Academic Year by Educational Attainment Level (1996 Dollars)

| Education Attainment Level | Total Students | Median Annual Earnings Worked Four Quarters | | Percent Change (%) |
		First Year Out of College*	Third Year Out of College	
All Male	18,257	$26,792	$31,148	16.3
.01–11.99 Units	309	$23,937	$28,439	18.8
12–23.99 Units	4,182	$25,985	$30,127	15.9
24 + Units	7,261	$23,257	$27,579	18.6
Certificate	2,884	$27,761	$31,506	13.5
A.A. or A.S. Degree	2,538	$28,203	$32,509	15.3

*Excluded from this table is the 0 units or noncredit category ($n = 1,083$).

ʼIn order to make comparisons of earnings from First Year Out of College to Third Year Out of College, the California Consumer Price Index for Urban Consumers was used to adjust earnings for changes in inflation. For the purpose of this study, all earnings were adjusted to 1996.

Source: California Community Colleges Chancellor's Office Management Information System.

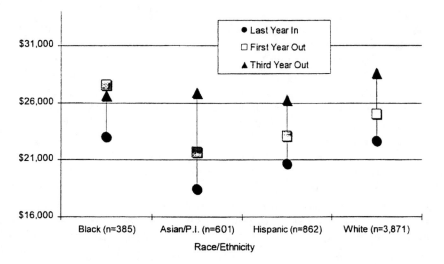

FIG. 6. Median earnings of vocational students from California community colleges with certificate by racial/ethnic background ($n = 5,806$).

three age-group categories were 18 to 25 years old, 25+ to 35, and 35 and over. In analyzing the data by age group (who are these students), among associate-degree completers students in the 18- to 24-year-old category had the highest percent gain (+ 27%) from first year out of college to third year, followed by students 25 to 34 years old (+ 10%), and 35 years old and over (+ 9%). Although 18- to 24-year-olds experienced the highest change, they had substantially lower third-year earnings ($23,000 versus $33,000). There is over a $10,000 gap between younger students (under 25) and nontraditional students (over 25).

Limitations

Although there are advantages in utilizing the EDD-UI and MIS student data files, there are some methodological concerns with respect to studying California community college students. The accuracy of the data is dependent on the reliability and uniformity of data submitted to the Chancellor's Office by individual colleges and districts for the 1992–93 academic year. Although UI wage records are tagged with students' educational data, the data set is strictly an administrative data set, not a research data set.

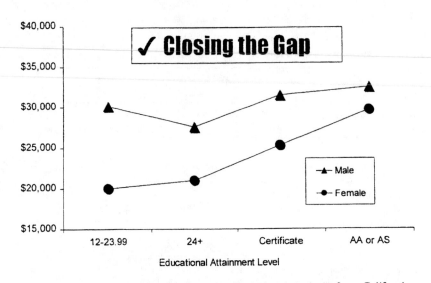

FIG. 7. (third year out). Median earnings of vocational students from California community colleges by sex and educational attainment.

The data only report students who had UI wage record matches with their MIS student files and do not control for students' educational experience and their place of employment in the workforce. As a result, the link between type of program completed at the community college and the extent to which the student is employed in the field studied is currently not possible. Although collaborative efforts have been formalized between CCC and CSU, which have resulted in identifying and removing students who transferred to one of the 23 campuses, students who transferred to the University of California or private four-year institutions in California are currently included in these reports. Students who transferred to out-of-state institutions are also included. As a result, the data still include a proportion of students who transferred to a four-year institution.

The percent matched is strictly a match rate for social security numbers found in the UI wage data files and thus is not an employment rate. Students not found in the wage records are not accounted for. Individuals who were employed by the military or federal government, self-employed, unemployed, or not in the workforce were not part of the data set. In California, there are several colleges that are located near military installations. Students who previously attended these institutions and who were later employed by the military are excluded in the UI wage data. As a result, the data do not accurately reflect the postcollege earnings of these students because

a successful match does not occur. Furthermore, it is estimated that individuals who are self-employed range from as little as 3% to 5% (Stevens et al., 1992) to a high of 10% to 15% (U.S. Department of Commerce, 1996).

The analysis for this study was restricted to students who worked all four quarters in the three time periods (i.e., last year in college, first year out of college, and third year out of college). These students were more likely to be employed in the labor force for a full year. The rationale for employing this methodology (i.e., worked four quarters) extends from the limitation that employers are not required to report the number of hours worked per quarter to EDD. As a result, it is impossible to calculate hourly wages and part-time or full-time status.

Finally, the data are descriptive in nature. That is, the data can only be used to answer the "what" and "how" questions relating to students' earnings during the last year and third year out of college. The aggregate data currently available to districts and individual colleges do not allow the researcher to conduct statistical analysis beyond descriptive statistics. In order to conduct parametric statistics (i.e., statistical test or significance, multivariate analyses, etc.), unitary records must be obtained.

Discussion and Conclusion

Similar to Friedlander's (1993a, 1996) earlier studies, analysis of the 1992–93 cohort confirms that the matching process between EDD and the Chancellor's Office MIS student data is a cost-effective mechanism in beginning to understand former California community college students' progress in the workforce. Of the 700,564 students in the study, UI wage record data were available for 64% of students in their last year in college; of those, 61% matched first year out of college, and over 56% of former students were in the UI wage data three years out of college. The decline in match rates is consistent with declines in match rates from other studies utilizing the UI files, usually around 3% per year.

The results in this study support the notion that there is a positive relationship between formal education and earnings. Thus, as students complete more education, they increase the likelihood of experiencing greater gains in their postcollege earnings. However, completing a vocational certificate or associate degree greatly increases students' postcollege earnings compared with taking a handful of units.

For all students, the greatest gains were among certificate completers (+ 14%), followed by A.A. or A.S. degree holders (+ 13%). Completing a formalized educational program such as the certificate or associate degree positively impacts not only an individual's future earnings but also the marketability of professional skills and technical abilities. Given the competitive economy and job market, employers are now becoming very demanding in terms of the type and quality of workers most suited for highly technical positions.

When examining the data by age (under 25 or 25 and over), younger students who completed a certificate experienced a 29% gain compared with students over 25 (9%). This finding suggests that for younger students, pursuing higher education impacts their postcollege earnings. Because younger students would not have any work experience under their belt, possessing educational credentials to some extent serves as a proxy for work experience. Although the data in this study show that younger students make substantially lower earnings compared with older students, there are substantial positive gains from last year in college, first year out of college, and third year out when more education is attained. Although the finding that older students (25 and over) have smaller gains is not surprising, these students were already making substantially higher wages in the workforce. In other words, given their age and time

spent in the work arena, completing a formalized education program, such as the certificate or associate degree, has positive affects on their postcollege earnings. However, when older students return to the community college to take a handful of units, their gains are small. Figure 3 illustrates that students in the .01–11.99 category have slightly higher earnings across all three time periods. A possible explanation for their higher wages is that these students are most likely individuals who are returning to the two-year college for skills upgrade or retraining. Also, they may be returning to the college for a career change and are thus pursuing other technical careers that require completion of a handful of courses.

When the data were analyzed by age group among vocational students, younger students (18 to 24) were more likely to have higher percent gains from first year out of college to third year out (+30%), compared with older students. Students between 25 and 34 years old had a 14% gain compared with 9% for students 35 and older three years out. This finding suggests that younger students will more likely experience the long-term economic benefit for completing the associate degree upon making the transition from education to work. In other words, having credentials at the start of a new job will give the young professional a jump-start in terms of salary and position level compared with non-subbaccalaureate-degree recipients.

For students who were identified as vocational students (i.e., completed 12 units or more in the same program area), positive gains were evident across educational attainment levels. The gains from first year out to third year out range from 14% to 17%. Students who completed a certificate had a 14% gain while associate-degree completers had a 15% gain. The results show that although students who completed 24+ or 12–23.99 units had slightly higher gains three years out, the actual earnings among completers (associate and certificate) in their first year out of college and third year out of college were substantially higher. An important finding is that during their last year in college, certificate and associate-degree completers had lower earnings compared with leavers. Given this finding, the results suggest that vocational students identified as completers increased their earnings the first year out and three years out. This finding suggests that students who complete a vocational program area and earn a certificate have an edge in the workforce. By possessing the credentials that provide a basis for employers to evaluate prospective employees, these individuals will likely start at higher levels in their positions and in salary schedules. This finding supports Grubb's (1996) assertion that the chance of obtaining a job that requires technical skills is highly increased with an associate degree or vocational certificate and the likelihood of becoming a laborer or having an unskilled position is reduced.

With the recent legislation both at the federal and state levels, the initiative to assist individuals to move from welfare to work has become a major policy issue in California. Education has always been used as a way to explain the relationship between the level of education attained and earnings. The results from this study provide empirical evidence that for students who are economically disadvantaged, completing more education is positively related to higher percent gains and actual earnings. Specifically, completing the associate degree or certificate will impact their long-term sustainable economic worth. Thus, as economically disadvantaged students complete more education, they will not only have substantial gains in their postcollege earnings but will also have higher earnings. Moreover, when these students complete a certificate they experience a 33% gain and 25% among A.A. and A.S. degree completers, respectively. This finding is important for policymakers, higher education leaders, and faculty in terms of not only acknowledging the contribution of a community college education but also as a tool to inform students about the value of attending and completing a program of study at a community college in California.

When examining the effects of a community college education by gender, interesting patterns arise. Female vocational students who completed the certificate ($25,288) or associate degree ($29,694) had higher third year out of college earnings compared with students completing some units ($20,000 to $21,000). Conversely, male vocational students who completed the certificate ($31,506) or associate degree ($32,509) experienced substantial gains from first year to third year postcollege earnings. The findings show that men were more likely to have higher earnings across the three time periods. Although not surprising, this is in support of what is found in the literature about the disparity between the earnings of men and women in the workforce. However, a significant finding is that the earnings gap is narrowed when women complete the certificate or associate degree. In other words, completing some units will not have a substantial effect on their marketability in the labor market. However, when they complete the certificate or A.A. or A.S. degree, not only will they possess a credential or meet the certification hypothesis, but they will also experience higher earnings. This finding suggests that women are most likely going to benefit in terms of future earnings if they are encouraged to complete formalized programs and obtain the academic awards.

Policy Implications and Future Research

Because community colleges in California are now required to utilize the EDD-UI wage data for final performance reports and program evaluation, there is a need to establish standard procedures to assess, understand, analyze, and interpret the data. Specifically, the data can be analyzed to assess colleges' program-level enrollment, completion, and follow-up employment of students. Given the availability of the data, colleges and districts can use the data for local programming, evaluation, and student advising. Individuals responsible for the data management, analysis, interpretation, and reporting must be acutely aware of specific "contextual information" required to adequately interpret the raw data displayed in these reports. Having an informed background of the local economy as well as the regional economy will assist in providing a framework to interpret the data to achieve meaningful results. California's efforts in developing a follow-up strategy using the UI wage records are considered to be comprehensive in nature. Given the size of the cohort and the different classification of enrollment concentrations, the results have significant policy implications. Further, unlike the other states' efforts, California examines all students served by the colleges who left in any given year since 1990–91 to the current academic year.

On January 1996, Senate Bill (SB) 645 became law in California. Referred to as "performance-based accountability," the mandate gives the State Job Training Coordinating Council (SJTCC) the responsibility for designing and implementing a system to evaluate the performance of publicly funded workforce preparation programs in California. Accountability will be assessed with the use of a "report card," which will be issued to workforce preparation programs. Since one of the functions of California's 107 community colleges is to provide vocational education and/or workforce preparation, this system will be held accountable to several measures of performance. In the wake of the new Report Card bill, colleges will be required to utilize the data to provide various student outcomes, namely earnings of their graduates and placement in the workforce. Future research studies should consider utilizing unitary records to design a methodology beyond descriptive statistics. Studies that consider the background characteristics and institutional environmental factors should be explored to better explain the relationship between earnings and education attainment.

In conclusion, the descriptive data reveal that obtaining an associate degree or vocational certificate positively affects students' postcollege earnings three years out. The data from this study provide evidence of the economic value of completing a subbaccalaureate credential awarded by community colleges. It is important for higher education administrators, policymakers, and society at large to acknowledge that a community college education positively contributes to an individual's long-term sustainable economic benefit. Moreover, completing formalized programs enables graduates to meet the certification or screening requirements maintained by employers upon embarking into the world of work. Further, by investing in their education, these students not only develop certain skills and abilities but also foster their human capital—intellectually, professionally, and personally.

Note

1. The definition of each SAM code is as follows: A = apprenticeship (offered to apprentices only); B = advanced occupational (not limited to apprentices); C = clearly occupational (but not advanced); D = possibly occupational; and E = nonoccupational.

References

Adams, W., and Jaffee, A. (1971). Economic returns on the college investment. *Change* 3: 8.

Astin, A. W. (1985). *Achieving Educational Excellence.* San Francisco: Jossey-Bass.

Becker, G. S. (1964). *Human Capital: A Theoretical and Empirical Analysis, with Special Reference to Education.* New York: Columbia University Press.

Becker, G. S. (1975). *Human Capital: A Theoretical and Empirical Analysis, with Special Reference to Education,* 2nd ed. New York: Columbia University Press.

Becker, G. S. (1992). Why go to college? The value of an investment in higher education. In W. E. Becker and D. R. Lewis (eds.), *The Economics of American Higher Education* (pp. 21–120). Boston: Kluwer Academic Publishers.

Becker, G. S. (1993). *Human Capital: A Theoretical and Empirical Analysis with Special Reference to Education,* 3rd ed. Chicago, IL: The University of Chicago Press.

Blaug, M. (1970). *An Introduction to the Economics of Education.* London: Allen Lane, Penguin Press.

Blaug, M. (1972). The correlation between education and earnings: What does it signify? *Higher Education* 1: 53–76.

Elam, S. (1983). The Gallup education surveys: Impressions of a pool watcher. *Phi Delta Kappan* 64: 14–22.

Friedlander, J. (1993a). *Using Wage Record Data to Track the Post-College Employment and Earnings of Community College Students* (ERIC Document Reproduction Service No. 360007).

Friedlander, J. (1993b). *Post-College Employment Rates and Earnings of Students Who Participated in SBCC Occupational Education Programs* (ERIC Document Reproduction Service No. 361022).

Friedlander, J. (1996). *Using Wage Record Data to Track the Post-College Employment Rates and Wages of California Community College Students* (ERIC Document Reproduction Service No. 390507).

Froeschle, R. (1991). *Pilot Study Findings of the Use of the Texas Employment Commission Unemployment Insurance Wage Records to Document Outcomes of Technical-Vocational Education and Training.* Austin, TX: Texas Higher Education Coordinating Board.

Grubb, W. N. (1996). *Working in the Middle. Strengthening Education and Training for the Mid-Skilled Labor Force.* San Francisco: Jossey-Bass.

Haller, A. (1982). Reflections on the social psychology of status attainment. In R. Hauser, D. Mechanic, A. Haller, and T. Hauser (eds.), *Social Structure and Behavior.* New York: Academic Press.

Head, R. B. (1994). *The Economic Impact of Piedmont Virginia Community College Upon Its Service Region.* Research Report Number 2–94. Charlottesville: Piedmont Virginia Community College (ERIC Document Reproduction Service No. 368437).

Henderson, C., and Ottinger, C. (1985). College degrees—still a ladder to success? *Journal of College Placement* 45: 35.

Jencks, C., Bartlett, S., Corcoran, M., Crouse, J., Eaglesfield, D., Jackson, G., McClelland, K. I., Mueser, P., Olneck, M., Schwarts, J., Ward, S., and

Williams, J. (1979). *Who Gets Ahead? The Determinants of Economic Success in America.* New York: Basic Books.

Katsinas, S. G. (1994). A review of the literature to economic development and community colleges. *Community College Review* 21(4): 67–80.

McIntyre, C. (1996). *Trends of Importance to California Community Colleges.* Sacramento: Office of the Chancellor, California Community Colleges (ERIC Document Reproduction Service No. 401956).

Merano, M. A. (1990). *On-the-Job-Training-Programs in JTPA: A Quality of Service Report to the Illinois Job Training Coordinating Council.* Illinois Department of Commerce and Community Affairs.

Occupational Outlook Quarterly (1992). Washington, DC: U.S. Department of Labor, Bureau of Labor Statistics. Spring 1992, p. 40.

Pace, C. (1979). *Measuring Outcomes of College: Fifty Years of Findings and Recommendations for the Future.* San Francisco: Jossey-Bass.

Pascarella, E., and Terenzini, P. (1991). *How College Affects Students.* San Francisco: Jossey-Bass.

Pfeiffer, J. J. (1990). *Florida Education and Training Placement Program. Annual Report.* Tallahassee, FL: Florida Department of Education.

Piper, L. S. (1990). *Feasibility Study Using Employer Wage Records to Determine Vocational Completer Labor Market Outcomes.* Indianapolis, IN: Indiana Commission on Vocational and Technical Education.

Psacharopoulos, G. (1973). *Returns to Education.* San Francisco: Jossey-Bass.

Psacharopoulos, G. (1985). Returns to education: A further international update and implications. *Journal of Human Resources,* 20: 538–604.

Seppanen, L. J. (1993). *Using Administrative Data Matches for Follow-up.* Technical Report No. 93–5. Olympia: Washington State Board for Community and Technical Colleges (ERIC Document Reproduction Service No. 382250).

Seppanen, L. J. (1994). *Job Placement Rates for Graduates of Washington Community and Technical College Vocational Programs.* Research Report No. 94–7. Olympia: Washington State Board for Community and Technical Colleges (ERIC Document Reproduction Service No. 382255).

Smith, G. P. (1989). *A Longitudinal Tracking Study of Short-Term Education and Employment Outcomes of Colorado Community College Graduates.* Colorado Community College and Occupational Education System.

Stevens, D. W., Richmond, P. A., Haenn, J. F., and Michie, J. S. (1992). *Measuring Employment Outcomes Using Unemployment Insurance Wage Records.* Washington, DC: Research and Evaluation Associates, Inc.

Stout, R. J. (1996). *Community Attitudes About Economic Impacts of Colleges: A Case Study.* Paper presented at the 1996 Association for Institutional Research Annual Forum, Albuquerque, NM (ERIC Document Reproduction Service No. 397737).

U.S. Department of Commerce, Bureau of the Census (1996). *Current Population Survey: Historical Income Tables—Persons.* Washington, DC.

Vanderheyden, B. (1994). *Employment of Community College Completers.* Research Brief No. 1994–01. North Carolina: North Carolina State Department of Community Colleges (ERIC Document Reproduction Service No. 375896).

Weitzman, S. M. (1991). *The Economic Impact of the Community College System on the State of Florida.* Gainesville: Florida University, Interinstitutional Research Council (ERIC Document Reproduction Service No. 336145).

Winter, G. M., and Fadale, L. M. (1991). *The Economic Impact of SUNY's Community Colleges on the State of New York. Spring 1991—Update.* Albany: State University of New York, Two Year College Development Center (ERIC Document Reproduction Service No. 337239).

Yang, X., and Brown, J. K. (1998). Using unemployment insurance data and job record data to track the employment and earnings of community college students. Paper presented at the annual forum of the Association for Institutional Research. Minneapolis, MN, May.

Jorge R. Sanchez, Director, and **Frankie Santos Laanan,** Senior Research Analyst, Vocational Education and Institutional Research, Coast Community College District; **W. Charles Wiseley,** Information Systems Specialist, California Community Colleges Chancellor's Office.

Paper presented at the 38th Annual Forum of the Association for Institutional Research, Minneapolis, MN, May 20, 1998.

Address correspondence to: Jorge R. Sanchez, Director, Vocational Education and Institutional Research, Coast Community College District, 1370 Adams Avenue, Costa Mesa, CA 92626; e-mail: jsanchez@cccd.edu

CHAPTER 38

RACIAL AND GENDER DIFFERENCES IN THE RETURNS TO 2-YEAR AND 4-YEAR DEGREES

SUSAN AVERETT & SHARON DALESSANDRO*

ABSTRACT *Using data from the 1993 National Longitudinal Survey of Youth, this paper documents differences in the rate of return to 2-year and 4-year degrees across race and gender. We find for each race and gender group that a baccalaureate degree is more valuable than an associate's degree, and the return to an associate's degree is greater than attending some college, which is in turn more valuable than simply finishing high school. Our results indicate that these effects are statistically different for black and white men. Finally, according to our research, one avenue of low-cost education for women and black men is to attend a 2-year school and then finish the degree at a 4-year institution.*

Introduction

Public concern about rising tuition costs, an increasingly high-tech job market, and the growing earnings differential between college graduates and those who only complete high school has led researchers and policy-makers to examine once again the issue of access to a college education and the value of that education. Recently, the Clinton Administration enacted the HOPE Scholarship that provides a tuition tax credit for 100% of the first $1000 of tuition for 1 year and for 50% of up to $1000 for a second year. According to a 26 September 1997 White House Press Release, this tax credit cuts tuition and fees at community colleges by 88% and in several states by up to 100%. Thus, the first 2 years of an education, or a 2-year degree, are available to virtually anyone who desires one. Several natural questions arise from this scholarship that we address in this research: What is the value of a 2-year versus a 4-year degree? Does it matter if one starts at a 2-year school and then finishes a degree at a 4-year institution? Is obtaining an associate degree more important than simply attending some college but not graduating? Do the returns to 2-year and 4-year degrees vary by race and gender?

While a substantial literature exists on the returns to higher education in general, and a small but growing literature on the value of 2-year versus 4-year degrees, we still know relatively little about how the returns to 2-year and 4-year education vary by race and gender. Yet, the community college (throughout the paper, we use the terms community college and 2-year school interchangeably) remains an important source of education for many Americans, particularly those who have historically had less access to 4-year schools, typically women and minorities.

For the past 20 years, community colleges have had a significant place in society; not only by consistently enrolling approximately one-half of all first-time students, but also because their growth has been at a higher rate than for 4-year colleges over the same 20-year period (Snyder, 1997, Table 173). Many students find that the out-of-pocket costs of an education can be significantly reduced if one starts at a 2-year school and then transfers and finishes at a 4-year institution (Hoover, 1998;

McCabe, 1998). In addition, community colleges are increasingly recognizing the need to have a curriculum that is readily transferable to a 4-year college (Franey, 1998; Hoover, 1998).

Two-year institutions were first created to provide increased access to higher education without creating a burden on existing 4-year institutions. Traditionally, the role of the community college has been to provide: (a) the first 2 years of a higher education, (b) vocational and career training for its community, and (c) continuing education (Morrison, 1961). Given this broad range of responsibilities, the community college as an institution must be diverse and flexible, including having open-door admissions policies. Administrators must be ready to respond to changes in market needs with curriculum enhancements, and faculty must be able to adapt teaching styles to the wide variation in student levels. It is these diverse qualities, and possibly also the decline in transfer rates to 4-year institutions (Grubb, 1991), that cause the community college, as an institution of higher education, to be looked on in a different light to traditional 4-year institutions. Many have questioned whether a 2-year education is a good investment from an economic point of view and whether it impedes a student's progress toward a 4-year degree (Dougherty, 1992). Rouse (1995) examines the probability that an individual who attends a 2-year school will graduate with a baccalaureate degree, and finds that community colleges do not appear to change the likelihood of eventually earning a baccalaureate degree.

Through its provision for diversity in education, the community college is in a position to provide higher education to those groups, such as minorities or women, who may traditionally face more financial or competitive barriers to obtaining a college education. Recent literature (McCartan, 1983; Grubb, 1991; Dougherty, 1992; Rouse, 1994) indicates that those who now attend 2-year schools are more often female, come from families with lower family income, and have lower levels of academic achievement than their 4-year counterparts. In addition, President Clinton indicated that he expected a considerable number of welfare recipients to receive training from community colleges as they begin their transition to the labor market (Burgos-Sasscer, 1998). There is also increasing discussion over the role of the community college in training individuals for a more technologically advanced workforce (Leigh & Gill, 1997; Bates, 1998; Burgos-Sasscer, 1998; Naughton, 1998).

In the present research, our goal is to examine the returns to 2-year versus 4-year degrees with a focus on racial and gender differences in the returns to education. The paper is organized as follows. In the next section, we review the relevant literature to place our work in context. We then discuss our data in the third section. The fourth section details our results and we end with some concluding remarks.

Literature Review

Numerous econometric studies of the returns to higher education have been published; many of these have focused on racial differences in these returns (Welch, 1973; Hoffman, 1984; Ashraf, 1994). A growing literature focuses specifically on the sub-baccalaureate market, which includes those in community colleges and junior colleges, whether they are pursuing an associate degree, certificate, or simply additional vocational training. It is the market for those with at least a high school diploma but less than a baccalaureate degree, and is estimated to account for nearly three-fifths of all workers (Grubb, 1997).

Early literature that examined sub-baccalaureate market returns had a very specific focus. Carroll and Ihnen (1967) examined the returns for an investment of 2 years in a technical school. Heinemann and Sussna (1977) examined returns to education at a large, Midwestern urban community college. It was not until the past 10 years that the literature addressing the rate of return to a community college education began growing.

Monk-Turner (1994) examines how the first type of college entered affects future earnings. She uses data from the Parnes National Longitudinal Survey on Labor Market Experiences. In her models, which are not run separately by race and gender, she includes a control for academic ability to overcome potential bias in the returns across type of institution. She finds that those entering a 4-year college when first starting college enjoy a 6.4% return over those first entering a community college. She concludes that those entering a community college as their first higher education institution are penalized in the long run; their future returns are actually lower in comparison with 4-year college attendees. She notes that community college attendees should not expect to earn as high a rate of return since they invest less in their education as compared with those who attend a 4-year school.

In a comprehensive study, Kane and Rouse (1995) compare the economic returns to 2-year and

4-year colleges using two data sources, the 1990 wave of the National Longitudinal Survey of Youth (NLSY) and the Class of 1972 National Longitudinal Study (NLS-72) across men and women, although not across race. They note that there are differences in the average family backgrounds between students in 2-year and 4-year colleges. Their regressions based on the NLSY data reveal similar returns for men and women to completing an associate degree (20%) and completing a baccalaureate degree (33%). They do find that the returns to some college (attending with no degree receipt) vary between men and women, with the returns typically lower for women. From the NLS-72 data, which has detailed information on credits, they find that completing the baccalaureate degree is important for men while the same is true of the associate degree for women.

Belman and Heywood (1991) were some of the first researchers to examine whether sheepskin effects (effects of completing the degree) vary by race and gender. They use data from the 1978 Current Population Survey to confirm that there is evidence of larger sheepskin effects for women and minorities, although they do not test to see if the differences are statistically significant. They also note that, theoretically, sheepskin effects may vary across demographic groups if degrees provide a stronger productivity signal for some groups than for others. Jaeger and Page (1996) continue Belman and Heywood's work by estimating sheepskin effects for all levels of education for blacks and whites by gender. They use the 1991 and 1992 Current Population Survey to obtain a matched sample of blacks and whites, aged 25–64 years, who were not enrolled in school. One drawback of these data is that they do not include information on ability, family background, or previous work experience. Corresponding to the findings reported by Kane and Rouse (1995), Jaeger and Page (1996) find that for white women associate degrees have statistically significant positive returns, for both vocational and academic degrees. The effect for vocational degrees is substantial when compared with the other groups and is attributed to the nursing programs that women often enroll in, which typically lead to relatively high paying jobs. They also find that white men benefit from academic associate degrees; however, the same finding does not hold for black men. They find little evidence to suggest the existence of different sheepskin effects across gender and race. However, they do find different sheepskin effects by type of degree (e.g., between occupational associate

degree and a bachelor's degree) and conclude that sheepskin effects appear to be important.

Building from the empirical findings of Kane and Rouse (1995), Leigh and Gill (1997) examine whether the returns estimated by Kane and Rouse hold for adults who return to attend a community college after several years in the workforce. Leigh and Gill use data from the 1993 wave of the NLSY, when respondents are between the ages of 28 and 35 years, and find that for associate degree recipients the returns are positive and significant. They find no difference in the return to a degree for those students who continue straight from high school and those who return after several years of work experience, despite the fact that the latter are more likely to have families and other responsibilities that might make studying difficult. Finally, they also note that community colleges are increasingly offering non-degree programs to help workers increase their skills. For men, there exists a positive and relatively large (8–10%) return to attendance in these non-degree programs.

Grubb has also carried out extensive work in the area of educational returns in the sub-baccalaureate market over the past decade. Grubb (1997) uses the Survey of Income and Program Participation for 1984, 1987, and 1990 to examine several issues. These include questions regarding the existence of economic returns to community college, how those benefits are determined by the credential earned, and whether there are returns above and beyond that due to sheepskin effects or, as Grubb refers to them, program effects. He finds that returns to associate degrees are significant for both men and women, although the rates are lower than a baccalaureate degree. He also finds that the difference in returns between the two degrees is smaller for women than men and that there do appear to be program effects for having degrees or credentials. However, his work suggests that there are substantial variations in the returns to different programs or courses of study for both 2-year and 4-year degrees, and that one must use caution when generalizing returns to a 2-year education since the programs offered are so varied.

Data

For our analysis, we use data from the NLSY, a large survey of 12 686 individuals who have been interviewed since 1979, at which time they were 14–21 years old. Data was available for as recently as 1994 at the time this research was completed. This data set was chosen because it contains extensive labor force, demographic, and schooling information. In addition, minorities and disadvantaged whites are over-sampled, making it possible to estimate the models separately by race.

These data also contain excellent work history information, in particular an accurate measure of previous work experience. Researchers have documented how important a precise measure of previous work experience is in studies of women's earnings (Filer, 1993). In addition, we have information on family background (measured by parental education) and ability (measured by the respondent's score on the Armed Forces Qualifications Test (AFQT), a test of academic ability and achievement administered in 1980). Family background and ability are particularly important when considering race and gender differentials in earnings.

We use data from the 1993 survey when the individuals are aged 28–35 years; sample members would have graduated from high school between 1976 and 1983. Thus, they have had ample time to complete an education and to develop an attachment to the labor force, although they are in the early years of their careers. Although data from 1994 are available, previous work experience and earnings are measured for the previous calendar year, necessitating the use of the 1993 survey year. We thus limit our sample to those who were interviewed in 1993, are working, report earnings, and completed high school. Rather than using years of education completed and lacking actual transcript information, we use self-reported information on degree receipt to test for program (sheepskin) effects. We do so recognizing that self-reported degree receipt may bias our estimates of the return to schooling upward (Grubb, 1997).

Following a similar procedure to that outlined by Leigh and Gill (1997), we work backward from 1993 to record the highest degree obtained. For those who did not obtain a degree, we determine whether they attended any college and classify them by the type of college attended. We use six mutually exclusive categories of educational attainment: (1) receipt of an associate degree as the highest degree earned, (2) receipt of a bachelor degree as the highest degree earned without ever having attended a 2-year school, (3) receipt of a bachelor degree as the highest degree earned and also attended a 2-year school, (4) attended only a 2-year school but never completed a 2-year degree, (5) attended only a 4-year school but never completed a 4-year degree, and (6) attended both a 2-year and a 4-year institution without ever completing either degree. The reference category is high school graduates who have never obtained any additional education. Our reason for separating the baccalaureate degree holders into two groups is to see if there is any penalty in the wage return for those who start at a community college and then transfer to finish at a 4-year school. It is possible that some of those earning a baccalaureate degree returned to a 2-year college after earning their 4-year degree to obtain specific skills, such as computer skills. However, our sample sizes do not permit us to separate out those who had their 2-year schooling before their 4-year schooling and those who had it after. We also cannot separate out the baccalaureate degree holders who went on to earn graduate or professional degrees for the same reason.

Our final sample consists of 6413 individuals. Table 1 presents sample means by race and gender. Blacks and whites in the sample attended 2-year schools (and did not earn an associate degree) at fairly similar rates, ranging from 12 to 18%, while blacks were more likely to attend a 4-year school and not earn the baccalaureate degree when compared with whites. Black women were the most likely to attend both a 2-year and a 4-year institution without finishing either degree (about 10%), while about 6.3% of the other groups attended but did not finish at both types of schools. About 22% of the white men and white women earned their baccalaureate degree compared with 16% of black women and 12.5% of black men. Of those obtaining a baccalaureate degree, 4.3% of black men, 4.1% of black women, 7.6% of white women, and 6.5% of black men had also attended a 2-year institution at some time. Very few (< 2%) of baccalaureate degree holders had also earned an associate degree; therefore, we cannot control for having received both degrees in our models. Individuals who received both degrees are classified as having the baccalaureate degree while also having attended a 2-year institution.

We specify and estimate a human capital model where the dependent variable is the natural log of the hourly wage.[1] We estimate two models for each race/gender group. In model 1, the control variables are a set of basic human capital variables including the dummy variables for various levels of educational attainment,

TABLE 1
Sample Means (Standard Deviations)

Variable	Black Women	Black Men	Women	Men
Sample size	830	907	2167	2509
Education				
Earned an associate degree	0.098	0.051	0.095	0.069
Earned baccalaureate degree, no 2-year school	0.123	0.084	0.158	0.157
Earned baccalaureate degree, also 2-year school	0.041	0.043	0.076	0.065
Attended a 2-year school	0.180	0.116	0.159	0.124
Attended a 4-year school	0.130	0.115	0.084	0.078
Attended both types of schools	0.099	0.063	0.062	0.063
Demographic (all pertain to 1993)				
Live in North Central region	0.170	0.168	0.252	0.270
Live in the Southern region	0.625	0.592	0.325	0.303
Live in the Western region	0.066	0.079	0.246	0.242
Unsure of region where living	0.004	0.003	0.005	0.009
Live in an Urban Area	0.860	0.830	0.763	0.767
Do not know if live in an Urban Area	0.013	0.021	0.049	0.044
Live in area with > 9% unemployment	0.024	0.024	0.095	0.090
Live in area with < 9% unemployment	0.345	0.353	0.266	0.265
Live in area where unemployment unknown	0.004	0.003	0.005	0.009
Age in 1993 (years)	31.929	31.822	31.908	31.799
	(2.225)	(2.217)	(2.257)	(2.238)
Have a child	0.687	0.398	0.631	0.485
Married	0.370	0.387	0.643	0.632
Separated, divorced or widowed	0.243	0.169	0.187	0.135
Family background				
AFQT score	25.954	23.645	48.995	48.822
	(19.527)	(21.704)	(26.109)	(28.319)
Missing AFQT score	0.020	0.036	0.036	0.052
Mother is a high school graduate	0.435	0.447	0.595	0.615
Do not know mother's education	0.067	0.093	0.039	0.056
Father is a high school graduate	0.383	0.366	0.566	0.585
Do not know father's education	0.201	0.223	0.084	0.081
Employment (all pertain to 1993)				
Hourly pay	9.940	11.030	11.800	15.150
	(20.050)	(14.120)	(34.380)	(37.100)
Employed by government	0.263	0.172	0.162	0.112
Do not know if employed by government	0.000	0.001	0.000	0.000
Member of a labor union	0.166	0.186	0.104	0.141
Experience in 1993 (years)	10.022	10.717	11.236	12.145
	(3.665)	(3.288)	(3.395)	(3.003)
Industry				
Agriculture, forestry and fisheries	0.002	0.026	0.013	0.037
Finance, insurance and real estate	0.073	0.037	0.089	0.048
Manufacturing	0.133	0.232	0.138	0.23
Mining and construction	0.007	0.096	0.015	0.145
Public administration	0.082	0.067	0.053	0.056
Trade	0.133	0.161	0.179	0.172
Transportation, communications and utilities	0.080	0.118	0.051	0.088
Occupation				
Precision production, craft and repair	0.019	0.122	0.024	0.205
Farming, forestry and fishing	0.004	0.035	0.008	0.034
Operators, fabricator and laborers	0.137	0.341	0.08	0.227
Service	0.229	0.198	0.183	0.096
Technical, sales and administrative support	0.418	0.168	0.417	0.2

years of previous work experience, age, AFQT score, region of residence, and residence in an urban area. Model 2 adds a richer set of controls, including local unemployment rates, child and marital status, union membership, government employment, parental education, industry, and occupation.[2] We recognize that selection effects are potentially quite important. In particular, it is possible that those who graduate from a 4-year college would have had higher earnings even without going to college. Thus, following Kane

and Rouse (1995) and Leigh and Gill (1997), we control for family background and ability in our models in an attempt to control for possible selection bias.[3]

Estimation Results and Discussion

Table 2 reports the estimation results by race and gender. Chow tests (see Greene, 1990, p. 218) confirm that the wage equations should be estimated separately for men and women. Within gender,

TABLE 2
Log-Wage Models of Education Returns (Standard Errors in Parentheses)

	White women (n = 2167)		Black women (n = 830)		Black men (n = 907)		White men (n = 2509)	
	Model 1	Model 2	Model 1	Model 2	Model 1	Model 2	Model 1	Model 2
Attended a 2-year school as highest institutional level attended	0.099* (0.034)	0.103* (0.034)	0.173* (0.051)	0.163* (0.049)	0.182* (0.054)	0.150* (0.051)	0.064† (0.035)	0.054† (0.033)
Attended a 4-year school as highest institutional level attended	0.147* (0.045)	0.085 (0.043)	0.187* (0.056)	0.172* (0.055)	0.089 (0.056)	0.093† (0.053)	0.079† (0.043)	0.06 (0.041)
Attended both types of schools but no degree earned	0.121** (0.050)	0.06 (0.048)	0.161* (0.062)	0.160* (0.061)	0.192* (0.070)	0.162** (0.068)	0.101** (0.046)	0.093** (0.045)
Associate degree as highest degree earned	0.241* (0.040)	0.173* (0.042)	0.322* (0.063)	0.286* (0.061)	0.164** (0.077)	0.175** (0.073)	0.174* (0.044)	0.163* (0.043)
Bachelor degree and did not attend a 2-year school	0.427* (0.048)	0.296* (0.042)	0.406* (0.064)	0.341* (0.066)	0.375* (0.069)	0.334* (0.070)	0.348* (0.038)	0.313* (0.040)
Bachelor degree and attended a 2-year school	0.447* (0.096)	0.306* (0.050)	0.398* (0.091)	0.375* (0.090)	0.471* (0.086)	0.473* (0.085)	0.294* (0.048)	0.251* (0.048)
Age (years)	-0.025* (0.005)	-0.017* (0.005)	-0.012 (0.008)	-0.012 (0.018)	-0.024* (0.008)	-0.018** (0.008)	-0.008 (0.006)	-0.006 (0.005)
AFQT score	0.002* (0.001)	0.002* (0.001)	0.004 (0.001)	0.003* (0.001)	0.004* (0.000)	0.002** (0.001)	0.004* (0.000)	0.003* (0.000)
Previous work experience	0.016 (0.017)	0.010 (0.016)	0.018 (0.020)	-0.002 (0.020)	0.054** (0.023)	0.051** (0.022)	0.041** (0.019)	0.047* (0.018)
Previous work experience squared	0.002** (0.001)	0.001† (0.000)	0.001 (0.001)	0.002† (0.001)	-0.000 (0.001)	-0.000 (0.001)	0.000 (0.000)	-0.001 (0.001)
Live in Northcentral US	-0.148* (0.039)	-0.140* (0.039)	-0.179* (0.064)	-0.118** (0.059)	-0.024 (0.059)	-0.002 (0.056)	-0.133* (0.035)	-0.130* (0.034)
Live in Southern US	-0.155* (0.037)	-0.176* (0.037)	-0.182 (0.052)	-0.114** (0.054)	-0.078† (0.049)	-0.044 (0.051)	-0.125* (0.034)	-0.084** (0.034)

Live in the Western US	-0.046 (0.039)	-0.050 (0.038)	0.018 (0.079)	0.098 (0.080)	0.127† (0.072)	0.149** (0.071)	-0.072** (0.035)	-0.028 (0.034)
Live in an Urban Area	0.190* (0.029)	0.166* (0.029)	0.077 (-.052)	0.043 (0.054)	0.147* (0.047)	0.133* (0.051)	0.185* (0.027)	0.177* (0.024)
Mother graduated from high school		-0.023 (0.027)		-0.019 (0.038)		0.019 (0.035)		0.035 (0.026)
Father graduated from high school		-0.020 (0.026)		-0.037 (0.041)		0.012 (0.038)		0.050† (0.025)
High unemployment in region of residence		0.008 (0.040)		-0.130 (0.121)		-0.085 (0.141)		-0.048 (0.038)
Low unemployment in region of residence		0.006 (0.027)		0.018 (0.038)		-0.045 (0.036)		-0.034 (0.025)
Have a child		-0.074* (0.025)		-0.012 (0.037)		0.055 (0.037)		0.063* (0.092)
Married		0.012 (0.032)		0.011 (0.038)		0.107* (0.041)		0.085* (0.028)
Separated, divorced or widowed		0.048 (0.038)		0.072† (0.042)		0.030 (0.044)		0.028 (0.035)
Work for federal, state or local government		-0.131* (0.038)		-0.057 (0.046)		-0.034 (0.052)		-0.141* (0.043)
Wages covered by collective bargaining (union member)		0.185* (0.038)		0.163* (0.048)		0.244* (0.042)		0.227* (0.031)
Adjusted R^2	0.275	0.347	0.289	0.354	0.248	0.353	0.202	0.286

P values and significance: $*P \leq 0.01$, $**P \leq 0.05$, $†P \leq 0.10$.

The dependent variable in all models is the natural logarithm of the hourly wage. Model 1 is the baseline specification that includes controls for education, experience, age, location and ability (AFQT). Not shown are coefficients on dummy variables for missing AFQT, SMSA and region variables. Model 2 adds controls for marital status, children, parental education, local unemployment rate, type of position (government or union), and industry and occupation. Dummy variables were included to control for missing variables on AFQT, SMSA, region and parental education. In the interest of parsimony, coefficients on the industry and occupation controls are not shown but are available from the authors on request. All education categories are mutually exclusive. The reference category consists of individuals who completed high school only.

Chow tests also verify that both models 1 and 2 should be estimated separately for black and white men, but only model 2 is statistically different for black and white women. Because we are presenting all the other models separately by race and gender, we also present model 1 estimated separately for white and black women; the coefficient estimates are similar when we pool and are available from the authors on request.

Beginning with model 1, there is clearly a value to continuing beyond high school, even if a degree is not earned. For women (black and white) and white men, earning a degree (either associate or bachelor) is always preferable to attending some college but not earning a degree. For black men, the results are less clear; attending both a 2-year and a 4-year institution yields a slightly higher return than an associate degree. Black women tend to get higher returns to all educational categories when compared with white men and white women, while the comparison between black women and black men does not yield any clear pattern. A 4-year degree yields a higher return than a 2-year degree for all groups. F tests confirm that 4-year degree recipients experience a higher return than those with a 2-year degree. Black women appear to benefit the most from the associate degree, followed by white women. For black men, attending a 2-year school is more valuable than obtaining the 2-year degree. This may be due to the type of programs they are enrolled in or to occupational choice. The returns to a 4-year degree are lowest for white men.

White and black women get essentially the same return to the baccalaureate degree whether or not they started at a 2-year school. However, this is not the case with the men. Interestingly, black men get a return nearly 10 percentage points higher if they get a baccalaureate degree and also attended a 2-year school, although this is not quite statistically significant ($P = 0.22$). However, the reverse is true for white men, who suffer a 5.4 percentage point reduction in the return to the 4-year degree if they also attended a 2-year school. These results are somewhat in contrast to Monk-Turner (1994) who found that those who started in a 2-year program and then transferred earned lower returns to the 4-year degree as compared with those individuals who obtain baccalaureate degrees without ever attending a 2-year institution. This may be related to occupational choice; black men may be in blue-collar occupations that are more

closely related to their 2-year schooling, thus this higher return may simply reflect a match between occupation and schooling. Grubb (1997) notes that field of study is an important component to the return to a credential.

In model 2, which has the complete set of controls including occupation and industry, we see that the general pattern of results is the same, although the magnitude of the rates of returns has been dampened somewhat. The coefficients for white women arc reduced more than those for the other groups, which may be due to the fact that white women often pursue nursing, a relatively lucrative field (Jaeger & Page (1996) and Kane & Rouse (1995) also note a similar finding). One interesting difference is that for white women after controlling for industry and occupation the return to attending both a 2-year and a 4-year school but earning no degree is no longer statistically significant, although it remains significant for the other groups. Another change is that, for black men, controlling for occupation and industry makes the coefficient on obtaining the 2-year degree larger than that of simply attending a 2-year school. The other results are similar to those obtained in model 1. In particular, earning an associate degree is more valuable than attending a 4-year institution without earning a degree, and earning a baccalaureate degree is more beneficial than an associate degree. As before, F tests confirm that the return to a 4-year degree is significantly higher than the return to a 2-year degree for all groups. Finally, controlling for occupation does not change the finding that black men with baccalaureate degrees who attended 2-year schools do better than those who just attended 4-year institutions, whereas the reverse is true for white men.

Although Chow tests confirm that blacks and whites and men and women should be studied separately, to determine whether the returns for blacks and whites are statistically different we pooled the male and female samples by race and interacted race with the education controls. F tests on the race/education interactions reveal that for women the returns are not statistically significantly different by race ($P = 0.8141$ for model 1, $P = 0.7072$ for model 2). For men, the returns are statistically different for model 1 ($P = 0.0842$) but not for model 2 ($P = 0.4464$). Thus, there is some evidence that black and white men have statistically different returns to education, although this is sensitive to the inclusion of occupation and industry controls.

Conclusions

Community colleges have a long history in the United States of providing education for individuals who either lack access to a 4-year college, are looking for a vocational set of skills, or are in need of re-training or additional training after having been in the workforce for some time. The HOPE scholarship provides an economic incentive to earning an associate degree or the first 2 years of a college degree, and it may prove to be an important entry into higher education for segments of the population with fewer financial resources and/or lower academic ability. In this paper, we have documented differences in the returns to education across gender for blacks and whites. We consistently find for each race and gender group that a baccalaureate degree is more valuable than an associate degree, and the return to an associate degree is greater than attending some college. Our results indicate that the returns are statistically different for black and white men, with black men obtaining higher returns to the baccalaureate degree. We also find that for women and white men the return to the 4-year degree is greater when one has not also attended a community college. Interestingly, we find the opposite for black men. Black men who have 4-year degrees but also attended 2-year schools have a higher rate of return than if they had not also attended a 2-year school. We also find that controlling for occupation dampens the returns to education, indicating that some of the return to education is really a function of the occupation one selects. However, using occupation and industry as control variables may be problematic if occupational segregation is an issue and blacks and/or women are funneled into low-paying occupations.

With respect to policy implications, our research indicates that one avenue of low-cost education for women and black men is to attend a 2-year school and then finish the degree at a 4-year institution. We also find that for white men attending a 2-year school and then obtaining a 4-year degree yields lower returns than simply obtaining a 4-year degree, whereas the reverse is true for black men. This latter finding is not explained by differences in occupation and industry, and therefore deserves further scrutiny.

There are many logical extensions of this research. Perhaps the most important is an investigation into why the returns are different across races. We leave this for future research.

Acknowledgments

The authors thank Howard Bodenhorn and Michele McLennan for helpful comments. All errors are our own.

Notes

1. We also ran all of our models with annual earnings as the dependent variable. The pattern of results is similar to those presented here, and these results are available on request from the authors.

2. We started by running four models. The first was the specification labeled model 1 in Table 2. To this we added controls for children, marital status and parental education. The third model built on the second by adding controls for local unemployment rates, government job, and union membership, and the final model further built on this by adding controls for occupation and industry. We found that the first three models produced virtually identical coefficients for the education variables but when controls for occupation and industry were added the returns to education were smaller. Therefore, in the interest of parsimony, we report only the coefficients from model 1 and the most detailed specification that we label model 2 in Table 2.

3. We do not correct our wage equations for the possible selection bias resulting from selection into employment (and hence observed wages). Other studies (including Leigh & Gill (1997) and Kane & Rouse (1995)) do not correct for selection bias from employment either, and we want our results to be comparable with theirs.

References

Ashraf, J. (1994) Differences in returns to education: an analysis by race, *American Journal of Economics and Sociology, 53*, pp. 281–290.

Bates, S. (1998) Building better worker's, *Nations Business,* June, p. 18.

Belman, D. & Heywood, J. S. (1991) Sheepskin effects in the returns to education: an examination of women and minorities, *The Review of Economics and Statistics, 73*, pp. 720–724.

Burgos-Sasscer, R. (1998) Path to Houston's job future through HCCS doors, *The Houston Chronicle,* 4 May, p. A21.

Carroll, A. B. & Ihnen, L A. (1967) Costs and returns for two years of postsecondary technical schooling: a pilot study, *The Journal of Political Economy, 75,* 6, pp. 862–873.

Dougherty, K. J. (1992) Community colleges and baccalaureate attainment, *Journal of Higher Education, 63*, pp. 188–214.

Filer, R. (1993) The usefulness of predicted values for prior work experience in analyzing labor market outcomes for women, *Journal of Human Resources, 28,* pp. 518–537.

Franey, L. (1998) State and community colleges seek closer ties: University of Missouri hopes to end transfer students' problems, *The Kansas City Star,* 27 March, p. C4.

Greene, W H. (1990) *Econometric Analysis* (New York, Macmillan).

Grubb, W. N. (1991) The decline of community college transfer rates: evidence from national longitudinal surveys, *The Journal of Higher Education, 62,* pp. 194–222.

Grubb, W. N. (1997) The returns to education in the sub-baccalaureate labor market, *Economics of Education, 16,* pp. 231–245.

Heinemann, H. N. & Sussna, E. (1977) The economic benefits of a community college education, *Industrial Relations, 16,* pp. 345–354.

Hoffman, S. D. (1984) Black-White difference in returns to higher education: evidence from the 1970s, *Economics of Education Review, 3,* pp. 13–21.

Hoover, R. (1998) Local colleges a bridge to universities: shunned by school of choice? Keep trying, pick transfers, *The Detroit News,* 10 July, p. C1.

Jaeger, D. A. & Page, M. E. (1996) Degrees matter: new evidence on sheepskin effects in the returns to education, *The Review of Economics and Statistics, 78,* pp. 733–739.

Kane, T. J. & Rouse, C. E. (1995) Labor-market returns to two- and four-year college, *The American Economic Review, 85,* pp. 600–614.

Leigh, D. E. & Gill, A. M. (1997) Labor market returns to community colleges: evidence for returning adults, *The Journal of Human Resources, 32,* pp. 334–353.

McCabe, C. (1998) Community colleges earn credit; best students save on tuition and find transfers are easy, *The Boston Globe,* 8 February, p. 1.

McCartan, A. M. (1983) The community college mission: present challenges and future visions, *The Journal of Higher Education, 54,* pp. 676–692.

Monk-Turner, E. (1994) Economic returns to community and four-year college education, *The Journal of Socio-Economics, 23,* pp. 441–447.

Morrison, D. G. (1961) What is the place of the community college among higher education institutions, *The Journal of Higher Education, 32,* pp. 462–463.

Naughton, K. (1998) From the frying pan to the factory, *Business Week,* 1 June, p. 106.

Rouse, C. E. (1994) What to do after high school: the two-year versus four-year college enrollment decision, in: Ehrenberg, R. G. (Ed.) *Choices and Consequences: Contemporary Policy Issues in Education* (Ithaca, NY, ILR Press), pp. 59–88.

Rouse, C. E. (1995) Democratization or diversion? the effect of community colleges on educational attainment, *Journal of Business and Economic Statistics, 13,* pp. 217–224.

Snyder, T. D. (1997) *Digest of Education Statistics 1996,* NCES 98–015 (Production Manager, C. M. Hoffman; Program Analyst, C. M. Geddes) (Washington, DC, US Department of Education, National Center for Education Statistics).

Welch, F. (1973) Black-White difference in returns to schooling, *The American Economic Review, 63,* pp. 893–907.

Susan Averett & Sharon Dalessandro, Department of Economics and Business, Lafayette College, Easton, PA 18042, USA. E-mail: averetts@lafayette.edu

CHAPTER 39

DOES COMMUNITY COLLEGE VERSUS FOUR-YEAR COLLEGE ATTENDANCE INFLUENCE STUDENTS' EDUCATIONAL PLANS?

ERNEST T. PASCARELLA
LINDA SERRA HAGEDORN
MARCIA EDISON
PATRICK T. TERENZINI
AMAURY NORA

In this study researchers tested the hypothesis that community college attendance lowers students' pre-college plans to obtain a bachelor of arts degree. In the presence of controls for precollege plans, other background factors, and college academic and nonacademic experiences, community college students initially planning to obtain a bachelor of arts degree were between 20% and 31% more likely than similar four-year college students to lower their plans below a bachelor of arts degree by the end of the second year of college.

A major critique of the two-year community college posits that, although it may largely guarantee equality of opportunity for access to postsecondary education, it has not, in relationship to four-year colleges and universities, provided equal opportunity in terms of the outcomes of postsecondary education (Brint & Karabel, 1989; Grubb, 1984; Karabel, 1986). A recent body of research, however, has called into question the notion that two-year college students are at a distinct disadvantage in terms of the cognitive or labor market outcomes of postsecondary education. For example, when initial ability and other important confounding influences were controlled statistically, students in two-year colleges appeared to make about the same gains in standardized measures of reading comprehension, mathematics, critical thinking, writing skills, and science reasoning as their student counterparts in four-year institutions (Bohr et al., 1994; Pascarella et al., 1995, 1995–1996; Terenzini et al., 1994). Similarly, the weight of evidence suggests that, when individuals of equal educational attainment and background characteristics are compared, there is a general parity between those initially enrolling in two-year and four-year colleges in such areas as job prestige, earnings, job stability, unemployment rate, or job satisfaction (Anderson, 1984; Pascarella & Terenzini, 1991; Smart & Ethington, 1985; Whitaker & Pascarella, 1994).

There seems to be little debate, however, that in the particularly crucial area of educational attainment students initially enrolling in two-year colleges are in fact significantly disadvantaged relative to similar students starting at four-year institutions (Kinnick & Kempner, 1988). Here the weight of evidence has indicated that two-year college students seeking a bachelor of arts degree are about 15% less likely to complete that degree in the same amount of time as similar students who begin postsecondary education at a four-year college or university (e.g., Alba & Lavin, 1981; Dougherty, 1987, 1992, 1994; Lavin & Crook, 1990; Nunley & Breneman, 1988; Pascarella & Terenzini, 1991; Velez, 1985). Because educational attainment plays such a central role in the labor-market returns of postsecondary education (e.g., Knox, Lindsay, & Kolb, 1993; Pascarella & Terenzini, 1991; Whitaker & Pascarella, 1994), such a finding would appear to have deleterious consequences for the occupational and economic mobility of students in two-year colleges.

Scholars have suggested a number of explanations for why beginning postsecondary education at a two-year college tends to inhibit degree attainment. One explanation tends to be largely structural and focuses on the difficulties involved in transferring from a two-year to a four-year institution to complete one's degree. Problems in securing acceptance, obtaining financial aid, and transferring credits can pose nontrivial administrative obstacles in transferring from two-year to four-year institutions (Dougherty, 1992, 1994; Grubb, 1991; Nora, 1993; Nora & Rendon, 1990). A related problem involves adjusting to the academic demands and unfamiliar social milieu of a four-year institution subsequent to transfer. Problems in such adjustment perhaps partially explain why a significant number of two-year college students experience a drop in grades after transferring (Dougherty, 1992, 1994; Kintzer & Wattenbarger, 1985).

A second explanation, and one which precipitated the research reported in this paper, concerns the role that two-year colleges themselves play in lowering students' educational attainment. In a major sociological critique of two-year colleges, Clark (1960, 1980) hypothesized that public two-year college systems are essentially a form of *tracking* in which the disproportionate numbers of non-White, working-class, and lower-middle-class students who attend two-year institutions are *cooled out* and led away from the path to a bachelor of arts degree. Specifically, the cooling-out process is one in which the curriculum, the socializing agents of the college (i.e., faculty and peers), and administrative procedures combine to lower students' educational

aspirations and goals (Brint & Karabel, 1989; Hunt, Klieforth, & Atnell, 1977; Karabel, 1972, 1974). Thus, the social-psychological reality of two-year college attendance itself functions to manage the ambition of lower socioeconomic status students in the American postsecondary education system (Brint & Karabel, 1989). As a result, instead of fostering social mobility for these students, two-year college attendance tends to contribute to the reproduction of existing class differences (e.g., Grubb, 1984; Karabel, 1974, 1986).

As an explanation for the negative influence of two-year college attendance on bachelor of arts degree completion, the cooling-out hypothesis has a considerable logical appeal. A review of existing literature, however, suggested that the hypothesis has yet to be tested directly. In this paper we report the results of a study in which we sought to test, at least preliminarily, the cooling-out hypothesis by estimating the extent to which two-year college attendance is linked to the lowering of educational plans. Specifically the study had two purposes. First, we attempted to determine the net impact of two-year versus four-year college attendance on students' lifetime educational plans after 1 and after 2 years of college. Second, we sought to determine if the net impact on lifetime educational plans of two-year versus four-year college attendance differed in magnitude for different kinds of students (e.g., students differing in ethnicity, gender, family socioeconomic origins, precollege academic ability, and precollege educational plans).

Method

Institutional Sample

The sample was selected from incoming first-year students at 18 four-year and 5 two-year institutions located in 16 states throughout the country. Institutions were selected from the National Center on Education Statistics Integrated Postsecondary Education Data System (IPEDS) to represent a variety of colleges and universities in terms of institutional type and control (e.g., private and public research universities, private liberal arts colleges, private and public comprehensive universities, historically Black colleges, and two-year colleges), size, location, commuter versus residential character, and the ethnic distribution of the undergraduate student body. The two-year colleges included three located in large metropolitan areas (one on the West Coast, one in New England, and one in the Carolinas), and two located in or near smaller communities (one in a Midwestern state and one in a Rocky Mountain state). The four-year college sample included: three public research universities (two located in urban areas and one in a small town); one private research university located in an urban area; four liberal arts colleges (three located in a small town and one located near an urban area; eight regional colleges and universities (four in urban areas and four in smaller towns); and two historically Black colleges (both located in urban areas). The 18 four-year institutions were located in 15 states from across the country.

Student Sample and Instruments

The individuals in the overall sample were 1,645 students who participated in both the first-year and second-year follow-ups of the National Study of Student Learning (NSSL). The initial sample was selected randomly from the incoming first-year class at each participating institution. The students in the sample were informed that they would be participating in a national longitudinal study of student learning and that they would receive cash stipends for their participation in each data collection ($25, $35, and $45, respectively). They were also informed that the information they provided would be kept confidential and would never become part of their institutional record.

An initial 3-hour data collection was conducted in the Fall of 1992, with 3,840 students from the 23 institutions participating. The data was collected using an NSSL-designed precollege survey that gathered information on student demographic characteristics and background, student lifetime educational plans, student expectations of college, and a series of items assessing the students' orientations toward learning. Participants also completed the reading comprehension, mathematics, and critical thinking modules of the Collegiate Assessment of Academic Proficiency (CAAP). The CAAP was developed by the American College Testing Program (ACT) specifically to assess selected general skills acquired by students during the first 2 years of college (ACT, 1991). Each of the CAAP modules requires 40 minutes, and we employed a composite score based on all three tests as an estimate of a student's level of academic preparation, or aptitude, upon entrance to postsecondary education.

The first follow-up testing of the NSSL sample took place in the Spring of 1993. This data collection required about 3 1/2 hours and included different forms of the CAAP modules, Pace's (1984, 1990) College Student Experiences Questionnaire (CSEQ) to measure students' first-year experiences in college, and a specially designed NSSL survey form assessing aspects of students' first-year experiences and lifetime educational plans not covered by the CSEQ. Of the original sample of 3,840 students who participated in the Fall 1992 data collection, 2,685 participated in the Spring 1993 follow-up, for a response rate of 69.9%.

A second follow-up testing of the NSSL sample took place in the spring of 1994. This data collection required about 2 1/2 hours and closely paralleled the first follow-up data collection. Students completed the writing skills and science reasoning modules of the CAAP, the CSEQ to measure students' second-year experiences in college, and a specially designed NSSL survey form assessing aspects of students' second-year experiences and lifetime educational plans not covered by the CSEQ. Of the 2,685 students who participated in the first follow-up (Spring 1993), 1,761 participated in the second follow-up (Spring 1994), for a response rate of 65.6%.

Testing the major hypothesis of the study essentially involved asking whether or not students, over time, lower their initial plans to obtain a bachelor of arts degree. Consequently, the sample employed in all our analyses was limited to those two-year and four-year college students who, upon entrance to postsecondary education (i.e., on the Fall, 1992 precollege testing), indicated that they planned to obtain at least a bachelor of arts degree in their lifetime. The sample was further limited to those students who participated in both the first and second follow-up data collections. Thus, the final sample was 1,645 students, 119 of whom attended the 5 two-year colleges and 1,526 of whom attended the 18 four-year colleges in the NSSL database.

Over the 2 years of the investigation the drop-out rates for the two-year and the four-year college samples differed. Two-year college students were more likely to drop out of the study than were four-year college students. (Indeed, the average response rates across the 2 years of the study were 69.68% for the four-year college sample and 54.25% for the two-year college sample.) However, no evidence indicated that the differential drop-out rates between institutional types led to any significantly greater bias by race, gender, or precollege ability in the two-year college sample than it did in the four-year college sample. Nevertheless, to adjust for potential response bias by gender, ethnicity, and institution, a sample weighting algorithm was developed for each year of the study.

Weighted Sample.   Specifically, within each of the 23 instituions participants in the follow-up data collection were weighted up to the institution's population by gender (male or female) and ethnicity (African American, Caucasian, Hispanic, other). (The *other* category consisted of Asian, Pacific Islander, Native American, etc.) Thus, for example, if an institution had 100 African American men in the first-year class and 25 African American men in the sample, each African American male in the sample was given a sample weight of 4.00. An analogous weight was computed for participants falling within each gender x ethnicity cell within each institution. The purpose of weighting the sample in this manner was to apply an adjustment for response bias, not only by gender and ethnicity, but also by institution. Thus, where necessary within each gender x ethnicity cell, two-year college students were given greater weight in the analyses to adjust for the higher drop-out rate in the two-year college sample. An analogous weighting algorithm was developed in the second year of the study that also adjusted for sample response bias by gender, ethnicity, and institution.

Because a sample based on only 23 institutions (even if representative of those institutional populations) could be biased with respect to the national populations of students in American two-year and four-year institutions, an additional weighting algorithm was developed. This algorithm weighted the sample up to the national populations of students entering American postsecondary institutions in Fall 1992 by gender, ethnicity (African American, Caucasian, Hispanic, other) and institutional type (two-year and four-year). The template for this weighting algorithm was *Enrollment in Higher Education: Fall 1986 Through Fall 1994* (National Center for Education Statistics, 1996).

Table 1 compares the percentage distributions by ethnicity, gender, and institutional type for the weighted samples from this study and the national populations estimated by the National Center for Education Statistics. As the Table indicates, the study sample weighted up to the 23 institutional populations tended to have somewhat lower percentages of Caucasian students and somewhat higher percentages of students of color than the national populations. On the other hand the study sample weighted up to the national populations tended to have ethnic percentages by gender and institutional type reasonably close to those of the national population.

Another indication of the representativeness of the weighted two-year samples is indicated by the distribution of students from different income levels. According to Dougherty (1994, p. 4), 10.1% of students in two-year colleges had 1991 family incomes of less than $15,000, and 11.1% came from families having 1991 incomes of over $75,000. In the two-year sample weighted up to the institutional populations 8.6% reported family incomes less than $15,000 and 12.6% reported family incomes of $75,000 or more. In the two-year sample weighted up to the national population 8.1% reported family incomes less than $15,000 and 13.6% reported incomes of $75,000 or more.

Unweighted sample.   The unweighted sample did not differ dramatically from the sample weighted up to the institutional populations. For four-year colleges the final unweighted sample was 12.2% African American, 67.8% Caucasian, 9.2% Hispanic, and 10.8% Other. For the two-year colleges the final unweighted sample was 14.5% African American, 63.3% Caucasian, 15.4% Hispanic, and 6.8% Other.

Variables

The dependent variables in the study were end-of-first-year and end-of-second-year lifetime educational plans dichotomized into two categories: bachelor of arts degree or above (coded 1) and less than a bachelor of arts degree (coded 0). The independent variable in the study was whether or not a student attended a two-year institution (coded 1) or a four-year institution (coded 0).

Guided by conceptual models for validly assessing college impact (e.g., Astin, 1993; Chickering, 1969; Tinto, 1975), we also introduced a number of salient confounding variables into our model for testing the cooling-out hypothesis. These were: initial or precollege lifetime educational plans, precollege academic ability,

TABLE 1
Percent Distributions for Weighted Sample Estimates and the National Population of Full-Time and Part-Time Students Entering Postsecondary Education in 1992

Ethnicity	Sample Weighted to Institutional Populations				Sample Weighted to National Populations				National Population[a]			
	4-Year		2-Year		4-Year		2-Year		4-Year		2-Year	
	M	W	M	W	M	W	M	W	M	W	M	W
African American	11.8	14.2	12.2	15.5	8.7	11.5	8.3	10.4	8.1	10.5	9.4	11.6
Caucasian	69.7	69.4	67.1	67.3	79.1	77.6	75.0	75.5	81.1	79.5	73.3	73.4
Hispanic	8.8	7.5	15.3	10.6	5.8	6.0	9.3	8.3	4.8	4.9	10.2	9.3
Other[b]	9.7	8.9	5.4	6.6	6.4	4.9	7.4	5.8	6.0	5.1	7.1	5.7

[a] Source: National Center for Education Statistics (1996); excluding nonresident aliens

[b] e.g., Asian American, Native American

precollege academic motivation, gender, ethnicity, age, family socioeconomic origins, cumulative credit hours taken, hours worked per week, on-campus or off-campus residence, and cumulative self-reported grades. Although its constituent items were based on existing research on academic motivation (e.g., Ball, 1977), the precollege academic motivation scale had an internal consistency reliability of only .65. We included it in the regression models, however, for two reasons: first, we felt that it was important to control for differences in students' academic motivation; and second, a reliability of .65 is acceptable for the kinds of group comparisons we were making in the study (Thorndike & Hagen, 1977). Additionally, we thought that some students entering two-year colleges who indicated that they planned to obtain at least a bachelor of arts degree might not be enrolled in academic programs that adequately prepared them to transfer to a 4-year institution. Consequently, the study also sought to control for differences in the content and emphasis of students' academic programs. This was operationalized by the cumulative number of courses taken during the first 2 years of college in five areas (social science, mathematics, technical or preprofessional, arts and humanities, and natural sciences and engineering). Place of residence and cumulative self-reported grades for the first and second year of the study were taken from the College Student Experiences Questionnaire. All other information was taken either from the NSSL pre-college survey or the NSSL first or second follow-up surveys. Operational definitions of all variables are provided in Table 2.

Analytic Procedures

The data analysis was carried out in three stages. In the first stage simple 2 x 2 cross-tabulations were computed to determine any relationship between attending a two-year versus a four-year college and the likelihood of lowering one's life-time educational plans below a bachelor of arts degree at the end of the first and second years of college. The second stage of the analyses employed logistic regression procedures to determine if any nonchance relationships between attending a two-year versus a four-year college and end of first-year and second-year educational plans persisted in the presence of controls for the 16 confounding variables specified above. In the third stage of the analyses we added a series of cross-product terms to the logistic regression model to determine if the magnitude of the impact on educational plans of attending a two-year versus a four-year college differed for students with different background (precollege) characteristics. The background or precollege characteristics considered were: gender, ethnicity, age, academic ability, family social origins, and precollege educational aspirations.

Parallel analyses were conducted with the weighted and unweighted samples with essen-

TABLE 2
Variable Definitions

Precollege Educational Plans: A single-item measure asking students to indicate the highest academic degree they intended to obtain in a lifetime. Coded: 1 = *bachelor of arts degree*, 2 = *master of arts degree*, 3 = *Ph.D., Ed.D. or advanced professional degree* (e.g., LLB or JD, MD, DDS, DVM).

Precollege Academic Ability: A composite of the reading comprehension, mathematics, and critical thinking modules of the Collegiate Assessment of Academic Proficiency (CAAP), developed by the American College Testing Program, alpha reliability = .83.

Precollege Academic Motivation: An 8-item, Likert-type scale (5 = *strongly agree* to 1 = *strongly disagree*) with an internal consistency reliability of .65. The scale items were based on existing research on academic motivation (e.g., Ball, 1977). Examples of constituent items are: "I am willing to work hard in a course to learn the material, even if it won't lead to a higher grade," "When I do well on a test it is usually because I was well prepared, not because the test was easy," "In high school I frequently did more reading in a class than was required simply because it interested me," and "In high school I frequently talked to my teachers outside of class about ideas presented during class."

Female: Coded: 1 = *female*, 0 = *male*.

Non-White: Coded: 1 = *non-White*, 0 = *White*.

Age: A continuous variable calculated by subtracting year of birth from 1992.

Family Social Origins: A combination of standardized measures of mother's and father's level of formal education and combined family income.

Total Credit Hours Completed: Cumulative number of credit hours completed through the first or through the second year of college.

Hours Worked Per Week: Combination of average number of hours of on-campus and off-campus work per week during the school year. Coded: 1 = *none* to 9 = *more than 35* (computed separately for the first and second years of college).

On-Campus Residence: 1 = *lived on campus*, 0 = *lived off campus* (computed separately for the first and second years of college).

Self-Reported Grades: Self-reported cumulative grades through the first or through the second year of college. Coded: 5 = *A* to 1 = *C, C–, or lower.*

Social Sciences Courses Taken: Cumulative number of courses taken through the first or the second year of college in anthropology, audiology/speech pathology, child and family studies, communications, economics, geography, history, political science, psychology, sociology, or social work.

Mathematics Courses Taken: Cumulative number of courses taken through the first or the second year of college in prealgebra, algebra, calculus, statistics, computer science, geometry, matrix algebra, accounting, or business math.

Technical or Preprofessional Courses Taken: Cumulative number of courses taken through the first or the second year of college in drawing, drafting, architectural design, criminology, education, agriculture, business, physical therapy, pharmacy, physical education, nursing, or computer programming.

Arts and Humanities Courses Taken: Cumulative number of courses taken through the first or the second year of college in art history, art appreciation, studio art, dance, theater, music appreciation, music performance, composition or writing, English literature, foreign language, humanities, philosophy, linguistics, classics, or religious studies.

Natural Sciences and Engineering Courses Taken: Cumulative number of courses taken through the first or through the second year of college in astronomy, botany, biology, chemistry, physics, geology, zoology, microbiology, and engineering.

Attended a Two-Year College: Coded: 1 = *attended a two-year college*, 0 = *attended a four-year college.*

Dependent Measures

End-of-First-Year or End-of-Second-Year Educational Plans: A single-item measure asking students to indicate the highest academic degree they intended to obtain in a lifetime. Recoded to: 1 = *bachelor of arts degree or above* (i.e., bachelor of arts, master of arts, doctorate, or advanced professional degree) and 0 = *less than a bachelor of arts degree* (i.e., associate degree, vocational certificate, or none).

tially the same results. The remainder of the paper, however, focuses on the results from the two weighted samples (adjusted to the actual unweighted sample size to obtain correct standard errors). Because of the relatively large unweighted sample size (N = 1,645) the critical alpha was set at 0.01 for all analyses. (Results of the unweighted analyses are summarized in a separate section.)

Results

Cross Tabulations (Sample Weighted to Institutional Populations)

With the sample weighted up to the 23 institutional populations the cross-tabulations for end-of-first-year and end-of-second-year educational plans both indicated significant relationships with two-year versus four-year college attendance. At the end of the first year of postsecondary education (Spring 1993) 11.8% of two-year college students who at entrance to college (Fall 1992) had planned to obtain at least a bachelor of arts degree reported that they now planned on obtaining less than a bachelor of arts degree in their lifetime. This compared to 5.2% of students attending a four-year institution (X^2 = 8.98 with 1 degree of freedom, $p < .01$). The same comparison at the end of the second year of postsecondary education was even more dramatic. Of the two-year college students who initially planned to obtain a bachelor of arts degree or higher 22.8% lowered their lifetime educational plans to less than a bachelor of arts degree by the end of the second year of college. This compared to 4.2% of the students attending a four-year college or university (X^2 = 66.54 with 1 degree of freedom, $p < .001$).

Thus, at the end of the first year of postsecondary education students attending a two-year college were slightly more than twice as likely as four-year college students to lower their lifetime educational plans below a bachelor of arts degree. By the end of the second year of postsecondary education two-year college students were more than five times as likely as their four-year college counterparts to plan on obtaining less than a bachelor of arts degree in their lifetime.

Cross-Tabulations (Sample Weighted to National Populations)

Cross-tabulation results with the sample weighted up to the national population were quite similar to those obtained with the sample weighted to the institutional populations. At the end of the first year of college 15.97% of the two-year college students who at entrance to college had initially planned to obtain a bachelor of arts degree reported that they now planned on obtaining less than a bachelor of arts degree in their lifetime. This compared to 4.9% of students attending four year colleges (X^2 = 25.03 with 1 degree of freedom, $p < .001$). At the end of the second year of college 21.0% of the two-year college students lowered their lifetime educational plans to less than a bachelor of arts degree. This compared to 4.3% of students in four-year institutions (X^2 = 58.84, with I degree of freedom, $p < .001$).

Logistic Regression Analyses (Sample Weighted to Institutional Populations)

Of course the relationships shown by the cross-tabulations can be substantially inflated because they do not take into account differences among the kinds of students who attend two-year and four-year institutions. The logistic regression procedures we employed permitted us to estimate the relationship between two-year versus four-year college attendance and changes in educational plans while statistically controlling for potential confounding influences. The results of the logistic regression analyses with the sample weighted to the institutional populations are summarized in Table 3. As Table 3 shows, the effect of two-year versus four-year college attendance on end-of-first-year educational plans became nonsignificant when potential confounding influences were taken into account. This did not hold, however, for the prediction of end-of-second-year educational plans. As Table 3 further indicates, two-year college students were significantly more likely than their four-year college counterparts to lower their lifetime educational plans below a bachelor of arts degree by the end of the second year of college. This association persisted even in the presence of controls for such confounding influences as precollege educational plans, academic ability, and academic motivation, gender, ethnicity, age, social origins, work responsibilities, full- or part-

TABLE 3
Logistics Regression Summaries for the Prediction of End-of-First-Year and
End-of-Second-Year Educational Plans (Sample Weighted to Institutional Populations)

Predictor	End-of-First-Year			End-of-Second-Year		
	Logistic Regression Coefficient	Standard Error of Coefficient	Coefficient divided by Std. Error	Logistic Regression Coefficient	Standard Error of Coefficient	Coefficient divided by Std. Error
Precollege educational plans	.806	.166	4.86*	0.406	.159	2.55
Precollege academic ability	.003	.064	0.05	0.132	.056	2.36
Precollege academic motivation	−.537	.234	−2.29	−0.239	.219	−1.09
Female	−.504	.223	−2.26	−0.290	.204	−1.42
Non-White	−.344	.244	−1.41	−0.255	.238	−1.07
Age	−.025	.017	−1.47	0.002	.017	0.12
Family social origins	−.018	.037	−0.49	−0.185	.052	−3.56*
Total credit hours completed	−.172	.080	−2.15	0.046	.064	0.72
Hours worked per week	−.091	.036	−2.53	−0.004	.032	−0.13
On-campus residence	−.092	.263	−0.35	0.775	.255	3.04*
Self-reported grades	.342	.102	3.35*	−0.053	.051	−1.04
Social sciences courses taken	.180	.072	2.50	0.010	.031	0.32
Mathematics courses taken	−.062	.089	−0.70	−0.084	.036	−2.33
Technical/preprofessional courses taken	.412	.128	3.22*	0.106	.041	2.59*
Arts and humanities courses taken	.078	.065	1.20	−0.025	.030	−0.83
Natural sciences and engineering courses taken	−.019	.089	−0.21	−0.084	.034	−2.47
Attended a two-year college	−.318	.265	−1.20	−1.937	.246	−7.87*
Constant	.912			−0.200		
Model df	17			17		
Model χ^2	98.03*			163.86*		

*$p < .01$.

time enrollment, place of residence, college grades, and type of coursework taken.

To estimate the magnitude of the effect of two-year (versus four-year) college attendance on the lowering of educational plans we converted the logistic regression coefficients for two-year college attendance shown in Table 3 to Delta-p, using a procedure outlined by Cabrera (1994). In the prediction of end-of-first-year educational plans the resultant Delta-p for the two-year college attendance was -.023. This means that, net of other influences in the prediction

model, two-year college students are only about 2.3% more likely than four-year college students to lower their lifetime educational plans below a bachelor of arts degree after 1 year of college. In the prediction of end-of-second-year educational plans, however, the estimated net effect of two-year college attendance was much larger, Delta-p = -.311. Net of other influences in the model, two-year college students initially planning to obtain at least a bachelor of arts degree were about 31% more likely than similar four-year college students to lower their lifetime educational plans below a bachelor of arts degree by the end of the second year of college.

Logistic Regression Analyses (Sample Weighted to National Populations)

Table 4 shows the results of the logistic regression analyses for the sample weighted up to the national populations. As the Table indicates, the results of these logistic regression analyses closely parallel those yielded when the sample was weighted up to the institutional populations (Table 3). When the influence of potential confounding influences was taken into account, the effect of two-year versus four-year college attendance on end-of-first year educational plans was nonsignificant. However, by the end of the second year of college two-year college students were significantly more likely than their four-year college counterparts to lower their lifetime educational plan below a bachelor of arts degree. Once again this significant association persisted in the presence of controls for all other variables in the prediction model (shown in Table 4).

Converting the logistic regression coefficients to Delta-p yielded -.034 for the effect of two-year college attendance in the prediction of end-of-first-year educational plans and -.198 for the effect of two-year college attendance in the prediction of end-of-second-year educational plans. Thus, net of other influences in the prediction model, two-year college students were about 3.4% more likely than four-year college students to lower their lifetime educational plans below a bachelor of arts degree after 1 year of college. After 2 years of college two-year college students were 19.8% more likely than students in four-year colleges to lower their lifetime educational plans below a bachelor of arts degree.

Conditional Effects (Sample Weighted to Institutional Populations)

None of the cross-product terms added to the logistic regression model shown in Table 3 (sample weighted up to the institutional populations) significantly improved the prediction of end-of-second-year educational plans. Thus, the negative effect of two-year college attendance on end-of-second-year educational plans appeared to be essentially similar in magnitude for students differing in precollege educational plans and academic ability, gender, ethnicity, age, and family social origins.

Basically the same results were found in the prediction of end-of-first-year educational plans, with one exception. Net of other influences, the cross product of attending a two-year (versus a four-year) college x precollege educational plans had a significant logistic regression coefficient at $p < .01$. This indicated that the modest (and nonsignificant) negative effect of two-year college attendance on end-of-first-year educational plans differed in magnitude for students with different levels of precollege educational plans. To determine the nature of this conditional effect we divided the total sample into two subsamples: (a) students who initially planned to obtain a bachelor of arts degree, and (b) students who initially planned to obtain a master of arts, doctorate, or advanced professional degree. (Recall that the sample was limited to those students who on entrance to college planned to obtain at least a bachelor of arts degree.) We then reestimated the logistic regression model predicting end-of-first-year educational plans for the two subsamples and compared the magnitude of the regression coefficients for attendance at a two-year (versus a four-year) college.

For students who initially planned to obtain a graduate or advanced professional degree two-year college attendance actually had a small and positive, but not statistically significant, effect on end-of-first-year educational plans (logistic regression coefficient =.653, $p > .20$). However, for students who initially planned to obtain only a bachelor of arts degree, two-year college attendance had a substantial, and statistically significant negative effect on end-of-first-year educational plans (logistic regression coefficient = -2.38, $p < .01$). Thus, the higher one's precollege educational plans the less likely was two-year college attendance to lead to a lowering of educational plans after 1 year of postsecondary education. Conversely, for students with relatively low levels of precollege educational plans (i.e., only a bachelor of arts degree), attendance at a two-year college produced a significant negative influence on end-of-first-year educational plans.

Conditional Effects (Sample Weighted to National Populations)

When the sample was weighted up to the national populations the conditional effects findings closely paralleled those found when the sample was weighted up to the institutional populations. None of the cross-product terms added

TABLE 4
Logistics Regression Summaries for the Prediction of End-of-First-Year and
End-of-Second-Year Educational Plans (Sample Weighted to Institutional Populations)

Predictor	End-of-First-Year			End-of-Second-Year		
	Logistic Regression Coefficient	Standard Error of Coefficient	Coefficient divided by Std. Error	Logistic Regression Coefficient	Standard Error of Coefficient	Coefficient divided by Std. Error
Precollege educational plans	.817	.158	5.17*	0.180	.149	1.21
Precollege academic ability	.039	.053	0.73	0.216	.051	4.23*
Precollege academic motivation	−.739	.221	−3.35*	−0.119	.198	−0.60
Female	−.529	.214	−2.47	−0.089	.193	−0.46
Non-White	.035	.269	0.13	0.158	.259	0.61
Age	−.017	.017	−1.03	−0.007	.016	−0.45
Family social origins	−.040	.054	−0.74	−0.153	.074	−2.07
Total credit hours completed	−.278	.405	−2.47	0.026	.059	0.44
Hours worked per week	−.084	.024	−3.61*	−0.016	.031	−0.52
On-campus residence	.137	.249	0.55	0.351	.211	1.66
Self-reported grades	.276	.096	2.86*	−0.053	.051	−1.03
Social sciences courses taken	.240	.063	3.82*	0.062	.027	2.27
Mathematics courses taken	−.114	.074	−1.54	−0.101	.031	−3.29*
Technical/preprofessional courses taken	.552	.111	4.98*	−0.034	.027	−1.24
Arts and humanities courses taken	.106	.061	1.75	0.070	.034	2.05
Natural sciences and engineering courses taken	−.091	.069	−1.32	−0.078	.032	−2.47
Attended a two-year college	−.463	.262	−1.77	−1.144	.251	−4.56*
Constant	1.196			1.275		
Model df	17			17		
Model χ^2	201.24*			202.50*		

*$p < .01$.

to the logistic regression mode) shown in Table 4 significantly improved the prediction of lifetime educational plans at the end of the second year of college. However, in the prediction of lifetime educational plans at the end of the first year of college the same cross product (attending a two-year versus a four-year college x precollege educational plans) was significant at $p < .01$. For students who initially planned to obtain a graduate or advanced professional degree the effect of attending a two-year college on end-of-first-year educational plans was small and non-

significant (logistic regression coefficient = -.333, $p > .40$). However, for students who initially planned to obtain only a bachelor of arts degree two-year college attendance had a substantial, and statistically significant negative effect on end-of-first-year educational plans (logistic regression coefficient = -2.060, $p < .01$).

Results of Unweighted Sample Analyses

Results of cross-tabulations with the unweighted sample were quite similar to those obtained with the weighted samples. At the end of the first year of college 15.9% of the two-year college students and 5.5% of the four-year college students lowered their lifetime educational plans below a bachelor of arts degree (X^2 = 20.97, 1 degree of freedom, $p < .001$). At the end of the second year of college 20.2% of the two-year college students and 4.26% of the four-year students lowered their lifetime educational plans below a bachelor of arts degree (X^2 = 54.61, 1 degree of freedom, $p < .002$).

The logistic regression results for the unweighted sample were also quite similar to those obtained with the weighted samples. In the prediction of lifetime educational plans at the end of the first year of college the logistic regression coefficient for two-year college attendance was -.673, $t = -1.97$, $p > .01$. In the prediction of educational plans at the end of the second year of college the logistic regression coefficient for two-year college attendance was -1.473, $t = -4.45$, $p < .01$. The Delta-p estimates were -.054 and -.253 for the impact of two-year college attendance on end-of-first-year and end-of-second-year educational plans, respectively.

Finally, the results of the conditional effects analyses with the unweighted sample closely paralleled those using the weighted samples. No significant conditional effects were found in the prediction of lifetime educational plans at the end of the second year of college. However, the two-year/four-year x precollege educational plans cross-product was significant in the prediction of lifetime educational plans after the first year of college. For students who initially planned to obtain a graduate or advanced professional degree the effect of attending a two-year versus a four-year college was small and nonsignificant (coefficient = .237, $p > .30$). However, for students initially planning to obtain only a bachelor of arts degree the effect of two-year college attendance on end-of-first-year educational plans was negative and statistically significant (coefficient = -2.261, $p < .01$).

Conclusions

This study sought to test Clark's (1960, 1980) hypothesis that two-year college attendance actually contributes to lower levels of educational attainment by cooling out or lowering students' lifetime plans to obtain a bachelor of arts degree. We found at least some correlational, if not causal, support for the cooling-out hypoth-

esis after 2 years of postsecondary education. Our estimates based on two different weightings of the study sample suggest that two-year college students who initially planned to obtain a bachelor of arts degree in their lifetime were between 20% and 31% more likely than similar four-year college students to lower their lifetime educational plans below a bachelor of arts degree by the end of the second year of college. This association persisted in the presence of controls for precollege educational plans, academic ability and academic motivation, gender, ethnicity, age, family social origins, credit hours taken, work responsibilities, grades, and the kinds of courses taken. The corresponding association during the first year of college was in the same direction, though much smaller in magnitude and not statistically significant. Overall the negative association of two-year college attendance with educational plans tended to be general rather than conditional. That is, it had essentially the same magnitude for students with different precollege characteristics. The only exception to this was in the prediction of end-of-first-year educational plans, where the association with two-year college attendance depended on level of precollege educational plans. For students who initially planned to obtain a master of arts, doctorate, or advanced professional degree, attending a community college did not have a significant negative association with end-of-first year educational plans. However, community college attendance did have a significant negative association with end-of-first-year educational plans for those students who initially planned to obtain to only a bachelor of arts degree in their lifetime. Although the interpretative burden was placed on estimates obtained from samples weighted up to the institutional populations and the national populations, essentially the same estimates of two-year college effects were obtained with parallel analyses of the unweighted sample.

Much of the criticism of two-year, community colleges probably has its basis in fact that students who attend them are significantly less likely to complete a bachelor of arts degree than are similar students at four-year colleges and universities. The results of this investigation suggest that the lower likelihood of degree completion may not be solely a function of the structural obstacles placed in the path of community college students as they seek to transfer to a four-year institution (i.e., securing acceptance, obtaining financial aid, transferring credits). Rather, our findings suggest at least the possibility that attendance at a community college may actually contribute to a lowering of precollege plans to complete a bachelor of arts degree. Of course there is a need for caution in making strict causal inferences from the findings of the study. First, the findings were based on correlational data, and second, the data do not allow us to identify the specific environmental factors in two-year colleges that might cause students to lower their initial educational plans.

In his trenchant analysis of the societal role of the two-year institution Dougherty (1994) employs the term *contradictory college*. Considered within the context of the body of research on the impact of two-year versus four-year institutions our findings would tend to support his description. On the one hand students initially aspiring to a bachelor of arts degree are less likely to obtain it if they start at a community college, in part, perhaps, because community college attendance is linked to a lowering of educational plans. On the other hand recent evidence (reviewed earlier in this paper) indicates that the cognitive or intellectual impact of community colleges may be the equal of many four-year institutions. This suggests that any cooling out of educational plans by community colleges may not be related to the quality of the teaching received or the rigor of the academic programs at those institutions. Rather, researchers may have to look to other aspects of the social-psychological environment of community colleges to understand how they may function to change students' educational plans; clearly this is an important direction for additional research.

Of course, a very real competing explanation for our results that must be taken quite seriously is that a substantial number of students who initially enter two-year colleges for the ostensible purpose of obtaining a bachelor of arts degree have unclear or undeveloped educational plans to begin with. Manski (1989) and Grubb (1996) have both suggested that many students in community colleges are *experimenters* who may indicate that they want a bachelor of arts degree but are actually somewhat unsure of what they want to do, and they have no way of finding out except by experimenting with postsecondary education in low-cost institutions. For these students community college attendance may function not so much to cool out genuinely held

aspirations or plans, but rather to assist them in clarifying aspirations or plans that may be undeveloped, unclear, or perhaps even unrealistic. Those who decide that a bachelor of arts degree is not for them may look as though they have been cooled out by the community college. However, from another perspective "they could be considered successes in the sense that they have gotten the information necessary to make informed decisions" (Grubb, 1996, p. 62). Unfortunately, the cooling-out hypothesis as tested by this investigation cannot make a definitive distinction between such alternative explanations for the findings.

Policy Implications

The findings of the current study underscore the need for community colleges to provide sufficient support or mentoring to students who enroll primarily to complete their first 2 years of postsecondary education and then transfer to a four-year institution to finish their bachelor of arts degree. Simply providing offices and services, such as a transfer center, may not be sufficient to encourage students to make effective use of them. The disproportionately large numbers of minority and first-generation college students enrolling in community colleges may warrant a more proactive system of student affairs programs and support services that actively encourages their aspirations and plans. For example, evidence reported by Nora and Cabrera (Cabrera & Nora, 1992, 1993; Nora, 1987; Nora & Cabrera, 1994, 1996) indicates that active support and encouragement by significant others, including faculty and professional staff, are particularly crucial to the persistence of minority and nonminority students in two-year and commuter institutions. Similarly, Rendon (1994) found that active validation of non-traditional student worth and competence in the classroom has an important impact, not only on how those students come to perceive themselves socially and academically, but also on their subsequent aspirations and plans.

Second, from a more general environmental perspective, community college administrators and student affairs professionals may have to focus particular effort on eliminating the aura of second class status often attached to community colleges and their students in American society (e.g., Brint & Karabel, 1989; Dougherty, 1994; Zwerling, 1976). This second-class or second-best mind-set may never quite be overcome, either by the students who enroll, or by the professional counseling staff who work at community colleges. Clearly, it is important to help ease students' transition from secondary to post-secondary education, and to assist them in developing a realistic view of their academic skills and resources in relationship to what will be required to complete a bachelor of arts degree. At the same time, however, community college advisors and counselors must take care not to turn the cooling-out hypothesis into a self-fulfilling prophecy through behaviors and attitudes that needlessly undermine a student's confidence and discourage him or her from pursuing educational goals that are potentially achievable.

Limitations

This investigation has several major limitations that should be kept in mind when interpreting the findings. First, although the sample consisted of a broad range of institutions from around the country, the fact that the analyses were limited to 18 four-year and only 5 two-year institutions means that we cannot necessarily generalize the results to all two-year and four-year institutions. Similarly the sample from the two-year institutions consisted of only 119 students followed over a 2-year period. This is a rather slender thread on which to hang definitive test of the cooling-out hypothesis. For this reason the findings of this study should be regarded as constituting only a preliminary test of the cooling-out hypothesis.

Second, although attempts were made in the initial sampling design, and subsequent sample weighting to make the sample as representative as possible at each institution, the time commitment and work required of each student participant undoubtedly led to some self-selection. We cannot be sure that those who were willing to participate in the study responded in the same way as would those who were invited but declined to participate in the study. Weighed against this, however, is the fact that we found no significant conditional effects involving such factors as precollege academic ability, age, gender, ethnicity, or family social origins. Thus, even if the sample had some bias on these factors, it did not appear to have an appreciable influence on the study findings.

Third, we could not track individuals who left their institution during the study. Conse-quently, some students in the two-year college sample who dropped out of the study may have actually transferred to a four-year college to pursue their bachelor of arts degree. Although this is clearly a possibility, at least some evidence suggests that students who dropped out of the study had characteristics that made them less likely to have been successful transfer students than those who remained in the study for years. Compared to those two-year college students who persisted in the study for two years those who dropped out of the study tended to have lower average precollege educational plans, lower average precollege academic ability, lower average self-reported grades during college, and were enrolled for a lower average number of credit hours.

Correspondence concerning this article should be addressed to Ernest T. Pascarella, Planning, Policy, and Leadership Studies, 491 Lindquist Center North, University of Iowa, Iowa City, IA 52242.

References

Alba, R., & Lavin, D. (1981). Community colleges and tracking in higher education. *Sociology of Education, 54,* 223–237.

American College Testing Program. (1991). *CAAP technical handbook.* Iowa City, IA: Author.

Anderson, K. (1984). *Institutional differences in college effects.* Unpublished paper, Florida International University, Miami, FL.

Astin, A. (1993). *What matters in college: Four critical years revisited.* San Francisco: Jossey-Bass.

Ball, S. (Ed.). (1977). *Motivation in education.* New York: Academic Press.

Bohr, L., Pascarella, E., Nora, A., Zusman, B., Jacobs, M., Desler, M., & Bulakowski, C. (1994). Cognitive effects of two-year and four-year colleges: A preliminary study. *Community College Review, 22,* 4–11.

Brint, S., & Karabel, J. (1989). *The diverted dream: Community colleges and the promise of educational opportunity in America, 1900–1985.* New York: Oxford University Press.

Cabrera, A. (1994). Logistic regression in higher education: An applied perspective. In J. Smart (Ed.), *Higher education: Handbook of theory and research.* (Vol. 10, pp. 225–256). New York: Agathon.

Cabrera, A., & Nora, A. (1992). The role of finances in the student persistence process: A structural model. *Research in Higher Education, 33,* 571–594.

Cabrera, A., & Nora, A. (1993). College persistence: The testing of an integrated model. *Journal of Higher Education, 64,* 123–139.

Chickering, A. (1969). *Education and identity.* San Francisco: Jossey-Bass.

Clark, B. (1960). The "cooling-out" function in higher education. *American Journal of Sociology, 65,* 569–576.

Clark, B. (1980). The "cooling-out" function revisited. In G. Vaughan (Ed.), *Questioning the community college role.* (New Directions in Community Colleges No. 32, pp. 15–31). San Francisco: Jossey-Bass.

Dougherty, K. (1987). The effects of community colleges: Aid or hindrance to socioeconomic attainment? *Sociology of Education, 60,* 86–103.

Dougherty, K. (1992). Community colleges and baccalaureate attainment. *Journal of Higher Education, 63,* 188–214.

Dougherty, K. (1994). *The contradictory college.* Albany: SUNY Press.

Grubb, N. (1984). The bandwagon once more: Vocational preparation for high-tech occupations. *Harvard Educational Review, 54,* 429–451.

Grubb, N. (1991). The decline of community college transfer rates: Evidence from national longitudinal surveys. *Journal of Higher Education, 62,* 184–217.

Grubb, N. (1996). *Working in the middle: Strengthening education and training for the mid-skilled labor force.* San Francisco: Jossey-Bass.

Hunt, T., Klieforth, A., & Atwell, C. (1977). Community colleges: A democratizing influence? *Community College Review, 4,* 15–24.

Karabel, J. (1972). Community colleges and social stratification. *Harvard Educational Review, 43,* 521–559.

Karabel, J. (1974). Protecting the portals: Class and the community college. *Social Policy, 5,* 12–18.

Karabel, J. (1986). Community colleges and social stratification in the 1980s. In L. Zwerling (Ed.), *The community college and its critics* (pp. 13–30). San Francisco: Jossey-Bass.

Kinnick, M., & Kempner, K. (1988). Beyond "front door" access: Attaining the bachelor's degree. *Research in Higher Education, 29,* 299–318.

Kintzer, F., & Wattenbarger, J. (1985). *The articulation/transfer phenomenon.* Washington, DC: American Association of Community and Junior Colleges.

Knox, W., Lindsay, P., & Kolb, M. (1993). *Does college make a difference?* Westport, CT: Greenwood.

Lavin, D., & Crook, D. (1990). Open admissions and its outcomes: Ethnic differences in long-term educational attainment. *American Journal of Education, 98,* 389–425.

Manski, C. (1989). Schooling as experimentation: A reappraisal of the college dropout phenomenon. *Economics of Education Review, 8,* 305–312.

National Center for Education Statistics. (1996, May). *Enrollment in higher education: Fall 1986 through fall 1994.* Washington, DC: U.S. Department of Education.

Nora, A. (1987). Determinants of retention among Chicano college students: A structural model. *Research in Higher Education, 26,* 31–51.

Nora, A. (1993). Two-year colleges and minority students' educational plans: Help or hindrance. In J. Smart (Ed.), *Higher education: Handbook of theory and research* (Vol. 9, pp. 212–247). New York, NY: Agathon.

Nora, A., & Cabrera, A. (1996). The role of perceptions of prejudice and discrimination in the adjustment of minority students to college. *Journal of Higher Education, 67,* 119–148.

Nora, A., & Cabrera, A. (1994, November). *The role of significant others in the adjustment and persistence of minorities and non-minorities in higher education.* Paper presented at the annual meeting of the Association for the Study of Higher Education, Tucson, AZ.

Nora, A., & Rendon, L. (1990). Determinants of predisposition to transfer among community college students: A structural model. *Research in Higher Education, 31,* 235–255.

Nunley, C., & Breneman, D. (1988). Defining and measuring quality in community college education. In J. Eaton (Ed.), *Colleges of choice: The enabling impact of the community college* (pp. 62–92). New York: American Council on Education.

Pace, C. (1984). *Measuring the quality of college student experiences.* Los Angeles: University of California, Higher Education Research Institute.

Pace, C. (1987). *Good things go together.* Los Angeles: University of California, Center for the Study of Evaluation.

Pace, C. (1990). *The undergraduates: A report of their activities and progress in college in the 1980s.* Los Angeles: University of California, Graduate School of Education, Center for the Study of Evaluation.

Pascarella, E., Bohr, L., Nora, A., & Terenzini, P. (1995). Cognitive effects of two-year and four-year colleges: Some new evidence. *Educational Evaluation and Policy Analysis, 17,* 83–96.

Pascarella, E., Edison, M., Nora, A., Hagedorn, L., & Terenzini, P. (1995–96). Cognitive effects of community colleges and four-year colleges. *Community College Journal, 66,* 35–39.

Pascarella, E., & Terenzini, P. (1991). *How college affects students: Findings and insights from twenty years of research.* San Francisco: Jossey-Bass.

Rendón, L. (1994). Validating culturally diverse students: Toward a new model of learning and student development. *Innovative Higher Education, 19*(1), 33–51.

Smart, J., & Ethington, C. (1985). Early career outcomes of baccalaureate recipients: A study of native four-year and transfer two-year college students. *Research in Higher Education, 22,* 185–193.

Terenzini, P., Springer, L., Yaeger, P., Pascarella, E., & Nora, A. (1994, November). *The multiple influences of college on students' critical thinking skills.* Paper presented at the annual meeting of the Association for the Study of Higher Education, Tucson, AZ.

Thorndike, R., & Hagen, E. (1977). *Measurement and evaluation in psychology and education.* New York: John Wiley & Sons.

Tinto, V. (1975). Dropout from higher education: A theoretical synthesis of recent research. *Review of Educational Research, 45,* 89–125.

Velez, W. (1985). Finishing college: The effects of college type. *Sociology of Education, 58,* 191–200.

Whitaker, D., & Pascarella, E. (1994). Two-year college attendance and socioeconomic attainment: Some additional evidence. *Journal of Higher Education, 65,* 194–210.

Zwerling, L. (1976). *Second best: The crisis of the community college.* New York: McGraw-Hill.

Ernest T. Pascarella is the Mary Louise Petersen Professor of Higher Education at the University of Iowa. Marcia Edison is a Postdoctoral Research Fellow in Medical Education at the University of Illinois at Chicago. Amaury Nora is Professor of Higher Education at the University of Houston. Linda Serra Hagedorn is Assistant Professor of Higher Education at the University of Southern California. Patrick T. Terenzini is Professor and Senior Scientist in the Center for the Study of Higher Education at Pennsylvania State University.

This study was conducted as part of the National Study of Student Learning (NSSL) at the University of Illinois at Chicago. NSSL is supported by Grant No. R117G10037 from the U.S. Department of Education to the National Center on Postsecondary Teaching, Learning, and Assessment.

CHAPTER 40

COGNITIVE EFFECTS OF 2-YEAR AND 4-YEAR COLLEGES: NEW EVIDENCE

ERNEST PASCARELLA
LOUISE BOHR
AMAURY NORA
UNIVERSITY OF ILLINOIS AT CHICAGO
PATRICK TERENZINI
PENNSYLVANIA STATE UNIVERSITY

This study investigated the freshman-year cognitive impacts of five 2-year and six 4-year colleges drawn from all sections of the United States. Controlling for individual precollege ability, there was a general parity between 2-year and 4-year college students on end-of-freshman year reading comprehension, mathematics, critical thinking, and composite achievement. This general parity, however, masked conditional effects based on gender and ethnicity. Men benefited cognitively more from 2-year colleges, whereas women realized greater cognitive returns from 4-year colleges. Non-White students benefited more from a 2-year college, whereas the reverse was true for their White counterparts.

Since its inception, the 2-year community college has developed into one of the major institutional configurations in the American postsecondary educational system. There can be little doubt that, in an absolute sense, the existence of 2-year institutions has substantially increased both the access to higher education as well as the social mobility of numerous individuals whose education would otherwise have ended with high school (Cohen & Brawer, 1982, 1989; Nunley & Breneman, 1988). However, a major critique of the 2-year college posits that, although it may largely guarantee equality of opportunity for access to higher education, it has not, in relationship to 4-year colleges and universities, provided equal opportunity in terms of the outcomes or benefits of higher education (Astin, 1977; Brint & Karabel, 1989; Grubb, 1984; Karabel, 1986; Zwerling, 1976).

A modest, but growing, body of research has sought to answer the question of the relative impacts of initial attendance at a 2-year versus a 4-year college or university. The preponderance of this inquiry has focused on the relative socioeconomic payoffs linked to initial enrollment in these different types of postsecondary institutions. The findings of this research with respect to educational attainment are reasonably clear. With controls made for important individual background differences, students who initially enroll in 2-year colleges seeking a bachelor's degree are about 15% less likely to complete that degree in the same period of time as similar students who begin postsecondary education in 4-year institutions (e.g., Alba & Lavin, 1981; Astin, 1977; Crook & Lavin, 1989; Dougherty, 1987, 1992; Hilton & Schrader, 1986; Temple & Polk, 1986; Velez, 1985). The findings are more ambiguous with respect to actual labor-market outcomes. Although exceptions exist (e.g., Monk-Turner, 1988), the weight of evidence would suggest that, when individuals of equal educational attainment and background characteristics are compared, there is a general parity between those initially enrolling in 2-year and 4-year colleges in such areas as occupational status, earnings, job stability, unemployment rate, or job satisfaction (e.g., Anderson, 1984; Breneman & Nelson, 1981; Smart & Ethington, 1985; Whitaker & Pascarella, 1994).

Although we have learned much from the inquiry on socioeconomic outcomes conducted over the past decade, little research has directly addressed the relative intellectual or cognitive effects of attendance at 2-year versus 4-year colleges. It has been argued that we might expect 2-year institutions to have a less powerful impact on the cognitive growth of students because such institutions admit students with lower levels of academic preparation and motivation than those admitted to 4-year colleges. This can lead to the development of a normative peer culture that offers little support for intellectual or academic effort, paired with a faculty that has lower expectations and places less rigorous demands on student academic performance (e.g., Dougherty, 1987; London, 1978; Neuman & Reisman, 1980). Consistent with this argument there is at least modest evidence that 2-year college students find it difficult to perform as well academically after transferring to 4-year colleges and universities (Cohen & Brawer, 1982; Kintzer & Wattenbarger, 1985). Although it is tempting to conclude that this reflects the less rigorous academic preparation in 2-year colleges, such a finding could also simply reflect the normal problems inherent in becoming socially and academically integrated in a new institutional setting (Pascarella & Terenzini, 1991).

Research focusing directly on the relative cognitive effects of attendance at 2-year and 4-year colleges is almost nonexistent. The evidence that does exist, however, does not support the argument that students are less challenged intellectually at 2-year institutions than they are at 4-year colleges and universities. Bohr et al. (1994) compared 35 students from a 2-year college located near a large urban area and 169 students from a nearby research university on first-year gains in standardized measures of reading comprehension, mathematics, and critical thinking. Statistically controlling for precollege cognitive skills, age, work responsibilities, and full- or part-time enrollment, 2-year college students made first-year gains on all three cognitive measures that were equal in magnitude to those made by students at the 4-year institution. We know of no other work, however, that addresses this issue (see, for example, Astin, 1993; Pascarella & Terenzini, 1991).

Clearly, it is risky to draw conclusions from a body of evidence consisting essentially of a single study, Bohr et al. (1994), that is based on a small sample from only two institutions. The small sample ($N = 204$), with attendant limited statistical power, means that the study ran at least some risk of a type II error (i.e., failing to identify statistically significant 2-year/4-year cognitive differences when they actually existed). More serious, perhaps, is the fact that the sample was drawn from only one 2-year and one 4-year institution, both located in the same metropolitan area. Thus, the evidence may also be quite limited in terms of generalizability. One might anticipate that the populations of 2-year and 4-year institutions would not be completely homogeneous in their educational impacts (e.g., Astin, 1993; Chickering & Reisser, 1993; Kuh, 1993). Consequently, it may be imprudent to assume that a single 2-year and a single 4-year institution adequately represent those respective populations.

The present study sought to contribute to a better understanding of the relative cognitive impacts of 2- and 4-year colleges by means of an investigation that was both longitudinal and multi-institutional. Specifically, the study had two purposes. First, employing a matched sample of five 2-year and six 4-year colleges from nearly all geographical regions of the country, the study sought to estimate the net impact of attending a 2-year versus a 4-year college on students' freshman-year development in reading comprehension, mathematics, critical thinking, and composite achievement. In doing so it employed instruments specifically designed to assess cognitive and intellectual skills acquired during the first 2 years of college. Second, the study attempted to determine the extent to which the cognitive effects of attending a 2-year versus a 4-year college differ in magnitude for students with different backgrounds and other precollege characteristics.

Method

Institutional Sample

The sample was selected from incoming freshman students at eighteen 4-year and five 2-year colleges and universities located in 16 different states throughout the country. Institutions were selected from the National Center on Education Statistics Integrated Postsecondary Education Data System (IPEDS) database to represent differences in colleges and universities nationwide on a variety of characteristics including institutional type and control (e.g., private and public research universities, private liberal arts colleges, public and private comprehensive universities, 2-year colleges, historically Black colleges), size, location, commuter versus residential character, and the ethnic distribution of the undergraduate student body. In aggregate, the student population of those 23 schools approximated the national population of undergraduates by ethnicity and gender.

Student Sample and Instruments

The individuals in the overall sample were 2,685 freshman-year students who participated in the National Study of Student Learning (NSSL), a large longitudinal investigation of the factors that influence learning and cognitive development in college. The research was sponsored by the federally funded National Center on Postsecondary Teaching, Learning, and Assessment. The initial sample was selected randomly from the incoming freshman class at each participating institution. Because voluntary cooperation was required from each randomly selected participant, however, the sample could not be judged as random in the strictest sense. The students in the sample were informed that they would be participating in a national longitudinal study of student learning and that they would receive a stipend for their participation. They were also informed that the information they provided would be kept confidential and would never become part of their institutional record.

An initial data collection that lasted approximately 3 hours was conducted in the fall of 1992. Students were paid a stipend of $25 by the National Center on Postsecondary Teaching, Learning, and Assessment. Students were reminded that the information they provided would be kept in the strictest confidence and that all that was expected of them was that they give an honest effort on tests and a candid response to all questionnaire items. The data collected included a precollege survey that gathered information on student demographic characteristics and background, as well as aspirations, expectations of college, and a series of items assessing their orientations toward learning. Participants also completed Form 88A of the Collegiate Assessment of Academic Proficiency (CAAP). The CAAP was developed by the American College Testing Program (ACT) specifically to assess selected general skills typically acquired by students during the first 2 years of college (ACT, 1989). The total CAAP consists of five 40-minute, multiple-choice test modules, three of which—reading comprehension, mathematics, and critical thinking—were administered during the first data collection.

The CAAP reading comprehension test is comprised of 36 items that assess reading comprehension as a product of skill in inferring, reasoning, and generalizing. The test consists of four prose passages of about 900 words in length that are designed to be representative of the level and kinds of writing commonly encountered in college curricula. The passages were drawn from topics in fiction, the humanities, the social sciences, and the natural sciences. The KR-20 internal consistency reliabilities for the reading comprehension test range between .84 and .86. The mathematics test consists of 35 items designed to measure a student's ability to solve mathematical problems encountered in many postsecondary curricula. The emphasis is on quantitative reasoning rather than formula memorization. The content areas tested include pre-, elementary, intermediate, and advanced algebra, coordinate geometry, trigonometry, and introductory calculus. The KR-20 reliability coefficients for the mathematics test ranged between .79 and .81. The critical thinking test is a 32-item instrument that measures the ability to clarify, analyze, evaluate, and extend arguments. The test consists of four passages that are designed to be representative of the kinds of issues commonly encountered in a postsecondary curriculum. A passage typically presents a series of subarguments that support a more general conclusion. Each passage presents one or more arguments and uses a variety of formats, including case studies, debates, dialogues, overlapping positions, statistical arguments, experimental results, or editorials. Each passage is accompanied by a set of multiple-choice items. The KR-20 reliability coefficients for the critical thinking test ranged from .81 to .82 (ACT, 1989). In pilot testing various instruments for use in the National Study of Student Learning on a sample of 30 college students the critical thinking test of the CAAP was found to correlate .75 with the total score on the Watson-Glaser Critical Thinking Appraisal.

Each of the 23 institutions was given a target sample size relative in magnitude to the respective sizes of the freshman class at each institution. The overall target sample for the fall 1992 data collection at the 23 institutions was 5,000. The overall obtained sample size, (i.e., those students actually tested) for the fall 1992 data collection was 3,840, a participation rate of 76.8%.

A follow-up testing of the sample took place in the spring of 1993. This data collection required about 3½ hours and included an extensive set of measures of students' freshman-year experience and Form 88B of the CAAP reading comprehension, mathematics, and critical thinking modules. Students were paid a second stipend of $35 by the National Center on Postsecondary Teaching, Learning, and Assessment for their participation in the follow-up data collection. Of the original sample of 3,840 students who participated in the fall 1992 testing, 2,685 participated in the spring 1993 data collection, for a follow-up response rate of 69.92%.

Given the high response rates at both testings it is not particularly surprising that the sample was reasonably representative of the population from which it was drawn. However, to adjust for potential response bias by gender, ethnicity, and institution, a sample weighting algorithm was developed. Specifically, within each individual institution participants in the follow-up data collection were weighted up to the institution's freshman population by gender (male or female) and ethnicity (White, Black, Hispanic, other). Thus, for example, if an institution had 100 Black men in its freshman class and 25 Black men in the sample, each Black male in the sample was given a sample weight of 4.00. An analogous weight was computed for participants falling within each Gender × Ethnicity cell within each institution. The effect of applying sample weights in this manner was to adjust not only for response bias by gender and ethnicity, but also for response bias (i.e., differential response rates) by institution.

Final Matched Sample

Because of the broad diversity of institutions in the overall sample, comparing 2-year colleges with all 4-year colleges seemed unrealistic. For example, the 4-year college sample contained a private university and a private liberal arts college that were among the most academically selective in the country, and enrolled almost totally residential, full time, and predominantly White student bodies. Similarly, the 4-year college sample also contained two historically Black colleges that enrolled almost no non-Black students. Consequently, rather than using a comparison group of all eighteen 4-year institutions we selected a matched group of six 4-year institutions whose incoming student bodies reasonably resembled those of the five 2-year colleges in academic preparation. The matching was based on a composite scale consisting of the three fall 1992 precollege scores on the CAAP reading comprehension, mathematics, and critical thinking tests. The 4-year colleges selected were those in the sample that were closest to falling within the range of average student precollege academic preparation of the 2-year colleges. The five 2-year colleges were located in five different states throughout the country (New England, the Carolinas, the Midwest, the Mountain States, and the Pacific Coast). Similarly, the six matching 4-year colleges were also distributed throughout the same parts of the country in six different states. The 4-year sample contained a liberal arts college, urban commuter institutions, comprehensive universities, and a research university. The final sample on which all analyses were conducted consisted of 811 students, 280 attending the five 2-year colleges and 531 attending the six 4-year institutions.

Design and Data Analysis

The study design was a pretest-posttest quasi-experimental design, in which comparison groups were statistically equated on salient precollege (fall 1992) and other variables. The comparison groups were students attending the five 2-year colleges and students attending the matched sample of six 4-year colleges and universities. The dependent variables were spring 1993 scores on the CAAP reading comprehension, mathematics, and critical thinking tests, in addition to a measure of freshman year composite achievement that combined all three tests.

The composite achievement measure was constructed in two steps. First, each of the three CAAP tests (i.e., reading, math, and critical thinking) was standardized to put each on the same metric. Subsequently, the composite achievement score was computed by summing across standardized scores and assigning an arbitrary scale mean of 0 and standard deviation of 1 for the entire followup sample ($N = 2,685$). The alpha, internal consistency, reliability for the composite achievement measure was .83.

To statistically control for precollege and other salient differences between students attending 2-year and 4-year institutions, we used least-squares analysis of covariance as the basic analytic approach. Individuals were the unit of analysis. Guided by the existing body of evidence on the factors independently influencing learning and cognitive development during college (e.g., Astin, 1968, 1977, 1993; Astin & Panos, 1969; Kuh, 1993; Pascarella & Terenzini, 1991), we used the following individual level covariates in the study:

1. Individual fall 1992 (precollege) CAAP reading comprehension, mathematics, critical thinking, and composite achievement scores [each employed in analysis of the appropriate end-of-freshman year (spring, 1993) CAAP reading comprehension, mathematics, critical thinking, and composite achievement score]

2. Sex

3. Ethnicity: White or non-White

4. Family social origin: the combination of standardized measures of mother's and father's level of formal education and combined family income

5. Fall 1992 (precollege) academic motivation: an eight-item, Likert-type scale (4 = strongly agree to 1 = strongly disagree) with an internal consistency reliability of .65. The scale items were developed specifically for the NSSL, and were based on existing research on academic motivation (e.g., Ball, 1977). Examples of constituent items are: "I am willing to work hard in a course to learn the material, even if it won't lead to a higher grade," "When I do well on a test it is usually because I was well prepared, not because the test was easy," "In high school I frequently did more reading in a class than was required simply because it interested me," and "In high school I frequently talked to my teachers outside of class about ideas presented during class."

6. Age: age in years in fall 1992

7. Credit hours taken: total number of credit hours for which the student was enrolled during the freshman year

8. Work responsibilities: average number of hours worked, on- or off-campus, during the freshman year

9. On- or off-campus residence: a dichotomous variable indicating whether the student resided on-campus or lived off-campus and commuted to college during the freshman year.

Because the existing body of evidence suggests that institutional context can often shape the impact of college in indirect, if not direct, ways, we also included one institutional-level variable as a covariate in the analytic model. This was:

10. The level of academic aptitude of the freshman class: estimated by the average fall 1992 CAAP reading, mathematics, critical thinking, or composite achievement score for the freshman class at each of the 11 institutions. Each student in the sample was given the mean of his or her institution on all three CAAP tests plus the composite, and each of the institutional mean scores was employed in analysis of the appropriate end-of-freshman-year (spring, 1993) individual-level reading comprehension, mathematics, critical thinking, or composite achievement score.

The analysis of covariance for each of the four dependent measures employed a least-squares regression solution, and was conducted in a hierarchical manner. The influence of attending a 2-year versus a 4-year institution was estimated while controlling for the effects of all 10 covariates. The results of this analysis provided estimates of the effects of 2- versus 4-year college attendance on end-of-freshman-year reading comprehension, mathematics, critical thinking, and composite achievement, net of the influence of the covariates. Because precollege (fall, 1992) reading, mathematics, critical thinking, and their composite were included among the covariates, a significant effect attributable to attending a 2-year versus a 4-year college permits one to conclude that there are significant net differences between students attending 2- and 4-year colleges, not only in end-of-freshman-year reading comprehension, mathematics, critical thinking, and composite achievement but also in the gains made on those cognitive dimensions during the freshman year (Linn, 1986; Linn & Slinde, 1977; Pascarella & Terenzini, 1991).

In the second stage of the analyses we tested for the presence of Covariate × 2- versus 4-year college conditional effects, one of the assumptions of the analysis of covariance model (Elashoff, 1969; Kerlinger & Pedhazur, 1973). A series of cross-product terms was computed between 2- versus 4-year college attendance and each of the 10 covariates. These were then added to the regression model containing the covariates and a dummy variable representing attendance at a 2-year versus a 4-year institution (i.e., the main-effects model). A statistically significant increase in the explained variance (R^2) attributable to the set of cross-product terms (over and above the main-effects model) indicates that the net effects of attending a 2- versus a 4-year college vary in magnitude for individuals at different levels of the respective covariates.

The weighted sample, adjusted to the actual (unweighted) sample size to obtain correct standard errors, was used in all analyses. Although a set of supplementary unweighted analyses yielded results essentially the same as those with the weighted sample, we report weighted sample estimates in the remainder of the article.

Results

Table 1 shows the analysis of covariance summaries, and Table 2 reports the weighted covariate-adjusted means and standard deviations on all four cognitive outcomes for students attending 2-year and 4-year institutions. (Regression coefficients for all covariates and main-effects are shown in the Appendix.) As shown in Table 1, when the influence of all 10 covariates was controlled there were no statistically significant differences between 2- and 4- year college students on any of the four end-of-freshman-year cognitive outcomes. As previously indicated in the methods section, this is essentially the same as saying that there were no significant 2-year/4-year college differences in the freshman-year gains made in reading comprehension, mathematics, critical thinking, or composite achieve-

ment. Only one analysis approached statistical significance. On mathematics the null hypothesis for the 2-year versus 4-year college difference could be rejected at $p < .10$

As shown by the covariate-adjusted means in Table 2, there was no clear group trend in the nonsignificant results. Four-year college students had slightly higher end-of-freshman-year reading comprehension and critical thinking scores, whereas 2-year college students had higher end-of-freshman-year mathematics and composite achievement.

The second stage of the analyses sought to determine if the cognitive effects of attending a 2-year versus a 4-year college are general or conditional. The addition of the set of cross product terms to the main-effects model was associated with small (i.e., 1.2–2.2%) but statistically significant increases in explained variance for all four cognitive outcomes. This suggested the presence of statistically significant Covariate × 2- versus 4-year college conditional effects. To determine the nature of these conditional effects each of the four freshman-year cognitive outcomes was regressed on the 10 covariates separately for the 2-year and the 4-year college samples. T tests for the significance of a difference in regression coefficients between independent samples were then used to determine which conditional effects were statistically significant (Cohen & Cohen, 1975).

In all cases the significant conditional effects involved student race or gender. That is, the cognitive effects of attending a 2- versus a 4-year college differed in magnitude for women versus men and for non-White versus White students. Table 3 shows the respective partial metric regression coefficients that were significantly different ($p < .05$) between women (coded 1) and men (coded 0), or between non-White students (coded 1) and White students (coded 0). In all cases the regression coefficients shown are with the influence of all other covariates in the model controlled statistically.

In the gender conditional effects women appeared to benefit more in first-year reading, critical thinking, and composite achievement from attending a 4-year college than their male counterparts. Conversely, men appeared to benefit somewhat more on those same three dimensions from attending a 2-year college. In the conditional effects involving ethnicity non-White students appeared to derive the greatest cognitive benefits in reading, mathematics, and criti-

TABLE 1

Analysis of Covariance Summaries of the Effects of Attending a Two-Year Versus a Four-Year Institution on End-of-Freshman Year Reading Comprehension, Mathematics, Critical Thinking, and Composite Achievement

Source	Reading comprehension		Mathematics		Critical thinking		Composite achievement	
	df	F	df	F	df	F	df	F
Covariates[a]	10	80.06*	10	123.04*	10	142.54*	10	229.68*
Attended a 2-year versus a 4-year institution	1	1.83	1	2.68	1	.30	1	.39
Residual	799		799		799		799	
Total	810		810		810		810	

[a] Individual fall 1992 reading, math, critical thinking, or composite achievement score; average fall 1992 reading, math, critical thinking, or composite achievement score for each institution; gender; ethnicity; age; family social origins; fall 1992 academic motivation; freshman year credit hours taken; work responsibilities; on- or off-campus residence.

*p < .01.

TABLE 2
Covariate-Adjusted Means and Standard Deviations for End-of-Freshman-Year Reading Comprehension, Mathematics, Critical Thinking, and Composite Achievement

Group	Reading comprehension	Mathematics	Critical thinking	Composite achievement[a]
Attended a 2-year institution				
M	59.80	56.25	59.85	− .37
SD	5.75	3.87	6.05	.77
Attended a 4-year institution				
M	60.25	55.64	60.02	− .39
SD	5.44	3.67	5.72	.73

[a] Z scores (mean = 0, standard deviation = 1 for the entire sample of 2,685 students) were used to form composite achievement from the combination of reading comprehension, mathematics, and critical thinking.

cal thinking from first-year attendance at a 2-year college. For their White counterparts, however, the reverse was true. White students appeared to benefit more on those same three dimensions from attendance at a 4-year college.

Summary

The findings of this study run contrary to several prevailing notions about the relative academic rigor of 2- and 4- year college programs. Replicating previous findings, the evidence from this longitudinal investigation suggests a parity in the relative cognitive impacts of 2- and 4-year colleges that enroll first-year students of generally similar academic preparation. Previous research, employing small student samples drawn from one 2- and one 4-year college, found only trivial differences in the relative first-year gains in reading comprehension, mathematics, and critical thinking made by these two respective student groups (Bohr et al., 1994). The present study employed a multi-institutional sample of students from five 2-year and six matched 4-year colleges located throughout the country. (All eleven institutions were different than those studied by Bohr et al.) With controls made for precollege cognitive skills, precollege academic motivation, age, sex, ethnicity, family social origins, credit hours taken, work responsibilities, place of residence, and the average student body academic aptitude of the institution attended, no significant differences were found between 2- and 4-year college students in end-of-freshman-year reading comprehension, mathematics, critical thinking, or a composite measure of all three tests. This is the equivalent of saying that there were no significant differences between the 2-

and 4-year college samples in the freshman-year gains made on the four cognitive measures.[1,2] Furthermore, there was no clear general trend in the nonsignificant differences in end-of-freshman-year scores (or freshman-year gains) favoring either the 2-year or the 4-year sample. The 2-year college sample had slightly higher end-of-freshman-year scores (or gains) in mathematics and composite achievement, whereas the 4-year sample had slight advantages in reading comprehension and critical thinking.

A second major question of this study concerned whether or not the cognitive effects of attending a 2- versus a 4- year college differed for different kinds of students. The findings of analyses addressing this question suggest that the overall parity in cognitive effects associated with 2- versus 4-year college attendance, while significant in its own right, may mask the presence of differential effects based on sex and ethnicity. Irrespective of ethnicity and other characteristics, women appear to derive greater cognitive benefits than men from 4-year college attendance, whereas men appear to derive somewhat greater cognitive benefits than women from 2-year college attendance. Similarly, irrespective of sex and other characteristics, non-White students appear to receive greater cognitive benefits than their White counterparts from first-year attendance at a 2-year college. Conversely, White students appear to derive relatively greater cognitive benefits from 4-year college attendance than do non-White students.

It is important to point out that conditional effects in nonexperimental research on college impacts do not replicate particularly well (Pascarella & Terenzini, 1991). Consequently, it is probably prudent to regard the

TABLE 3
Regression Coefficients for Significant Conditional Effects

Group	Reading comprehension		Mathematics		Critical thinking		Composite achievement	
	2-year	4-year	2-year	4-year	2-year	4-year	2-year	4-year
Sex								
(Female = 1; Male = 0)	-.151[a]	1.276[a]			-.736[d]	.596[d]	-.146[c]	.736[c]
	(.274)	(.358)			(.423)	(.266)	(.069)	(.309)
Ethnicity								
(Non-White = 1; White = 0)	1.534[b]	-1.339[b]	.548[c]	-.547[c]			.317[f]	-.608[f]
	(.725)	(.408)	(.323)	(.225)			(.073)	(.362)

Note. Top number is the metric (unstandardized) regression coefficient. bottom number is the standard error. Regression coefficients with the same superscript are significantly different in magnitude at $p < .05$ with the influence of all other covariates in the model controlled statistically.

sex- and ethnicity-based conditional effects uncovered in this study as preliminary and suggestive rather than confirmatory or conclusive. They await replication, but they also underscore the importance of investigating the presence of conditional effects in studies that examine the relative impacts of different kinds of postsecondary institutions. Failure to do so could, as the findings of this study suggest, mask the presence of significant institutional impacts for different subgroups of students.

Policy Implications

The findings of this study are consistent with a growing body of evidence suggesting that, when educational attainment and background are controlled, students initially attending 2-year colleges can compete on equal terms with their 4-year college counterparts in such areas as occupational status, earnings, job stability, and job satisfaction. In their national study of the occupational and economic consequences of where one begins postsecondary education, Whitaker and Pascarella (1994) conclude that, when one considers its relatively lower tuition costs, the 2-year college may represent a cost-effective way of obtaining the first 2 years of college without sacrificing job-market competitiveness. The present findings would suggest further that the relatively lower tuition costs of attending a 2-year (versus a 4-year) college may not necessarily come at the price of a less intellectually rigorous academic program. At least during the first year of attendance, the cognitive impacts of 2-year colleges may be essentially indistinguishable from those of a substantial segment of 4-year institutions that enroll students of generally similar academic preparation.

The specific institutional contexts accounting for this parity in academic outcomes are difficult to pinpoint from the data available in our study. However, the findings do underscore and reinforce an important policy-relevant generalization from research on the relative cognitive impacts of different kinds of postsecondary institutions. Specifically, differences in institutional resources such as library size, money spent per student, faculty-student ratio, campus physical and recreational facilities, etc., may have little influence on the cognitive and intellectual outcomes of college. More salient may be such proximal influences as the quality of teaching, curricular experiences and effective general education, and the pattern of coursework taken. In these areas 2-year colleges may not be at a distinct disadvantage relative to a substantial segment of 4-year institutions.

For secondary school guidance counselors, these findings may have nontrivial implications for how they advise seniors with college aspirations, particularly those with limited financial resources. Obtaining the first year or two of postsecondary education at a 2-year college may not necessarily provide an inferior academic experience when compared to the 4-year college alternative. This is not to say that a student would necessarily be wise to choose a 2-year college over a selective, residential, liberal arts college if the latter were an academic and financial possibility. However, many of those less selective 4-year institutions that such a student might more realistically consider may not offer an academic experience that is markedly more rigorous or cognitively influential than a less expensive, and perhaps more geographically convenient, 2-year college.

The findings may also have implications for how state higher education planners and legislators view 2-year colleges, which in turn may influence funding priorities. In a tight economic scenario there may be a tendency among state-level policymakers to protect the state's flagship and other major 4-year institutions, without regard to the likelihood that the largest numbers of financially needy and minority students may be receiving their postsecondary instruction at 2-year colleges. To the extent that 2-year colleges provide those students with an academically rigorous and viable alternative to many 4-year institutions, state planners might rethink where funding has its greatest social utility.

In a related sense the findings may also have implications for alternative ways of funding the postsecondary education of minority and financially needy students. Rather than depending exclusively on the awarding of individual financial aid and scholarships to such students, it may be more effective to use some of the resources targeted for financial aid to increase the funding of those 2-year institutions at which minority and low socioeconomic status students are most likely to begin postsecondary education.

Finally, the study may also have implications for the focus of future program evaluation and policy research on community colleges. As noted earlier in this article, most research has focused on the relative socioeconomic outcomes of attendance at, or graduation from, a 2-year college. Little evidence is available that examines the relative intellectual and cognitive impacts of 2-year college (vs. 4-year college) attendance. Until such evaluation and policy-oriented inquiry is conducted, state and federal funding policies and priorities are likely to be shaped by an educational status structure founded on beliefs and stereotypes rather than any empirical evidence.

Limitations

This investigation has several limitations that should be kept in mind when interpreting the findings. First, although the overall sample is multi-institutional and consists of a broad range of 2- and 4-year institutions from around the country, the fact that the analyses were limited to a matched sample of five 2-year and six 4-year colleges means that we cannot necessarily generalize the results to all 2- and 4-year institutions. It is important to reiterate that we purposefully excluded historically Black colleges that enrolled almost no non-Black students and two highly selective, private, residential institutions from the 4-year comparison sample. Other 4-year institutions were excluded that had composite CAAP precollege scores either lower or higher than the range included by the 2-year colleges. When the 2-year college sample was compared with the entire 4-year college sample, the latter had somewhat higher covariate-adjusted end-of-freshman-year reading comprehension and critical thinking scores. However, these differences disappeared when the two selective, private, residential institutions, and particularly the selective liberal arts college, were removed from the 4-year sample. Such a finding is consistent with previous evidence, suggesting that it may only be a few of the most selective, residential, liberal arts-oriented, 4-year institutions that have a truly distinctive impact on student cognitive growth (Pascarella & Terenzini, 1991). The relative net intellectual impacts of the vast majority of other institutions in the American postsecondary system, both 2- and 4-year, may be essentially homogeneous and largely indistinguishable from each other.

Second, although attempts were made in the initial sampling design and subsequent sample weighting to make the sample as representative as possible at each institution, the time commit-

APPENDIX
Metric Regression Coefficients for Covariates and Main Effects

Variable	Reading comprehension	Mathematics	Critical thinking	Composite achievement
Individual fall, 1992 score	.616**	.657**	.735**	.281**
	(.032)	(.024)	(.027)	(.008)
Average fall, 1992 score for each institution	.177	.557**	.390**	.060**
	(.119)	(.153)	(.101)	(.014)
Female	.421	−.682**	−.006	.003
	(.289)	(.183)	(.256)	(.027)
Non-White	−.331	−.099	−.645*	.031
	(.370)	(.210)	(.329)	(.037)
Age	.077**	−.041**	.016	.001
	(.023)	(.014)	(.021)	(.002)
Family social origins	.102	−.056	−.111	−.009
	(.070)	(.046)	(.064)	(.007)
Fall, 1992 academic motivation	−.239	.099	−.136	−.009
	(.265)	(.165)	(.238)	(.026)
Credit hours taken	.447**	.117*	.428**	.039**
	(.091)	(.057)	(.082)	(.009)
Work responsibilities	.072	−.038	−.051	−.004
	(.050)	(.032)	(.046)	(.005)
On-campus residence	.870*	.577*	−.326	.055
	(.370)	(.215)	(.329)	(.036)
Attended a 4-year (versus a 2-year) institution	.469	−.618	.187	−.021
	(.338)	(.370)	(.297)	(.037)

Note. Top number is the metric (unstandardized) regression coefficient, number in parentheses is the standard error.
*p < .05. **p < .01.

ment and work required of each student participant undoubtedly led to some self-selection. We cannot be sure that those who were willing to participate in the study responded in the same way as would those who were invited but declined to participate in the study. Weighed against this, however, is the fact we found no significant conditional effects involving such factors as age, family socioeconomic status, pre-college academic aptitude, credit hours taken, or work responsibilities. Thus, even if the sample had some bias on these factors, it did not appear to have an appreciable influence on the study results. Third, although we looked at several different measures of cognitive development in college (specifically, standardized, multiple-choice tests of reading comprehension, mathematics, and critical thinking), these are certainly not the only dimensions along which students develop intellectually during the college years. Alternative conceptualizations or approaches to the assessment of cognitive development (e.g., essay tests of content-knowledge, tests that focus on application and problem solving, or writing skills) might have produced findings different from those yielded by this investigation. Finally, this study is limited by the fact that it was only able to trace cognitive growth over the first year of college. We cannot be sure that the apparent overall parity in freshman-year cognitive growth demonstrated by 2-year and 4-year college students in these particular institutions would persist over the next year of college.

Notes

This investigation was conducted as part of the National Study of Student Learning (NSSL) at the University of Illinois at Chicago. NSSL is supported by Grant No. R117G10037 from the U.S. Department of Education to the National Center on Postsecondary Teaching, Learning, and Assessment. The first author also received support for his work on this article as the University of Illinois Foundation "James F. Towey University Scholar."

[1]It is sometimes risky to apply a substantive interpretation to nonsignificant differences because they can be caused by statistical and measurement artifacts. However, those particular artifactual conditions are unlikely to hold in the present study for four reasons. First, the unweighted (actual) sample size of 811 is sufficiently large to detect rather small between-group effects (Cohen & Cohen, 1975). Second, each of the four dependent measures had more than adequate reliability (.80 or higher) to detect between-group differences (Thorndike & Hagen, 1977). Third, the use of strong covariates, including a parallel precollege measure of each dependent variable, substantially lowered the error term and dramatically increased the probability of finding any real between-group differences that existed (Pedhazur, 1982). Finally, the dependent measures employed in the study each tap cognitive dimensions shown to be significantly influenced by exposure to postsecondary education (Pascarella & Terenzini, 1991).

[2]By definition the absence of between-sector (2- versus 4-year) differences suggests that there may be substantially greater between-institution differences *within* the 2- and 4-year samples. We tested this possibility by replicating the main analyses separately for the 2- and 4-year samples with individual institutions as the comparison groups. In both analyses there were substantial differences among individual institutions on the four cognitive outcomes. However, these became statistically nonsignificant when the influence of the covariates was taken into account. The range of covariate-adjusted institutional differences on the cognitive outcomes was approximately the same for the 2- and 4-year samples. Thus, it is unlikely that the overall nonsignificant cognitive differences found between the 2- and 4-year samples are the result of one or two outlier institutions.

References

Alba, R., & Lavin, D. (1981). Community colleges and tracking in higher education. *Sociology of Education, 54,* 223–237.

American College Testing Program. (1989). *Report on the technical characteristics of CAAP: Pilot year 1: 1988–89.* Iowa City, IA: Author.

Anderson, K. (1984). *College effects on the educational attainment of males and females.* (Res. rep.). Florida Atlantic University.

Astin, A. (1968). *The college environment.* Washington, DC: American Council on Education.

Astin, A. (1977). *Four critical years.* San Francisco: Jossey-Bass.

Astin, A. (1993). *What matters in college: Four critical years revisited.* San Francisco: Jossey-Bass.

Astin, A., & Panos, R. (1969). *The educational and vocational development of college students.* Washington, DC: American Council on Education.

Ball, S. (Ed.). (1977). *Motivation in education.* New York: Academic Press.

Bohr, L., Pascarella, E., Nora, A., Zusman, B., Jacobs, M., Desler, M., & Bulakowski, C. (1994). Cognitive effects of 2- year and 4-year colleges: A preliminary study. *Community College Review, 22,* 4–11.

Breneman, D., & Nelson, S. (1981). *Financing the community college: An economic perspective.* Washington, DC: Brookings Institution.

Brint, S., & Karabel, J. (1989). *The diverted dream: Community colleges and the promise of educational opportunity in America, 1900–1985.* New York: Oxford University Press.

Chickering, A., & Reisser, L. (1993). *Education and identity* (2nd ed.). San Francisco: Jossey-Bass.

Cohen, A., & Brawer, F. (1982). *The American community college.* San Francisco: Jossey-Bass.

Cohen, A., & Brawer, F. (1989). *The American community college* (2nd ed.). San Francisco: Jossey-Bass.

Cohen, J., & Cohen, P. (1975). *Applied multiple regression/correlation analysis for the behavioral sciences.* Hillsdale, NJ: Lawrence Erlbaum.

Crook, D., & Lavin, D. (1989, April). *The community-college effect revisited: The long-term impact of community-college entry on B.A. attainment.* Paper presented at the Annual Meeting of the American Educational Research Association, San Francisco.

Dougherty, K. (1987). The effects of community colleges: Aid or hindrance to socioeconomic attainment? *Sociology of Education, 60,* 86–103.

Dougherty, K. (1992). Community colleges and baccalaureate attainment. *Journal of Higher Education, 63,* 188–214.

Elashoff , J. (1969). Analysis of covariance: A delicate instrument. *American Educational Research Journal, 6,* 383–401.

Grubb, N. (1984). The bandwagon once more: Vocational preparation for high-tech occupations. *Harvard Educational Review, 54,* 429–451.

Hilton, T., & Schrader, W. (1986, April) *Pathways to graduate school: An empirical study based on national longitudinal data.* Paper presented at the Annual Meeting of the American Educational Research Association, San Francisco.

Karabel, J. (1986). Community colleges and social stratification in the 1980s. In L. Zwerling (Ed.), *The community college and its critics* (pp. 13–30). San Francisco: Jossey-Bass.

Kerlinger, F., & Pedhazur, E. (1973). *Multiple regression in behavioral research.* New York: Holt, Rinehart & Winston.

Kintzer, F., & Wattenbarger, J. (1985). *The articulation/transfer phenomenon.* Washington, DC: American Association of Community and Junior Colleges.

Kuh, G. (1993). In their own words: What students learn outside the classroom. *American Educational Research Journal, 30,* 277–304.

Linn, R. (1986). Quantitative methods in research on teaching. In M. Witrock (Ed.), *Handbook of research on teaching* (2nd ed., pp. 92–118). New York: Macmillan.

Linn, R., & Slinde, J. (1977). The determination of the significance of change between pre- and posttesting periods. *Review of Educational Research, 47,* 121–150.

London, H. (1978). *The culture of a community college.* New York: Praeger.

Neumann, W., & Riesman, D. (1980). The community college elite. In G. Vaughn (Ed.), *Questioning the community college role* (pp. 53–71). San Francisco: Jossey-Bass.

Monk-Turner, E. (1988). Educational differentiation and status attainments: The community college controversy. *Sociological Focus, 21,* 141–151.

Nunley, C., & Breneman, D. (1988). Defining and measuring quality in community college education. In J. Eaton (Ed.), *Colleges of choice: The enabling impact of the community college* (pp. 62–92). New York: American Council on Education.

Pascarella, E., & Terenzini, P. (1991). *How college affects students.* San Francisco: Jossey-Bass.

Pedhazur, E. (1982). *Multiple regression in behavioral research: Explanation and prediction* (2nd ed.). New York: Holt, Rinehart & Winston.

Smart, J., & Ethington, C. (1985). Early career outcomes of baccalaureate recipients: A study of native 4-year and transfer 2- year college students. *Research in Higher Education, 22,* 185–193.

Temple, M., & Polk, K. (1986). A dynamic analysis of educational attainment. *Sociology of Education, 59,* 79–84.

Thorndike, R., & Hagen, E. (1977). *Measurement and evaluation in psychology and education* (4th ed.). New York: Wiley.

Velez, W. (1985). Finishing college: The effects of college type. *Sociology of Education, 58,* 191–200.

Whitaker, D., & Pascarella, E. (1994). Two-year college attendance and socioeconomic attainment: Some additional evidence. *Journal of Higher Education, 65,* 194–210.

Zwerling, L. (1976). *Second best: The crisis of the community college.* New York: McGraw-Hill.

ERNEST T. PASCARELLA is a Professor of Higher Education at the University of Illinois, 1040 W. Harrison St., (m/c 147), Chicago, IL 60607-7133. His specialization is research on the impact of college.

LOUISE BOHR is an Assistant Professor in the Reading Department at Northeastern Illinois University, 5500 North St. Louis Ave., Chicago,

IL 60625-4699. Her area of specialization is reading.

AMAURY NORA is an Associate Professor of Higher Education at the University of Illinois. His specialization is student persistence in higher education.

PATRICK TERENZINI is a Professor of Higher Education at the Center for the Study of Higher Education at Penn State University, 403 South Allen St., Suite 104, University Park, PA 16801-5202. His specialization is research on the impact of college.

Received June 6, 1994
Revision received
September 7, 1994
Accepted October 15, 1994

CHAPTER 41

COMPARING STUDENT PERFORMANCE AND GROWTH IN 2- AND 4-YEAR INSTITUTIONS

LINDA C. STRAUSS AND J. FREDERICKS VOLKWEIN

This study examines the organizational characteristics of 51 higher education institutions in relationship to student performance and growth. The study first finds that organizational measures of mission, size, wealth, complexity, and selectivity are statistically represented by the 2-year versus 4-year college mission. Findings indicate that 2-year and 4-year campuses indeed do exert significantly different influences on undergraduate GPA and self-reported intellectual growth. Next, the study uses both OLS regression and HLM to examine these influences. High school percentile rank and college classroom experiences are better predictors of Cum GPA at 4-year institutions, while student effort is a better predictor of GPA at 2-year institutions. Whereas the most important predictors of Cum GPA include precollege measures such as high school percentile rank and SAT score, the most influential predictors of student intellectual growth are campus experiences including classroom vitality, peer support, student effort, commitment, and involvement. Controlling for all other variables, students at 2-year institutions receive higher grades, and students at 4-year campuses experience more growth.

KEY WORDS: *institutional commitment; hierarchical linear modeling; 2-year institutions; 4-year institutions.*

Introduction and Need for the Study

In discussing his "input-environment-output" (IEO) model, Astin (1977, 1984) notes the lack of empirical studies analyzing multicampus data and the important contribution of structural/organizational influences on student outcomes. Several causal models have been developed hypothesizing that campus structural characteristics and college organizational climates produce environments that impact student outcomes (Berger and Milem, 2000; Pascarella, 1985; Weidman, 1989). Pascarella and Terenzini (1991) note the inconsistency in the evidence about organizational influences and discuss the difficulties of using institution level variables to predict individual level outcomes. Many studies that examine organizational impact on student outcomes fail to consider individual students as the unit of analysis (Berger and Milem, 2000). These concerns combined with newly developed software have stimulated higher education researchers to undertake multilevel modeling in their college effects research (Ethington, 1997; Patrick, 2001; Porter and Umbach, 2001). In theory, hierarchical models allow researchers to arrive at more accurate results by taking into account the nested structures of the institution's subenvironments. In reality, multilevel modeling adds complexity and density to the analysis, possibly overstates the strength of the evidence, and may not be necessary

(Ethington, 1997). Some researchers question the uncritical use of complicated modeling and believe that traditional OLS approaches perform equally well under most conditions (Busing, 1993; Draper, 1995; de Leeuw and Kreft, 1995; Morris, 1995).

This is an important and timely issue in higher education because of government, trustee, and accreditation interest in institutional performance. Concern about the student outcomes of college has become quite intense in the past decade. The guidelines and mission statements of both regional and program-specific accrediting agencies reveal that student outcomes evidence is an important component of today's accreditation standards. Regional accrediting agencies such as the North Central, Middle States, Southern, and Western Associations for Schools and Colleges now demand evidence of student learning and other outcomes in their reviews. This has resulted in greater campus attention to policies and practices that improve these student outcomes (Carnevale, 2000; McMurtrie, 2000; Ratcliff, Lubinescu, and Gaffney, 2001; Semrow et al., 1992). Research has documented the effect that accreditation, state characteristics, and institutional dynamics have on the kind of student assessment evidence that is collected (Peterson & Augustine, 2000).

Trustees and government officials have become results-oriented and reach for performance indicators as signs of institutional effectiveness and as justifications for higher education funding (Burke and Serban, 1998; Burke, 2000; Ewell, 1998). Student outcomes evidence can be used for both internal and external purposes. Institutions can use performance evidence to make internal budget adjustments or to benchmark against other institutions for improvement initiatives (Massy 1994). Performance indicators also help institutions demonstrate their performance to stakeholders such as legislators, employers, parents, media, and accreditation agencies (Cabrera, Colbeck, and Terenzini, 2001; Ewell, 1998). To attract sufficient state funding, public 2-year and 4-year institutions increasingly must meet criteria set by their state governments. Thus, it is especially important to know if particular structural/organizational characteristics are significantly associated with positive student performance, learning, and growth.

States vary not only in the types and number of performance indicators but also in the ways they apply them to 2-year versus 4-year

institutions. Both Burke (2000) and Ewell (1998) call for the distinction between indicators at 2- and 4-year institutions, but many states attempt to create indicators that are applicable to all institutional types. Specific indicators developed from 4-year institutional models may not be appropriate for the 2-year sector. Without adequate research evidence, the dominant 4-year models may be inappropriately applied to the two-year sector (Strauss, 2000).

This study is an attempt to close the gap in the research comparing 2-year and 4-year institutions. Outcomes from research on 4-year institutions cannot automatically be generalized to 2-year institutions, and compared to studies of 4-year institutions, there is a relative dearth of research on the 2-year sector (Cohen and Brawer, 1996; Layzell, 1997; Pascarella and Terenzini, 1991).

Thus, using a population of several thousand students at 23 four year and 28 two year institutions, this study has two goals:

1. To examine the structural/organizational characteristics that influence student performance and intellectual growth.

2. To compare the results of this examination using both traditional OLS regression and HLM.

Conceptual Frameworks

Higher education scholarship has produced an array of theories and models that explain the relationship between students and their colleges. Drawing from this pool of available models, at least four major assertions regarding the interactions between students and their colleges and the influences on student outcomes can be cited (Pascarella and Terenzini, 1991; Volkwein, Szelest, Cabrera, and Napierski-Prancl, 1998; Volkwein, Valle, Blose, and Zhou, 2000). The most traditional view is that precollege characteristics such as student backgrounds, academic preparedness for college, and clear goals are the main factors accounting for differences in academic performance, persistence behavior, and other educational outcomes (Astin, 1991; Feldman and Newcomb, 1969; Stark et al., 1989).

A second group of alternative yet complementary perspectives fall under the general description of student-institution fit models (Pascarella and Terenzini, 1991). Perhaps the most widely researched of these models claims that student persistence and growth depends on the degree of successful integration into the academic and social structures of the institution (Spady, 1970, 1971; Tinto, 1987, 1993). Another student-institution fit model focuses on the importance of student involvement and effort (Astin, 1984; Pace, 1984). Also within the student-institution fit perspective is the importance of support from friends and family in college adjustment (Bean, 1980; Bean and Metzner, 1985; Nora, 1987; Nora, 1990). Yet another branch of this literature emphasizes the importance of financial variables and the student's ability to pay (Cabrera, Nora, and Castaneda, 1993; St. John, 1992). While the majority of these models have been constructed to explain one outcome, student persistence, several researchers have successfully used these and similar models to explain other outcomes including student growth and satisfaction (Kuh, Race, and Vesper, 1997; Terenzini, and Pascarella, 1980; Terenzini, Pascarella, and Lorang, 1982; Terenzini, Theopbilides, and Lorang, 1984; Terenzini and Wright, 1987; Terenzini, Springer, Pascarella, and Nora, 1995; Terenzini, Springer, Yaeger, Pascarella, and Nora, 1996; Volkwein, King, and Terenzini, 1986, Volkwein and Lorang, 1996; Volkwein et al., 2000). More recently, one model has been presented to explain the learning and cognitive outcomes of community college students (Voorhees, 1997). More than the others, the Voorhees model emphasizes the competing demands of family, work, and community.

A third set of assertions emphasizes the importance of campus climate in student adjustment (Bauer, 1998). Perceptions of prejudice and discrimination have gained increased attention as factors accounting for the differences in persistence rates between minorities and nonminorities (Cabrera and La Nasa, 2000; Fleming, 1984; Hurtado, 1992, 1994; Hurtado, Carter and Spuler, 1996; Loo and Rolison, 1986; Murgufa, Padilla, and Pavel, 1991; Nora and Cabrera, 1996; Smedley, Myers and Harrell, 1993). All students need to be able to function in a safe environment, without fear of oppression, stigma, and violence, in order to maximize their chances of success (Reynolds, 1999). Even beyond the literature on prejudice and discrimination, there is general agreement that creating an affirming campus climate for all students, one that allows for optimal development, is a major factor in successful student outcomes (Upcraft and Schuh, 1996).

Fourth, structural/functional perspectives drawing from the literature on organizations, encourage researchers to give greater attention to those variables that reflect the influence of organizational characteristics (Hall, 1991). Studies of colleges and universities, as particular types of organizations, have shown that campus mission, size, wealth, complexity, and selectivity exert significant influences (ranging from small to large) on a variety of internal transactions and outcomes including student values, aspirations, educational and career attainment (Pascarella and Terenzini, 1991; Volkwein et al., 1986; Volkwein et al., 1998). In their recent synthesis of the literature, Berger and Milem (2000) conclude that an array of organizational features and behaviors influence student experiences and outcomes. The Berger and Milem Conceptual Model integrates the Pascarella Model (1985) and the Weidman Model (1989). These are the only models that give prominence to campus organizational behaviors and structural characteristics as influences on student outcomes.

These four types of theoretical perspectives and their models provide the conceptual foundation for the research reported here. In constructing the data and measures for the current study, however, two models are used more heavily than the others—the Cabrera, Nora, and Castaneda (1993) Integrated Model of Student Persistence, and the Pascarella (1985) General Causal Model. (The Berger and Milem 2000 model was formulated after the instrumentation and data collection for this study in the mid-1990s.)

The Cabrera model merges the best elements of Tinto's (1987) Student Integration Model and Bean's (1980) Student Attrition Model (Cabrera, Castaneda, Nora, and Hengstler, 1992). Cabrera et al. recognized the similarity between the two models and tested their overlap. The two models were found to be significantly related and were quantitatively amalgamated through structural equation modeling, thereby producing this Integrated Model of Student Persistence. Many of the concepts in these models and the survey items used to reflect those concepts were incorporated into the Albany Outcomes Model and subsequently into the State University of New York Student Outcomes Survey (Volkwein, 1992; Volkwein et al., 2000).

The Pascarella (1985) General Causal Model specifies five elements influencing student learning and cognitive development. These elements are student background/precollege traits (such as aptitude, personality, ethnicity, high school preparation), structural/organizational characteristics of institutions, (such as size, mission, wealth, complexity, and selectivity), interactions with agents of socialization (faculty and peers), institutional environment (such as classroom experiences, student services, tolerance, safety), and quality of student effort. Whereas the Pascarella model assumes that the structural and organizational variables contribute only indirectly to learning and cognitive development, this study has made these characteristics a central focus of the investigation. There are few empirical studies using the Pascarella model as a conceptual framework, and the most rigorous of these found no direct effects and only trivial indirect effects between institutional characteristics and two academic outcomes (Franklin, 1995).

Thus, there are only a few models that have been put forward in the literature, and they have not been thoroughly tested. We do not know which organizational characteristics have the greatest influence on which outcomes, and under what conditions, and for what types of students. Also of interest to this study is Pascarella's call for multilevel analysis of student outcomes. He finds fault with exclusive use of either the institution or the individual as the single level of analysis. "One helpful direction for future research in this area would be to analyze data at both levels of aggregation (institution and individuals) whenever possible" (1985, p. 51).

Method

Using the concepts and models discussed above, this research examines student performance and intellectual growth at 51 public institutions of higher education in a single state (23 4-year and 28 2-year campuses). There are 7,658 students in the database who completed the assessment instrument at the end of their second year (2,576 at four-year campuses and 5,082 at two-year campuses). The study is limited to students identifying themselves as sophomores, ensuring that they have spent approximately the same amount of time at their respective 2-year and 4-year institutions. The database contains both institutional and student level data.

Data Collection

This research undertakes a secondary analysis of data collected by a consortium of 51 participating institutions and the State University of New York System. The institutional data were gathered from multiple sources, all for the 1996–1997 academic year. A committee of cooperating researchers and administrators from participating institutions developed the survey instrument, based in part on the Albany Outcomes Model and the student surveys developed by the State University of New York at Albany (Volkwein, 1992). The variables and scales used in the analysis draw directly from the constructs from the literature in general and from the Cabrera and Pascarella outcomes models in particular. The survey was administered across the SUNY System in spring 1997 under conditions that varied slightly from campus-to-campus, but which resulted in a representative group of respondents. The survey for the database was printed and scored by the American College Testing program. Student level variables are drawn from the survey instrument. Institutional level data are generated from the 1996–1997 Integrated Postsecondary Education Database System (IPEDS). The database is stored and analyzed using SPSS PC version statistical software and hierarchical linear modeling (HLM) (version 5.02) statistical software.

Analytical Technique

Based on the Cabrera Integrated Model of Student Retention and the Pascarella General Student Outcomes Model, there are many variables and constructs hypothesized to influence the two outcomes selected for this study—student cumulative grade point average (Cum GPA) and self-reported intellectual growth. Previous studies using this dataset have conducted factor analysis to see if the items clustered consistently with the outcomes theory and the models (Volkwein and Cabrera, 2000; Volkwein et al., 2000). Since those efforts were successful, we are able to forego principal components analysis in this study, and instead move directly to scale construction. The alpha reliabilities for the multiitem scales are recalculated for this population; all exceed .70 and the majority exceed .80. The descriptive statistics for the scales and other variables are shown in Table 1.

We began the research with a larger number of variables, but using diagnostics, we reduced the original list down to those shown in Table 1. For the final model, we tested for multicollinearity by computing variance inflation factors (VIFs). For the GPA model, the VIF scores ranged from 1.02 to 1.929 with all but one being under 1.40. For the growth model, the VIF scores again were under 1.4, with the exception of institutional commitment having a VIF of 2.155. Specifically, the following variables are included in the study.

Dependent Variables-GPA and Growth

For the purposes of this study, student performance, learning, and growth are taken from two perspectives: students and faculty. First, student perceptions of growth are obtained from students' self-assessment of their own intellectual growth (acquiring information, ideas, concepts, and analytical thinking) on a 5-point growth scale (1 = none and 5 = extremely high). Second, faculty perceptions of student learning are measured by the Cum GPA reported for each student.

Independent Variables

Student Precollege Characteristics. Student characteristics include age, male/female, racial/ethnic group membership, employment, marital status, dependent children, socioeconomic background, SAT score, high school percentile rank, and high school average.

Structural/Organizational Characteristics of Institutions. Key indicators for structural/organizational characteristics used in previous literature have included size, wealth, complexity, mission, and selectivity (Volkwein et al., 2000). Mission is a dummy variable where 1 = 4-year, 0 = 2-year. Size is represented by the total undergraduate headcount enrollment at the institution. Wealth includes measures of revenues and expenditures per annual full-time equivalent (FTE) enrollment. The complexity measure reflects the number of organizational units headed by a vice president or dean (or equivalent). Selectivity includes the percentage of applicants admitted.

Financial Need/Aid. The amount of financial aid generally is an objective measure of student need and socioeconomic status. Research demonstrates that unmet need and student aid influence college academic performance (Nora, 1990; Voorhees, 1985). This study asks students to indicate the extent to which their education is being supported by Federal and state grant funds

(zero, minor, or major support). As shown in Table 1, this financial aid scale has an alpha of .88. Equal opportunity funding and college work-study data, asked in the same format, were originally included as single items in the model but later dropped after diagnostics identified them as weak contributors.

Goal Clarity and Encouragement. A scale of educational and occupational goal clarity was constructed with a Cronbach's alpha of .84. Encouragement from significant others includes perceived support from family and friends to pursue and continue in college.

Academic Experiences and Interactions with Agents of Socialization. The academic environment of each campus is reflected in the measures of classroom experiences (an 8-item scale reflecting stimulation in class, faculty preparation, classroom satisfaction, quality of instruction; alpha = .87) and interactions with faculty outside of class (amount of direct contact with faculty, satisfaction with faculty and advisers). Other "agents of socialization" include student peers, and the scale measuring the extent and value placed on peer interactions has an alpha of .86.

Institutional Environment/Climate. The climate and social environment of each campus is reflected in the measures of openness and tolerance (e.g., the atmosphere of understanding, freedom from harassment, racial harmony, and security/safety), perceptions of low prejudice (by peer students, faculty, and administrators), a climate that fosters diversity, satisfaction with various student services, and satisfaction with various academic support services and facilities. These scales are shown in Table 1 and the alphas range from .74 to .90.

Student Effort and Involvement. Student effort is measured by student perception of good study habits and giving a high priority to studying. This scale has an alpha of .80. The scale of student involvement has an alpha of .76.

Institutional Commitment. Institutional commitment in this study is a scale of four items reflecting the student's overall impression of, sense of belonging to, satisfaction with, and willingness to attend the institution again (alpha = .77).

Thus, we assembled a rich and large dataset that allows us to examine the many potential

TABLE 1
Descriptive Statistics and Scale Alphas

	Mean	Std. Deviation	Scale Alpha	Number of Scale Items
Dependent Variables				
Grade Point Average (Cum GPA)	2.963	0.601	n/a	n/a
Intellectual Growth (Scale)	3.569	0.860	0.89	6
Independent Variables				
Age	3.775	1.673	n/a	n/a
Being Female	0.423	0.494	n/a	n/a
Member of an Underrepresented Group (African American, Hispanic American, Native American)	0.109	0.311	n/a	n/a
High School Rank	605.115	234.104	n/a	n/a
Total SAT Score	911.965	184.765	n/a	n/a
Marital Status	0.118	0.323	n/a	n/a
Number of Dependent Children	1.349	0.847	n/a	n/a
4-Year Mission	0.334	0.472	n/a	n/a
Size	6436.297	5343.574	n/a	n/a
Wealth	13459.154	18013.857	n/a	n/a
Complexity	5.428	3.753	n/a	n/a
Selectivity	0.873	0.107	n/a	n/a
Family Strong Support	3.865	1.248	n/a	n/a
Friends Strong Support	3.494	1.213	n/a	n/a
Receiving Federal and State Financial Aid (Scale)	2.539	1.272	0.88	2
Goal Clarity (Scale)	4.062	0.937	0.84	3
Classroom Experiences (Scale)	3.720	0.815	0.87	8
Interaction with Faculty Outside the Classroom (Scale)	3.606	0.794	0.77	4
Peer Support (Scale)	3.758	1.043	0.86	2
Social and Community Involvement (Scale)	3.288	0.704	0.76	2
Hours Worked Per Week	2.769	1.611	n/a	n/a
Perceived Climate of Low Prejudice (Scale)	3.613	0.957	0.90	3
Perceived Climate of Openness and Tolerance (Scale)	3.357	0.630	0.74	5
Perceived Climate for Fostering Diversity (Scale)	3.404	0.676	0.77	4
Satisfaction with Academic Facilities (Scale)	3.476	0.565	0.83	11
Satisfaction with Registration and Billing (Scale)	3.372	0.939	0.75	2
Student Effort (Scale)	3.566	0.994	0.80	2
Institutional Commitment (Scale)	3.689	0.792	0.77	4

influences on the two outcomes. We set out to use both HLM and the more traditional OLS multivariate analysis to see if the results differ. The study includes both institutional level and individual student level data that is nested within 51 the campuses. The structural/organizational characteristics from each campus comprise the institutional level data. HLM is normally recommended to respond to the multilevel nature of the measures. However, there is some skepticism about the need to engage in such complicated analysis when the more traditional

OLS regression analysis may produce the same results.

HLM varies from traditional OLS regression in that the regression coefficients can be treated as random effects by including an error term for the level 1 (student effects) in the level 2 (institution) model, resulting in a decomposition of the variance of the dependent variable into within institution and between institution effects (Bryk and Raudenbush, 1992; DiPrete and Forristal, 1994).

HLM uses regression equations from both level 1 and level 2 data to derive a fitted value for the dependent variable. In the case of the present study, the level 1 variables are all the student precollege characteristics and campus experiences identified in Table 1. The level 2 variables are the institutional structural/organizational characteristics of mission, size, wealth, complexity, and selectivity. The level 1, or student variables, are "nested" within the level 2 units, the individual institutions.

Using HLM, the researcher first designates the dependent variable. Next, the student variables are selected. For each student variable, and the regression intercept, institutional variable(s) can be selected to determine if the institutional characteristic has an effect on the relationship between the student variable and the dependent GPA or self-reported growth.

Simply stated, HLM determines the regression equation by calculating the beta weight for each student variable from the sum of the level two variables and random error. The resulting coefficients for each student variable are used to calculate the final regression equation by substituting the level 2 equations back into the level 1 equation (Bryk and Raudenbush, 1992; Singer, 1998; Von Seckor and Lissitz, 1997).

Results

Grade Point Average Analysis

OLS Regression Model

We first used a traditional OLS regression model to predict cumulative grade point average. The independent variables were entered in blocks according to the Pascarella Model with listwise deletion of missing cases. The variables were entered with precollege variables in the first block, structural organizational characteristics in the second, interactions with agents of social-

ization and institutional environment in the third, and institutional commitment and student effort in the final block.

The results, shown in Table 2, indicate that high school rank, total SAT score, number of hours worked per week, being female, being at a 2-year, classroom experiences, and effort are all significant positive predictors of grade point average. The adjusted R^2 for this model is .272, indicating that this model accounts for 27% of the total variance in Cum GPA.

The beta weights reveal that high school rank and total SAT scores account for as much variance in Cum GPA as all the other variables combined. Together they are more than twice as influential as student effort, three times as influential as classroom experiences, and four times as influential as being at a 2-year college. Additionally, the results reveal that being female and working more hours per week are associated with a slightly higher grade point average. The mission variable explains only about 3% of the variation in student GPA.

HLM Analysis

Unconditional Model.   HLM assumes that some of the variation in student grade point average is contained in the between institution (level 2) model. Indictors of this variance are shown in Table 3. An unconditional model (a model with no level 1 or level 2 predictors, analogous to a one-way ANOVA) was conducted to test this assumption (Bryk and Raudenbush, 1992; Singer, 1998).

Table 3 indicates that the maximum likelihood point estimate for the grand-mean grade point average is 2.92 with a standard error of .02, indicating a 95% confidence interval of $2.92 \pm 1.96(.02) = (2.88, 2.95)$. The estimated value of the variance at the school level (i.e., between individual institutions) of grade point average, represented by tau, is .02. The estimated value of the variance at the student level, or within schools, of grade point average, represented by sigma squared, is .42. These estimates indicate that most of the variation in the outcome is at the student level, although a substantial and statistically significant portion ($p < .01$) exists between individual schools.

Intraclass Correlation.   A second way of examining the variance between institutions is to estimate an intraclass correlation (Bryk and Raudenbush,

TABLE 2
OLS and HLM Analyses for Cumulative Grade Point Average

Adjusted R^2 = .272	OLS Beta	HLM Beta	Change in Tau = .50
(Constant)	2.174	2.952	(Constant)
		0.106	2-YEAR MISSION
Age			Age
Being Female	0.052	.067	Being Female
Underrepresented group member			Underrepresented group member
High School Percentile Rank	0.255	0.000272	High School Percentile Rank
		0.000299	4-year mission
Total SAT Score	0.251	0.000304	Total SAT Score
Marital Status			Marital Status
Number of dependent children			Number of dependent children
2-year mission	0.124		
Size			Size
Wealth			Wealth
Complexity			Complexity
Selectivity			Selectivity
Family strong support for academic goals			Family strong support for academic goals
Friends strong support for academic goals			Friends strong support for academic goals
Receiving Federal and State Financial Aid (Scale)			Receiving Federal and State Financial Aid (Scale)
Goal clarity (Scale)			Goal clarity (Scale)
Classroom experiences (Scale)	0.136	0.115	Classroom experiences (Scale)
		0.049	2-year mission
Interaction with faculty outside the classroom (Scale)			Interaction with faculty outside the classroom (Scale)
Hours worked per week	0.052	0.013	Hours worked per week
Social and Community Involvement (Scale)			Social and Community Involvement (Scale)
Perceived climate of low prejudice (Scale)			Perceived climate of low prejudice (Scale)
Perceived climate of tolerance (Scale)			Perceived climate of tolerance (Scale)
Perceived climate fostering diversity (Scale)			Perceived climate fostering diversity (Scale)
Satisfaction with registration and billing (Scale)			Satisfaction with registration and billing (Scale)
Student effort (Scale)	0.193	0.137	Student effort (Scale)
		0.063	2-year Mission
Institutional Commitment (Scale)			Institutional Commitment (Scale)

$p < .05$.

1992; Kennedy, Teddlie, and Stringfield, 1993; Singer, 1998). An intraclass correlation indicates the proportion of the total variance occurring between schools. As Table 3 indicates, 5% of the total variance in grade point average is accounted for by institution to institution differences.

The HLM Model

After entering all of the level 1 and level 2 variables, the HLM model did not reach conver-

gence. Thus, the large number of variables included in the HLM analysis needed to be reduced to allow the model to converge. To reduce the number of variables, we were guided by the correlation tables and the results from the OLS regression equation. The variables correlated with grade point average at the $p < .05$ level were retained for use in the HLM analysis.

To build the HLM model, all of the level 1 and level 2 variables were grand centered. Centering when using level 2 variable to predict level

TABLE 3
HLM Unconditional Model: Dependent Variable Cum GPA

Fixed Effect	Coefficient	Standard Error	T ratio	df	P value
Intercept for GPA, B0					
INTRCPT2, G00	2.919995	0.021198	137.749	47	0.000

Random Effect	Standard Deviation	Variance Component	df	Chi-square	P value
Intercept for GPA, U0	0.13542	0.01834	47	315.92982	0.000
level-1, variance R	0.64881	0.42095			

Intraclass Correlation
Tau = .02
Sigma Squared = .42
Tau/(tau + sigma squared) = .02/(.02 + .42) = .05

1 coefficients is an effective strategy due to the nature of the interaction term when the level 1 and level 2 equations are combined. When the equations are combined, an interaction term is created consisting of the level 1 variable multiplied by the level 2 variable. This interaction term is correlated with both the level 1 and level 2 variables. By centering the variables, the correlation is eliminated because the equation now reflects the random variance that should not be correlated (Singer, 1998). The results are shown in Table 2.

Interpretation of the Model

One way of measuring the impact of mission on Cum GPA is to compute how much the variance between institutions (tau) has changed between the unconditional model and the final model (Bryk and Raudenbush, 1992; Singer, 1998). This is computed by the formula: tau (unconditional)—tau (final model) / tau (unconditional) or [(.02-.01)/.02 =.50], indicating that 50% of the change in variance between the two GPA models is explained by the student level variables. The model statistics indicate that the intercept coefficient is 2.95 ($p < .01$ level), and the value of student GPA at the intercept for 2-year institutions is .11 higher than the value for GPA for 4-year institutions. The intercept value for 2-year institutions is 3.06 and for 4-year institutions it is 2.95.

Structural/Organizational Characteristics. Of the five structural/organization characteristics (mission, size, wealth, selectivity, and complexity)

only mission is a significant predictor in the final model. Because mission is significant, the HLM equation can be rewritten into a pair of fitted models, one for each sector, substituting the values for the 2-year and 4-year institutions (Singer, 1998). These equations are shown in Table 4, and the regression lines are shown in Figure 1 with the values for the 25th, 50th, and 75th percentiles. The regression lines in Figure 1 depict the higher value for student grade point average at the intercept for students at 2-year institutions, with this trend increasing as the values of the student variables increase.

The final HLM models, shown in Tables 2 and 4, show that six variables plus mission are significant—female, high school rank, total SAT score, hours worked, classroom experiences, and student effort. Of these six significant HLM variables, three of them are influenced by institutional mission: percentile rank, classroom experiences, and student effort. The statistics in Tables 2 and 4 indicate that rank in class and classroom experiences are better predictors at 4-year institutions, but student effort is a better predictor at 2-year institutions. We draw these conclusions from the average slopes representing the relationship between Cum GPA and each of the predictor variables. For high school rank and classroom experiences, the slope is steeper at 4-year than at 2-year institutions, indicating a stronger relationship. For student effort, the slope is .06 higher at 2-year institutions.

All seven variables in the OLS model also appear in the HLM model. The OLS and HLM Models for Cum GPA are nearly identical. Both techniques identified the same variables and

TABLE 4
HLM Sector Equations for Cum GPA

2-Year Equation
 Grade Point Average = 3.06 + (.06 × Female) + (.000272 × high school rank)
  +(.000304 × SAT score) + (.11 × classroom experiences)
  + (.13 × hours worked) + (.13 × effort)

4-Year Equation
 Grade Point Average = 2.95 + (.06 × Female) + (.000571 × high school rank)
  + (.000304 × SAT score) + (.16 × classroom experiences)
  + (.13 × hours worked) + (.07 × effort)

nearly the same magnitudes of influence. Using OLS, the mission variable explains about 3% of the variance in GPA, whereas using HLM the mission variable explains about 2% of GPA variance.

Student Growth Analysis

OLS Regression

As with GPA, we first used a traditional OLS regression model to predict student intellectual growth. The independent variables were entered in blocks according to the Pascarella Model with listwise deletion of missing cases. We entered precollege variables in the first block, structural organizational characteristics in the second, interactions with agents of socialization and institutional environment in the third, and student effort, involvement, and commitment in the final block.

 The results for this growth model, as shown in Table 5, are more robust than the corresponding OLS model for GPA. Student classroom experiences, along with student commitment, effort, and involvement, constitute the most powerful contributors to student growth. Other positive influences on intellectual growth include being at a 4-year institution, having good facilities, receiving strong peer support, receiving financial aid, being female, and having goal clarity. Table 5 shows two significant negative influences on growth: a perceived climate of tolerance, and satisfaction with registration and billing procedures. The adjusted R^2 indicates that this model accounts for 42% of the total variance in growth scores. The mission variable accounts for only about 2% of the explained variance.

HLM Analysis

Unconditional Model. As with the previous HLM, we constructed an unconditional model to examine the variance between institutions; the results are displayed in Table 6. This table indi-

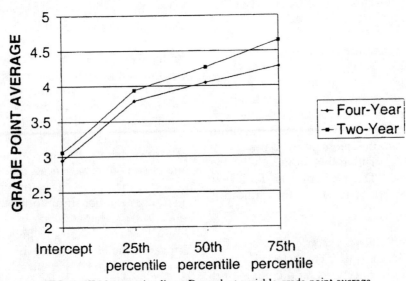

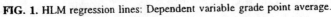

FIG. 1. HLM regression lines: Dependent variable grade point average.

TABLE 5
OLS and HLM Analyses for Intellectual Growth

Adjusted R^2 = .423	OLS Beta	HLM Beta	Change in Tau = .93
(Constant)	3.005	3.579	(Constant)
		0.089	4-year mission
Age			Age
Being Female	0.038		Being Female
Member of an underrepresented group			Member of an underrepresented group
High School Rank			High School Rank
Total SAT Scores			Total SAT Scores
Married			Married
Number of dependent children			Number of dependent children
4-year mission	0.068		4-year mission
Size			Size
Wealth			Wealth
Complexity			Complexity
Selectivity			Selectivity
Family strong support for academic goals			Family strong support for academic goals
Friends strong support for academic goals			Friends strong support for academic goals
Receiving Federal and State Financial Aid (Scale)	0.038		Receiving Federal and State Financial Aid (Scale)
Goal Clarity (Scale)	0.041	0.060	Goal Clarity (Scale)
Classroom experiences (Scale)	0.266	0.274	Classroom experiences (Scale)
Interaction with faculty outside the classroom (Scale)			Interaction with faculty outside the classroom (Scale)
Peer Support (Scale)	0.082	0.086	Peer Support (Scale)
Hours worked per week			Hours worked per week
Climate of perceived low prejudice (Scale)			Climate of perceived low prejudice (Scale)
Climate of perceived tolerance (Scale)	−0.072	−0.049	Climate of perceived tolerance (Scale)
Perceived climate fostering diversity (Scale)			Perceived climate fostering diversity (Scale)
Satisfaction with registration and billing (Scale)	−0.062		Satisfaction with registration and billing (Scale)
Satisfaction with campus academic facilities (Scale)	0.091	0.047	Satisfaction with campus academic facilities (Scale)
Social and Community Involvement (Scale)	0.058	0.044	Social and Community Involvement (Scale)
Student effort (Scale)	0.113	0.094	Student effort (Scale)
Institutional Commitment (Scale)	0.325	0.348	Institutional Commitment (Scale)

$p < .05$.

cates that the maximum likelihood point estimate for the grand-mean grade point average is 3.57 with a standard error of .02, indicating a 95% confidence interval of $3.57 \pm 1.96(.02) = (3.53, 3.69)$. The estimated value of the variance at the school level (i.e., between individual institutions) of institutional commitment scores, represented by tau, is .02. The estimated value of the variance at the student level, or within schools, of intellectual growth scores, represented by sigma squared, is .72. These estimates indicate that most of the variation in the outcome is at the student level, although a substantial and statistically significant portion ($p < .01$) exists between individual schools. An intraclass correlation was used to again test the variance between institutions. As Table 6 indicates, 3% of the total variance in growth is accounted for by institution to institution differences.

The HLM Model

Again, the HLM model suffered from a lack of convergence, and the number of predictors in the

TABLE 6
HLM Unconditional Model: Dependent Variable Intellectual Growth

Fixed Effect	Standard Coefficient	Standard Error	T ratio	df	P value
Intercept for Growth, B0 INTRCPT2, G00	3.571145	0.023653	150.983	47	0.000

Random Effect	Standard Deviation	Variance Component	df	Chi-square	P value
Intercept for Growth U0	0.14592	0.02129	47	242.45879	0.000
level-1, variance R	0.85248	0.72672			

Intraclass Correlation
Tau = .02
Sigma Squared = .73
Tau/(tau + sigma squared) = .02/(.02 + .73) = .03

model needed to be reduced. The significant correlations and predictors from the OLS regression equation were used for the final HLM analysis. Of the five organizational characteristics (mission, size, wealth, selectivity, and complexity), only mission is a significant predictor in the final model. The variables were again grand mean centered. The statistically significant coefficients for all of the variables are listed in Table 5.

The change in variance accounted for in the model was again calculated using the formula tau (unconditional)—tau (final model) / tau (unconditional) or [(.02129-.00151)/.02129 = 93], indicating that 93% of the change in variance between the two growth models is explained by the student level variables. Institutional mission is the only significant level 2 organizational variable having an impact on the intercept for intellectual growth. The value for growth at the intercept for 4-year institutions is 3.67, or .09 higher than the 3.58 value for growth at the 2-year institutions.

Thus, student intellectual growth is reportedly higher at 4-year institutions. Again, two

equations, contained in Table 7, were written, one for the 2-year sector, and one for the 4-year sector. As suggested by the tau calculation, the two models are virtually identical, except for the differences in the intercepts based on mission. Figure 2 shows these regression lines with the values for the 25th, 50th, and 75th percentiles.

Consistent with the Pascarella Model and the previous OLS results, the strongest student level predictors of intellectual growth in this HLM model include classroom experiences, along with student commitment, effort, and involvement. Other positive influences on student growth include receiving strong peer support, having goal clarity, and having good facilities. Table 5 shows one significant negative influence on growth: a perceived climate of tolerance.

These findings are largely congruent with the OLS regression results. In both HLM and OLS models, the mission variable explains about 2% of the variance in student intellectual growth. With three exceptions, the significant variables and the magnitudes of their importance are nearly identical using OLS versus HLM. How-

TABLE 7
HLM Sector Equations for Intellectual Growth

2-Year Equation
Growth = 3.58 + (.06 × goal clarity) + (.27 × classroom experiences) + (.086 × peer support) + (.04 × involvement) − (.05 × tolerance) + (.05 × facilities satisfaction) + (.09 × effort) + (.35 × institutional commitment)

4-Year Equation
Growth = 3.67 + (.06 × clarity) + (.27 × classroom experiences) + (.086 × peer support) + (.04 × involvement) − (.05 × tolerance) + (.05 × facilities satisfaction) + (.09 × effort) + (.35 × institutional commitment)

ever, this HLM model for student self-reported growth excludes being female, receiving financial aid, and satisfaction with registration and billing as being relevant. While significant under OLS, these three measures are not significant contributors to this HLM model.

Discussion and Conclusions

This study examines two student outcomes in relation to the structural/organizational characteristics of 51 campuses. The study first finds that organizational measures of mission, size, wealth, complexity, and selectivity are statistically represented by the 2-year versus 4-year college dimension. The different missions of 2-year and 4-year campuses indeed do exert significantly different influences on undergraduate GPA and intellectual growth. The study uses both OLS regression and HLM to examine these influences, and finds similar results.

Grade Point Average

Similarities Between OLS and HLM

The same student level variables predict Cum GPA in both the OLS and the HLM models. In both models, high school rank and total SAT scores account for as much variance in Cum GPA as all the other variables combined. The next most influential predictors are student effort followed by the vitality of classroom experiences and being at a 2-year institution. Additionally,

the results reveal that being female and working more hours per week are associated with a slightly higher GPA.

The relationships between high school rank and total SAT scores and grade point averages are in the expected direction and magnitude, based on the past 40 years of research in higher education. Following the Pascarella Model (1985) and dating back to the research synthesis by Feldman and Newcomb (1969), precollege academic achievement is the best predictor of college achievement. Similarly, most literature reviewed by Pascarella and Terenzini (1991) finds that females tend to earn modestly higher GPAs than males.

The positive impact of classroom experiences on Cum GPA is consistent with several studies by Volkwein finding that the classroom plays an essential part in the learning experience of students (Volkwein and Cabrera, 2000; Volkwein and Carbone, 1994; Volkwein and Lorang, 1996; Volkwein et al., 1986, 2000). Better classroom experiences result in higher GPAs, as well as in greater student effort as reported by students.

One surprise is the positive relationship between number of hours worked and Cum GPA. This may be due to characteristics of the students. Students who earn higher grades may also be students who work harder and longer. This work ethic may apply to both academic work and occupational work. Another possible explanation is that sophomores in general, and older community college sophomores in

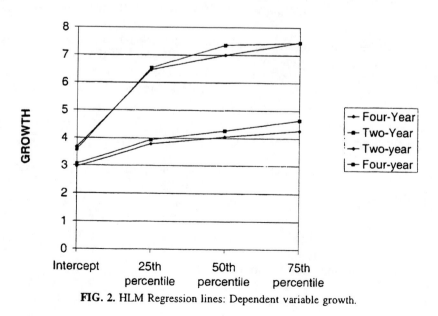

FIG. 2. HLM Regression lines: Dependent variable growth.

particular, may be more experienced at balancing work and school obligations. While a reviewer of this manuscript was kind enough to offer this latter explanation as a possibility, the models suggest that the positive connections between work and Cum GPA hold up, even controlling for all other variables in the analysis.

Another clear similarity in the OLS and HLM models for GPA is the positive influence of attending a 2-year campus, controlling for all other variables. Students with the same demographic and family profiles, the same work patterns and effort, the same goal clarity, and the same campus experiences inside and outside the classroom will earn higher grades by attending a 2-year institution. Whether this is evidence for greater student learning or for grade inflation at 2-year campuses is a matter for further study, but the finding is clearly indicated in both models. With the 2-year population reporting lower growth but higher GPAs, we believe the evidence suggests that students tend to be graded more generously by the faculty at 2-year campuses, all other things being equal.

Differences Between OLS and HLM

Despite sharing the same set of OLS predictors, the HLM analysis reveals a more precise picture of the interaction between three of the variables and Cum GPA. The differences between 2-year and 4-year Cum GPA in the HLM models is a function of differences in high school rank, classroom experiences, and effort. Specifically, the HLM model indicates that attending a 4-year institution results in a steeper slope for percentile rank and classroom experiences. This means that high school rank and classroom experiences are more predictive of Cum GPA at 4-year institutions than at 2-year institutions. On the other hand, attending a 4-year institution results in a flatter slope for student effort, meaning that student effort is more strongly associated with Cum GPA at 2-year institutions, and less so at 4-year campuses.

Intellectual Growth

Similarities Between OLS and HLM

The OLS and the HLM analyses share a number of similarities. Eight variables of similar magnitude contribute to both models: classroom experiences as well as student effort, commitment, and involvement are large and significant predictors of growth in both models. Smaller but significant contributors also include goal clarity, peer support, satisfaction with facilities, and a climate of intolerance. Thus, greater intellectual growth appears to occur when students with clear goals attend institutions that provide favorable classroom experiences, good facilities, and where the student's own effort and involvement are reinforced by a supportive peer group. This academic and social profile is consistent not only with the Pascarella and Cabrera models, but also with the work of Spady (1970, 1971) and Tinto (1993).

One surprise in the results is the negative relationship between growth and perceiving a climate of tolerance. Students who perceived a less tolerant environment are more likely to experience more intellectual growth. According to the Cross model (1991), students exploring their identity become immersed in the issues of identity formation and consequently become more sensitive to environmental circumstances. Subsequently, these students may perceive their campus environment to be less tolerant of differences. Thus, students experiencing tremendous amounts of personal growth may also report a more problem filled environment.

Differences Between OLS and HLM

The OLS model has three additional predictors of growth that are not present in the HLM model. These predictors are receiving federal and state aid, being female, and satisfaction with registration and billing. We looked for, but did not find, structural and organizational characteristics that impact student growth. Mission is significant only for the intercept, indicating that intellectual growth at 4-year institutions is slightly higher than at 2-year institutions.

Comparing the Grade Point Average Models to the Growth Models

Both intellectual growth models are more robust than the corresponding GPA models. Regardless of using OLS or HLM models of estimation, the intellectual growth model exhibits higher statistics ($R^2 = .42$, tau change = .93) than the corresponding Cum GPA model ($R^2 = .27$, tau change = .50).

One implication for administrators as well as faculty is that we can have a bit more confidence in knowing and influencing what it is that enhances student intellectual growth than in knowing what leads to a high student grade point average. We know from this and other studies that intellectual growth is most strongly associated with many things that happen after students enter the institution; the vitality of the classroom experience as well as a rich array of other campus variables, most prominently the student's own effort, involvement, and peer support. On the other hand, the strongest predictors of college Cum GPA are high school class rank and SAT scores. Less variance in Cum GPA is contributed by campus experiences such as student effort and classroom vitality, even though they are highly significant contributors.

These results call for caution in using Cum GPA to measure student performance (Pascarella and Terenzini, 1991). Grade point average may be subject to inflation or may vary considerably discipline-by-discipline, instructor-to-instructor. Moreover, the most talented students tend to gravitate toward the most rigorous majors (science, math, accounting, premedicine, prelaw, etc.), thus diminishing the relationship between prior performance and college GPA. Additionally, we find evidence in this study that 2-year faculty may grade students more generously than those at 4-year and research institutions. The results of this study support the contention that college GPA should not be used as a single measure of college performance, and whenever possible other measures should be identified.

Comparing 2-Year Institutions to 4-Year Institutions

College mission turns out to be the only organizational variable exerting differential influences on student GPA and intellectual growth. Both OLS and HLM models indicate that growth and GPA are influenced by the 2-year versus 4-year mission. The regression tables, figures, and equations show the many similarities and a few differences between student GPA and growth at 2-year versus 4-year campuses. For Cum GPA the models are similar, except that rank in class and classroom experiences are better predictors of GPA at 4-year institutions, while student effort is a better predictor of GPA at 2-year institutions. Moreover, controlling for all other variables, students at 2-year institutions receive higher grades. For intellectual growth, the two HLM models are

almost identical, except that, controlling for all other variables, students report more growth at 4-year campuses.

Limitations

While this study draws from a rich outcomes dataset of 7,658 sophomores at 51 public college campuses in a single state system, the study has limitations that should be considered. First, the results may not be completely transportable to nonpublic institutions and to other states. Additionally, the robustness and consistency of the 2-year versus 4-year differences may obscure the important effects of organizational size, wealth, complexity, and selectivity that would be more apparent in the wider population of public and private campuses. Future studies should examine organizational influences on student outcomes using an even more diverse and representative range of institutions.

Another possible limitation is the population of students who self-identify as being sophomores. This study does not control for part-time or full-time attendance, or degree versus non-degree seeking. Further delineation of the sample into these categories might reveal interesting differences in future research. Additionally, these sophomores represent only those who have successfully persisted at their respective institutions. Results from this study may not be generalizable to students who do not persist into their second year, and these persistence patterns may also vary by institution type.

The study examines both student GPA and self-reported intellectual growth as important outcomes of the collegiate experience. Although Cum GPA and self-reported growth have become accepted as measures of student performance and learning, these may not be the best measures (Franklin, 1995; Pascarella, 1985; Pascarella and Terenzini, 1991). A better outcome variable reflecting student learning might be a standardized achievement test. However, such a measure was not available for this population.

Another limitation of the current study is the use of self-report measures to reflect financial need. One question asked students to indicate whether federal and state grants were a major, moderate, minor, or no source of assistance. While this scale does not provide a direct dollar value that can be compared across students and institutions, the scale roughly reflects financial need. Other student perceptions of financial difficulty were dropped from the analysis after diagnostics identified them as weak contributors.

This study also was limited to a 2-level HLM analysis using organizational variables and student experiences. A 3-level HLM may better capture important within and between campus influences due to the student's major field of study or membership in a particular subpopulation. Future analyses with this or other similar datasets should attempt 3-level HLM to explore these effects.

Nevertheless, for all its limitations, this study does indicate that the distinctive missions of 4-year versus 2-year campuses indeed do exert important and significantly different influences on undergraduate GPA and self-reported intellectual growth. While the student level predictor variables in the OLS and HLM models are substantially similar, the HLM results bring greater visibility to the precise interaction effects between campus mission and student experiences. High school percentile rank and college classroom experiences are better predictors of Cum GPA at 4-year institutions, while student effort is a better predictor of GPA at 2-year institutions. Moreover, controlling for all other variables, students at 2-year institutions receive higher grades, and students at 4-year campuses experience more growth.

Whereas the most important predictors of Cum GPA include precollege measures like high school rank and SAT score, the most influential predictors of student intellectual growth are campus experiences such as classroom vitality, peer support, student effort, commitment, and involvement. Moreover, since these same campus experiences contribute significantly to both outcomes, faculty and administrators should focus their actions and energies in these directions.

Acknowledgments.   This paper was presented at the Annual Forum of the Association for Institutional Research, Long Beach, CA, June 2001. The authors gratefully acknowledge the database building work contributed by two researchers in the State University of New York, Gary Blose and Kelli Parmley.

References

Astin, A. (1977). *Four Critical Years.* San Francisco: Jossey-Bass.

Astin, A. W. (1984). Student involvement: a developmental theory for higher education. *Journal of College Student Personnel* 24(5): 207–308.

Astin, A. W. (1991). *Assessment for Excellence: The Philosophy and Practice of Assessment and Evaluation in Higher Education.* New York: Macmillan.

Bauer, K. B. (1998). Campus climate: understanding the critical components of today's colleges and universities. *New Directions for Institutional Research, Number 98.* San Francisco: Jossey-Bass.

Bean, J. P. (1980). Dropout and turnover: the synthesis and test of a causal model of student attrition. *Research in Higher Education* 12: 155–187.

Bean, J. P., and Metzner, B. S. (1985). A conceptual model of nontraditional undergraduate student attrition. *Review of Higher Educational Research* 55(4): 485–540.

Berger, J. B., and Milem, J. F. (2000). Organizational behavior in higher education and student outcomes. In J. C. Smart (ed.), *Higher Education Handbook of Theory and Research,* Vol. 15, pp. 268–338. New York: Agathon Press.

Bryk, A. S., and Raudenbush, S. W. (1992). *Hierarchical Linear Models: Applications and Data Analysis Methods.* Newbury Park, CA: Sage.

Burke, J. C. (2000). Performance funding: popularity and volatility. Paper presented at the National Association for Institutional Research Forum, May 2000, Cincinnati, Ohio.

Burke, J. C., and Serban, A. M. (1998). Performance funding for public higher education: fad or trend? *New Directions for Institutional Research, 97.* San Francisco: Jossey-Bass.

Busing, F. M. T. A. (1993). Distribution characteristics of variance estimates in two-level models. (Technical Report No. PRM 93–04). Leiden, The Netherlands: University of Leiden, Department of Psychometrics.

Cabrera, A. F., Castaneda, M. B., Nora, A., and Hengstler, D. (1992). The convergence between two theories of college persistence. *Journal of Higher Education* 63(2): 143–164.

Cabrera, A. F., Colbeck, C. L., and Terenzini, P. T. (2001). Developing performance indicators for assessing classroom teaching practices and student learning: the case of engineering. *Research in Higher Education* 42(3): 327–352.

Cabrera, A. F., and La Nasa, S. M. (2000). *On the Path to College: Three Critical Tasks Facing America's Disadvantaged.* Penn State University: Center for the Study of Higher Education.

Cabrera, A. F., Nora, A., and Castaneda, M. B. (1993). The role of finances in the persistence process: a structural model. *Research in Higher Education* 33(5): 571–593.

Carnevale, D. (2000). Accrediting bodies consider new standards for distance-education programs. *The Chronicle of Higher Education* XLVII(2): A58-A59.

Cohen, A. M., and Brawer, F. B. (1996). *The American Community College.* San Francisco: Jossey-Bass.

Cross, W. E. (1991). *Shades of Black.* Philadelphia: Temple Press.

de Leeuw, J., and Kreft, I. G. G. (1995). Questioning multilevel models. *Journal of Educational and Behavioral Statistics* 20; 171–189.

DiPrete, T. A., and Forristal, J. D. (1994). Multilevel models: method and substance. *Annual Review of Sociology* 20; 331–357.

Draper, D. (1995). Inference and hierarchical linear modeling in the social sciences. *Journal of Educational and Behavioral Statistics* 20; 115–147.

Ethington, C. A. (1997). A hierarchical linear modeling approach to studying college effects. In J. C. Smart (ed.), *Higher Education Handbook of Theory and Research* Vol. 12, pp. 165–194. New York: Agathon Press.

Ewell, P. T. (1998). National trends in assessing student learning. *Journal of Engineering Education* 87(2): 107–103.

Feldman, K., and Newcomb, T. (1969). *The Impact of College on Students.* San Francisco: Jossey-Bass.

Fleming, J. (1984). *Blacks in College: A Comparative Study of Students' Success in Black and in White Institutions.* San Francisco: Jossey-Bass.

Franklin, M. (1995). The effects of differential college environments on academic learning and student perceptions of cognitive development. *Research in Higher Education* 36(2): 127–154.

Hall, R. H. (1991). *Organizations: Structure and Process.* Englewood Cliffs, NJ: Prentice-Hall.

Hurtado, S. (1992). The campus racial climate: contexts of conflict. *Journal of Higher Education* 63: 539–569.

Hurtado, S. (1994). The institutional climate for talented Latino students. *Research in Higher Education* 35: 21–41.

Hurtado, S., Carter, D. F., and Spuler, A. (1996). Latino student transition to college: assessing difficulties and factors in successful college adjustment. *Research in Higher Education* 21(3): 279–302.

Kennedy, E., Teddlie, C., and Stringfield, S. (1993). Multilevel analysis of phase II of the Louisiana School Effectiveness study. Paper presented at the annual meeting of the International Congress for School Effectiveness and Improvement. November 3, 1993, Norrkoping, Sweden.

Kuh, G. D., Race, R. C., and Vesper, N. (1997). The development of process indicators to estimate student gains associated with good practices in undergraduate education. *Research in Higher Education* 38(4): 435–454.

Layzell, D. L. (ed.). (1997). Forecasting and managing enrollment and revenue: an overview of current trends, issues, and methods. *New Directions in Institutional Research* 93: 81–93. San Francisco: Jossey-Bass.

Loo, C. M., and Rolison, G. (1986). Alienation of ethnic minority students at a predominately white university. *Journal of Higher Education* 57: 58–77.

Massy, W. F. (1994). Measuring performance: How colleges and universities can set meaningful goals and be accountable. In W. F. Massy, and J. W. Meyerson (eds.), *Measuring Institutional Performance in Higher Education*, pp. 38–58. Princeton, NJ: Peterson's Guides.

McMurtrie, B. (2000). Accreditors revamp policies to stress student learning. *The Chronicle of Higher Education* 46: A29–A31.

Middle States Association of Colleges and Schools (1994). *Characteristics of Excellence in Higher Education: Standards for Accreditation.* Available: *www.msache.org.*

Morris, C. N. (1995). Hierarchical linear models for educational data: an overview. *Journal of Educational and Behavioral Statistics* 20: 190–200.

Murguía, E., Padilla, R. V., and Pavel, M. (1991). Ethnicity and the concept of social integration in Tinto's model of institutional departure. *Journal of College Student Development* 32(5): 433–454.

Nora, A. (1987). Determinants of retention among Chicano students: a structural model. *Research in Higher Education* 26(1): 31–59.

Nora, A. (1990). Campus-based programs as determinants of retention among Hispanic college students. *Journal of Higher Education* 61(3): 312–331.

Nora, A., and Cabrera, A. F. (1996). The role of perceptions of prejudice and discrimination on the adjustment of minority students to college. *Journal of Higher Education* 67: 119–148.

North Central Association of Colleges and Schools (2000). *Shaping the Commission's Future: Mission Statement 2000.* Available: *www.ncacihe.org.*

Pace, C. (1984). *Measuring the Quality of College Student Experiences.* Los Angeles: University of California, Higher Education Research Institute.

Pascarella, E. T. (1985). College environmental influences on learning and cognitive development: a critical review and synthesis. In J. Smart (ed.), *Higher Education: Handbook of Theory and Research*, Vol. 1, pp. 1–61. New York: Agathon.

Pascarella, E. T., and Terenzini, P. T. (1991). *How College Affects Students.* San Francisco: Jossey-Bass.

Patrick, W. J. (2001). Estimating first-year student attrition rates: An application of multilevel modeling using categorical variables. *Research in Higher Education* 42(2): 151–170.

Peterson, M. W., and Augustine, C. H. (2000). Organizational practices enhancing the influence of student assessment information in academic decisions. *Research in Higher Education* 41(1): 21–52.

Porter, S. R., and Umbach, P. D. (2001). Analyzing faculty workload data using multilevel modeling. *Research in Higher Education* 42(2): 171–197.

Ratcliff, J. L., Lubinescu, E. S., and Gaffney, M. A. (2001). Two continuums collide: accreditation and assessment. *New Directions for Higher Education* 113: 5–21.

Reynolds, A. L. (1999). Working with children and adolescents in the schools: Multicultural counseling implications. In R. H. Sheets and E. R. Hollins (eds.), *Racial and Ethnic Identity in School Practices: Aspects of Human Development*. Mahwah, NJ: Lawrence Erlbaum.

Semrow, J. J., Barney, J. A., Fredericks, M., Fredericks, J., Robinson, P., and Pfnister, A. O. (1992). *In Search of Quality: The Development, Status, Forecast of Standards in Postsecondary Accreditation*. New York: Peter Lang.

Singer, J. D. (1998). Using SAS PROC MIXED to fit multilevel models, hierarchical models, and individual growth models. *Journal of Educational and Behavioral Statistics* 24(4): 323–355.

Smedley, B. D., Myers, H. F., and Harrell, S. P. (1993). Minority-status stresses and the college adjustment of ethnic minority freshmen. *Journal of Higher Education* 64: 434–452.

Spady, W. G. (1970). Dropouts from higher education: an interdisciplinary review and synthesis. *Interchange* 1(1): 64–85.

Spady, W. G. (197 1). Dropouts from higher education: toward an empirical model. *Interchange* 2(3): 38–62.

St. John, E. P. (1992). Workable models for institutional research on the impact of student financial aid. *Journal of Student Financial Aid* 22(3): 13–26.

Stark, J., et al. (1989). Student goals for college and courses: a missing link in assessing and improving academic achievement. *ASHE-ERIC Higher Education Report 6*. (ed317121, 132 pages)

Strauss, L. (2000). *Policy Analysis: Funding of Community Colleges in Pennsylvania*. Unpublished manuscript.

Terenzini, P. T., and Pascarella, E. T. (1980). Student/faculty relationships and freshman year educational outcomes: A further investigation. *Journal of College Student Personnel* 21: 521–528.

Terenzini, P. T., Pascarella, E. T., and Lorang, W. (1982). An assessment of the academic and social influences on freshmen year educational outcomes. *Review of Higher Education* 5: 86–110.

Terenzini, P. T., Springer, L., Pascarella, E. T., and Nora, A. (1995). Influences affecting the development of students' critical thinking skills. *Research in Higher Education* 36: 23–39.

Terenzini, P. T., Springer, L., Yaeger, P., Pascarella, E. T., and Nora, (1996). First generation college students: characteristics, experiences, and cognitive development. *Research in Higher Education* 37: 1–22.

Terenzini, P. T., Theophilides, C., and Lorang, W. (1984). Influences on students' perception of their personal development during the first three years of college. *Research in Higher Education* 21: 178–194.

Terenzini, P. T., and Wright, T. (1987). Students' personal growth during four years of college. *Research in Higher Education* 26: 161–179.

Tinto, V. (1987). *Leaving College: Rethinking the Causes and Cures of Student Attrition*. Chicago: University of Chicago Press.

Tinto, V. (1993). *Leaving College: Rethinking the Causes and Cures of Student Attrition*, 2nd ed. Chicago: The University of Chicago Press.

Upcraft, M. L., and Schuh, J. H. (1996). *Assessment in Student Affairs: A Guide for Practitioners*. San Francisco: Jossey-Bass.

Volkwein, J. F. (1992). Albany outcomes model. *Assessment Research Report #12*. Office of Institutional Research, State University of New York at Albany. Available: <http://www.albany.edu/ir/reports.html>

Volkwein, J. F., and Cabrera, A. F. Antecedents and consequences of classroom vitality among college seniors. Research Paper presented at the ASHE Annual Meeting, November 2000, Sacramento, CA.

Volkwein, J. F., and Carbone, D. A. (1994). The impact of departmental research and teaching climates on undergraduate growth and satisfaction. *Journal of Higher Education* 65(2): 147–167.

Volkwein, J. F., King, M. C., and Terenzini, P. T. (1986). Student faculty relationships and intellectual growth among transfer students. *Journal of Higher Education* 57: 413–430.

Volkwein, J. F., and Lorang, W. G. (1996). Characteristics of extenders: full-time students who take light credit loads and graduate in more than four years. *Research in Higher Education* 37(1): 43–68.

Volkwein, J. F., and Malik, S. M. (1997). State regulation and administrative flexibility at public universities. *Research in Higher Education* 38(1): 17–42.

Volkwein, J. F., and Szelest, B. P. (1995). Individual and campus characteristics associated with student loan default. *Research in Higher Education* 36: 41–72.

Volkwein, J. F., Szelest, B. P., Cabrera, A. F., and Napierski-Prancl, M. R. (1998). Factors associated with student loan default among different racial and ethnic groups. *Journal of Higher Education* 69(2): 206–237.

Volkwein, J. F., Valle, S., Parmley, K., Blose, G., and Zhou, Y. (2000). *A multi-campus study of academic performance and cognitive growth among native freshman, two-year transfers, and four-year transfers.* Paper presented at the meeting of the Association for Institutional Research Forum, Cincinnati, OH.

Von Secker, C. E., and Lissitz, R. W. (1997). Estimating school value-added effectiveness: consequences of respecification of hierarchical linear modeling. Paper presented at the Annual Meeting of the American Educational Research Association, Chicago, IL, March, 24–28, 1997. (ED 410243).

Voorhees, R. A. (1985). Financial aid and persistence: do the federal campus-based aid programs make a difference? *Journal of Student Financial Aid* 15: 21–30.

Voorhees, R.A. (1997). Student learning and cognitive development in the community college. In J. C. Smart (ed.), *Higher Education Handbook of Theory and Research,* Vol. 12, pp. 313–370. New York: Agathon Press.

Weidman, J. (1989). Undergraduate socialization: a conceptual approach. In J. Smart (ed.), *Higher Education: Handbook of Theory and Research,* Vol. 5, 289–322. New York: Agathon Press.

Linda C. Strauss, Institutional Research Associate, Office of Undergraduate Education, and J. Fredericks Volkwein, Director and Professor, Center for the Study of Higher Education, Penn State University.

Address correspondence to: J. Fredericks Volkwein, Center for the Study of Higher Education, Penn State University, 400 Rackley Building, University Park, PA 16801-3203; volkwein@psu.edu.

CHAPTER 42

RECOMMENDED READINGS AND WEB-BASED READINGS

Recommended Readings

Kim, K. A. (2003). ERIC review: Exploring the meaning of "nontraditional" at the community college. *Community College Review 30*(1), 74–89.

Laanan, F. S. (2003). Degree aspirations of two-year college students. *Community College Journal of Research and Practice, 27,* 495–518.

Shaw, K. M. (1999). Defining the self: Constructions of identity in community college students. In K. Shaw, J. Valadez, & R. Rhoades (Eds.), *Community colleges as cultural context* (pp. 153–171). Albany: SUNY Press.

Strauss, L. C., & Volkwein, J. F. (2004, March/April). Predictors of student commitment to two-year and four-year institutions. *The Journal of Higher Education, 75*(2), 203–227.

Grubb, W. N. (1997). The returns to education in the sub-baccalaureate labor market, 1984–1990. *Economics of Education Review, 16*(3), 231–245.

Grubb, W. N. (2002, August). Learning and earning in the middle, part I; National studies of pre-baccalaureate education. *Economics of Education Review, 21*(4), 299–321.

Deil-Amen, R., & Rosenbaum, J. E. (2003, March). The social prerequisites of success: Can college structure reduce the need for social know-how? *Annals of the American Academy of Political and Social Science, 586,* 120–143.

Lin, Y., & Vogt, W. P. (1996). Occupational outcomes for students earning two-year college degrees: Income, status, and equity. *The Journal of Higher Education, 67*(4), 446–475.

Leigh, D. E., & Gill, A. M. (2003, February). Do community colleges really divert students from earning bachelor's degrees? *Economics of Education Review, 22*(1), 23–30.

Mobley, C. (2001, Spring). The impact of community colleges on the school-to-work transition: A multilevel analysis. *Community College Review, 28*(4), 1–30.

Voorhees, R. A. (1997). Student learning and cognitive development in the community college. In J. C. Smart (Ed.), *Higher Education: Handbook of Theory and Research,* Vol. 12 (pp. 313–370). New York: Agathon Press.

Web-Based Resources

Hamm, R. E. (2004). Going to college: Not what it used to be. In K. Boswell & C.D. Wilson (Eds.), *Keeping America's promise* (pp. 29–33). Denver, CO: Education Commission of the States. *http://www.league.org/league/projects/promise/download.html*

Wilson, C. D. (2004). Coming through the open door: A student profile. In K. Boswell & C.D. Wilson (Eds.), *Keeping America's promise* (pp. 25–27). Denver, CO: Education Commission of the States. *http://www.league.org/league/projects/promise/download.html*

VanDerLinden, K. (2002, April). Faces of the future: Credit student analysis, 1999 to 2000. Research Brief. Washington, DC: Community College Press. *http://www.aacc.nche.edu/Template.cfm? Section=Research_Briefs&template=/Content Management/ContentDisplay.cfm&ContentID=7738 &InterestCategoryID=221&Name=Research%20 Brief&ComingFrom=InterestDisplay*

Bailey, T., Kienzl, G., & Marcotte, D. (August, 2004). *CCRC Brief. Who benefits from postsecondary occupational education? Findings from the 1980s and 1990s*, No. 23. New York: Community College Research Center. *http://www.tc.columbia.edu/ Publication.asp?UID=251*

Bailey, T. (January, 2003). CCRC Brief. *Community colleges in the 21st century: Challenges and opportunities.* New York: Community College Research Center. *http://www.tc.columbia.edu/ Publication.asp?UID=88*

Bailey, T., Alfonso, M., Scott, M., & Leinbach, T. (August, 2004). CCRC Brief. *Educational outcomes of postsecondary occupational students.* New York: Community College Research Center. *http://www. tc.columbia.edu/Publication.asp?UID=4*

Dougherty, K. J., & Bakia, M. F. (2000). Community colleges and contract training: Content, origins, and impact. *Teachers College Record, 102*(1), 197–243. *http://www.tcrecord.org/PDF/10445.pdf*

Jenkins, D., & Fitzgerald, J. (September, 1998). *Policy paper. Community colleges: Connecting the poor to good jobs.* Denver, CO: Education Commission of the States. *http://www.communitycollegepolicy.org/ html/top.asp?page=/html/publications_main.asp*

Rubin, S., & Autry, G. (September, 1998). Policy paper. Rural community colleges: Catalysts for economic renewal. Denver, CO: Education Commission of the States. *http://www.communitycollegepolicy.org/ html/top.asp?page=/html/publications_main.asp*

ABOUT THE EDITORS

Barbara Townsend is a former community college faculty member and administrator who is currently Professor of Higher and Continuing Education at the University of Missouri-Columbia. She has been a faculty member and administrator at Thomas Nelson Community College in Virginia, Loyola University of Chicago, and the University of Memphis. While at the University of Memphis, she was the senior vice provost's faculty associate for transfer and articulation issues with two-year colleges. She has also served in several leadership positions in the Council for the Study of Community Colleges, including as its president. She has published extensively about the community college, including the edited books, *Community Colleges: Policy in the Future Context* (2000) and *Two-Year Colleges for Women and Minorities* (1999). Additionally, she has edited four *New Directions for Community Colleges* issues: *The Role of Community Colleges in Teacher Education* (2003); *Understanding the Impact of Reverse Transfers upon Community Colleges* (1999), *Gender and Power in the Community College* (1995), and *A Search for Institutional Distinctiveness* (1989) and is co-editor (with Kevin Dougherty) of an upcoming volume tentatively titled *Community College Missions in the 21st Century*. Her current research interests include access to higher education through the community college, community college faculty, and the baccalaureate degree offered by community colleges.

Debra Bragg is Professor of Higher Education at the Department of Educational Organization and Leadership in the College of Education at the University of Illinois at Urbana-Champaign (UIUC). Her specializations include postsecondary education, school-to-college transition, policy analysis and evaluation, and community college leadership development. She directs the Office of Community College Research and Leadership as well as the Higher Education program and Community College Executive Leadership graduate program at UIUC. Dr. Bragg's research on the community college focuses primarily on various policies associated with college access for underserved populations, including studies assessing the impact of dual enrollment, school-to-work transition, and tech prep on college readiness and retention. Her national evaluation of tech prep programs, funded by the U.S. Department of Education, provides the most extensive results on student participation and outcomes linked to date. She has published in the *Peabody Journal on Education, Community College Review, Community College Journal of Research and Practice, New Directions for Community Colleges, Journal for Vocational Education,* and numerous other scholarly journals. From 2001-02, Dr. Bragg served as president of the Council for the Study of Community Colleges, and from 1996–1998 served on the Council's board. She also served on the editorial boards of the *Journal of Vocational Education Research* and *Journal of Career-Technical Education* from 1996–1998, serving as associate editor of the *Journal of Vocational Education Research* in 1997. She has been the special issue editor of two *Journal of Vocational Education Research* issues, both examining high school to college transition policies, and she is the editor of a 2001 *New Directions for Community Colleges* volume titled *The New Vocationalism in Community Colleges.*

ABOUT THE ASSOCIATE EDITORS

Kevin J. Dougherty is Associate Professor of Higher Education in the Department of Organization and Leadership and Senior Research Associate at the Community College Research Center at Teachers College, Columbia University. He received his doctorate in sociology from Harvard University in 1983 and his undergraduate degree in political science from Washington University (St. Louis) in 1972. His research has examined the historical origins and current social role of community colleges, their impact on student educational and economic attainment, the transfer process between community colleges and four-year colleges, contract training in the community college, and the impact of performance accountability systems on community colleges. He is now principal investigator on a Lumina Foundation for Education-funded project, "Assessing State Policies Affecting Access, Opportunity, and Success in Community Colleges," that is examining what policies states have in place to encourage access to and success in community colleges on the part of minority and low-income students. He recently finished a report for the Community College Research Center entitled *Performance Accountability and Community Colleges: Forms, Impacts, and Problems.* He also has a paper (with Greg Kienzl) forthcoming in the *Teachers College Record,* entitled "It's Not Enough to Get Through the Open Door: Inequalities by Social Background in Transfer from Community Colleges to Four-Year Colleges." His research on contract training is reported in "Community Colleges and Contract Training" (*Teachers College Record,* February 2000) and a CCRC report, *The New Economic Role of the Community College* (1999). Dougherty's research on the community college's impact on student educational and economic attainment and on the historical development of the institution is summarized in *The Contradictory College: The Conflicting Origins, Impacts, and Futures of the Community College* (SUNY Press, 1994). The book was awarded the American Sociological Association's Willard Waller Award for best book in the sociology of education for the years 1994 to 1996.

Frankie Santos Laanan is an assistant professor in the Department of Educational Leadership and Policy Studies at Iowa State University (ISU). Prior to joining ISU, he held various faculty and administrative positions, including serving as senior research scientist and associate director of the Bill J. Priest Center for Community College Education, and as assistant professor in the community college leadership program at the University of Illinois at Urbana-Champaign. Prior to these positions, he was senior research analyst in the Office of Vocational Education and Institutional Research at Coast Community College District in Costa Mesa, California. His research focuses on access and equity, minority students' transition to the baccalaureate and beyond, and the impact of community colleges on society and individuals. He has authored book chapters and articles that have appeared in *Community College Journal of Research and Practice, Community College Review, Educational Gerontology, New Directions for Community Colleges,* and *Research in Higher Education.* He has edited two issues of *New Directions for Community Colleges,* including *Transfer Students: Trends and Issues* (2001) and *Determining the Economic Benefits of Attending Community Colleges* (1998). Laanan has served on national advisory boards, including that of the Council for the Study of Community Colleges, and is currently a member of the ASHE Reader Series Board. In 2004 he was appointed Chair of the Council on Ethic

Participation (CEP). During his tenure as Chair of CEP (2004–07) he is also a member of the ASHE Board of Directors.

Berta Vigil Laden is an associate professor in the Department of Theory and Policy Studies in the Ontario Institute for Studies in Education at the University of Toronto. She teaches in the community college leadership program and in the higher education program. In her research, she focuses on issues of transition within the educational pipeline related to access, equity, race, and gender from high school to under-graduate and graduate studies. Dr. Laden's research focuses on both students and faculty of color. Her current research also focuses on His-panic-Serving Institutions and on the baccalau-reate degree in the community college. Prior to becoming a university faculty member, she was a faculty member and department chair at Mis-sion College in California for ten years. She has published in the *Community College Review, Community College Journal of Research and Practice,* the *New Directions for Community Colleges* series, the *New Directions for Institutional Research* series, and published chapters in numerous books. Dr. Laden has served as editor for a special issue of *Community College Journal of Research and Practice* on Hispanic-Serving Community Colleges, editor of a *New Directions in Community Colleges* issue on serving minority populations, and a co-editor of the *ASHE Reader on Multiculturalism in Higher Education* (2nd ed.). She served on the boards of the Council for the Study of Community Colleges (CSCC) and the Association for the Study of Higher Education and is currently on the boards for the Institute for Higher Education Policy and the Status of Women. Dr. Laden currently chairs the committee for the Dissertation of the Year award for CSCC.